AF650231

Indian Numismatics

Its Bearing on History, Culture, Art
and Iconography

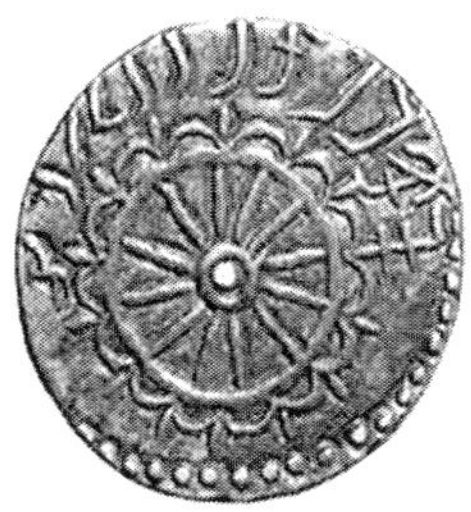

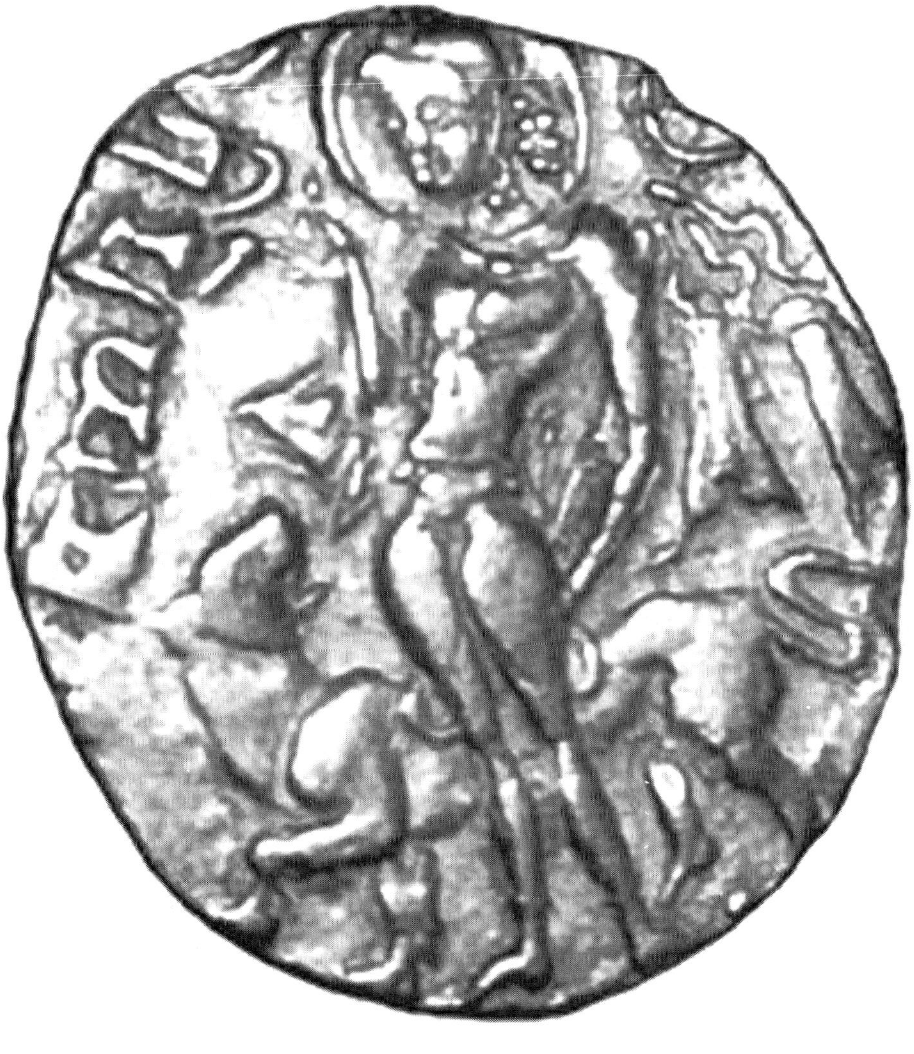

Indian Numismatics

Its Bearing on History, Culture, Art and Iconography

Select Essays

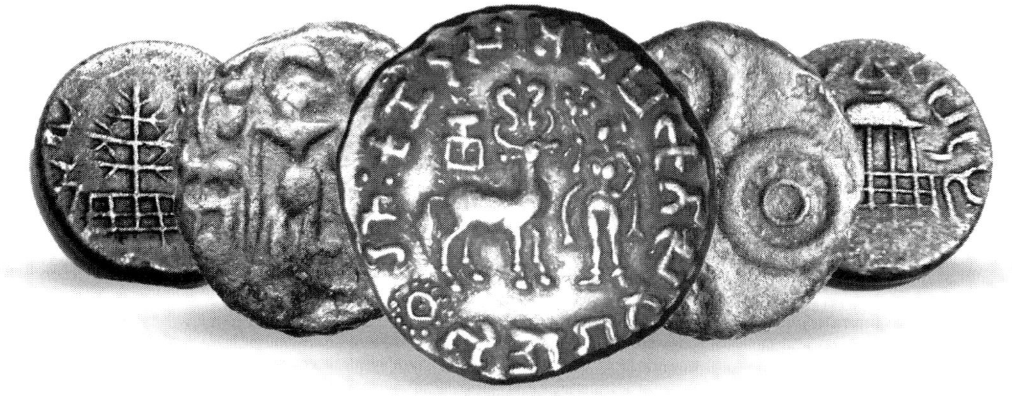

Devendra Handa

Aryan Books International
New Delhi

Books That Live!

Aryan Books International was established in 1992. Though it began as a commercial venture, business was only a part of the whole. The primary aim was to bridge the gap between the history taught and the real history of our country, and also to present its lesser known and sometimes deliberately neglected facets. In academia, the legacy of our art, culture and ethos was being undermined to perpetuate a narrative which left us looking weak, soft and lagging behind the so-called progressive West.

It was this narrative that we sought to contest. The journey over the last thirty years has not been an easy one. However, it gives us a sense of satisfaction to have possibly made a small difference by publishing over 750 titles written by the most acclaimed authors in the field. We have specialized in publishing ingenious and outstanding scholarship, both established as also fresh. While we focus on our long forgotten history, we also bring to the fore certain extremely important aspects of Indian art, culture and traditions.

Apart from pioneering content, we also ensure that our production quality remains the best in the business, as we continue with the mission to publish books that **Live Forever**!

We are also aware that this is just the beginning of a long journey. A long road lies ahead. A lot more needs to be said. A lot more needs to be explored. We assure you that we're on it with renewed commitment!

www.aryanbooks.com
@AryanBooksInt

Aryan Books International 30 Years

Aryan@30

Preface

During the last about half a century the popularity of coin-collecting has grown by leaps and bounds in India inciting awareness to preserve every bit as valuable and important item of our heritage and as documents of historical value. This in turn has resulted in the preservation of coins which generally used to be melted down earlier for their metallic value. Realizing the importance and value even of allied items like seals, sealings, tokens, proto-monetary items, etc., a substantial number of intelligent and enterprising persons have also started collecting, preserving and dealing in them. Consequentially there has grown a large number of sellers and buyers, and to cater to the needs of which quite a few auction-houses have come up providing an opportunity to the bulk collectors to dispose off their duplicate or bulk pieces and for others to get items of their choice and preference. Generally collectors want to know the value and importance of the items they acquire. Though development of technology and means of communication, mobiles and internet in particular, have brought the acquisition of information and knowledge to our fingertips yet everything we want to know is not accessible to everybody because of the immense flow and rapidity of knowledge and the variety of sources thereof. Availability of handy thematic volumes has therefore not lost their relevance and is welcome to many.

The present volume contains 31 articles on miscellaneous aspects of numismatics, a field to which I have been contributing for about the last more than 50 years now, bringing to light many significant new coins, seals, sealings, tokens, official and personal signet-rings and allied objects and presenting fresh interpretations thereof. The study also includes numerous pieces brought to light by other fellow beings for which I have my own interpretations and views. There are numerous numismatic groups on WhatsApp and Facebook whose members put the scans of their acquisitions and finds on the internet. The present volume illustrates as to how many of these items put on the internet besides those published earlier and/or in private collections and museums in India and abroad have a bearing on our history, culture, religion, art, architecture, iconography, language, palaeography, geography, metallurgy, coin-technology, movement of peoples, migrations of motifs, etc. I owe my gratitude to all those earlier writers and past and present collectors whose numismatic items have been discussed and commented upon by me. I feel specially beholden to Sarvashri Girish Sharma, R.K. Aggarwal and his son Vaibhav Aggarwal, Gulshan Bhardwaj and his son Kapil Bhardwaj, Jan Lingen, (late) Nicholas Rhodes, Murthi Macherla, Bhushan Kapadia, Kamal Vaid, Rajnarayan Maurya, Vishal Parikh, Karan Singh, Daulal Johri, Ranvijay Singh, Jeevandeep Singh, Sanjeev Chagti, Vishal Bumb Jain, Deepak Jain, Sanjay Godbole, Sharad Sharma; Drs. Wilfried Pieper, D.L. Neema, R.C. Thakur, Prashant Kulkarni, Nilaish, Akshay Jain, Satish Karandikar, (late) N.P. Joshi, Major M.K. Gupta, S.K. Bhatt, Shailendra Bhandare, Advocate Shailesh Jain and many other friends whose scans besides those of some auction houses have been utilized in this work. For sake of clarity the illustrations have generally been enlarged and are not to scale.

Besides the works of great stalwarts like R.C. Majumdar, A.S. Altekar, D.C. Sircar, V.V. Mirashi and numerous others the recent publication of Daniel Balog on the inscriptions of the Aulikaras and their associates has helped me a lot to associate numerous recently recovered seals, sealings and signet-rings to them. Drs. K.K. Maheshwari, Satya Vrat Varma, Manmohan Kumar and Suken Shah have been helpful in various ways and owe my gratitude.

Many of the articles published earlier and relevant today have also been incorporated in the present volume and I express my gratitude to the editors and other relevant authorities for that: Himachal State Museum, Shimla for IX* (* asterisk mark has been used for revised articles) (*Manimahesh* VII: 52-61); Jñāna-Pravāha, Varanasi for X and XXIV published in the *Research Journal* Nos. XXIII: 1-8 and XIV: 17-19, Fig. 4.1-4 respectively; Indian Institute of Research in Numismatic Studies (now Indian Numismatic, Historical and Cultural Research Foundation), Anjaneri/Mumbai for III* (*ND* 20: 25-32), XI* (*ND* 38: 1-35), XVI* (*ND* 39: 1-26), XVII (*ND* 32-33: 7-18), XX (*ND* 36-37: 45-54), XXII* (*ND* 27-28: 39-42) and XXV* (incorporating material from *ND* 40: 78-85, 42: 79-84; *The Journal of Academy of Indian Numismatics & Sigillography*, Indore, XXXII: 91-94 and from *History Today* 21: 122-25); NSI/*JNSI* for XV* (*Studies in Indian Numismatics*: 109-35), XIII (*JNSI* LXXIV: 145-50), XIX (*JNSI* LXII: 16-18), XXVII (*JNSI* LXX: 60-64), XXVIII (*JNSI* LXXII: 94-97); *Prāgdhārā* (25: 87-88) for XIV; Indian History and Culture Society for XXIX* & XXXI* (*History Today* 20: 135-36 & 18:144-45 respectively) and XXX [*Spink Numismatic Circular*, CI (5), June 1993, p. 154]. Since new material trickles every now and then and research is a continuous process, many of the articles published earlier have been revised in the light of new and recent data. I therefore hope that the contents will be useful not only to the growing numbers of coin-collectors and dealers of numismatic items but also to the students and savants of Indology and its various branches.

The credit for bringing out the volume in its present form goes to Shri Vikas Arya and his experienced team of ABI. However, for the omissions and commissions if any, I owe the responsibility and beg to be excused.

Devendra Handa

Contents

Transliteration Table

अ A, a	आ Ā, ā	इ I, i	ई Ī, ī	उ U, u
ऊ Ū, ū	ऋ Ṛi, ṛi	ऌ Ḷ, ḷ	ए E, e	ऐ Ai, ai
ओ O, o	औ Au, au	अं Aṃ, aṃ	अः Aḥ, aḥ	
क् K, k	ख् Kh, kh	ग् G, g	घ् Gh, gh	ङ् Ṅ, ṅ
च् Ch, ch	छ् Chh, chh	ज् J, j	झ् Jh, jh	ञ् Ñ, ñ
ट् Ṭ, ṭ	ठ् Ṭh, ṭh	ड् Ḍ, ḍ	ढ् Ḍh, ḍh	ण् Ṇ, ṇ
त् T, t	थ् Th, th	द् D, d	ध् Dh, dh	न् N, n
प् P, p	फ् Ph, ph	ब् B, b	भ् Bh, bh	म् M, m
य् Y, y	र् R, r	ल् L, l	व् V, v	श् Ś, ś
ष् Sh, sh	स् S, s	ह् H, h	क्ष् Ksh, ksh	त्र् Tr, tr
ज्ञ् Jñ, jñ	Jihvāmūlīya x	Upadhamānīya ≍	Avagraha ('), ऽ	

Common words and modern names are usually written without diacriticals.
In the original titles and quotations, Ṛ/ṛ, C/c and Ṣ/ṣ have also been used for ऋ, च्, ष्, etc.

Abbreviations

AA	*Arts Asiatique*
ABORI	*Annals of the Bhandarkar Oriental Research Institute*
Æ/AE	Copper/Copper alloy
AIN	*Ancient Indian Numismatics* by S.K. Chakrabortty
AMH	*Ancient Mints of Haryana* by Swami Omanand Saraswati
ASH	*Ancient Seals of Haryana* by Swami Omanand Saraswati
AR	Silver
ASI	Archaeological Survey of India
BCE	Before Common Era
BDCRI	*Bulletin of the Deccan College Research Institute*
BM	British Museum
BMCAI	*British Museum Catalogue of Coins of Ancient India* by John Allan
BSOAS	*Bulletin of the School of Oriental and African Studies*
C/c	*C/circa*
CAI	*Coins of Ancient India* by Cunningham
CAGI	*Ancient Geography of India by Cunningham*
CASR	*Cunningham's Archaeological Survey Report*
CE	Common Era
CII	*Corpus Inscriptionum Indicarum*
DHI	*Development of Hindu Iconography* by J.N. Banerjea
g	gram
GH	Gupta and Hardaker
gr	grains
IAR	*Indian Archaeology - A Review*
ICSNL	*Indian Coin Society Newsletter*
IHQ	*Indian Historical Quarterly*

IIRNS	Indian Institute of Research in Numismatic Studies, Anjaneri (Nashik)
IMC	*Indian Museum Catalogue* by V.A. Smith
INC	*Indian Numismatic Circular*
INS	*Indian Numismatic Studies*
ISNI	*Indigenous States of Northern India* by Bela Lahiri
JA	*Journal Asiatique*
JASB	*Journal of the Asiatic Society of Bengal*
JBORS	*Journal of the Bihar and Orissa Research Society*
JAINS	*Journal of the Academy of Numismatics and Sigillography*, Indore
JNSI	*Journal of the Numismatic Society of India*
JISOA	*Journal of the Indian Society of Oriental Art*
JONS	*Journal of the Oriental Numismatic Society*
JPRJ	*Jñāna-Pravāha Research Journal*
JRAS	*Journal of the Royal Asiatic Society*
JRASB	*Journal of the Royal Asiatic Society of Bengal*
JUPHS	*Journal of the United Provinces Historical Society*
Mbh.	*Mahābhārata*
ND	*Numismatic Digest*
NHHP	*Numismatic History of Himachal Pradesh* by P.L. Gupta
NL	*Newsletter*
NS	*Numismatic Supplement*
NSI	Numismatic Society of India
ONS	Oriental Numismatic Society
Rām.	*Rāmāyaṇa*
SAIS	*Studies in Ancient Indian Seals* by K.K. Thaplyal
SPTCAI	*Seminar Papers on the Tribal Coins of Ancient India*
TCAI	*Tribal Coins of Ancient India* by Devendra Handa
THAI	*Tribal History of Ancient India – A Numismatic Approach* by K.K. Dasgupta
ZDMG	*Zeitschrift der Deutschen Morgenländischen Gesellschaft*

List of Illustrations

I

Identification of the Crested Figure of Punch-marked and Ujjain Coins

An important innovation of the second urbanization in India which took place sometime about the middle of the first millennium BCE was the evolution of coinage, the earliest examples of which show certain naturalistic, geometrical, floral, faunal and very rarely anthropomorphic marks punched on them. The earliest of these silver punch-marked coins were probably issued by the *Soḷasa* (sixteen) *Mahājanapadas* 'great states/tribes' of Buddha's time, and also probably by some lesser important *Janapadas*. A silver punch-marked coin of the Aurihar hoard weighing approximately 3.24 g depicting Sun figure (Fig. 1a, …) and bearing three other symbols first noticed by Dr. P.L. Gupta[1] and later illustrated by Dilip Rajgor[2] and Paul Murphy[3] was dated to 525 – 465 BCE. Rajgor also published silver coins of 8-*rattis* (*Pāda-kārshāpaṇas*) from Saurashtra bearing figures of Lakshmī/Gaja-Lakshmī (Fig. 1.a-f) over struck on cut down Imperial *kārshāpaṇas* of thin flans of Series III and IV (discussed below) datable to 5th – 4th century BCE.[4] Michael Mitchiner[5] and Van't Haaff[6] too came across such coins and dated them likewise. Shinji Hirano, however, doubts such an early date for the emergence of these iconic forms.[7] Terry Hardaker[8] described and analyzed all the early coins belonging to the *Janapada* series of India north of the Deccan, including the coins mentioned above as also coins from the Bijnor Series showing elephant with rider (Fig. 1.g-i), known from Shamiwala hoard in district Bijnor of Uttar Pradesh which had been published earlier by Durga Prasad.[9] Hardaker has dated them to the period after the decline of the Mauryas.[10]

A coin from Bijnor Series bearing a Śivaliṅga like symbol (…) was put under the 'Uncertain' coins by Hardaker[11] but Sharad Sharma and Shinji Hirano have recently published a hoard of 29 coins from Loni in district Ghaziabad of Uttar Pradesh which contains 24 coins of this type weighing between 1.52 and 1.98 g as well as 5 of another type weighing between 0.29 to 0.40 g showing a crudely executed human

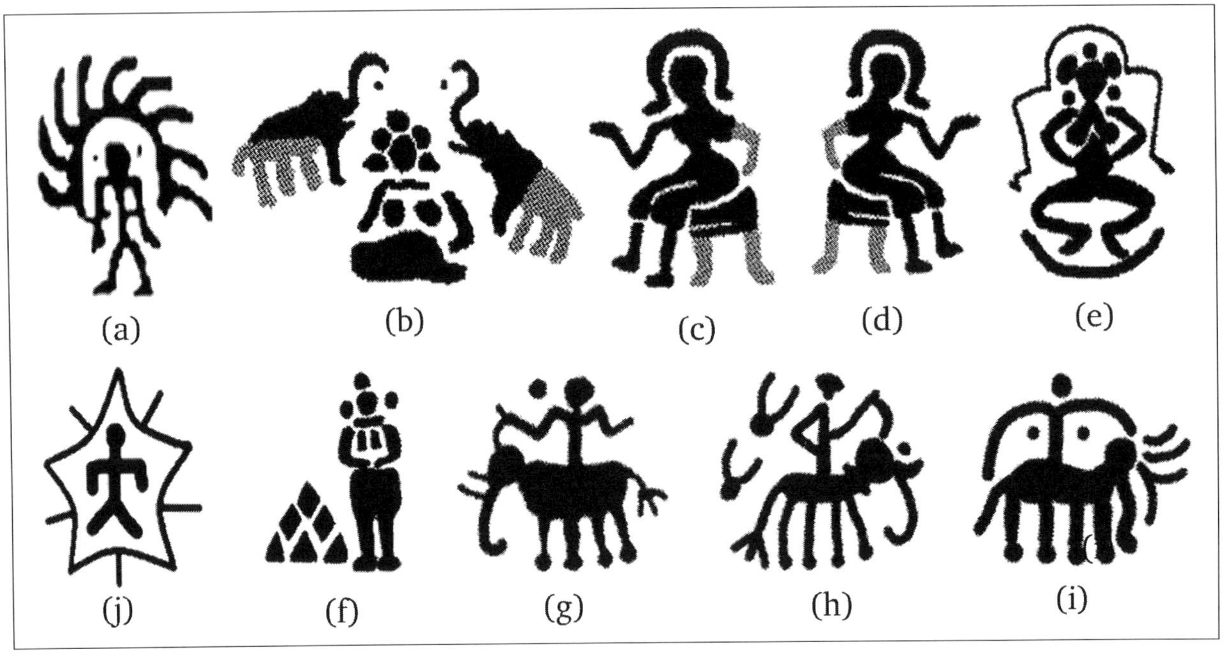

Fig. 1. Punch-marked coins of Saurashtra and Bijnor Series.

figure (Fig. 1j 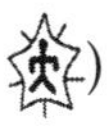) and date this hoard to the first half of the fourth century BCE.[12] It must, however, be admitted that this human figure is not properly identifiable. The crude linear figures of the elephant-riders of Shamiwala hoard (Fig. 1.g-i) too remain unidentified.

Earlier, Gupta and Hardaker had classified the Magadha-Maurya silver punch-marked coins which bear varied symbols including sun, six-armed marks, arches, animals (bull, elephant, dog, deer, lion, camel, horse/donkey, etc.), birds, aquatic beings, beetles, insects, squares, wheels, etc. into nine series (Series 0-VIII): Series 0 is associated with Bimbisāra or the period of the *Mahājanapada* states; I/II-IV with the Nandas; Va and VIa with Chandragupta Maurya's accession; Vb, VIb and VII with Aśoka's accession and VIII with post-Mauryan states. Coins of Series 0 bear one to four marks and belong to non-*kārshāpaṇa* series while Series I-VII, sometimes called Imperial Series, bear five symbols and a weight standard of 32 *rattīs* (approximately 3.6 g) and are known as *kārshāpaṇas* as alluded to above. Coins of Series VIII are mostly of base metal and belong to the local political units following the fall of the Mauryan Empire.[13]

Early Indian art being basically symbolic in nature, the earliest of these series show only symbols and the portraiture of anthropomorphic figures is very rare. Of a total of 625 odd varieties of these punch-marked coins, human figures punched on them are as follow (Fig. 2).

Gupta and Hardaker hold that all these figures "are intended to represent deities rather than living individuals." They opined that symbol numbers 264 and 362 may be Vishṇu or Kṛishṇa, 142 may be Kārttikeya or Śiva, and 266, showing a female with a small child, may be mother goddess.[14]

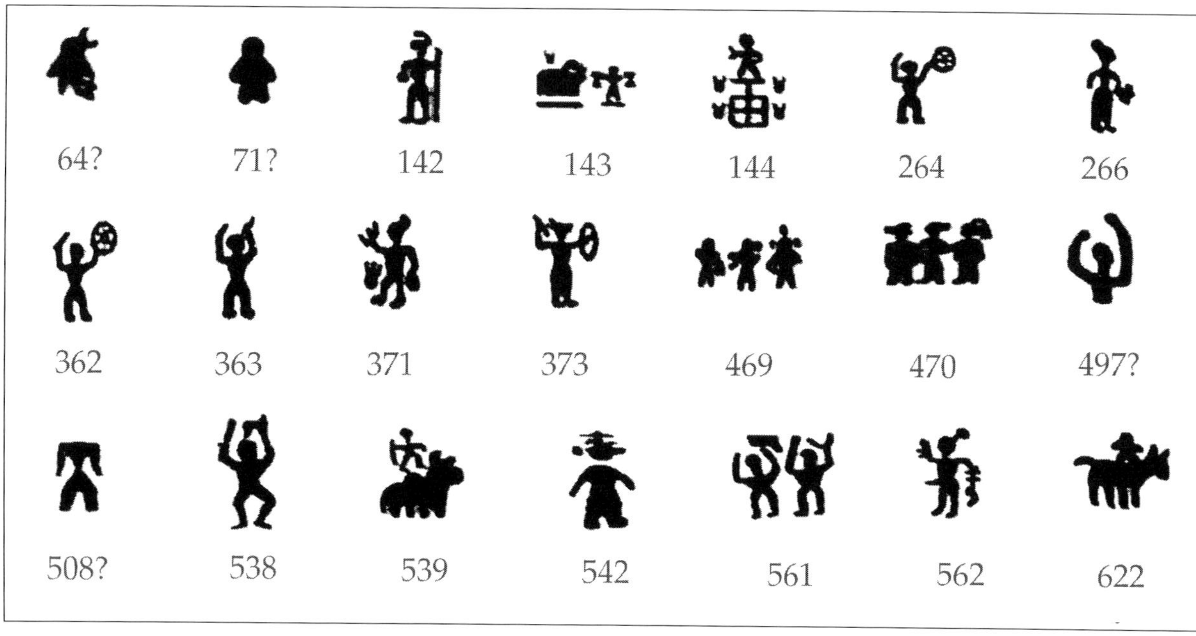

Fig. 2. Anthropomorphic figures on punch-marked coins.

It may be mentioned here that symbol 142 (Fig. 3) occurs for the first time on Type 566 of Series VIb associated with the accession of Aśoka indicating that the deity was depicted in human form for the first time sometime during the reign of Aśoka. It is also found on the base metal/brass punch-marked coins of Malwa region (Fig. 4.e-f) which issued abundant copper coinage based on Type 566 in the post-Mauryan period (GH Types 613-15).

The crested figure is generally seen turned slightly to his right but specimens showing him turned to his left also exist though rare. *Daṇḍa* 'staff' and *kamaṇḍalu* 'water-pot' in his right and left hands sometimes swap their sides. Bewildering number of varieties of Malwa or Ujjain copper coins which continue to betray Mauryan legacy show numerous variations in the depiction of the crested, mono-cephalous and tri-cephalous god. Ujjain coins representing the god with matted locks whether mono-cephalous or tri-cephalous, however, always show him as holding the staff in his right hand and water vessel in the left hand. The different types of matted locks; tight-fitting hemmed upper garment; the size, angle and position of attributes in his hands are indicative of the large number of dies used for striking these coins and the huge corpus produced over a long period of time.[15]

Allan[16] associated the helmeted or crested figure found on punch-marked and Ujjain coins with mono-cephalous and tri-cephalous figures bearing top-knots and holding a staff and water pot (Fig. 4.a-g), Wakankar[17] found sixteen variations of these coins (Fig. 4.1-16), Sethi[18] recognized numerous others, some with an animal (Fig. 4.i-xvi & xviii-xix), and Kothari[19] noted some new variations also on Ujjain coins (Fig. 4.xx-xxxiii).

Cunningham suggested that the three-headed standing figure (Fig. 4.d) "is probably intended for the Brahmanical god *Mahākāla*, who had a famous temple at

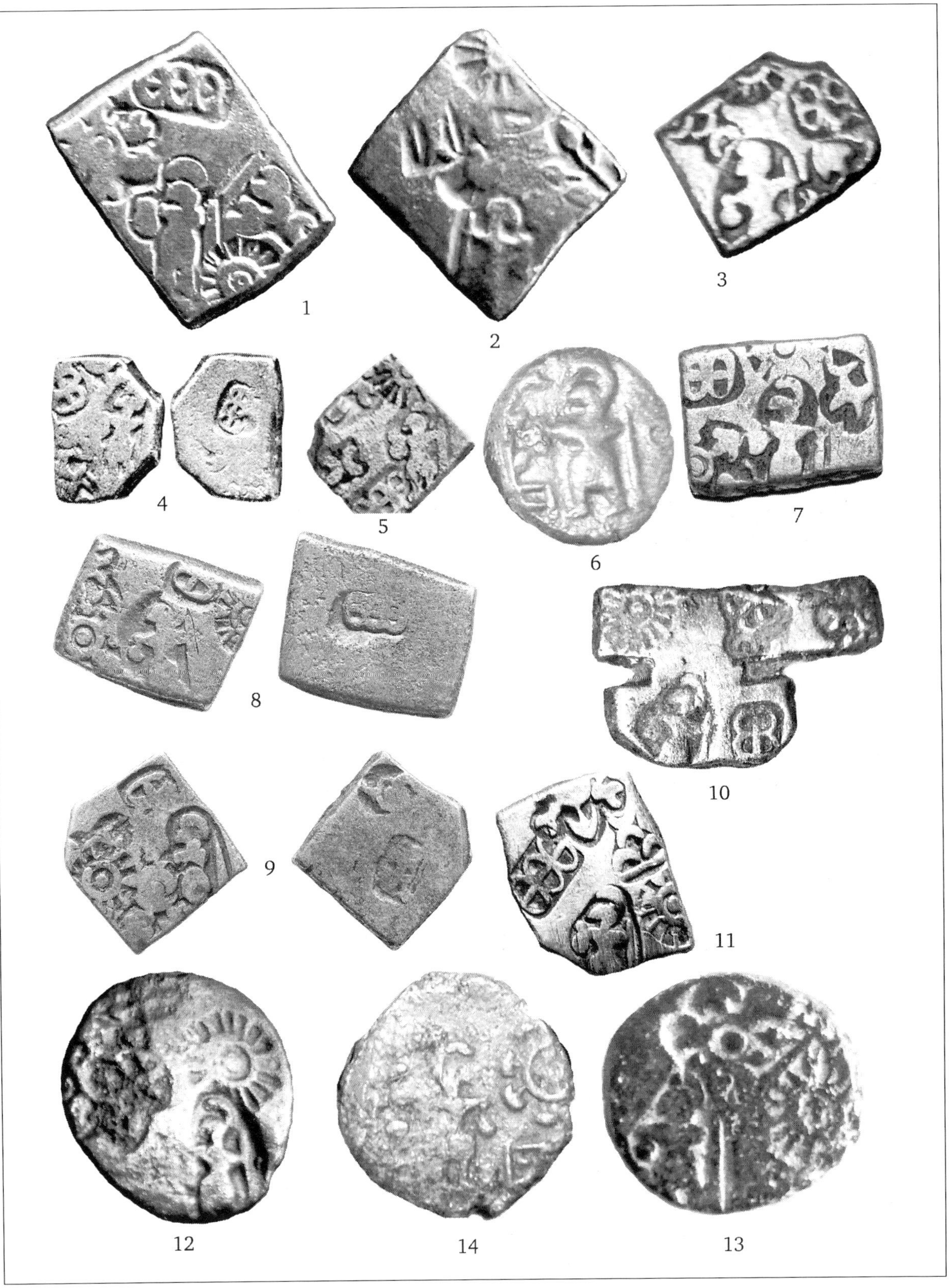

Fig. 3. Crested figures.

Ujain". He found that "The figure on the coins seems to carry a club in one hand, and a water vessel in the other, both of which symbols are characteristic of Śiva".[20] Allan, however, differed and identified all the seven forms of human figures (Fig. 4.a-g) as Kārttikeya since he holds a spear. About the three-headed figure he stated that "the other three heads are behind and naturally not represented because they cannot be seen, so that he is six-headed – which identifies him as Kārttikeya" but also observed that "The possibility that he is Śiva, whose plurality of heads would be indicated in the same way, must not be overlooked; the absence of the trident or other symbol of Śiva, and the fact that he has only two arms – although this need not be stressed – is against this. The importance of the cult of Śiva Mahākāla at Ujjayinī is well known; it is of course not impossible that, as on the coins of the Yaudheyas, both deities are represented".[21] Sethi[22] also thought that the deity depicted is four-headed Śiva Mahākāla, the fourth head being at the back and hence not visible.

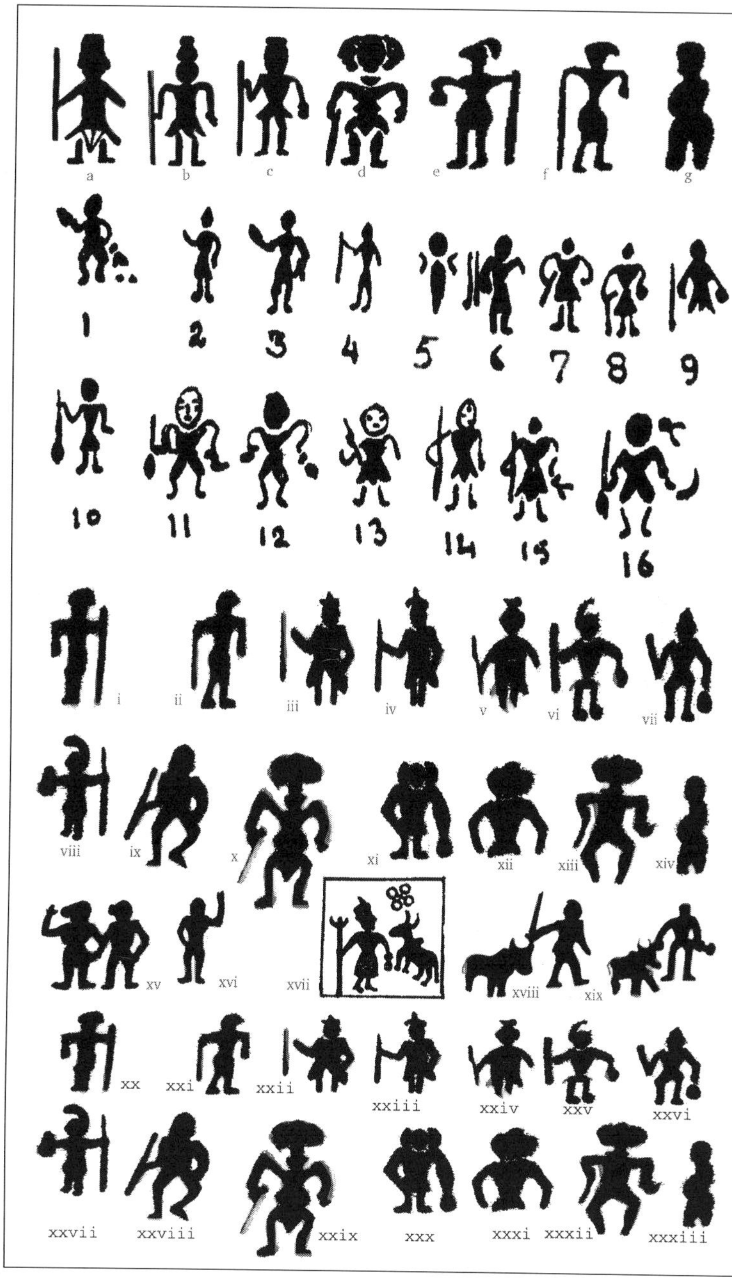

Fig. 4. Crested and other figures on punch-marked and Ujjain coins.

Referring to the phallic emblem of Śiva on an Ujjayinī coin (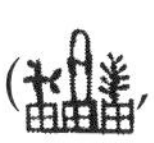, actually 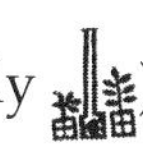) and the mono-cephalous and tri-cephalous figures cited above, Banerjea[23] took the helmeted figure also as that of Śiva for it too carries the same attributes of *daṇḍa* and *kamaṇḍalu*. He observed that "Śiva appears for the first time in an anthropomorphic form on the coins hailing from Ujjayinī and its environs. . . . Any doubt whatsoever is set at rest by the testimony of another variety of the same series of coins which shows a bull slightly prancing up and looking at the deity (cf. the *Matsyapurāṇa* passage which enjoins that Viśākha,

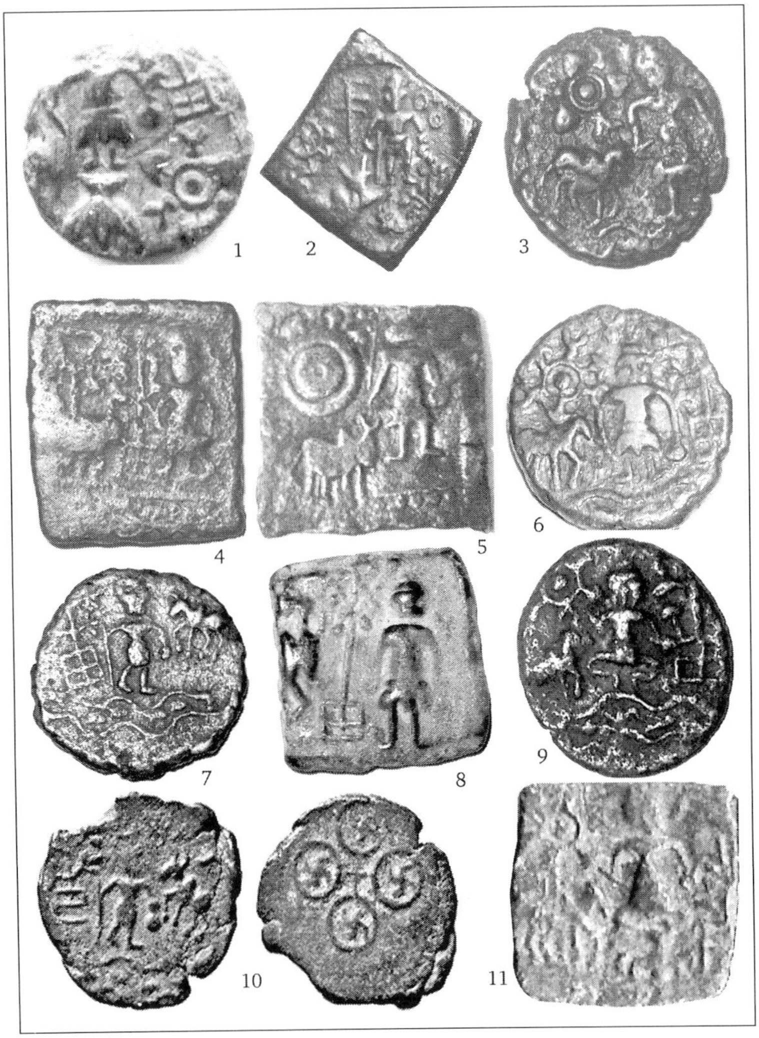

Fig. 5. Śiva standing on a lotus seat (1) and with Nandī (2-11).

the mount of Śiva, should be in the attitude of looking at the god, *devavīkṣaṇatatparaḥ*" (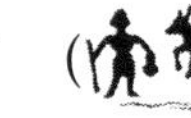). Numerous coins show the bull (Nandī) with the god who invariably holds the staff in his right hand and water vessel in the left (Fig. 5). In one case he is depicted as standing on an inverted lotus seat betraying divinity (Fig. 5.1). Bull as the vehicle of Śiva is well known in Indian iconography. Following Banerjea other scholars like Mahalingam[24] Shastri[25] and many others[26] also identify these figures as Śiva.

Altekar and Diskalkar observed that the deity standing beside a trident 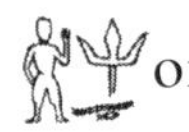on a diminutive cast coin weighing only 8 grains from Kasarwad hoard of 130 Ujjain coins obtained in the excavations conducted in 1939-40 represented Mahākāla.[27] Shastri regarded this as the sure proof of the identity of the figure with Śiva.[28] Some coins from Ujjain too show the trident in the hand of the god or trident-battleaxe as a motif and the god with bull which should be regarded as the definite evidence of the depiction of Mahākāla Śiva (Fig. 6.1-3).

However, Bhaskar Chattopadhyay[29] has observed that, "The hypothesis put forward by Dr. Banerjea with regard to the identification of the deity on Ujjainī series is no doubt strengthened by the occurrence of the bull on certain variety of the Ujjainī series" but he cautions that "we may not also overlook the absence of the trident or other symbols of Śiva".

It may also be pointed out that many of the Ujjain coins no doubt show the bull as the vehicle of the deity in anthropomorphic form but there are specimens in which the human figure is depicted as holding the bull by its horn (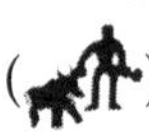), or driving away the animal (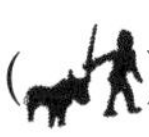)[30] or showing him standing by the side of two animals (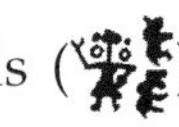)[31]

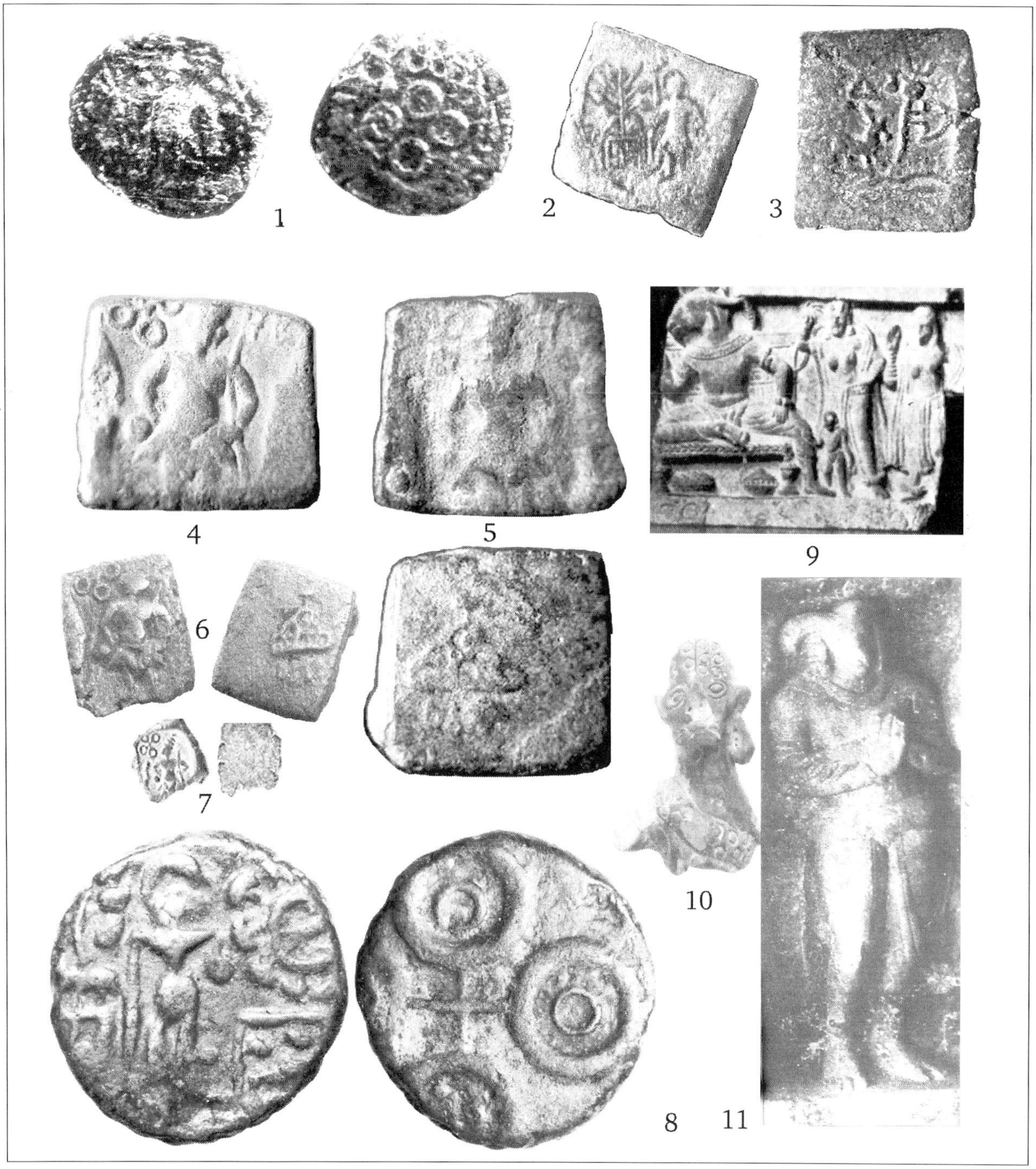

Fig. 6. Coins showing Śiva holding trident (1-3), Brahmā (4-7), goat-headed crested figure (8), stone and terracotta images of goat-headed Naigamesha.

which would hardly justify the identification of the human figure with Śiva. The animal here may be cow/s grazed and driven home by the cowherd (Gopāla, Kṛishṇa?).[32] There are some Ujjain coins which show the human figure holding staff and *kamaṇḍalu* but accompanied by an ass or horse instead of the bull (), sometimes even with a crested figure (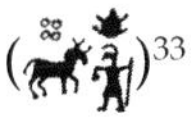)[33] and it will be difficult to accept the figure as that of Śiva.

Sethi[34] feels that the helmeted figure "may be a representation of Ganga issuing from the head of Shiva". Allan had referred to the object in the other hand as bag-like object, bag (?) and pouch which can better be identified as *kamaṇḍalu* or water vessel. Sethi identifies the round object in the hand of some of the figures as begging bowl or human head (*kapāla*) though *kamaṇḍalu* seems to be the right option.

These coins thus indicate that though the deity holding staff and water-pot in his two hands and sometimes depicted with a bull as depicted on the Ujjain coins is generally regarded as Śiva, some difference of opinion exists regarding the position of the attributes in his two hands, the vehicle and even the identification of the deity. Pieper has observed that "For the numismatic depiction it is important to observe that the rule that Śiva is holding the stick in his right and *kamaṇḍalu* in his left appears to be quite strictly followed but when it comes to the deity with crested hairstyle the *kamaṇḍalu* changes sides and it is now being placed in the right hand of that deity. This fact alone could already be taken as one argument for the identity of the deity with crested hairstyle to be different from Śiva. . . ."[35] Some coins in the collection of Girish Sharma, Pieper and Daulal Johri show a similar deity but with the two attributes swapped in the right and left hands (i.e., water-pot in right hand and staff in left hand), some bearing the label inscription in early Brāhmī characters of *circa* second century BCE reading 'Bramhā' (Fig. 5.4-7)[36], thus portraying Brahmā instead of Śiva. There are some coins where we see a similar figure without any legend, but the stance of the figure, the attributes in the two hands and associated symbols leave little doubt to the figure being that of Brahmā. Revising his earlier view of identifying the crested figures as Śiva, Pieper too has postulated that the *daṇḍa* and *kamaṇḍalu* in the right and left hands of the crested figures swap their places in the *kārshāpaṇas* as well as in Ujjain coins where the god is shown with matted locks and that there are some examples where the deity is shown in association with an ass/horse (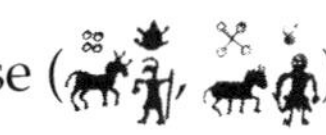). He takes the horse as symbolizing Hayagrīva who helped Brahmā get back the Vedas. So he feels inclined to identify all these figures as Brahmā.[37] The arbitrariness of regarding the ass-like animal as horse and to regard it as symbolizing Hayagrīva is purely imaginary as during the period of these coins Brahmā was losing his importance and the cults of Śiva and Vishṇu were gaining ascendancy and becoming more popular. Ass/horse facing the crested figure holding water pot in his right hand and staff in the left when compared with mono-cephalous god with matted hairstyle holding staff in the right and water pot in his left hand as illustrated above also renders this possibility as doubtful. I feel that it was the curved staff which distinguished the deity and not the swapping of the attributes which was important as Kothari has published a coin which shows similar curved staff in the right hand of the god and *kamaṇḍalu* in the hanging left hand (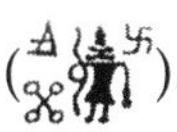).[38] Though the legend is missing the god depicted seems to be Brahmā as indicated by subsidiary symbols also.

Definitely Kārttikeya too has been depicted on Ujjain coins. It is interesting to note that Altekar and Diskalkar have also described the human figure appearing on the obverse of Class I, Var. F of the Kasarwad hoard of Ujjain coins as Kārttikeya holding *śakti* 'lance'.[39] We thus see that both Śiva and Kārttikeya have been shown on Ujjain coins and to generalize that the figures holding staff and water-pot exclusively represent Śiva or Kārttikeya will be a mistaken conclusion. There is thus no doubt that various deities have been depicted on Ujjain coins.[40]

The Ujjayinī coins published by Kothari show a variety of such figures: 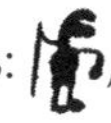, 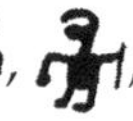, 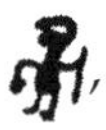, , . A goat-like face and helmet or horn-like flourish on the head characterize all these figures. So they have to be distinguished from the simple headed figures. The crest or horn is sometimes shown backwards as on the head of a goat and more commonly turning forward as seen on the head of a ram. A coin documented in trade actually shows the animal face with crested hairstyle (Fig. 5.8) removing all doubts to this figure being animal or ram-headed. A parallel to this may be found in the representation of Naigamesha (Fig. 5.9) in a Mathura sculpture[41] and numerous terracotta figurines of early historic centuries found from different sites of the country (Fig. 5.10). Naigamesha is a counterpart of Kārttikeya. The Rameshwar Cave 21 at Ellora also contains a figure of the acolyte of Kārttikeya as bearing a goat or ram-head with horns standing with folded hands (Fig. 5.11).[42] I would therefore identify this horned figure generally referred to as crested or helmeted figure as that of Naigamesha, the Jaina version of Kārttikeya as I had suggested it in 2008-2009.[43]

NOTES AND REFERENCES

1. This coin was originally assigned to Series I of Magadha Imperial coins by P.L. Gupta to Type XX in his thesis [Gupta, P.L. (1959), *Punchmarked Coins of Ancient India*, Unpublished Ph.D. Thesis submitted to the Banares Hindu University].
2. Rajgor, Dilip (1996), 'History and Coinage of Saurashtra Janapada (c. 400-350 BCE)', *Journal of the Oriental Institute*, Baroda, Vol. 45 (3-4), pp. 195-214; (2001), *The Punch-marked Coins of Early Historic India*, California: Reesha Books International, p. 209, symbol no. 621.
3. Murphy Paul (2001), *Kosala State Region, c. 600-470 BCE: Silver Punchmarked Coinage*, Nasik: IIRNS Publications, Type IIId-3.
4. Rajgor (2001), symbol nos. 622-625, pp. 68 & 155.
5. Mitchiner, Michael (2004), *Ancient Trade and Early Coinage*, Vol. 2, Hawkins Publication, nos. 1099, 4485-86.
6. Van't Haaff, P.A. (2004), *Saurashtra and Surasena Silver Punchmarked Coinage*, Nasik: IIRNS Publications, Type 20.0.1.
7. Hirano, Shinji (2007), *The Ghaghra-Gandak River Region: c. 600 – 300 BC Archaic Silver Punchmarked Coinage*, Anjaneri: IIRNS, p. 7.
8. Hardaker [Hardaker, Terry (2019), *Punchmarked Coinage of the Indian Subcontinent Non-Imperial Series North of the Deccan*, Nasik: IIRNS Publications, p. 202] thinks that "It represents an anomaly in that the human figure, which appears to be surrounded by a halo-like arc or canopy, is rendered in a style that is not seen as an official mark until the later Mauryan coinage. It is however most likely that the human figure has been punched as a bankers

mark on top of a sun symbol, because the outline of the human figure punch appears to show up as an arc round the top and as straight line along the bottom, thus defining the edges of a separate punch."

9. Prasad, Durga (1939), 'Shamiwala (Bijnor District) Hoard of Punch-marked Coins', *Journal of the Numismatic Society of India*, Vol. I, pp. 1-4.
10. Hardaker (2019), *op. cit.*, pp. 266-69.
11. *Ibid.*, p. 284, Type-UN 11.
12. Sharma, Sharad and Shinji Hirano (2018), 'Two New Local Types of Silver Punchmarked Coins From Loni', *Numismatic Digest*, Vol. 42, pp. 1-7.
13. Gupta, P.L. and T.R. Hardaker (2014), *Punchmarked Coinage of the Indian Subcontinent: Magadha-Maurya Series*, Mumbai: IIRNS Publications.
14. Gupta, P.L. and T.R. Hardaker (1985), *Ancient Indian Silver Punchmarked Coins of the Magadha-Maurya Kārshāpana Series*. Anjaneri (Nashik): IIRNS; (2014), p. 59.
15. Pieper, Wilfried (1994), "The Local Copper Currency of Ujjain in Ancient Central India (ca. 200 BC – ca. 50 BC)", *ONS Newsletter*, No. 142, pp. 6-9; (2013), *Ancient Indian Coins Revisited*, Lancaster/London: CNG, pp. 33-37.
16. Allan, John (1936), *Coins of Ancient India*, London: British Museum, pp. cxli-cxliv & 241 ff., Class 2, varieties *f* and *g*; Pl. II.1-3. Allan also classed them with their crude version (occurring on Class 1, variety *i* and Class 3, vars. *a-g*) which are also depicted on his Ujjayinī coins besides some others (Class 2, variety *a*) respectively.
17. Wakankar, V.S. (1975), 'Coins of Mitra Dynasty from Ujjain', *The Journal of the Numismatic Society of Madhya Pradesh*, Vol. II, vol. 25, Pl. II.17-20.
18. Sethi, R.R. (1985-86), 'Ring and Ball Symbol on Ujjayini Coins' in Bhatt, S.K. (Ed.). *Professor Ajay Mitra Shastri Felicitation Volume: Journal of the Academy of Indian Numismatics & Sigillography*, Vol. VI. Indore: Academy of Indian Numismatics & Sigillography, pp. 45-57, Pl. II.28-29.
19. Kothari, Narendra. 2006. *Ujjayini Coins*. Edited by Dilip Rajgor. Mumbai: Reesha Books International.
20. Cunningham, Alexander. 1891. *Coins of Ancient India*, London (reprint, Varanasi, 1963), p. 96.
21. Allan (1936), *op. cit.*, p. cxliii.
22. Sethi (1985-86), *op. cit.*, p. 50.
23. Banerjea, J.N. (1956), *Development of Hindu Iconography*, 2nd edition, Calcutta, 1956, pp. 114-17.
24. Mahalingam, T.V. 1968. 'The Bearing of the Local Coins on the Religious Conditions of Central India', in Narain, A.K (Ed.), *Seminar Papers on the Local Coins of Northern India: C. 300 B.C. To 300 A.D.* Varanasi: Department of Ancient Indian History, Culture & Archaeology, Banaras Hindu University. pp. 54-58.
25. Shastri, Ajay Mitra (1968), 'Religious Study of Symbols on the Local Coins of Central India', *Ibid.*, pp. 70-86.
26. See also Srivastava, Prashant (2012), *Encyclopedia of Indian Coins*, Vol. II, Delhi, pp. 360 ff.
27. Altekar, A.S. and D.B. Diskalkar (1946), 'Kasarwad Hoard of Ujjain Coins', *JNSI*, VIII (ii), p. 104, Pl. VI.17.
28. Shastri (1968), *op. cit.*, p. 74.
29. Chattopadhyay, Bhaskar (1977), *Coins and Icons A Study of Myths and Symbols in Indian Numismatic Art*, Calcutta: Punthi Pustak, p. 209.
30. Sethi (1985-86), p. 50.

31. Kothari (2006), p. 112, Type 65.
32. Handa, Devendra (2013), 'Divinities on Ujjain Coins', *Indian Coin Society Newsletter*, No. 51, pp. 25-27.
33. Kothari (2006), p. 100, #RB 233B and #RB 135; Pieper (1994), p. 7; (2015), 'The Earliest Śaivite Images on Ancient Indian Coins', *Numismatic Digest*, Volume 39, pp. 66-71; (2016), 'The deity with crested hairstyle and the first identification of the serpent goddess Manasā Devi on ancient Indian coins', *Ibid.*, Vol. 40, pp. 21-26.
34. Sethi (1985-86), *op. cit.*, pp. 50-51.
35. Pieper (2016), p. 22.
36. Handa, Devendra (2011-2012), 'The Earliest Representation of Brahmā: Numismatic Evidence', *Jñāna-Pravāha Research Journal* (*JPRJ*), No. XV, pp. 38-45.
37. Pieper, Wilfried (2015), pp. 66-71; (2016), pp. 21-26.
38. Kothari (2006), p. 104, RB# 268.
39. Altekar and Diskalkar (1946), *op. cit.*, p. 102.
40. Handa (2013), *op. cit.*, pp. 1-58.
41. Tiwari, M.N.P. 1981. *Jaina Pratimā-vijñāna* (Hindi). Varanasi: Pārśvanātha Vidyāśrama Śodha-Saṃsthāna, p. 34, Fig. 39.
42. Berkson, Carmel. 2000. *The Life of Forms in Indian Sculpture*. New Delhi: Abhinav Publications, p. 153, Ill. 148.
43. Handa, Devendra (2008-2009), 'Numismatic Imagery and Beyond: Some Observations', *JPRJ*, Volume XII, p. 61.

II

Vaṭāśvaka Coins

The round copper coins bearing the Brāhmī legend *Vaṭasvaka* on left written perpendicularly from bottom upwards in characters of the early second century BCE were found from Taxila along with some other coins of Taxila.[1] The uniface coins show a human figure to left with hands folded in worship (*añjali-mudrā*) towards a crescented three-arched hill or *chaitya* symbol below which is a pile of six balls (mentioned as bales by Cunningham[2]) in three tiers (of three, two and one ball respectively). Under the female figure is a horizontally placed taurine with arms opening to right. Allan[3] listed six coins of this type (Fig. 7.1-6). Two more coins, one procured by Shri Girish Sharma of Indore (Fig. 7.7) and the other by Shri Jeevandeep Singh of Ludhiana (Fig. 7.8), have surfaced in the recent years.[4]

Allan described the three-arched *chaitya* with crescent ( ) as a mountain and takes the human figure as female, not as a worshipper but as a city goddess. Bühler took the inscription *Vaṭasvaka* in Prakrit as equivalent of the nominative plural of Sanskrit *Vaṭāśvakāḥ*, the Vaṭāśvakas or 'Aśvakas of the Vaṭa (fig-tree) division'.[5] But Allan has observed that "As the language of the Shāhbāzgaṛhī Edicts[6] shows, Vaṭasvaka could be a nominative plural in the Prākrit of the north-west, but the objection to Bühler's interpretation is that we should expect a genitive plural in a coin-legend. It is therefore better to take Vaṭāśvaka as a singular and as a place-name, which preserves the memory of the Aśvakas, the Assakenoi of the Greeks (Arrian, *Anabasis*, IV, 27)". Regarding its location, Allan points out that "If not in the territory of Taxila, it was near enough to be in close commercial relations with it".[7]

The Aśvakas[8] were a people who lived in the region of north-eastern Afghanistan and the Peshawar valley. The area occupied by them was also known as Aśvaka.[9] The name Aśvaka may be derived from the Sanskrit word 'aśva' meaning horse. The

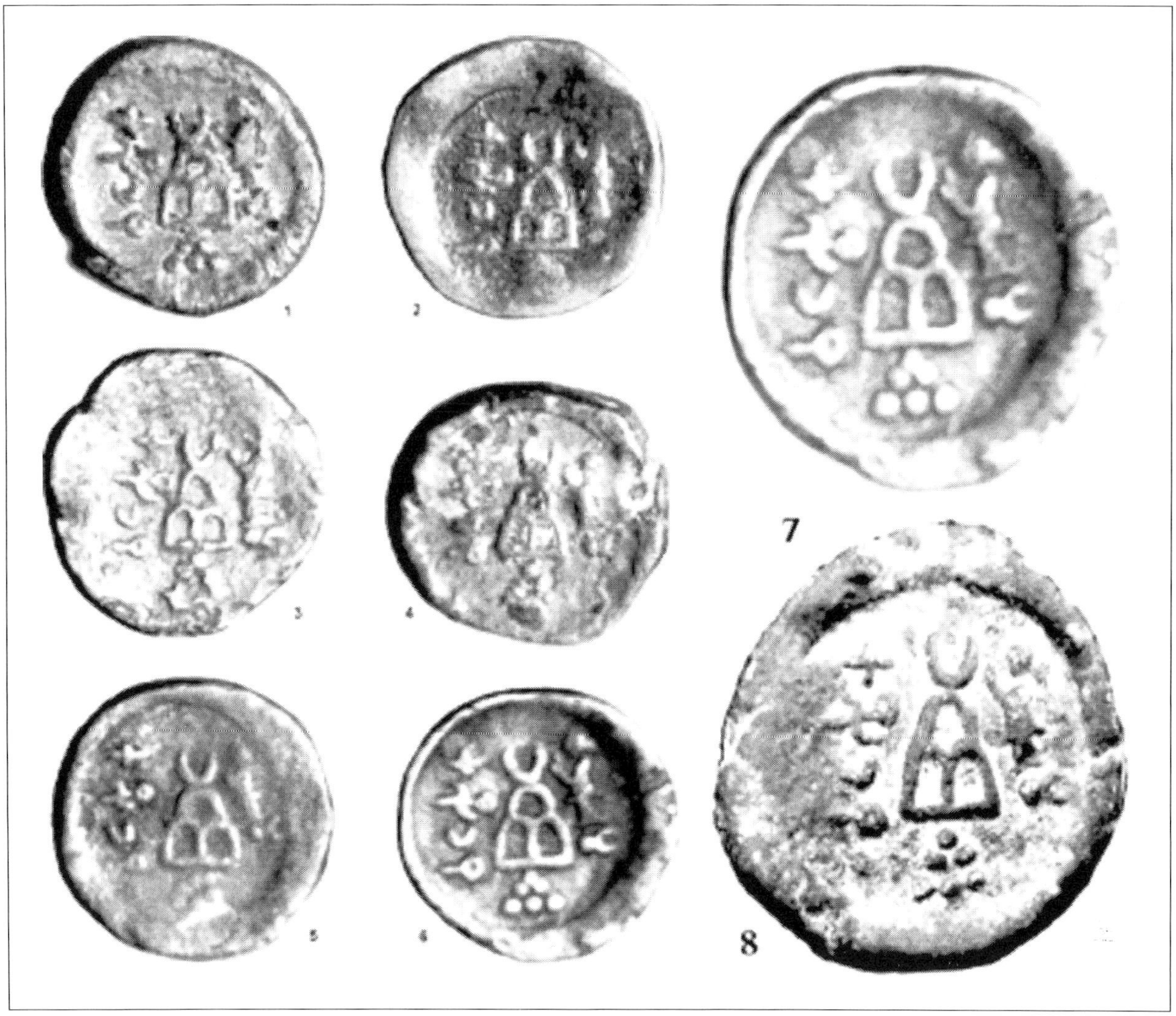

Fig. 7. Vaṭāśvaka coins.

Aśvakas may have been horsemen, or cavalrymen, horse-breeders or trainers.[10] S.K. Chakrabortty[11] felt that Allan rightly took Aśvakas to be the Assakenoi of Arrian, the people who dwelt in the Swat valley and were the first Indian people to fight bravely against Alexander, with 2000 cavalry, 30 elephants and 30,000 infantry with their womenfolk also taking up arms preferring "a glorious death to a life of dishonor."[12] Pāṇini has also referred to the Āśvakāyanas who lived in the Swat valley and highlands, with their capital at Maskavati.[13]

Chakrabortty did not accept Bühler's interpretation of Vaṭa being a fig-tree clan of the Aśvakas and pointed out that Vaṭa also means a cowry shell and might mean a 'coin'. So he interpreted the legend *Vaṭasvaka* as *Vaṭāśvakaḥ* (*Aśvakānāṃ Vaṭaḥ*, according to Pāṇini II.2, 31), 'the coin of the Aśvakas'.[14] K.K. Dasgupta has pointed out that "we have no instance in early Indian numismatics where the issuers are found to have put the name of a coin-denomination on their issue" and feels inclined to accept Bühler's interpretation.[15] It may, however, be noted that the names of the tribes exist on the coins in genitive plural only. The tribal name may however occur in genitive singular only when compounded with the word *'gaṇa'* or *'janapada'*. Here the tribal name Aśvaka is not suffixed by *'gaṇa'* or *'janapada'* and therefore the legend cannot be accepted to mean 'the coin of the Aśvaka tribe'. The names in the case of monarchical issues are given in genitive singular on coins. City issues have the legends in nominative or genitive singular. So the coins with the legend *Vaṭasvaka* have to be taken as the city issues only.

As far as the symbols are concerned some other coins from Taxila also show the use of these symbols and may be linked with the Vaṭāśvaka coins. Actually Cunningham[16] had found the following two varieties[17] also along with Vaṭāśvaka coins and coins of Pantaleon and Agathocles of Taxila fabric in one pot:

Var. *h* 

Var. *i* 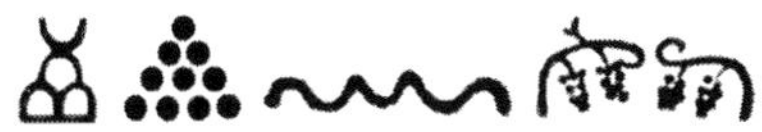

There is thus little doubt to these coins having been in circulation during the first quarter of the second century BCE, may be from earlier period. The female figure on his Var. *h*, however, is not depicted in profile in worshipping attitude as on Vaṭāśvaka coins but is shown as standing between the pile of balls and the three-arched symbol with crescent above. She is holding a flower in her right hand with left akimbo. She resembles the deity on the gold half stater of Azes of Pushkalavati mint bearing the Kharoshṭhī legend *Pukhalāvatidevatā* (and *Drupayasa*) on the reverse with the figure of a bull having the Greek legend Tauros above and *Ushabhe* in Kharoshṭhī below on the other side.[18] Pushkalāvatī (Greek Peukelaotis), has been referred to as Peukelas by Arrian who mentions it as a very large and populous city and the capital of king Astes, perhaps Hasti. A large stupa was erected here by Aśoka.[19] A coin-type of Eukratides shows 'Zeus sitting on throne to front holding wreath and palm with forepart of an elephant on right and a pilos on left having an indistinct monogram above, bearing the Kharoshṭhī legend *Kavi(/pi) śiya nagara-devatā*.[20]

Kapiśā is the Kipin of the Chinese travelers and Kapiśī of Pāṇini (IV.2, 99). According to Lassen, Kapisa is the valley of the Ghorbund river.[21] Sten Konow identified it with modern Begram, about 80 km north of Kabul on the basis of a Kharoshṭhī inscription found there naming the city.[22] According to Pliny Kapiśī was destroyed by the Achaemenian emperor Cyrus in the sixth century BCE. It was well known in Pāṇini's time for its wine known as *Kāpiśāyana* which was widely exported. Kauṭilya's *Arthaśāstra* too refers to *Kāpiśāyana* which was prepared from green grapes as distinguished from *hārahūraka* prepared from black grapes in the Kandhar region. Excavation at Begram has yielded numerous glass flasks, fish-shaped wine jars and drinking cups which were used in wine trade.[23] The grape vines on Var. *i* seem to represent the abundant production of grapes for which the Chaman Huzuri area of Afghanistan is well known. Even Pāṇini mentioned Āśvakāyana about the middle of the first millennium BCE as the region must have been famous for its production of grapes at that early time. The undulating line represents the Ghorbund River. Xuanzang also visited Kapis and states that "To the south-west of the capital was the *Pi-lo-sho-lo* Mountain. This name was given to the mountain from its presiding genius who had the form of an *elephant* and was therefore called *Pi-lo-sho-lo*."[24] Dhavalikar traces the origin of Gaṇeśa as the city god of Pushkalāvatī (present-day Charsadda in Afghanistan), initially as a local deity in the Gandhāra region, then raised to the status of a demigod (Yaksha) and as a minor Śaivite divinity, ultimately developing into a cult deity when the number of his worshippers increased substantially.[25]

Allan takes the 'pile of nine balls' (actually ten balls 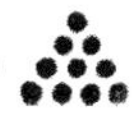 in four lines of four, three, two and one respectively) and the three-arched symbol with a crescent atop (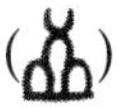) on these coins as 'two forms of mountain'.[26] The occurrence of two symbols representing one object as well as of the same symbol twice is rather an unusual and unnoticed phenomenon in numismatics. And as we have noticed above the pile of nine balls occurs below the three-arched symbol with a crescent above. If we take both the symbols as representing mountain, the depiction of a mountain above (or below) a mountain does not seem to be logical at all. I therefore take the symbol consisting of three, six or ten balls as representing the mountain, the tiers indicating the height perhaps. This mountain may be identified with Pi-lo-sho-lo or Pilusara as referred to by Xuanzang: "To the southwest of the capital (Kapisa) was the *Pi-lo-sho-lo* mountain. This name was given to the mountain from its presiding genius who had the form of an elephant and was therefore called *Pil-lo-sho-lo*."[27]

Though the origin of this symbol has been traced back to the trefoil decorations on the shawl of the bearded figure of the priest-king found from Mohenjodaro and similar designs on beads and other antiquities found from Mohenjodaro, Harappa and other sites[28] yet the great gap between the Indus civilization and the early historic period pushes this possibility in the background.

Cunningham regarded the three-arched symbol with a crescent above as a *stūpa*. Theobold[29] also took it so. Smith[30] and Spooner called it a *chaitya* probably because its shape resembled the *gavākshas* (windows) of the *chaityas* (Buddhist shrines or temples). The identification of the symbol with a *stūpa* or *chaitya* was disproved long back by Ananda Coomaraswamy who pointed out that the mountain represented by arches (Peaks) is found in Mesopotamia and throughout the ancient world as well as in later Indian and central Asian Chinese art.[31] S.K. Chakrabortty described it as a hill.[32] Allan, as noted above, also accepted it as a mountain.[33] Bhagwanlal Indraji explained the symbol as Meru with a crescent at the top.[34] In Indian mythology, Meru is the fabulous mountain of gold situated in the centre of Jambūdvīpa and is the residence of Brahmā in allusion to which the temple top is also known as Meru. Durga Prasad questioned these views and pointed out that the three arches cannot be a *stūpa* and that there is no reference of the moon with Meru in Paurāṇic mythology.[35] It may be pointed out here that some Indian Śilpa-śāstras also compare a Hindu temple with Mount Meru and establish the identity of the two. According to the *Bṛihatsaṃhitā* (LV.17 f.) and the *Matsyapurāṇa* (CCLXIX, 28 f.), Meru (the axis of the world or pole of the earth), Mandara (planted as the churning rod on Vishṇu's back in his tortoise incarnation at the time of the Samudra-manthana 'churning of the ocean' by gods and demons in search of *amṛita* 'elixir') and Kailāśa (the abode of Śiva in the Himalayas), which are all the names of the mountains, are the three names amongst the twenty types of great temples described in these early texts.[36] The *Samarāṅgaṇasūtradhāra* (LV.3) refers to Meru as the 'king of temples'. It is notable that in Cambodia (Myanmar) and Bali (Indonesia) the words 'Giri' (mountain) and Meru denote a temple.[37]

The beginning of the symbol may be traced to the early Indian coins themselves. Some early punch-marked coins of the Golakpur hoard in the Patna Museum and Aurihar hoard in the Lucknow Museum, classified by P.L. Gupta and T.R. Hardaker as belonging to Series I of the punch-marked silver *kārshāpaṇas* datable to the period of the Bṛihadratha dynasty (*circa* 500-430 BCE) contain a triangular symbol (), or three dots placed one over the two in a triangular fashion (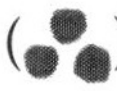), or sometimes three dots or pellets placed in three angles of the triangle () or in a flat-topped quadrilateral (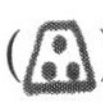) or a circle (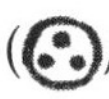, )[38] which may have been the precursors of the three-arched *chaitya* or hill symbol as referred to above. The three angles of the triangle and/or three dots in it (or even in a circle) seem to represent some triad – the Trinity of Hinduism or the *triratnas* (Three Jewels) of Buddhism (Buddha, Dhamma and Saṃgha 'community') or the three constituent properties of nature or created things (*sattva*, *rajas* and *tamas*), or some such concept.[39] The first proposition was supported by Durga Prasad who held that the symbol "represents the abode or the temples of Brahmā, Vishṇu and Śiva, the upper cell with the crescent on top indicating the abode of Śiva."[40] It, however, certainly cannot be the Hindu Trinity as the worship of Brahmā at least is not known to have been practiced at that period. The worship of the 'three jewels' recalls to our mind a rare Gandhāran aniconic representation – a pillar with three large wheels on top being worshipped by monks and others[41] – a form which is similar to the three-arches placed one upon the two. But the arched symbol actually precedes and may have inspired the Gandhāran relief and as such this representation cannot be taken as the proto-type of the arched symbol. One, however, cannot be certain about the representation of the three *guṇas* of *sattva*, *rajas* and *tamas* in the form of three dots, circlets or peaks of a triangle. But why was a crescent placed on the top as we get on the punch-marked silver *kārshāpaṇas* cannot be explained satisfactorily.

A single-die silver *dvi-māshaka* (0.6 g) coin of the Saurashtra *Janapada* Series (No. 19) dated to *c.* 450-300 BCE shows six triangular symbols placed on a base line in three tiers of three, two and one respectively and capped by a crescent (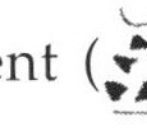).[42] Saurashtra is famous for its temple of Somanātha (Śiva). Śūrasena Mahājanapada is one of the Sixteen *Mahājanapadas* of the Buddhist chronicles. Coins of the Śūrasena *Mahājanapada* (400-350 BCE) having its capital at Mathura also issued coins before its annexation by Mahāpadma Nanda in *circa* 350 BCE showing the three-arched *chaitya* or hill with crescent before an animal (perhaps lion)  and 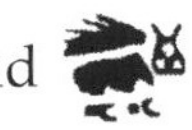 on the half

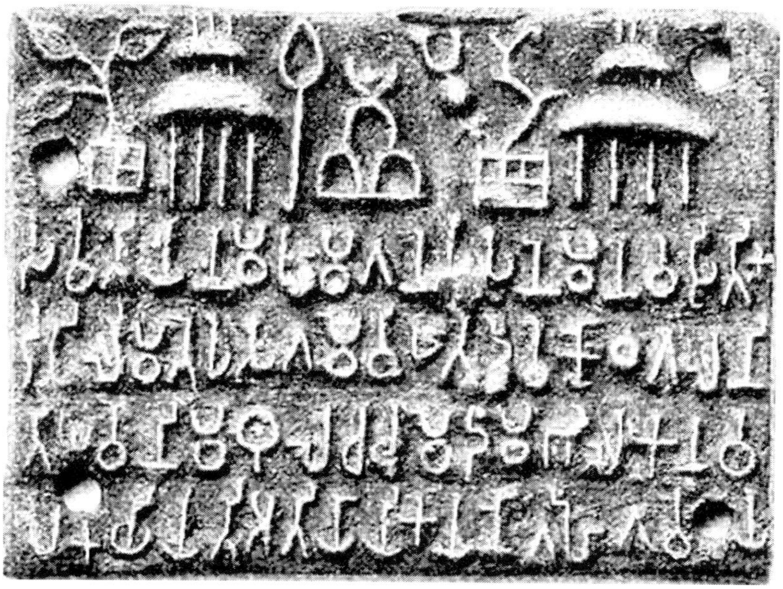

Fig. 8. Sohagaura copper plate.

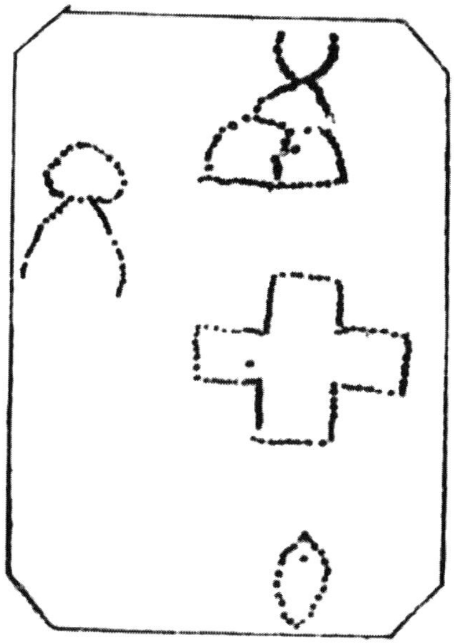

Fig. 9. Rampurva copper bolt.

kārshāpaṇa series bearing the single punch.[43] The arched symbols which appear for the first time on the silver punch-marked coins of Series IVa ascribed to the early Śiśunāga dynasty (*c.* 410-400 BCE) are , 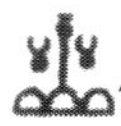, 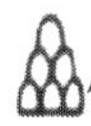, 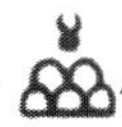, ,  and 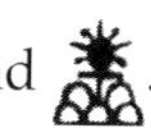.[44] The arched symbol with crescent appears for the first time in Series VIa (320-270 BCE) of the punch-marked coins. This symbol was also witnessed on the Sohagura copper plate (Fig. 8)[45], on one of the pillars of the hall of Chandragupta Maurya at Kumrahar during the excavations of Pāṭaliputra (Patna) by D.B. Spooner, on a terracotta matrix from the same place, on terracotta dishes from Bulandibagh and on the copper bolt connecting the Rampurva lion capital with the monolith (Fig. 9).[46] Thus the three-arched symbol with a crescent appears for the first time on the silver *kārshāpaṇas* of Series IVa (320 BCE onwards) during the reign of Chandragupta Maurya and continued subsequently during the rule of the Mauryas and even later.

Quite often the symbol has a wavy line below which is generally interpreted as representing river. Cunningham had observed that some of the kings also placed on their money punning allusions to their names, e.g. Sūryamitra and Bhānumitra depicted Sun, Chandragupta a crescent, king Hasti an elephant on his coins.[47] Durga Prasad suggested that Chandragupta Maurya may have adopted the three-arched symbol by adding a crescent to it.[48] We have seen above that a three-tiered hill with a crescent atop occurs on the coins of the Saurashtra Janapada Series (No. 19). So the crescent above the hill symbol had come into existence quite some time before Chandragupta Maurya and he cannot be credited to have put the crescent above the arched hill symbol. Durga Prasad regarded Kauśāmbī coins showing crescent above hill and a cross as a passport *Mudrā* of Aśoka.[49] Such coins are well known from Taxila[50] and have also been discovered from Andhra[51] and Vidarbha.[52] A coin from Taxila portraying a lion with a *svastika* on its back licking the three-arched hill with crescent on the obverse and an elephant to right with hill symbol on its back on the reverse[53] has been connected by K.P. Jayaswal with a story of Chandragupta Maurya mentioned in connection with the invasion of Alexander the Great by McCrindle which says that he was licked by a lion while asleep and that a wild elephant mounted him on its back when he got up. Jayaswal tried to identify the symbol as the royal insignia (*Rājāṅka*) of Chandragupta Maurya.[54] Elsewhere he offered another fascinating interpretation of this symbol basing his conclusion on a far fetched palaeographic explanation. He interpreted it as an abbreviation of Chandagutta (Chandragupta), the founder of the Mauryan Empire. He takes the crescent to be 'Chandra' and the remaining hill-like combination to be 'gutta' – the upper loop standing for the letter '*ga*' and the lower two for '*tta*' in Brāhmī.[55] F.R. Allchin points to the ubiquity of this symbol during the Mauryan period and regards it as a mark of far-reaching authority extending from at least Patna to Taxila and concludes that "the hill-with-crescent appears to have been the specific invention of either Chandragupta or Aśoka and has every right to be regarded as a 'hall-mark' originating in the Mauryan period".[56] The suggestion is too speculative to be relied upon. Since the three-arched hill with a crescent continues even subsequent to the Mauryas, on the coins of the tribal republics, Sātavāhanas, Western Kshatrapas, etc. it cannot be regarded as an exclusive mark of Chandragupta Maurya or Aśoka.

Banerjea had made an important observation that even when iconism had come to be accepted by the majority of the Indian people, the earlier practice of using the symbols on coins continued and 'the three-arched mountain symbol with a crescent above it may typify the aniconic representation of the same god (who) is sometimes described as *triśṛṅga paravata* . . . with the lunar crescent on his crest, *Śaśāṅkaśekhara* . . .'[57] The suggestion is fascinating as we know that in Indian mythology Mount Kailāśa, a peak of the Himalayas, is regarded as the abode of Śiva, who is also called Girīśa, the Lord of the Mountain. The lower ranges of hills between the Yamunā and the Beas are still called Shiwalak Hills (Śiva+*alaka* 'locks', i.e. hills resembling the locks of Śiva with their winding streams). Banerjea also observed that "some of the animals appearing on them may stand for theriomorphic representations of deities while others appearing on mountain symbols, three-, five- or six-arched ones, may also have some cult significance".[58] The suggestion, however, like most of the views discussed above, is based on the hypothesis that the arched-hill symbol represents the mountain for which no definite or corroborative evidence has been adduced by any of the scholars so far.

While studying the Yaudheya coins I have come across very interesting data and a clue to the understanding of the arched symbol. It is well-known now that Yaudheya coins of Shaḍānana-Deer type show a temple before or above the deer on the reverse.[59] In some varieties of these coins the deer faces an arched symbol indicating clearly that the arched symbol is the alternative depiction of the temple. In some examples this symbol is depicted at the back of the deer indicating the return of the deer (representing perhaps the ruling authority - the *Saṃgha* or the *Gaṇa*) after paying obeisance to the Lord. If the symbolic representation is earlier than the depiction of

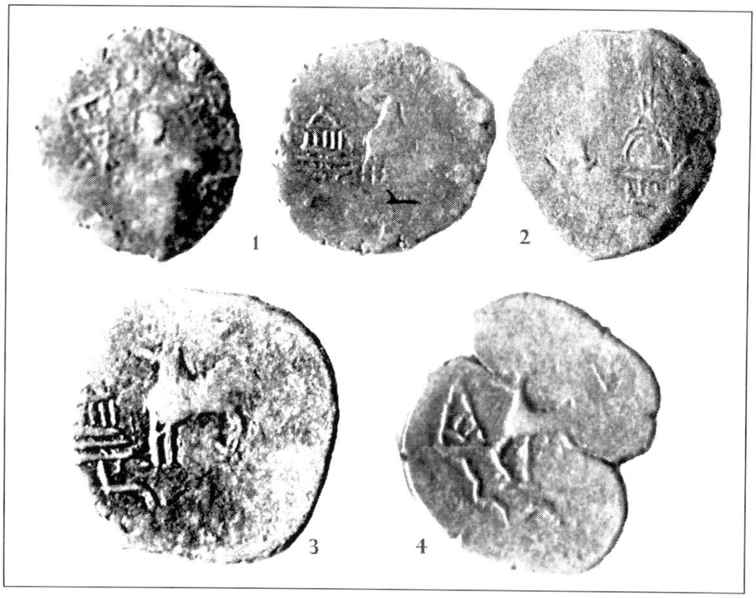

Fig. 10. Temples/arched symbols on coins.

the temple, coins with the arched symbol may have been struck earlier but as yet no stratigraphic or any other evidence to this effect is available, though a great desideratum. On those varieties where Shashṭhī is shown on the reverse in stead of the deer, the arched symbol is depicted in front or by the side of the goddess. Since the arched and tree symbols and the deer have been adopted from the Kuṇinda coins along with many other subsidiary devices, the arched symbol shown thereon also seems to signify a temple. The arched symbol there as well as on many of the Yaudheya coins bears a *chhatra* (parasol), a sign of honor and respectability in which the shrine or the deity was held. Providing a parasol to a shrine or deity is an age-old tradition in India and is continuing to date. The cult association of the shrine on these coins is sometimes betrayed by the attributes, emblems or vehicles of the deities which surmount the multi-arched symbol with a parasol.

I have studied Yaudheya coins of the Shaḍānana-Deer type in the British Museum, in private collections and in a hoard probably found from Tehri-Garhwal (belonging to the Birla Archaeological and Cultural Research Institute, Hyderabad, henceforth referred to as Garhwal Hoard) which furnish very interesting and corroborative evidence. The deer faces temple building on some varieties as noted above. The temples in certain cases show the emblems or the attributes of the enshrined deities and I have distinguished the temples of Śiva, Sūrya or Vishṇu (or Kṛishṇa), Saṃkarshaṇa (Balarāma), Kubera, and Indra on these coins.[60]

Some temples show a trident (*triśūla*) atop the building (Fig. 10.1-2) or a channel of water flowing from beneath it (Fig. 10.3). There are examples where an arched structure is capped by a trident or has a water-channel flowing from beneath (Fig. 10.4).

Coin nos. 223, 358, etc. in the Garhwal Hoard represent three-arched *chaitya* with a parasol (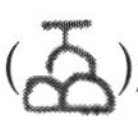); no. 374 has four triangular compartments within the triangle and is capped by a parasol (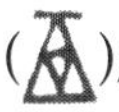); no. 232 has a multi-arched *chaitya* with a *chhatra* above (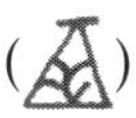) and no. 329 has a trident above (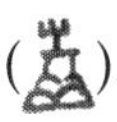). These examples allay all doubts to the arched symbol being the temple. Obviously the arched symbols on these coins represent the temple with *chhatra* (parasol). The last coin carries even the attribute of

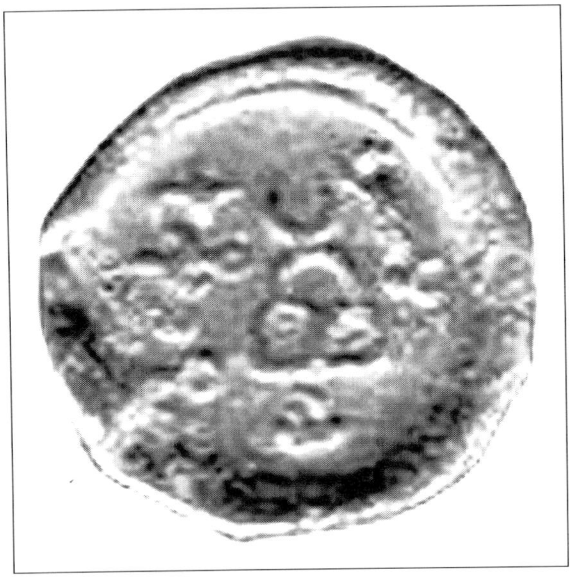

Fig. 11. Enlargement of Jeevandeep Singh's coin.

Śiva atop. The cult affiliation of coin no. 209 in the said hoard is indicated by the presence of the *nandipada* atop the three-arched symbol with a parasol, a symbol which occurs on some other tribal coins also belonging mostly to the mountainous region where the worship of Śiva was quite dominant.

If we take the arched symbol as representing a *chaitya* or shrine, the 'pile of nine bales or balls' may be taken to stand for a mountain as suggested by Allan. In the case of Vaṭāśvaka coins, the shrine seems to have existed atop a mountain and the female figure in *añjali-mudrā* seems to be performing worship. It is an age-old custom to approach and enter a temple with folded hands. Kauṭilya refers to the *chaityas* as the houses of gods and states that people used to perform worship at the *chaityas* in order to avert the evil attacks of demons.[61] Dasgupta[62] regards the pile of balls below the *chaitya* 'as representing *piṇḍas* (balls) of food which the *chaitya* worshipper has to offer to the *chaitya* as a mark of devotion' but the Vaṭāśvaka coins do not depict the scene of offering *piṇḍas* (generally seven in number) but of worshipping with folded hands. One does not offer *piṇḍas* in a standing posture. We thus take the device 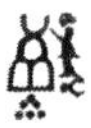 of the Aśvaka coins as representing the scene of worship by a female at a Śaiva temple located on the top of a hill or mountain.[63] And since the legends on most of the coins of the city-states are in nominative or locative singular, Vaṭāśvaka should not be taken as the name of any tribe or ruler. Allan had rightly observed that "A name in the nominative singular like Tripurī, Ujeni, &c., usually indicates a town, and one naturally expects Vaṭāśvaka to be the name of a town or district".[64] The legend on the coin of Jeevandeep Singh is clearly *Vaṭasvake* '(coin struck/circulating) at/in Vaṭāśvaka' (Fig. I.8 & its enlargement Fig. 11) which like the legends Ajudhe, *Madavike*, Agodake, Hathodake, etc. on certain city-state coins further supports the view that Vaṭāśvaka was the name of a city and that the coins under consideration are the city issues.

NOTES AND REFERENCES

1. Cunningham, Alexander, *Archaeological Survey Report* (henceforth *CASR*), Vol. XIV, p. 18.
2. Cunningham, Alexander (1891), *Coins of Ancient India*, London (Reprint, Varanasi, 1963) (*CAI*), p. 61, Pl. II.17.
3. Allan, John (1936), *Catalogue of the Coins of Ancient India*, British Museum, London (*BMCAI*), pp. cxlvi and 264, nos. 1-6. The weights and diameters of these coins are as follow: (1) 9.029 g, 22.12 mm; (2) 9.364 g, 23.75 mm; (3) 9.175 g, 24.75 mm; (4) 8.937 g, 22.57 mm; (5) 9.047 g, 24.34 mm and (6) 8.741 g, 22.10 mm. Allan illustrated only 4 coins in his Pl. XXXIX.1-4.

4. Mr. Girish Sharma's uniface Vaṭasvaka coin weighs 10.66 g (Fig. 1.7). The details of Jeevandeep Singh's coin (Fig. 1.8) are not known. Recently Wilfried Pieper (*Ancient Indian Coins: A Comprehensive Catalogue*, Mumbai: IIRNS, 2021, p. 239, No. 1578) has illustrated a coin (AE, 8.01 g, 24 mm) from the collection of Aman Ur-Rahman.
5. *Indische Studien*, Vol. III, p. 46. Smith, Vincent A. (1906), *Indian Museum Catalogue*, I, Oxford, p. 157) followed Bühler's interpretation of the legend.
6. *Corpus Inscriptionum Indicarum*, I, p. 90.
7. *BMCAI*, pp. cxlvi-cxlvii.
8. Dasgupta, K.K. (1972), 'The Aśvakas: an Early Indian Tribe," *East and West*, Vol. 22 (1-2), pp. 33-40.
9. However, it was to be distinguished from Assaka (<Aśvaka) *janapada* 'state, tribe' of South India referred to in some Buddhist texts [Gupta, Parmanand (1989), *Geography from Ancient Indian Coins and Seals*, Kurukshetra: Concept Publishing Company, pp. 17-18].
10. Choudhury, S.B. (1955), *Ethnic Settlements in Ancient India, A Study on the Puranic Lists of Peoples of Bharatavarsa*, General Printers and Publishers, p. 51; Majumdar, R.C. & A.D. Pusalkar (Eds.), *The History and Culture of the Indian People*, Vol. 2, Bombay: Bharatiya Vidya Bhavan, p. 45.
11. Chakrabortty, S.K. (1931), *Ancient Indian Numismatics*, Mymensingh (*AIN*), p. 157 & (1935-36), 'The Tribal Coins of Northern India', *Numismatic Supplement* (*NS*), XLVI, pp. 69-70. See also Majumdar, R.C. (1952), *Ancient India*, Delhi: MLBD (Reprint, 1977), p. 99.
12. Dani, Ahmad Hasan *et al.* (1999), *History of Civilizations of Central Asia*, UNESCO, p. 76. Barbara A. West [(2009), *Encyclopaedia of the Peoples of Asia and Oceanica*, Infobase Publishing, p. 359], however, cites Assakenoi force as consisting of 20,000 cavalry with 30 elephants and 30,000 infantry.
13. Agrawala, V.S. (1963), *India As Known to Pāṇini*, 2nd ed., Varanasi, p. 456.
14. *AIN*, p. 157 & (1935-36), *NS*, XLVI, pp. 69-70.
15. Dasgupta, K.K. (1974), *Tribal History of Ancient India A Numismatic Approach, Calcutta* (*THAI*), pp. 29-30.
16. *CASR*, XIV, p. 18, Pl. X.
17. Allan's Vars. *h* and *i* of Class I of un-inscribed Taxila coins (*BMCAI*, pp. cxxxiv, 221-22, Pl. XXXII.5, 6, 9 & 10.
18. CNG 91, Lot 446, September 2012; Kulkarni, Prashant P. (2016), 'Earliest Gold Coins of India and Bactria', *Numismati Digest*, Vol. 40, p. 45, Fig. 33.
19. Cunningham, Alexander (1963), *The Ancient Geography of India*, Varanasi: Indological Book House (*CAGI*), pp. 42-44.
20. The bronze square coin of Eucratides bears the diademed and hemeted bust of the king to right with Greek legend ΒΑΣΙΛΕΩΣ ΜΕΓΑΛΟΥ ΕΥΚΡΑΤΙΔΟΥ on the obverse and Zeus seated on throne to left holding wreath and palm with forepart of elephant to right in front and conical object behind and monogram to right with Kharoshṭhī legend *Kaviśiye nagaradevatā* [Gardner, Percy (1966), *Coin of Greek and Scythic Kings of Bactria and India in the British Museum*, Chicago (reprint), p. 19, Pl. VI.8].
21. *Journal of the Asiatic Society of Bengal*, 1840, p. 484.
22. *Epigraphia Indica*, XXII, 1933, p. 11.
23. Agrawala (1963), *op. cit.*, p. 120
24. Watters, Thomas (1961), *On Yuan Chwang's Travels in India*, Delhi: Munshiram Manoharlal, p. 129.
25. Dhavalikar, M.K. (1987), "Ganesa in Mathura," in Pande, B.M. & B.D. Chattopadhyaya (Eds.), *Archaeology and History: Essays in Memory of Sh. A. Ghosh*, 2 vols, Delhi: Agam Kala

Prakashan, Vol. II, pp.471-78; (1990), "Origin of Gaṇeśa", *Annals of the Bhandarkar Oriental Research Institute*, Vol. LXXI pp. 1-24; (2016), *Gaṇeśa the God of Asia*, New Delhi: Aryan Books International.

26. Allan, *BMCAI*, p. cxxxiv. Chakrabortty (*NS*, XLVI, p. 70) also feels that "both are perhaps the different varieties of the Hill Symbol".
27. Watters, *op. cit.*, p. 129.
28. Marshall, John (1931), *Mohenjodaro and the Indus Civilization*, London, Vol. III, Pl. XCVIII.2; Vats, M.S. (1940), *Excavations at Harappa*, New Delhi, Pl. CXXXII.2a,-c, -e; Mackay, E.J.H. (1938), *Further Excavations at Mohenjodaro*, Delhi, Pl. CXXXVI.57, 66, 71, etc.
29. *Journal of the Asiatic Society of Bengal*, 1890, pp. 194-95.
30. *IMC*, I, pp. 156 f.
31. Coomaraswamy, Ananda K. (1927), *History of Indian and Indonesian Art*, New York, p. 44, fn.4. See also Chattopadhyay, Bhaskar (1977), *Coins And Icons – A Study of Myths and Symbols in Indian Numismatic Art*, Calcutta, p. 32.
32. *AIN*, pp. 157-58; *NS*, XLVI, p. 70.
33. *BMCAI*, p. xxiv, fn. 1.
34. *NS*, XLVII, p. 61.
35. *Ibid.*, XLV, p. 44.
36. Kramrisch, Stella (1976), *The Hindu Temple*, Calcutta, 1946 (reprinted Delhi), Vol. I, p. 161. There are numerous inscriptions also which compare temples or their spires with mountains.
37. *Ibid.*, p. 171.
38. Gupta, P.L. and T.R. Hardaker (1985), *Ancient Indian Silver Punch-marked Coins of the Magadha-Maurya Kārshāpana Series*, Anjaneri.
39. Upasak believes that "this symbol is the representation of three full size stūpas crowned with a half size stūpa like a *Chatra* at the top" [Upasak, C.S. (1977), "Some Buddhist Symbols on Punch-marked Coins", *JNSI*, XXXIX, pp. 24-25].
40. Prasad, Durga (1934), "Classification and Significance of the Symbols of the Silver Punch-marked Coins of Ancient India", *Journal of the Asiatic Society of Bengal, Numismatic Supplement*, No. XLV, XLV (1934), pp. 16-55, Pl. 9; (1937-38), XLVII, pp. 63 ff, Pls. 7-19. Durga Prasad tried to explain the significance of the symbols with the help of some late texts and suggested that most of these were Tantric in character. See also Chandra, R.G. (1968), "The Symbol of Hillocks", in A.K. Narain (Ed.), *Seminar Papers on the Local Coins of Northern India: C. 300 B.C. to 300 A.D.*, Varanasi, 1968, pp. 193-202.
41. Marshall, John (2012), *The Buddhist Art of Gandhāra*, Cambridge, 1960 (Reprint, Delhi: Munshiram Manoharlal).
42. Rajgor, Dilip (2001), *Punch-marked Coins of Early Historic India*, California, p. 69, Type 424b. Haaff, P. Anne van't (2004), *Saurashtra (c. 450 – 50 BC) Surasena (c. 500 – 350 BC) Silver Punchmarked Coinage*, Anjaneri: IIRNS, pp. 10-11 and 29-31) has also referred to six-arched hill or multiple Lingam, six-dot hill, etc. on Saurashtra coins.
43. Rajgor (2001), pp. 177-79, Series 76, types 1189-1190.
44. Gupta & Hardaker (1985), pp. 62-63. I have explained the meaning and significance of these and many other allied symbols [Handa, Devendra (2007), *Coins and Temples: Numismatic Evidence on the Evolution of Temple Architecture*, Reesha Books International, Mumbai].
45. *JASB*, 1894, p. 44; Spooner, *loc. cit.*
46. *Ibid.*; Durga Prasad, *NS*, XLVII, p. 62, Pl. VIII.1-2 & 5.
47. *CAI*, pp. 57-58.
48. Durga Prasad, *NS*, XLVII, *op. cit.*, pp. 65 & 75.

49. *Ibid.*, p. 62.
50. *CAI*, Pl. XI.15-16; *BMCAI*, Pl. XXXIII.10-15.
51. Maheshwari, K.K. (June 1977), "Some Interesting Coins from Andhra Pradesh", *ND*, Vol. 1, Part 1, pp. 5-6, Pl. I.7-11.
52. Gupta, Chandrashekhar (October 2004), "Uninscribed Cast Copper Coin from Pauni, District Bhandara", *Indian Coin Society Newsletter*, No. 34, pp. 3-4.
53. *CAI*, Pl. III.2.
54. *ABORI*, XX, p. 28.
55. *Epigraphia Indica*, XXII, p. 3.
56. *Bulletin of the School of Oriental and African Studies*, XXII, pp. 548 ff.
57. Banerjea, J.N. (1956), *Development of Hindu Iconography*, 2nd ed., Calcutta (*DHI*), pp. 108-09.
58. *Ibid.*
59. *BMCAI*, p. 275, var. h, Pl. XL.12; *THAI*, p. 207, Class IV, Var. G. See also *JNSI*, II (1940), pp. 111-12, nos. 19-20 & 95-96; XLVII (1985), pp. 14-17, Pls. I.1-18, II.1-9; *ND*, VIII (1984), pp. 32-33.
60. I have discussed and illustrated numerous Yaudheya coins bearing the temple building showing cult attributes [Handa, Devenndra (2007), *Tribal Coins of Ancient India*, New Delhi, Pls. XLII-LXIX].
61. *Arthaśāstra*, I.20; XII.5.
62. *THAI*, p. 33.
63. The female thus cannot be taken as the *nagara-devatā* or city-goddess as held by Allan. The *nagara-devatā* being the city-deity cannot be expected to perform worship. The female figure here may therefore be the queen, princess, mayor or administrator of the city.
64. *BMCAI*, pp. cxxxviii-cxxxix.

III

Kāḍa Coins

Coins popularly known as Kāḍa coins, were first published by Sir Alexander Cunningham in 1891.[1] Cunningham did not record the find spots of his coins but mentioned the discovery of a Kāḍa coin with the coins of the Kuṇindas.[2] This indicated Punjab (i.e. old Punjab which included modern Haryana and parts of Himachal Pradesh) as the provenance for the Kāḍa coins. The specimens in the British Museum from the collections of Rodgers and Whitehead confirm this.[3] Allan distinguished six varieties (Var. *a-f*) of "the very rude cast copper coins bearing a legend Kāḍasa in early Brāhmī characters, probably of the latter half of the third or early second century B.C."[4]

The details of the coins of the six varieties of Kāḍa coins published by Allan are as given below.

KĀḌA
(Third Century BCE)

VAR. *a*

No.	Wt. gr/g	Metal	Size	Obverse	Reverse
1.	116/7.576	Æ	.9 ″	Large rayed circle (sun) around	Tree in railing in centre; uncertain rectangular object on l., 𑀓𑀸𑀟𑀲 put perpendicularly on r.[5] (Fig. 12.1)

VAR. *b*

No.	Wt. gr/g	Metal	Size	Obverse	Reverse
2.	124/8.o35	Æ	.95 ″	Undulating line  𑀓𑀸𑀟𑀲	As obverse

3.	164/10.626 Æ	.95 ″	Same	Same
4.	166/10.756 Æ	.9 ″	Same	Same
5.	157/10.173 Æ	.9 ″	Same	Same
6.	125/8.100 Æ	.9 ″	Same	Same (Fig. 12.2-6)

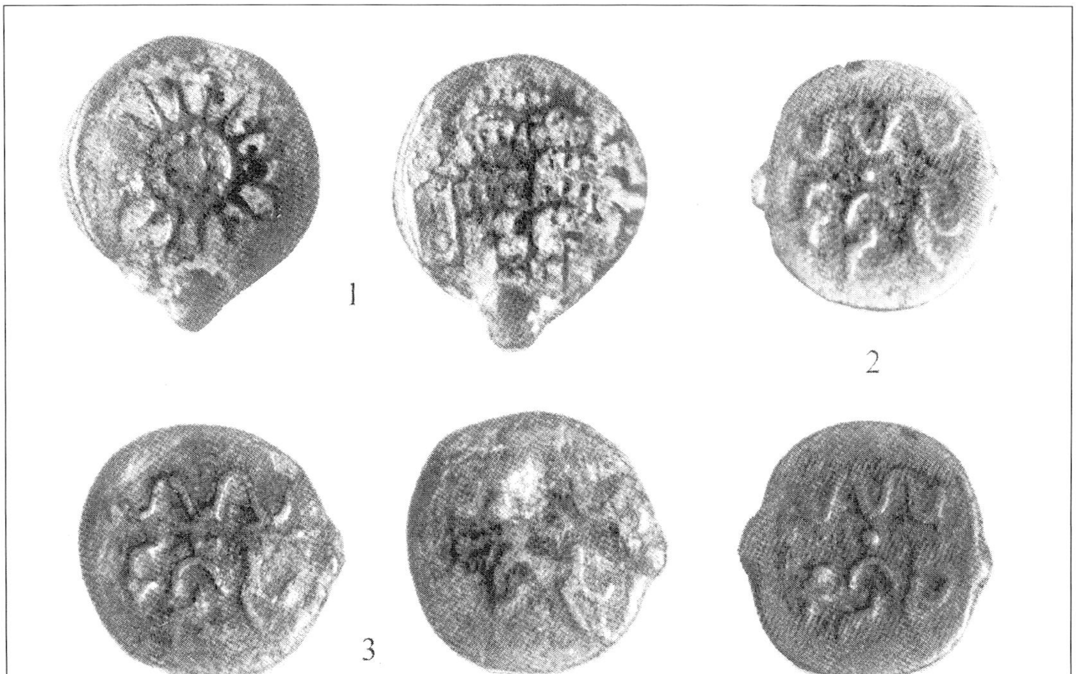

Fig. 12. Kāḍa coins: variety *a* 1; var. *b* 2-6.

No.	Weight	Metal	Size	Obverse	Reverse
VAR. *c*					
7.	143/9.265	Æ	.95 ″	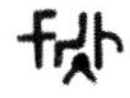 wavy line below	Rude figure on r. holding staff in left hand; uncertain object on l., ? *kalaśa* with flowers.  Below on l. (Fig. 13.2)
8.	166/10.756	Æ	.85 ″	Same	Same (Fig. 13.1)
VAR. *d*					
9.	181/9.784	Æ	1.0 ″	Undulating line 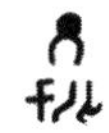	Elephant l. (square, cast) (Fig. 13.3)
10.	211/13.672	Æ	1.0 ″	Same	Same (Fig. 13.4)
VAR. *e*					
11.	52/3.362	Æ	.5 ″	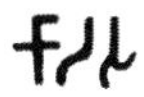	*Kalaśa* with flowers (Fig. 13.5)
VAR. *f*					
12.	76/4.924	Æ	.7 ″	Rayed circle (sun) as on no. 1	Horse r.[7] (Fig. 13.6)
13.	69/4.471	Æ	.8 ″	Same	Same (Fig. 13.7)
14.	64/4.146	Æ	.65 ″	Same	Same (Fig. 13.8)

Of these fourteen coins in the British Museum, eleven are inscribed and three (var. *f*) anonymous, which are connected with var. *a* by the obverse design 'Sun'.[7] Vars. *a-c* and *f* are round while others (Vars. *d* and *e*) are square.

Some time back Dr. Shailendra Bhandare pointed out to cast fakes of variety *c* citing the following example (Fig. 14.1).[8]

The collectors should therefore be careful while acquiring such coins. The size of the coins varies from 0.5 to 1.0 inch and the weight from 52 to 211 grains (3.362 to 13.672 g). Allan assigns these coins to the latter half of the third century or early second century BCE in the introduction, but in the *Catalogue* (p. 145) all these coins are dated to the third century BCE. K.K. Dasgupta[9] has classified these coins into four classes consisting of six varieties (vars. *a-f*) as listed above. Variety *g* is a new addition to the known copper coins.

VARIETY *g*

15. A square copper coin with elephant to right on the reverse constituting a new variety (Var. *g*) has also come to our notice (Fig. 14.2). Its size and weight were, however, not available.

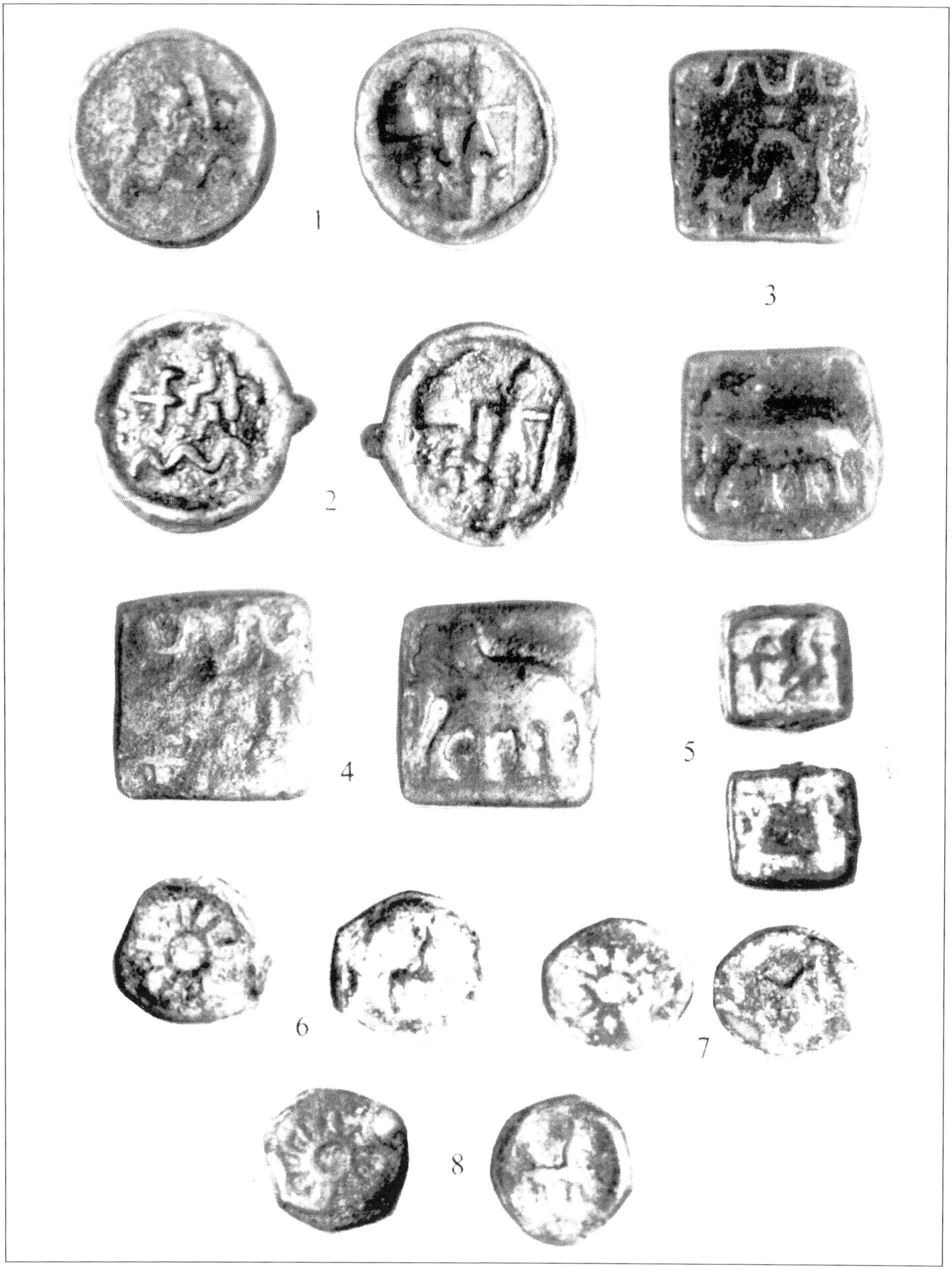

Fig. 13. Kāḍa coins: var. *c* 1-2, var. *d* 3-4, var. *e* 5, var. *f* 6-8.

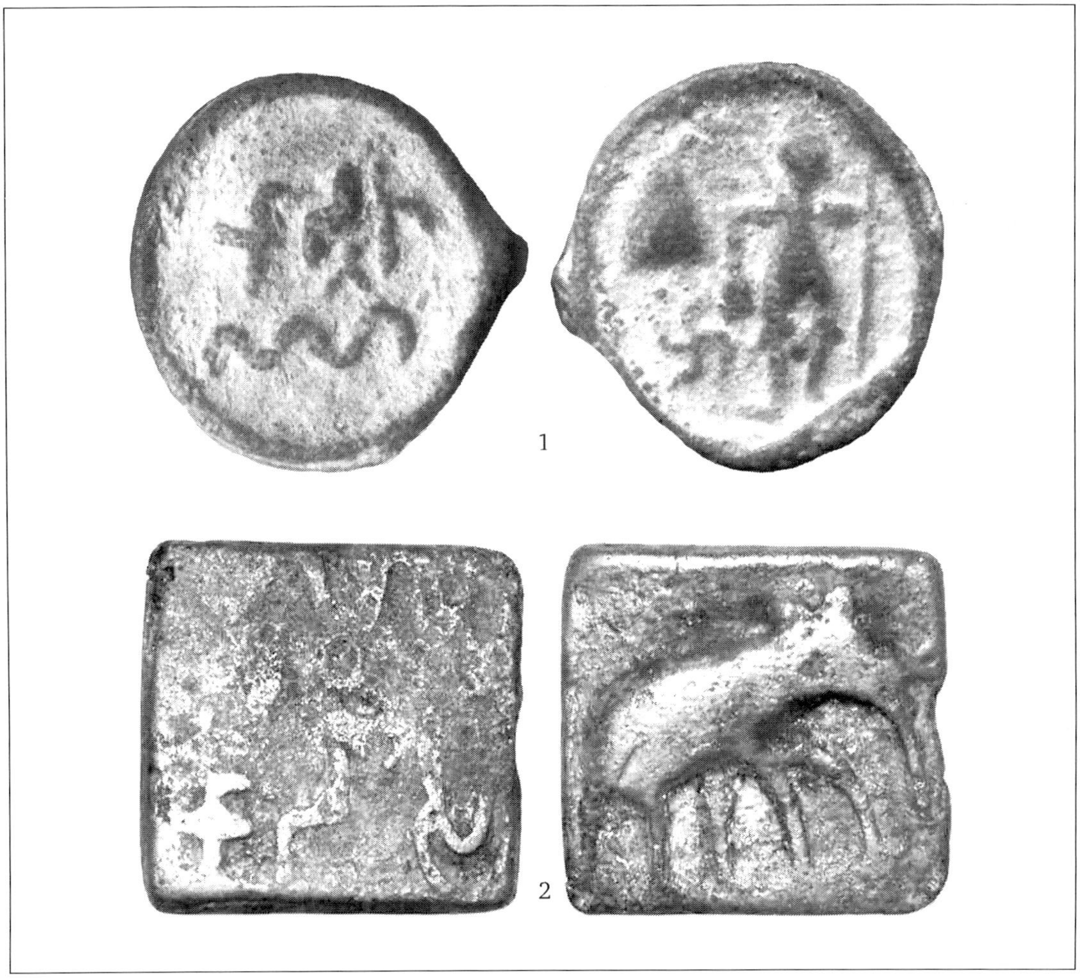

Fig. 14. Fake Kāḍa cast coin of variety *c* 1 and square variety *g* 2.

Obv. Undulating line in the centre with *svastika,* taurine and tree in railing from left to right above and the legend 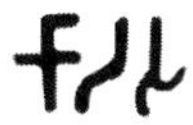 below.

Rev. Elephant walking to right.

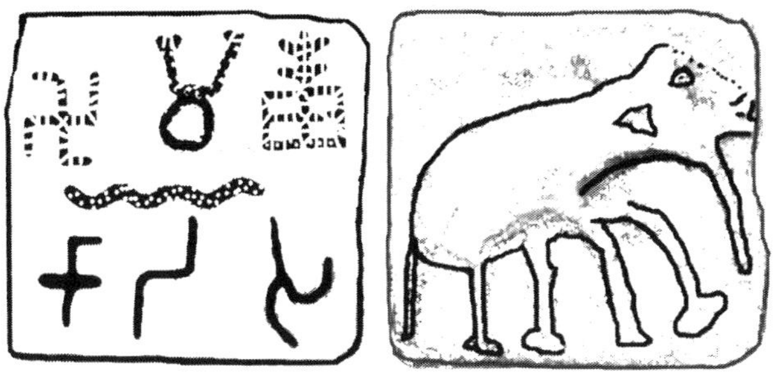

(Fig. 14.2)

Variety *h*

To the published varieties of Kāḍa coins was added another variety represented by a solitary specimen recovered from archaeological excavations at Sugh, a well known archaeological site near Jagadhari in district Yamunanagar of Haryana.[10] The coin may be described as follows:

16. Copper alloy[11], round, 2.325 cm, thickness 4.75 mm, wt. 15.9227 g.

Obv. *Kāḍasa* in early Brāhmī characters, snake[12] to left in the centre; tree in railing[13], inverted *nandipada* and *svastika* in a row from left to right below.

Rev. An elephant with a rider to right[14] (Fig. 15.1).

The coin is a cast one. The protuberance of the edge indicates that at least two coins were cast simultaneously. The obverse is flat, but the reverse is convex, the devices being carved in an unusually high relief, which reminds us of the coins of early Seleucid rulers. The mould used for casting these coins appears to have been prepared by a master artist, copying in all probability, some early Bactrian coins which might have been known in northwest India then.[15]

To the above-mentioned fifteen coins may now be added fifteen more specimens in copper, lead and potin, all collected from Sugh and forming part of Mr. R.K. Aggarwal's collection. The details thereof are given below.

17. Æ; round, 2.6 X 2.4 cm, 8.3745 g

Obv. Undulating line with serpent-head on left, Brāhmī legend (*Kāḍasa*) above with inverted taurine symbol () below the letter *ḍa* of the legend.

Rev. Rude human figure on right holding staff in left hand, uncertain object (*Kalaśa* with flowers?) on left and *svastika* 卐 below on left. (Fig. 15.2)

The coin is a cast one as indicated by the protuberance of the edge and belongs to vatiety *c*. On the obverse may also be seen a small dot below the thick one above – almost in the centre, probably for the adjustment and orientation of the moulds. The Brāhmī letter *sa* is unusual but an exactly similar form exists on the two coins of this variety (Var. *c*) illustrated by Allan.[16]

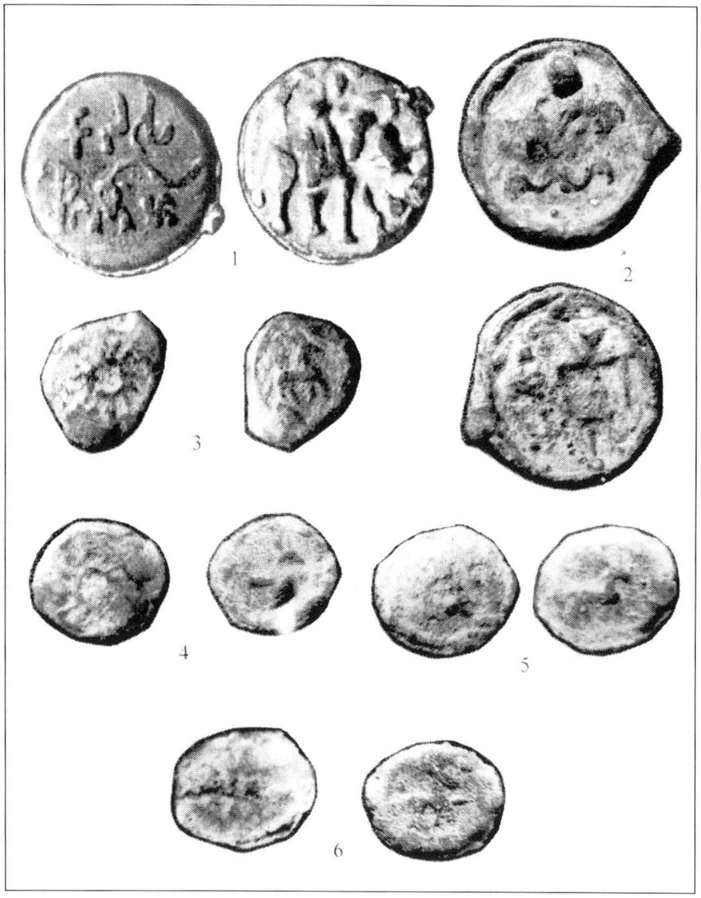

Fig. 15. Additional Kāḍa coins: var. *h* 1, var. *c* 2, var. *f* 3-6.

18. Æ, roundish, 1.7 X 1.45 cm, 4.0983 g.
Obv. Rayed sun.
Rev. Deer to right (Fig. 15.3).

19. Æ, roundish, 1.7 X 1.4 cm, 2.9783 g.
Obv. Similar.
Rev. Similar (Fig. 15.4).

20. Æ, 1.75 X 1.6 cm, 6.0021 g.
Obv. Similar.
Rev. Similar (Fig. 15.5).

21. Æ, 1.8 X 1.4 cm, 3/9381 g.
Obv. Similar.
Rev. Similar (Fig. 15.6).

VARIETY *i*

Shri Kamal Vaid of Raipur (Chhattisgarh) possesses the following lead coin which constitutes a new variety:

Lead, square, 3.57g, 12 x 12 mm, thickness 2.26 mm.

Obv. Brāhmī legend 𑀓𑀸𑀟𑀲 above the snake or undulating line and *svaastika*, inverted taurine and tree in railing from left to right below.

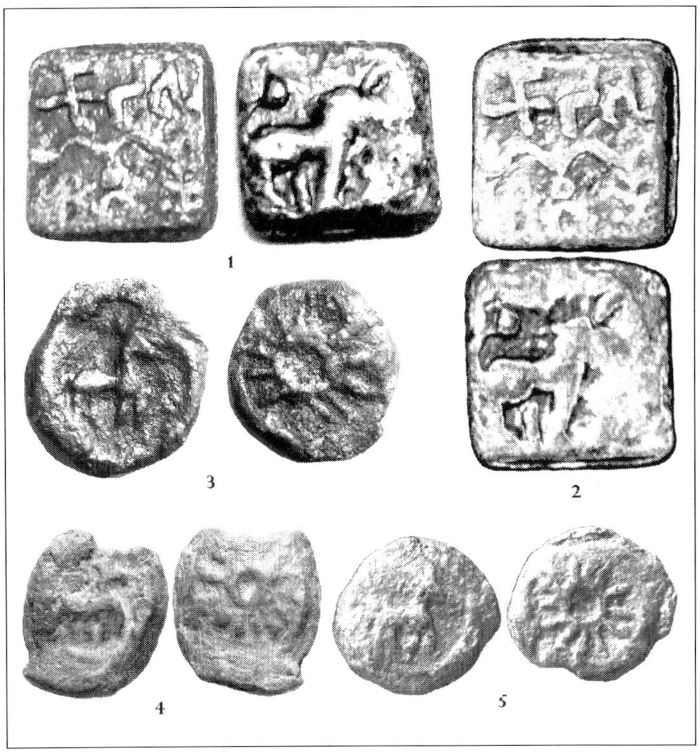

Fig. 16. Miscellaneous Kāḍa coins.

Rev. Lion with upcurled tail to right, other symbols if any obliterated (Fig. 16.1).

The protuberances on the edges and joining lines throughout in the middle of these coins are the clear evidence of casting. These coins are similar to the coins of Var. *f* published by Allan. Some more coins of variety *f* have appeared on the Facebook in recent years by Sanjeev Chagti (Fig. 16.3), Murthy Macherla (Fig. 16.4, 8.43 g) and Ashok Kataria (Fig. 16.5) while one copper coin (6.72 g, 19 mm) of this type is preserved in the collection of Kamal Vaid (Fig. 16.2).

VARIETY *j*

22. Lead, squarish, 1.85 X 1.7 cm, 10.7051 g.

Obv. Undulating line (with cobra head to left?), inverted taurine symbol below in the centre, *dakshiṇāvarta svastika* 卐 on left and traces of tree in railing on right and Brāhmī legend above.

Rev. Lion wit upcurled tail (looks like elephant) to right (Fig. 17.1).

Allan had published two square copper coins under Var. *d* showing undulating line with inverted taurine and the Brāhmī legend *Kāḍasa* (𑀓𑀸𑀟𑀲) below on the obverse and the elephant to left on the reverse.[17] To those we added another variety (Var. *g*) in copper showing undulating line with *svastika*, taurine and tree in railing from left to right above and the legend 𑀓𑀸𑀟𑀲 below on the obverse and elephant walking to right on the reverse. Our coin differs in the arrangement of the legend and device on the obverse and the direction of the elephant on the reverse. Variety *i* is similar to variety *g* but it is in lead and thus constitutes another variety. Another difference to be noted is that the rider on the elephant on the reverse of this square coin may have been there originally as indicated by a partially visible right leg of the rider just behind the head of the tusker and the blank space of the flan above. The body structure of the elephant also differs from that of the elephant on the reverse of variety *g*. The reverse of the two coins seems to be similar but have the difference in the arrangement of the three subsidiary symbols below the snake or undulating line. Their metals too differ as indicated above.

VARIETY *k*

23. Lead; rectangular; 1.15 X 0.95 cm; 2.869 g.

Obv. Similar.

Rev. Similar but the depiction and stance of the animal is slightly different (Fig. 17.2).

VARIETY *l*

24. Lead, square, 1.2 cm, 3.3288 g.

Obv. Similar.

Rev. Animal figure is different and has upcurled tail above its body, probably a horse or lion (Fig. 17.3).

The legend above the snake on the obverse, however, is fairly preserved and so also the inverted *nandipada* below. Tree in railing on the right and *svastika* on left are visible only in traces. The obverse of this coin thus confirms and corroborates the description of the preceding pieces. The variations in sizes and weights obviously indicate denominational differences.

VARIETY *m*

25. Lead; round; 1.4 cm; 3.8589 g.

Obv. Brāhmī legend *Kāḍasa* above; snake in the centre, traces of some symbols below.

Rev. An animal with long legs and up-curled tail to right (probably a horse or lion) (Fig. 17.4).

Two lead coins of this type in a better state of preservation exist in the collection of Mr. Kamal Vaid of Raipur (Fig. 16.1-2). The second coin seems to depict a lion on the reverse.

VARIETY *n*

26. Lead; round; 1.1 X 1.05 cm; 1.6255 g.
Obv. Eight-petalled lotus.
Rev. Deer to left with some object in front (Fig. 17.5).

VARIETY *p*

27. Lead, octagonal, 1.5 cm, weight not recorded.

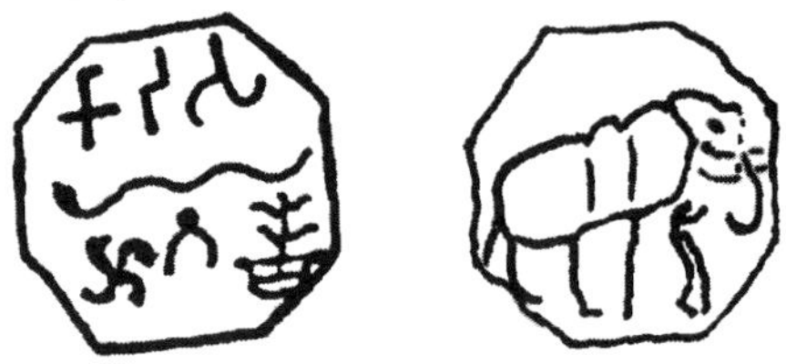

Obv. *Kāḍasa* in early Brāhmī characters above, snake to left and *svastika*, inverted taurine and tree-in-railing from left to right below.
Rev. Elephant to right (Fig. 17.6).

VARIETY *q*

28. Lead, octagonal, 1.6 X 1.4 cm, weight not recorded.

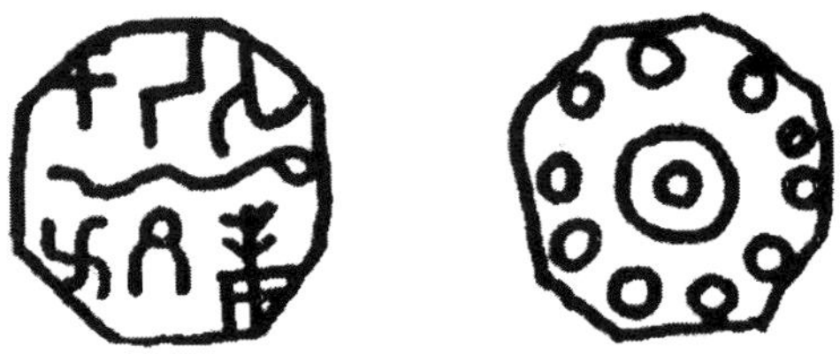

Obv. Similar but with snake to right.
Rev. A circle with a prominent pellet in the centre and ten circlets around.

VARIETY *r*

29. Lead, octagonal, 1.9 X 1.7 cm, weight not recorded.

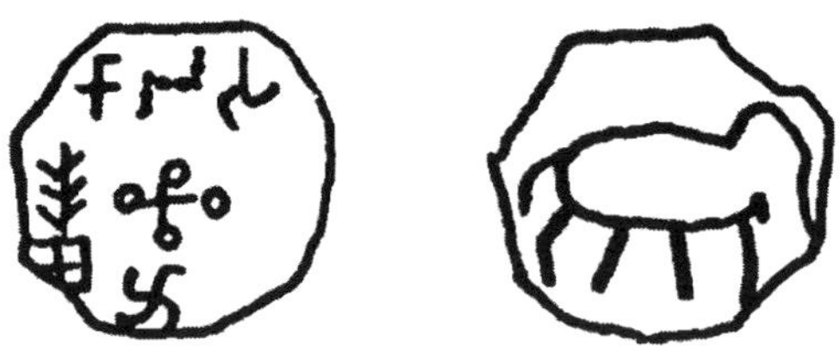

Obv. *Kāḍasa* in early Brāhmī letters above, tree-in-railing on left, Ujjain symbol in the centre and *svastika* below the Ujjain symbol.
Rev. Elephant to right.

The space to the left of the Ujjain symbol on the obverse is worn out and may have carried some other symbol/s.

VARIETY *s*

30. Lead, round, 2.2 cm, 7.044 g.

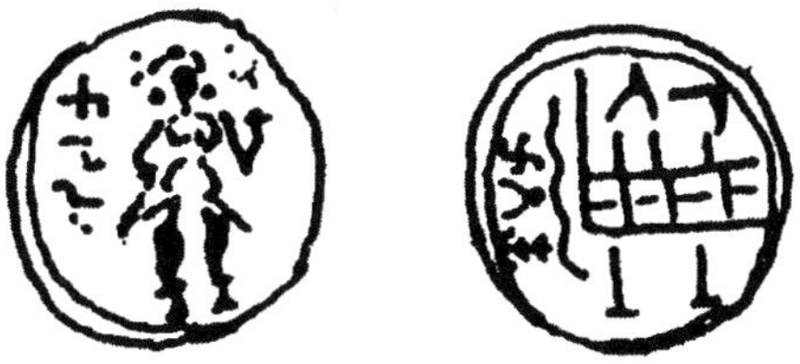

Obv. Female figure standing to front, holding a flower (lotus?) in the upraised left hand and a flywhisk (?) in the *kaṭyavalambita* right hand; Brāhmī legend *Kāḍasa* placed perpendicularly on left.

Rev. A railed structure standing on two pillars with upper portions off the flan, snake and the usual three symbols, viz. *Svastika*, taurine and tree-in-railing placed perpendicularly on the left (Fig. 17.7).

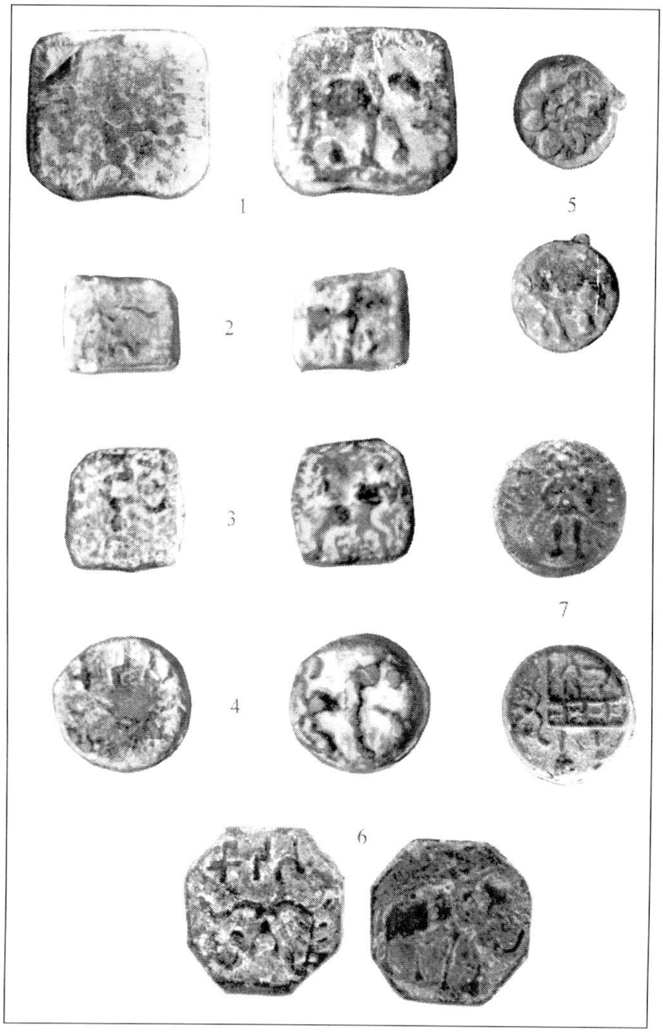

Fig. 17. Newer varieties of Kāḍa coins: vars. *i* 1, *j* 2, *k* 3, *l* 4, *m* 5, *n* 6, *r* 7.

VARIETY *t*

31. Lead, oval, 1.7 X 1.5 cm, weight not recorded.

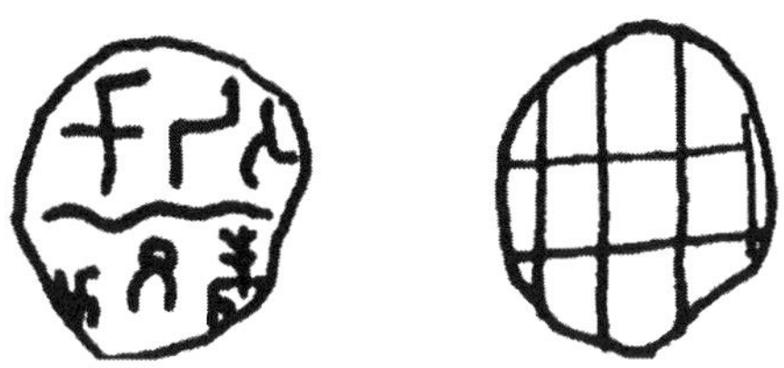

Obv. As on no. 28.

Rev. Four vertical lines crossed by two horizontal lines.

It is interesting to note that coin nos. 27-29 are the earliest specimens of octagonal shape. Coin nos. 16 and 22-31 represent newer varieties. Lead used for many of the Kāḍa coins also constitutes its earliest and perhaps the most copious use for coinage at such an early age particularly for coinage.

The devices found on the Kāḍa coins include variably an undulating line[18], a tree in railing, a large rayed circle (sun), an upturned taurine symbol, vase with flowers, *svastika*, elephant with or without a rider, horse[19] and a rude standing figure holding a scepter or spear[20] in the right hand and a small bag[21] or *Kamaṇḍalu* (water-vessel)[22] in the left.[23] The symbols like taurine, sun, tree in railing, undulating line, elephant, etc. (which are seen on punch-marked coins also), the early Brāhmī characters, the shape and fabric of these coins suggest them to be of a fairly early date.

It is very difficult to definitely ascertain the chronological order of different varieties listed above. They contain uninscribed and inscribed varieties of irregular, square, round and octagonal shapes and are made of copper, potin or alloys and lead. I think that the uninscribed coins, which are mostly of irregular shapes and fractional in nature, are the earliest. I also regard the side depicting deer to be the obverse. Thes coins may have been followed by the double obverse cast round coins. Square and slightly rectangular coins may have been partly coeval with them followed by octagonal shaped coins. This chronological order is only subjective and tentative and may be amended with more definite evidence coming to light in the future.

ATTRIBUTION

The legend *Kāḍasa* has been explained as a genitive singular of Kāḍa, the name of king[24], place[25] or a tribe.[26] Cunningham attributed these coins to the descendants of Kadru who is described as the mother of snakes in Hindu mythology.[27] S.K. Chakrabortty identified *Kāḍasa* with Cadrusi of Cadrusia[28], a town near Alexandria on the north bank of the river Panjshir under the Caucasus.[29] B.R. Mani has rejected these attributions as being 'imaginative or mythic in character' and based on phonetic sound analogy in disregard of all numismatic sequences.[30] He has assigned these coins to the Kaṭha tribe of the Punjab, Hyphasis (Beas), which gave a stiff resistance to Alexander, who ultimately overcame them with the help of Porus.[31] Later the Kaṭhas were subjugated by Chandragupta Maurya. Mani opines that they regained their independence sometime after Aśoka in 232 BCE and issued coins.[32] He derives *Kāḍasa* from (*Kāṭhasya*) and assigns the following connotation to the word:

(1) An offspring of Kaṭha[33]
(2) Kaṭhas as a class (*Kaṭhānāṃ*) and
(3) A territorial determinant[34]

Finally Mani concludes, "the fabric and symbols, and early Brāhmī character found on these coins suggest that these are assignable to the Kaṭhas and that they cannot be later than the 2nd century B.C.".[35] Thus he seems to be inclined to assign these coins to the Kaṭha tribe rather than to a king or territorial unit.

Now let us proceed from the known to the unknown and examine the issue of the attribution of the Kāḍa coins in the light of the early Indian coins belonging to various cities, tribes and kings.

City coins constitute one of the earliest classes of India's inscribed issues and are found generally associated with the punch-marked and un-inscribed cast coins from layers datable to about the third and second centuries BCE.[36] They are generally of a purely indigenous fabric and character containing Brāhmī legends in the Prakrit form of the name of the city in the nominative in contradistinction to the dynastic or tribal issues which are in the genitive.[37] City issues of Bhāgilā, Erakina, Kauśāmbī, Kurarā, Mahishmatī, Tripurī, Ujjayinī, Vārāṇasī and Vidiśā are known to us.[38]

As far as Kāḍa coins are concerned, the only exact find spot known so far is Sugh, the ancient Srughna, mentioned as many as six times by Patañjali[39] who has also referred to, among others, Kauśāmbī, Mahishmatī, Ujjayinī, Vārāṇasī, etc., whose city-issues are known to us. The Kāḍa coins from Sugh are in copper, lead, and potin, an alloy of copper and cast in the indigenous way. According to the excavator, it comes from the mid-levels of Period I B which be dates between 'c. 400 B.C. and the close of the 1st century B.C.'[40] The excavator tells us that "there has been found from the late levels of the period a hoard of silver coins buried in small earthen pot containing 26 punch-marked coins and one each of Antimachus and Menander, the Indo-Greek kings".[41] Evidently, the coin belongs to the second century BCE or perhaps earlier. The characters of the legend also indicate an early date. But the coin, unlike other city-issues, betrays alien influence as we have noted above. The legend also is in genitive. No city of the name Kāḍa is known from any source. Sugh as the find spot of the Kāḍa coin also indicates that the Kāḍa coins are not city-issues as there is copious literary evidence that the present name of Sugh has come down to us from its ancient name Srughna mentioned by Pāṇini, Patañjali, *Mahāmāyurī*, *Bṛihatsaṃhitā*, etc.

The inscribed tribal issuers, when they bear the name of the tribe, refer to it in the genitive. A noteworthy point in this connection, however, is that the legend does not consist of a single word and if it does,[42] it is always in the genitive plural and not singular. In so far as the coin bearing the legend *Upagodasa*[43] is concerned, we do not know whether it belongs to a city, tribe or king.[44]

We are thus left only with the last possibility, i.e., Kāḍa coins are dynastic issues like many others which bear legends in the genitive singular. But there is no source of knowing who was this Kāḍa. This however does not negate the possibility of the Kāḍa coins being monarchical issues, as we know many other coins bearing names of kings about whom nothing is known to us from any other source. Therefore, till the availability of more definitive evidence it will be better to regard the coins in question as monarchical issues rather than tribal or territorial.

NOTES AND REFERENCES

1. *CAI*, p. 62, Pl. II. 21-22 and p. 71, Pl. V. 6.
2. *Ibid*. *CASR*, II, p. 71.
3. *BMCAI*, pp. xcii-xciii and 145-46, Pls. XIXL, 14-20 and XX.III. 10-11.
4. *Ibid*.
5. I feel that the side bearing the legend should be regarded as the obverse and the coin has been doubly struck on the other side as the tree device appears vertically and laterally crossing each other.

6. Though Allan described the animal in the Catalogue as horse, he had observed in the Introduction (*BMCAI*, p. xciii) that "it may be meant for a deer which is more natural to find on coins of this period".
7. To me the animal seems to be deer.
8. Since amny other varieties of Kāḍa coins including the one illustrated as Fig. 15.1 which was recovered in regular excavations at Sugh discussed in this paper are cast varieties, I don't feel that the cast varieties are fake. Also I prefer to take the deer device on obverse and sun device on reverse on the evidence of Allan's coin no. 1 as suggested in fn. 5 above.
9. *THAI*, pp. 236-39, Pls. VII-IX. Nos. 136-40.
10. Bhan, Suraj (1977), "Report of Excavations at Sugh (1964 and 1965)", *Journal of Haryana Studies*, Vol. IX, Nos. 1-2, pp. 1-49; Handa, Devendra, 'Sugh' in Dilip K. Chakrabarti and Makhan Lal (Editors), *History of Ancient India-III, The Texts, Political History and Administration Till c. 200 BC*, New Delhi: Vivekanand Research Foundation and Aryan Books International, no date, pp. 635-42; (2021), *Facets of Indian Art, Iconography and Numismatics*, New Delhi: Aryan Books International, pp. 18-50.
11. The coin has been described as that of lead and potin at two different places by Suraj Bhan (*Ibid.*, pp. 6 and 43 respectively). It is definitely not lead but on ally of copper which has turned blackish in color now. The exact nature of the alloy can, however, be determined only after its metallographical examination.
12. It differs from a mere undulating line and has a thickened head.
13. Not very clear. It seems to override the snake.
14. It is difficult to ascertain the identity of the rider satisfactorily.
15. Foreign coins seem to have been known in northwestern India since Alexander's time.
16. Allan, *BMCAI*, p. 146, nos. 7-8, Pl. XIX. 19 and 17.
17. *Ibid.*, p. 146, nos. 9-10, Pl. XIX. 18.
18. Cunningham (*CAI*, p. 62) took it to be a snake. On our coin it is definitely serpentine symbol.
19. Allan (*BMCAI*, p. xciii) states, "it may be meant for a deer".
20. *Daṇḍa* according to Ajay Mitra Shastri ("Symbols on tribal Coins: An Interpretative Study", in Narain, A.K., Jai Prakash Singh and Nisar Ahmad {Eds.) (1977), *Seminar Papers on the Tribal Coins of Ancient India*, Varanasi:NSI, p. 97, fn. 3.).
21. Allan, *loc. cit.*
22. Shastri, *loc. cit.*
23. Allan (*loc. cit.*) equated the human figure with the one found on Ujjayinī coins and identified it with Kārttikeya. Ajay Mitra Shastri (*loc. cit.*) however, takes the figure to that of Śiva - "one of the earliest representations of Śiva in human form so far as the historical period is concerned".
24. Bühler held Kāḍa to be a king. See Rapson, E.J. (1970), *Indian Coins*, Varanasi (Indian reprint).
25. *AIN*, p. 180.
26. Allan, *op. cit.* Jai Prakash Singh (*SPTCAI*, p. 97, note to fn. 3) has, however, expressed himself against taking these coins as tribal. Cunningham (*CAI*, p. 71) equated Kāḍasa with Kāḍaik, "A subdivision of the Kunets". Dasgupta (*THAI*, p. 236 ff.) puts them in doubtful series.
27. *Mahābhārata* (Gita Press ed.), Ādi Parva, XVI, 5-8: LXV. 1, etc.
28. *AIN*, p. 180.
29. Cf. *CAGI*, p. 11.
30. Mani, B.R. (1978), 'Determining the Type and Substantival Attribution of Kadasa Coins', *JNSI*, XL, pp. 9-12.
31. *Ibid.*, pp. 9-12.

32. *Ibid.*
33. *Ibid.* Mani observes, "the singular ablative of the Kāḍasa legend is important, as reminiscing the forbears Kaṭhas whose descendant the king claims himself to be. The rude figure found on these coins may be that of the king of the Kaṭhas". It was the custom among the Kaṭhaiois to elect the most handsome person as the king [McCrindle, J.W. (1901) *Ancient India as described in Classical Literature*, Westminster, p. 38]. Should we then regard the rude figure on some of the Kāḍa coins to be that of the king? The figure holding a staff and water vessel has rightly been identified with Śiva by Ajay Mitra Shastri (*Seminar Papers*, *op. cit.*)
34. Explanations offered for taking Kaṭha as a territorial determinant are (I) *Kaṭhāḥ santyasmin deśe kaṭho deśaḥ* and (ii) *Kaṭhānāṃ nivāso deśa Kaṭhaḥ.*
35. *JNSI*, XI, p. 12.
36. Lahiri, Bela (1976), "India's Earliest Inscribed Coins: The City Issues". *JNSI*, XXXVIII, Part II.
37. *Ibid.*, p. 37
38. *Ibid.*, pp. 37 ff.
39. *Mahābhāshya* VI. 2. 15. Manmohan Kumar refers to a Kāḍa coin from Rattakhera in tahsil Gulha of district Kaithal also but does not give any details of the coin [Manmohan Kumar, 'Historical Geography of Some Tribes of Ancient India', *Numismatic Studies*, Vol. 6 (2001), p. 125].
40. Bhan, *op. cit.*, p. 14. Elsewhere in the same report (p.43). However, the coin is stated to have been obtained "from the upper levels of Period 1B".
41. *Ibid.*, p. 13.
42. As in the case of some Mālava coins.
43. Allan, *BMACAI*, pl. XXXV. 18.
44. Lahiri (1976), *op. cit.*, p. 38; Dasgupta, *THAI*, p. 245.

IV

Coins of Sujyeshṭha

Mr. Raj Kumar Aggarwal has collected the following interesting coins from Sugh during the last more than fifty years.

1. Lead, round, 2.0 cm, 7.044 g.

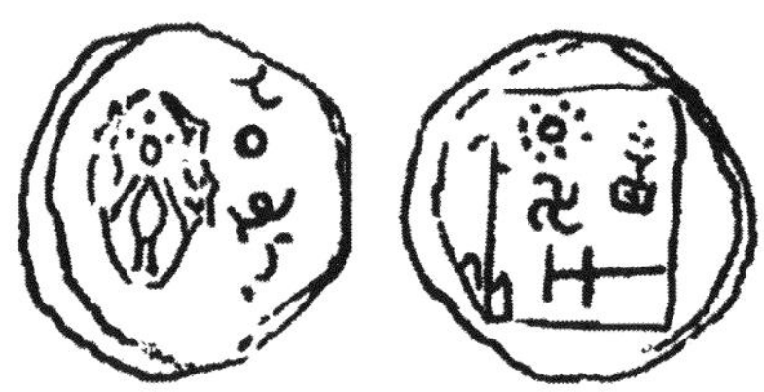

Obv. Gaja-Lakshmī on left, perpendicular legend in early Brāhmī characters on right *Sujeṭhasa.*

Rev. Within a square incuse laterally placed banner (*dhvaja* or *patākā*) symbol below, sacrificial or śūlagava symbol on left, *svastika* in the centre with a circlet having eight pellets around and probably a tree in railing on right (Fig. 18.1).

2. Lead, round, 1.85 cm, 2.377 g.

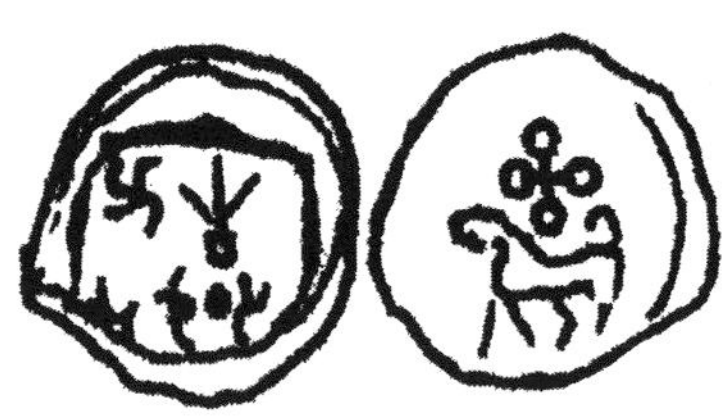

Obv. Within a squarish incuse with rounded corners *svastika* on left and tree in railing on right above and legend below *Sujeṭhasa.*

Rev. Lion with up curled tail to left with Ujjain symbol above (Fig. 18.2).

3. Lead, round, 1.0 cm, 1.175 g.

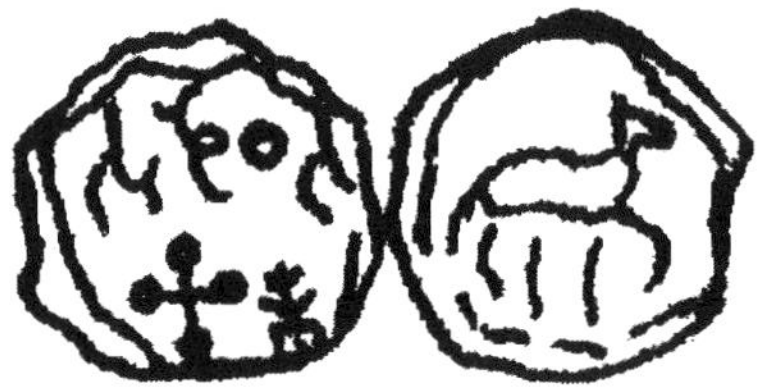

Obv. Legend *Sujeṭhasa* above, Ujjain symbol and another symbol (tree in railing) below.
Rev. Horse or deer to right (Fig. 18.3).

4. Lead, roughly circular, 1.2 X 1.1 cm, weight not recorded.

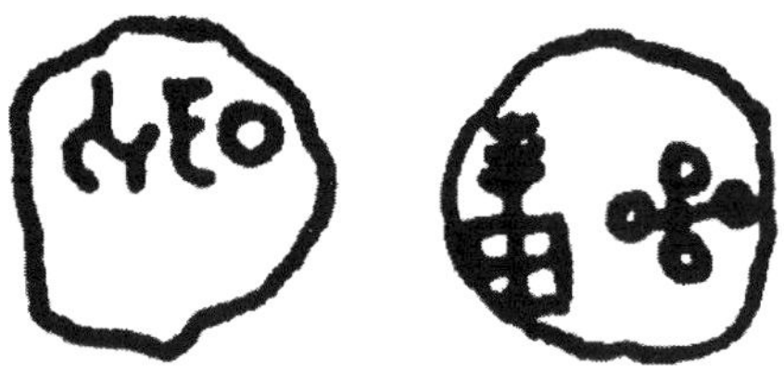

Obv. Early Brāhmī legend *Sujeṭhasa* in the upper portion.
Rev. Tree in railing on left, Ujjain symbol on right.

5. Lead, square, 1.1 cm, 1.650 gm.

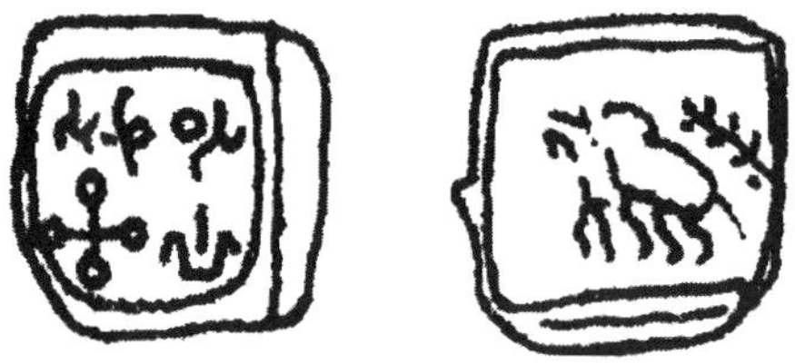

Obv. Within a squarish incuse legend *Sujeṭhasa* above and Ujjain symbol on left and an *agni-kuṇḍa* on right below.
Rev. Elephant to left with a branch (or tree?) placed slantingly on its back, probably some object in front (Fig. 18.4).

6. Lead, square, 1.05 cm, 0.947 g.

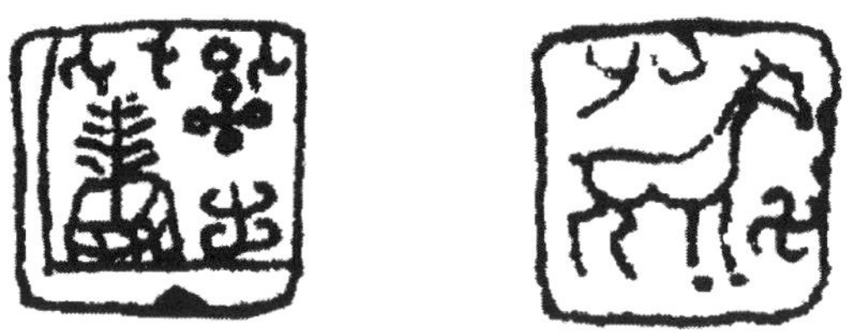

Obv. *Sujeṭhasa* above; tree in railing on left below, Brāhmī *yya*-like *śrīvatsa* with Ujjain symbol above it on the right.
Rev. Horse or deer to right with *svastika* in front, some symbol (or symbols) above on the back (Fig. 18.5).

7. Lead, square, 1.8 cm.

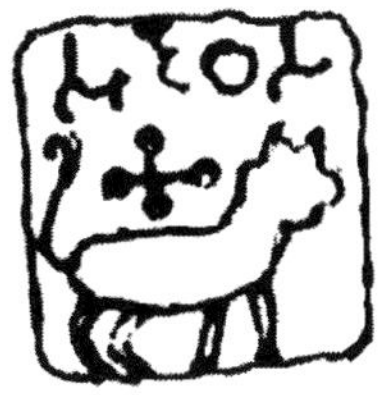

Obv. Lion with up curled tail back, legend *Sujeṭhasa* above.
Rev. Obliterated.

8. Lead, octagonal, 1.8 cm.

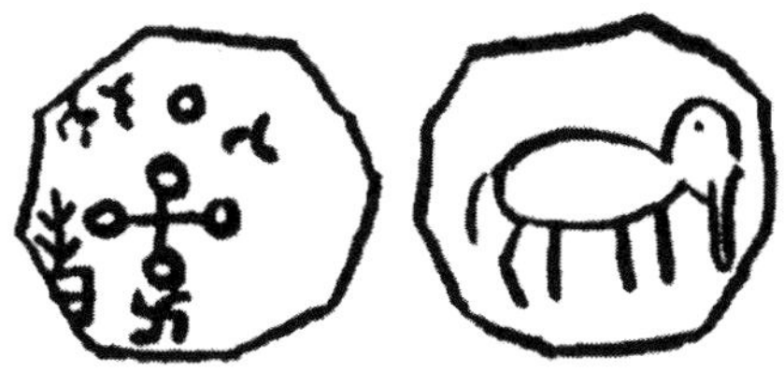

Obv. Ujjain symbol in the centre, legend *Sujeṭhasa* above, tree in railing, *svastika* and probably inverted *nandipada* in a row from left to right below.
Rev. Elephant to right.

All the eight coins are made of lead, three being round, one is roughly circular, three are square and one is octagonal in shape. All show joining lines on the edges indicating clearly that the planchets were cast. All the three round coins show protuberances also on their edges. The deep incuses on the reverse of coin no. 1 and obverse of coins nos. 2 and 4 indicate that the cast planchets were struck by dies. This is an interesting feature of these coins. The octagonal shape of coin no. 8 is also very interesting.

Each of the eight coins represents a different variety. All of them, however, bear the name of Sujeṭha (Sujyeshṭha) in early Brāhmī characters which may be assigned to the first half of the second century BCE, if not earlier.

The letter *ja* is interesting. It is not the usual English letter E type but somewhat typical with looped centre, the like of which may be seem in the Kalsi version of the Aśokan edicts. Kalsi is nearly 75 km northeast of Sugh and both the sites seem to have been connected by an ancient trade route running along the Yamunā River. Both the sites are known to have Aśokan connections.

It is interesting to note that a copper coin bearing similar legend in early Brāhmī characters as well as Gaja-Lakshmī motif, of an unknown provenance, was published by Ajit Ghose of Calcutta in 1954 from an unknown provenience.[1] This rectangular die-struck coin (0.95" in size and 120 gains in weight) bore the following details -

Obv. King riding a prancing horse to left preceded by a person with a water-pot in his right hand, Ujjain symbol on top. On left corner and eight-petalled lotus-shaped *Chakra* with spokes at top right corner, legend *Sujeṭhasa* between the two symbols.

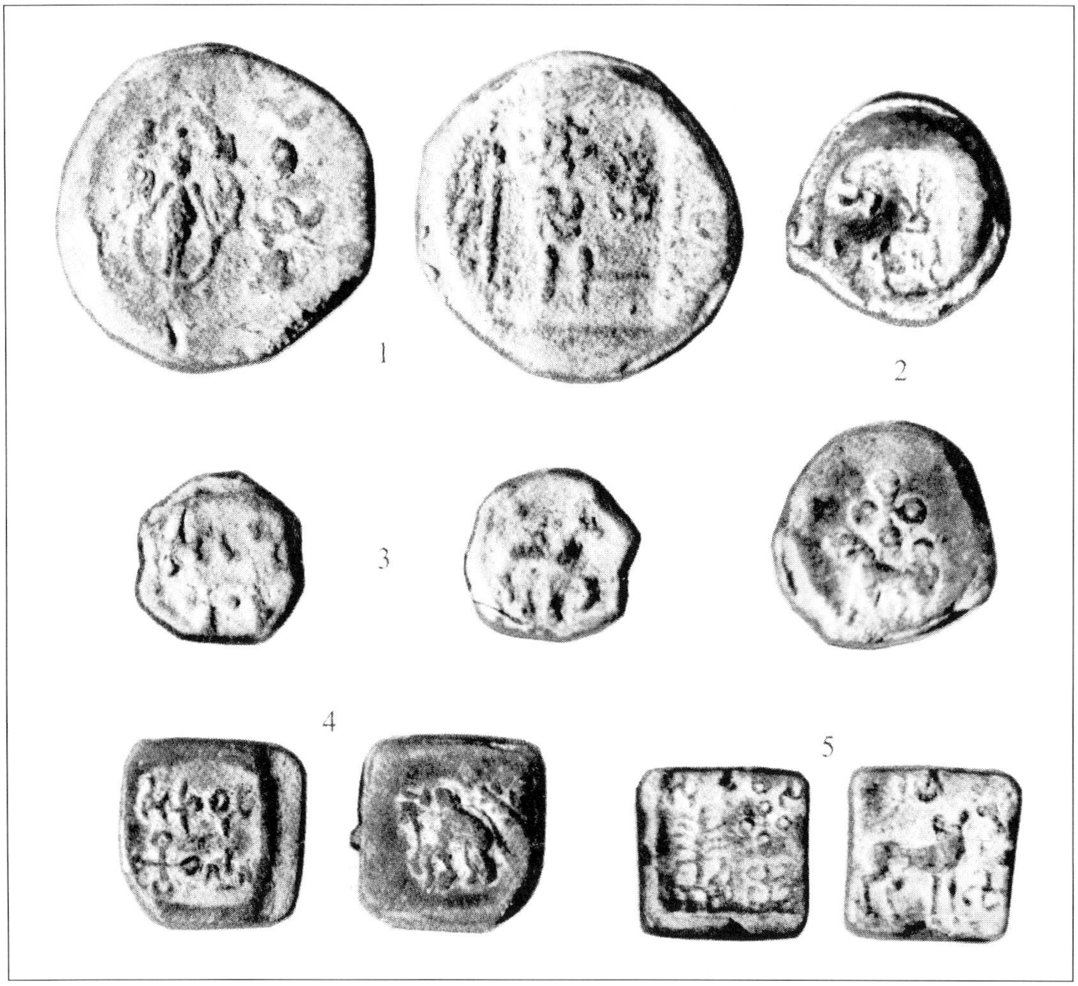

Fig. 18. Coins of Sujeṭha (Sujyeshṭha).

Rev. Lakshmī standing facing on lotus and holding flower in raised right hand anointed by elephants on circular raised area, traces of border lines to left and above circle.

Ajit Ghose observed that, "Here, however, we have a coin of a ruler whose name was Sujeṭha = Sujyeshṭha, and we may with a reasonable degree of probability, identify him with Sujyeshṭha, who is the third in the line of Śuṅga kings as given in the Vishṇupurāṇa".[2] The learned editor (Prof. V.S. Agrawala) also endorsed this attribution ". . . . The attribution of the present coin to a ruler of the Śuṅga dynasty who ruled at Vidiśā may be very likely, as suggested by the author".[3]

Sujyeshṭha (variants Jyeshṭha and Vasujyeshṭha) is said to be a son of Agnimitra in the *Bhāgavatapurāṇa* and all the Purāṇas assign him a reign of seven years.[4] Jayaswal[5] had identified Sujyeshṭha with Jeṭhamita (Jyeshṭhamitra) of Kauśāmbī coins as k manuscript of the *Vishṇupurāṇa* calls him Jyeshṭha and because Jyeshṭhamitra of the said coin is also connected with an Agnimitra.[6] Commenting on the dynastic lists of the Śuṅga kings and the issuers of the Pañchāla series of coins,

Allan observed, "The only name found in both lists is Agnimitra, which is too common a name for any deduction to be made from it. Sujyeshṭha or Vasujyeshṭha has been identified with Jyeshṭhamitra (Jeṭhamitra), but the latter has no connection with the Pañchāla series, even if we were to accept the possibility of this connection".[7]

Bela Lahiri, too, has shown the un-tenability of the identification of Sujyeshṭha with the Jeṭhamitra of Kauśāmbī or Pañchāla coins.[8] Referring to the coin of Sujyeshṭha published by Ajit Ghose she has observed that, "we cannot be sure of this attribution until a definitely assignable Śuṅga coinage comes to light".[9] Another coin of Sujeṭha (Sujyeshṭha) from Atranjikhera in district Etah of U.P. was published by M.D.N. Sahi[10] in 1968 and has also been subsequently described and discussed by R.C. Gaur.[11] Bela Lahiri did not take notice of this coin. Found from the upper phase (Sub phase B) of the NBPW Period from a deposit (ARJ 78/62), which is stratigraphically earlier in the same trench than that which yielded the coin of Kshatrapa Hagāmaśa (ARJ 71/62). This coin bears the following details —

Atranjikhera, lead, 1.5 x 1.75 cm, maximum thickness 0.4 cm, weight 8.818 g.[12]

Obv. Lakshmī standing on lotus in the centre with twin stalk and lotus on either side of the deity. On each flower stands an elephant holding together a *Chhatra* (parasol) over the head of the goddess. Around her head is a girdle of dots. On her left towards the outer edge is a tree with multiple branches and thick leaves. Between the *Chhatra* and the apex of the tree over the back of the left elephant is the Ujjain symbol of which two orbs are out of flan. In the lower left margin runs the legend *Sujeṭhasa*.

Rev. Large Ujjain symbol with Brāhmī '*ya*' in one orb. The signs in other orbs are indistinct.

Probably taking a clue from the coin published by Ajit Ghose, Sahi and Gaur have also attributed the lead coin from Atranjikhera to the Śuṅga ruler Sujyeshṭha.[13]

Some time back Dr. O.P.L. Srivastava too has published the following coin from Erach (25° 47′ N & 79° 7′ E) located on the right bank of the Betwa in district Jhansi in Uttar Pradesh –

Erach, bronze, rectangular (9 x 12 mm, 0.72 g), cast coin.

Obv. Forepart of an animal (elephant) to right, inverted *Indradhvaja* and Ujjain symbol in the upper row with early Brāhmī legend *Sujeṭhasa* below.

Rev. Taurine, *svastika* with elephant to right under these two symbols and a *Indradhvaja* along the right edge.

Srivastava too identifies the issuer as the scion of Pushyamitra – son of Agnimitra.[14]

Though these coins betray some common symbols like *svastika*, *Indradhvaja*, Ujjain symbol, elephant, Gaja-Lakshmī, etc. yet the popularity of all these symbols on early Indian coins does not help us to ascertain the identity of their issuers with certainty as they all show typological differences. Typological, metallic, proveniencial and metrological differences indicate that all of these coins may not have been issued by the same potentate. The possibility of these coins to have been issued by a scion of Pushyamitra seems to be little as neither Sugh nor Atranjikhera and Erach may have formed part of Śuṅga dominions after Pushyamitra. The coin of Ajit Ghosh was made of copper and Srivastava mentions his coin as that of bronze while all coins from Sugh and the one from Atranjikhera are of lead. In spite of some symbols which were popularly used in those times Atranjikhera coin does not betray similarity to any of the lead coins from Sugh and may have been issued by a different ruler. The exact provenance of the coin of Sujyeshṭha published by Ajit Ghose is not known and this coin too differs substantially from Sugh coins. It therefore seems more likely that this coin too was issued by another local ruler. Just like the names of Agnimitra, Sūryamitra, Gomitra, etc. which were very popular in those times Sujyeshṭha was another popular name during the second century BCE and was borne by different rulers who held sway in different territories.

Pliny had recorded that "India has neither brass nor lead but exchanges precious stones and pearls for them".[15] Sahi, therefore, thinks that the lead coin from Atranjikhera is perhaps the earliest lead coin of Northern India.[16] We may mention here that Allan had published fourteen Kāḍa type coins and about a dozen more have been collected from Sugh half of which are made of lead as described in the foregoing pages. These coins were dated to third century BCE or early second century BCE by Allan.[17] These coins must have preceded the lead coins of Sujyeshṭha at Sugh. Lead seems to have been used very commonly at Sugh and many other places in India as discussed in a following paper in the 3rd - 2nd century BCE. A lead human figure ascribable to *circa* 2nd century BCE has also been obtained from the site of Sugh and is preserved in Mr. Aggarwal's collection besides certain undetermined objects and even lead lumps. Recent studies have disproved Pliny's observation also. The process of the crystallization of lead from argentiferous galena leaving silver-rich residue seems to have been discovered in the third millennium BCE and lead objects from Mohenjodaro and Lothal containing 99.2% and 99.54% lead indicate that the metal workers could achieve a high degree of purity of lead. The (argentiferous) lead ore may have been obtained from Faranjal mine in Afghanistan and Rajpura-Dariba (80 km NE of Udaipur), Rampura-Aguncha (25° 50′ N and 74° 44′ 15" E, 15 km SE of Gulabpura near Ajmer) and Zawar (30 km SW of Udaipur) in Rajasthan.[18] Wadia had referred to ores of lead in the Himalayas.[19] Referring to the vast heaps of mine debris and a lead piece recovered from the slag dump containing 97.5% lead and 150 ppm silver at Rajupura-Dariba, A.K. Biswas has observed that "The evidences show 'the gregarious nature of working' of the Lead-Silver ore in the area during the successive Pre-Maurya, Maurya, Śuṅga and Kuṣāṇa periods of the Indian history".[20] Possibly, therefore, the lead for these coins may have been obtained from Rajpura-Dariba mines in Rajasthan or the Himalayas.

These lead coins seem to have been the local currency of Sugh. It is doubtful if Sugh and Atranjikhera were included in the Śuṅga dominions during the reign of Sujyeshṭha. Sugh has not yielded any definitely attributable Śuṅga coins. Śuṅga Sujyeshṭha ruled for seven years but the eight coins published here and two coins published earlier belong to different types indicating a longer rule of the king. The palaeography, too, seems to point an earlier date than that of the Śuṅga Sujyeshṭha. Ajit Ghose himself had observed that "in fact the epigraphy looks more Aśokan then Śuṅga".[21] In the light of all these facts, it is difficult to accept this local coinage of Sujyeshṭha to have been issued by the Śuṅga ruler of this name.

Some historians believe that the Mauryan Empire had started disintegrating after Aśoka's death. The Indo-Greek invasions during the reign of Pushyamitra too seem to have decimated his dominions. Pushyamitra's grandson Vasumitra had led the imperial army against the Yavanas during the lifetime of his grandfather and defeated them on the Sindhu, which probably formed the boundary of the Śuṅga Empire. Many scholars identify this Sindhu with the Kali Sindhu in Central India. If this were so, the area northwards must have been out of the pale of Pushyamitra's empire. P.L. Gupta has shown that Mathurā, Kauśāmbī and various north Indian republican states had started issuing their coinages from about the middle of the second century BCE.[22] Sugh thus must have definitely been out of the Śuṅga dominions during Sujyeshṭha's rule. Coins bearing the legend *Kāḍasa* in the early Brāhmī characters of late third-early second century BCE found from Sugh[23] furnish corroborative evidence in this connection.

Who issued these coins then? Probably a local ruler Sujyeshṭha. In fabric, shapes, metals, palaeography, etc. these coins betray affinities with Kāḍa coins but more evidence is required to establish a definite link between the two.

NOTES AND REFERENCES

1. *JNSI*, XVI, pp. 59-60, pl. V. 2.
2. *Ibid.*, p. 60.
3. *Ibid.*
4. Lahiri (1974), *ISNI*, p. 51.
5. *Journal of Bihar and Orissa Research Society*, III, p. 147 and X, p. 206.
6. Lahiri (1974), *ISNI*.
7. *BMCAI*, p. cxx.
8. *ISNI*, chs. IV and V.
9. *Ibid.*
10. *JNSI*, XXX, pp. 56-60.
11. *Ibid.*, LVI, pp. 1-3.
12. Gaur has mentioned the weight as 8.85 gm.
13. *Loc. cit.*
14. Srivastava, Om Prakash Lal (2017), 'A Rare Coin of Sujyeshtha from Erach', *ND*, Vol. 41, pp. 10-12; (2020), *Erach Rediscovered: Coins, Inscriptions, Seals and Sealings*, Mumbai: Rajgor's Heritage Hub, p. 54.
15. Schoff, W.H. (1912), *The Periplus of the Erythrean Sea*, New York, XXXIV. 17, p. 22.
16. *JNSI*, XXX, p. 59.
17. *BMCAI*, pp. xcil and 145.
18. Biswas, Arun Kumar (1996), *Minerals and Metals in Ancient India*, Vol. I, New Delhi, pp. 61, 110 and 329 ff. See also Reedy, C.L. (1997), "Technical Studies of Gandhāran Art", in

Bridget Allchin *et al.* (Eds.), *Gandhara Art in Contaxt: East West Exchange at Cross-roads of Asia*, New Delhi, pp. 267-81.

19. Wadia, D.N. (1975), *Geology of India*, Delhi, p. 351.
20. Biswas, *op. cit.*, p. 331.
21. *JNSI*, XVI, p. 60.
22. *IHQ*, XXVII, pp. 197-207; "The Bearing of the Local Coins on the History of Northern India," in *Seminar Papers on the Local Coins of Northern India* (Ed. A.K. Narain), Varanasi, 1968, pp. 147-56.
23. *BMCAI*, pp. xcii - xciii and 145-46, pls. XIX. 14-20 and XLIII. 10-11; *ND*, VI (1962), pp. 12-16; Handa (1985), *op. cit.*, ch. 6.

V

Lead Coins of Gomitra and Vishṇumitra

Some very important lead coins of two Mitra kings, Gomitra and Vishṇumitra, unknown from any other source, have also been obtained from Sugh.

DESCRIPTION OF THE COINS

1. Lead, square, 1.1 cm.

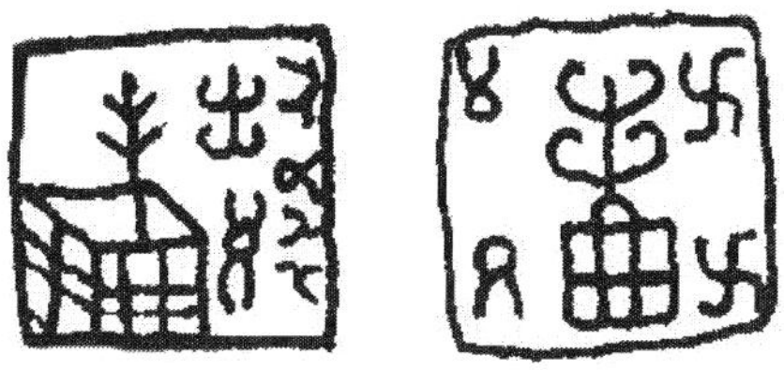

Obv. Tree in railing on left, Brāhmī *yya* like symbol (*śrīvatsa?)* in the upper field in centre and perpendicularly placed legend *Gomitasa* in early Brāhmī characters on right.

Rev. *Śrīvatsa* (Brāhmī *yya* like symbol) placed on a railed platform in the centre, a normal and an inverted *nandipada,* in the corners on left and svastika symbol in the corners on right.

2. Lead, round, 1.2 cm.

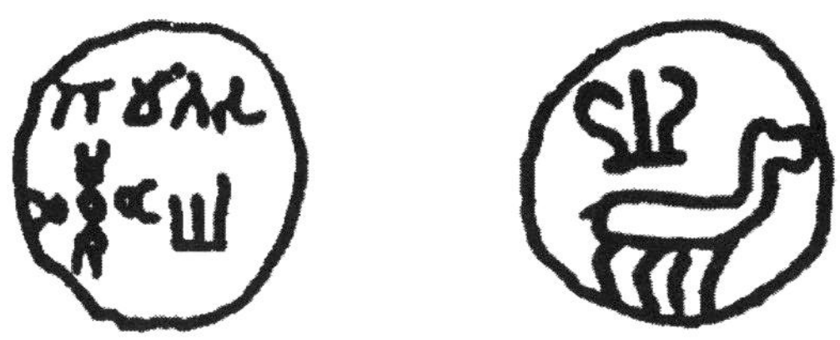

Obv. *Gomitsa* in early Brāhmī characters above, a pellet with four *nandipada* symbols in four cardinal directions around on left and Brāhmī *gha* like symbol on right below. The lower part seems to have been obliterated.

Rev. An animal (deer?) to right with *śrīvatsa* (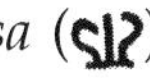) at the back.

3. Lead, round, 1.2 x 1.1 cm.

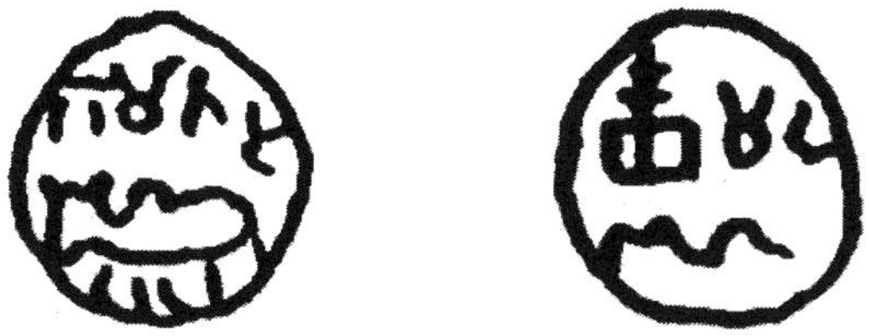

Obv. Humped bull to left with early Brāhmī legend *Gomitasa* above.

Rev. Tree in railing, *nandipada* and an unidentifiable partly visible symbol from left to right above, partially visible humped bull to left below.

4. Lead, rectangular, 1.4 x 1.6 cm, weight not recorded.

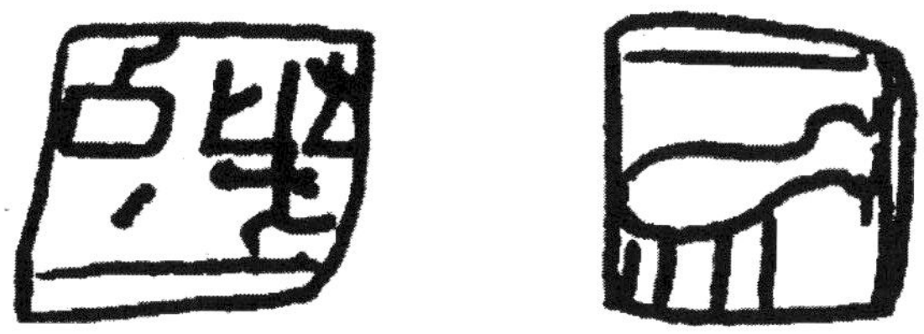

Obv. Brāhmī legend in two lines: *Bishṇu-mi / [ta]sa.*

Rev. Animal (perhaps elephant or bull) to right.

These lead coins, like the other lead coins of Kāḍa and Sujeṭha from Sugh, are struck on cast planchets as indicated by the joining lines of the moulds on the edges and may be placed in the second century BCE on palaeographic grounds. They, thus, seem to have followed the Kāḍa and Sujeṭha lead coins at Sugh. Tree-in-railing, *svastika*, *śrīvatsa* and *nandipada* symbols are connecting links. Ujjain symbol, found on the coins of Kāḍa and Sujeṭha, is not seen on the known three types of these Mitra coins. Also the octagonal shape of the Kāḍa and Sujeṭha coins is missing, though the square and round shapes continue. The depiction of humped bull, not seen on the earlier coins, seems to have been introduced by Gomitra, probably in consonance with his personal name. Tree-in-railing, *śrīvatsa*, *nandipada* and bull symbols occur on the coins of Gomitra(s) of Mathura also. But the shapes of these symbols on the Mathura coins are so different that it is difficult to establish their identity with the symbols on the Sugh coins of Gomitra. Mathura coins are of copper and die-struck whereas Sugh coins of Gomitra are struck on cast lead planchets, Moreover, no coin of any Gomitra of Mathura has ever been found at Sugh and no lead piece resembling those of Gomitra of Sugh has ever been obtained from any site except Sugh. Gomitra of Sugh, thus, seems to have been a local ruler who may have belonged to the line of Kāḍa and Sujeṭha and ruled sometime during the second century BCE.

The only known coin of Vishṇumitra is interesting not only for showing the legend in two lines but spelling the name with *Ba*, presenting an example of Pāṇini's *sūtra* (aphorism) *Bavayorabhedaḥ*, i.e. there is no difference between *ba* and *va*. The rectangular shape has been given by cutting the edges. Being the only known coin of Vishṇumitra of Sugh, it is important. The paucity of his coins indicates that he may not have ruled for a long time.

As is well known, there were many rulers with Mitra-ending names ruling in various parts of north India during the second and subsequent centuries. Since these lead coins of Gomitra and Vishṇumitra do not show any kinship with their namesakes in other parts of the country, they have to be taken as the Mitra rulers of Sugh, known from these coins for the first time. They, however, seem to have belonged to the family of Kāḍa as noted above.

NOTES AND REFERENCES

1. Being made of lead and blackish in color, and in an indifferent state of preservation, these coins did not give a good photograph and hence only their eye copies have been given here.
2. It shows some affinity with the symbol which occurs on the Taxilian coins of uninscribed Class 1, var. e of Allan (*BMCAI*, pp. cxxxiv and 220, nos. 50-51, pl. XXII.12-13.

VI

Coins of Pratishṭhāna

More than a decade and a half back, two lead coins, one square (19 x 20 mm, 4.62 g) and another round one (16 x 18 mm, 2.32 g), said to have been 'found somewhere in District Hisar of Haryana' seen with a collector of Jind (Haryana) were published by Prashant P. Kulkarni.[1] The square coin bears the early Brāhmī legend *Pusamitasa* on the obverse and a wheel, club, Ujjayini symbol, plough and pestle on the reverse, the first three in the upper row and the last two in the lower row while the round piece bears a human figure and the legend *Patithana* in early Brāhmī characters on the obverse and a tree in railing flanked by an arched hill symbol on left and *svastika* on right on the reverse counter struck on both sides[2] (Fig. 19).

Wilfried Pieper too possesses a similar coin with the only differences that the countermark on the obverse is bigger and the wheel or lotus countermark is struck on the upper left branch of the tree on the reverse. There is an indistinct device visible above the counter mark. It may have been a lotus held by the female figure in her raised right hand indicating it to be goddess Lakshmī. The coin may have probably the same provenance. The three-arched symbol drawn by Kulkarni seems to have been inverted *triratna*. Pieper's coin also shows the Brāhmī letters 'ga' and 'na' at about 7 and 10 o'clock positions and 'patiṭhāne' placed between 1 and 4 o'clock posiition on the obverse (Fig. 20.1).

Mr. Gulshan Bharadwaj of Jind, the original procurer of the lead coins published by Kulkarni, told me personally that these pieces were found from Uklana in district Hisar. I have seen similar lead coins in the collection of Shri R.K. Aggarwal of Ambala who confirms the provenance of these coins to be Mughalpura near Uklana in district Hisar.

Prashant had referred to a coin of this type on which he deciphered the legend 'Trinanam'. Originally found from Mughalpura and belonging to Mr. Gulshan Bharadwaj this coin appeared in trade and was put on the net by Sarvashri Girish

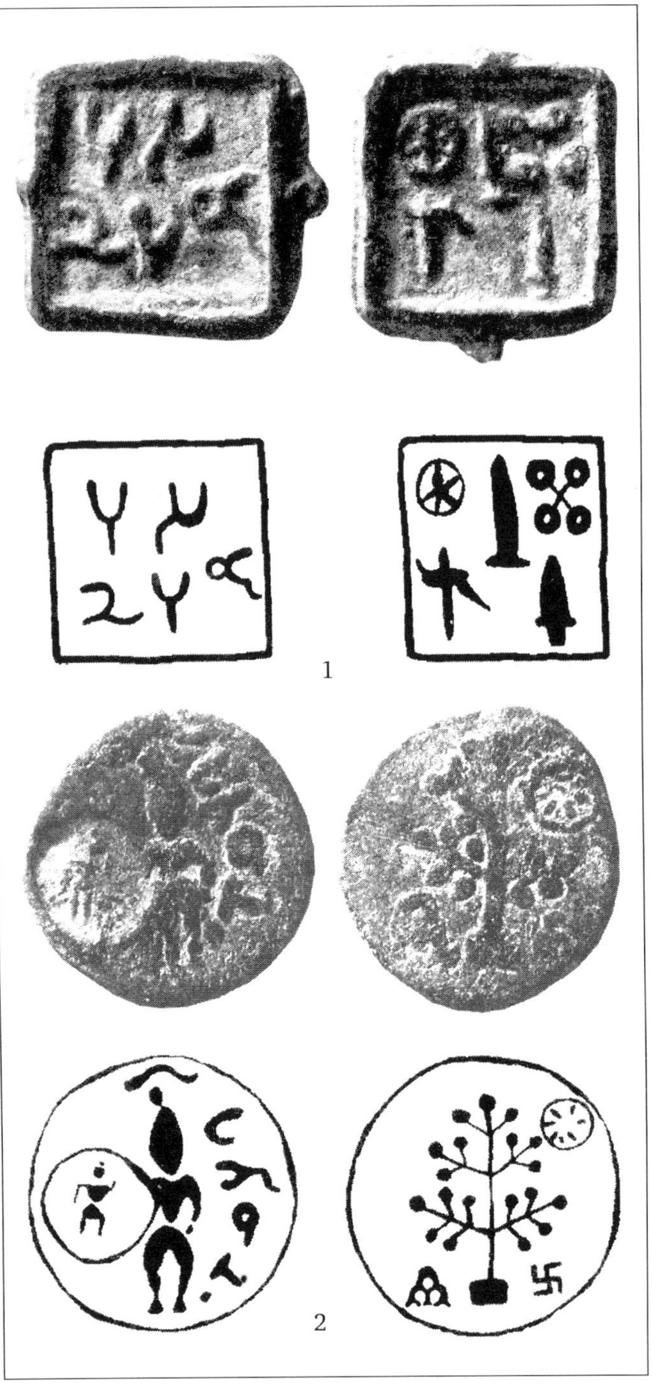

Fig. 19. Lead coins of Pushyamitra and Pratishṭhāna.

Sharma, Vijay Solanki, Kapil Bharadwaj (son of Shri Gulashan Bharadwaj), etc. at different times some years back and was finally procured by Dr. Nilaish (Fig. 20.2). This lead coin weighs 2.23 g. In the centre on the obverse is a female figure standing facing wearing earrings, necklace, wristlets, puffed anklets, dhoti secured by waistband and a scarf with her right hand raised to hold an object (lotus?) and left hand akimbo. Finer details are not visible because of the indifferent state of preservation but an end of her scarf seems to flutter away to left touching the first letter of the legend at about 7 o'clock position. The legend reads as *Gaṇānaṃ* from 7 to 10 o'clock and *Patiṭhānaṃ* from about 2 to 4 o'clock in early Brāhmī letters may be seen along the edge in a round die impression. The reverse shows a big tree in railing with more than three branches on either side of the trunk and having leaves on both sides. On the left of the railing is an inverted *triratna* symbol while a *svastika* may be seen on the right of it. The round die mark is very clear even on this side. The legend on Pieper's coin too may have originally been similar but the countermark concealed the middle letter.

Kapil Bharadwaj has procured a number of Pratishṭhāna coins from Mughalpura and nearby sites. Amongst these was a very badly mutilated, worn out and broken piece of the preceding type (1.650 g, 15 mm) recovered from Daulatpur, another ancient site close to Mughalpura (Fig. 20.3). Female figure with her right hand raised and left on hip with traces of legend on her right and left like the preceding example may still be seen. *Patiṭhānaṃ* on her left is comparatively better preserved and may be discerned on the original coin. Though the tree in railing on the reverse is almost completely obliterated yet the round countermark of wheel or lotus has survived in fairly good condition.

Kapil Bharadwaj put on the net another badly worn out coin which shows the female figure with a vertical indulating line (serpent?) on the right of the female figure on the obverse and a faintly visible device of tree in railing and inverted *nandipada* on viewer's left on the reverse (Fig. 20.4), similar to the preceding example but without visible countermark.

A very much worn out coin of this type showing only the female figure and the legend *patiṭhānaṃ* from 1 to 4 o'clock position on her left and snake or undulating river line above on the obverse and with a similar reverse has recently been acquired by Dr. Nilaish from a dealer of Haryana.

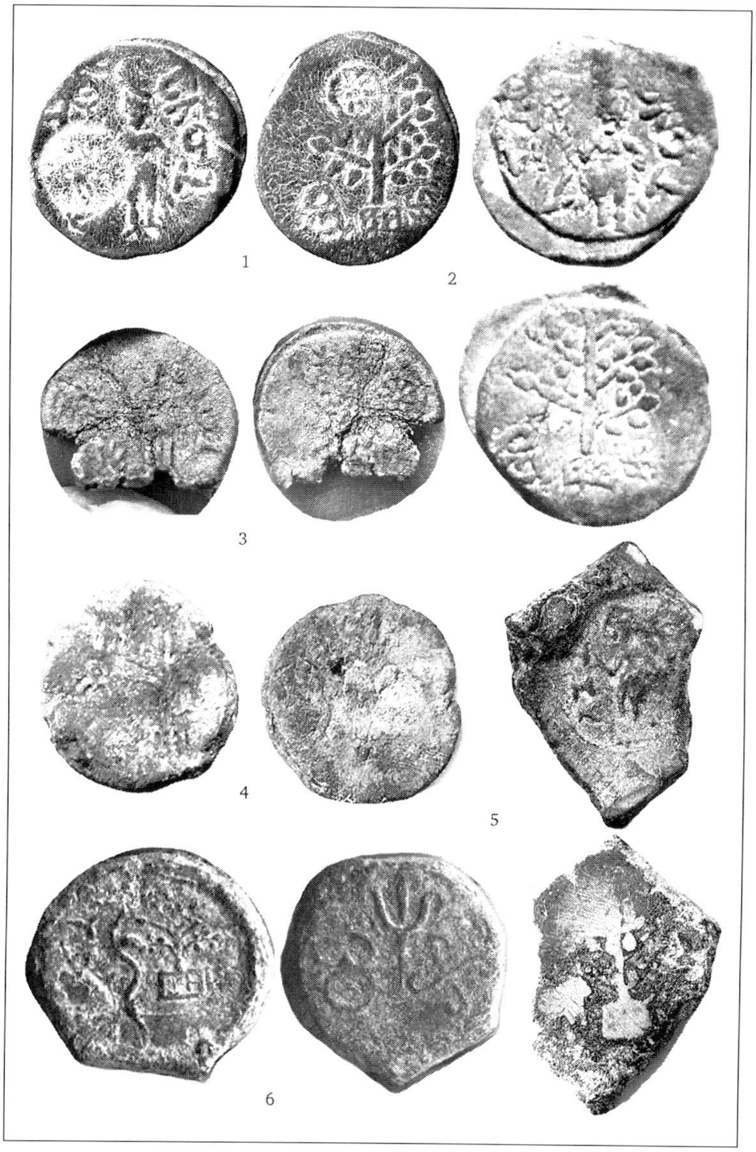

Fig. 20. Pratishṭhāna coins.

Kapil Bharadwaj possesses another slightly broken square coin from Mughalpura which has preserved the female figure with the legend *Gaṇānaṃ* on her right in a deep roundish incuse on the obverse and tree in railing with inverted *triratna* symbol near the railing on the reverse. Another coin in his possession from the above-mentioned site shows tree in railing with vertically placed snake or river line on (viewer's) left and the Brāhmī letter *na* at 10 o'clock position on the obverse and trident flanked by a *nandipada* on left and *svastika* on viewer's right on the reverse (Fig. 20.6). It may also be attributed to Pratishṭhāna on the basis of symbology and the existence of letter *na* on the obverse. Recently he has recovered a new elephant type Pratishṭhāna coin of lead from the same site showing the tree rising from an eight-compartented railing with vertically placed undulating line on its right (i.e. viewers' left) and part of the early Brāhmī legend along the right edge from bottom upwards from about 3.30 to 1.30 o'clock reading *patiṭhāna* on the obverse and a tusker walking to left with anti-clockwise placed similarly reading Brāhmī legend along the right edge from bottom upwards from about 2.30 to 11.30 o'clock:

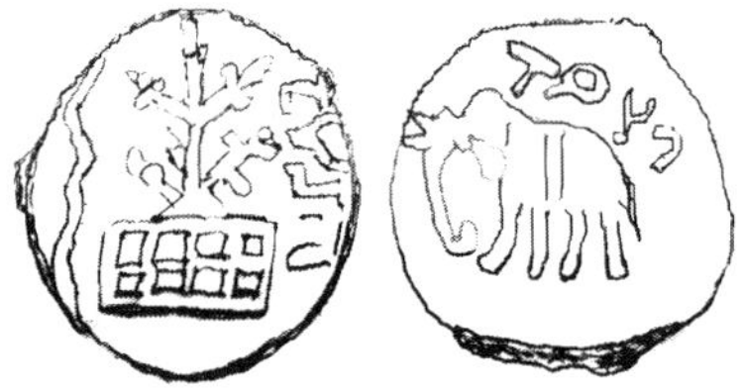

Recently Dr. Akshay Jain has acquired a small (approximately 1.0 g) lead coin showing the elephant to right.

Some years back Shri Vaibhav Aggarwal had obtained from this site a newer type of Patishṭhāna coin:

Lead, round, 2.35 g, 16 mm.

Obv. A horse to left facing a vertically placed snake, Brāhmī legend *Patiṭhāna* in characters of late third or early second century BCE above and *svastika* and taurine(?) below the horse.

Rev. Tree-in-railing on right, inverted taurine with an indistinct symbol above on left (Fig. 21.1).

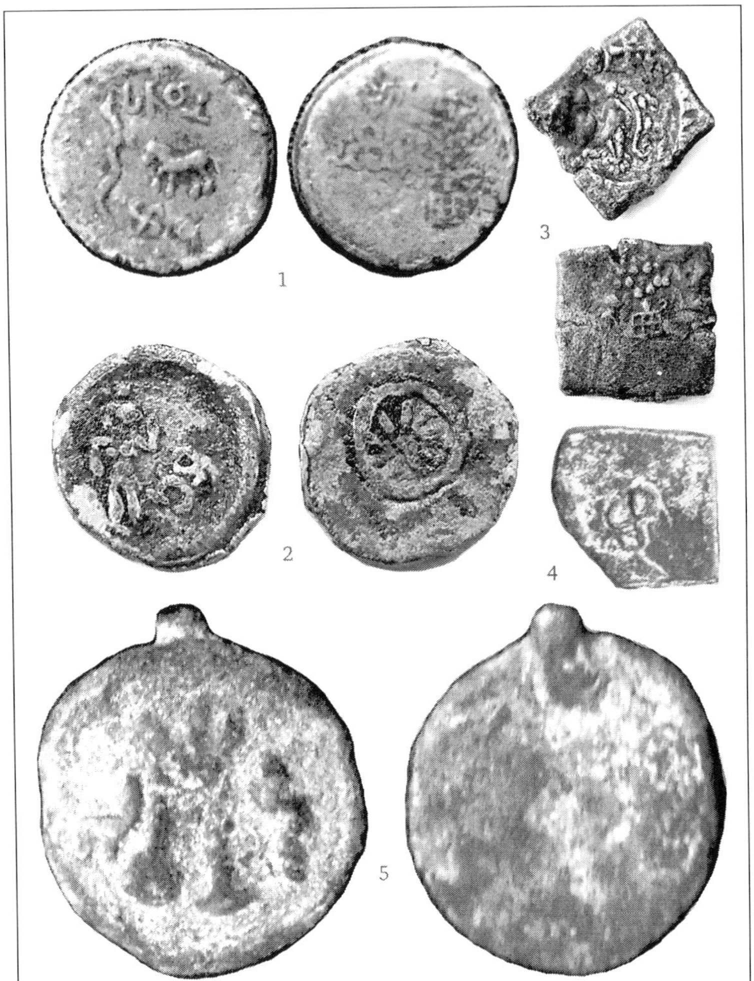

Fig. 21. Pratishṭhāna and allied coins 1-4, coin of Bhavanandi 5.

This thus is a new type of lead coin bearing the legend *Patiṭhāna* (Sanskrit Pratishṭhāna) from Mughalpura. The weight indicates that it was of the same denomination as that of Kulkarni's coin.

A small lead coin from Daulatpur near Mughalpura weighing 0.410 g bears wheel or lotus symbol as seen in the countermark on figures 19 and 20 illustrated above exclusively on the reverse side and a female standing with her left hand raised to the level of the shoulder with right suspended to the waist with two bold letters (- *tiṭhā*?) in the right field on the obverse seems to be connected with Pratishṭhāna coins because of the female figure and the wheel/lotus symbol which we generally find struck on some Pratishṭhāna coins (Fig. 21.2).

Another small coin from this site (Fig. 21.3) shows on the obverse in a deep round incuse a female wearing a chignon and dhoti standing on a lotus slightly turned to her right holding a lotus in her extended right hand with left hand holding perhaps a bunch of fruits and resting it on hip. On viewers' left seems to be a *kalaśa* 'pot' while a vertically placed curved frame representing perhaps a pond with fishes. The reverse shows a fruit tree with six-compartment base. Other motifs or legend are irretrievably lost. This may have been an allied coin. Another squarish lead piece from the site shows a *svastika* resembling the symbol as seen on a coin (Fig. 20.6) too may have belonged to the Pratishṭhāna specie (Fig. 21.4).

The ancient site of Mughalpura (29° 30' 99" N / 75° 82' 88" E) spread over about 60 acres and nearly 13 – 15 m high from the road level lies very close to the town of Uklana, almost adjoining it, nearly 50 km north-northeast of the district headquarters of Hisar on Uklana-Sirsa road (Fig. 22).

Dilip K. Chakrabarti and Sukhdev Saini picked up painted potsherds and goblet bases belonging to Late Harappan or Hakra ware besides brickbats strewn over the

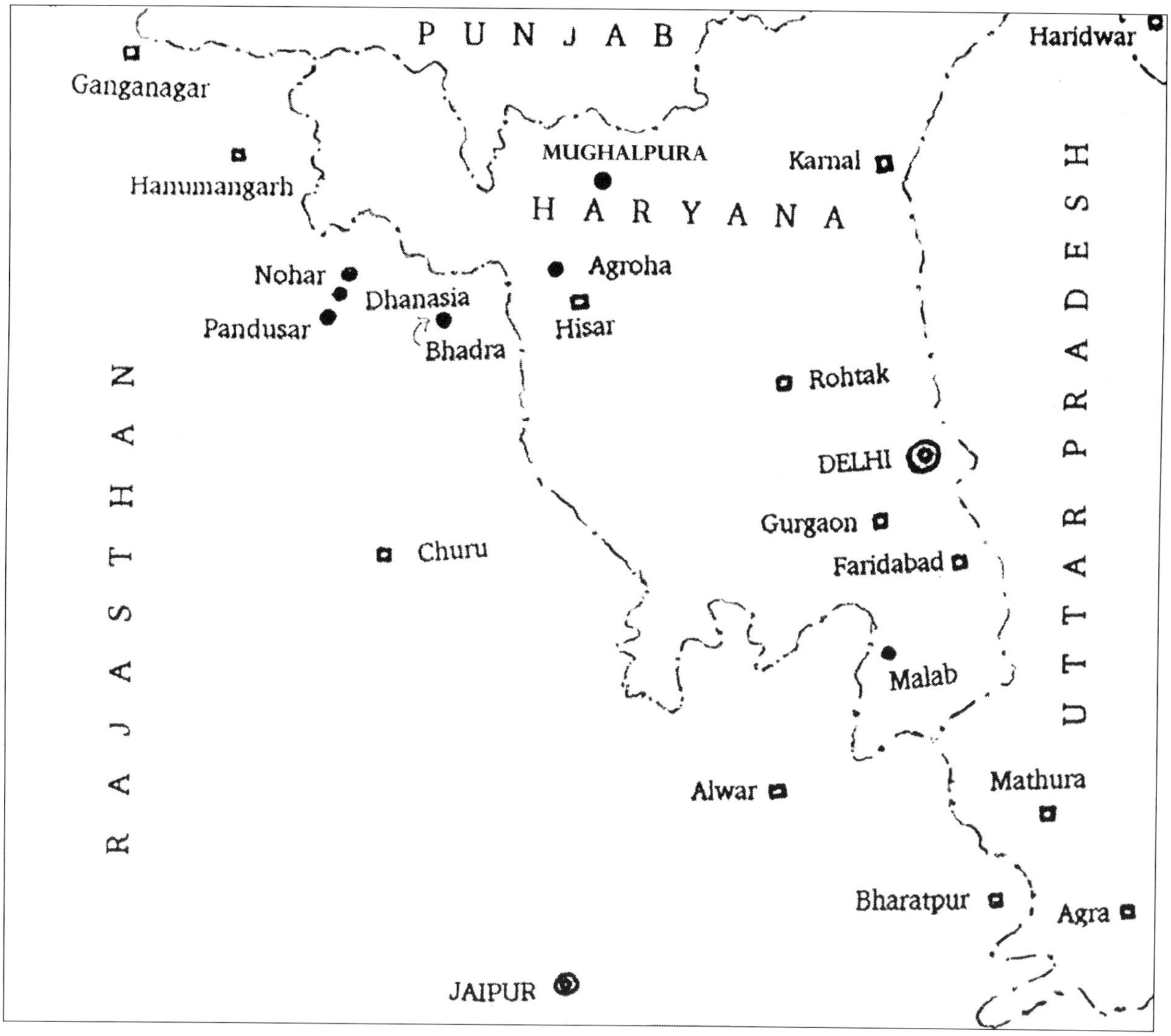

Fig. 22. Map showing the location of Mughalpura.

surface of the mound and have observed that "apart from Rakhigarhi and probably Nachar Khera and Bhirrana, this is the largest protohistoric mound of Haryana."[3] The site yields early historic and medieval relics also.[4]

Besides the coins described above the site of Mughalpura has also yielded a lead coin belonging to Bhavanandi bearing the legend in Brāhmī characters of late third or early second century BCE (Fig. 21.5). Nothing is known about Bhavanandi from any other source. The reverse is obliterated completely: It is preserved in Shri R.K. Aggarwal's collection at Ambala.[5]

The coins from the site suggest that Mughalpura was probably known as a big market (Pratishṭhāna) of the empire over which Pushyamitra and Bhavanandi ruled during the late third or early second century BCE. The discovery of quite a good number of lead coins of Kāḍa, Sujyeshṭha, Gomitra and Vishṇumitra from Sugh as discussed in the foregoing pages suggests that this region had slipped from the hands of Aśoka's successors and become independent.

In ancient times there were quite a few well-established towns bearing the name of Pratishṭhāna.[6] The *Harivaṃśa*[7] refers to Pratishṭhāna as the capital of Purūravā, still called Pratishṭhānapura, on the northern bank of the Gaṅgā and identified with Jhusi opposite Prayāga or Allahabad) on the confluence of Gaṅgā and Yamunā. It was the capital of the kings of the lunar race. A town of this name on the Godāvari River in district Aurangabad (modern Paithan) was the capital of the Sātavāhana rulers. Pathankot on the Ravi in Punjab was also known as Pratishṭhāna in ancient times.[8] It was the capital of the Udumbaras. It is interesting to note that Garibnath Temple Inscription of Pehowa (ancient Pṛithūdaka) of the time of King Bhoja Pratihāra refers to the place as *Pṛithūdaka-sthāne* and *Pṛithūdakādhishṭhāne* at two different places. It was a big market for horse-trade.[9]

It is interesting to note that like the prefixes *adhi, upa*, etc. 'prati' was used with *sthāna* (meaning place) in the sense of 'against', 'in opposition to' or 'at par with' implying that Pratishṭhāna was in the sense of 'a town or place founded or used against or in opposition to an earlier town or place'. The commonness of use of the term Pratishṭhāna suggests that it was not a regular place-name but was a descriptive epithet.[10]

The romance of King Purūravā, grandson of Manu, with nymph Urvaśī and his excursions in the Himalayas are well known through literature. Tradition depicts Purūravā as an illustrious monarch of great achievements who conquered all the seven continents.[11] Bharadwaj has observed that "Manu Vaivasvata had laid the foundation of his kingdom in Brahmāvarta where his capital was probably at some place located centrally in the Sarasvatī-Dṛishadvatī region. Sudyumna extended it westward across the Sarasvatī or Ghaggar and moved from the original seat of his predecessor to a more strategic place on the western bank, which being a new settlement, was called Pratishṭhāna in contradistinction to the old capital."[12] Jaichandra Vidyalankar suggested the location of this new Pratishṭhāna somewhere near the Sarasvatī[13] and Mughapura fits into this proposal. Though there is no definite evidence to ascertain it, the possibility of the tradition of being so cannot be ruled out altogether.

So the term Pratishṭhāna here seems to have been used not only for the capital cities but also for big towns and market places.The old mound of Mughalpura spread over 60 hectares of land and rising to a height of about 50 feet bears witness to its being one of the very extensive and important places. It is therefore no surprise if Mughalpura adjoining Uklana (old Ulūkhalāyana) was also known as Pratishṭhāna in the early historic period. The coins bearing the legend *Patiṭhāna* found from this place thus indicate it to be a big market place for goods exported to Rajasthan as its location indicates.

NOTES AND REFERENCES

1. *Indian Coin Society Newsletter*, No. 38, Jan-March 2006, pp. 4-7. Kulkarni felt inclined to attribute the square lead coin to Pushyamitra who was the commander-in-chief of the last Maurya emperor Bṛihadratha and had founded the Śuṅga dynasty after assassinating him in circa 185 BCE. To me, however, this seems to be a Vṛishṇi coin issued by some local ruler named Pushyamitra carrying the usual five Vṛishṇi symbols but with the half-lion and half-elephant symbol substituted by the Ujjain symbol.
2. *Ibid.*; Kulkarni (2009-2010), "Coinage of Pushyamitra Śuṅga", *The Journal of Academy of Indian Numismatics & Sigillography*, Indore, Vol. XXIII-XXIV, pp. 5-9 and "Recent discoveries in early inscribed coins of Vidarbha", *Supplement to the Journal of the Oriental Numismatic Society*, No. 205, pp. 4-15.
3. Chakrabarti, Dilip K. and Sukhdev Saini (2009), *The Problem of the Sarasvati River and Notes on the Archaeological Geography of Haryana and Indian Panjab*, New Delhi: Aryan Books International, p. 73.
4. *Indian Archaeology – A Review*, 1980-81, p. 18.
5. *JONS*, 216 (2013), pp. 23-24. My thanks are due to Shri R.K. Aggarwal and Kapil Bharadwaj for information, scans and details of the coins from Mughalpura and Daulatpur in their collections.
6. Dey, Nundo Lal (1971), *The Geographical Dictionary of Ancient and Medieval India*, 3rd ed., New Delhi: Oriental Books Corporation, Reprint, p. 159. Many of these sites have been mentioned in the Puranas, Jatakas, inscriptions and secular literature.
7. *Harivaṃśa* (Gita Press edition), I.26, 49: *Rājyaṃ sa kāryamāsa Prayāge pṛithavīpatiḥ / Uttare Jāhnavītīre pratishthānaṃ mahāyaśāḥ / /*
8. *Kangra District Gazetteer*, Lahore, 1926, p. 89; Chaudhuri, S.B. (1955), *op. cit.*, pp. 57 and 117.
9. *Śrī-pṛithūdakādhishṭhāne piśāchī-chaturddaśyāṃ ghoṭaka-yātrāyāṃ*. . . (Line 3 of the inscription) and *Pṛithūdaka-sthānāya tathā ghoṭaka-saṃgrāhakair...* (line 14). For details see Handa, Devendra (2004), *An Epic Pilgrimage History and Antiquity of Pehowa: Ancient Pṛithūdaka*, New Delhi: Aryan Books International, pp. 86-87.
10. Bharadwaj, O.P. (1986), *Studies in the Historical Geography of Ancient India*, Delhi: Sundeep Prakashan, 1986, p. 46.
11. *Matsyapurāṇa* (*Ānandāśrama Series*), XXIV.11.
12. Bharadwaj, *op. cit.*, p. 46.
13. AS quoted by Bharadwaj, *loc. cit.*

VII

Two Interesting Coins of King Gomitra of Mathura

The earliest inscribed coins of Mathura belong to Gomitra who has been dated to late third century BCE on palaeographic grounds. These copper coins of 0.6-0.7 inch square weighing between 66 and 89 grains (4.28-5.77 g) bear four symbols in the centre with *Gomitasa* in early Brāhmī characters above and *yaranam*? below on the obverse and tree in railing in a square of dots on the reverse.[1] This ruler was named as Gomitra I as some more square and round copper coins of a crude fabric showing an enface standing female figure identified as Lakshmī holding a lotus in her uplifted right hand with typical Mathura tree[2] on left, and on right with below and the legend *Gomitasa* along the edge above the goddess, the whole in a circular die on the obverse and depicting a facing elephant with rider holding goad flanked by similar ones in three-quarters profile on the reverse had also come to light from Mathura. This latter king was named as Gomitra II.[3] Variety b of this type showed the goddess holding lotus in her left hand and Var. c showed the goddess facing to left and tree in centre with Ujjain symbol below the tree and the Brāhmī legend *Gomitasa* reading downwards on right.[4] Base metal (potin) round coins weighing between 32 and 46 grains (2.073 to 2.980 g) of Gomitra II constitute Var. d and show bull to right before tree in railing and Ujjain symbol at the end of the legend.[5] The different symbology of the coins of Gomitra I and II certainly distinguishes them as separate entities. Allan has also listed a square copper coin of another Gomitra which he believed to have belonged to a different dynasty. It carries a rude figure with arms uplifted, a taurine symbol on right and the legend *Gomitasa* on the obverse with a three-branched tree in railing on the reverse.[6] Bela Lahiri, however, thought that the palaeography of the legend on the square coins of Gomitra (I) and that of Gomitra of another dynasty as visualized by Allan is similar to that of Mora Well inscription, so these coins should belong to a similar date

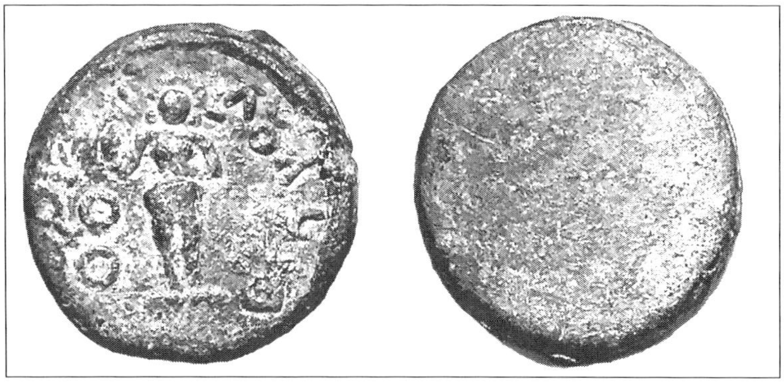

Fig. 23. Copper coin of Gomitra.

of first century BCE and that "the two Gomitras seem to be identical."[7] Allan's Gomitra II who issued both square and round coins seems to be the earliest amongst the Mathura rulers who struck the regular Mathura type coins of round shape. He was followed by some other rulers like Brahmamita, Dṛiḍhamita, Satamita, Sūryamita and Vishṇumita who all bore *mitra*-ending names. These Mitra rulers were followed by kings bearing *data*-ending names (Bhavadata, Kāmadata, Purushadata, Rāmadata, Śeshadata and Uttamadata) who replaced the Ujjain symbol with Brāhmī palatal sibilant *śa*-like symbol (ᕱ) on their coins.[8]

Two new round copper coins of Gomitra have come to my notice and are published here.

(1) Æ, round, 2.0 cm, 8.0 g approximately (Fig. 23).

Obv. Goddess Lakshmī standing enface with right hand holding a lotus at the level of the shoulder and left hand akimbo, feet splayed completely sideways, halo of dots around the head, Ujjain symbol with inverted triangle-headed symbol (*Indradhvaja*) above on left, tree in railing on right and Brāhmī legend *Gomitasa* from 1 to 4 o'clock position.

Rev. Blank.

The coin shows some interesting features. The goddess is shown with feet turned to right angles and bears an aureole of dots, the earliest depiction of the nimbus known so far. The Ujjain symbol is shown with multiplication-like cross having two circles horizontally placed at top and the other two below rather than with circles in cardinal directions as seen on other coins. An inverted *Indradhvaja* is shown above it, These symbols are shown on the proper right of the goddess whereas all known coins of this ruler show Ujjain symbol placed above the *Śrivatsa* to the proper left of the goddess. *Śrivatsa* has been replaced by an inverted *Indradhvaja* on our coin. The tree in railing also occurs on the proper left of the goddess and not on her right as seen on published specimens known so far. It is not the standard Mathura type tree in railing which shows the fruits above the horizontal branches but shows them as hanging from the branches. The Brāhmī characters are almost similar to Mauryan letters and betray an early date. Obviously this coin seems to have been struck before the standardization of the type. As such the coin may have been the earliest round coin-type of Gomitra.

(2) Æ, round, 1.5 cm, 2.34 g (Fig. 24).

Obv. Bull to right facing tree in railing, traces of Ujjain symbol at the back at 9 o'clock position, Brāhmī legend in early Mauryan characters *Gomitasa* along the edge from 10 to 1 o'clock position.

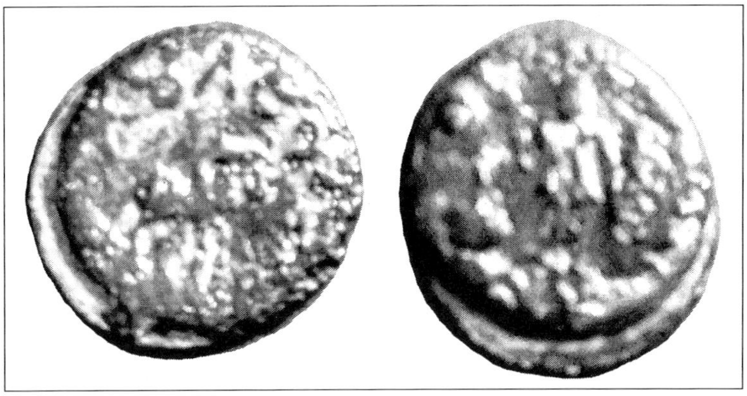

Fig. 24. Copper coin of Gomitra.

Rev. Human figure with right hand raised to the level of the shoulder and left hand suspended, symbols on right and left are blurred and not clear.

The coin gives the impression of having been over struck but the under type with legend is quite clear on the obverse which resembles the Var. d potin specie of Allan's Gomitra II.[9] Gomitra's potin coins are of plain reverse but our coin shows a human figure with some symbols on the reverse. This thus constitutes a newer variety of his round copper coins. Another very important fact revealed by this coin is that the obverse and reverse were prepared separately on thin flans and then joined together by adding baser material between the two layers to bring them to a standard weight. In this case the faulty joining of the obverse and reverse layers is very clear. Through the courtesy of Dr. Vasant Swarnkar who conducted excavations in the Purana Qila (Inderpat< Indraprastha), New Delhi in the recent years I had the opportunity of examining coins recovered in excavations and I saw this phenomenon in some cases of Mathura and Yaudheya coins of Bahudhāñake type with different layers clearly distinguishable (Fig. 25). A Pañchāla coin in possession of Gautam Jantakal of Pune also shows split thick edge.

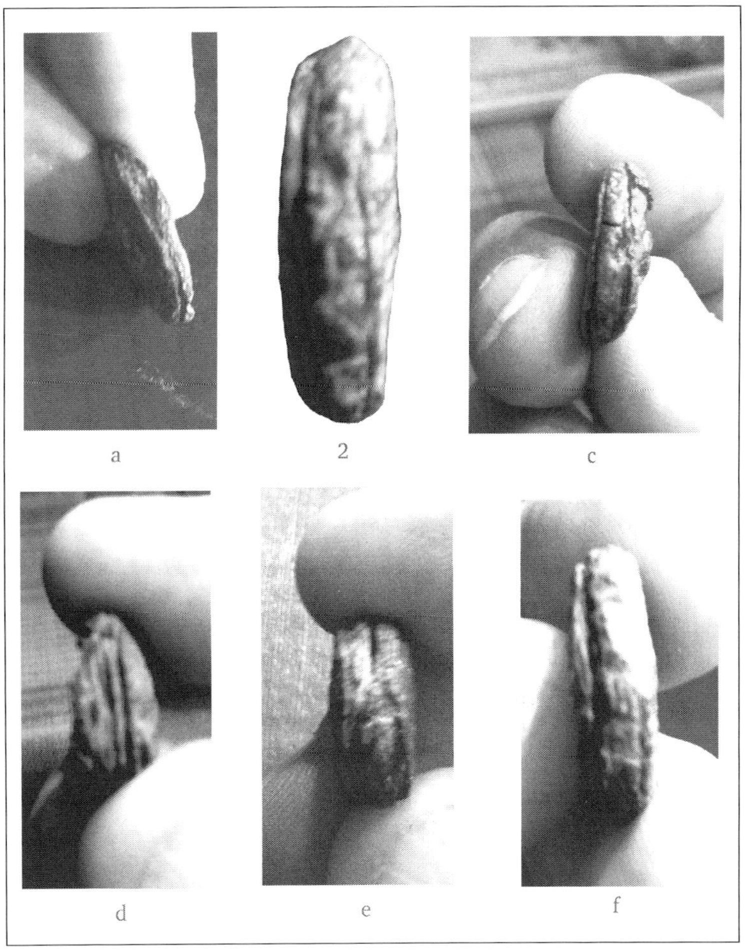

Fig. 25. Split edges of coins.

These coins cannot therefore be regarded as modern forgeries. If at all these were forgeries they may have been contemporary ones.

The coins are important as showing us the hitherto

unknown types, furnishing evidence of the earliest example of a deity having an aureole around the head and a new technique of manufacture.

NOTES AND REFERENCES

1. *BMCAI*, pp. cviii and 169, nos. 1-4, Pl. XXIV.20-21. Cunningham had obtained these coins at Bulandshahr and had read the legend below the main device on the obverse as *Baranaye* (*CASR*, XIV, p. 147; *CAI*, p. 88, Pl. X.8.
2. This typical type of tree is seen on punch-marked and other local coins and is now recognized as symbol of Mathura as a mint-town.
3. *BMCAI*, pp. cix and 170-72, Pl. XXV.1-11.
4. *Ibid.*, p. 171, no. 18, Pl. XLV.1.
5. *Ibid.*, p. 172, Pl. XXV.8-11.
6. *Ibid.*, p. 169, no. 5, Pl. XXV.3.
7. *ISNI*, p. 153.
8. *BMCAI*, pp. cx and 176-82; Lahiri, *ISNI*, pp. 155 ff.
9. *Ibid.*, p. 172, nos. 19-25, Pl. XXV.8-11.

VIII

Legends on Kuṇinda Silver Coins

Numismatic Evidence of the Transition from Prakrit to Sanskrit

In their study of the Western Kshatrapa coinage Amiteshwar Jha and Dilip Rajgor[1] made a very important observation regarding the use of Sanskrit on these coins:

> With a few exceptions, the Brāhmī coin-legends of the Western Kṣatrapas are in hybrid Sanskrit. These are characterized by the dominance of Sanskrit forms and an admixture of Sanskrit inflexions. Sanskrit feature is particularly reflected in the regular use of compound akṣaras, *viz. kṣa* and *tra* in *kṣatrapasa;* jño in rājño; sva in svāmi, tra in putrasa, pra in prathame, dvi in dvitīye; sva and śrī in svaśrīya and also ṣṭa in Chaṣṭana; tya in Satya; pṛ in pṛthvī-; śva in Viśva; tṛ in Bhartṛ, and so on. But along with this, some Prakrit features are also found. The one distinct Prakrit form noticed is –sīha, which is used in place of Sanskrit –siṃha. The most important Prakrit feature, however, is the regular use of Prakrit genitive –sa in place of Sanskrit –sya. The only exceptions to this are the few coins where the legend is in almost pure Sanskrit. But such coins are extremely few. Even those rulers, whose coins with Sanskrit legend are known, issued most of their coins with the usual hybrid Sanskrit legend. In fact, there is not a single ruler in the history of the dynasty who issued coins with Sanskrit legend only. Those rulers whose coins are known with Sanskrit legend are Chaṣṭana, Rudradāman, Dāmajadaśriya I, Satyadāman, Dāmasena and Rudrasena III.

We thus see that experimentation was going on in western India with the use of hybrid Sanskrit. Efforts were made to leave the use of Prakrit and follow Sanskrit. Does it indicate that people were getting literate now and an educational development was taking place? We have the first official use of Sanskrit on the coins of Chashṭana who came to hold possession of the state after the defeat and demise of Kshaharāta Nahapāna at the hands of Gautamiputra Sātakarṇi. Some scholars believe that Chashṭana started the Kushan era in 78 CE. The Junagarh Praśasti of his grandson Rudradāman (Year 72 = 150 CE) is believed to have been the earliest royal panegyric in chaste Sanskrit. In various other parts of India during the first two centuries the situation was not much different and Prakrit or hybrid Sanskrit continued to be used on the coins.

While studying Kuṇinda coins I found that they show the transition from Prakrit to Sanskrit legends. These coins have generally been described as following:

Obv. A deer or stag to right with a female figure (generally identified with goddess Lakshmī) standing facing on right, holding flower/s in uplifted right hand. Between the horns, above and sometimes also below the deer are symbols like *śrīvatsa* (or two cobras), tree-in-railing, crescented hill (or *chaitya*), *svastika*, etc. and the Brāhmī legends around from about VII o'clock reads as discussed below.

Rev. Six-arched hill surmounted by an umbrella and a *nandipada* in the centre, tree-in-railing having three or four horizontal branches with drooping leaves on the right, *svastika* above an *Indradhvaja* (triangle-headed standard) on the left and a wavy line below. The Kharoshṭhī legend from about V o'clock along the border is *Raña Kunidasa Am[o]ghabh[u]t[i]sa* with *Maharajasa* in the exergue.

I have, however, noticed and distinguished the following types of the Brāhmī legends on the obverse of silver coins as following (Fig. 26)[2] –

1. *Raña Kuṇi(ṃ)dasa Am(o)ghabh(u)tisa Maharajasa* (coins 1-2)
2. *Rañaḥ Kuṇi(ṃ)dasa Am(o)ghabhūtisa Maharajasa* (coin 3)
3. *Raño Kuṇi(ṃ)dasa Am(o)ghabhūtisa Maharajasa* (coin 4)
4. *Rājña Kuṇi(ṃ)dasa Am(o)ghabhūtisa Maharajasa* (coin 5)
5. *Rājña Kuṇi(ṃ)dasya Am(o)ghabhūtisa Maharajasa* (coin 6)
6. *Rājña Kuṇi(ṃ)dasya Am(o)ghabhūtisya Maharajasya* (coin 7)
7. *Rājñaḥ Kuṇi(ṃ)dasa Am(o)ghabhūtisa Mahārājasa* (coin 8)
8. *Rājñaḥ Kuṇi(ṃ)dasya Am(o)ghabhūtisa Mahārājasa* (coin 9)
9. *Rājñaḥ Kuṇi(ṃ)dasya Am(o)ghabhūtisya Mahārājasya* (coin 10)

We *thus* see that these coins show successive attempts towards Sanskritization till the legend becomes almost fully Sanskritized. In the instances cited above the word *Amoghabhūtisya* instead of *Amoghabhūteḥ* betrays the impact of Prakritism which persisted even though the suffix *-sya* has been used as in Sanskrit considering Amoghabhūti as the stem. There is evidence that even *i*-ending names were popularly treated as stems and genitive suffix *sya* was added to them as late as the Gupta period. Shri Girish Sharma of Indore possesses a square sectioned rectangular copper seal bearing the legend *Kumāradevasya Sogisya. . . .* and *Yaśadevasya Sogisya. . . .* in Gupta Brāhmī characters (see Figs. 102-104 below) on its different facets[3] betraying the use of the genitive case-ending with the clan name Sogi known to us from the Nandsa Pillar Inscription of Kṛita year 282 (= 225-26 CE).[4] Such aberrations may be seen even in some Sanskrit works like the Yoga-Vāsishṭha. It is, however, very difficult to ascertain whether they represent temporal successiveness or were issued contemporaneously from different mints or for different regions within the Kuṇinda dominions which extended over a large territory. Definite knowledge of the provenance of coins with these legends will help us to determine their temporal succession or contemporaneity. Let us hope that collectors and numismatists will

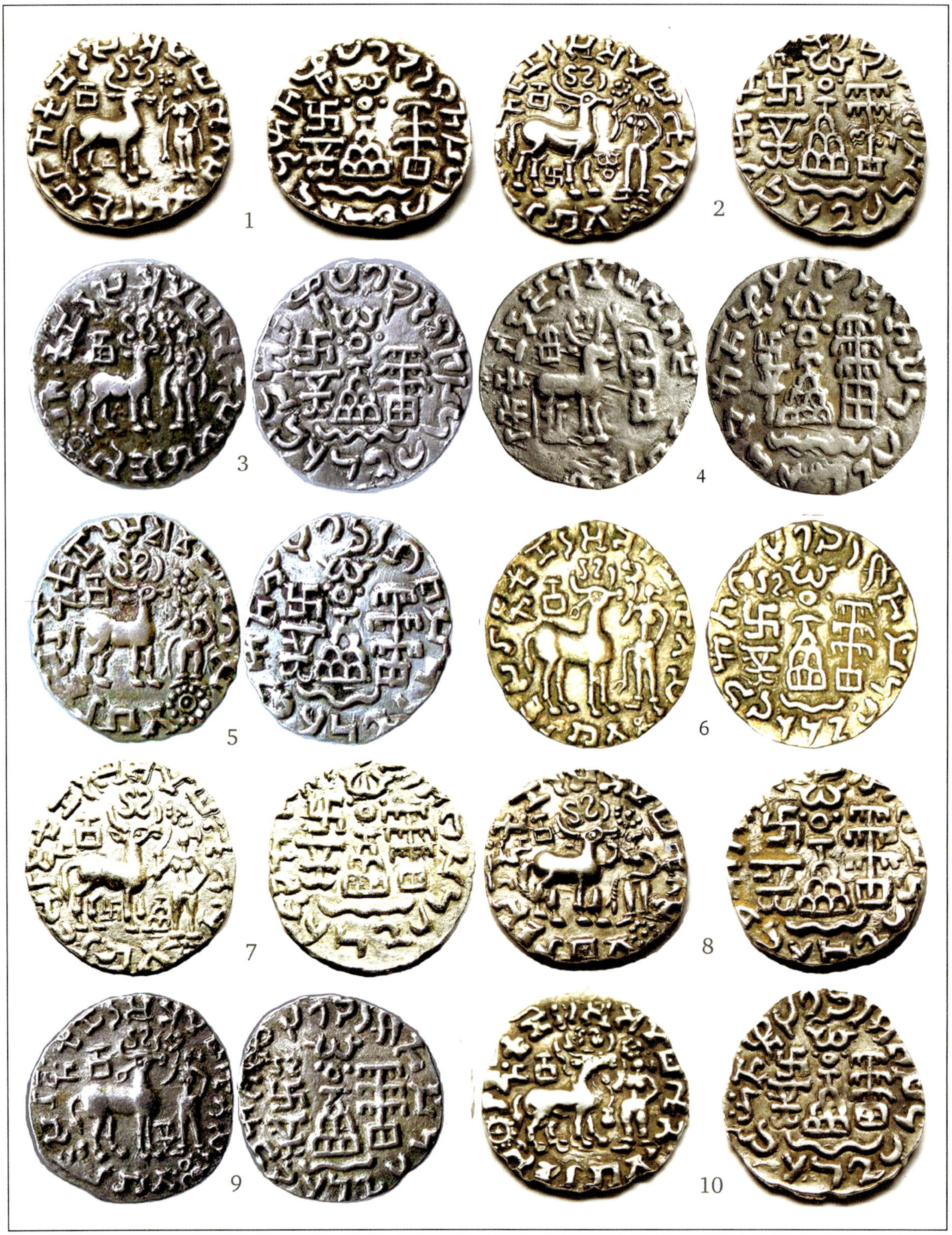

Fig. 26. Legends on Kuṇinda silver coins.

take care to record the find spots of all coins in future which will help us to determine the extent of dominions of the issuers and types and varieties circulating at those places.

The study of the Kuṇinda coins, however, betrays the earliest official use of Sanskrit by the Kuṇindas who mainly occupied the hilly tracts of Himachal Pradesh and Uttarakhand and adjoining plains during the second-first centuries BCE. Parts of this region still preserve the linguistic remnants of Sanskrit in the tribal hill areas. It may thus be concluded that the complete transition from Prakrit to Sanskrit took place sometime during first century BCE. The numismatic evidence thus corroborates Sircar's observation that "Sanskrit is first noticed in the inscriptions of North India from about the second half of the first century B.C."[5]

NOTES AND REFERENCES

1. Jha, Amiteshwar and Dilip Rajgor (1994), *Studies in the Coinage of the Western Kṣatrapas*, IIRNS, Anjaneri, p. 48.
2. The illustrated coins are enlarged and not to scale.
3. Handa, Devendra (2018), 'Some Recently Discovered Aulikara Seals', *JAINS*, Vol. XXXII, pp. 91-94. The use of genitive suffix with *ikārānta* names was an old practice as indicated by the legend *Dhanabhūtisa* on a clay seal of first century BCE from Kaushambi [Thaplyal, K.K. (1972), *Studies in Ancient Indian Seals*, Lucknow, p. 27].
4. Altekar, A.S. (1948), 'Nandsa Yupa Inscription', *Epigraphia Indica*, 27, pp. 252 ff.
5. Sircar, D.C. (1965), *Indian Epigraphy*, Delhi: Motilal Banarsidass, p. 39.

IX

Revisiting Trigarta Coins

ANTIQUITY, HISTORY AND HABITAT

The Trigartas are known to us from literary and numismatic sources. The earliest reference to their name occurs in Pāṇini's *Ashṭādhyāyī* (V.3, 116) where they are mentioned as an *'āyudhajīvī Saṅgha'*, i.e., a republic living by the profession of arms and as a confederation of six states known as Trigarta-Shashṭha.[1] Literally meaning 'three pits', Trigarta denotes the region drained by the three rivers – Ravi, Beas and Satluj – corresponding to the Jālandhar group of states. Pāṇini has also mentioned Jālandharāyaṇa in the Rājanyādi group (IV.2, 53). He has also made special mention of the Bhārgāyaṇa *gotra* (sept) in the Trigarta (IV.1, 111). The Trigartas are referred to by Patañjali also in his *Mahābhāshya* (IV.1, 178). The Trigarta country was partitioned into smaller territorial divisions or *janapadas*. The *Kāśikā* mentions the six members of the confederacy as –

Āhustrigarttashashṭhāṃstu Kauṇḍoparatha-Dāṇḍakī /
Kraushṭakir=Jālamāniścha Brāhmagupto'tha Jānakiḥ //

i.e., (1) Kauṇḍoparatha, (2) Dāṇḍaki, (3) Kraushṭaki, (4) Jālamāni, (5) Brāhmagupta, and (6) Jānaki (or Jālaki as read by Bhaṭṭoji Dīkshit). Of these, V.S. Agrawala[2] thinks that king Jānaki born of the demon Chandravināśana (*Mahābhārata*, Ādiparva 67.39) who was invited by the Pāṇḍavas to join them before the Great War (Udyogaparva 4.20) represents the Jānakis. They were the helpmates of king Suśarmā of Trigarta. He also refers to the possibility of Brāhmagupta being Bhramor (Chamba).

The *Mbh.* contains numerous references to the Trigartas whose king Suśarman too is referred to quite often.[3] They are described as wonderful charioteers (*rathodārāḥ*, *mahārathāḥ*), knowing the 'science of bow' (*dhanurvedavida*), invincible by the enemies (*ajeyāḥ śatrubhiḥ*) and preeminent fighters (*dhurandhara-kshatriyas*). They have been mentioned along with the Śibis, Yaudheyas, Rājanyas and Madrakas at one place[4] and were conquered by Arjuna during his conquest of the northern quarter

(Sabhāparvan 27.18) and by Nakula during his conquest of the western quarter (Sabhā 32.7). At the time of his Rājasūya they had brought presents for Yudhishṭhira (Sabhā 52.14). The rulers of Trigarta were five brothers and all of them were great charioteers, the best being Satyaratha (Udyoga 166.9-11). The Great Epic, however, contains the description of their defeat at the hands of the five Pāṇḍavas, Karṇa, Kṛishṇa, Parśurāma and others.[5]

The *Vishṇupurāṇa* mentions them with the Audumbaras and the Kulindas.[6] Audumbara coins have been found from Pathankot in Punjab at almost the entry point to Himachal; Jwalamukhi, Irrippal and probably in the lost Palampur hoard in Kangra district. The Kulindas are identified with the Kuṇindas who occupied an extensive area from Mandi in Himachal Pradesh to Kashipur in Uttarakhand. The mention of the Trigartas with these tribes clearly indicates their connection to the hilly region which is corroborated by the *Mārkaṇḍeyapurāṇa* (LVII.57) which refers to them along with the people living in the (Himalayan) hills (*parvatāśriyaṇaḥ*).[7] The *Brahmāṇḍa* (I.16, 68), *Matsya* (114.56), *Vāmana* (13.58), *Vāyu* (45.136), etc. also refer to the Trigartas.[8] The *Chāndravyākaraṇa* (c. CE 470 or sixth century) mentions Trigarta and the country of the Trigartas as Traigartaka (IV.3, 93 & III.2, 39). The *Bṛihatsaṃhitā* refers to not only the Trigarta,[9] but also Traigarta[10] and Traigartaka.[11] Xuanzang refers to the Trigarta country under the name of She-lan-t'olo (i.e. Jālandhara) whence he proceeded to the Kulūta country[12] indicating clearly the proximity of the two. The *Vaijayantī* (Bhūmikāṇḍa, verse 26) and the *Abhidhānachintāmaṇi* (IV.24) also equate Jālandhara with Trigarta. Daṇḍin's *Daśakumāracharita* (seventh century) also refers to the Trigarta *janapada*.[13] According to Kalhaṇa's *Rājataraṅgiṇī* king Śreshṭhasena of Kāśmīra conferred the territory of Trigarta on Pravareśa (III.100), Mātṛigupta conquered Trigarta (III. 285), king Pṛithvīchandra of Trigarta fled before the arms of Śaṅkaravarman in ninth century CE (V.144), minister Keśava of Trigarta served king Ananta (1028-63 CE), and so on.[14] The Chamba Copper Plate Inscription (1050 CE) of Somavarmadeva and Āsaṭadeva mentions a king of Trigarta along with the Kulūta king as a friend and presumably as a neighbor of Sāhilla, the founder of the Chamba line.[15] Trigarta finds mention in the *Sarasvatīkaṇṭhābharaṇa* (IV.2, 87) and *Gaṇaratnamahodadhi* (V.144) also. All these references make it amply clear that Trigarta and Jālandhara were used synonymously (*Jālandhrāstrigartāḥ syuḥ*) and that the state of Trigarta was located in the hills. Cunningham located Trigartadeśa in the country lying between the Ravi and the Satluj – 'the land watered by three rivers' - the Ravi, Beas and Satluj.[16] It has, however, to be noted that Trigarta was a synonym for Kangra region down to the early nineteenth century and the name applied only to the lower Beas valley.[17] It is interesting to note that the name Trigarh (Trigarta) still applies to the conjunction of the three tributaries of the river Beas – Bānagaṅgā, Kurali and Nayagula – which unite at Haripur and fall into the Beas opposite Śibi fort.[18] We may thus pinpoint the old Trigarta country to have been located between the present Jalandhar and Kangra cities comprising of Fatehpur-Chintpurni-Dera Gopipur-Shahpur area to the northeast of Jalandhar and Hoshiarpur in close vicinity of the Audumbaras and Kuṇindas with whose coins they share the use of both Brāhmī and Kharoshṭhī on their coins. This small area is still maintaining its heroic tradition through its recruits in the military corps.

THE COINS

Only one square copper coin which could be attributed definitely to the Trigarta tribe was known till recently (Fig. 27 & 28.1). It is preserved in the British Museum and was described by Allan[19] in 1936 as follows.

Æ, 0.7 inch (1.798 cm), 43.0 grains (2.780 g)

Obv. Four-tiered stupa; traces of Kharoshṭhī legend on right

Rev. Brāhmī legend *Trakataja* above, three symbols in centre, and part of the legend *napadasa* below.[20]

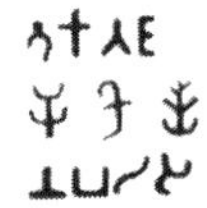

Allan read the legend correctly as "*Trakatajanapadasa* 'of the tribe of Trigarta' in Brāhmī characters of probably the first half of the second century B.C." and observed that "There are traces of this same inscription in Kharoṣṭhī on the obverse, but only the end . . . *padasa* is legible".[21] The enlarged scan of the coin, however, shows that there are traces of '*jana*' also before '*padasa*' and that there also existed the name of the tribe in Kharoshṭhī along the left margin of the coin. Both '*Trakata*' and '*janapadasa*' have been placed perpendicularly along the left and right margins and are to be read from inside, i.e. by turning the left and right margins towards the top. What Allan referred to as stupa on this coin may have actually been a multi-storeyed building (Fig. 29.a).

It has been regarded as a four-storied pavilion with a circular finial by K.K. Dasgupta[22] and P.L. Gupta[23] has described it as "a four-storeyed pillar structure with a dome at the top and a curvilinear eave around the ground floor' and observed that "it is not possible for us to say if it represents a religious or a secular building. Not unlikely, it represents a multi-storeyed residence or a palace." The structure is supported by a high railing and probably also a gate or pillared-post in the front.

I had examined the original coin in the British Museum and feel that the structure depicted on this Trigarta coin is only three-tiered and the pillared-post in front has a bird, probably a cock, perched on it. As such, it is probably a Kukkuṭa-dhvaja. Such *dhvajas* carrying a weapon or the vehicle of the deity was a usual thing in ancient times. We know of some other Garuḍa- and Kukkuṭa-dhvajas also. This observation goes well with the description of the Trigarta *janapada* as an *āyudhajīvī-saṃgha* by Pāṇini and

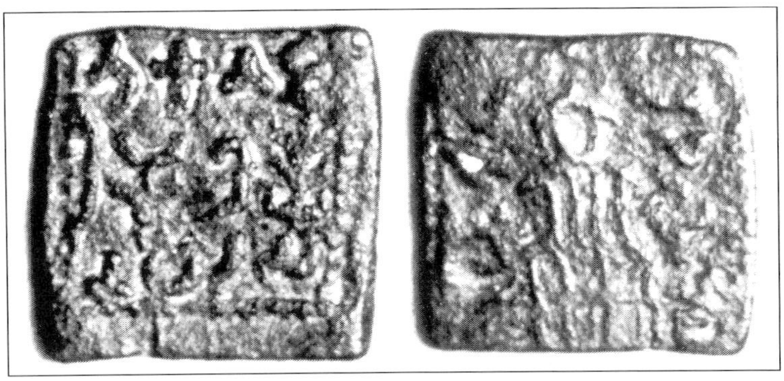

Fig. 27. Trakata coin, British Museum.

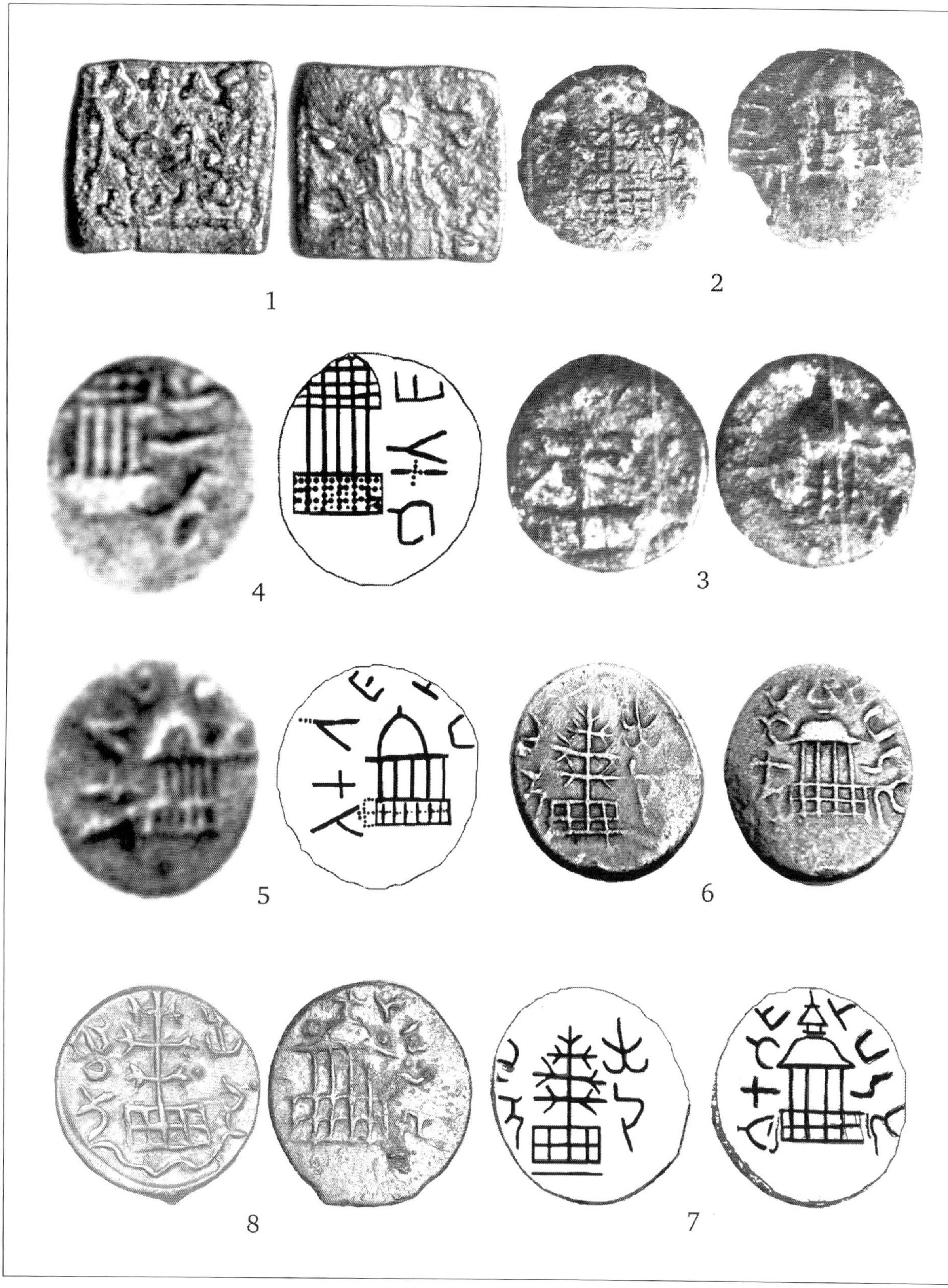

Fig. 28. Coins of the Trigartas.

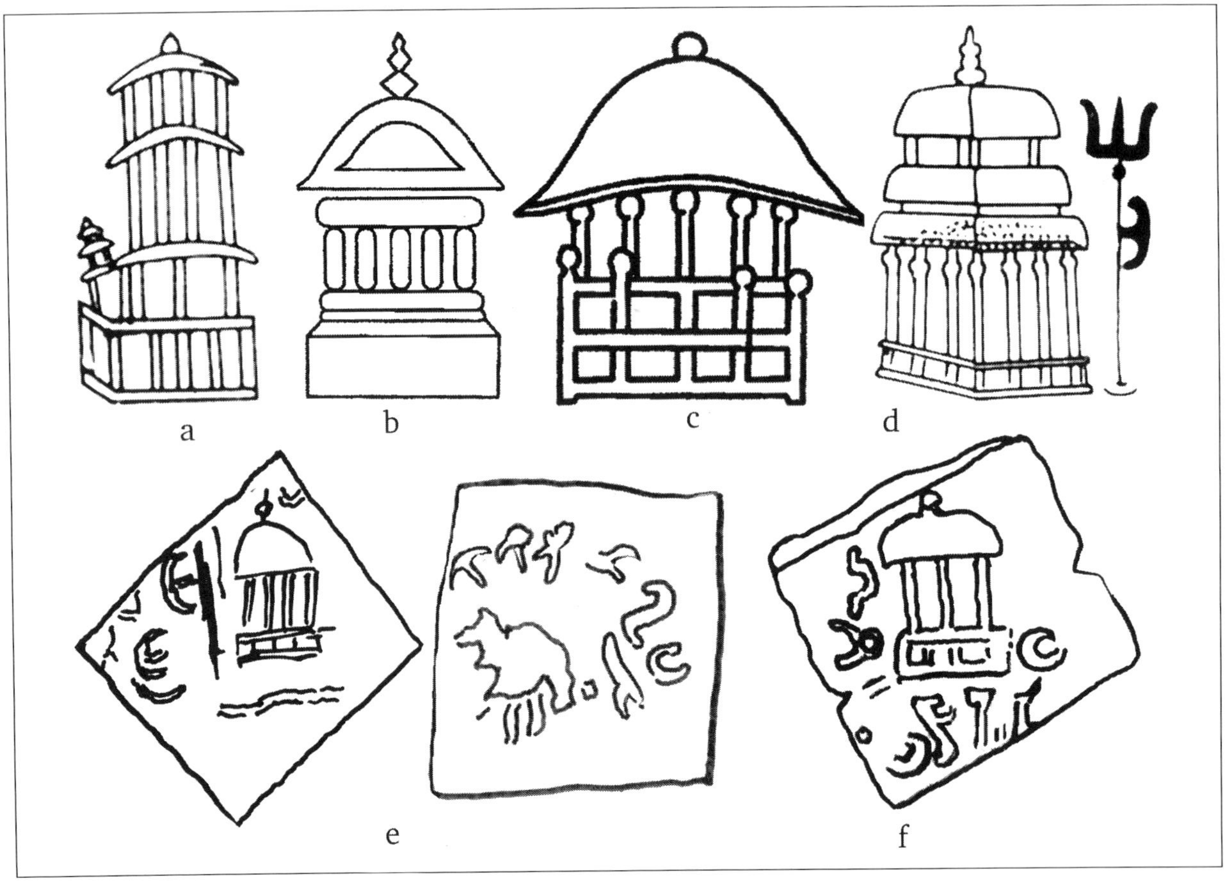

Fig. 29. Temples on Trigarta and Audumbara coins.

as wonderful warriors- *rathodārāḥ, mahārathāḥ, dhurandhara-kshatriyas, śatrubhiḥ ajeyāḥ, dhanurvedavidaḥ*, etc. in the *Mbh*. It is well known that *kukkuṭa* is the emblem of the war-god Kārttikeya. It will therefore be no wonder if the valiant Trigartas living by the profession of arms, like the Yaudheyas, may have been the worshippers of Kārttikeya.[24]

While studying numismatic evidence on the evolution of temple architecture a copper coin bearing a railed and pillared pavilion on the obverse and tree in railing on the reverse came to my notice bearing on the two sides Brāhmī and Kharoshṭhī legends which being not very clear could not be deciphered properly at that time.[25] A better photograph accessed subsequently has enabled me to decipher the legend satisfactorily and identify it as a coin of the Trakata *janapada* (Fig. 28.6-7).

The Brāhmī legend on the obverse can be read as *Trakata janapadasa* without any doubt though the building seems to be a pavilion. On the reverse we have only blurred traces of letters on the left of the tree but the Kharoshṭhī letter *sa* is very clear under the *śrīvatsa* symbol. This is another type of Trigarta coin not known earlier. We also notice the change from square/rectangular type to the round one. The pillared pavilion seems to have a railing not to allow animals to let inside where there might have been placed the image or emblem of the deity, probably Vaishnavite if the *śrīvatsa* symbol on the reverse provides the clue. But since this symbol has been employed as an auspicious symbol on varied types of objects we cannot be sure of the affiliation to any particular cult. This type of structures were used in ancient times also for worshipping images or symbols of divinities and may still be seen in parts of the country.

A similar copper coin in a good condition of preservation was allegedly discovered from beneath a stupa at Katlang, district Mardan of Khyber Pakhtunkhwa province of Pakistan and its scan was documented in trade sometime back (Fig. 28.8). Katlang is the tehsil headquarter and an expanding town and the remnants of the nearest stupa with monastic establishment exist on the spur of a 500-feet high hill overlooking the Jamal Garhi village about 5 km south of it. Jamal Garhi is about 45 km northeast of Charsadda and may have been located on the old Mathura–Pushkalāvatī (Purushapura, Peshawar) trade route. Cunningham has left a detailed account of this site and the stupa.[26] Though it is somewhat surprising to find a Trigarta coin from such a distant region yet its undoubted identity furnishes evidence of long distance trade or pilgrim activities and religious proclivities of the people of Trigarta (Jālandhara) like their neighbours the Kulūtas of Kulu whose eleven coins were found from Sirkap (Taxila).[27] On the basis of this discovery of Kulūta coins from Sirkap P.L. Gupta theorised the existence of two monarchy-based tribal states of the Kulūtas, one in Gandhara region and the other in the Himalayan rgion near Kangra.[28] It may be mentioned here that even a Rājanya coin has been documented in trade from ths Gandhara region. It is thus clear that these tribal coins reached Gandhara through travelers as Taxila and Charsadda wer great centres of trade, art and culture and it will be preposterous to imagine the existence of different branches of the tribal people.

The obverse or tree side of the coin described above clearly shows an undulating line below the main device and *śrīvatsa* on the right of the tree and a *triratna* or *nandipada* symbol on its left. The pavilion as seen on these coins had been observed on two coins in the British Museum which were listed by Allan as 'uncertain coins' put under the Audumbaras (Fig. 28.2-3).[29] Both these coins have a tree in railing with some subsidiary symbols on the obverse and depict a pillared pavilion having a domical superstructure and square railing. The reason for putting them under uncertain category may have been the difference between the pavilions on those two coins as drawn by Gupta[30] (Fig. 29.b-c) and the architecture of the temple on Audumbara coins (Fig. 29.d). It is, however, interesting to note that similar pavilions have been depicted on Audumbara coins also which were brought to light by me sometime back.[31] One coin is square in shape (1.1 x 1.15 cm) and weighing 1.87 g shows on the obverse the temple or pavillion with trident on left to which battleaxe has been attached facing outwards and undulating line is shown below as generally found on square temple type Audumbara coins. In the left corner may be seen some letters of which *Śi* is very prominent, probably followed by *va* of which only the lower triangular part has survived. The coin therefore seems to have been struck by a ruler having the first part of his name as Śiva. Since this side generally carries the tribal denomination of *Odu(ṃ)barisa*, it seems that the coin was struck when the legend pattern was not strictly followed. The reverse, however, is very interesting as it shows a complete elephant to left with traces of a *svastika* on its back and fairly visible Kharoshṭhī legend of which *Mahadeva*[*sa raña**] may be made out on the back of the elephant, *ghosha*[sa*] above and [*Odu(ṃ)bari**]*sa* below (Fig. 23.e). The coin may thus be attributed with fair amount of certainty to a king whose name ended in *ghosha*. We know of Dharaghosha but the part of the Brāhmī legend *Śiva* on the obverse indicates that the issuer could be Śivaghosha, unknown from any other source till now. We do not know whether he was an ancestor or descendant of Dharaghosha but the degradation noticeable on the coin indicates that he may have been Dharaghosha's successor. Only future discoveries may provide clinching evidence. It represents a hitherto unreported variety published here for the first time.

Equally interesting is another square coin (Fig. 29.f) measuring 1.3 x 1.3 cm and weighing 1.96 g as the usual temple is substituted on its obverse by a three-pillared pavilion in railing and having a vaulted roof with a pitcher-shaped finial with pointed top. The planchets were cut from the metal stripes and the blanks do not seem to have been heated properly before striking as is indicated by the impact of the hammer which has resulted in cracks on the sides. No care was taken even for a proper adjustment of the dies. On the left of the pavilion may be seen bold Brāhmī letters *Maha* which seem to have been parts of the legend *Mahadevasa*. Below the pavilion are also visible some Brāhmī letters reading *risa* which form the end-part of the tribal name in genitive *Odu(ṃ)barisa* as found on Audumbara copper coins. On the right are traces of Brāhmī letters which I feel inclined to decipher as [Śi]va. It may have been the part of the name of the same ruler who issued the preceding coin, i.e., Śivaghosha. The reverse gives a jumbled impression, probably resulting from careless double striking. Tree in railing with upper part of the trident on right may be made out. The Kharoshṭhī legend below may fairly be deciphered as *Mahadeva*[*sa**] vouching for its being a coin of the Audumbaras. We may recall here that Allan's two copper coins listed as 'Uncertain' under the Audumbaras show a pavilion with un-deciphered legends (Fig. 28.2-3) and the present piece corroborates their attribution to the tribe. Better specimens in future may help us in retrieving the name of the issuer of such coins.

Śivaghosha, the issuer of these coins, was probably the last ruler of the dynasty.[32] The similarity of the railed domed pavilion on the coins of this ruler and that of the Trigartas illustrated above seems to be significant. These coins of Śivaghosha show degradation of manufacturing technique, are square and bear Brāhmī and Kharoshṭhī legends like the Audumbara coins of his ancestors but instead of the temple they show the railed domed pavilion like those of the Trigartas. Did he accept subjugation of the Trigartas or the Trigartas adopted this device after having defeated capturing some of his territory and issued coins adopting the device of the vanquished enemy? To me it seems more likely as the Trigartas continued striking coins with this device as evidenced by the uncertain Audumbara coins of the British Museum which can now be identified as Trigarta coins with some certainty as the name of the tribe may be read on these coins in Brāhmī script on the obverse (Fig. 28.4-5).

We thus see that now we know the Trigartas not only from one unique square coin but also from three round copper coins.

DATE OF THE COIN

Allan had noted that "The square shape of the coin is further evidence of its early date".[33] Bela Lahiri, however, regarded the side with the Brāhmī legend as obverse (to which I also concur) and felt that "the traces of Kharoshṭhī legend on the reverse suggests (sic.) a date not earlier than the first half of the first century B.C., before which period the Kharoshṭhī script does not appear on indigenous coins".[34] The BM coin comes from the collection of J.P. Rawlins (1922) who had collected coins from district Hoshiarpur and probably from adjacent areas and corroborates our location of the Trigarta tribe to the northeast of Hoshiarpur. In spite of copious literary references the Trigarta *janapada* seems to have attained political importance only for some time in a limited area after the decline of the Indo-Greeks.[35]

NOTES AND REFERENCES

1. Pāṇini has also referred to Trigarta amongst *garta*-ending names in *Ashṭādhyāyī* (IV.2, 137).
2. Agrawala (1963), *op. cit.*, pp. 54, 68, 446-47, 453, etc.
3. Udyogaparvan 164.8; 166.9-13; Bhīshmaparvan 56.4, 61.12-13. 72.7, 102.9-23; Droṇaparvan 4.8, 11.17, 17.16-17, 19.16, 70.12, 141.2-8, 157.28; Karṇaparvan 4.8; Śalyaparvan 27.31-48; etc. See also Law, B.C. (1973), *Tribes in Ancient India*, 2nd ed., Poona.
4. *Mbh.* II.48, 13:
   Kāśmīrāḥ Kundamānāścha Paurakā Haṃsakāyanāḥ /
   Śibi-Trigarta-Yaudheyā Rājanyā Madra-Kekayāḥ //
   The *Garuḍapurāṇa* (II.52, 14) repeats this verse.
5. For details see *Mahābhārata kī Nāmānukramaṇikā*, Gita Press, Gorakhpur, VS 2016, pp. 132-33.
6. *CASR*, XIV, p. 116.
7. *Mārkaṇḍeyapurāṇa*, Eng. Tr. By Pargiter (1904), pp. 346-47.
8. For details see D.C. Sircar, *Studies in the Geography of Ancient and Medieval India*, Delhi, 1960, p. 37, fn. 1.
9. IX.19: *Draviḍābhīrāmbashṭhatrigartasaurāshṭrān*; and XIV.19: *Ādarśāntardvīpitrigartaturgānanāḥ*. Trigarta occurs in *Samāsasaṃhitā* (29.31) also.
10. X.11: *Aindramākhye traigarta-chīna-kaulūta-kuṅkumaṃ lākshā /*
    Sasyānyatha māñjishṭhaṃ kausumbhaṃ cha kshayaṃ yāti //
    XVI.22: *Traigartapauravāmbashṭhapāratā Vāṭadhānayaudheyāḥ /*
    Sārasvatārjunāyanamatsyārddhagrāmarāshṭrāṇi // and
    XVII.16: *Traigartapārvatīyāḥ pīḍyante kampate cha mahī /*
    Traigarta occurs in the *Kāśyapasaṃhitā* also –
    Traigartasindhusauvīrāḥ śatadrūmathure api /
    Srughnaudīchyavipśāścha pāratāmbashṭhakāstathā //
11. IV.24: *Traigartakān Mālavān.*
12. Watters, *op. cit.*, pp. 296-300.
13. *Daśakumāracharita* (Nirṇaya Sāgara Press ed., Bombay, 1906), Bk. VI, p. 216.
14. *Rājataraṅgiṇī*, Eng. Tr. by Ranjit Sitaram Pandit, Sahitya Akademi, New Delhi, 1977.
15. *Indian Antiquary*, XVII, pp. 7 ff.
16. Cf. *CASR*, II, p. 16; V, p. 148; XIV, p. 116; *CAGI*, pp. 115-19.
17. Moorecraft, *Travels*, I, pp. 140-41 (as quoted by Gupta, P.L. (1988), *Numismatic History of Himachal Pradesh* (*NHHP*), Delhi, p. 49, fn. 36.

18. Hutchison, J. and J. PH. Vogel (1933), *History of the Punjab Hill States*, Lahore, 1933, p. 112. See also *NHHP*, p. 12.
19. *BMCAI*, p. 212, no. 19, Pl. XXIX.10. Allan missed to describe the pellet border.
20. *Ibid.*, p. cxl.
21. *Ibid.*.
22. *THAI*, p. 170.
23. Gupta, P.L., "Bearing of Numismatics on Early Indian Art History in the Background of Epigraphy", *Indian Epigraphy: Its Bearing on the History of Art*, Ed. Asher, F. and G.S. Gai, New Delhi, pp. 6-11, Fig. 15; *NHHP*, pp. 13-14.
24. Handa (2007), *TCAI*, p. 122; (2016), 'Revisiting Trigartas and their Coins', *Manimahesh*, Vol. VII, pp. 52-61.
25. Handa, *Coins and Temples*, Pl. XXX.
26. *CASR*, V, pp. 46-53, Pls. XIV-XV.
27. Marshall (1975), *Taxila*, II, p. 793; III, Pls. 252-57.
28. *NHHP*, pp. 9-12.
29. *BMCAI*, p. 125, nos. 24-25, Pl. XV.11-12.
30. Gupta, *loc. cit.*
31. Handa, Devendra (2015), 'Some Square and Apsidal Audumbara Coins', *Manimahesh*, Vol. VI, pp. 30-40.
32. *Ibid.*
33. *BMCAI*, p. cxl.
34. ISNI, p. 255.
35. *Ibid.*

X

Orthographical Peculiarities of Yaudheya and Some Other Tribal Coins

The Yaudheyas are well known to the numismatists for having issued the largest number of species of different types issued over nearly half a millennium from about the second century BCE to about the middle of the fourth century CE with an interregnum of Scythian-Kushan supremacy during the first-second century CE. Besides a unique gold coin struck on the Kushan module (in a private collection) showing hex-cephalic Kārttikeya with a long legend in Brāhmī on the obverse and Gaja-Lakshmī standing on a lotus with some subsidiary symbols on the reverse and a slightly damaged silver coin preserved in the British Museum depicting six-headed Kārttikeya holding a lance in his right hand with the Brāhmī legend *Bhagavata-svāmino Brahmaṇya Yaudheya* (भगवत स्वामिनो ब्रह्मण्य यौधेय) on the obverse and six-headed Shashṭhī standing on a lotus with undulating line below flanked by six-arched parasoled symbol surmounted by a *Nandipada* on her right and four-branched railed tree on her left in a dotted border on the reverse, the Yaudheyas issued copper coins of various types in the regions they occupied in different phases of their historical existence. After the disintegration of the Maurya and Śuṅga empires they seem to have been located at and around Rohtak in Haryana with their area of influence extending to northeastern Rajasthan touching Narnaul district in the southwest and Bijnor district of Uttar Pradesh in the northeast as indicated by their coin-finds showing a bull with railed Śūlagava (sometimes without it) and the Brāhmī legend *Yaudheyānāṃ Bahudhāñake* (यौधेयानाँ बहुधाञके) along the margin above and below the bull on the obverse and the reverse carrying the figure of an elephant with a *nandipada* and banner-like symbol at its back. There are quite some variations in the known specimens. Under the Scytho-Kushan pressure the Yaudheyas had to leave their original home and find safer refuge in the Garhwal region where they seem to have dedicated their state to their tutelary deity Kārttikeya striking their copper coins showing his effigy and bearing the Brāhmī legend *Bhagavata-svāmino Brahmaṇyadevasa Kumārasa* (भगवत स्वामिनो

ब्रह्मण्यदेवस कुमारस), sometimes shortened without the last word. The reverse depicted his spouse six-headed Shashṭhī with subsidiary symbols. These coins are generally rudely struck and show many variations. Their regime seems to have touched and perhaps occupied some area where Kuṇinda coins were the popular currency. They had thus issued coins copying the Kuṇinda symbols of deer standing facing a female holding a lotus in her upraised right hand, generally identified as Lakshmī. Perhaps later, the goddess was substituted by a deer and/or temple. Generally it is on the cumulative evidence that the legend can be restored as a marked degradation took place in striking these coins. There are numerous variations in the figures of the goddess and the temple types resulting into a large number of varieties of these coins. Variation in weights is also large and fractions too may have been struck. And finally when they were instrumental along with some other factors perhaps to force the Kushans out of their native region they descended to the plains and occupied not only their original territory but also a very large area comprising parts of the present day western U.P., Uttarakhand, Himachal Pradesh, southern Punjab (in present day India and Pakistan), Bahawalpur, and northern Rajasthan as shown in the map (Fig. 30):

From the viewpoint of orthography, it is the legends of their coins which interest us here. Their earliest coins of bull-elephant type, as noted above, show *Yaudheyānāṃ*

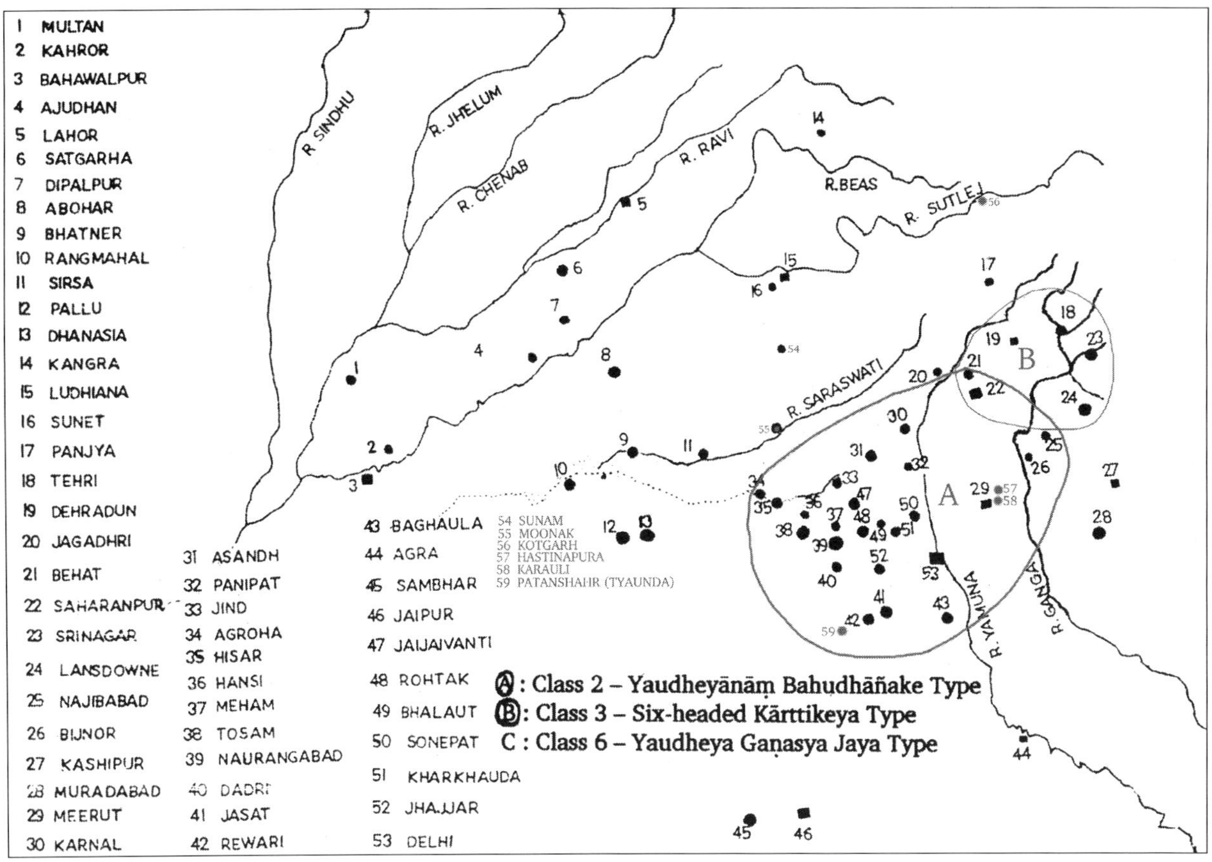

Fig. 30. Map showing the distribution of Yaudheya coins.

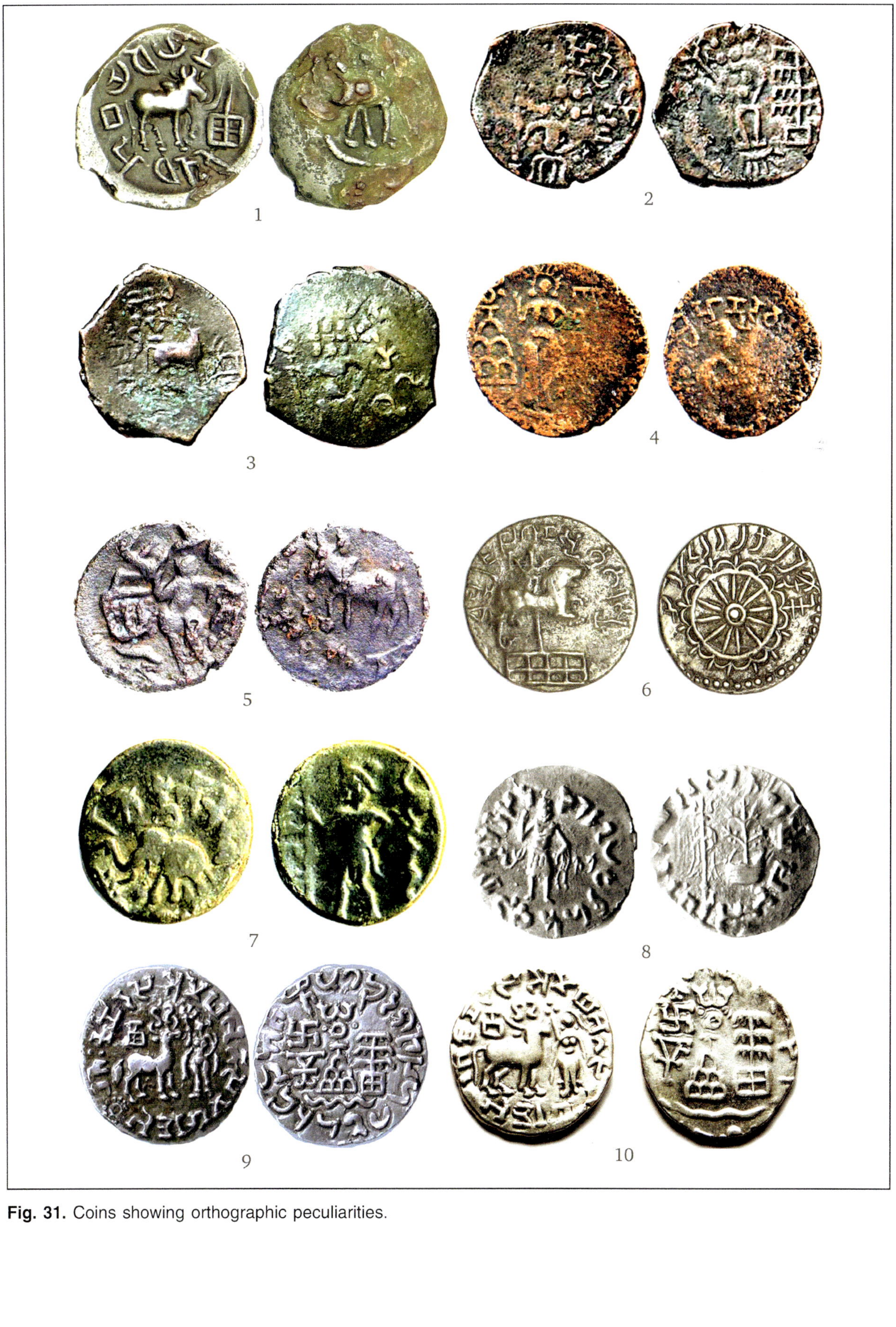

Fig. 31. Coins showing orthographic peculiarities.

Bahudhāñake (sometimes with indistinct or truncated vowel marks) as the commonest legend with palatal nasal used for the conjunct of dental nasal with first semi-vowel, i.e. *Yaudheyānāṃ Bahudhāñake* (यौधेयानाँ बहुधाञके) used for *Yaudheyānāṃ Bahudhānyake* (यौधेयानाँ बहुधान्यके) (Fig. 31.1).

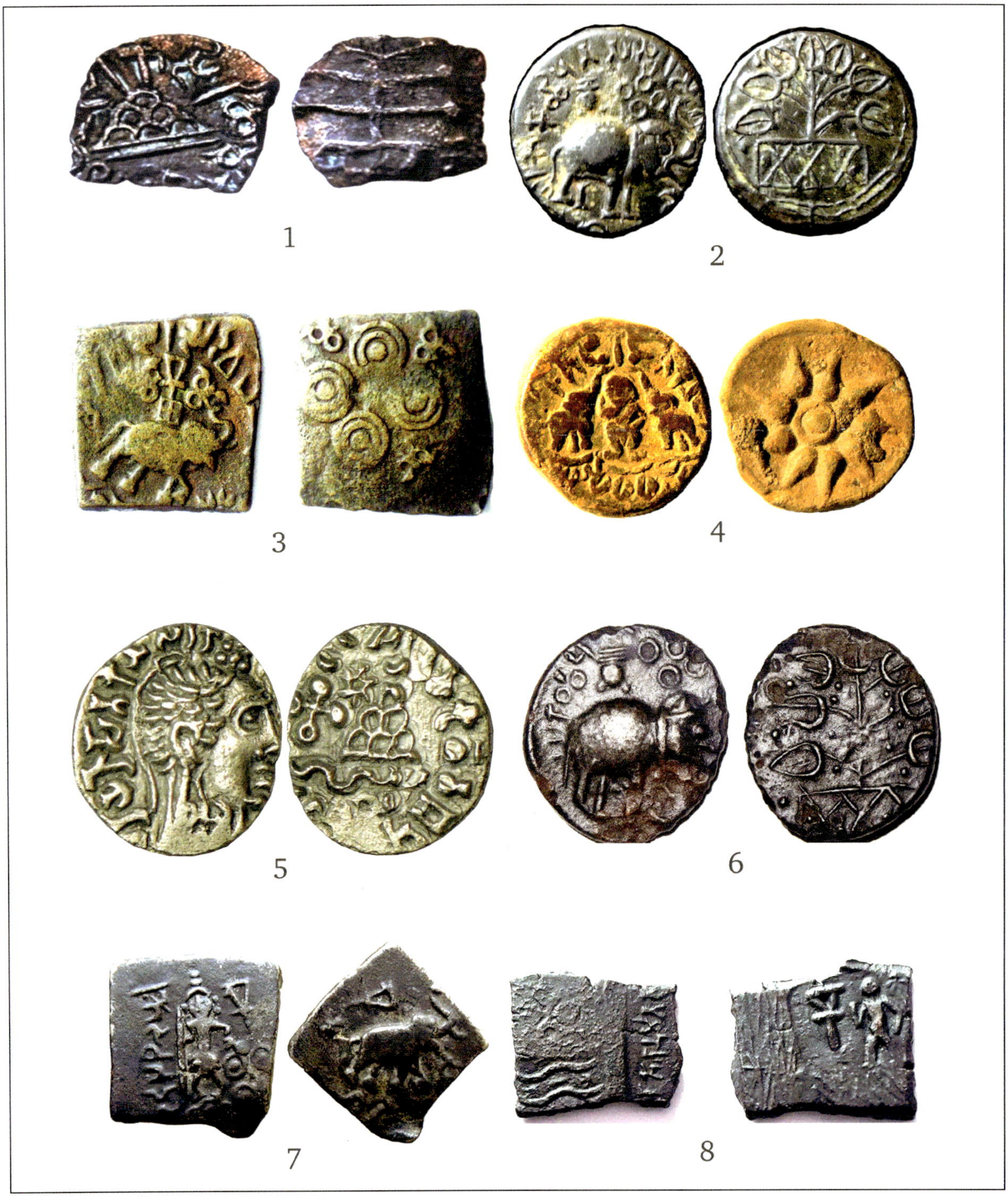

Fig. 32. Orthography of Sātavāhana and central Indian coins.

Another class of coins carries the legend *Bhagavata-svāmino Brahmaṇyadevasa Kumārasa* or a shorter version thereof. The legends are seldom found complete on individual examples and have been reconstructed on the cumulative evidence of the coins of the particular type. It is the word Brahmaṇya on these coins which betray anomalous spellings like *Brahmaña, Brahmañya, Brahmanya* (ब्रह्मञ, ब्रह्मञ्य, ब्रह्मन्य) and *Brahmaṇya* (ब्रह्मण्य) (Fig. 31.2-5).

These different types of orthography reveals that the Yaudheyas pronounced the words like Bahudhānyaka and Brahmaṇya in different ways or did not distinguish the *ña, ñya, nya* (ञ, ञ्य, न्य) and *ṇya* (ण्य) sounds. Another question arises here whether these different spellings were used in different regions or at different times. We have noted above that during second-first century BCE the bull-elephant type coins were used at Rohtak and the area around and it was the nucleus region of their settlement. No distinction was made here between *ña* (ञ) and *nya* (न्य) at that period. They used the Kārttikeya-Shashṭhī and Kārttikeya-deer type coins when they moved to the hill region of Garhwal during first-second century CE. Even here they spelled the word *Brahmaṇya* differently as *Brahmaña, Brahmañya, Brahmanya* (ब्रह्मञ, ब्रह्मञ्य, ब्रह्मन्य) as noted above. So it is clear that they not only made any difference between *ña* and *nya* (ञ and न्य) but also confused the sound with *ñya* and *ṇya* (ञ्य and ण्य).

That *ña* and *nya* (ञ and न्य) were not distinguished during this period is revealed by Rājanya coins also which circulated mostly north of the Satluj river in old Hoshiarpur district which now comprises of Shahid Bhagat Singh Nagar district also. These coins also spell the word *Rājanya Janapadasa* (राजन्य जनपदस) as *Rājaña Janapadasa* (राजञ जनपदस) (Fig. 31.6).

The Vṛishṇi silver coins too spell the word *Rājanya gaṇasya* (राजन्य गणस्य) as *Rājajña gaṇasya* (राजज्ञ/ज्ञ गणस्य) indicating further that *nya* (न्य) was confused as *jña*/ (ज्ञ/ज्ञ) (Fig. 31.7).

The use of *ña* (ञ) for *jña* (ज्ञ/ज्ञ) may also be seen in the titles prefixed to the names of Bhānumita and Mahimita of the Mitra rulers of Punjab: *Raño Bhānumitasa* (रञो भानुमितस) (Fig. 31.8) and *Raño Mahimitasa* (रञो महिमितस) as well as in the legends on Audumbara and Kuṇinda coins, e.g. *Mahādevasa raño Dharaghoshasa Odubarisa* (महादेवस रञो धरघोषस ओदुबरिस) (Fig. 31.9) and *Raña Kuṇi(ṃ)dasa Amoghabhutisa mahārājasa* (रञ कुणिंदस अमोघभुतिस महाराजस) (Fig. 31.10).

Not only the tribal and some other north Indian states were using *Raña/ Raño* (रञ/रञो) as the regal title but also the Sātavāhana and some other rulers in central and south India were doing so. Coins of Chhimuka, Kautsīputra, Sādavāhana and Sātakarṇi show the title *Raño* prefixed to their names (Fig. 32.1-4 & 6 respectively). The name of Yajña Sātakarṇi has been spelt as *Yaña Sātakanisa* on his coins (Fig. 32.5). Similarly the names of Sachabhadra (Fig. 32.7) and Bhānumitra of central India (Fig. 32. 8) have also been preceded by the regal title *Raña/ Raño*. This very title has been used by the Mahārathis, Kuras and others also in south India.

The use of *Raña/ Raño* (रञ/रञो) for *Rājñaḥ / Rājño* (राज्ञः/राज्ञो) was thus the result of the use of Prakrit in that period which prevailed almost in the whole of the sub-continent. But the indiscriminate use of *ña* (ञ), *ñya* (ञ्य) and *nya* (न्य) for *ṇya* (ण्य) by the Yaudheyas and *ña* (ञ) for *nya* (न्य) by the Rājanyas, *jña* (ज्ञ/ज्ञ) for *nya* (न्य) by the Vṛishṇis is a peculiar orthographic feature of the tribal coins of north India coming mainly from the ancient Punjab (which comprised part of Himachal Pradesh, the whole of the present Punjab and Haryana) along with some adjoining parts of Uttarakhand and Uttar Pradesh. All the tribes including the Mitras and except the Yaudheyas were issuing biscriptual coins with Brāhmī and Kharoshṭhī legends. The Yaudheyas were living in close proximity to these tribes and in all probability belonged to the same socio-cultural zone and were impacted by Prakrit language and Kharoshṭhī orthography. When the Kharoshṭhī disappeared from this region after third century CE probably with the exit of the Imperial Kushans this confusion also vanished and the Brāhmī legends and inscriptions show the use of appropriate alphabets and conjuncts for relevant sounds.

The peculiar orthographic feature of the use of *ña, ñya, nya* (ञ, ञ्य, न्य) for *ṇya* (ण्य) by the Yaudheyas is interesting and calls for explanation. Does it indicate different regional pronunciations or a successive temporal difference towards Sanskritisation? Since the exact provenances of the coins showing the use of *ña, ñya, nya* (ञ, ञ्य, न्य) for *ṇya* (ण्य) are not definitely known, it is very difficult to be sure of regional pronunciations within the small territory occupied by the tribe in Garhwal region. Does the use of these different sounds betray temporal progress then? It is equally difficult to be affirmative even on this point. I think that the Yaudheyas (and of course other tribes and states) were coming out of the shackles of the use of Prakrit and Kharoshṭhī and stepping towards Sanskritisation and adjusting the pronunciation and orthography accordingly.

XI

Coins from Maheshwar

HISTORY AND ARCHAEOLOGY

Maheshwar (Maheśvara, 22° 11' N & 75° 36' E), is located 65 km southwest of Indore on the right (northern) bank of the Narmadā (Fig. 33) in district West Nimar of Madhya Pradesh.

It formed part of Avanti, one of the sixteen *Mahājanpadas* 'Great States' of Buddha's time (Fig. 34). Avanti corresponded roughly to western central Indian region with a part of the Narmadā valley from Māndhātā to Maheshwar, with its capital at Ujjain, the famous site of a Jyotirliṅga of Śiva and well-known as the capital of king Vikramāditya of debated historicity.[1] The *Janapada* was divided into two parts by the Vindhyas; the northern part with its capital at Ujjain drained by the Śiprā and other streams and the southern part washed by the Narmadā having its centre at Māhishmatī) (Māhissatī of the Buddhists, sometimes mentioned as its capital).

Māhishmatī is said to have been founded by king Māhishmat, a descendant of Haihaya king Kārtyavīrya Sahasrabāhu (*lit.* having a thousand arms) Arjuna of the Yadu family who was killed by Paraśurāma. It is one of the ancient cities of India and was the capital of Anūpadeśa which formed part of southern Avanti. Its location on the right (northern) bank of the Narmadā on the trade route from Pratishṭhāna (Paithan) to Ujjayinī and further to Vaiśālī endowed it with commercial importance and made it a flourishing city as reflected in Patañjali's reference to it.[2]

After the decline of the Maurya empire, Māhishmatī seems to have grown independent as a city state like Bhadravatī, Bhadrapurikā, Bhāgilā, Bharukachchha, Erikachchha, Erakina, Hathodaka, Kauśāmbī, Kurara (Kurarāya or Kuraghara), (Kura-)Purikā, Madāvika, Śuktimatī, Tripurī, Ujjayinī, Vārāṇasī, Vidiśā, etc.[3] and issued its own currency.

Mahāgovinda Sutta refers to Māhissatī as the capital of Avanti[3] indicating that there were certain occasions when Māhishmatī was more important than Ujjain.

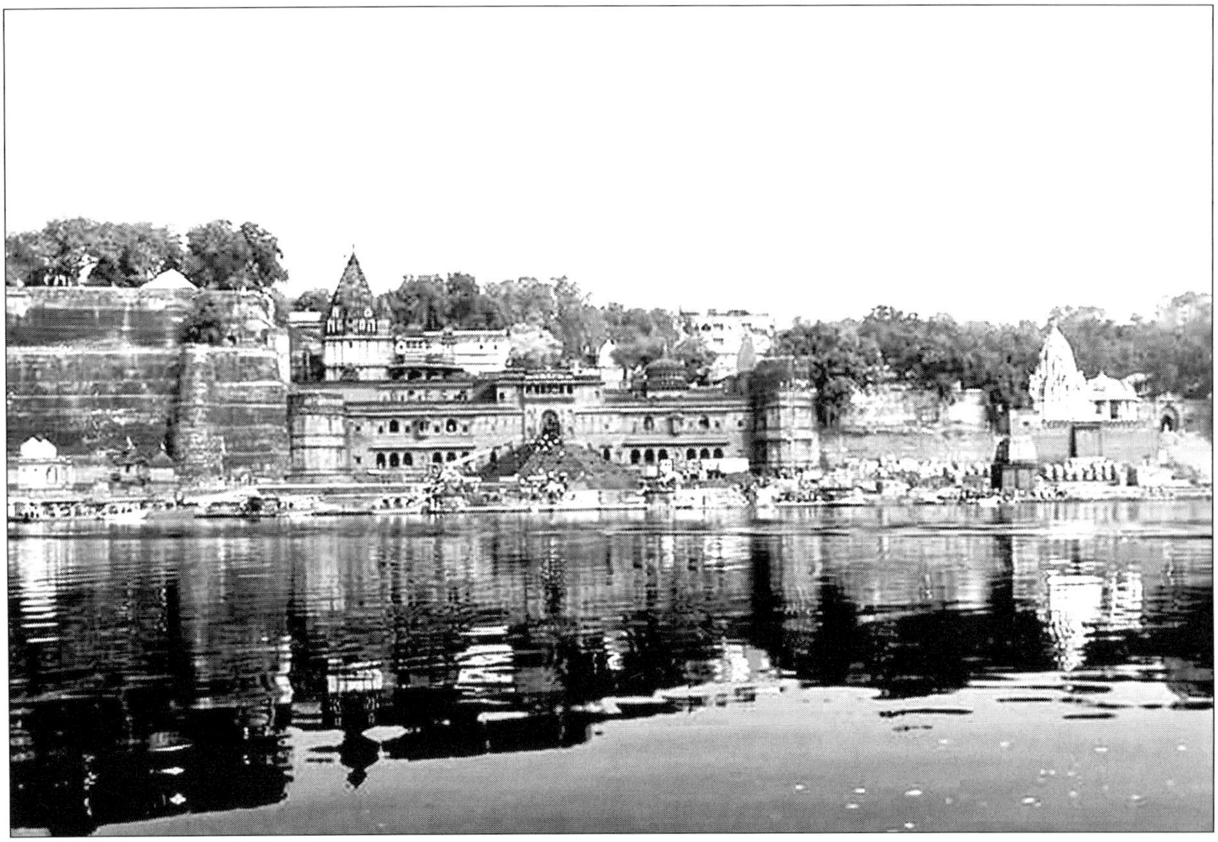

Fig. 33. Maheshwar on the right bank of the Narmadā.

Some donatory inscriptions of Sanchi mention it as Mahisati and Māhisati.[4] The *Mahābhārata* (II.31, 10), however, distinguishes between the kingdom of Avanti and Māhishmatī locating the former near the Narmadā. The southern part was known as Haihaya, Mahisha, Māhishaka[5], Anūpadeśa[6], Ākara[7], etc. The *Matsya* (XLIII.8-29) and *Vāyu* (XCIV.5-26) purāṇas attribute the foundation of Māhishmatī to the Haihayas after overthrowing the Nāga aborigines of the Narmadā valley. The *Harivaṃśa* (I.33, 4-5) names its founder as Mahishmān while the *Padma Purāṇa* (Uttara, chapter 75) names him Mahisha.

The *Mahābhārata* (Karṇa Parva, 33-34) and many Purāṇas[8] narrate the story of Śiva's victory over Tripurāsura, a demon, Bāṇa by name, residing at Tripura, generally and rightly identified with the archaeological site of Tewar near Jabalpur or Bhedaghat. This demon (or three demons named Tārakākshya, Kamalāksha and Vidyunmālī, the three sons of the demon Tāraka, according to other sources) was (/were) in possession of three forts or *puras* made of gold, silver and iron, which were almost invincible. Śiva, in order to overpower the demon by destroying his three forts, made necessary preparations on the bank of Narmadā. The *Matsya Purāṇa* (187.2) and the *Padma Purāṇa* (Svarga-khaṇḍa, 15.2)[9] tell us that the event took place at Maheśvara (Maheshwar). Maheshwar is traditionally identified with Māhishmatī which is also supported by the discovery from here of coins bearing the name of the city as we shall see in the sequel.

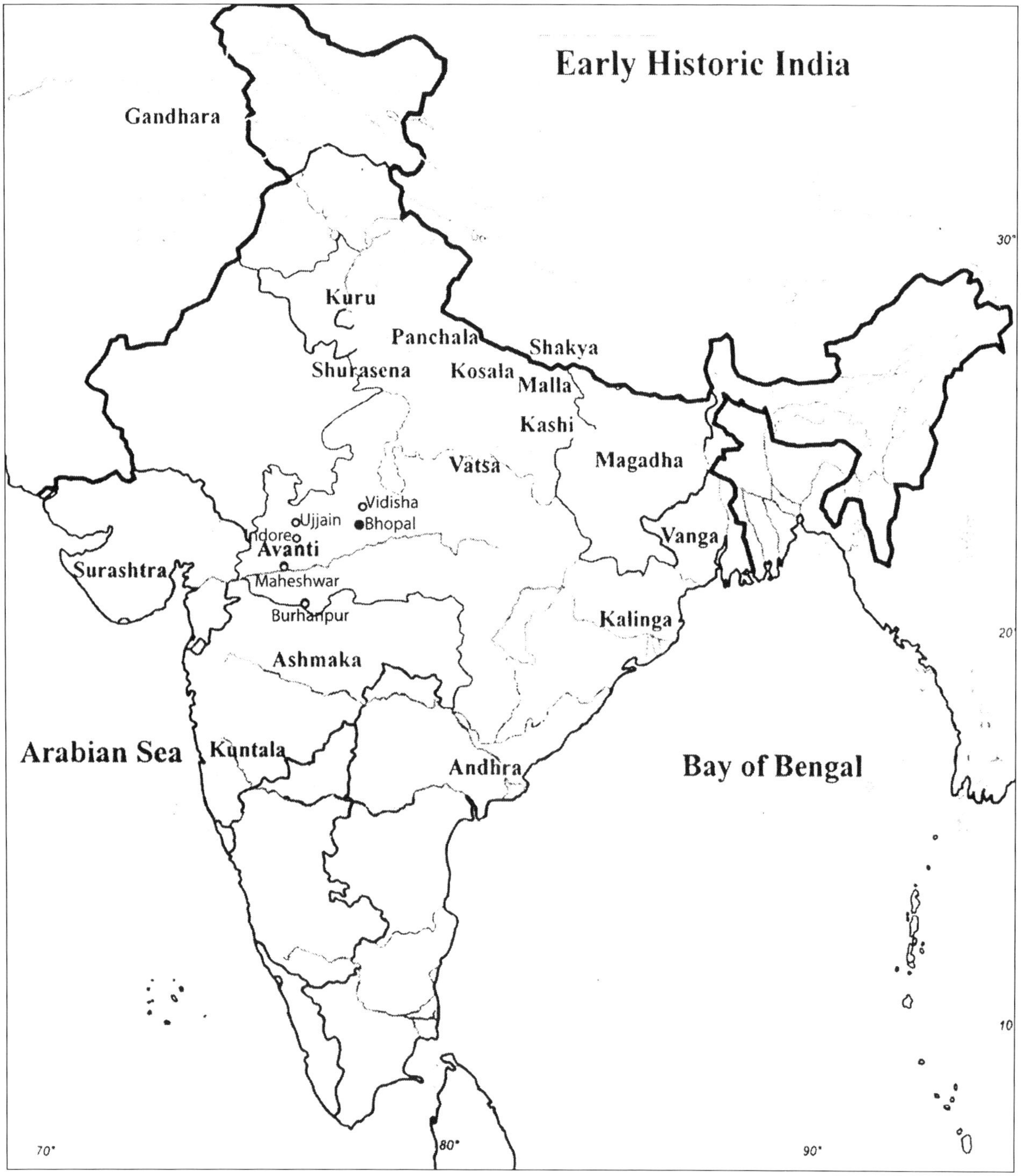

Fig. 34. Map showing the location of Maheshwar and sixteen *Mahājanapadas.*

Maheshwar and Navdatoli opposite Maheshwar, on the southern bank of the river, have provided the story of human habitation on the Narmadā with certain gaps from prehistoric to late medieval times. Excavations by Dr. H.D. Sankalia *et al.* have revealed that both these sites were inhabited almost at the same time during the Early Stone Age (Period I) and continued to be occupied during the Middle Stone

Age (Period II) and the proto-historic period (Period III) which ended in about the fifteenth century BCE. Both the sites were, however, re-occupied after a long gap and the people used a characteristic pottery known as Northern Black Polished Ware along with black-and-red ware, iron objects, terracottas, beads of semi-precious stones, bangles and early coins (Period IV) dated from *circa* 400 to 100 BCE (but more probably datable to 500 BCE – 150 BCE). A *stūpa* at Navdatoli with some kiln-burnt bricks inscribed in the Brāhmī characters of third century BCE was washed away by a flood. The habitation at Navdatoli ended but the occupation of Maheshwar lasted longer though during the subsequent period (Period V: 150 BCE – 200 CE) a general decline is noticeable. During this period the black-and-red ware diminished considerably and burnished red wares became more popular. Period VI at Maheshwar is characterized by Red Polished Ware which is generally associated with the Kshatrapa period in western India. The black-and-red ware shows further decline while the use of coarse red and black wares increases. Period VII at Maheshwar is dated to late medieval times marked by Muslim and Maratha antiquities and buildings.[10]

Excavations and explorations at the twin sites of Maheshwar and Navdatoli yielded punch-marked silver and copper coins, 37 un-inscribed cast and local coins, 32 came from Maheshwar and 5 from Navdatoli, 12 of them being stratified, 1 coming from a layer of Period IV and all others from later periods. Two un-inscribed cast copper coins found from Maheshwar came from regular layers and 5 were un-stratified, two Taxilian coins were stratified and four were surface finds, six Ujjayinī coins were stratified and eleven un-stratified while two coins of Māhishmatī were also surface finds.[11]

It must be pointed out here that Maheshwar and Kasarawad[12], an historical site less than 10 km south of the former, besides Ujjain are so rich in numismatic finds that they have been attracting from far and near numerous archaeologists and collectors who have made rich hauls from these sites. There are numerous collectors at Indore in particular and other places in general who have collected very large number of coins from Maheshwar or purchased them in the market at Indore. Most of these collectors, however, hardly bother to know and keep a record of the exact provenance of their coins. Much of the important historical evidence has thus got lost. Noteworthy amongst the old stalwarts who have collected and/or studied coins from Maheshwar being members of Dr. Sankalia's team, Dr. Nagu, Dr. V.S. Wakankar, Sarvashri N.R. Advani, S.L. Pardeshi, R.K. Sethi, Umrao Singh Babel, Tikekar, Daulal Johri, Gopaldas Mangaldas, Dr. S.K. Bhatt, Prof. Dau Lal Neema and the younger generation of Girish Sharma (all belonging to Indore), Major Dr. M.K. Gupta (Burhanpur), (Late) Shri Narendra Kothari (Jaipur) and numerous other individuals in various cities of the country. Prof. Dau Lal Neema of Indore has been a keen collector of coins, particularly from Maheshwar, and possesses hundreds, perhaps thousands, of coins from this site recording their provenance very meticulously. Drs. Michael Mitchiner (U.K.) and Wilfried Pieper (Germany) are the foremost amongst the foreign scholars who have procured and studied coins from Malwa including Maheshwar.

PUNCH-MARKED COINS

Punch-marked coins are said to have been found from the strata of Period IV (Early Historic-I, *circa* 400-100 BCE) which yielded Northern Black Polished sherds and other early historic antiquities. Besides a round silver *kārshāpaṇa* (No. 1036, MHSR II.A.I, Layer 15 (- 37 ft 6 inches) of 2.722 g (approximately 24 *rattīs* or 42 grains) bearing the five symbols of sun, *shaḍara-chakra* (six-armed symbol), rabbit on arched hill, bull to right and thick knobbed circle between two taurines on the obverse and faint traces of sun-like symbol on the reverse[13], two copper punch-marked coins, nine silver and two copper minuscule pieces (Nos. 1006a-j, MHSR V) ranging between 4 and 5.25 mm in size and 0.099 to 0.159 g in weight were discovered from the site of Maheshwar.[14] One copper punch-marked coin obtained from a depth of only about six inches from the surface (No. 161) shows the sun, six-armed and an animal-like symbol partially on the obverse and a caduceus on the reverse[15] while the other (No. 1006, 14 x 10 x 3 mm, 2.66 g) was recovered from a depth of about 33 feet from the surface from Layer 13 of Trench II and shows sun, *shaḍara-chakra* 'six-armed wheel', hill with crescent at top and two other unidentified symbols and have stratigraphically been placed between the end of third to the beginning of the second century BCE.[16]

Illustrated below are some good specimens of one silver and six copper punch-marked coins from this site in Dr. Neema's collection (Fig. 35)[17]:

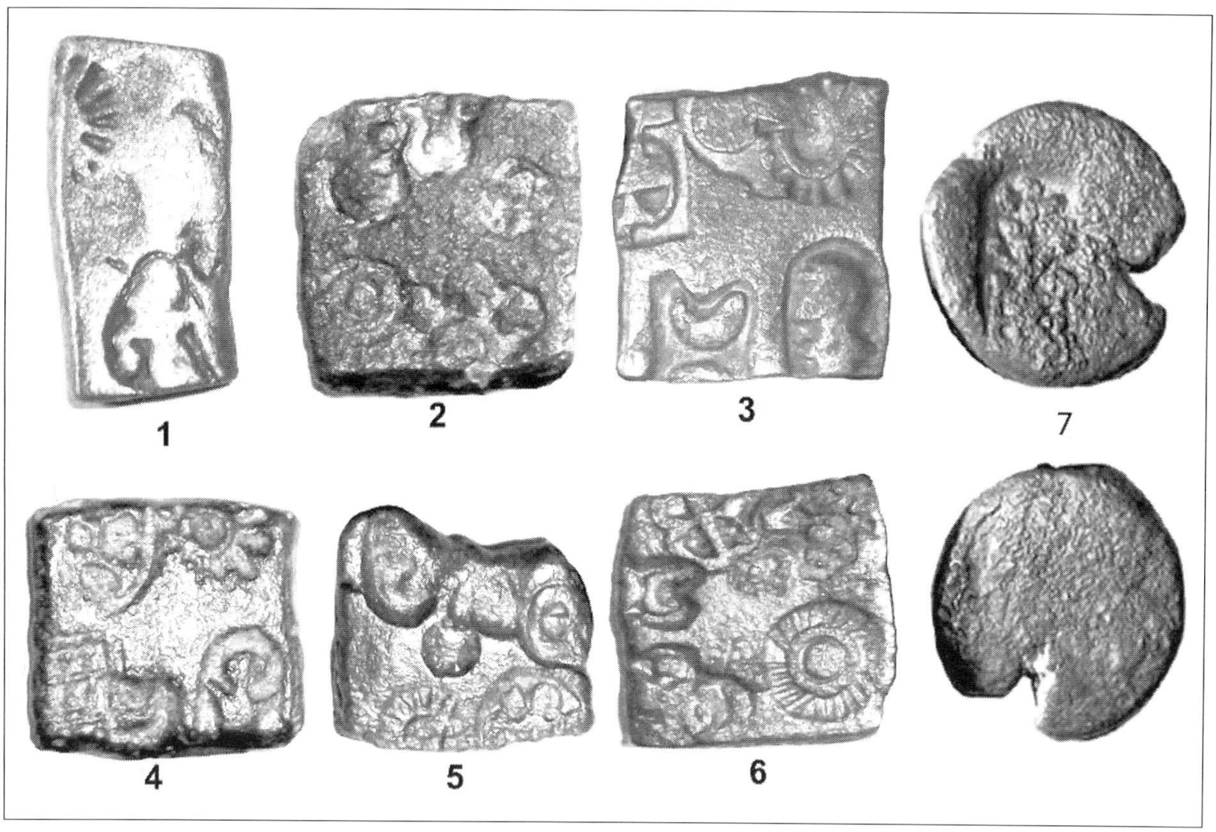

Fig. 35. Maheshwar: Punch-marked coins: silver (1), copper (2-6) and single-punch copper (7).

Pieper has listed six copper coins from northern and central India bearing only one punch, elephant and lion being the important devices on them.[18] Dr. Neema has procured a copper coin from Maheshwar bearing only one punch of tree in railing.

A seal impression on a glass tablet, datable to *circa* 4th century BCE, was recovered from Mandalkho mound at Maheshwar.[19]

MINUSCULE SILVER COINS

Numerous minuscule silver coins have also been recovered from Maheshwar. Possibly many of the coins bearing 6-armed symbol with alternating arrow-heads and taurines and those showing a *patākā* 'banner' with two taurines placed one over the other on either side of its shaft referred to by Mitchiner as coming from Indore may have actually belonged to Maheshwar.[20] Major Dr. Gupta of Burhanpur (now shifted to Indore) too has a very large collection of diminutive silver coins (still unpublished) many of which, if not most, come from Maheshwar.

Except the silver *kārshāpaṇa* bearing five symbols belonging to the Imperial Series of the Magadhan Empire which represents the circulation of the pan-Indian currency used for long distance trade, all the light-weight punch-marked coins served the purpose of lower denomination local currency to facilitate the day-to-day needs of the people in this part of the country. Though the excavators dated the strata of Period IV to *circa* 400-100 BCE, Nisar Ahmad assigns Period IV to *circa* 800 BCE to 150 CE and layer 15 from which the punch-marked coin was found to about the first half or middle of the 5th century BCE.[21] The coins bearing the sun symbol with straight rays, however, are generally believed to belong to the Magadhan Empire and their pre-Mautyan date may not hold good. What is important, however, is the use of minuscule local currency which may have been the legacy of the local low denomination coinage of the *Mahājanapada* period which bore less than five symbols. We know of single-die quarter units (*pāda-kārshāpaṇas*) and *Māshaka* (0.45 g) coins and even of smaller denominations of the Avanti Mahājanapada also.[22]

Of the diminutive un-inscribed coins procured by Sankalia *et al.* listed below P.L. Gupta identified the last one as 'Raupya Ardha-Māshaka'[23] though all of them weigh approximately one *rattī* and may therefore have been the *ardha-māshaka* coins. Their reverses are blank or have obliterated beyond recognition. They may be briefly described as following.

1. No. 1006a, AR, round, 5 mm, 0.121 g.
   Obv. Triskeles and probably a taurines.
2. No. 1006b, AR, round, 5 mm, 0.099 g.

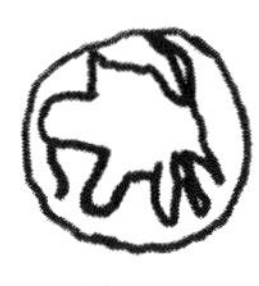

Obv. Probably a bull to left with two taurines above and two below.

3. No. 1006c, AR, round, 5 mm, 0.121 g.

Obv. Bull or elephant with similarly placed taurines.

4. No. 1006d, Æ?, round, 4 mm, 0.131 g.
Obv. Crown or shield-like symbol.

5. No. 1006e, Æ?, round, 4-4.5 mm, 0.150 g.

Obv. Crown-like symbol.

6. No. 1006f, AR, round, 4 mm, 0.159 g.

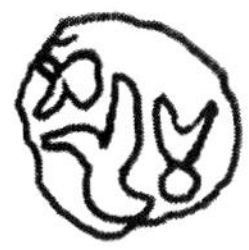

Obv. Triskeles and taurines(/s).

7. No. 1006g, AR, round, 5-5.25 mm, 0.130 g.

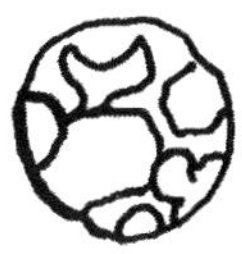

Obv. Six-armed symbol.

8. No. 1006h, AR, round, 4 mm, 0.127 g.

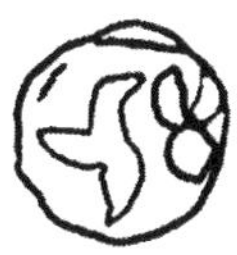

Obv. Triskeles and taurines.

9. No. 1006i, AR, round, 4 mm, 0.114 g.
Obv. Similar.

10. No. 1006j, AR, round, 4.5 mm, 0.148 g.
Obv. Similar?

LEAD COINS

Prof. Dau Lal Neema has been gracious enough to send the scans of numerous of his coins from Maheshwar and allowed me to publish them. Many of his coins are similar to those recovered by Sankalia *et al.* and corroborate the fact of their existence and circulation at Maheshwar during the latter half of the first millennium BCE. Some of these coins both square and round in shape, are made of lead (Fig. 36) and seem to be quite early ones.

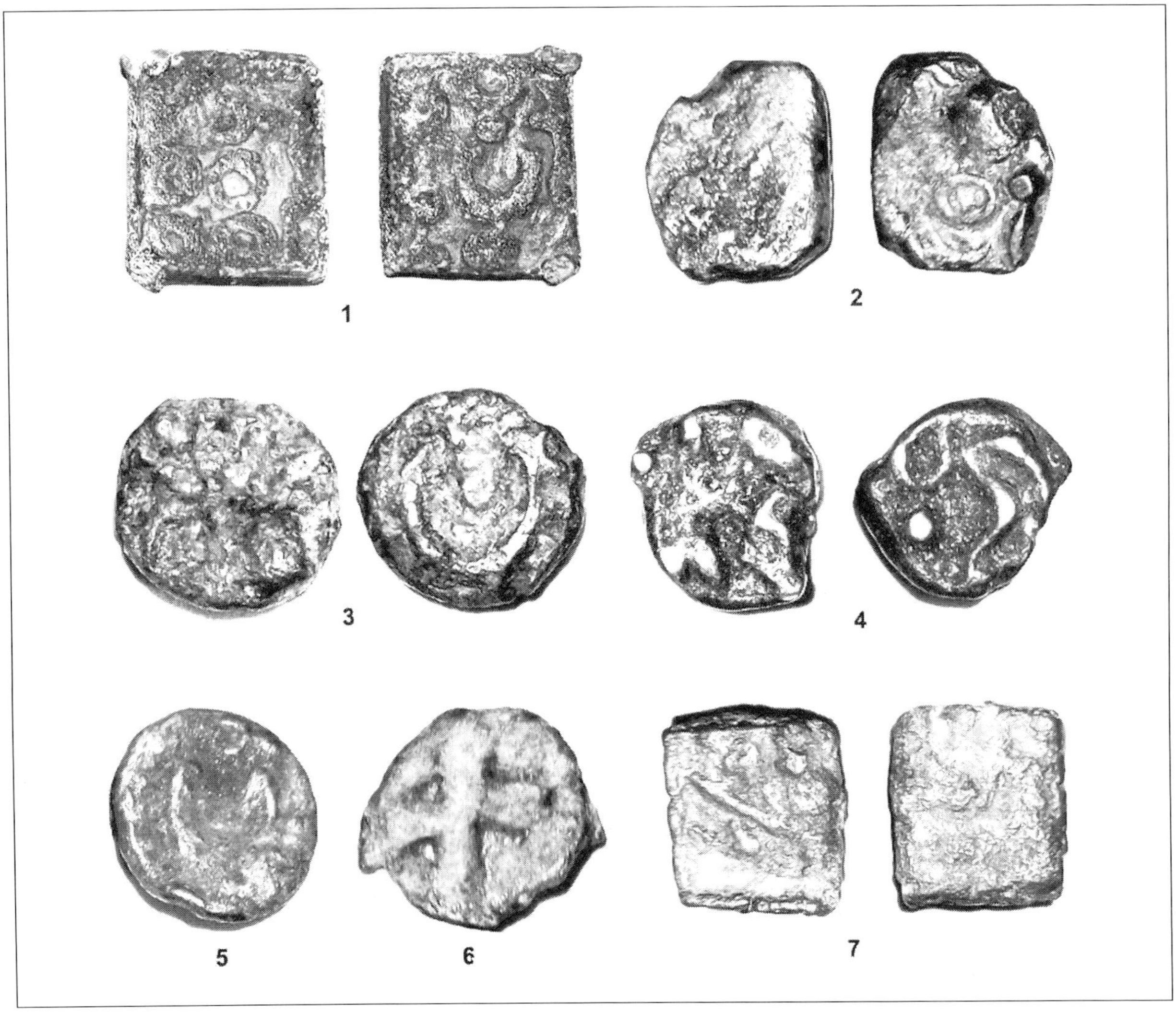

Fig. 36. Lead coins from Maheshwar.

Mostly they are in an indifferent state of preservation and it is rather difficult to make out the symbols and motifs on them satisfactorily. One coin is square in shape carrying un-connected four circlets and a laterally placed taurine on the obverse and two taurines symbols one upon the other with undetermined linear symbols or motifs which look like *svastika* and probably triangle-headed symbols on railed posts on the reverse (Fig. 36.1). A rectangular piece is uniface with rounded corners, one chipped off slightly, and shows a whorl-like symbol akin to the symbol as found on a variety of four-symbol silver *kārshāpaṇa* coins of the Avanti *Mahājanapada* dated to 500-400 BCE.[24] This symbol of four un-connected circlets may be a precursor of the Ujjayinī symbol and is met with on the early coins of the Avanti *mahājanapada*[25] which had issued besides the four-symbol *kārshāpaṇas* their half (1.8 g), quarter (0.9 g) and *dvi-māshaka* (0.45 g)[26] and perhaps even smaller denominations of one *rattī* subsequently.[27] One more square lead coin of this type (2.2 cm, 13.05 g) with four circlets and parts of some other indeterminate symbols on the obverse and a big taurines with two small *svastikas* in the top corners on the reverse, probably from Ujjain or Maheshwar, has appeared in the catalogue of an auction house recently.[28] The obverse motif on another lead coin from Neema collection is not clear but the reverse seems to carry a taurine within a bigger taurine (Fig. 36.2). A round piece shows a blossomed lotus flower on the obverse and a smaller taurine placed above a bigger taurine on the reverse (Fig. 36.3). One piece carries the depiction of a taurine on left with crescent shaped linear tank probably with fishes on right on one side while the motif on the other side can not be made out clearly (Fig. 36.4). A uniface piece shows part of a big taurine symbol (Fig. 36.5) while another carries a cross-like symbol (Fig. 36.6). The obverse device of a square piece is not clear but the reverse seems to carry a *svastika*, perhaps with taurine ends on the reverse (Fig. 36.7). A square lead coin showing unconnected four circlets and a taurine and another with smaller taurines above one of a bigger size flanked by railed triangle-headed and *svastika* standard also exist in the collection of Shri Girish Sharma of Indore. These lead coins are thus quite in line of the small denomination coins of the *mahājanapada*. I would attribute these coins also to Avanti and date them to fourth century BCE, when Maheshwar formed part of the *mahājanapada*. We know of the lead punch-marked coins from Ujjain region, but some of these pieces perhaps precede them and may be the earliest specimens of lead coins in India.

UN-INSCRIBED CAST COPPER COINS

Interesting amongst the un-inscribed cast copper coins found in the excavations[29] are pieces showing an elephant with rider walking to left on the obverse and three-arched hill (sometimes with dots in the arches) and crescent above on the reverse (Fig. 37.1-6). In many cases they have the protruding ledges also on the sides indicating that they were cast in groups. Coins of this type have been recovered from Tripuri also.[30] One coin (16 mm, 2.929 g) shows the crescented hill with a water-chute coming out from its base on the obverse and a hollow cross on the reverse (Fig. 37.7).[31] Another coin of this type (round, 21.25 mm, 74 grains or nearly 4.9 g) was brought to light by Trivedi from the collection of S.L. Paradeshi of Indore.[32] A uniface interesting piece (16 mm, 2.065 g) shows a railed post on left and hollow cross with arrow-heads protruding from it in cardinal directions on right (Fig. 37.8). Its typical symbol helps us in determining the provenance of similar coins. A coin (15 mm, 2.2 g) of this type exists in the collection of Major Dr. Gupta also (Fig. 39.1).[33] Trivedi[34] published a 13 mm roughly square copper coin weighing 47.5 grains (approximately 2.9 g) picked from Jwaleshwara Bedi mound at Maheshwar from the collection of V.S. Wakankar showing three-arched hill with crescent on the obverse and tree in railing on the reverse the likes of which had earlier been published by Allan.[35] Wakankar classified his family collection of more than six thousand coins of the Ujjain region preserved in Bharat Kala Bhavan, Ujjain into 33 major classes and 475 varieties[36] but unfortunately he could not publish their details and illustrate all the varieties in his life time. Recently Pieper has listed about 150 varieties of Ujjain and Narmadā valley coins which he has divided into 12 main classes, viz., (1) Standing

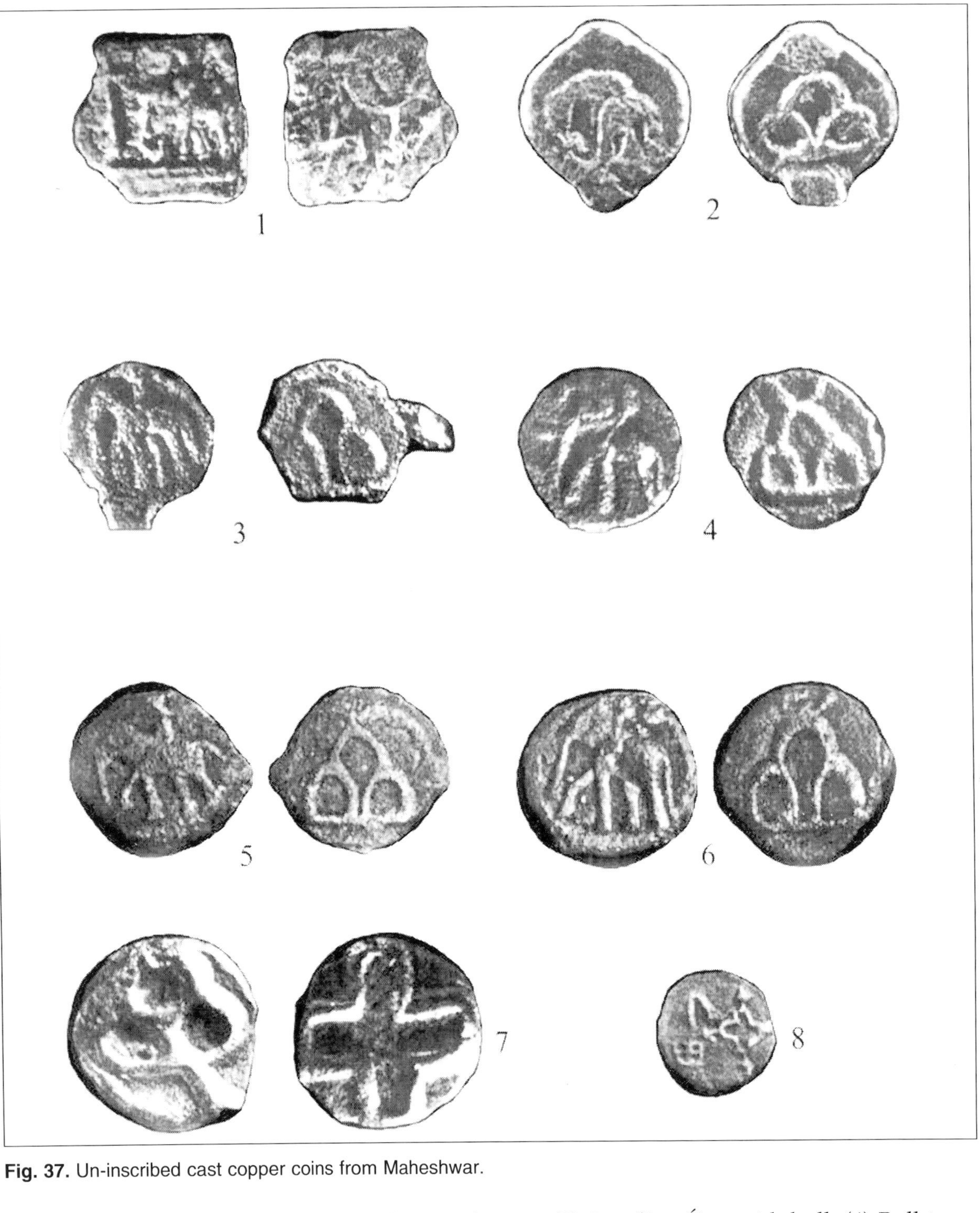

Fig. 37. Un-inscribed cast copper coins from Maheshwar.

human figures, (2) Seated human figures, (3) Standing Śiva with bull, (4) Bull type, (5) Horse type, (6) Elephant type, (7) Lion type, (8) Tortoise type, (9) Multi-symbol type, (10) Diverse single-symbol type, (11) Tree type, and (12) Inscribed Ujjain type.[37] Many other coins have been put under different classes in the absence of definite information of their provenance.

COINS WITH A HOLLOW CROSS

Amongst the coins illustrated in Fig. 37 above the last two coins show hollow cross. The motif of hollow cross was especially popular at Taxila and has also been noticed

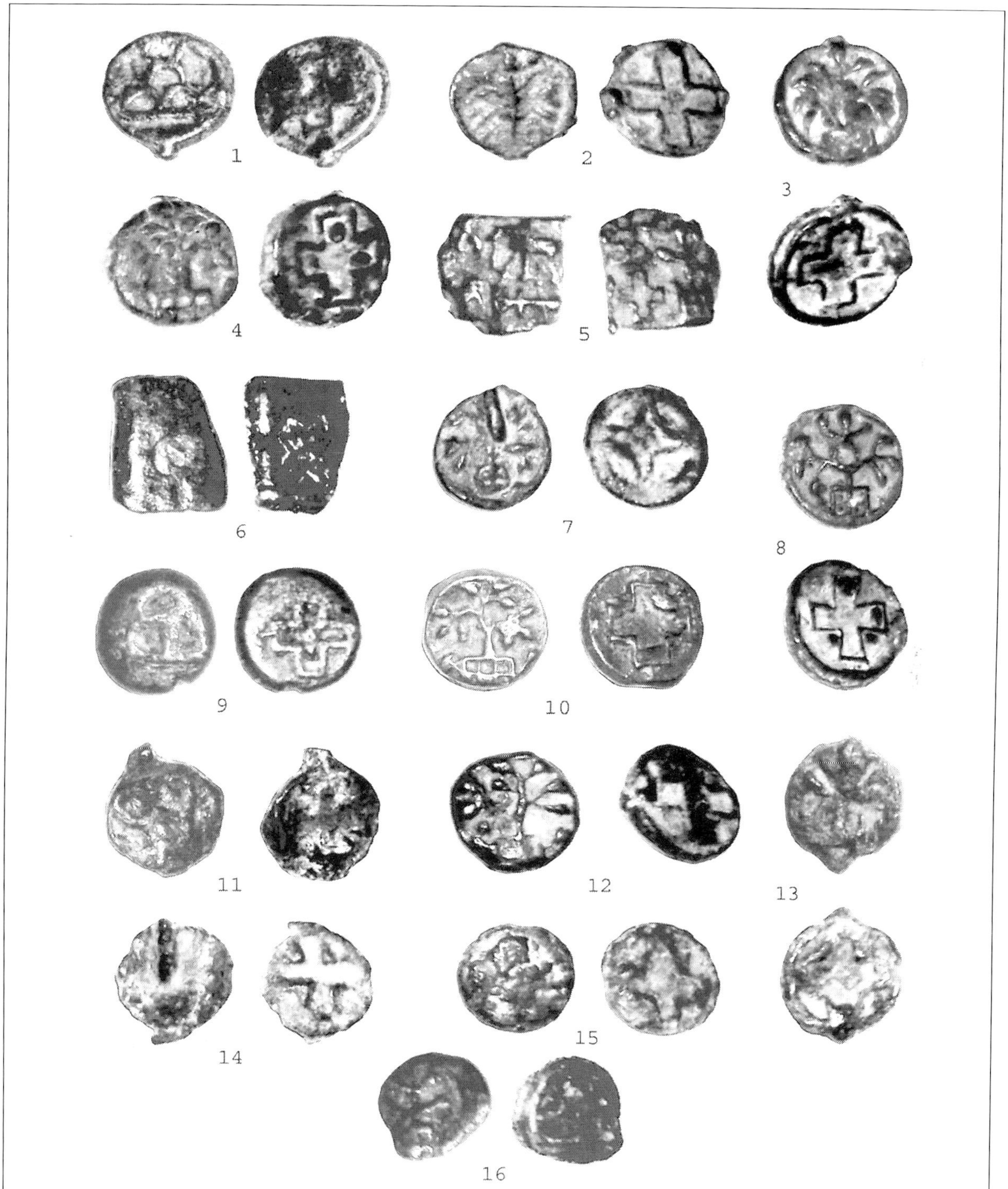

Fig. 38. Coins with hollow cross.

on the coins of Kauśāmbī, some city-states like Kuraghara/Kurarāya and Tripuri, central India and the Deccan. Dr. Neema has a good number of coins picked up from Maheshwar which show this motif. Sixteen of these pieces are illustrated here (Fig. 38).

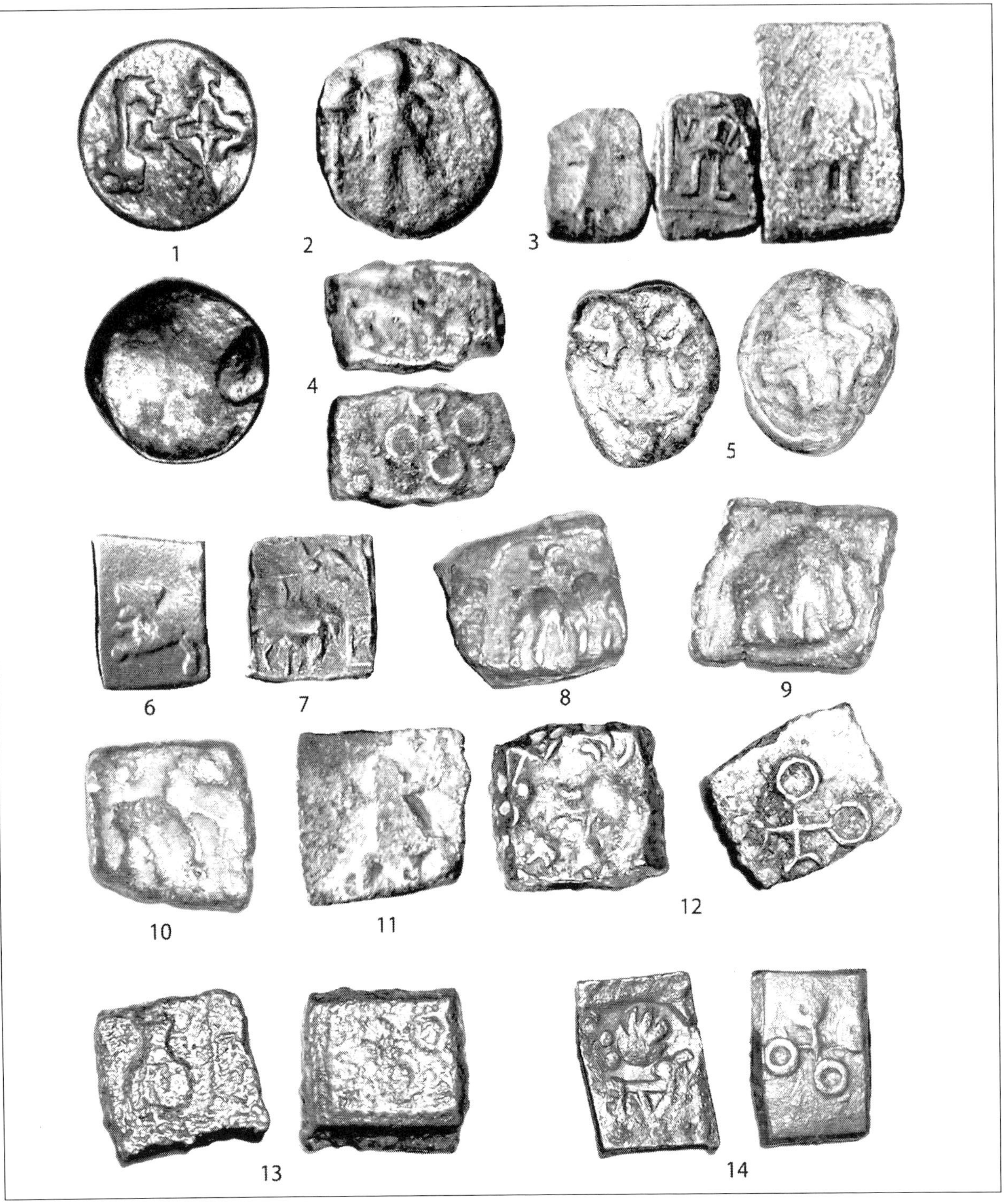

Fig. 39. Miscellaneous coins from Maheshwar.

The respective weights of these coins in grams are: (1) 9.29, (2) 1.55, (3) 1.30, (4) 3.46, (5) 2.19, (6) 5.30, (7) 1.61, (8) 1.41, (9) 4.10, (10) 3.66, (11) 2.15, (12) 1.62, (13) 1.31, (14) 3.660.65, (15) 0.80 and (16) 0.36. They are square/rectangular as well as

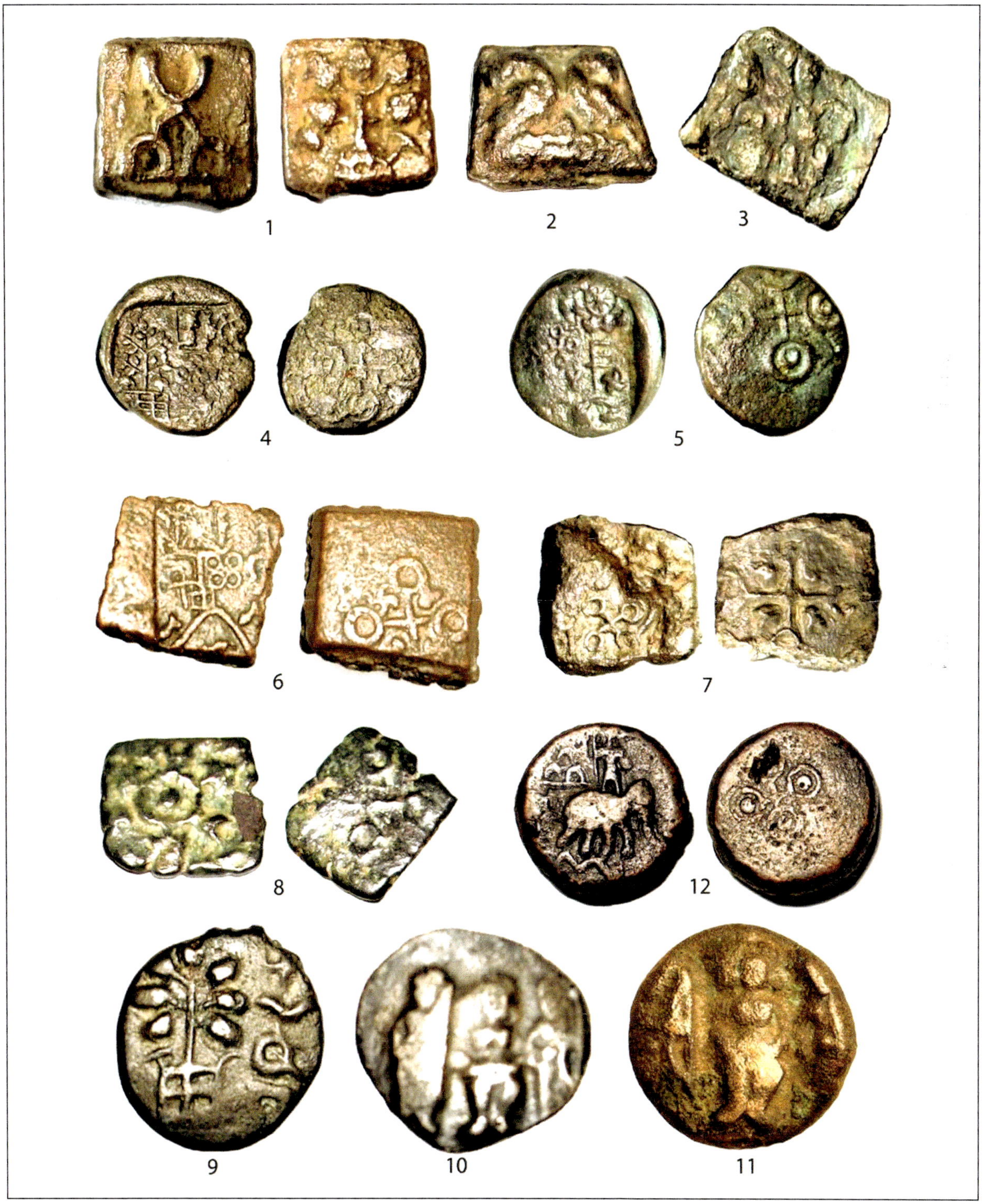

Fig. 40. Coins of various types from Maheshwar.

round in shape. Three-arched hill with crescent and tree in railing are the commonest motifs of the obverse. Most of the coins are cast but some give the impression of being die-struck also. Their weights vary and do not seem to be in any definite proportion. Perhaps the coins were issued for a long time and in different fractions.

Coins collected by Dr. Neema from Maheshwar include many varieties of Ujjain coins showing helmeted human figure, standing monocephalous Śiva holding a staff on different denominations (Fig. 39.2-3), human figure with an animal (Fig. 39.4), crude human figure with taurine on a standard in front, lion (Fig. 39.5-6), bull (Fig. 39.7), elephant (Fig. 39.8-9), horse (Fig. 39.10) or ass, tortoise, frog (Fig. 39.11), scorpion? (Fig. 39.12), vase (Fig. 39.13), *śrīvatsa*, *svastika*, hand with fingers (*pañchāṅgulaka*) (Fig. 39.14), three-arched hill with crescent/tree in railing (Fig. 40.1), retrorse birds (Fig. 40.2), male and dancing female figure (Fig. 40.3), multi-symbols (Fig. 40.4-7), eight-armed wheel with alternating arrow-heads and taurines (Fig. 40.8), etc. many of which types are known from Ujjain coins.

A coin of the city state of Hathodaka (Fig. 40.9) indicates contemporary trade and interaction between the cities of the Narmadā valley. Very interesting, however, is a potin (?) coin showing three human figures (Fig. 40.10) which I have identified as Rāma, Sītā and Lakshmaṇa. A copper coin in the collection of Major Dr. M.K. Gupta also shows similar figures and probably had the same provenance (Fig. 40.11).[38]

COINS OF THE CITY-STATE OF MĀHISHMATĪ

Though the important state of Avantī had already been conquered by the Śiśunāgas and annexed to the Magadhan empire, the Nandas consolidated their control over this area by defeating the Haihayas. It seems that at the weakening of the Maurya power in late third century or early second century BCE Vidiśā, Ujjain and Maheshwar became independent as city states and issued their own coinages with the legends *Vedisasa*, *Ujeni/ya* and *Mahismati*. The coins of Mahismati/Māhishmatī may be classified as following.

CLASS I: SQUARE/RECTANGULAR COINS

VARIETIES 1-5

Two uniface square copper coins weighing 64 and 16 grains (approximately 1.04 and 4.15 g) and measuring 0.65 and 0.4 inch (16.25 and 10.0 mm) showing a standing human figure and a symbol consisting of a pellet with four crescents around 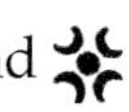 with the legend *Mahās*[- -] put under 'Uncertain Coins' were published in 1936 by Allan who proposed to restore the legend as Mahāsenasa attributing the coins to a king named Mahāsena.[39] In 1951 T.N. Ramchandran also published a similar coin obtained from the bed of the river Śiprā at Ujjain showing the lower portion of the draped human figure to left with the legend *Mahisa* below.[40] It was, however, P.L. Gupta who first read the legend correctly and identified the coins as belonging to the city of Māhishmatī.[41] We thus have a variety (1) like this –

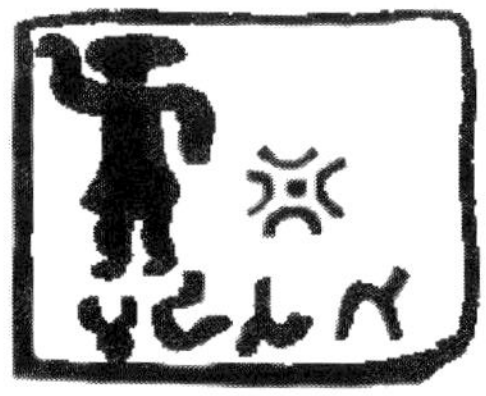

Wakankar[42] had picked up two coins of Māhishmatī from Maheshwar in course of surface exploration in 1953-54. These coins were first published in the Excavation Report of Maheshwar and Navdatoli[43] and later in an article by Dr. H.V. Trivedi.[44] Wakankar seems to have obtained more coins from Maheshwar from time to time. Allan's coin described above is quite similar to what may be seen on one of the four coins (no. III) published and illustrated in the form of sketches, without the details of their size and weight, along with the symbols and the legends by Wakankar[45] in 1971 (Fig. 41).

Wakankar's coin nos. I and II are also single type (with blank reverse). They were purchased from the local market by Umarao Singhji of Indore who handed them over to Wakankar. Coin no. I shows a three arched hill or *chaitya*, a pellet flanked by four crescents (called *chatushmakāra* by Wakankar), tree in railing (actually taurine standard as known from better specimens) with the Brāhmī legend below reading *Māhisati* (transcribed as *Mahīsatī* in Devanāgarī in the details of symbols).

Wakankar's coin no. II has in the top row a three arched *chaitya* with a crescent above, triangle-headed standard (*Indrayashṭi*, more popularly known as *Indradhvaja*) and what looks like the lower part of a human figure (or may have been the two arms of an inverted taurine symbol); in the middle row again from left to right, a couchant lion and an inverted lotus within a railing with minute dots and four crescents around and a taurine above it; in the third row, the legend to be read upside down, *Mahisati*; and at the bottom, river with tortoise and two fishes. The earliest coins of Māhishmatī thus seem to have been square in shape and uniface.

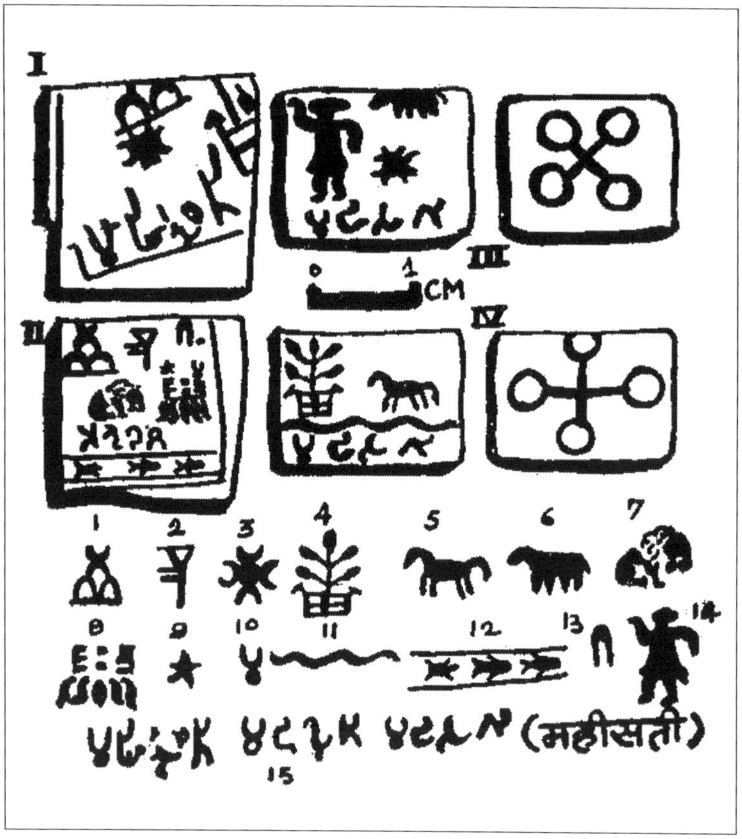

Fig. 41. Coins of Mahis(m)ati.

Wakankar had picked up his coin no. III from Jwaleshwar

mound (located on the east of Maheshwar on the confluence of Māhishmatī Nālā and the Narmadā). It is similar to his coin no. 1 and its better preserved examples as illustrated above but for the stance of the female figure which shows her with her right hand raised and left akimbo. His coin number IV was found from Dhanbedi mound of Maheshwar in course of surface exploration in 1953-54 during the excavations at Maheshwar and Navdatoli. Coin no. III bears on the obverse, a standing human figure with right hand raised and left hanging down on left, an animal (identified as horse by Wakankar) walking to left along the upper margin and a pellet with four crescents in the centre with Brāhmī legend *Mahisati* below. Coin no. IV shows a tree in railing and a horse walking to left in the upper portion with an undulating line below and the legend *Mahisati* at the bottom.[46] We thus see that all these coins – two of Allan and one published by Ramchandran, and four pieces brought to light by Wakankar – are square or rectangular in shape and represent five different varieties (Class I, Var. 1-5).

Quite a few pieces of the city-state exist in the private collections of various persons in Indore and elsewhere, the notable amongst these being Sarvashri Dau Lal Neema, Girish Sharma and Daulal Johri of Indore, Major Dr. Gupta (Fig. 43)[47], Karan Singh and Advocate Shailesh Jain, the well-known numismatists. It is presumable that many of these coins if not all may have come from Maheshwar.

Variety 6

A uniface rectangular coin similar to Wakankar's coin no. I exists in Girish Sharma's collection also but is better preserved to reveal that the topmost row contains triangle-headed standard, three-arched hill with crescent and the taurine on standard from left to right, the middle portion contains a lotus flower-like four crescents around a central pellet and the railing on right from which rise the standard of the taurine while the lowest row on the base carries the legend *(Ma)hismat(i)* in early Brāhmī characters of second century BCE (Fig. 42.1). The clearly visible three symbols in the topmost row, however, distinguish it as variety 6 of square/rectangular coins.

Variety 7

A beautiful coin of Māhishmatī picked up from Maheshwar in the same collection (Fig. 42.2) shows the complete figure of the female with left hand raised and right akimbo though the taurine standard has gone out of flan. It further supports the identification of this place with Māhishmatī. It shows the female figure standing facing with her left hand raised and right akimbo, triangle-headed standard and crescented three arched symbol on right top corner, four crescents around a pellet () below these and the Brāhmī legend *Mahismati* below on the obverse. The reverse is blank. With the female figure this coin represents variety 7 of square/rectangular coins.

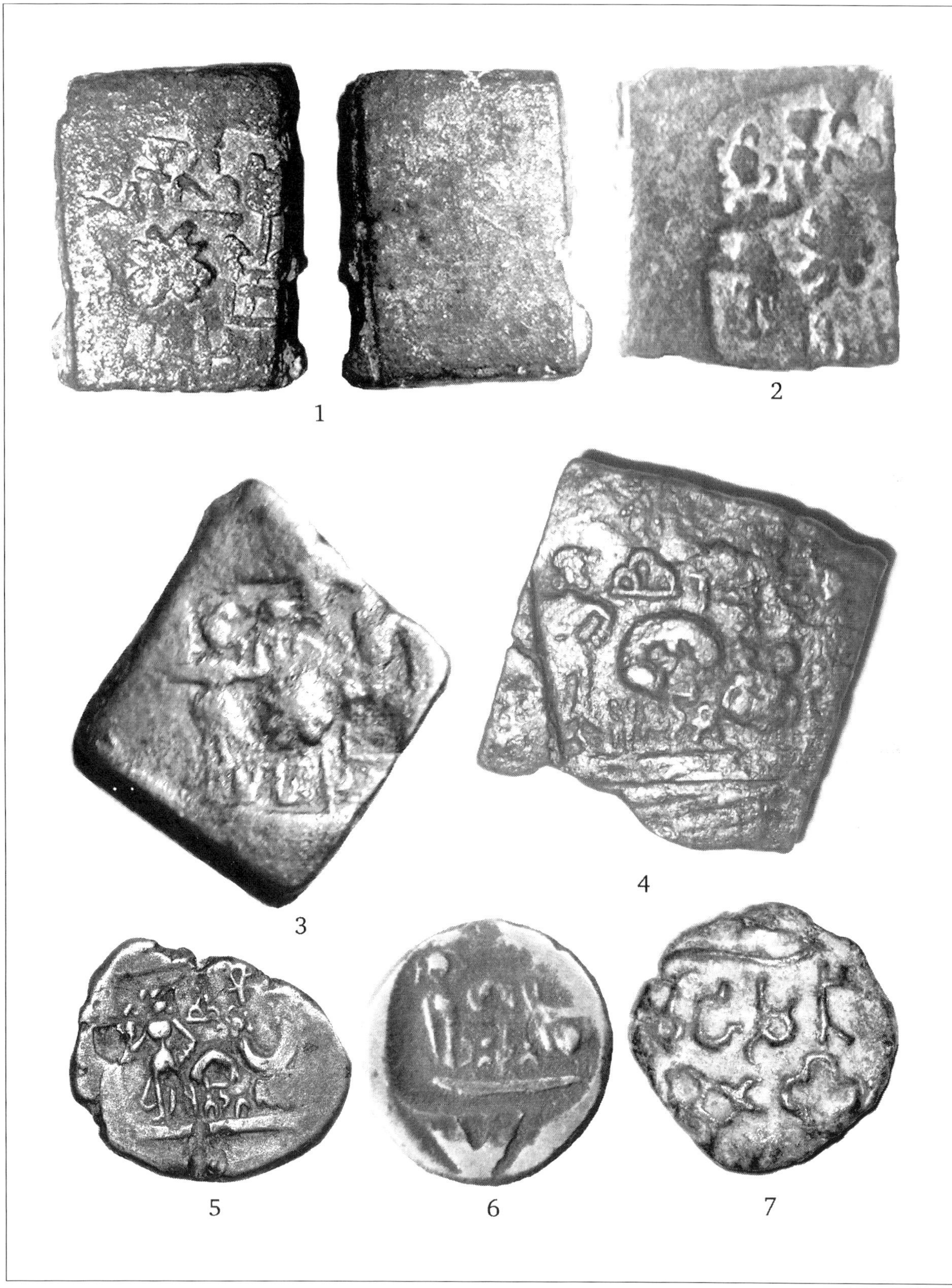

Fig. 42. Māhishmatī coins: Girish Sharma collection 1-3, 6-7; Dau Lal Neema collection 4; Daulal Johri collection 5.

VARIETY 8

The deep incused impression on Fig. 42.3 presents a combination of the the preceding two coins with much better preserved legend and the female figure with both hands raised and thus constituting variety 8.

CLASS II: RE-STRUCK SQUARE/RECTANGULAR COIN

VARIETY 1

A beautiful coin obtained from Maheshwar in the collection of Dr. Dau Lal Neema (Fig. 42.4) appears to have been struck on an earlier coin. It bears a similar deep incuse as in the preceding example but shows the graceful female figure wearing an exquisite coiffure, *karṇa-kuṇḍalas* 'earrings', bodice and *sārī* 'female dhoti'. She has multiple bangles on her left arm resting on the hip. The central device looking like the placenta with a fetus in the womb is clearer than other known specimens. The motif on the right is not very clear and looks like a couple. Better specimens in future may, however, reveal its true nature. The arched hill symbol above is very well struck. The triangle-headed symbol has suffered some diminution and the taurine which may have existed on the right in the top line is now completely obliterated. The legend, however, is fully intact and may be read by inverting the coin.[48]

VARIETY 2

A rectangular or wedge-shaped (0.7 x 1.4 cm, 7.0 g) coin of copper alloy (bronze?) in the collection of Major Dr. Gupta constituting the tenth variety of rectangular coins (Fig. 43.1) may be described as follows.

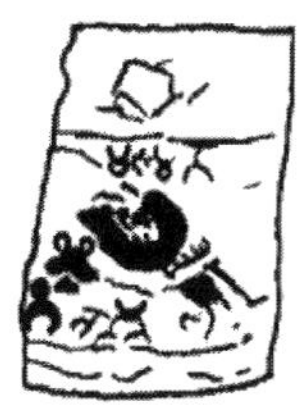

Obv. Jumbled impression of a doubly struck coin on an earlier piece which still shows traces of a hollow square or pentagon on the original top, symbol called lion or tiger (but having no resemblance to these animals actually) in the incused portion in the centre with the legend *Ma[his]mati* above, lower part of a female figure to the southeastern side of the so-called animal and the head of an animal (perhaps a buffalo) with hooked horns and bell hanging from the neck on the corresponding southwestern side and a three-arched hill with crescent below on counterstruck portion. On turning the coin upside down, we see traces of river (perhaps with fishes) on the top (perhaps legend *Mahismati* visible partially below it), a bold taurine symbol on right, etc.

Rev. Obliterated.

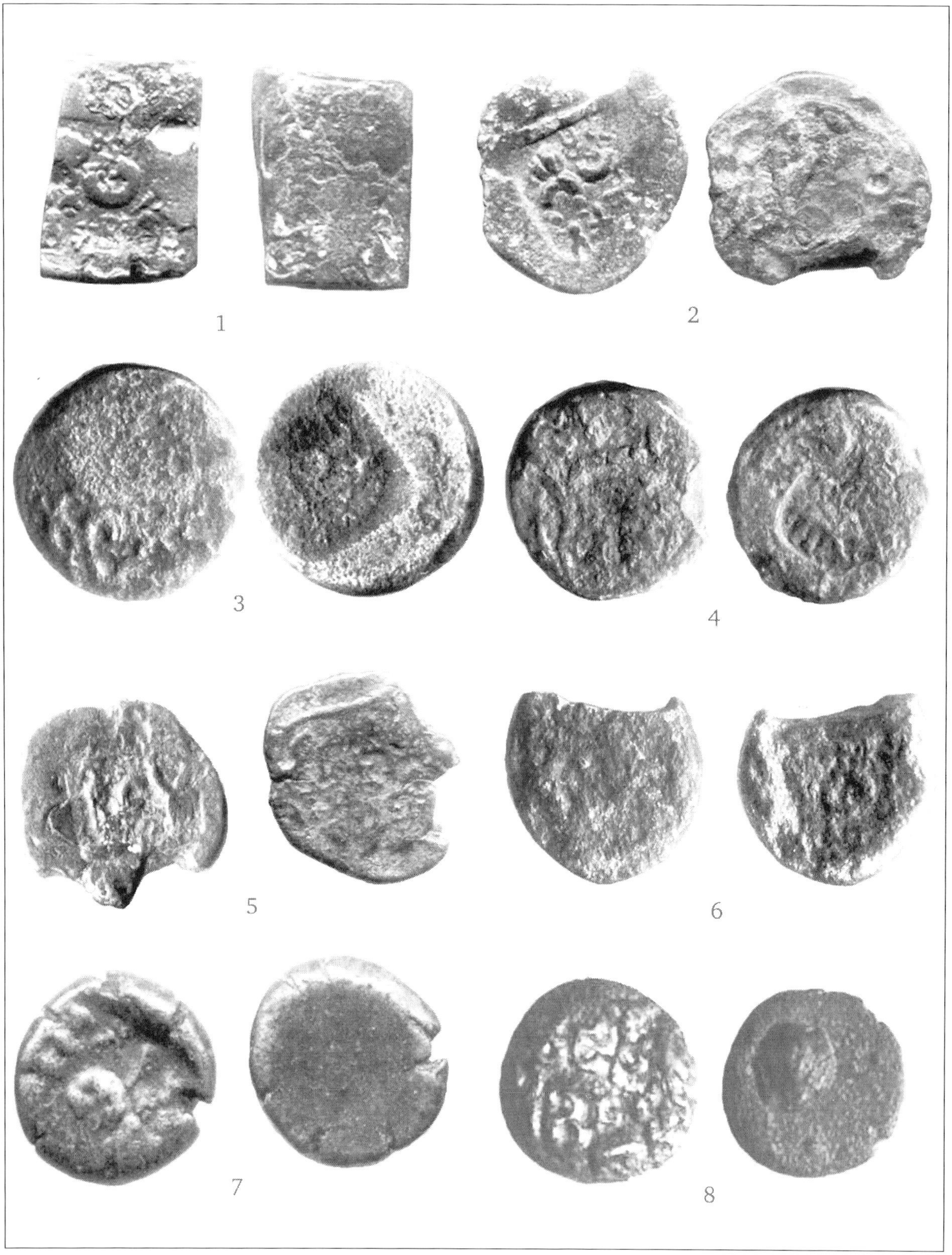

Fig. 43. Māhishmatī coins, Major Dr. M.K. Gupta's collection, 1, 3-8; Dau Lal Neema collection 2.

CLASS III: CIRCULAR COINS

VARIETY 1

A round copper coin of this city state was published by Ajay Mitra Shastri. This coin weighing 7.1 g and having a diameter of about 20 mm formed part of the collection of Shri Daulal Johri of Indore and showed a line (river symbol) at the top and the Brāhmī legend below it reading *Mahismati*.[49] Below the legend, in a row from left to right, a taurine over a vertical line, probably *nandipadadhvaja* 'taurine-topped post', a horizontally laid three-peaked hill surmounted by a crescent and a hollow cross; and at the bottom a fish. The reverse is blank. The coin showed the conjunct *sma* in the name of Māhishmatī for the first time as also the *nandipadadhvaja*, hollow cross and single fish. Shastri rightly dated the coin to second century BCE.[50]

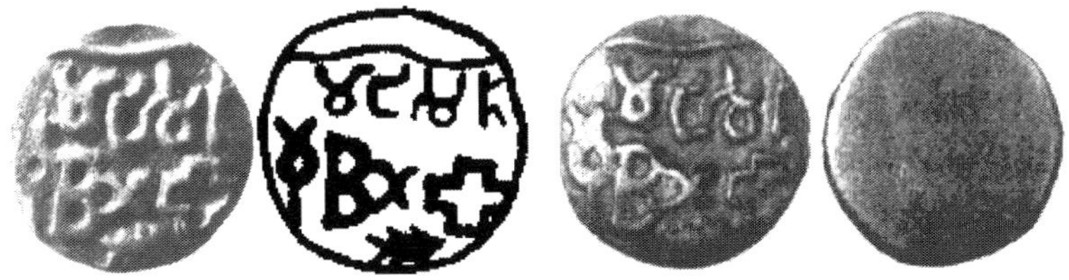

Prashant P. Kulkarni re-examined this coin and identified the wavy line above the legend with river Narmadā and read the legend as *Māhismatī*.[51] He has studied and republished some other coins also with very significant observations and notes.

VARIETY 2

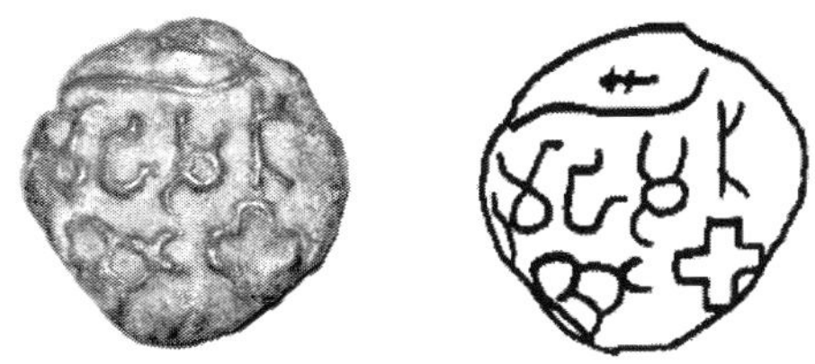

Recently Girish Sharma has acquired a similar copper/bronze round piece (1.95 cm, 7.8 g) which does not show the *nandipada* standard on left (Fig. 42.7). Sharma identifies the line at the top as the river Revā but has wrongly spelled the legend as *Mahishmati*[16] in stead of *Māhismatī*. Sharma has described the fish symbol below (not clear in his illustration) but seems to have missed a symbol above the river line on the top which too may have been the fish. Perhaps the *nandipada* standard is out of flan or only partially accommodated.

VARIETY 3

Another coin in the collection of Major Dr. M.K. Gupta, though similar to Shastri's coin, substitutes the fish symbol by an *Indradhvaja*, forming the third variety. Its details are given below.

Bell metal, circular, 2.1 cm, 7.5 g, Fig. 43.8.

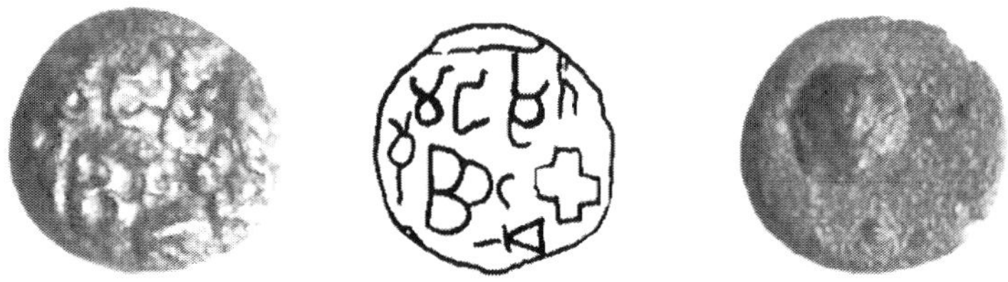

Obv. *Nandipada* standard, horizontally laid three arched hill with crescent and hollow cross from left to right, horizontally laid *Indradhvaja* below and Brāhmī legend *Māhismat(i)* above with linear representation of Narmadā at the top.

Rev. Blank with a round protrusion.

This is a very interesting coin of Māhishmatī which varies slightly from the coin-types published by Shastri and Kulkarni from the collections of Shri Daulal Johri described and illustrated above. Here we find the fish symbol substituted by a horizontally placed *Indradhvaja* with triangle-head on right. The legend also shows an altogether new form of the conjunct *sma* with the left hand stroke coming under the rounded base of *ma* rather than appended on the left of the vertical limb of the superscript *sa* as usually found on other coins.

Variety 4

Shri Girish Sharma possesses another uniface round coin of a new variety as it shows the female figure with elongated legs standing facing raising her right hand with left akimbo on left, placenta-like orb in the centre under which seems to be the legend (to be read by turning the coin upside down) and an unrecognisable symbol or motif on right having a track-like thick line below. A bold triangle-head of the *Indradhvaja* may be seen below the thick track line (Fig. 42.6).

Variety 5

Shri Daulal Johri, however, possesses the best preserved specimen, though slightly broken on the upper edge, depicting in a deep rectangular incuse with broken peripheral lines in their middle, female figure standing to front with strayed feet wearing usual garments and multiple bangles on the right wrist resting on hip and holding some object (flower?) in the right hand raised above. To the left of her shoulder and above the placenta-like symbol is the three-arched hill. At about I o'clock position is shown *Indradhvaja* with taurine below it. On viewers' right is depicted a bold symbol showing the mountain with crescent and sun above (Fig. 42.5).

CLASS IV: RE- (OR COUNTER-) STRUCK CIRCULAR COINS

On a re-examination of the counter struck coins of Māhishmatī from Daulal Johri's collection one of which was published earlier by S.K. Bhatt[52] on which he had read the legend *Madamae* which he connected with the town of Māṇḍu or the Māṇḍavya tribe mentioned in the *Bṛihatsaṃhitā* (XIV.2, 22 &27), Kulkarni[53] has noted some interesting features. He has given the details of two coins as follow.

VARIETY 1

Bell metal, 8.22 g, 22 mm.

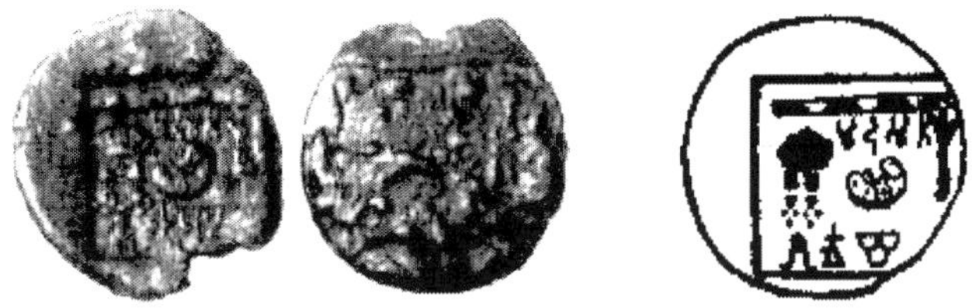

Obv. Counter marked with a square die on the reverse of a coin-type published by Shastri described and illustrated above. The counter striking shows the representation of a river with fish at the top and the legend *Mahasmatī* below. The rest of the symbols are to be viewed by holding the coin upside down. The top line shows three symbols in a row – three arched hill, *Indradhvaja* and a *nandipada* from right to left, 'the second line has three formalized drawings of a standing lady, a crouching tiger and a large lotus with two deities seated on a pedestal'.

Rev. Traces of the above-mentioned variety of the Māhishmatī coin published by Shastri.

VARIETY 2

Bell metal, 6.72 g, 19 mm.

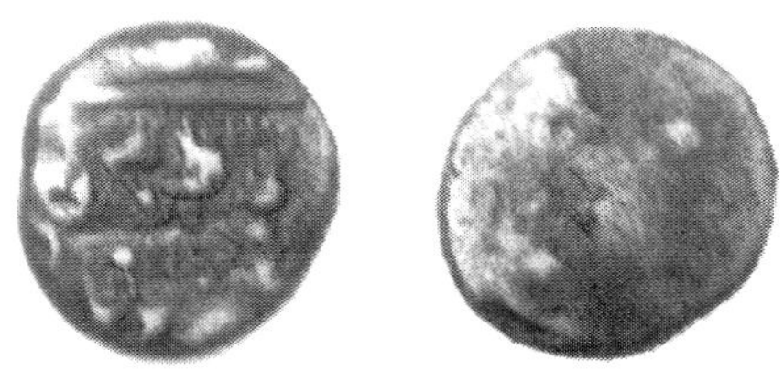

Obv. Counter mark of square punch of the preceding coin on the obverse symbols as on Shastri's coin making it highly obliterated and jumbled.

Rev. Blank.

It may be pointed out that the square punch on these coins resembles the device of Wakankar's coin no. II as illustrated above. In his list of symbols, Wakankar drew the second letter of the legend almost similar to what has been regarded by Kulkarni as *da* to give the reading *Madasmatī* 𑀫𑀤𑀲𑁆𑀫𑀢𑀻. It seems that because of the constricted space the left hand stroke of the following conjunct *sma* has joined the base end of the letter *hi* to give it the appearance of *da*. The limitation of available space may have been the reason for turning the axis of the letter *ha* which inspite of its natural lateral position has been placed sideways. The letter *ha* looking like *da* may be seen on some Western Kshatrapa coins also.

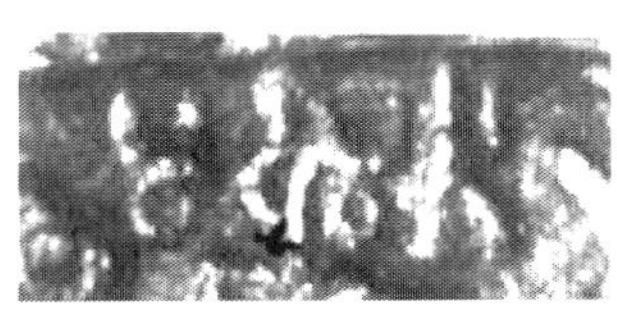

It certainly is not *da* but *hi* as found on other coins of Māhishmatī. Kulkarni himself has read a similar letter as *ha* on the third coin of Hathodaka illustrated by him.[54] The reading *Madasmatī* is fallacious and unwarranted and to connect it with Māndhātā because of the existence of *ma*, *da* and *ta* as believed by Kulkarni[55] and transgresses all rules of linguistics. Madasmatī does not figure as the name of a city anywhere in literature or epigraphs and none of the alleged Madasmatī coins have been found from Māndhātā. There is no evidence that the city-states embarked on the policy of expansion and conquered each other.

Published here are some more coins of the city from the collection of Major Dr. M.K. Gupta which conform to not only the above-mentioned varieties but also reveal new ones.

Variety 3

Alloy of copper (bronze?), circular (broken), 2.3 cm, 3.1 g, Fig. 43.2.

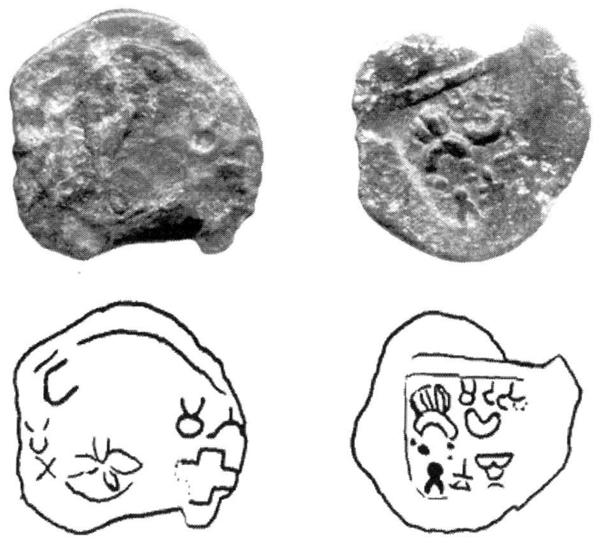

Obv. Badly obliterated original obverse of which the bold letters of the legend *M(ā)[hi]smat(ī)*, *nandipada* standard on left, (a round flower with petals? in place of the arched hill with crescent symbol) and a hollow cross on right may still be made out.

Rev. In an incused portion a very bold inverted taurine with trifurcated roundel and having equally bold dots at the ends of the leg strokes (giving the impression even of a human figure), the so-called lion or tiger symbol resembling a crescent in the centre with Brāhmī legend *Mahis(matī)* above. On turning the coin upside down, may be seen perhaps the usual three symbols of which the arched hill is only faintly visible but *Indradhvaja* and taurine are fairly clear.

Curved line running along the margin as seen from about X-III and again under the petals of a flower at about VII o'clock position indicates that it perhaps ran all along the border enclosing the obverse legend and devices. It is much different from the line interpreted as the river line seen on other coins of Māhishmatī and is thus a new feature. So is the existence of the four petals of a flower at the place of horizontally laid three arched hill with crescent as usually seen on other coins. A flower with similar petals or even only four petals may be seen counter struck on coins attributed to Ravibhūti (Revabhūti) of Daśārṇa (eastern Malwa region watered by Narmadā and its tributaries) by Alka Tiwari[56] who also refers to numerous other similarly counter struck coins of this king in the collection of her father (Prof. K.B. Tiwari). The coin under discussion also bears marks of counter striking. The coins of the city-states are generally recognized by scholars to be the earliest inscribed coins.[57] Ravibhūti seems to have counter struck this coin like others referred to above by Alka Tiwari resulting in the occurrence of the flower mark (or four petals of the flower) on the originally existing horizontally laid three arched hill with crescent.

Variety 4

Bronze?, circular, 2.1 cm, 6.4 g, Fig. 43.3.

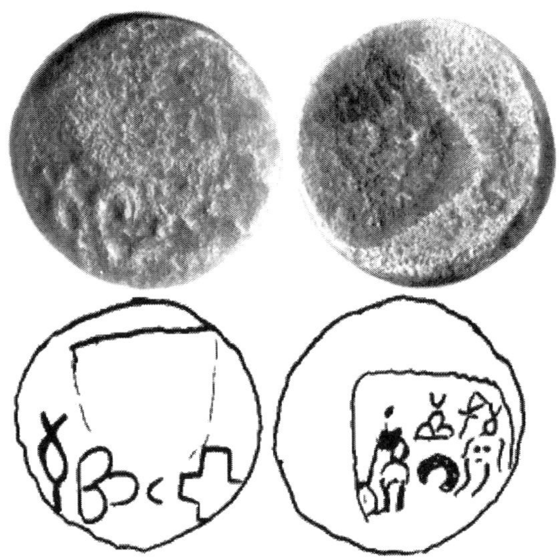

Obv. Badly obliterated but part of the *nandipada* standard, horizontally laid arched hill and hollow cross are visible. The incuse struck forcibly on the reverse is also looking out vaguely and has obliterated the legend above.

Rev. Square incuse with perhaps a female figure on left holding some round object in her hanging (*pralamba*) right hand and left akimbo (*kaṭihasta*), inverted curved symbol (so-called lion of Wakankar and tiger of Kulkarni) in the centre and perhaps another human figure on right with traces of a three arched hill with crescent, *Indradhvaja* and perhaps taurine in a row on the top.

VARIETY 5

Bronze?, circular, 2.2 cm, 9.8 g, Fig. 43.4.

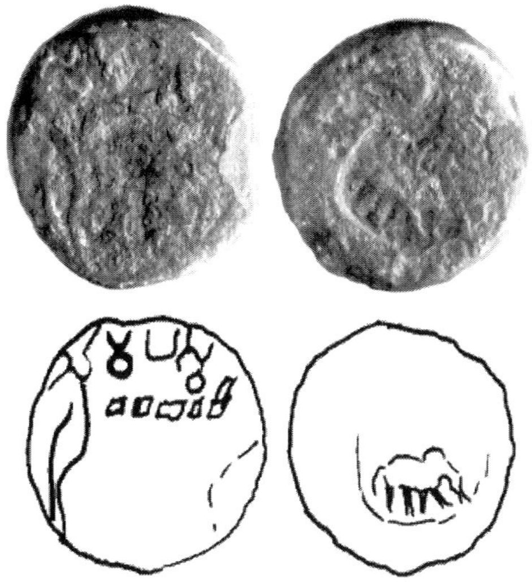

Obv. Traces of *nandidhvaja* and another standing curved line on left, Brāhmī legend *Ma*[his*mati*] above, and traces of other.

Rev. An elephant to right with trunk hanging down in an incuse probably struck on an earlier flan.

VARIETY 6

Bronze?, circular (broken), 2.4 cm, 4.9 g, Fig. 43.5.

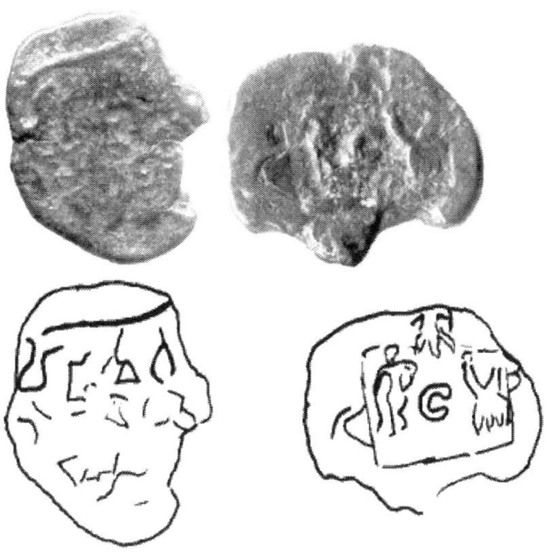

Obv. Jumbled impressions of some symbols and Brāhmī letters of which only a river line and *Maha* can be made out presumably followed by [*smatī*].

Rev. A square or rectangular incuse showing a female figure as on the preceding coin, curved symbol resembling the English letter C in the centre and a bold taurine on the right.

VARIETY 7

Bronze?, circular (broken), 1.9 cm, 4.0 g, Fig. 43.6.

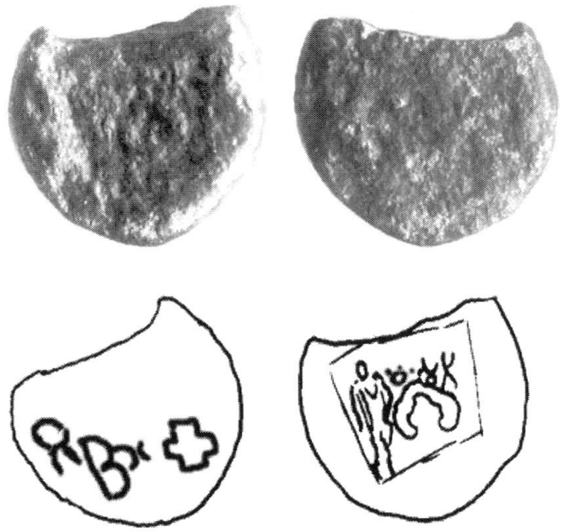

Obv. Faint traces of an inverted *nandipada* (or perhaps *nandipada* standard), horizontally laid three arched hill with crescent and hollow cross.

Rev. In a square incuse a female standing on left, curved symbol in the centre, the symbol on right completely worn out, above the central curved symbol Brāhmī legend *Ma*[*his*]*mat*[*ī*].

VARIETY 8

Bronze?, 1.8 cm, 5.5 g, Fig. 43.7.

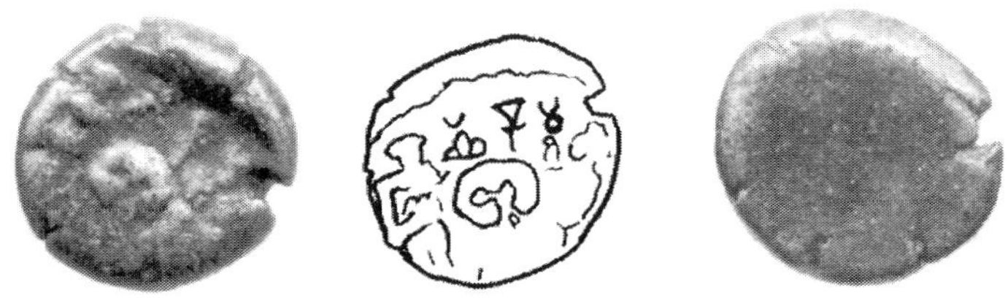

Obv. Female figure slightly turned to her left with left hand raised and right akimbo, curved object in the centre, three arched hill with crescent, *Indradhvaja* and taurine above.

Rev. Obliterated.

VARIETY 9

Much better preserved than all the above-mentioned coins, however, has been acquired recently by Advocate Shailesh Jain (Fig. 44.1) which is an addition to the known repertoire of Māhishmatī specie. It has been struck on an earlier coin as indicated by the existence of very bold and prominent lines of the now unrecognizable devices. The die-impression of Mahishamati coin too has come out clearly showing the enface standing female figure with splayed feet holding some object (flower?) in the raised right hand and also perhaps in her akimbo left hand. Placenta-like object with three arched hill above may be seen on her left with the legend below (to be read by inverting the coin) and partially visible crescent on mountain (?) along the right edge at 3-4 o'clock position. The reverse carries traces of multiple *svastikas*.

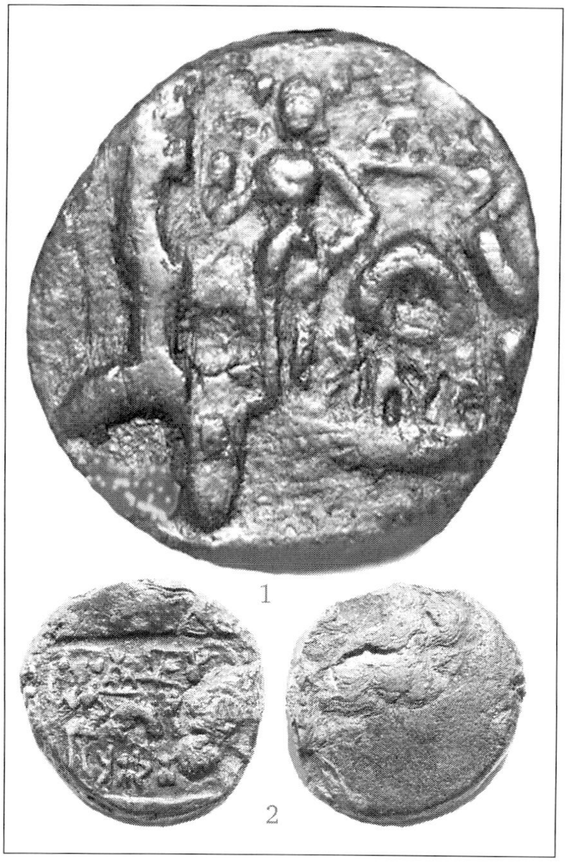

Fig. 44. Māhishmatī coins of Advocate Shailesh Jain (1) and Karan Singh (2).

Variety 10

Karan Singh's coin (Fig. 44.2) shows similar die-impression in a rectangular incuse with arched hill, *Indradhvaja* and taurine symbols in the top line. The symbol/motif on the right has been concealed by a thick metal appendage but the bold track line below is present. The reverse seems to have carried the figure of a horse to right.

We thus see that the coins of Māhishmatī show four different classes and twenty-five varieties as under –

Class I: Square or rectangular coins of eight different varieties.
Class II: Re-struck or counter struck square and rectangular coins of two varieties.
Class III: Circular coins of five varieties.
Class IV: Circular re-struck or counter struck coins of ten different varieties.

Many of these varieties are brought to light for the first time here. The paleographic variations indicate long use of these coins which is corroborated by their re-striking and numerous varieties also. Kulkarni has observed that "The fact that the coins of Māhiṣmatī are counter struck with those of Madasmatī itself shows that they may not be very far off each other. There might have been frequent battles between such city-states resulting into the privilege of countermarking coins of the defeated city by the victor". We have stated above that the reading Madasmatī is based on false decipherment and there is no evidence that it was the name of Oṃkāreśvara Māndhātā located about 50 km east of Maheshwar. Māhishmatī coins were re-struck by Māhishmatī after a time gap on the blank reverse or on the obverse because of the wearing out of the die impressions or may be because of certain other unknown reason. Re-striking on the blank reverse in most of the cases seems to have affected the obverse designs obliterating them wholly or partially. Later they seem to have been counter struck by king Ravibhūti who probably held sway over the area of the circulation of Māhishmatī coins.

Though probable, it is difficult to determine in the present state of our knowledge whether square or rectangular currency preceded the circular one. The bifacial coins

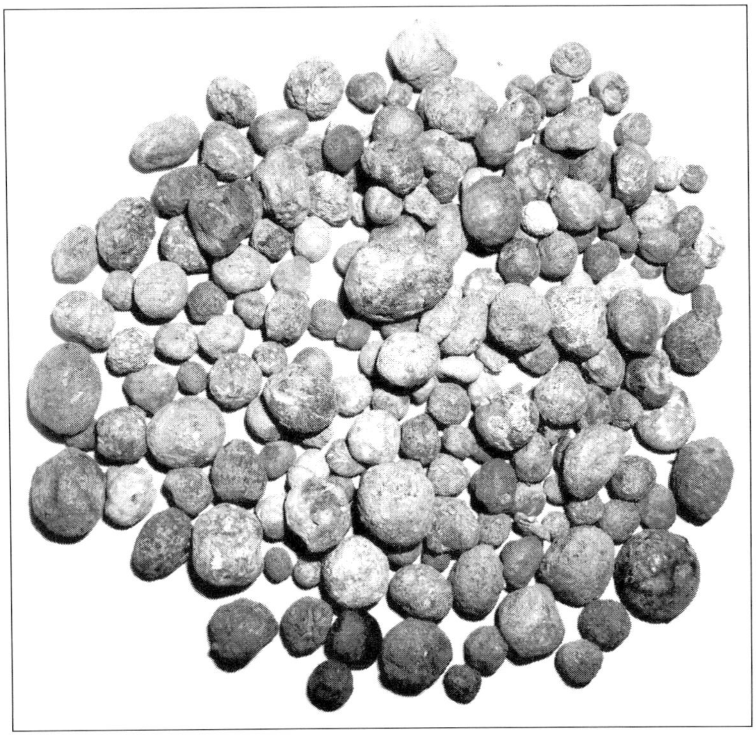

Fig. 45. Metal globules and bits from Maheshwar.

with Ujjain symbol on the reverse hint at the connection of Māhishmatī with Avanti and Ujjayinī, but such coins are rare. The weight of Māhishmatī coins ranges between 1.04 and 9.8 g and though no definite conclusion can be drawn on the meager data available, it seems that four different denominations were struck in the range of 1.25, 5.0, 7.5 and 10.0 g, i.e., 1, 4, 5 and 8 units. The use of bell metal, like the currency of most other city states of the Narmadā valley, is another characteristic of these coins though some coins show the use of bronze or some alloy of copper the exact nature of which can only be determined by their scientific assaying. The known provenance is only Maheshwar-Navdatoli and no coin is known to have come from Māndhātā. So Māhishmatī has to be identified with Maheshwar and no other place. Systematic survey and excavation of the different city states of the Narmadā valley, however, is a great desideratum and the State Department of Archaeology and Museums and/or the Archaeological Survey of India should accomplish this urgently needed task.

These coins attest to the existence of a mint at Maheshwar. A large number of copper globules and bits have been collected by Prof. Neema from the site which too may have been used to prepare planchets for striking coins (Fig. 45).[58]

Bhatt has probably rightly observed about the operation of a silver mint here that "there is no direct evidence forthcoming in this direction, yet keeping in view of its significant position at Dakshiṇāpatha and a very old sea trade traditions (sic.), internal as well as external, also keeping in view of variety of silver punch mark coin hoard from Pati, not far off from Maheshwar, the possibility of a silver mint at Maheshwar cannot be ruled out".[59] The ancient trade route which connected Mathura with Paithan and other places in the south passed through Ujjain, Maheshwar, Burhanpur, etc. Maheshwar being located on the northern bank of the Narmadā was connected with Bhṛigukachchha (Barygaza) which was an important port in ancient times. Most of India's trade with the western world was carried out through this port and it is well known that supremacy over this port was a bone of contention between Nahapāṇa and the Sātavāhanas in the early historic period.

The discovery of coins bearing the name of Māhishmatī (Mahismati) from Maheshwar clearly indicates that it was this place which in ancient times was known as Māhishmatī and not Māndhātā (Oṃkāreśvara), an island in the Narmadā situated about 50 km northwest of Khandwa where is located the temple of Oṃkāranātha, one of the famous Jyotirliṅgas of Śiva, which has not yielded even a single coin bearing the name of Māhishmatī.

The deity depicted on Māhishmatī coin in the British Museum and the one found from Jaleshwar Bedi mound at Maheshwar was referred to as male by Allan[60] and Wakankar[61] and some other scholars continue to do so. [62] Some coins illustrated above, however, clearly show the deity to be a female. No scholar has tried to identify the deity. I feel inclined to identify her as Māheśvarī (Durgā) who may have been regarded as the city-goddess by the people.

UN-INSCRIBED DIE-STRUCK COPPER COINS

There is ample evidence now to aver that the age-old techniques of punching and casting continued in the Malwa region even after the introduction of die-striking technique. Sankalia *et al.* discovered quite a good number of un-inscribed die-struck coins during excavations and surface explorations at Mahshwar-Navdatoli, generally with Ujjain symbol and sometimes also with tree in railing, *svastika*, bull, eight-armed symbol, etc. which are usually ascribed to Ujjain.[63] Narendra Kothari[64] and Wilfried Pieper[65] have listed numerous types of die-struck coins which they ascribe to Ujjain and central India. Amongst Sankalia's coins obtained from surface exploration at Maheshwar is a typical rectangular piece (19-20 x 17-20 mm, 8.235 g) showing on the obverse tree in railing to left, elephant walking to right with a human figure (deity) holding staff in his left hand as if standing on the back of the elephant, Ujjain symbol on the right top corner and hand symbol in a square frame on top left corner. Another symbol in front of the elephant is truncated. The reverse shows a

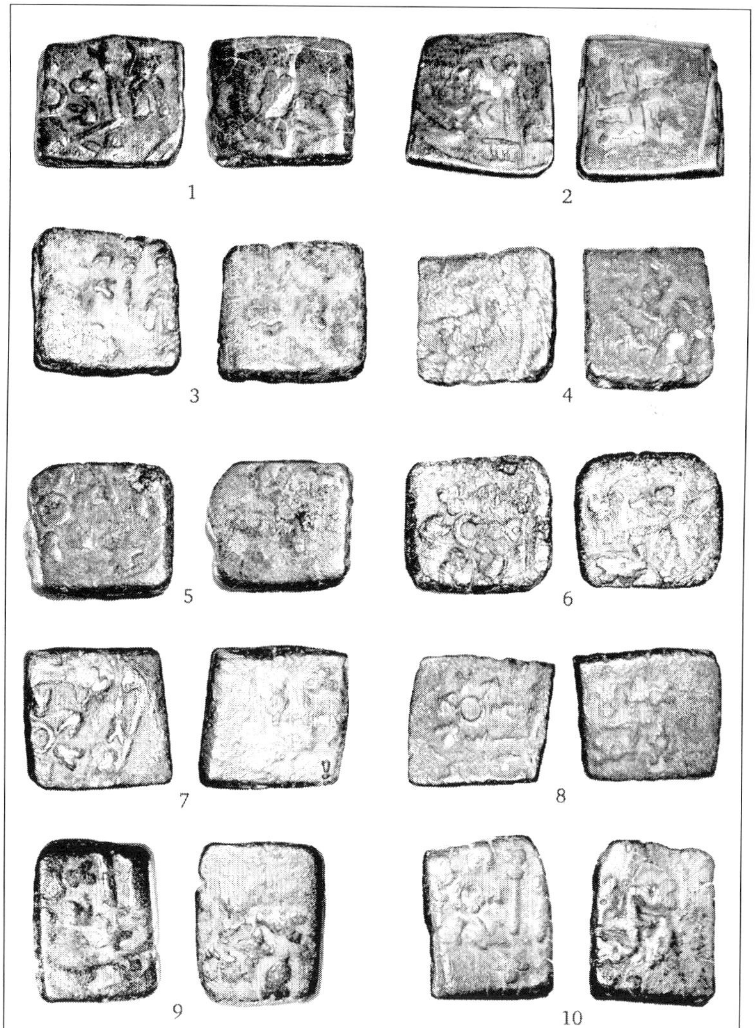

Fig. 46. Coins with crude human figure.

double-orbed Ujjain symbol. A round copper coin showing similar devices exists in Girish Sharma's collection (Fig. 39.12) which may have the same provenance.

Allan had ascribed coins showing a crude human figure with a standard with taurine above, triangle-headed standard, six-armed or tree symbol with river having fishes below on the obverse with a *svastika* or a double *svastika* having taurine ends or a frog or a peculiar symbol on the reverse to Ujjayinī.[66] Kothari followed him to regard such coins as belonging to Ujjain[67] but Pieper mentions Gujarat as the provenance of these coins.[68] Numerous coins carrying the crudely depicted human figure with a staff surmounted by a taurines, *Shaḍara-chakra* (six-armed symbol), *Jayadhvaja* or *Indradhvaja* (triangle-headed standard) and river with fishes on the obverse and *svastika* with taurines at the ends on the reverse found from Maheshwar are preserved in the Neema collection (Fig. 46) furnishing evidence of Maheshwar as the source of such coins. Since trade of the Malwa region with the west was conducted through the sea-port of Barygaza (Bhṛigukachchha) in Gujarat it is not surprising if they are also found from Gujarat.

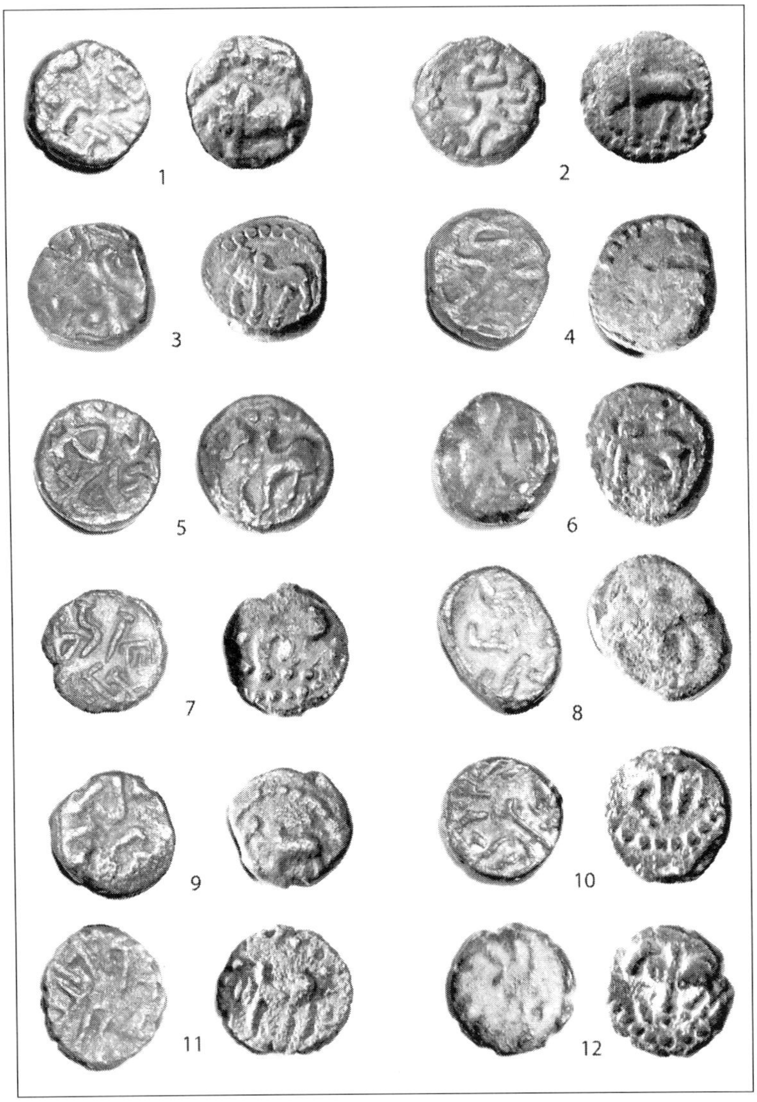

Fig. 47. Nāga coins.

NĀGA COINS

The political hegemony of Gaṇapati-nāga of Padmāvatī extended to Dhāra in the south-southwest and he is called *Dhārādhīśa* 'Lord of Dhārā' in the *Bhāva Śataka*. A number of Nāga coins, those of Gaṇapati Nāga in overwhelming number amongst them, are said to have been collected from the bed of the Śiprā at Ujjain by V.S. Wakankar but unfortunately never published.[69] Kothari also refers to several coins of Nāga rulers, especially of Gaṇapati-nāga, in quite a good number collected from Ujjain.[70] A large number of diminutive Nāga copper coins have been collected by Dr. Neema from Maheshwar (Fig. 47). The exclusiveness and predominance of the coins of Gaṇapati indicate clearly that it was he who extended his sway up to Ujjain and Maheshwar.

COINS OF JISHṆU

Diminutive copper coins of Jishṇu (Fig. 48) resembling light-weight specie of the Nāga kings of Padmāvatī[71] are well known to the numismatists now. They were first brought to light by S.C. Upadhyaya[72] and H.V. Trivedi[73] in 1951. The former published legible five of the twelve coins purchased from a dealer and said to have been obtained from the river-panners of Śiprā at Ujjain. He pointed out that the coins of Jishṇu obtained from Malwa cannot be assigned to any Nāga ruler. Trivedi selected five of the thirty pieces from the collection of N.R. Advani made largely from Ujjain-Bhilsa region and observed that the issuer of these coins was obviously a devotee of Vishṇu like most Gupta monarchs. P.L. Gupta[74] also published some coins of Jishṇu having conch on the reverse reportedly obtained from Bhilsa and referred to having seen similar coins in the collection of V.S. Wakankar. Gupta published some coins bearing the name of Jishṇu found from Punjab also and suggested that all these coins were issued by a king who flourished after Yaśodharman and ruled over extensive kingdom from Punjab to Malwa. But the coins of Jishṇu from Punjab differ in fabric, metrology, typology and palaeography and have rightly been pointed out to be different from the coins of Jishṇu of Malwa.[75] Jai Prakash Singh has rightly observed that "the coins from the Punjab seem to be of a much later date than the coins concerned from Malwa. Hence it appears more likely that the two Jishṇu's (sic.) were in all probability local rulers of Malwa and the Punjab and issued their coins in conformity with the local numismatic traditions of the period and the areas of their rule."[76]

Trivedi later published three of Wakankar's coins and two from the collection of S.L. Pardeshi.[77] All the coins mentioned above depicted either a conch or a wheel within a dotted border on the reverse but one coin published by Trivedi showed on the reverse a vase 'with foliage as found on the coins of Gupta monarchs' and some others having a *nandipada* above with its top bifurcated.[78] Amongst the light weight small coins recovered from Maheshwar by Prof. Dau Lal Neema of Indore are five coins of Jishṇu (Fig. 39.5-9) as well as a piece which also shows a vase with foliage on one side and theri-anthropomorphic Garuḍa in a flying posture on the other (Fig. 39.10). It is a unique un-inscribed coin and its ascription is only tentative. It may be noted that Garuḍa-type coins weighing 0.8, 0.5, 0.4 and 0.2 g issued by Jishṇu have been published by Kothari amongst the coins of Ujjain.[79]

P.K. Jayaswal placed Jishṇu of Malwa soon after Samudragupta and stated that "Jishṇu was probably a kinsman of Rāmagupta – also a local king of Malwa who had accepted the suzerainty of the Guptas, and probably with the help of the Śakas defeated and killed him. Consequently, Chandragupta II, who was on the throne of Magadha, by now, hastened to control the situation and was probably successful in defeating Jishṇu and his allies soon".[80] This hypothesis, however, goes against the tradition and generally held view that Rāmagupta was killed by his own brother Chandragupta II. Trivedi, who had pointed out the similarity of Jishṇu's coins with those of the Nāgas earlier[81] suggested that "the size, shape and the fabric of the present coins, and those of published earlier, connect them with Mālava coins, and here we have also to take into account the symbol of vase, appearing on one of them".[82]

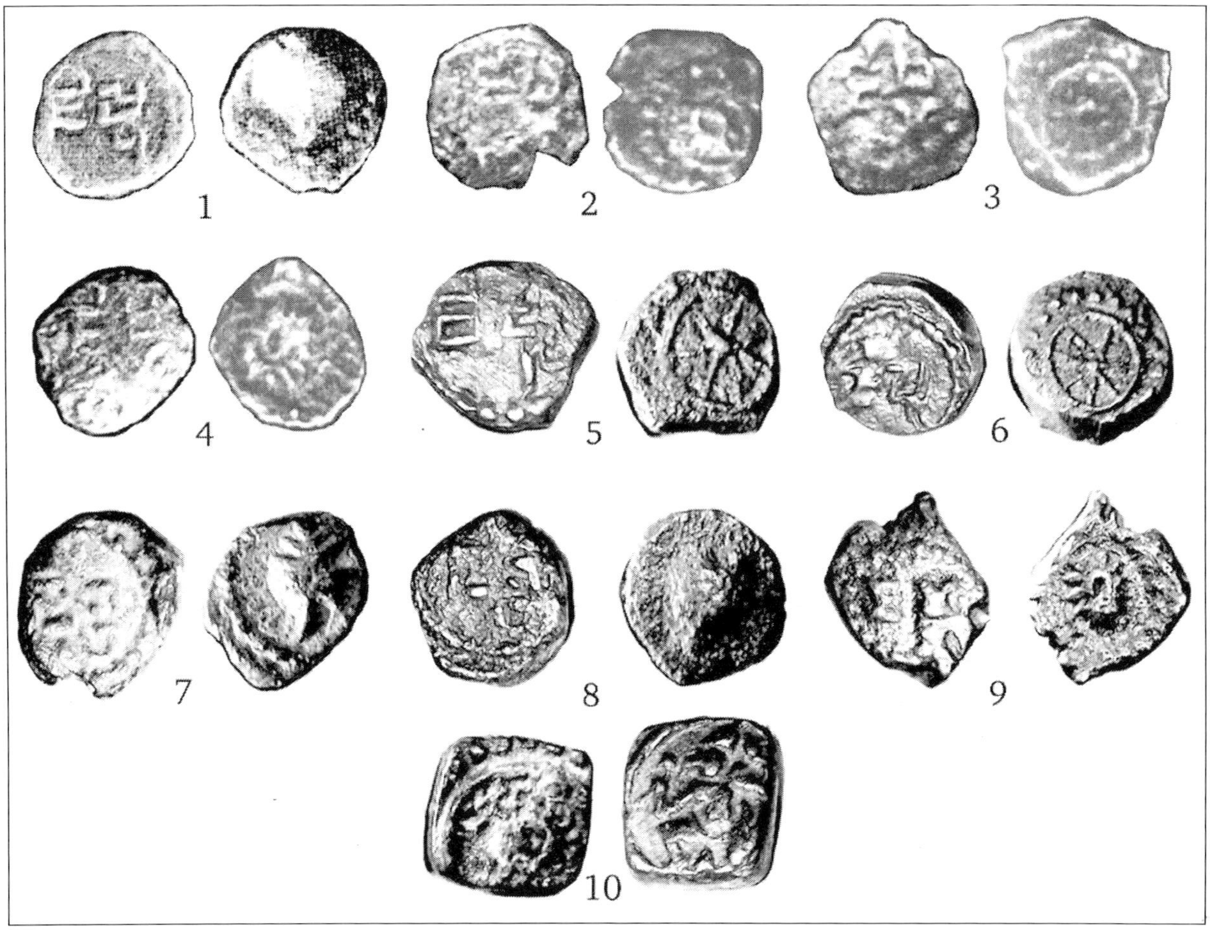

Fig. 48. Coins of Jishṇu.

The diminutive size, light weight, shapes, fabric, etc. of Jishṇu's coins show similarities with the coins of the Nāgas, Mālavas and Rāmagupta. These characteristics are shared even by some Ujjain coins.[83] Since most of these coins belong to southern Rajasthan and parts of central India continuing from early centuries to about the Gupta period, these characteristics may be said to have resulted from spatial-temporal numismatic tradition. Kothari has published eight different reverse types of Jishṇu's coins[84] reading wrongly Jishaṇa, Jija, Jishṇaja or Jiṇshja, Jimaṇa and Jima on Types 90 – 94. *Ja* has been engraved in a number of ways with some differences in their forms (Pl. XLVII.1 & 5), (Pl. XLVII.4), (Pl. XLVII.7), (Pl. XLVII.2), (Pl. XLVII.6) and (Pl. XLVII.9); *sha* as (Pl. XLVII.4), (Pl. XLVII.1), (Pl. XLVII.7), (Pl. XLVII.2) and (Pl. XLVII.6). *Ṇa* is engraved as (Pl. XLVII.7), (Pl. XLVII.5), (Pl. XLVII.2-4) and as *na* (Pl. XLVII.1). Kothari seems to have misread *sha* on some coins as *ma*. The difference has resulted because of die-engravers' hand, faulty striking and wear and tear because of which the legend is not visible completely on some specimens. The three letters *ja*, *sha* and *ṇa* forming part of the name of the issuer show palaeographic differences no doubt but the name can be read on the coins without much difficulty and the cumulative evidence leaves little doubt to the legend having been engraved as Jishnu and Jishṇu indicating that *na* and *ṇa* were confused because of slight difference in pronunciation. It is interesting to note that Mālava coins show the use of lingual instead of the dental nasal[85] and the lingual nasal has been replaced by its dental form on the coins of Gaṇapati-nāga.[86] Jishṇu's coins share this orthographic characteristic with the coins of Gaṇapati to which they seem to have been spatially and temporally related. Gaṇapati-nāga was forcibly uprooted by Samudragupta as we know from the Allahabad Praśasti. His influence extended from Mathura in the north to Ujjain and Maheshwar in the southwest. It seems that Rāmagupta, whether he was a son of Samudragupta or a local ruler[87], got the opportunity to rule over parts of eastern Malwa. His light-weight coins bearing lion and Garuḍa devices recovered from Vidisha-Eran area resembling those of the Mālavas and the Nāgas, palaeographically datable to fourth-fifth century CE[88] indicate that he filled the vacuum created by the defeat of Gaṇapati in eastern Malwa. Rāmagupta was killed by Chandragupta II. Jishṇu's diminutive coins found from Maheshwar, Ujjain, Vidisha and Padmāvatī[89] bearing Vaishṇavite devices of *śaṅkha*, *chakra*, Garuḍa, vase with foliage, etc. in contrast to the generally found Śaivite devices of bull, trident, Śiva-*liṅga*, etc. on Nāga coins and following the tradition of some of Rāmagupta's issues indicate that he may have risen to fill the vacuum in central India after Rāmagupta's assassination. That he was not a Nāga ruler is borne out amply by his coins which show Vaishṇavite devices in contrast to the Śaivite devices of Nāga coins. The clear and straight-lined legend pattern on Jishṇu's coins also differs from the often jumbled and longer legends running along the margins of round coins on the latter. He may have borne allegiance to the Gupta rulers as indicated by the vase and Garuḍa devices which are also noticeable on Gupta copper coins of Chandragupta II.[90] Numerous diminutive copper coins with these devices belonging to Chandragupta II (and probably of Kumāragupta I also) found from excavations at Ahichhatra bearing these devices are now preserved in the Central Antiquities Section of the Archaeological Survey of India in the Purana Qila in Delhi. I have seen such small coins in a private collection also.

All the coins illustrated here seem to have been struck from different dies. The differences in engraving the same letters as noted above indicate that Jishṇu's rule was not a short-lived one. This could happen in a peaceful time after the dislocation of Gaṇapatināga. The reverse devices of conch, wheel, sun and Garuḍa certainly suggest Vaishṇavite affiliation and palaeography indicates a fourth-fifth century date. In all likelihood, Jishṇu may have ruled in parts of Malwa and central India as a feudatory of the Guptas.[91]

COINS OF ARAB GOVERNORS

Like many other collectors, Prof. Neema has made a rich collection of coins from the region. His collection from Maheshwar includes diminutive silver pieces of the Arab governors of Sindh which generally carry the partially accommodated Kufic legend *La ilah il Lillah wahdat la sharik Allah Muhammad Rasul Allah al Amir* (with the name of the Amir hardly legible).

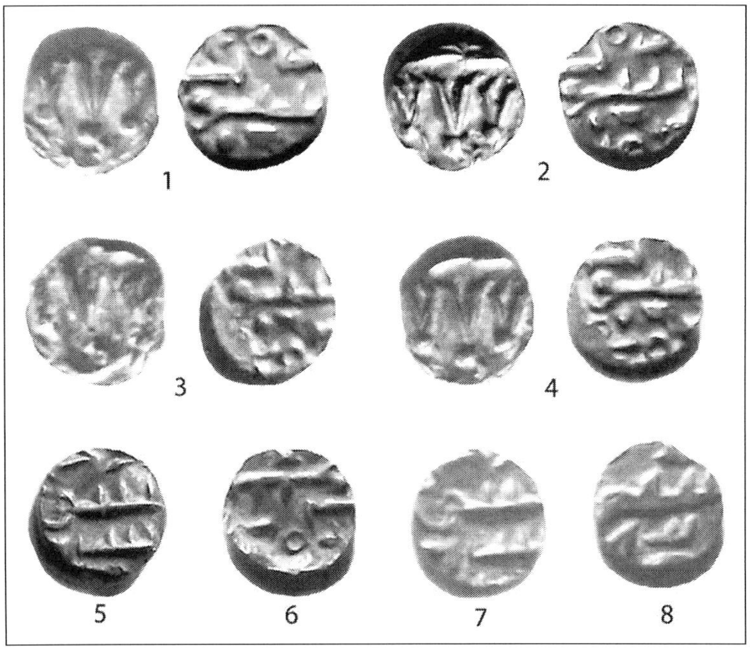

Fig. 49. Diminutive silver coins of Arab Governors.

In the early eighth century the Arabs, under the leadership of Junaid, the governor of Sindh, and his lieutenants, had led raids into the interior of India after conquering Sindh and Multan, and spreading fanwise, they overran Marwar, Malwa and Baroach.[92] A big hoard of 3.260 kg silver coins belonging to Arab governors and issuers of Indo-Sassanian (Gadhaiya) types was discovered at Thane in Maharashtra in 1972-73.[93] Large hoards of 6585 diminutive silver pieces of the Arab governors found from Mandor and Chohtan near Jodhpur were published long back by Reu.[94] 135 such pieces found from near a temple of Bhopal Sagar road (Udaipur)[95] and 368 from elsewhere in Rajasthan were published by R.C. Agrawala.[96] A big hoard was unearthed at Osian of which 373 pieces are preserved in the Jain Temple Trust, Osian.[97] Stray finds have been made from Bagor, Degana, Pallu and elsewhere in Rajasthan.[98] Thin and tiny, Reu found his coins measuring around a centimeter in size and weighing from 7 to 9 grains. Coins from Osian measure from 7.5 mm to 1.0 cm and weigh from 393 to 523 mg. Eight good specimens from the collection of Dr. Neema (Fig. 49.1-8) are around 7 mm in size and have an average weight of 320 mg. These coins belong to eighth through tenth century and their discovery in large hoards from Marwar, Mewar, Malwa, Gujarat and Maharashtra indicates not only their temporal sway but also commercial relationships between these areas during the time of their use. It is for this reason that the discovery of these diminutive coins from Maheshwar is so important. More so as they bear evidence to the continued existence and occupation of Maheshwar during the early medieval period during which trade continued with the Arab world through the Tapti and Baroach and also probably land routes.

During 10th-11th centuries the region was under the Paramāras of Malwa as indicated by monumental remains, but after the decline of Paramāra power it passed into the hands of the Yādavas of Devagiri. Long back a hoard of 800 Padmaṭaṅkas from Maheshwar was reported by the local jewelers during floods.[99]

We thus see that Maheshwar has yielded very significant evidence bearing on the history and culture of not only the city but also of the Malwa region. It was the capital of the Haihayas and served as an important mint of Anūpadeśa. It was through this city that most of the trade was carried out with the western world via the port-town of Bhṛigukachchha (modern Baroach) in ancient times and continued even during the early medieval period. Lead coins found from Maheshwar indicate that it was one of the earliest places to make use of this base metal for coins. The identification of ancient Māhishmatī has been a vexed question but the coins bearing the Brāhmī legend *Mahismati* found in good numbers from this site furnish evidence of the identity of Maheshwar with Māhishmatī. This metropolis has yielded the earliest numismatic evidence of the portrayal and deification of Rāma. The numismatic material obtained from the site helps us in fixing the provenance of some coin types with certainty. It is for the first time that diminutive copper coins of Nāga king Gaṇapati and those of Jishṇu have been brought to light from this site along with the minuscule silver coins of the Arab governors. A careful study of the collections of various collectors of the region may bring to light many more important facts and is a great desideratum.

NOTES AND REFERENCES

1. Raychaudhuri, Hemchandra (1953), *Political History of Ancient India*, 6th edition, Calcutta, pp. 95-96 and 144-46. See also *Skanda Purāṇa*, Avanti-khaṇḍa, chapter 40; *Brahma Purāṇa*, chapter 43; *Anargharāghava*, Act VII.109; Davids, Rhys, *Buddhist India*, p. 28; De (1971), p. 13; etc. It is notable that Cunningham had identified the *Mo-hi-shi-fu-lo-pu-lo* or Maheśvarapura of the Chinese pilgrim Xuan Zian with Maheshwar (*CAGI*, pp. 411-12).
2. *Mahābhāshya* on Pāṇini III.1, 26. See also Rapson, E.J. (Ed) (1922), *Cambridge History of India*, Vol. I, (reprint, Delhi, 1968), pp. 516-17; Sircar, D.C. (1971), *Studies in the Geography of Ancient and Medieval India*, 2nd ed., Delhi, p. 106; Lahiri, Bela (1976), "India's Earliest Inscribed Coins: the City Issues", *JNSI*, XXXVIII (II), p. 49.
3. *Dīgha Nikāya*, XIX, 36.
4. Bühler, G. (1894), 'Votive Inscritions from the Sanchi Stupas', *Epigraphia Indica*, Vol. II, p. 109; 'Further Inscriptions from Sanchi', *ibid.*, pp. 389-90.
5. *Śiva Purāṇa*, Dharma-saṃhitā, chapter 56; *Harivaṃśa*, chapters 5, 33, 112 and 114. R.G. Bhandarkar placed the Mahishaka country on the Narmadā with Māhishmatī as its capital [Utgikar, N.B. (Ed.) (1929), *Collected Works of Sir R.G. Bhandarkar*, III, Poona: BORI, pp. 13-14.]
6. *Mahābhārata*, Vana Parva, ch. 114; *Skanda Purāṇa*, Nāgara-khaṇḍa, ch. 66.
7. 'Pūrv-āpar-Ākar-Āvanti' are mentioned in the Junagarh inscription of Rudradāman I [Sircar, D.C. (1965), *Select Inscriptions*, Vol. I, p. 172, line 11.] for the eastern and western division of Malwa. Ākara occurs in Varāhamihira's *Bṛihatsaṃhitā* (XIV.12) also and Kern, H. (1895), *Bṛihatsaṃhitā of Varāhamihira with Utpala Bhaṭṭa's commentary*, Benares, p. 235 suggested its identification with modern Khandesh.
8. *Liṅga*, Pūrvārdha, 71-72; *Matsya*, 186-87; *Padma*, Svarga-khaṇḍa, 14-15; *Śiva*, Rudra-saṃhitā, I.7-10; *Skanda*, Revā-khaṇḍa, 26-28; etc.
9. *Nāmnā Maheśvara-sthānaṃ trishu lokeshu viśrutam/ Tasmin sthāne Mahādevaḥ chintayana Traipure vadham//.*
10. Sankalia, H.D., B. Subbarao and S.B. Deo (1958), *The Excavations at Maheshwar and Navdatoli*, Poona-Baroda; Sharma, Y.D. (1961), "Protohistoric Remains" and "Remains of early historical cities" in *Archaeological Remains Monuments and Museums*, Part I, New Delhi, pp. 20-22 and 72-73 respectively.
11. Sankalia *et al.* (1958), pp. 68-79; Ahmad, N. (1968), "On the Local Coins of Maheshwar and Navdatoli Excavations", in Narain, A.K., J.P. Singh and Nisar Ahmad (Eds.), *Seminar Papers*

on the Local Coins of Northern India c. 300 B.C. to 300 A.D., Varanasi, pp. 89-93. See also Sharma, R.K. (2011), *Coinage of Central India With Special Reference to Early Coins from the Narbada Valley*, New Delhi, pp. 9, 14, 19, 38, 45-47, 62-63, 80-82, 98-100, etc.: *JNSI*, XV, pp. 197-201; XVI, pp. 36-39; XVII, pp. 42-44 and 94-96.

12. Altekar, A.S. and D.B. Diskalkar (1946), "Kasarawad Hoard of Ujjain Coins", *JNSI* (VIII), pp. 99-106.
13. Corresponding to Allan's Class 6, Group III coins. See *BMCAI* for details and illustrations.
14. Sankalia *et al.* (1958), pp. 66-70, Pl. XII. See also Sharma (2011), pp. 46-47.
15. Sankalia, *et al.* (1958), p. 70.
16. Ahmad, Nisar (1966), "The Bearing of the Archaeological Evidence from Maheshwar on the Chronology of Punch-Marked Coins", in *Seminar Papers on the Chronology of the Punch-Marked Coins* edited by Narain, A.K. Varanasi, pp. 48-50.
17. Coins illustrated with this article are not to scale.
18. Pieper, Wilfried (2013), *Ancient Indian Coins Revisited*, Lancaster-London, pp. 182-84, nos. 221-26.
19. *JNSI*, XV (1953), pp. 201-202.
20. Mitchiner, Michael (1983), "India: Minute Silver Coins of the Early Mauryan Empire", *East and West*, New Series, Vol. 33, Nos. 1 4, pp. 113-23 and (July 1994), "Mauryan-Sunga Punch-marked One Ratti Coinage: 128 Silver-Plated Copper Specimens", *ICSNL*, No. 27, pp. 1-4. See also Hardaker, T.R. (1999), *The Mashaka Fractional Coinage of Ancient India*, Nasik.
21. Ahmad, Nisar (1966), *op. cit.*, pp. 48-50.
22. Rajgor (2001), *op. cit.*, pp. 80-81.
23. Sankalia, *et al.* (1958), p. 70; *JNSI*, XVI (1954), pp. 36-39.
24. Rajgor (2001), p. 77, no. 430.
25. Cf. Kulkarni, Prashant P. (2006) in his foreword (p. 7) to Narendra Kothari's *Ujjayini Coins* (edited by Dilip Rajgor), Mumbai.
26. Rajgor (2001), pp. 75-81.
27. Mitchiner, Michael (1978), *Oriental Coins and Their Values, II: The Ancient and Classical World*, London, pp. 537 ff and (July 1994), pp. 1-4.
28. *Oswal Antiques' Auctions*, Auction No. 1 (11th January 2009, Pune, p. 5, no. 4. Shri Girish Sharma of Indore too possesses similar coins in his collection.
29. Sankalia *et al.* (1958), pp. 70-72; *JNSI*, XVII, pp. 42-44; Sharma (2011), pp. 80-82, Pl. XI.
30. Sharma (2011), pp. 73 ff.
31. Cf. Allan, *BMCAI*, p. 92, no. 65.
32. *JNSI*, VII, p. 43, Pl. II.
33. Handa, Devendra and Major Dr. M.K. Gupta (2012), *Numismatic Gleanings*, Delhi, pp. 51-53, Pl. VI.4.
34. *JNSI*, VII, p. 42, Pl. II.
35. *BMCAI*, pp. lxxvii & 93, Pl. XI.19-21.
36. Wakankar, V.S. (1964-65), "Coins from Ujjain", *The Indian Numismatic Chronicle*, Vol. III, Part II & Vol. IV, Part I, pp. 182-88, Pl. I.
37. Pieper (2013), pp. 192-222.
38. Handa, Devendra (2012-2013), "Portrayal and Deification of Hanumān and Rāma – Fresh Evidence", *Jñāna-Pravāha Resarch Journal*, No. XVI, pp. 1-16; (2013), "Divinities on Ujjain Coins", *ICSNL*, No. 51, pp. 29-30, Pl. X.
39. *BMCAI*, pp. cliv & 279. Allan took these coins as comparable to the inscribed issues of Ujjayinī.

40. Ramachandran, T.N. (1951), 'A Recent Find of Coins from Ujjayini', *JNSI*, XIII, p. 74, no. 1, Pl. V.6.
41. Gupta, P.L. (1953), 'Coins of the City of Mahiṣmatī', *JNSI*, XV, pp. 70-73, Pl. I.17 (enlarged version of Ramchandran's coin). Gupta, however, suggested (p. 72) that the complete legend may have been *Mahisatisa*.
42. Wakankar, V.S. (1971), "Coins Bearing Māhishamatī Legend", *INC*, Vol. IX, pp. 85-89.
43. Sankalia *et al.* (1958), p. 78, no. 49.
44. Trivedi, H.V. (1955), "Coins of the City of Māhishmatī", *JNSI*, XVII, pp. 94-95, Pl. VIII.5.
45. Wakankar (1971), *loc. cit.*
46. *Ibid.* The possibility of there being the legend Mahismati on one or more specimens of Wakankar cannot be ruled out altogether.
47. Handa, Devendra (2009), "Coins of the City-State of Māhiṣmatī", *Prajñādhara: Essays on Asian Art History Epigraphy and Culture in Honour of Gouriswar Bhattacharya* (edited by Gerd J.R. Mevissen and Arundhati Banerji), Vol. I, New Delhi, pp. 149-57, Pl. 15.
48. Handa, Devendra (2011), 'A Rare Coin of the City State of Mahishmati', *JNSI*, LXXIII, PP. 41-42.
49. Shastri, Ajay Mitra (1978-79), 'A New Variety of Mahishmati Coins', *JAINS*, II, pp. 1-5, Pl. IV (last coin at the bottom).
50. *Ibid.* The vowel marks with *'ma'* and *'ta'* are fairly clear and the legend should be deciphered as *Māhismatī*. Prashant P. Kulkarni (2005, 'New Discoveries in Coins from Narmda Valley: Geographical and Historical Implications', *ICSNL*, No. 17, pp. 1-2) has rightly deciphered the legend as *Māhismatī*.
51. Kulkarni (2005), *op. cit.*, p. 3.
52. Bhatt, S.K. (1988), 'A Unique Coin of Madamae', *JAINS*, VI, pp. xxxvi-xxxviii.
53. Kulkarni (2005), *op. cit.*, pp. 5-6.
54. *Ibid.*, pp. 1 &17.
55. *Ibid.*, pp. 6-8.
56. Tiwari, Alka (1981), 'Daśārṇa Kshetra kī Lipi-yukta Mudrāeṃ', *JNSI*, XLIII, pp. 38-44.
57. *BMCAI*, p. cliv; Lahiri, Bela (1976), 'India's Earliest Inscribed Coins: the City Issues', *JNSI*, XXXVIII/II, pp. 35-54.
58. Alternatively, however, these metal pieces may have been used for throwing in the river as it has been an age old tradition in India.
59. Bhatt, S.K. (2012), "The Ancient Avanti and its Coinage", *JAINS*, Vol. XXV-XXVI, p. 46.
60. *BMCAI*, pp. cliv and 279, Pl. XLV.11.
61. *JNSI*, XVII (1955), p. 94.
62. Sharma (2011), pp. 125 ff.
63. Sankalia *et al.* (1958), pp. 73-77, Pls. XIV-XVI.
64. Kothari, Narendra (2006), *Ujjayini Coins* (edited by Dilip Rajgor), Mumbai.
65. Pieper (2013), pp. 184 ff.
66. *BMCAI*, pp. cxliii-cxliv, 253-56 and plates.
67. Kothari (2006), pp. 114-15.
68. Pieper (2013), pp. 236-39.
69. Trivedi, H.V. (1957), *Catalogue of the Coins of Nāga Kings of Padmāvatī*, Gwalior, p. xxxix.
70. Kothari (2006), 21.
71. Trivedi (1957), *loc. cit.*
72. *JNSI*, XIII (II), pp. 150-51.
73. *Ibid.*, p. 192.
74. *Ibid.*, XV, pp. 89 ff.

75. Altekar's Editorial Note to Gupta's article, *JNSI*, XV (I), pp. 92-93. See also Jayaswal, P.K., *Ibid.*, XVII (I), p. 102.
76. Singh, Jai Prakash (1976), "Coinage of Jishṇu of Malwa", *JNSI*, XXXVIII (I), p. 67.
77. *JNSI*, XVI, pp. 105-06.
78. *Ibid.*, XVI (I), Pl. IV.14-18.
79. Kothari (2006), p. 118, RB# 360.
80. *JNSI*, XXVII (I), p. 102.
81. *Ibid.*, XIII (II), p. 192.
82. *Ibid.*, XVI (I), p. 106.
83. Kothari (2006), pp. 71 ff. Many diminutive Ujjain coins are preserved in the British Museum, London also.
84. *Ibid.*, pp. 118-19, RB# 358-65.
85. *BMCAI*, p. cvi.
86. Trivedi (1957), p. xxii.
87. For a discussion on the problem of Rāmagupta see Agrawal, Ashvini (1989), *Rise and Fall of the Imperial Guptas*, Delhi, pp. 153-60.
88. *JNSI*, XII, pp. 103-06, Pl. IX.1-6; XIII, pp. 128-30, Pl. VIII.1-8; XVII, pp. 108-09, Pl. VIII.1; XXIII, pp. 340 ff, Pl. X.1, 12. See also Sircar, D.C. (1968), *Studies in Indian Coins*, Delhi, pp. 221-29 for a critical appraisal of the attribution of these coins.
89. Trivedi (1957), p. xxxix.
90. Altekar, A.S. (1957), *The Coinage of the Gupta Empire*, Varanasi, pp. 160-64, Pl. XVI.18-21.
91. Jishṇu, literally meaning victorious, is a name of Vishṇu and it is just possible that *Mahārāja* Mātṛivishṇu and his brother Dhanyavishṇu, known from Eran stone pillar inscription (*Corpus Inscriptionum Indicarum*, III, 1989, pp. 339 ff.) were his scions.
92. Sharma, Dasharatha (Gen Ed.) (1966), *Rajasthan Through The Ages*, Vol. I, Bikaner, p. 106.
93. *Indian Archaeology – A Review*, 1972-73, p. 56.
94. Reu, B.N. (1946), *Coins of Marwar*, Jodhpur, p. 4; (1947), "Coins Struck by the early Arab governors of Sind", *JNSI*, IX, pp. 124-27.
95. Agrawala, R.C. (1955), "Some New Finds from Mewar", *JNSI*, XVII, p. 130.
96. Agrawala, R.C. (1959), "A Find of Arab Coins", *Ibid.*, XXI, p. 202.
97. Handa, Devendra (1984), *Osian History Archaeology Art and Architecture*, Delhi, pp. 233-34, Pl. 167.
98. *IAR*, 1970-71, p. 63.
99. *East Nimar Gazetteer*, Bombay, 1908, p. 87.

XII

Coins of the City State of Hathodaka

Though two copper coins from the collection of Major Dr. M.K. Gupta (Fig. 50.1 & 4), one complete and the other broken, showing a tree as the main device encircled by subsidiary marks of which fish to left on the top, *svastika* to the right of the railing, crescent (of the arched hill?) below, some marks resembling Brāhmī letters on the right or left (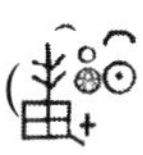 and 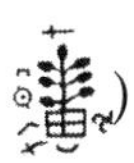) were published earlier[1] yet the credit to bring more coins of this type to light and decipher the legend correctly as Hathodaka and to attribute them to the city-state of this name goes to Prashant P. Kulkarni.[2] He had seen at least twenty coins of this type in the collections of M/s Govind Mangal, Daulal Johri and Pankaj Tandon, mostly made at Indore, showing varieties of style of inscription, of which he has brought to light four better specimens with almost complete legends (Fig. 50).

Svastika to the right and the sword-like or fish symbol[3] above the tree (if the coin is seen with right position of the tree) are, however, very clear on another coin of this type in the collection of Dr. M.K. Gupta (Fig. 50.4). Coins illustrated by Prashant Kulkarni reveal that all specimens are round in shape. He has given more importance to the legend and illustrated the coins with horizontal legend and tree placed laterally to right or left, always shown in a railing of four compartments. The tree is depicted with seven or five leaves and the legend is placed above or below the laterally placed tree. The letter *ha* is generally placed sideways as on the coins of Māhishmatī, with its mouth open to right, somewhat resembling *pa* and *da* letters. The letter *da* opens to right as well as left. The dot in the circular form of the letter *tha* is not visible on all specimens but being clear in some others it leaves little doubt to its being *tha*. Prashant felt that the "coins show variant legends such as Hathodaka, Hathodari and possibly Hathodato". As usual on most of the series of early Indian coins, the vowel marks on these coins are not always preserved and clearly visible. Even the form of individual

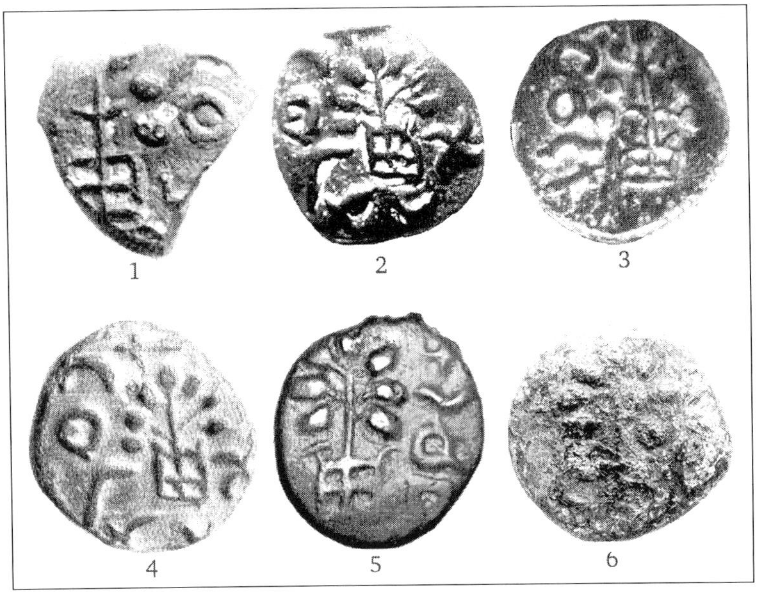

Fig. 50. Coins of Hathodaka City State.

letters on different coins varies. There, however, is little doubt that the legend on these coins is 'Hathodaka/Hathodakī' and not Hathodarī(/tī) or Hathodato as suggested by Prashant Kulkarni. What has been read as '*ka*' on the top of the tree on Coin 1 by him is actually a symbol, probably a fish, which is visible completely and clearly on similar coins published by us and referred to above (Fig. 50.2 & 4).

A close look at the illustrations of Prashant's coins, however, shows the first letter of the legend '*ha*' bears a medial *ā* vowel-mark on some of the specimens. It thus seems to have been '*Hā*'.[4] The next letter is '*tha*' which shows medial '*o*' mark on his Coin 4 and has thus been correctly read as '*tho*'. There cannot be any doubt regarding the following '*da*' though this letter shows variant forms. The last letter has been deciphered as '*ka*' on some specimens but on Coin 1 Prashant observes that "The last letter *rī* is a bit truncated. It could be *tī* if the stroke of *ta* existed at the lower middle portion of the letter which is out of flan."[5] But the cross-bar in the middle of the vertical stroke of this letter and the evidence of the other specimens rules out the possibility of its being *ti* (*tī*), it is certainly *ki* (*kī*). The whole legend thus seems to have been Hāthodaki(/ī), the Prakrit equivalent of Sanskrit Hāthodakīya. May be that the place was know both as Ha(/ā)thodaka and the coins bore the legend Ha(/ā)thodaki(/ī) in Prakrit derivable

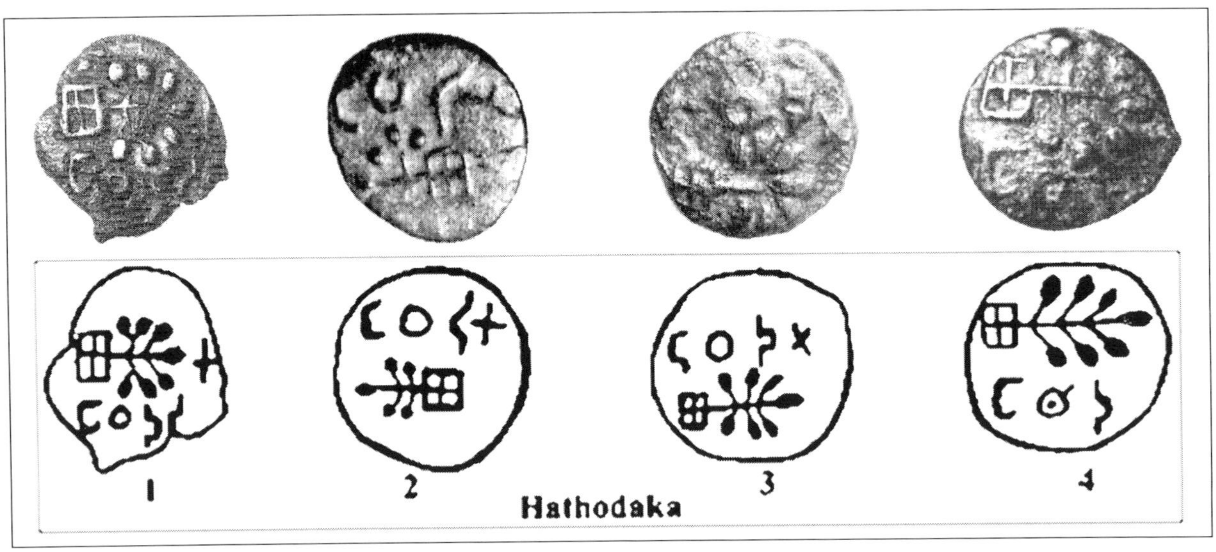

Fig. 51. Hathodaka coins.

from Sanskrit Hastodaka and Hastodakīya (i.e. '(coin) of or belonging to Hathodaka'). I think the legend on one of our coin (Fig. 41.4) is Hathodakiya, the letter *ka* shows a slight slant on its upper end to represent *i*-vowel. We have a comparable example of some coins of Bhaddavatiya (< Bhadravatīya) bearing the legend *Bhadvatīya*. The legend *Ujeniya* on some coins of the city-state of Ujjain may have been used for Ujjayanīya, i.e. (coin) of Ujjayana.

Prashant has referred to the metal of the coins as bell metal. All the illustrated specimens are uniface. The coins have been dated between third and second century BCE on palaeographic grounds. The broken cast coin published by us earlier (Fig. 50.1-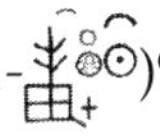)[6], however, seems to have been counter struck by Ujjain symbol. Four circlets in one of the visible orb of this symbol indicate that it may have originally been of the variety occurring on the reverse of the Ujjain coin bearing the Brāhmī legend *Bhūmimitasa* as published by Kothari (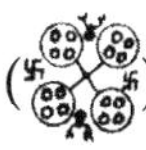).[7] If so, king Bhūmimitra may have annexed Hathodaka to the Ujjain kingdom some time in the second century BCE, a date supported by palaeography. The coins are roughly circular and their sizes have been given as 22 x 23, 20 x 23, 22 x 23 and 22 x 22 mm. The weight of Coin 1 only has been mentioned as 9.2 g. The coins published by us vary between 19 and 25 mm and weigh from 5.3 g (broken piece) to 9.3 g[8], the latter limit corresponding well to Prashant's Coin 1. The ledge on our broken coin indicates that the planchets were prepared by casting and the coins were then struck with a single die on one face after heating the blanks.

The true form of the legend and the location of the city-state can only be determined with the publication of more and clearer specimens from definite provenance/s. We have also noticed in the collection of Prof. D.L. Neema of Indore (Fig. 50.5) a very well preserved Hathodaka coin which shows a tree in railing divided into four compartments with its upper edges bearing parasol-like appendages. The stem of the tree has three leaves on either side and one at the apex. The Brāhmī legend *Hathodaka* is placed parallel to the tree on the right and is to be read from outside by turning the coin to right at right angle. The vowel mark with *tha* is clearly marked. The parasol-like appendages with the railing have not been found on any specimen noticed earlier and are thus a new feature. This form of tree in railing with parasols on top corners of the railing is found on coins bearing the legend *Madāvike* also.[9] The coin has been procured at Indore and its exact provenance may not have been far distant. Another coin (Fig. 50.3)[10] also shows parasol-like appendages on the top corners of the railing and also carries traces of *svastika* on the right of the tree.

The name Hathodaka reminds us of the name of Agrodaka (*Agodaka Agācha janapadasa*) on the coins of the Agra/Āgreya republic. Agrodaka finds mention in the *Mahāmāyūrī*[11], a Buddhist text of the early centuries of the current era, and a medieval inscription (as Agrotaka)[12] and was rightly identified with modern Agroha near Hisar (Haryana) by Przyluski in 1926.[13] Another well known *udaka*-ending place is Pṛithūdaka, modern Pehowa on the river Sarasvatī about 25 km west of

Kurukshetra (Haryana).[14] A *tīrtha* on the Sarasvatī named Kālodaka has been mentioned in the *Mahābhārata*.[15] There thus remains little doubt to there being *udaka*-ending places in ancient times. Hathodaka compares well with these names. In all probability all such places were located on the river banks or some other water-bodies or associated with them.

Prashant has rightly observed that since the coins belong "to the series of Narmada valley style coins of Tripurī, Māhishmatī and Kurarāya, I feel that there is more probability that Hathodaka was a city and not the name of a ruler. This is further supported by the fact that there are several places in India by the name Hatoda. One such Hatoda is only 50 km west of Indore."[16] But ignorant of the antiquity of this place he looked for another town on the banks of Narmadā for identification of the place and on Dr. S.K. Bhatt's suggestion he felt inclined to identify Hathodaka of the coins with Hathnāvar (22° 9' N and 75° 21' E) on the banks of River Narmadā in Manavar *pargana* of the district of Dhar which has been referred to in Sihore Grant dated VS 1272 of king Arjunavarman and is "full of antiquity (sic) and was famous for the elephants in that region.[17]

It does not seem to be logical to derive Hāthodaka(/kī) from or identify it with Hastināvara or Hastināvaragrāma of the medieval inscriptions. A place name like Hat(h)oda or Hat(h)odi is more likely to be its derivative and the place should be looked for on the bank of or near some river. Archaeological remains of the early historic period from such a site would further strengthen the identity. Hatod near Indore to its northwest has yielded microliths in association with the black-and-red, black-and-cream or grey ware[18] and as such it seems to have continued to be a place of significance from the early times down to the early historic period and may be identified with Hathodaka mentioned on the coins under discussion. Another possible claimant may be the site of Hathab on the bank of the river Maheshwari, about 1.5 km from the sea shore lying to the southwest of modern Bhavnagar. It was excavated by S. Pramanik and has yielded a large number of sherds of amphorae sherds found from the layers overlying the Mauryan level. These sherds indicate that Hathab was an ancient port used for Roman trade in the post-Mauryan period. It may have been well connected with some important towns inland also for trade purposes. The site has also yielded many seals and sealings indicating that it continued to flourish to the Valabhi period of sixth century CE and later.[19] The name-ending *udaka* may have been substituted during the medieval period by the word *āb* (cf. Punjab) which is the Persian synonym of the Sanskrit word *udaka* 'water'.

NOTES AND REFERENCES

1. Handa, Devendra & M.K. Gupta (April 2005), "Some Uniface Cast Copper Coins", *IIRNS Newsline*, Issue 46), pp. 4-5, nos. 6 and 10; (2012), *Numismatic Gleanings*, pp. 7-11, Pls. II.9 & III.1.
2. Kulkarni (July-Dec. 2005), *ICSNL*, No. 37, pp. 3-5.
3. Kulkarni (*Ibid.*) expressed the possibility of the symbol having a straight line with a small cross-bar (his plus sign) above the tree to be a *svastika* but we feel that the said sign represents a fish. It may well be compared with the fish symbol on some Māhishmatī coins.

4. This negates the possibility of the place-name having been derived from Hasti(n).
5. Kulkarni (July-Dec. 2005), *op. cit.*, p. 4.
6. *IIRNS NL*, 46, p. 4, no. 6, Pl. I.9.
7. Kothari (2006), p. 102, Type 58. Recently Dr. Akshay Jain has acquired a Hathodaka coin counter-struck by Revabhūti of Eran.
8. *IIRNS NL*, 46, p. 4, nos. 6 and 10, Pl. I.9 and 13 respectively.
9. Kulkarni (July-Dec. 2005), *op. cit.*, p. 17.
10. See Bhatt, S.K. (Ed) (2006), *Narmada Valley Culture and Civilization*, Indore, cover page.
11. *Agrodake Mālyadharaḥ* (Line 8) and *Agrodake Muñjakeśaḥ* (Line 70) of the *Mahāmāyūrī* edited by Sylvain Levi in *Journal Asiatique*, 1915, pp. 19-138. See also *Journal of the U.P. Historical Society*, Vol. XV, pp, 27-28, 33 and 45.
12. *Epigraphia Indica*, Vol. I, pp. 93-94.
13. *JA*, 1926, pp. 16 f; Przyluski, James (1962), *Ancient Peoples of the Panjab*, English tr. by Chitrabhanu Sen, Calcutta, p. 9.
14. Handa, Devendra (2004), *An Epic Pilgrimage - History and Antiquit of Pehowa: Ancient Pṛithūdaka*, New Delhi.
15. *Mahābhārata* (Gita Press ed.), XII.152, 12-13.
16. *ICSNL*, No. 37 (July-Dec. 2005), p. 4.
17. *Ibid.*, pp. 4-5.
18. *IAR*, 1958-59, p. 27.
19. Pramanik, S. (2004), 'Hathab: An Early Historic Port on the Gulf of Khambat', *Journal of the Indian Ocean Archaeology*, vol. I, pp. 133-40.

XIII

Coins of Kurarā(ya) and Kuraghara

Though S.L. Katare[1] had referred to coins bearing the legend *Kurarāya* while bringing to light the issues of the city-state of Bhāgilā in 1952 yet he could not publish their details in his life-time and it was Alaka Tiwari[2] who first illustrated and gave details of six copper pieces in 1980 from the collection of her father Prof. K.B. Tiwari of Hoshangabad, made mostly from Nandner, Obedullahgunj (both in district Sehore) and Vidisha in Madhya Pradesh. She divided them into three varieties (A – C) comprising respectively of two, three and one coins. The two coins of variety A are round and the remaining four square. Alaka Tiwari could not recognize the symbols properly and also read the legend on second coin of Variety A as Kuraya instead of Kuragha[ra], as confirmed by coins published later by I.K.S. Chauhan, S.K. Bhatt and others.[3] Prof. S.J. Mangalam and Pushpa Tiwari have corrected Alaka Tiwari's description and classification observing that "The two coins of Variety-A are in fact two different types. The first coin is of single- die, i.e. its reverse is blank. The second coin is of double-die having on its reverse a bold hollow cross with four or five pellets (not three) inside. The palaeography of these two coins is also different, the first being earlier and Mauryan type and the second at least a century later with shorter verticals and angular *YA* (sic. *gha*). The dwindling of the name to KURAYA is also an indication of its later origin. Even in weight these two are totally different. The three coins grouped in Variety-B, presuming depiction of three symbols in a row – Ujjain symbol, tree-in-railing and *Indrayaṣṭi*, can be of two varieties. The first and the third have below the legend, a tree-in-railing on left and *Indrayaṣṭi* to right. The second coin, also below the legend, has Ujjain symbol to left and tree-in-railing to right. The single specimen of Variety-C is totally a different type. Thus in all there are five different types reported by Alaka Tiwari."[4] We may say that the twig-like flourish shown by Alaka Tiwari under the legend of the first coin of Variety-A (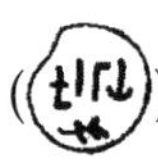) is the *kurara* bird 'osprey' lying on its back as found on some other varieties also (Fig. 52.1-2). Coin no. 2 of Variety-A which has been drawn erroneously as 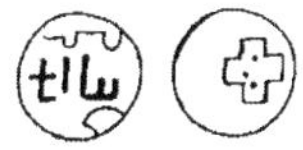 shows very clearly a hollow cross with pellets on right and a crescented three-arched hill symbol placed sideways with vertical base on right to the left of the cross above the legend. The *kurara* bird is depicted below the legend (Fig. 52.B: 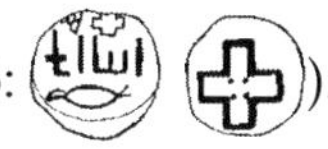). Most of the scholars have missed to notice the crescented hill symbol to the left of the hollow cross on this type of coins. These symbols are used commonly together or separately on these and many other city-state coins. On the coins of her Variety-B, Alaka Tiwari describes three symbols the existence of which is not borne out by the specimens illustrated by her. Mangalam and Tiwari have rightly pointed out that they belong to two types showing railed tree and triangle-headed symbols on one type (Fig. 53.3-4, 7 & 8) and Ujjain symbol accompanied by railed tree on its right on the other (Fig. 53.5-6 & 10). R.K. Sharma[5] has illustrated good specimens thereof from the collection of K.P. Pandey of Jabalpur noting that they were 'collected at Hoshangabad, where these must have come from Nandner or Jamunia' (Fig. 52.6 & 5 respectively). Wilfried Pieper has published a square die-struck coin of Kurarā (11 x 10 mm, 0.98 g) which has the obverse like that of Fig. 52.6 but shows a double-*yya* like *śrīvatsa* placed on a four compartmented railing (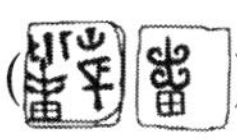) on the reverse.[6] Alaka Tiwari also failed to recognize the *nandipada* over the Ujjain symbol and described that as a crescent. *Nandipada* over the Ujjain symbol is very clear on the specimens illustrated by Amiteshwar Jha (Fig. 53.5-6)[7] and Sharma (Fig. 52.5) as well as on a square Kuraghara type coin auctioned some time back (Fig. 52.D and Fig. 53.9).[8]

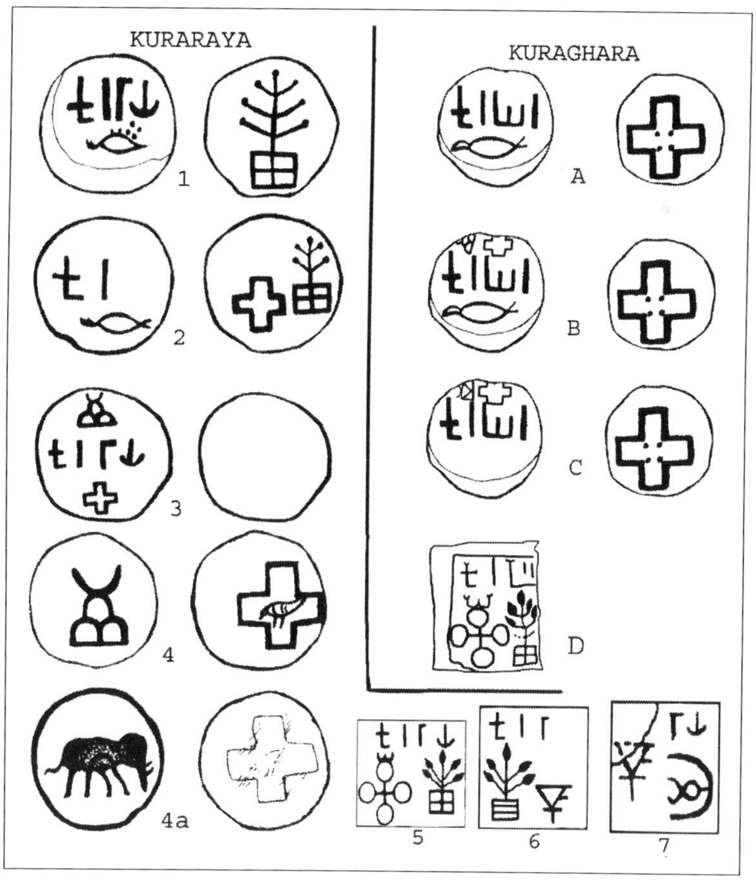

Fig. 52. Important Types of Kurarāya/Kuraghara Series.

Prof. K.B. Tiwari[9] added to the then existing repertoire a new variety showing a railed tree under the legend *Kurarāya* in 1981 when he translated his daughter's article in Hindi. While cataloguing the rich collection of Prof. Shankar Tiwari in 2001, S.J. Mangalam and Pushpa Tiwari

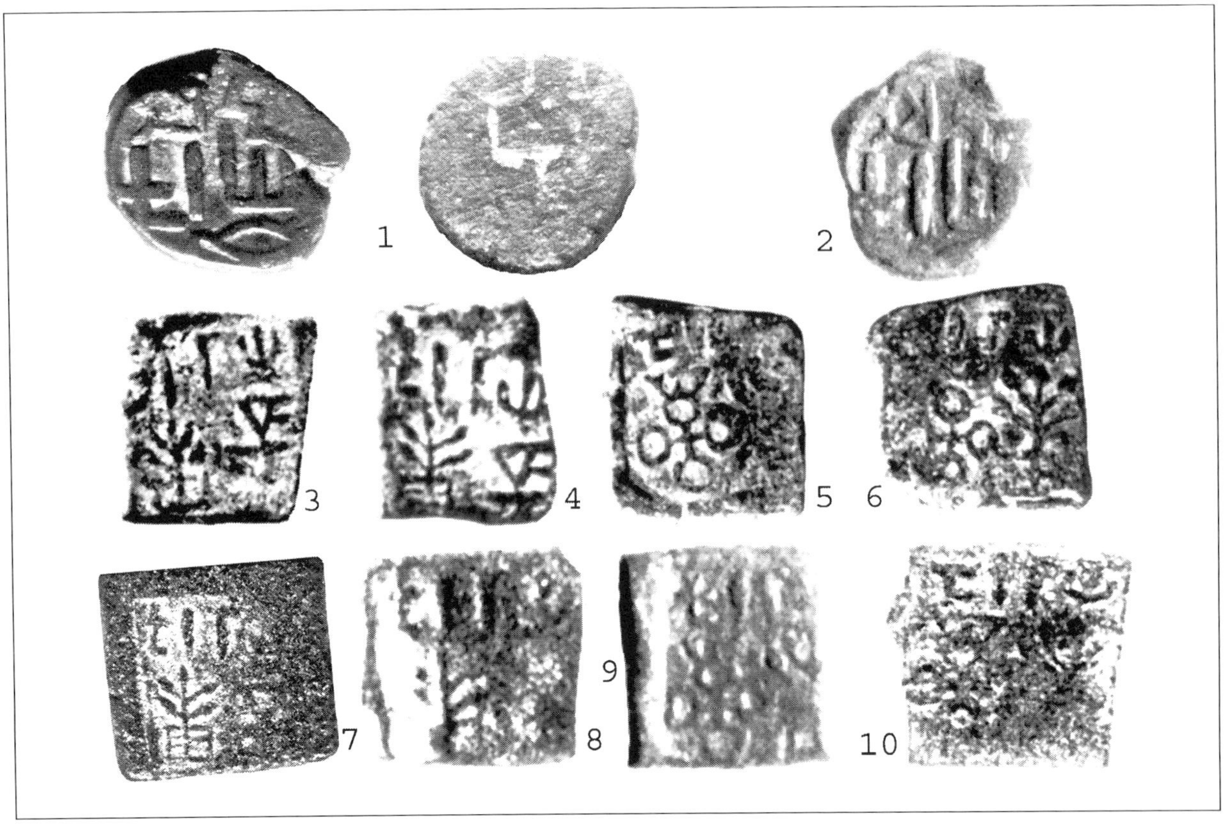

Fig. 53. Kuraghara/Kurarāya coins.

took stock of the existing specimens publishing several new varieties of Kurarāya and Kuraghara species unknown till then. The duo assigned these coins to the period ranging from late Mauryan period to the middle of the first century BCE.[10] In 2003 Amiteshwar Jha[11] made a brief reference to square copper coins bearing the legend 'Kuraraya' illustrating four specimens thereof (Fig. 53.3-6) belonging to two types of Variety-B of Alaka Tiwari. As noted above two specimens of Jha (Fig. 53.5-6) show very clearly the *nandipada* surmounting the Ujjain symbol which Alaka Tiwari had wrongly described as a crescent. Sharma also recognized the *nandipada* correctly on K.P. Pandey's coin as cited above.[12] In 2005, Prashant P. Kulkarni published the coins of city-states of Hathodaka, Māhishmatī, Madāvike, Tripurī, Kurapurikā, Kuraghara and Kurara from the Narmadā valley culling many literary and epigraphic references to these places and discussing their significance.[13] Kurarāya coin-types showing the crescented three-arched hill above and the hollow cross below the legend (Fig. 52.3), the bird in the hollow cross on the reverse (Fig. 52.4) and crescented hill obverse counter-struck by an elephant to right (Fig. 52.4a) constitute interesting examples. Kulkarni is reported to have seen nearly two hundred Kurara coins in various collections at Bhopal, Vidisha, Indore and Ujjain.[14] The most recent work from the pen of Prof. R.K. Sharma makes a reference to most of the earlier publications[15] and includes a Kuraghara coin collected from Hoshangabad from the collection of Ajay Jaiswal of Gadarwara which according to him belongs to a new variety and shows on the obverse triangle-headed standard placed horizontally to the left of the hollow cross in the top register above the legend and the *kurara* bird below while the reverse carries a mark in two wings of the hollow cross.[16] This is nothing but a sub-variety of the coin published by Chauhan in which the crescent-topped hill has been depicted differently with triangular arches, better specimens of which are illustrated here (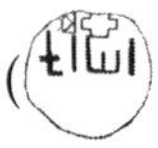 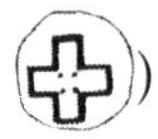) (Fig. 53.1-2).

Coins with the legend *Kurarāya* are met with more frequently than those with the legend *Kuraghara*. As noted above, many varieties of coins referred to above show the *kurara* 'osprey' bird and the city may have been known as Kurara/Kurarā or Kuraghara (abode of ospreys) because of the abundance of such birds as is indicated by literary references also referred to by some scholars. Numerous references to Kurara, Kurarā, Kurarī, Koraghara, etc. in Sanchi inscriptions[17] indicate that the place was located somewhere near it. Though Kurarāya has been identified with Kurawai along the river Betwa, about 25 km from Bina in Vidisha district of Madhya Pradesh[18] and Kuraghara with Kurwar (23° 38' N. Lat. & 77° 4' E. Long.)[19] yet the absence of any early historic archaeological remains and the non-association of these sites with ospreys renders the identifications somewhat uncertain.[20]

Kulkarni and Sharma have dealt with the coins of Kurarāya and Kuraghara under separate heads and the former has specifically observed that "the available evidence is not enough to prove whether Kurara and Kuraghara were one and the same town or two different places".[21] A comparison of the symbols (Fig. 52), indicates the two being the names of the same place. Whatsoever little doubt remains is, however, removed by the small square coin illustrated here (Fig. 53.9) which also carries the same symbols as found on coins bearing the legend Kurarāya (Fig. 52.5).[22]

Mangalam dates the Kuraghara type coins to the Mauryan period and those bearing the legend Kurarāya about a century later.[23] while Bhatt places the latter to *circa* and third-second century BCE and states that "At the second phase of mining, the legend ghar (sic.) on coin was dropped, reducing it to Kurar only."[24] The elongation of letters in both the types, however, indicates that they belong to second-first century BCE and it is very difficult to ascertain the exact date with certainty. As noted above, the Kurarāya coins square and the Kuraghara coins are round in shape. The former are of lighter and the latter of a higher weight. The development from square to round shapes and lighter to higher weights seems to be logical but difficult to prove in the present state of our knowledge. Both, however, may have been current simultaneously – the square ones of lighter weights for local and day to day transactions and the round pieces of higher weight for commercial use.

NOTES AND REFERENCES

1. Katare, S.L. (1952), 'Hitherto Unknown Coins of Bhāgilā City', *JNSI*, XIV, p. 12; XLIV (1982), pp. 29 ff.
2. Tiwari, Alaka (1980), 'Coins of Two Ancient City States of Madhya Pradesh', *ND*, IV (ii), pp. 1-3.

3. Chauhan, Indra Kumar Singh (1980), 'The Coins of Kuraraya', *JAINS*, III, pp. 3-5, Pl. IV.6-9a; Bhatt, S.K. (1981-82), 'Coins of Kurahara', *Ibid.*, IV, pp. 11-12, Pl. II.1-2; Mangalam, S.J. and Pushpa Tiwari (2001), *Shankar Tiwari Collection of Early Coins from the Narmada Valley*, Bhopal.
4. Mangalam and Tiwari, *op. cit.*, p. 170.
5. Sharma, R.K. (2011), *op. cit.*, p. 123.
6. Pieper (2013), *op. cit.*, pp. 242-43, no. 501.
7. Jha, Amiteshwar (2003), *Bhāratīya Sikke Eka Aitihāsika Parichaya* (Hindi), Anjaneri, pp. 26-27.
8. *Todywalla's Auctions Catalogue No. 14* (22nd April 2006, Mumbai), p. 5, lot no. 22.
9. Tiwari, K.B. (1981), 'Pūrva Mālavā ke Prāchīna Nagara Rājya (Bhāgilā evaṃ Kurara)' in *Malwa Through the Ages* (edited by M.D. Khare), Bhopal, pp. 221-23.
10. Mangalam and Tiwari, *op. cit.*, pp. 170-74.
11. Jha (2003), *op. cit.*, pp. 26-27.
12. Sharma (2011), *op. cit.*, p. 123.
13. Kulkarni (July-Dec. 2005), *ICSNL*, No. 37, pp. 1-21.
14. *Ibid.*, p. 15.
15. Sharma (2011), *op. cit.*, pp. 121-25.
16. *Ibid.*, p. 125.
17. For references see Kulkarni (July-Dec. 2005), *op. cit.*, p. 14.
18. Tiwari, *loc. cit.*
19. Bühler, George (1894), 'Votive Inscriptions from the Sanchi Stupas', *Epigraphia Indica*, Vol. II, p. 96.
20. Cf. Sharma (2011), *op. cit.*, pp. 124-25.
21. Kulkarni (July-Dec. 2005), *op. cit.*, p. 15.
22. Mangalam and Tiwari, *op. cit.*, pp. 170-74.
23. Bhatt, S.K. (2003), "Kurar Coins", *JAINS*, XVII-XVIII (2003), p. 56.
24. I am thankful to Drs. R.K. Sharma, M.K. Gupta, Amiteshwar Jha, Prashant P. Kulkarni and Todywallas for the coins illustrated here. The illustrated coins are not to scale.

XIV

Alleged Coin of Brāhmaṇa-nagara-sthāna

A unique round copper piece of approximately 15 mm diameter weighing 1.07 g datable to first century BCE and allegedly belonging to a new city state named 'Brahmana Nagara Sthan' in the Mathura region was offered for sale some time back by an auction house (Fig. 54). Its details as given in the printed catalogue[1] are as follow:

Obv. Female standing with one hand raised beside tree in railing, Brāhmī legend around 'brahmananagarasthan'.

Rev. Three dotted lines.

Fortunately enough, the catalogue has been printed and produced nicely and includes an enlargement of the obverse of the coin making it clear that the stylized linear figure of the female, goddess Umā or Lakshmī in all likelihood, is standing to front with right hand raised and the suspended left touching the corresponding shank. Over the head the goddess is a semicircular hood, simulating the depiction of the deity as on early inscribed Mathura coins and some Mathura sculptures.[2] The piece regarded as a coin seems to have been attributed to a new city state on the basis of the legend as read by the cataloguer. This city state is not known to us from any other source. The illustration of the coin carries the legend in a fairly preserved state and one can see the elongation of the vowel mark with the last two consonants as also the dot representing the *anusvāra* (nasalization) of the last syllable of *Brāhmaṇānāṃ*. The *i*-vowel marks with the following two letters, i.e. with *g* and *r*, making them *gi* and *ri*(ī)[3] and the next palatal sibilant *śa* are fairly visible on the coin. The cataloguer has completely missed the vowel marks and the palatal sibilant to read the legend correctly. He has, however, rightly restored the last word of the compound though the dental sibilant of the conjunct is totally out of the flan.

The legend, however, is amply clear and may be deciphered undoubtedly as [*Brā*]*hmaṇānāṃ giri*(*ī*)*śa*-(*s*)*th*(*ā*)*na*(*ṃ*), meaning 'temple of Śiva belonging to the

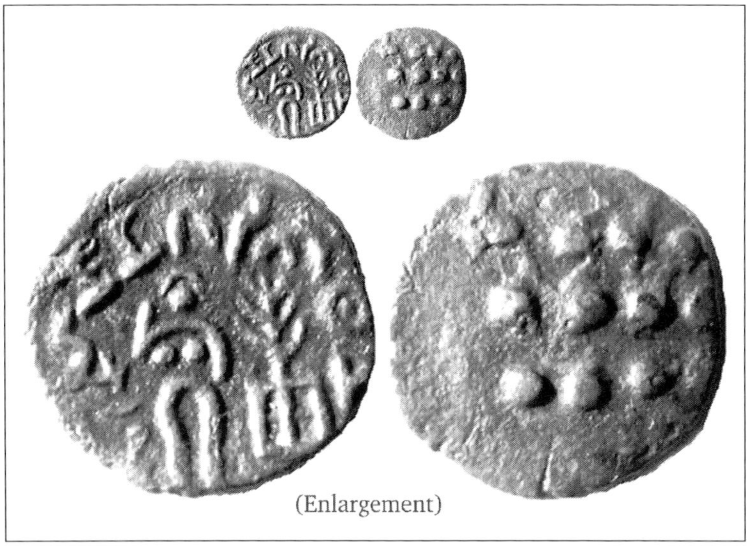

Fig. 54. An alleged coin of 'Brahmana Nagara Sthan'.

Brāhmaṇas'. The Sanskrit word *sthāna* has many meanings[4] and stands for a holy place or temple also. Sunet near Ludhiana in Punjab has yielded a clay sealing bearing the Brāhmī legend *Śrī-sthānasya*.[5] K.K. Thaplyal has rightly observed that "The legend suggests that the place was sacred and that a temple dedicated to Śrī-Lakshmī probably existed there."[6] Nandsa Yūpa Inscription of Kṛita Samvat 282 (=225 CE) also refers to the temples of Brahmā, Indra, Prajāpati, etc. by using the term *sthāna* (*Brahm=endra-prajāpati-maharshi=rvishṇu-sthāneshu kṛit=āvakāśasya*).[7] The light weight and almost mint-fresh state of preservation of the piece under discussion also suggest that in all probability it did not circulate as a coin and was given to some select devotees with *prasāda* 'propitiatory offering' by the priests as is the custom even now with some celebrated shrines. The obverse motif of female goddess standing facing with right hand raised to the level of the shoulder and left suspended downwards simulating the depiction of the goddess Lakshmī on Mathura coins hints at its provenance in the region if not this city itself which is well known to have been a great religious centre in the early historic period. The depiction of Lakshmī on this piece probably represents a stage when Lakshmī was regarded as the goddess of prosperity and welfare worshipped by all sections of society and not as a sectarian deity. Having studied various series of coins showing a goddess standing on a lotus and/or holding a lotus in her hand and quoting the Agamic verse describing the two-armed Durgā-Gaurī images (*Dakshiṇe chotpalaṃ haste vāmahastaṃ pralambitaṃ. . . .*), J.N. Banerjea had observed that "one will be justified to hold that some of these female figures on coins with lotus in their right hands and their left hands resting on hip are variants of goddess Durgā."[8] It may be mentioned here that the goddess on some coins of Māhishmati (Maheśvara) is shown similarly and may in all probability be Māheśvarī, i.e., Pārvatī or Durgā:

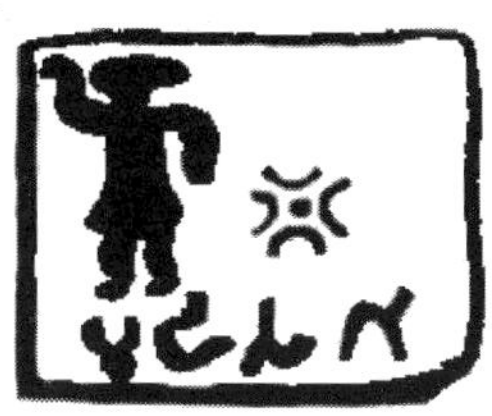

The goddess depicted here may thus be Durgā which seems to be quite appropriate for a propitiation gift of a Śaivite temple. Alternatively she may be Lakshmī also as she bestows wealth to all who visit religious shrines.

NOTES AND REFERENCES

1. *Kohinoor Auctions*, Auction # 1 (Friday, 20 December, 2013), Pune, p. 4, no. 15. It now forms part of Shri Girish Sharma's collection.
2. For example Kushāṇa Shashṭhī images in Mathura Museum, Nos. F 2, F 3, 54.3763, 1244, 15.739, etc.
3. Giriśa and Girīśa, both these names/epithets were used for Śiva. An example of the former may be seen in a verse of the *Bhāgavata Purāṇa* (VI.17, 8) which runs as following: *Giriśaṃ dadṛiśe gachchhan parītaṃ siddha-chāraṇaiḥ / Āliṃgyāṅgīkṛitāṃ devīṃ bāhunā muni-saṃsadi / /*.
4. Apte, V.S. (1959), *The Student's Sanskrit-English Dictionary*, Delhi-Patna-Varanasi, p. 622.
5. *JNSI*, XX (1959), p. 68, no. 3. Cf. Śrī-kshetra (Puri, Odisha), Śiva-thala (Śivasthala) *vide* Sircar (1965), *Select Inscriptions Bearing on Indian History and Civilization*, Vol. I, 2nd ed., Calcutta, p. 130.
6. Thaplyal (1972), *SAIS*, p. 178.
7. Altekar, Anant Sadashiv (1948), 'Nandsa Yupa Inscriptions', *Epigraphia Indica*, Vol. 27, p. 264.
8. Banerjea (1956), p. 134.

XV

Early Indian Lead Coins

Lead (*sīsaṃ, sīsakaṃ, nāgaṃ, yogeshṭaṃ, vapraṃ* in Sanskrit) is a metal which has been commonly used in the world for about the last seven thousand years because of its being widespread, easy to extract and easy to work with. It is highly malleable and ductile as well as easy to smelt. In the early Bronze Age, lead was used with antimony and arsenic which acted as the hardening agents. In alchemy, lead is thought to be the oldest metal and is associated with the planet Saturn 'Śani'. Pb as the symbol of lead is an abbreviation of its Latin name *plumbum* for soft metals.[1]

The word '*sīsam*' (lead) occurs in some of the Vedic texts, viz., *Atharvaveda* (I.16, 2 & 4; XII.2, 1, 19-20 & 53); *Yajurveda, Vājasaneyi Saṃhitā* (XVIII.13) where it has been mentioned along with the names of other metals like gold, silver, copper (*ayas*), iron and tin (*trapu*); *Maitrāyaṇī Saṃhitā* (II.4, 2; III.11, 9), *Taittirīya Brāhmaṇa* (III.12, 6, 5) and *Śatapatha Brāhmaṇa* (IV.1.2,14; XII.7.1,7; XII.7.2,10). We continue getting references to it in subsequent literature also, the important texts referring to it being the *Chhāndogya Upanishad* (IV.17.7-8), the *Sūtras, Vinaya Piṭaka, Nikāyas, Jātakas*, Pāṇini's *Ashṭādhyāyī* (IV.3, 154), Kauṭilya's *Arthaśāstra, Mahābhārata, Charaka and Suśruta Saṃhitās*, etc. We thus see that as far as literary sources in India are concerned they show almost continuous knowledge of lead in the country.

Metallic lead does occur in nature, but is rare. Lead is usually found in ore with zinc, silver and (most abundantly) copper, and is extracted together with these metals. The main lead mineral is galena (PbS), which contains 86.6% lead. Other common varieties are cerussite ($PbCO_3$) and anglesite ($PbSO_4$). Lead is obtained from galena by smelting it. In mining, the ore is extracted by drilling or blasting and then crushed and ground. Roasting the galena helps in removing sulphur from it and then coking results in lead bullion which contains impurities like gold, silver, antimony, arsenic, copper, tin and zinc. These impurities are then removed by various refining steps to obtain pure lead.

A soft, heavy, toxic and malleable poor metal, lead is bluish white when freshly cut but tarnishes to dull gray when exposed to air. Metallic lead is attacked only superficially by air, forming a thin layer of oxide that protects it from further oxidation. The metal is not attacked by sulfuric or hydrochloric acids. It does, however, dissolve in nitric acid. The melting point of lead is 327.46 degree Celsius. Its softness and low

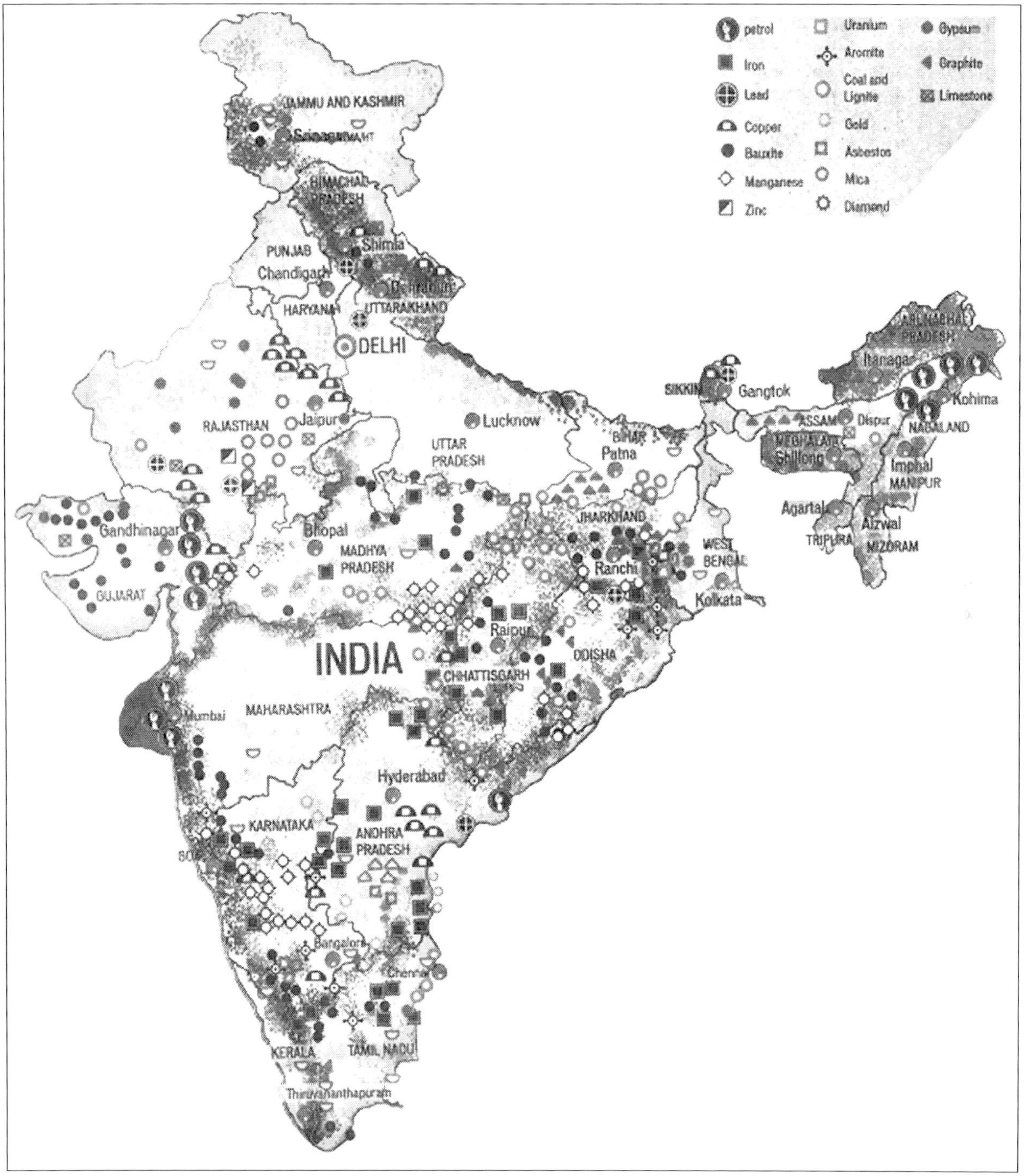

Fig. 55. Mineral resources of India including lead ores.

melting point make lead very easy to handle and fashion. Of the various isotopes of lead four – 204Pb (1.48%), 206Pb (23.6%), 207Pb (22.6%) and 208Pb (52.3%) - are stable and do not change during extraction, refining, environmental and industrial processes, i.e., the amount of each of these isotopes in a particular ore is determined when it is formed and remains unchanged throughout its life. The isotopes thus give lead of different ores its signature. In other words lead isotopic structure serves as its finger print and helps us to determine its parentage or provenance. Like all other metals, trace elements in lead also help in determining the source or mine from which galena was utilized.

In the Indian subcontinent, however, lead was generally obtained as a by-product of the extraction of silver from the argentiferous galena ores of the different mines. About a century and a quarter back Valentine Ball[2] had given us a comprehensive summary of the sources of lead ores in India and the results of various projects and investigations have been published some time back by the Geological Survey of India[3] and as we shall see in the sequel lead ores exist in India in a wide area (Fig. 55).

The earliest occurrence of lead in the form of a 'leaden slag' has been noticed at the pre-Harappan site of Nal[4] (second half of the third millennium BCE) the probable source for which may have been the nearby Baluchistan. While copper/bronze appeared earlier than silver in the sub-continental scenario, yet we see substantial use of these metals along with gold and lead during the period of the Harappan or the Indus-Sarasvati Culture.[5] Scientific analysis of lead objects from Mohenjo-daro and Lothal containing 99.2 and 99.54% lead indicates the extent of the high degree of the purity of lead the Harappan metal workers could achieve.[6] Pascoe thought that lead may have come to Mohenjo-daro from Ajmer or the Faranjal mine in Afghanistan or from Persia.[7] Except from Chalcolithic Navdatoli near Maheshwar on the Narbada in Madhya Pradesh (1700-1400 BCE)[8] which has yielded three small lead objects the source of metal for which may have been the nearby Zawar (Udaipur) mines of Rajasthan, the use of lead seems to have been forgotten for many centuries after the decline of the Harappan Culture to be rediscovered in the early historic period. Rajni Nanda and Dilip K. Chakrabarti[9] have dealt with geological, archaeological and literary study of lead in early India but a detailed survey and examination of its use for numismatic purpose remains a desideratum.

PUNCH-MARKED LEAD COINS

Lead has been used for coins in India from quite an early period. The earliest coins of India belong to various Mahājanapadas 'great states' of Buddha's time (6th-5th centuries BCE).[10] These coins are made of silver and bear one to four punches. Coins of the subsequent Magadha Empire are also predominantly made of silver but they bear five punches and have been struck only on the weight standard of *Kārshāpaṇa* (32 *rattīs* or approximately 3.6 g or 56 grains) whereas coins of the Mahājanapada series follow fractions or multiples of *kārshāpaṇa* or fractions of *Śatamāna* (100-*rattī* or 11.5 g or 180 grains). Simultaneous use of imperial punch-marked and cast copper coins at least during the Maurya period if not earlier is also generally accepted by scholars. The Jātakas mention *Sīsakahāpanas* (*sīsakārshāpaṇa*, i.e. lead *kārshāpaṇa*)[11] also the first example of which datable to *circa* 4th century BCE was published in 1991 from Paunar in Vidarbha by Chandrashekhar Gupta.[12] Two more specimens, one from Ujjain and the other from Pauni in Vidarbha, bearing four symbols have been published recently[13] indicating the use of lead punch-marked coins though only sporadically during the *Mahājanapada* phase. The Bhir Mound at Taxila yielded some minute lead coins bearing a single punch and these have been dated to the Mauryan period.[14] Some early lead coins have been obtained from Maheshwar as noted above (Fig. 36). The source of lead for these punch-marked coins may have been the same as for Navdatoli noted above. The discovery of a semi-circular heavy lead piece having a diameter of 13.10 cm of the plain surface weighing 2.97 kilograms from the stratified deposits of the Mauryan period confirmed by a rectangular seal incuse of 5.30 X 5.0 cm bearing Aśokan Brāhmī legend *raño Iṃ)dagutasa* in the characters of *circa* late 3rd or early 2nd century BCE from Eran in district Sagar (Madhya Pradesh) is of great importance as the evidence of the use of lead in the early period.[15] The use of lead coins in the post-Maurya period is evidenced from numerous finds most important of which have been listed and discussed in the following lines.[16]

POST-MAURYA LEAD COINS

After the decline of the Mauryan Empire, the people of the southern Deccan, more than elsewhere in India, developed a particular preference for lead as a coin metal. Perhaps the main reason for this was the easy availability of this metal through natural resources. Cunningham had described the lead coins of the Sātavāhanas, Kuras and Āndhras [1891.[17] Vincent Smith also listed coins of the Āndhras – Kuras and Sātavāhanas – in the Indian Museum, Calcutta[18] but it was Rapson who presented the most comprehensive and monumental work on the coins, including lead ones, not only of the Āndhras and their feudatories (Mahārathis and Ānandas), but also those of the Western Kshatrapas and the Bodhis.[19] Most of the coins of the Sātavāhanas and their feudatories come from the Deccan and quite often they are made of lead. The Ikshvākus, Kuras, Kadambas, Ānandas, Vishṇukuṇḍins and Hiraṇyaka rulers also took fancy to this metal. I.K. Sarma thinks that the Sātavāhanas developed a special liking for lead as a metal for currency because of its malleability in manufacturing coins of various shapes[20] but Bajpai's view that the Sātavāhanas' choice of lead was dictated by the prevailing local tradition[21] seems to be more logical as we find abundant use of lead for coinage in Malwa, Vidarbha, Andhra, Konkan and Karnataka by some pre-Sātavāhana dynasties also.[22]

ANDHRA PRADESH

Andhra Pradesh has yielded the largest number of lead coins. Excavations and surface finds at Kotalingala (district Karimnagar, Andhra Pradesh)[23], Sangareddy (district Medak)[24], Veerapuram[25], Satanikota[26] (Nandikotkur taluk of district Kurnool), Vaddamanu near Amaravati (district Guntur)[27], Thotlakonda (25 km from

Vishakhapatnam on Bhimli beach road), Bavikonda, Pavuralakonda, Peddabankur (Karimnagara district)[28], Kondapur[29], Salihundam[30], etc. include a large number of un-inscribed and inscribed coins from the post-Mauryan levels belonging to pre-, Sātavahana and post-Sātavahana dynasties containing almost pure lead.[31] A very large hoard of 5330 lead coins was found in district Ananthpur some time back.[32] A hoard of 1211 Sātavāhana potin coins has been obtained as Treasure Trove from Pulumavidi near Hyderabad.[33] Seven lead coins of the Sātavahanas were picked up from Gundlakamma in district Prakasam.[34] Sātavahana copper and lead coin types with lion, bull, three-arched *chaitya* or hill, *chakra* (wheel), conch, etc. continued to be issued by their immediate successors like the Ikshvākus[35], Śālaṅkāyanas[36], early Pallavas and Vishṇukuṇḍins in Coastal Andhra and Tondaimandalam between 4th-6th centuries CE. The Ikshvākus and the Meghavāhana rulers[37] issued coins only in lead. Nagarjunakonda yielded some Ikshvākụ coins and a hoard of 277 lead coins was found in the Ongole taluq of Guntur district.[38] It is however to be noted that lead coins generally cease to be issued after 5th century CE.

Hyderabad Museum is a big repository of Sātavāhana coins and it is to be noted that 21,529 out of 38,512 Sātavāhana coins in its cabinets are made of lead and 1742 of potin.[39] Even a majority of the coins of the predecessors, contemporaries and successors of the Sātavāhanas, viz. the Sadas, Kuras, Mahātalavaras, Mahārathis, Mahāsenāpatis, Sebakas, Ikshvākus and Śālaṅkāyanas were made of lead.[40]

Tamil Nadu

The earliest coins issued in lead from Tamilnadu (first or second century CE) come from Āṇḍipaṭṭi hoard (143 cast circular coins), Chengam taluk, North Arcot District.[41] K.V. Raman found eight lead coins in the post-Sātavahana deposits in his excavations at Kanchipuram with bull in a dotted border on obverse and minor symbols like *śrīvatsa, nandipada*, etc. on the reverse.[42] Variants with tree in railing on the reverse were noted from Tiruvanmiyur, the likes of which had earlier been published by Tuffnel, Walter Elliot, and C. Minakshi who ascribed them to the Pallavas.[43] Several large sized lead coins of Sangam period belonging to the Cheras and Cholas dated to about 3rd century BCE have been found from the bed of Amaravathi River near Karur.[44] Ship/Ujjain symbol type Sātavāhana lead coins are found mainly along the Coromandel coast between Chennai and Cuddalore.

Karnataka

Numerous Kura, Mahāraṭhi, Sātavāhana and allied coins of lead have been discovered from Karnataka. Wheeler's excavations at Chandravalli brought to light quite a few lead coins indicating the relationship of Sadakana Kalalaya family with the Mahāraṭhis which ruled in Mysore-Kanara region. This excavation also showed that the Chuṭukulānanda family was either the successor of Sadakana rulers or their contemporary in some neighboring region.[45] Excavations at Maski in Raichur district has also yielded a small 20 grain lead coin from the latest level of Period III (mid 1st century to 3rd century CE).[46] From Chitaldurga district come the large lead coins of

Humped bull/Tree & *chaitya* type bearing the legend *Sadakana Kalalaya Maharathisa* and from Karwar district in North Kanara are known similar large lead coins of Chuṭukulānandas. L.C. Gupta published some un-inscribed and inscribed (Mahāraṭhi) lead coins obtained by him at Belgam.[47] Numerous lead coins of the Chuṭus (Ānandas) of Banvasi and Karwar, Kuras of Belgaum (and Kolhapur), Sadakanas of Chandravalli and Hiraṇyakas of Karnataka have figured in Todywalla's auction catalogues and Oswal Antiques' fixed price lists in recent years.

Maharashtra

We have referred to the punch-marked lead coins from Paunar and Pauni in Vidarbha above. An un-inscribed lead coin from Vidarbha with goddess on obverse and Ujjayinī symbol on reverse, the like of which we are informed exist in the personal collections of various collectors, has been published by Ashok Singh Thakur and Rajesh Somkuwar who date it to *circa* 4th-3rd centuries BCE.[48] The Brahmapuri hoard discovered from near Kolhapur in Maharashtra in 1873 contained more than 600 coins of which nearly half were those of lead. Another hoard from the same site discovered in 1877 and now preserved in the Prince of Wales Museum, Mumbai contains 1865 coins of lead (and 100 copper coins along with a few other antiquities) belonging to Sātavāhana and Kura kings.[49] Excavations at Nevasa yielded numerous lead coins of the Sātavāhanas from the layers of Period IV associated with the Northern Black Polished Ware, and hence dated to *circa* second-first century BCE.[50] Sātavāhana lead coins from Paithan, Nasik and other sites are preserved in many private collections. Sātavāhana and Kura lead coins are known from Thane also.[51] Coins bearing Kura-ending names, found from various places including the Brahmapuri excavations, are now rightly recognized as belonging to a pre-Sātavāhana dynasty.[52] Kulkarni published a hoard of 40 small lead coins, all square or rectangular with the exception of two round pieces, bearing a three arched *chaitya* or hill, peacock, dog, elephant, human figure and some other devices, belonging to ten different varieties, ascribable to *circa* 2nd-1st century BCE discovered by an agriculturist while ploughing field near Amalner, a town in the Jalgaon district of Maharashtra.[53] A lead coin of Sātavāhana Mahākshatrapa Isamahisa (later corrected as Isimulasa) from Junnar was published by Shobhana Gokhale.[54] Subsequently some more specimens of this type were published. Junnar has yielded many lead coins of this type as well as those of the Sātavāhanas[55] and was a mint-site.[56] Sanjay Godbole has published three lead coins from Prakashe.[57] Finds from Paunar, Pavani, Arvi, Adam, etc. in Vidarbha indicate that the use of lead for coinage continued in the subsequent periods too. Adam has yielded quite a few specimens of Taxila and local type coins, 'The first ever reported lead portrait coins of the Satavahanas' and also a mould therefor.[58] Finds from Bhokardan[59] and Ter[60] also attest to the use of lead from 3rd-2nd century BCE onwards, though the coins at these sites appear a bit later. Un-inscribed lead coins like those of Bhokardan have been discovered from Sillod and neighbouring areas in district Aurangabad also.[61]

GUJARAT

Lead coins of the Western Kshatrapas were published by Rapson and have been referred to above. A hoard of nearly 5000 lead coins was reported from district Junagarh nearly half of which consisted of Bull/Hill type coins of the Western Kshatrapas.[62] Some stray finds have been made subsequently also.[63]

Moreshwar G. Dikshit published in 1951 a hoard of about 600 lead coins from Karvan which included un-inscribed coins of *circa* 1st century BCE onwards and also included Sātavāhana coins of Central Indian and Deccan fabrics and one Gupta coin.[64] Some unidentified lead coins have been found in excavations at Vadnagar in Mehsana district.[65] Amreli has yielded Sātavāhana and Kshatrapa lead coins.[66] Shamalaji in district Sabarkantha yielded some non-descript lead coins from Period II (50-400 CE).[67] Three lead coins of the Maitrakas (480-766 CE) and some lead objects were recovered in excavations at Devnimori[68] while lead objects have been found from Jokha in district Surat and Dhatva on the southern bank of the Tapi.[69]

MADHYA PRADESH

Punch-marked lead coins from Ujjain referred to above indicate the use of this metal for coinage in Madhya Pradesh at quite an early period. Subsequent discoveries of lead coins amongst uninscribed Ujjain series indicate its continuity in the early centuries before and after the start of the Current Era. Numerous early coins are preserved in the coin collections of Dr. D.L. Neema, sarvashri Girish Sharma, Dau Lal Johri, etc. at Indore.

During the season of 1960-61, excavations at Eran yielded a lead piece from the top layer of period II B bearing the impression of a die of king Indragupta in the Brāhmī characters palaeographically assigned to *circa* 200 BCE.[70] Two lead coins obtained from Tripuri near Jabalpur, one un-inscribed and the other issued by king Abhayadatta, datable to *circa* 1st century BCE, were published by R.R. Bhargava who latter brought to light another lead coin of Bhavadatta also from this site.[71] A lead coin obtained from somewhere in Madhya Pradesh bearing the legend 'Mugamukhe' in Aśokan Brāhmī characters was published by R.D. Bhatt in 1992 and quite a few more similar pieces have come to light subsequently.[72] An early un-inscribed round lead coin with elephant-rider and Ujjaini symbol has been published by Rahman Ali.[73] Some fish-shaped pieces of lead have recently been obtained from the Shivna at Mandsaur and Shipra river at Ujjain.[74] Lead coins found from Maheshwar have been detailed in the foregoing pages. Lead coins of Sātakarṇi, Gautamiputra Siri Puḷumāvi, Dāmabhadra, Maghasiri, etc. collected from Ujjain area have also been published recently.[75] Details of lead coins from Maheshwar have been given in the foregoing pages. Numerous lead coins have been found from Mandsaur also in the recent years.

CHHATTISGARH

Lead coins of various local types and a new series have also been discovered in the recent decades from Malhar in district Bilaspur of Chhattisgarh (earlier a part of

Madhya Pradesh).[76] Some coins of the new series issued by Silalusiri, Achaḍasiri, Maghasiri, Siriyamagha and Paramagha show 100% pure lead while some others show zinc and iron as the trace metals. Many specimens reveal that lead was alloyed with copper also.

Orissa

Excavations at Sisupalgarh by B.B. Lal had yielded 14 lead coins of which five came from the levels datable to *circa* 200 CE. Other objects indicated the use of lead up to 350 CE. Lal thought it probable that the availability of lead ore in the neighborhood of Sambalpur may have provided the metal but also referred to "other sources in the proximity being in Manbhum district of Bihar and in Surguja state and Raipur district of the Central Provinces" (now Chhattisgarh).[77]

Uttar Pradesh

Only one lead coin has been reported from Uttar Pradesh so far. It was a coin of Sujyeshṭha obtained in excavations at Atranjikhera in district Etah from second century BCE deposits.[78] It may, however, be added here that the earliest un-inscribed coins from Kauśāmbī show copper to the extent of 96.14 percent and the rest include impurities like tin, lead, nickel, sulphur, arsenic, iron, calcium, etc. There are, however, specimens containing 16.93% lead which seems to have been deliberately alloyed for lowering the melting point which would provide ease in casting.[79]

Rajasthan

In spite of the availability of galena from Zawar and Ajmer, Alwar, Pali, etc. it is surprising that Rajasthan has not yielded any lead coin though a lead seal with a perforated knob and bearing the Brāhmī legend 'Mālavajanapada(sa)' is known to have been found at Rairh.[81]

Haryana

"Very crude cast copper coins bearing the legend *Kāḍasa* in early Brahmi characters, probably of the third or early second century B.C.", now generally and popularly referred to as Kāḍa coins, were first brought to light by Alexander Cunningham in 1891.[80] He, however, did not record the find spots of his coins and mentioned their discovery along with the coins of the Kuṇindas.[82] This indicated Punjab (of the pre-partition days, i.e. including parts of present day Punjab states of India and Pakistan, Haryana and parts of Himachal Pradesh of the former) as the provenance of the Kāḍa coins. The specimens from the collections of Charles Rodgers and Whitehead confirm this.[83] The British Museum possesses 14 specimens of these coins distinguished into six varieties (Var. a – f) by Allan.[84] The legend *Kāḍasa* has been explained as a genitive singular of Kāḍa, the name of a king, place or tribe. Excavations at Sugh in district Yamunanagar of Haryana during 1964-66 yielded another specimen and I have brought to light fifteen more pieces collected from the site five of which are made of copper and the remaining ten of lead. Seven lead coins bearing the Brāhmī legend *Sujeṭhasa*, three issued by king Gomitra and one by Vishṇumitra, continuing the coin-devices of Kāḍa, have also been obtained from the same site which has also yielded a lead human figure of *circa* second century BCE, some indeterminate objects and even lead lumps as described in the foregoing pages.[85] Lead coins of Pusamita, Pratishṭhāna, Bhavanandi, etc. have been recovered from Mughalpura near Uklana in district Hisar in the recent years.[86] Some unidentified lead coins have been found from Agroha also.

Quite a few years back, a friend sent to me the photograph of a cast lead coin bearing a camel to right facing a railed post on the obverse and probably an elephant on the reverse (round, 2.0 cm, 3 mm, 2.66 g or 24 *ratti*) from Jind in Haryana. Two lead sigils of the Yaudheyas bearing the Brāhmī legend 'Yaudheyānāṃ' have been obtained from Naurangabad in Bhiwani district of Haryana.[87] Another lead signet of the tribe has also been published some time back.[88] Quite a good number of Yaudheya coins of Bull/Elephant type ascribable to *circa* second-first century BCE are made of potin indicating the availability of lead to the Yaudheyas.

Punjab

The earliest lead coin from Punjab is a small uninscribed coin of 1.65 g weight obtained from Charan on the northern bank of the Satluj about 25 km west-northwest of Ropar (Rupnagar). The site has also yielded a Rājanya coin of the same weight in this metal as also another 17 mm square piece of 7.1 g belonging to king Ajamitra of Punjab. It bears the symbol of a small circle with four crescents around on one side and a taurine placed on a wavy line on the other. Two lead coins showing a human figure on the obverse and a temple structure on the reverse obtained from Sunet thought to belong to the Audumbara tribe and a lead seal with 3-line Kharoshṭhī inscription of *circa* 1st century BCE belonging to one Spikalaka has been discovered from Sanghol in district Fatehgarh Sahib in Punjab.[89] It is to be noted that lead objects and 157 lead coins of Lion/Heracles type of Rajuvula and two lead coins of Strato (I or II) from Taxila brought to light by John Marshall provide ample evidence of the use of lead in early historic period.[90]

Spatial and Chronological Consideration

We thus see that except Kerala, all the states of south India are quite rich in lead coins. Maharashtra, Gujarat, Madhya Pradesh, Chhattisgarh and Orissa too have yielded lead coins in good numbers whereas only sporadic finds have been made from Uttar Pradesh, Haryana and Punjab. The eastern states of Jharkhand, Bihar, West Bengal and the North-East lack lead species. Even Rajasthan, Uttarakhand, Himachal Pradesh and Jammu & Kashmir are blank as far as the use of lead coins is concerned. Use of lead for coinage started in *circa* fifth century BCE but it was very rare. Kauṭilya's *Arthaśāstra* and evidence from Vidarbha indicates that lead was known and continued to be used during the Mauryan period also. Most of the un-inscribed cast copper and lead coins of Andhra Pradesh, Maharashtra and Madhya Pradesh may be dated to this period. Post-Mauryan, i.e., pre-, Sātavāhana and post-

Sātavahana coinage (together with those of their contemporaries and feudatories) shows a fair proportion of lead in almost the whole of the Deccan and other adjoining regions occupied by these dynasties. Post-Mauryan finds from Andhra Pradesh, Maharashtra and adjoining areas of Karnataka, Gujarat and Madhya Pradesh furnish evidence of the use of the malleable metal in the early centuries BCE to be continued in these and other parts of the country noted above. The Western Kshatrapas seem to have utilized lead for low denomination coinage for quite a long time from Bhūmaka and Nahapāṇa onwards to the Gupta period.

The Karvan hoard of lead coins published by M.G. Dikshit contained a lead coin of king Chandragupta II bearing the legend Vikrama.[91] Lead coins published by Jurgen Moller and M.B. Mitchiner[92] probably belonged to Junagarh hoard from which Dilip Rajgor also published lead coins of Chandragupta II, Kumāragupta I and Skandagupta.[93] The composition of the hoard pointed to the circulation of these coins in Malwa. We thus see that from about the middle of the first millennium BCE to the fifth century CE, lead continued to be used for coinage in parts of India as noted above. Lead coins issued by some of the Gupta rulers indicate that the metal was still available to them during the 4th-5th centuries. The use of lead thereafter seems to have dwindled in general but coins here and there continued to be struck on the basis of earlier available species and metal.

Scientific Studies and the Availability of Ores

In this age of science and technology, analysis of coins and their composition have assumed great importance as they provide information relating to the source of metals used in mints and technological trends in minting.[94] Unfortunately, however, systematic studies of Indian coins of various periods, dynasties, regions and metals are rather scarce.[95]

We do not know the source of lead for the punch-marked lead coins from Vidarbha and Malwa referred to above. Successful efforts have been made in the recent decades for the search of copper and lead-zinc ores in the Ran Mangli prospect, Nagpur district. Geophysical investigations have also been undertaken for lead, zinc and copper in the Chichgarh-Wadsa area, Bhandara district, Maharashtra. Geochemical sampling for copper, lead and zinc in Sukwari and Bagwari area, Sidhi district and polymetallic mineralisation in Imalia-Bhula-Navalia and adjoining areas, Jabalpur district, Madhya Pradesh make this area to be another possibility for being the source. In the absence of any chemical analysis, however, it is difficult to hazard even a guess.

There is another possibility. Though not certain, it is probable that the very source of silver which supplied the metal for punch-marked coins may have provided lead also as lead and silver occur invariably together. It has been noted above that in the process of extraction of silver from argentiferous galena a large amount of lead is produced as by-product. H.C. Bhardwaj has observed that "The Indian subcontinent is in general poor in mineral resources of silver except the Bawdwin mines (Shan state of Burma), where it occurs in the form of zinc-blend argentiferous galena. These mines are very rich and there is evidence of their early exploitation. The Bawdwin ore is primarily a lead-zinc sulphide with silver in substantial amounts and in addition it has cobalt, nickel, antimony and tin as minor impurities".[96] While pointing out to Zawar and other sources of argentiferous galena in Bihar and Mysore in India, Franjal mines of Afghanistan and Armenia and argentiferous lead mines of Persia, he states that "On the basis of the impurity pattern it is most likely that the silver punch-marked coins were obtained from the argentiferous galena ore of Bawdwin mines of Burma".[97] But the use of punch-marked coinage predates trade between India and Southeast Asia for which there is no evidence before 1st century BCE/CE. This trade flourished in the first millennium of our era.[98] A thorough probe into the source/sources of metal for punch-marked coinage still remains a desideratum.

K.T.M. Hegde who made chemical and spectrometric studies in Kshatrapa silver coins also concluded that the metal for these coins was imported.[99] But Bhardwaj has pointed out that there is a likelihood of exploitation of Zawar mines of Rajasthan as the source of Kshatrapa silver coins since both the Kshatrapa coins and Zawar mines have the common impurity of lead, zinc, manganese, aluminium and vanadium.[100]

Hegde's analysis of the lead coins from Nagara (Gujarat) determined the amount of lead and trace elements as following –

	Pb	Zn	Mg	Al	Others	Total
1.	97.40	1.26	0.26	0.38	0.70	100
2.	97.21	1.18	0.42	0.29	0.90	100

On the basis of the spectrographic analysis showing over 97% lead and zinc as the major impurity, Hegde[101] felt inclined to believe that the source of metal for these lead coins are the Zawar mines (25 km south of Udaipur in the Aravalli region) of Rajasthan. The lead coins got analysed by Jha and Rajgor, however, showed the presence of nickel which was not detected before, and only 0.02 percentage of zinc in comparison to Hegde's 1.0 percent.[102]

It may be pointed out that copper, lead, zinc, gold & associated minerals are abundantly found in Rajasthan from an area of over 15000 km.[103] Lead-zinc-copper deposits have been located in Dariba-Rajpura belt, Udaipur district; Dariba-Suras belt and Hirakhera blocks, Pur-Banera belt, Bhilwara district; Bajta-Maharani Mata-Ghatiali sector at the northern part of the Sawar-Bajta belt and Sawar-Ganeshpura area. Geophysical investigation has indicated the existence of lead and copper ore occurrence in Saradhna and Lohakhan Taragarh areas also in Ajmer district, Rajasthan. We thus see that the Udaipur-Bhilwara region contains zinc-blended argentiferous ore. Referring to the vast heaps of mine debris and a lead piece recovered from the slag dump containing 97.5% lead and 150 ppm silver from Rajpur-Dariba (80 km northeast of Udaipur in Rajasthan), A.K. Biswas has also observed that "The evidence show 'the gregarious nature of working' of the Lead-Silver ore in the area during the successive Pre-Maurya, Maurya, Śuṅga and Kuṣāṇa periods of Indian history".[104] Copper, lead and zinc have been located in the Khandia area, district

Baroda, Gujarat also but there is no evidence that the mineral wealth of this area was ever exploited in ancient times. A determination of the permanent isotopes in the Kshatrapa lead coins is desired to corroborate the evidence.

Referring to the use of lead coins in Tamilnadu, R. Krishnamurthy has observed that "Lead has been reported to have been found in Rajasthan and Bihar. But Myanmar endowed with large deposits of lead may have been the source to the Chola country and the metal would have arrived through Kaveri-poom-payyinam port".[105]

Seven lead coins each from Vaddamanu and Veerapuram have been analyzed by Ganorkar *et al.*[106] and the results of their compositions are given below.

S.No.	Coin no.	Pb (%)	Cu (%)	Fe (%)	Ag (%)
Vaddamanu					
1.	286	99.90	0.04	—	0.02
2.	569	99.92	0.03	—	0.05
3.	857	99.87	0.07	0.05	0.08
4.	1135	99.89	0.05	—	0.02
5.	1300	99.91	0.02	0.02	0.10
6.	1468	99.88	0.03	0.06	0.04
7.	1552	99.85	0.04	0.02	0.04
Veerapuram					
1.	4747	99.70	0.18	—	0.01
2.	5209	99.58	0.14	—	0.02
3.	4917	99.81	0.14	—	0.02
4.	4533	99.83	0.12	0.01	0.02
5.	4748	99.21	0.51	—	—
6.	5920	99.83	0.01	—	0.02
7.	5477	99.38	0.01	—	0.01

The excavation report states that the Roman lead coin or lead bullae (No. 4747) had a silver coating over it[107] but the analytical data do not show the presence of silver which may have been lost during the process of cleaning.[108] Lead was found alloyed with some copper coins also which had some quantity of tin as well. Smaller quantity (1.42% – 3.03%) may have been accidental or due to the reuse of scrap metal while the higher amount of lead (5.85 – 10.3%) suggests a deliberate addition to improve machinability and to lower the melting point of copper.[109]

Maritime trade between Rome and the Deccan in the early centuries before and after the beginning of the Current Era is a well known fact evidenced by numerous finds of Roman and other Western coins.[110] The export items included pearls, diamonds, ivory, spices, aromatics, tortoise shell, silk, peacocks, parrots, etc. while gold and silver coins, tin, lead, glass, coral and wine were the main imports. There is, however, no evidence of the Roman gold and silver coins to have entered India before the first century CE. Lead coins from Vaddamanu include un-inscribed Lion type,

Lion type of Sada, Sātavāhana, Elephant/Ujjain symbol type Ikshvāku and worn out pieces while those from Veerapuram belong to the Mahāraṭhis, Sātavāhana and Ikshvākus. All these coins thus may be put between 1st century BCE and 3rd century CE. D. Raja Reddy observes that "The singular properties of lead, such as low melting point of 327° C, ease of casting and fabrication, high density low strength, acid resistance, chemical stability in air, water and earth probably made the Andhra rulers prefer this metal for coins."[111]

The lead content of more than 99% in these coins, however, reveals that metal purification technology in those days had reached a high degree of perfection matching modern times. The adoption of lead for coinage indicates the availability of lead in large quantities in the post-Maurya period to the pre-Sātavāhana dynasties, to the Sātavāhanas and their feudatories and successors. Use of Roman gold (may be as bullion), silver, copper and lead (including potin) coins by the Sātavāhanas presents an interesting picture of the economic conditions of the times. Easy availability of the metal, ease of manufacturing and cheaper goods and the requirement for small local day to day transactions may have lead to the production of lead coins in the region. But it is difficult to determine whether these coins were made of indigenous or imported lead.

Andhra Pradesh has got quite large gold, copper, lead, zinc, silver, nickel, tungsten, antimony, bismuth arsenic, cobalt, molybdenum & platinum group of metals. Detailed investigations have been undertaken in the recent years for copper-lead-zinc deposits near Mamandur in South Arcot district; zinc, lead and copper ore minerals in Chelima area, Nandyal taluk, Kurnool district; copper-lead deposits of Agnigundala, Peddagavalakonda, Bandlamottu and Dhukonda blocks in Agnigundala mineralised belt, Guntur district in Andhra Pradesh. This indicates the availability of lead from indigenous sources. The presence of large number of pits and old habitation sites near some of these furnish evidence of the mining activity carried out in these mines in ancient times. The ore from Agnigundala has significant amount of tin which is generally not seen in un-inscribed lead coins of Andhra suggesting that this was not the ore for making those coins. Interestingly the lead isotopes of the ores of Zawar, Agnigundala and Bandlamottu do not match with the lead isotopes of some of the Sātavāhana and Ikshvāku lead coins indicating some other source of lead.[112] Only further investigations and testing of a large number of samples may lead us to a definite conclusion.

Numerous lead coins from Malhar in district Bilaspur of Chhattisgarh (1st century BCE to 4th century CE) indicate that the early rulers issued coins with high percentage of lead, even 100% in some cases, whereas it dwindles later. The coin-analysis reveals that the technique of alloying was not known to the local people although for the purpose of hardening they used zinc. Iron may have been natural or added deliberately for strengthening and/or increasing the weight.[113] It may also be mentioned that Malhar seems to have stood on a trade route connecting Kauśāmbī with Andhra as indicated by some Roman and Byzantine coins found from the region.[114] So even in this case we are not sure of the actual source of lead used for

Malhar coins though Sankera hills, Turee Pahar, Bairuki and Panch Pahar are the lead bearing localities in the Santhal Parganas and the ore is found at Chicholi in Raipur, Saleemanabad in Jabalpur and Joga in Hoshangabad also.

In Karnataka lead occurs in the Sandur hills of Bellary area. Recently successful drilling operations for the search of lead have been undertaken in Kadikangalbetta and Ramanahalli areas, Hassan district. In Uttar Pradesh copper, lead, zinc and associated minerals are found in an area of over 1000 square km. Lead is known to occur in Garhwal-Kumaun area of Uttarakhand. In Bihar detailed investigations in the recent decades have revealed the presence of copper, lead and zinc in Baraganda area; copper, lead and zinc around Ganganpur in Bengabad and Kusmarja and adjoining areas in Hazaribagh district; copper, lead and zinc in Bengabad, Jhalakdiha area; copper and lead deposits at Dondlo, Hazaribagh district; copper, lead and zinc in the Dudhijharana-Kharikhanda area, Bhagalpur district; copper-lead deposits in Bentanagar (Karaikela), Rajkharswan-Sini and Duarpuram-Kadamdiha area, Singhbhum district. West Bengal has shown deposits of copper, lead and zinc in parts of Midnapore district, and Mahulbani, Bengbuta areas and in the areas east of Gohalberia, Midnapore district, Bankura, Purulia and Midnapore districts.

Lead coin of Sujyeshṭha found from Atranjikhera in district Etah of Uttar Pradesh seems to have been a drift from Sugh in Haryana which is the only other known site yielding coins of this ruler.[115] But from where did the lead for un-inscribed Kauśāmbī coins come is only a matter of guess yet. Lead coins from Haryana have not been analyzed yet. Haryana has got some limited area of about 400 square km from which lead, zinc, copper, gold and associated minerals are being exploited but it is not sure if the mines were used in ancient times also. Sugh is located at the foot of the Himalayas near Jagadhari in district Yamunanagar. D.N. Wadia has referred to ores of lead in the Himalayas also[116] and Shimla (Subathu), Sirmur and Kullu are the areas where lead ore occurs. In Pakistan Hazara and Murree districts bear lead ores. An alternate source may have been Afghanistan. C.L. Reedy has observed that Afghanistan had an excess of metal available for export – copper, zinc, tin and lead – to adjacent regions.[117] The Himalayan source seems to be quite likely but in the absence of the determination of the permanent isotopes of lead in the Himalayan ores and coins from Haryana it remains only a guess.

Based on a statement in *The Periplus of the Erythrean Sea*[118] (which is a first century CE log book of an unknown Greek sailor in Egypt who steered his vessels into India) that lead was imported in India from the west through the ports of Barygaza (Bhṛigukachchha, modern Broach in Gujarat) and Muziris (modern Crangnore). Pliny told us that "India has neither brass nor lead"[119] and Warmington observed that "lead was imported along with copper into the chief western marts of India mainly for native coinages."[120] The data cited above, however, clearly indicates that lead was known from very early times and was available in most parts of India and used for coinage from about the middle of the first millennium BCE but it will be future scientific studies which will enlighten us about the sources of metal, whether alien or indigenous, down to about the middle of the first millennium of the Current Era that were utilized for minting of lead coins in India.

NOTES AND REFERENCES

1. Originaly it was *plumbum nigrum*, whereas *plumbum candidum* was used for tin. The English word 'plumbing' also derives from this this Latin root as plumbeous or lead bobs were generally used for maintaining vertical alignments.
2. Ball, Valentine (1881), *Manual of the Geology of India, Part III, Economic Geology*, Calcutta.
3. *Miscellaneous Publication, No. 27: Exploration and Development of Non-ferrous Metals in India*, Geological Survey of India, Calcutta, 1977.
4. H. Hargreaves in *Archaeological Survey of India – Annual Report 1925-26, Section II, Exploration and Research, Frontier Circle*, p. 70.
5. Marshall, John (Ed.) (1973), *Mohenjo-daro and the Indus Civilisation* (reprint, Delhi); Mackay, E.J.H. (1938), *Further Excavations at Mahenjo-daro*, New Delhi, and (1976), *Chanhu-daro Excavations 1935-36* (reprint, Varanasi); Vats, M.S. (1940), *Excavations at Harappa*, Delhi, 1940.
6. Biswas Arun Kumar and S. Biswas (1996), *Minerals and Metals in Ancient India*, Vol. I, New Delhi, pp. 61, 110 and 329.
7. Pascoe, E., "Mineral and Metals", in Marshall, Vol. II, pp. 676-77. In the early historic context, maximum evidence of lead came from Taxila, Sirkap and Sirsukh [Marshall, John (1975), *Taxila*, 2 vols, (reprinted Varanasi), pp. 169, 191, 509, 572, 585, 592, 649, 836, 838, etc.] the metal for which may have also been obtained from sources mentioned above for Mohenjo-daro and other Harappan sites.
8. Sankalia *et al.* (1971), p. 402. For radiocarbon dates of Chalcolithic Navdatoli see Agrawal, D.P. and S. Kusumgar (1974), *Prehistoric Chronology and Radiocarbon Dating in India*, Delhi, p. 116. Earlier excavations at Navdatoli had yielded some lead objects from Period V and VI datable respectively to 100 BCE – 100 CE and 100 – 500 CE (Sankalia *et al.*, p. 210. The source of lead slags of Navdatoli may have been from central Indian deposits, Rajasthan or Andhra.
9. See for details Nanda, Rajni and Dilip K. Chakrabarti (July 1981 – January 1982), "Lead in Early India: A Study of the Geological, Archaeological and Literary Data", *The Indian Historical Review*, New Delhi, Vol. III, Nos. 1-2, pp. 1-18. The authors have made a comprehensive study of lead in early India from different sources. I am thankful to Prof. Himanshu Prabha Ray (JNU, New Delhi) for kindly making available to me a zerox copy of this very useful article.
10. Rajgor (2001).
11. Bhandarkar, D.R. (1921), *The Carmichael Lectures on Ancient Indian Numismatics*, Calcutta (Reprint, Patna, 1984), p. 142; Fausboll, V. (1963), *The Jātaka*, London, Vol. IV, p. 12. According to Upendra Thakur "The *Nidānakathā* actually refers to lead *Kahāpaṇa*" but he does not cite the reference ["The First Coins: A Study in Evolution and Growth" in Sircar, D.C. (Ed.) (1970), *Early Indian Indigenous Coins*, Calcutta, p. 47].
12. Gupta, Chandrashekhar (January 1991), "Sīsa-Kahāpaṇa: The Lead Punch-marked Coin", *ICSNL*, No. 6, p. 1.
13. Sharma, Varsha S. (October 2007), "Lead Punch-Marked Coins from Central India", *Nidhi*, Nagpur, Vol. II, pp. 21-23. Some more specimens of lead punchmarked coins have also come to light in the recent years.
14. Agrawala, V.S., P.L. Gupta and T.R. Goirala (1954), "A Further Note on the Minute Silver Punchmarked Coins of the Raupya-Mashaka Series", *JNSI*, XVI, p. 19; Hardaker, Terry (1999), *The Mashaka Fractional Coinage of Ancient India: A Type Catalogue*, Anjaneri: IIRNS, p. 3.
15. *IAR*, 1960-61, p. 55; Bajpai, K.D. (October 1975), "New Excavated Numismatic Material bearing on the History of Malwa", *Research Journal: Humanities & Social Sciences*, University of Indore, Vol. IV, No. 2, p. 1, Pl. I-A.

16. Since it is not possible to list every find of lead coins, only important numismatic finds have been considered here. Many other finds of lead coins may be gathered from articles published in the *JNSI, ND, Studies in South Indian Coins, ICSNL, Numismatic Chronicle, JAINS, Chandrapur Coin Society News Bulletin* and various other numismatic publications.
17. *CAI*, pp. 109-11.
18. *IMC*, I, pp. 208-13, pl. XXIII.
19. Rapson, James (1908), *Catalogue of the Coins of the Andhra Dynasty the Western Kṣatrapas the Traikūṭaka Dynasty and the "Bodhi" Dynasty*, British Museum, London (reprinted 1967). For some stray important finds of Sātavāhana lead coins see also Mirashi, V.V. (1946), "A Lead Coin of Sātakarṇi", *JNSI*, VIII (i), pp. 18-21, pl. II.A-1; (1949), "A Lead Coin of Sātavāhana", *Ibid.*, XI (i), pp. 5-6, pl. II.11); (1983), *ND*, VII, pp. 24-26 for an oval lead coin (27 x 21 mm, 5.95 g) attributed to King Kṛishṇa, etc.
20. Sarma, I.K. (1980), *Coinage of the Sātavāhana Empire*, Delhi, pp. 56 ff.
21. Bajpai, K.D. (1976), *Indian Numismatic Studies*, New Delhi, p. 171.
22. Rapson, *op. cit.*, pp. lxxxi ff, clxxxii ff; Sastry, P.V. Parabrahma (June 1978), "Unknown Coins of Satavahanas and their Predecessors", *ND*, Vol. II, Part I, pp. 10-21; Gupta, P.L. (December 1978), "Kot-Lingala Find of Post-Mautyan Coins", *Ibid.*, Vol. II, Part II, pp. 24-33; Reddy, D. Raja and P. Suryanarayana Reddy (1987), *Kotalingala Coinage of the Satavahanas and other rulers – A Profile*, Hyderabad; etc.
23. Reddy and Reddy (1987), *Ibid.*; (1989), "Some Rare Coins of Satavahana Dynasty" in Handa, Devendra (Ed.), *Ajasya-Śrī - Recent Studies in Indology (Prof. Ajay Mitra Shastri Felicitation Volume)*, Vol. 1, Delhi, pp. 293-300, pls. 36-39; (2007), "Unpublished Kotalingala Coins and a Discussion on Ujjain Symbol", *JNSI*, LXIX, pp. 68-71; Reddy, D. Raja and T. Devender Rao (2007), "Kotalingala Coins: Further Observations", *Ibid.*, pp. 72-76.
24. *Ibid.* The same authors have published potin coins also from Sangareddy bearing the *svastika* device (1988-89), "Svastika Type Satavahana Coins", *ND*, vols. 12-13, pp. 17 ff.
25. Sastry, T.V.G. (1983), *Vaddamanu Excavations and Explorations in Krishna Valley*, BACRI, Hyderabad, pp. 1-11; Kamalkar, G. and M. Veerender, "Coins from Veerapuram Excavations", *Numismatic Bulletin*, No. 3, BACRI, Hyderabad, p. 29.
26. Ghosh, N.C. and Ajaya Mitra Shastri (June 1981), "A Coin of Kumara Sata from Satanikota", *ND*, V (I), pp. 8 ff.
27. Bai, M. Kasturi (1987), "Coins from Vaddamanu Excavations", in *Numismatics & Archaeology* (Eds. Gupta, P.L. and A.K. Jha), IIRNS, Anjaneri, pp. 102-13; (1991), "Archaeological Significance of Coins Unearthed at Veerapuram", *JNSI*, LIII, pp. 34-48. Reddy, D. Raja and P. Suryanarayana Reddy (1991, *JNSI*, LIII, pp. 49-51) have published five lead Sātavāhana Ship/Arched Hill type coins from Chebrolu near Amaravathi.
28. Ramalakshman, A. (2002), *Andhra Pradesh Archaeology – A Review, 1987 – 2001*, Dept. of Archaeology and Museums, Govt. of Andhra Pradesh, Hyderabad. See also *JNSI*, Vol. LXVI (2004), p. 29.
29. Rao, M. Rama (1961), *Satavahana Coins in the Andhra Pradesh Govt. Museum*, Hyderabad.
30. Subramanyam, R. (1964,), *Salihundam*, Hyderabad, p. 117, Pl. XLVI.
31. Reddy, D. Raja and P. Suryanarayana Reddy (1984), *Uninscribed Coins of Andhra*, Hyderabad Numismatic Society, Hyderabad, p. 22.
32. Reddy, D. Raja (2004), Presidential Address, *XIVth Annual Conference of the South Indian Numismatic Society*, Thiruvananthapuram, Feb. 13-14; Reddy, D. Raja and G.V.R.K. Acharyulu (2005), "Weights of Uninscribed Coins Found in Andhra", *JNSI*, Vol. LXVII, pp. 56-62.
33. *JNSI*, LVII, pp. 18-25, Pls. 1-III. The word 'potin', was the name given by 19th century metallurgists to a special alloy of bronze, which contained an unusually high percentage of

tin (up to 25%), and quite often an appreciable percentage of lead as well. It was its metallurgical composition that made it the choice of moneyers in Gaul, roughly the area of today's France and Belgium, between about 100 BC and the beginning of the Roman Empire under Augustus. In India this term has been used rather loosely to indicate coins having an alloy of copper with baser materials like lead, ash, etc.

34. *Ibid.*, XLVII (1985), pp. 26-28.
35. Subramayam, R. (1962), *A Catalogue of Ikshvaku Coins in A.P. Govt. Museum*, Museum Series, No. 5, Hyderabad. A hoard and many stray Ikshvāku lead coins were recovered in excavations at Vaddamanu (Kasturi Bai, *loc. cit.*). See also Veerender, M. (1996), "Coinage of Ikshvakus", in Maheshwari, K.K. and Biswajeet Rath (Eds.) (1996), *Numismatic Panorama (Essays in honour of Late Sh. S.M. Shukla)*, New Delhi, pp. 169-77 and Pieper (2013), pp. 288-91, nos. 722-38.
36. Thirteen lead and potin coins of the Śālaṅkāyanas were reported from Ghaṇṭaśāḷa (district Krishna, Andhra Pradesh). For details see Sarma, I.K. (1989), "Shalankayana Coins from Ghantashala, District Krishna (A.P.)", in *Ajaya-Śrī*, Vol. 1, pp. 313-17, Pl. 41.
37. Reddy, D. Raja and P. Suryanarayana Reddy (1993), *Coins of the Meghavahana Dynasty of Coastal Andhra*, Numismatic Society of Hydrabad, Hyderabad.
38. Nanda and Chakrabarti, *op. cit.*, pp. 11-12.
39. Rao, M. Rama (1961), p. 1; Reddy, D. Raja (2004), "Sources of Lead for Andhra Coins", *JNSI*, LXVI, pp.28-31.
40. Anantpur, Brahmagiri, Chandravalli, Guntur, Kondapur, Kurnool, Nelakondapalli, Sangareddy, Veerapuram, Zaheerabad, etc. are the important find spots of Mahāraṭhi coins. For details see Reddy, D. Raja and Reddy, P. Suryanarayana (1983), *Coins of the Satraps of the Satavahana Era*, Numismatic Society of Hyderabad, Hyderabad. Ten Mahāraṭhi lead coins of heavy weight (11 to 34 g) were also published by the same authors from Zaheerabad, Sangareddy and Anantpur in Andhra (*JNSI*, LIV, 1992, pp. 29-33 and by L.C. Gupta from Guntur (*Ibid.*, LV, 1993, pp. 31-39). See also Sastry, T.V.G. (1987), "Maharathi Coins & Their Chronology", *JNSI*, XLIX, p. 33 & Ahmad, Nisar (1990), "The Maharathi Coins of Karnataka", *Ibid.*, LII, pp. 74-80. Horse type Mahātalavara coins mostly come from Anantpur, Chandravaram, Cuddapah, Dhulikatta, Kalyanadurg, Kondapur, Kotalingala, Peddabankur, Phanigiri, Polakonda, Sangareddy and Warangal [Mirashi, V.V. (1953), "A Coin of Mahatalavara", *JNSI*, XV, p. 117; Reddy, D. Raja and P. Suryanarayana Reddy (1993), "New Mahatalavara Coins", *JNSI*, LV, pp. 42-43; (1991), "Mahātalavara and Mahāsenāpati Coins", *Studies in South Indian Coins*, Vol. I, pp. 71-80). Important find spots of Mahāgrāmika coins are Kondapur, Peddavengi and Veerapuram (Chaudhary, Krishnanand (1987), "On Mahāgrāmika Coins", *JNSI*, XLIX, pp. 34-35). Sebaka coins come from Hyderabad, Kotalingala, Pusad (district Yavatmal in Vidarbha), etc. (*ND*, I, ii, pp. 17-22; VII, pp. 27-31; *JNSI*, LIII, pp. 32-33; LXIX, pp. 172-86; *ICSNL*, No. 38, pp. 8-10; No. 39, pp. 45-48; etc.). It has also to be noted that because of the malleability of lead and ease of working it many forgeries of lead coins have also been detected recently.
41. Raman, K.V. (1987), "Numismatography of Tamil Nadu", *JNSI*, XLIX, p. 206; Krishnan, K.G. (1989) "Coins from the Andipatti Hoard", *Epigraphia Indica*, XL, Part IV, pp. 139-40; Krishnamurthy, R. (1996), 'Presidential Address: Coin Circulation in Ancient Tamil Region, c. 400 B.C. – C. 600 A.D', *JNSI*, Vol. LVIII, p. 11.
42. *IAR, 1962-63*, pp. 182-84; *JNSI*, XXXI (1969), pp. 185-86.
43. Raman, K.V. (1991), "South Indian Numismatics with Special Reference to Tamilnadu", *JNSI*, LIII, p. 18; Sarma, I.K. (1992), *South Indian Coinage – A Review of Recent Discoveries*, New Era Publications, Madras, p. 21.

44. *JNSI*, Vol. LVIII (1996), pp. 7-8. Ambasamudram in district Nellai Kattabomman of Tamilnadu has yielded a lead coin of the great Rājarāja Chola (*JNSI*, LVII, 1995, p. 57).
45. Wheeler, R.E.M. (1947-48), "Brahmagiri and Chandravalli 1947", *Ancient India*, Bulletin of the Archaeological Survey of India, New Delhi, No. 4, pp. 287 ff..
46. Thapar, B.K. (1957), "Maski 1954: A chalcolithic site of the southern Deccan", *Ibid.*, No. 13, p. 120, Pl. XXX.1.
47. Gupta, L.C. (1987), "Lead Coins from Karnataka", *ND*, XI, pp. 23-27. Some of these coins may have been modern forgeries. See Mitchiner, Michael (1996), "Forgeries of Ancient Lead Coins of Karnataka", *Ibid.*, Vol. 20, pp. 41-48.
48. Thakur, Ashok Singh and Rajesh Somkuwar (April, 2005), "An Un-inscribed Lead Coin of Vidarbha", *Chandrapur Coin Society News Bulletin*, Chandrapur, No. 3, p. 3.
49. Sankalia, H.D. and M.G. Dikshit (1957), *Excavations at Brahmapurī (Kolhapur), 1945-46*, Poona, p. 50; Gupta, P.L., (1955-57), "Sātavāhana Coins from Brahmapuri (Kolhapur)", *Bulletin of the Prince of Wales Museum*, No, 5, pp. 62 ff.; "Coins from Brahmaouri excavations (1945-46)", *Bulletin of the Deccan College Research Institute*, Poona, XXI, pp. 38-84; (1972), "Sātavāhana Coins from Excavations", in Shastri, Ajay Mitra (Ed.), *Coinage of the Sātavāhanas and Coins from Excavations*, Nagpur, pp. 128-40;; Rao, M. Rama (1955), "Coins of the Kura Kings from Brahmapuri", *JNSI*, XVII, pp. 55-88; Khandalwala, Karl, "Brahmapuri", *Lalit Kala*, no. 7, pp. 29-56; Dutta, Mala (1990), *A Study of the Sātavāhana Coinage*, New Delhi, pp. 142-60.
50. Sankalia, H.D. *et al.* (1960), *From History to Pre-history at Nevasa (1954-56)*, Poona, pp. 165 ff.
51. Dhopate, S.G. (1996), "Studies in Ancient Coins found in Thane", *JNSI*, Vol. LVIII, pp. 33-36, Pl. II.9 & III.1-5. Some lead coins picked up from Elephanta have doubtfully been assigned to the Konkan Mauryas by Mangalam (*ND*, Vol. 15, 1991, pp. 86-94) but P.L. Gupta, in his editorial note appended to the article, thinks that the coins may have been issued by the Portugese in their own territories in India.
52. Gupta, P.L., *BDCRI*, XXI, pp. 41-48; (1972), pp. 129-30. See also Rao, M. Rama (1955), *JNSI*, XVII, pp. 58 ff).
53. *ND*, VII, 1983, pp. 5-10.
54. *Numismatic Studies*, 2, pp. 63-68, pl. VII.1 & *ND*, 15 (1991), 31-40. Later it was rightly assigned to Isimula, a ruler of a local ruling family of Junnar by Radhakrishnan, P.V. and Chumble, P.D. (1999-2000), *ND*, 23-24, pp. 51-56.
55. *ND*, 15, pp. 48-49; 23-24, pp.51-56.
56. Shastri, Ajay Mitra (1996), "Junnar: A Mint-Town of the Sātavāhanas", *Studies in South Indian Coins*, V, pp. 51-56.
57. *JNSI*, LIX (1997), p. 31, Pl. IV.2-4.
58. Nath, Amarendra (1990), *Nidhi*, I, pp. 25-30; (1991), "A Lead Issue of Siva Skanda Satakarni", *Numismatic Studies*, Vol. 1, pp. 59-62; (1992), "A Portrait Coin Mould from Adam", *JNSI*, LIV, pp. 55-59.
59. Deo, S.B. (Ed.) (1974), *Excavations at Bhokardan*, Nagpur, p. 27, Pl. XVI.13, pp. 50 and 62, Pl. XXV.6 for coins and p. 184 for other lead objects.
60. Chapekar, B.N. (1969), *Report on the Excavation at Ter (1958)*, Poona, p. 128.
61. Jha, Amiteshwar (2012-2013), "Some Uninscribed Lead Coins from Sillod and Neighbouring Areas", *ND*, Vols. 36-37, pp. 55-61.
62. *ICSNL*, No. 2 (June, 1990), p. 2. Bull/Hill type lead coins published by Jurgen Moller and M.B. Mitchiner (*ONSNL*, No. 57, December 1978; *ND*, V, I, June 1981, pp. 19-23) probably belonged to this very hoard. Mitchiner attributes these coins to the Ābhīras [Mitchiner, M.B. (1976), *Indo-Greek and Indo-Scythian Coinage*, Vol. 9, London, type 1417].

63. Angal, Devadatta G. (1995),"An Early Kshaharāa (Nahapāṇa) Coin in Lead", *JNSI*, LVII, pp. 34-35. For a comprehensive list of hoards, stray finds and moulds of Western Kshatrapa coins see Jha and Rajgor (1994), Appendix I, pp. 68-77.
64. *JNSI*, XIII, I, pp. 22 ff.
65. *Ibid.*, LIV, 1992, pp. 34-43.
66. Rao, S.R. (1966), *Excavations at Amreli*, Baroda, p. 83, Pl. XXIV.7.
67. Mehta, R.N. and A.J. Patel (1967), *Excavations at Shamalaji*, Baroda, p. 50 & 59, Pl. IVB.
68. Mehta, R.N. and S.N. Chowdhary (1966), *Excavations at Devnimori*, Baroda, p. 104.
69. Nanda and Chakrabarti, *op. cit.*, pp. 6-7.
70. *IAR, 1960-61*, p. 18; Bajpai, K.D. (1992), "Coins from Eran Excavation", *Numismatic Studies*, Vol. 2, New Delhi, p. 24.
71. *ND*, 12-13, 1988-89, pp.6-8; *ICSNL*, No. 5 (December 1990), p. 2.
72. Bhatt, R.D. (1992), "Some Interesting Coins from Madhya Pradesh", *Ibid.*, pp. 37-38, Fig. 1, color plate I.1; *Todywalla's Auctions*, Catalogue No. 11 (September 2005), p. 7, no. 46; *Ibid.*, Catalogue No. 22 (October 2007), p. 4, no. 15.
73. *JNSI*, XLIX (1987), p. 21.
74. Pathak, H.D. and R.C. Thakur (2006), "Unique Fish Shaped Coins from Ujjain", *JNSI*, LXVIII, pp. 38-39, Pl. I.
75. *JNSI*, LXIX, 2007, pp. 38-40, Pl. II.11, 5 &14.
76. Bhargava, R.R. (1955), "Numismatic History of Malhar", *ND*, 19, pp.13-35; Majumdar, Sushmita Bose (2000), *Local Coins of Ancient India – a new series: Coins of Malhār*, IIRNS, Anjaneri.
77. Lal, B.B. (1949), "Sisupalgarh 1948", *Ancient India*, p. 91.
78. *JNSI*, XXX (1968), p. 56; LVI (1994), pp. 1-3.
79. Bhardwaj, H.C. (1987), "Review of Metallurgical Studies of Ancient Indian Coinage", in Gupta, P.L. and A.K. Jha (Eds.), *Numismatics & Archaeology*, IIRNS, Anjaneri, p. 135 & Table I on p. 137.
80. Puri, K.N. (no date), *Excavations at Rairh*, Jaipur, p. 54, Pl. XXVI.22.
81. *CAI*, p. 62, Pl. II.21-22 & p. 71, Pl. V.6.
82. *Ibid.*; *CASR*, II, p. 71.
83. *BMCAI*, pp. xcii-xciii and 145-46, Pls. XX.10-11 & XLIX.14-20.
84. *Ibid.*
85. Handa, Devendra (2006), *Early Indian Coins From Sugh*, New Delhi, pp. 72-98, Pls. XIII-XV.
86. *ICSNL*, No. 38 (Jan – March 2006), pp. 4-7.
87. Śāstrī, Yogānanda (1999), *Prāchīna Bhārata meṃ Yaudheya Gaṇarājya* (Hindi), New Delhi, pp. 127-28, Pls. 5-6.
88. Ahmad, Nisar and F.K. Nadooshan (1993), "A lead signet of the Yaudheyas and reappraisal of their certain published seals", *JNSI*, LV, pp. 152-54.
89. Kumar, Manmohan and Sudarshan Kumar (1980), "Some Interesting Tribal Coins From Sunt", *JAINS*, III, pp. 28-29, Pl. IV.4-5 and Sharma, G.B. & Manmohan Kumar (1966), *Coins Seals and Sealings from Sanghol*, Chandigarh, p. 55 respectively.
90. Marshall, *Taxila*, various pages.
91. *JNSI*, XIII, pp. 27 ff.
92. *ONSNL*, No. 57, December 1978; *ND*, V, I, June 1981, pp. 19-23.
93. *ICSNL, No. 2, June 1990, pp. 2-3.*
94. Goffer, Z. (1980), *Archaeological Chemistry*, John Willey and Sons, New York, pp. 252-83.
95. Mention must be made here of Satyaprakash and Rawat, N.S. (1965), *Chemical Study of Some Indian Archaeological Antiquities*, Bombay and Satya Prakash and R. Singh (1968), *Coinage of*

Ancient India, Delhi. Scientific studies of various coin series undertaken in India, however, remain confined to excavation reports or articles in research journals generally not available to numismatists.

96. Bhardwaj, H.C., *op. cit.*, p. 136.
97. *Ibid.*
98. Mitchiner, Michael, *"Early Trade between India and Mainland Southeast Asia, as Reflected by Coinage"*, in Gupta and Jha, *op. cit.*, pp. 62-83.
99. Hegde, K.T.M. (1967), "Chemical and Spectrometric Studies in Kshatrapa Silver Coins", *JNSI*, XXIX (i), pp. 63-66.
100. Bhardwaj, *loc. cit.*
101. Hegde, K.T.M. (1968), "Source of the metal in lead coins of Kshatrapa periods", *Current Science*, Vol. XXXVII, No. 18, p. 518.
102. Jha and Rajgor, *op. cit.*, pp. 61-67.
103. Geological Map of Agucha Lead-Zinc Mineral Belt, Bhilwara Distt., Rajasthan (Part Of Toposheet Nos. 45 K/9&13). Lead deposits are said to have beeen found from Ajmer lead-zinc zone, Jabalpur lead-zinc-copper belt, the Pur-Banera belt, the Basantgarh Deri belt, etc. besides the Zawar lead-zinc belt. For details see Raghunathan, K.R., B.K. Rao, Dhruva and M.L. Singhal (1981), "Exploration for copper, lead and zinc ores in India", *Bulletin of the Geological Survey of India Series A – Economic Geology*, No. 47, Calcutta.
104. Arun Kumar Biswas, *op. cit.*, p. 331.
105. *JNSI*, LVIII (1996), p. 8.
106. Ganorkar, M.C. *et al.*, "Scientific Study and Conservation of Coins", *Numismatics & Archaeology*, p. 117.
107. Sastry, T.V.G., M. Kasturibai and J.V.P. Rao (1984), *Veerapuram a type site for cultural study in the Krishna Valley*, BACRI, Hyderabad, pp. 73-103.
108. Ganorkar *et al.*, *loc. cit.*
109. *Ibid.*, p. 116.
110. Various articles in Gupta and Jha, *op. cit.*
111. Reddy, D. Raja (2004), "Sources of Lead for Andhra Coins", *JNSI*, LXVI, p. 28.
112. *Ibid.*, pp. 29-30.
113. Majumdar, Sushmita Bose, *op. cit.*, pp. 22-26.
114. *Ibid.*, pp. 20-21.
115. Handa (2006), *op. cit.*, pp. 86-94, Pl. XV.
116. Wadia (1975), *Geology of India*, p. 351.
117. Reedy, C.L., "Technical Studies of Gandhāran Art" in B. Allchin *et al.* (Eds.), *Gandhara Art in Context: East West Exchange at Cross-roads of Asia*, Regency Publication, New Delhi, pp. 267-81.
118. Schroff, W.H. (1912), *The Periplus of the Erythrean Sea*, London, XXXIV.17, pp. 15, 22, 190 etc.
119. Pliny, *Naturalis Historia*, edited by C. Mayhoff, Leipzig, 1892-1909.
120. Warmington, E.H (1974), *The Commerce between the Roman Empire and India*, Delhi, pp. 267 ff.

XVI

The Bull on Indian Coins

The bull 'an ault uncastrated male domestic bovine' has been one of the most useful animals for mankind and occupies an important place in the myths and mythology of various sects of the world. It is a vigorous animal used for tilling the land, riding, racing, carrying load, drawing carts and chariots, and a multitude of other activities which help people lead better life. As a symbol of strength and vigour it has been represented in art from the pre-historic period.

The bull has been a popular item of terracotta art in the Indian sub-continent from pre-Harappan times. Mehrgarh, Kulli, Mehi, etc. have yielded terracotta bull figurines and the tradition continued as revealed by finds from Harappa, Mohenjodaro, Kalibangan, Lothal, Rangpur and numerous other Harappan sites. Steatite seals depicting bull (with or without humps), elephant, etc. found from various sites of this culture are really a treat to the eyes. Terracotta bulls and elephants far outnumber other animals. Examples of bull-fights have also been met with.[1] Steatite seals showing the bull (Fig. 56) and other animals betray exquisite workmanship and the importance given to them. In the Late- and post-Harappan cultures we have terracotta bulls from Bhagwanpura, Daimabad, Dangwara, Kaytha, Eran, Atranjikhera, etc.[2] In the terracotta art of India the bull occupies a very important place from the period of the pre-Indus-Sarasvati Culture.

In the Vedic period also bull and cow continued to be recognized as important animals. In the *Ṛigveda*, Indra is constantly designated as a bull, a term applied much less frequently to Agni, Sūrya (V.45, 9 and X.189, 1) and occasionally to other gods like Dyaus. In the *Atharvaveda* (IX.4, 9) a bull is addressed as Indra and in the *Śatapatha Brāhmaṇa* (II.V.3, 18) the bull is stated to be Indra's form. Elsewhere it mentions cows and bulls as supporting everything. Indra was the most powerful deity in the Ṛigvedic period. So the bull was considered to be powerful and vigorous. Rudra is called a bull in the *Ṛigveda* (II.33, 7-8 & 15). In the Vājasaneyi-Saṃhitā

(VIII.8) of the *Atharvaveda* Prajāpati 'Lord of creatures' is invoked as a great bull, 'the male, bestower of seed' and in later literature often receives the epithet of Paśupati. In the early historic period, however, we find bull representing Śiva and also associated with him as his mount. The bull is regarded as a symbol of Dharma or righteousness. Nandi (meaning giving delight) is a *gaṇa* of Śiva who is loyal to his master and also serves as his doorkeeper. He is often represented in art as a bull or bull-headed acolyte of Śiva. In the *Rāmāyaṇa* (VIII.16, 14), however, he is referred to as a monkey having a terrific look, dwarfish size, short arms and very strong.[3] He is said to be the second Śaṅkara (*dvitīyamiva Śaṅkaraḥ*). According to the *Mahābhārata* (XIII.77, 27-28) Daksha Prajāpati gave to Śiva a bull which became his mount and banner-mark. The epic refers to Śiva as Govṛishāṅka, Govṛisha-dhvaja, Govṛishottama-vāhana, Ṛishabhaketu, Vṛisha, Vṛishāṅka, Vṛisha-dhvaja, Vṛishaketana, Vṛishavāhana, Vṛishabha, Vṛishabhāṅka, Vṛishabha-dhvaja, Vṛishabhaketans, Nandīśvara, etc.[4] indicating that by the time of the great epic, the bull had firmly been associated with Śiva as his banner-mark and mount. This must have happened sometime in the early first century BCE before the reign of Wema Kadphises from whose time Nandi is generally depicted with Śiva as his mount. In sculptures, however, a broken image of Ardhanārīśvara in the Mathurā museum (Acc. no. AMM, 15.800) belonging to the Kushāṇa period is the earliest specimen showing the bull standing to right behind the deity.[5] In Kṛishṇa-līlā scenes depicted on the walls of various temples in India demons Arishṭāsura and Vatsāsura are represented as bulls. Fighting and taming of bulls (Vṛishabhadamana) was actually a sport in ancient times (*Bhāgavata Purāṇa*, X.ii, 58, 33, 41-47). Taming of a bull was a common feat of strength and is mentioned among the games in the *Harivaṃśa* (Vishṇu-parva, XX.16) which tells us that Kṛishṇa organized a bull fight in Vraja (*Vṛishāṇāṃ jātadarpāṇāṃ yuddhāni samayojayat//*). The Jallikattu 'running of the bulls' of Tamilnadu which has been traditionally a part of the Pongal festival is a survival of the bull-taming sport celebrated as a thanksgiving festival for bountiful harvest of which bull or cattle-worship is a part.

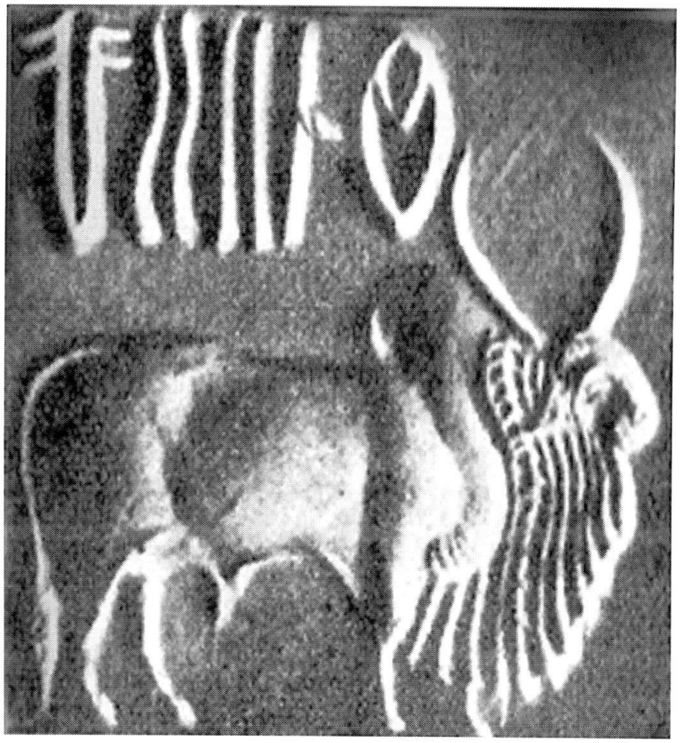

Fig. 56. Harappan steatite seal depicting bull.

Vṛisha and Vṛishabha are the Sanskrit words for bull and are also used as the name or epithet not only of Śiva but also of Vishṇu. It also means virile and in erotic works like *Rati-mañjarī* it is used for a class of men who are lustful and virile. The bull

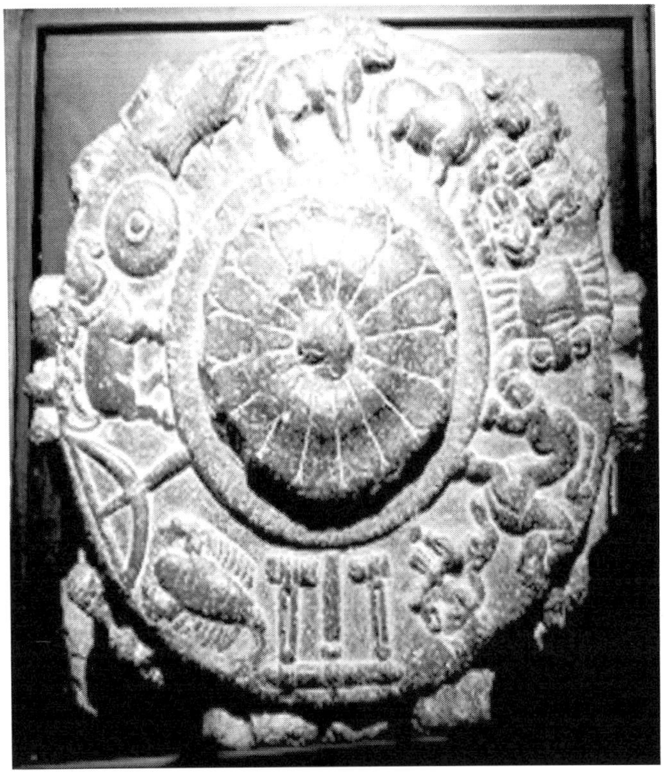

Fig. 57. *Rāśi-paṭṭa* (Chhatrapati Shivaji Maharaj Vastu Sangrahalaya, Mumbai).

also symbolizes morality, stability, fertility, strength, stamina, even-headedness, helpfulness, justice and virtue. The word is used for anything best or eminent in a class.[6] The representation of bull therefore signifies these qualities also and it is no wonder if some rulers represented themselves as bulls on their coins. White bull (*śveta-vṛisha*) was also considered as auspicious (*Harivaṃśa*, II.109, 98). As a constellation, the bull named Taurus, is associated with abundance resulting from the congenial season of spring. In astrology, therefore, Vṛishabha or Taurus is the zodiacal sign signifying spring and productivity, birth and life and is generally represented by the bull on Rāśi-paṭas 'zodiac boards' (Fig. 57) or face of a bull 'Nandi-mukha' in the zodiacal symbolism.

In Greek mythology the bull is identified with Zeus, Dionysos and Poseidon and has portentous significance. According to Greek mythology, Zeus felt enamoured to the Phoenician maiden named Europa and transformed himself into a tame white bull and mixed in with her father's herds to seduce her. In man-bull form with horns Dionysos was also honoured at fertility festivals. Zeus is sometimes represented in his bull form or just as the head of a bull on Greek coins.

Bull was a beast of prey and an animal of sacrifice in ancient times. A ritual called Śūlagava is described in details in the Gṛihyasūtras. The Gṛihyasūtras tell us that this sacrifice was performed to obtain heavenly rewards, sons, long life, renown and cattle. The ceremony of setting a bull at liberty (Vṛishotsarga) is described in the *Vishṇu-smṛiti*.[7]

Bull being a strong animal was used for pulling chariots and carts and also for yoking in agriculture. Bullock-carts still in use in Sind (Pakistan) and villages of Punjab and Haryana are a legacy of the tradition of the Harappan times as evidenced by the cartwheel-marks found on a road of Kalibangan in Rajasthan as revealed by excavations. Terracotta toy bullock-carts found from numerous early historic sites indicate their continued use through the centuries. Bullock-cart racing as as sport too may have been prevalent in ancient times and its continuity may still be seen in the present-day rural sports held every year at Raipur in district Ludhiana, Punjab and may be elsewhere also in other parts of India. Bulls were and continue to be yoked to the ploughs even now for tilling the land in many parts of the country. In an architectural piece of *circa* 5th-6th century CE obtained from Svāmīghāṭ at Mathurā representing the Mahāparinirvāṇa of Buddha, two bulls have been shown back to back with a *Bhāravāhaka* 'load bearing' yaksha.[8]

In the Sanskrit drama *Mudrā-Rākshasa* of Viśākhadatta, Kauṭilya addresses Chandragupta Maurya as Vṛishala. Owing to its great utility the cow too was held in great respect. The cow is addressed as Aditi and a goddess, also identified with Lakshmī. She was personified as the rain-cloud, beam of dawn, etc. Her bountifulness made her wish-fulfilling (*kāmadughā, kāmaduh, kāmadhenu*) and she continued to be personified and sung as such even subsequently. The term *Go* in Sanskrit stands both for the cow and the bull. The gods are sometimes called *gojātāḥ* 'cow-born'. *Go* or cow is a symbol of motherhood, life, sustenance, piety, purity, etc. *Go* is also identified with Earth, speech, goddess Sarasvatī and has numerous other connotations. Whatsoever moves is also calle *Go* (*gachchhati iti go*). It also connotes sense, and hence the designation of Gosvāmī for a person who has control over his senses. Kṛishṇa is well known as Gopāla. His Govardhanadhārī form often shows cows or cows and bulls taking refuge ubder the mountain lifted by the god to escape the fury of the rain-god Indra.

The bull and various other animals find place on the abacus of various monolithic pillars which represent the official art of Mauryan emperor Aśoka. The Sarnath and Sanchi pillars had four lions back to back on their haunches superposed over the abacus. At Salempur the abacus supported four bulls in a likewise fashion. Vaishali, Lauriya-Nandangarh and one of the two Rampurva columns are crowned by a single lion figure seated on its haunches. The Sankisa column is superimposed by a standing elephant, while the second Rampurva column is crowned by a standing bull. The Sarnath pillar capital adopted as India's National Symbol shows four addorsed lions which originally supported a *Dhamma-chakka*, or Wheel of Law, resting on an abacus bearing in relief an elephant, horse, bull and lion separated by four small *dharma-chakras*, below which is carved an inverted lotus forming the bell of purely indigenous type. D.R. Sahni[9] regarded the four animals as purely ornamental or as theriomorphic representations of Brahmanic deities subordinated to Buddhism. B. Majumdar[10] related them to the four prime events of the life of Buddha: elephant symbolizing Conception, bull Nativity, horse Renunciation and lion Buddha himself (Śākya-siṃha) or as representing the four quarters of the world. Coomaraswamy[11] and Bloch[12] explained these four figures as symbolizing the divinities Indra, Sūrya, Śiva and Durgā whose mounts these animals are and followed Sahni to regard them as indicating their subordination to the Buddha and his Law. Smith[13] also regarded these animals as the guardians of east, south, west and north respectively. The association of bull with Śiva, however, is established by Ujjain coins which show the mono-cephalous deity holding a staff and water-pot referred to by Banerjea[14] as 'devavīkshaṇatatparaḥ' as described in the *Matsya Purāṇa* (195.18). The coins belong to 2nd-1st centuries BCE. Epithets like Govṛishāṅka, Govṛisha-dhvaja, Govṛishottama-vāhana, Ṛishabhaketu, Vṛisha(bha)-dhvaja, Vṛisha(bha)-vāhana, etc. used for Śiva in the *Mahābhārata*[15], however, leave absolutely no doubt that the bull was associated with the god as his

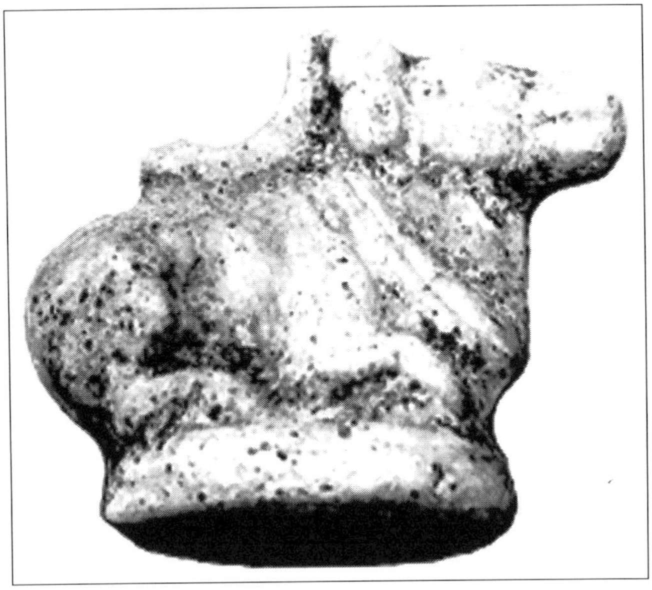

Fig. 58. Terracotta Nandī, Kurukshetra.

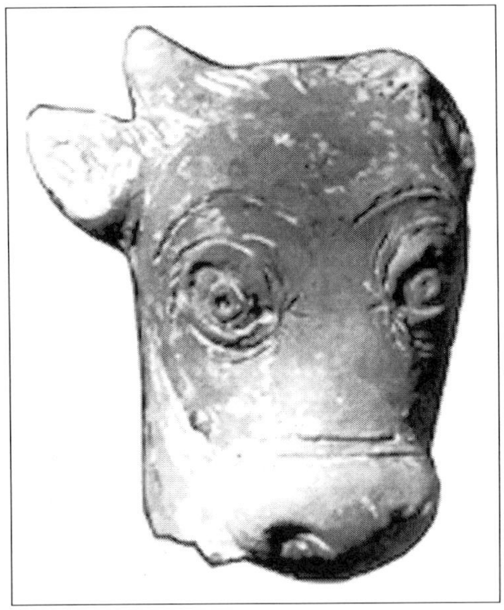

Fig. 59. Nandī head, Agroha.

mount as well as banner-mark. Depiction of bull in the terracotta art, most of them used as toys but some as of religious significance, continued in the early historic period as evidenced from the finds made at Ahichhatrā[16], Mathurā[17], Sugh[18], Agroha[19], etc.

In sculptures, the 3rd century Gandhāra image of Trimūrti Śiva – three-headed, three-eyed, six-armed, standing before the bull and holding *ḍamaru* 'dumb-bell' *triśūla* 'trident' and *kamaṇḍalu* 'ritual water-pot', is one of the early stone images of Śiva with Nandī. Independent images of bull, with or without ornamentation, are also often found. They represent the god himself or his vehicle (Figs. 58-59). Bull becomes an important adjunct of the images of Śiva, Hari-Hara, Ardhanārīśvara and Umā-Maheśvara in the later period. Māheśvarī, the *śakti* 'power' of Śiva, is also represented in Indian sculptures as seated on the bull or the animal is shown near her when depicted in a standing posture.

Some royal dynasties adopted the bull mark as their regal insignia. It was the *rājāṅka* of the Bṛihadratha dynasty.[20]

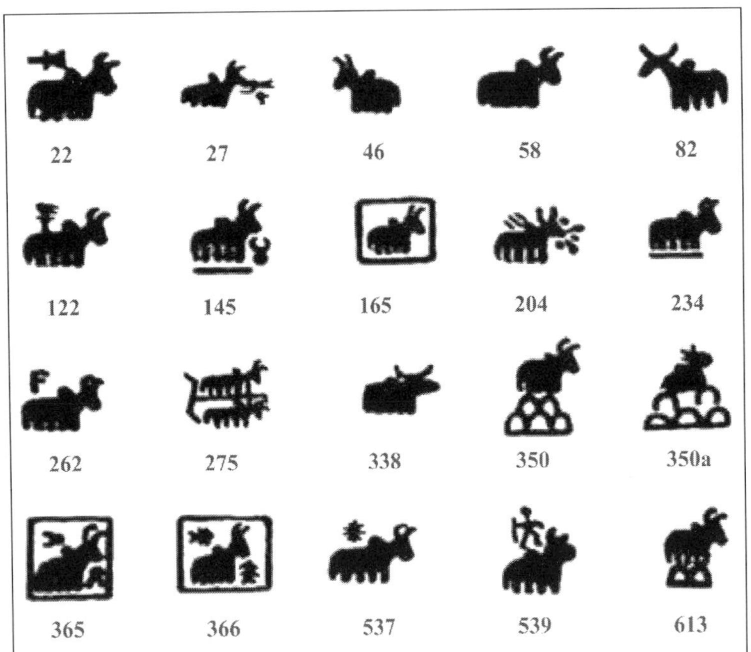

Fig. 60. Bulls depicted on Punch-marked coins.

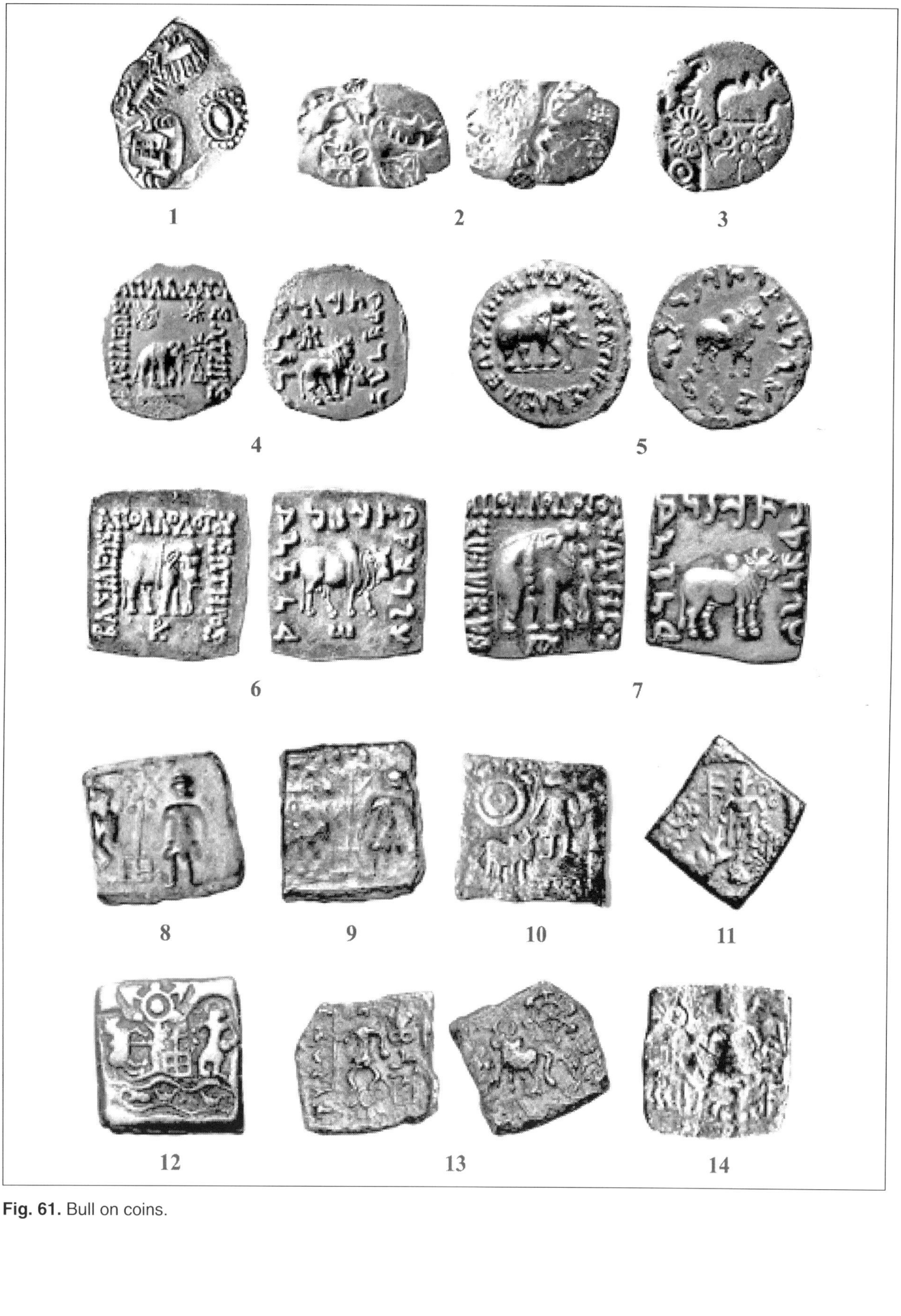

Fig. 61. Bull on coins.

Some cities like Pushkalāvatī adopted bull (Taurus, probably representing Śiva) as their city-deity. Sanghol in Punjab has yielded a terracotta sealing showing the bull to right and the Brāhmī legend *Nandipurasya* which indicates that Sanghol was known as Nandipura in ancient times and that it got this name from Śiva's vehicle who is represented on the glyptic (Pl. 63.9).

The bull and the elephant are the two animals which appear on the silver punch-marked coins of the earliest series (Series 0) bearing four symbols and continue to be depicted thereon till the last (Series VIII). There are numerous varieties of *kārshāpaṇas* showing both elephant and bull together. Though lion and horse too are depicted on punch-marked coins sometimes, the occurrence of bull and elephant far outnumbers them. P.L. Gupta and T.R. Hardaker have noted early (), variable early (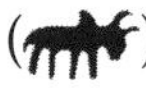) and late (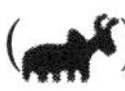) forms of the bull on these series. The early form of bull facing left or right has the head bowed down with horns almost parallel to the ground as if in a combative mood (Fig. 61.2) and occurs on Series 0-II while the late form which starts with Series I show the animal in a naturalistic form (Fig. 61.3), sometimes with a rider[21] or having additional subsidiary symbols or on an arched symbol (Fig. 60). On the silver coins of Vidarbha region bearing four punches and *kārshāpaṇas* of Series I[22] (Symbol no. 275 of Gupta and Hardaker) two bulls are shown as yoked to a plough indicating their popular use for tilling the land at that early period (Fig. 61.1).[23]

Bulls yoked to a plough (S-275), eating leaves (S-204), in a square frame without or with subsidiary marks like the taurines or fishes (S-165, 365, 366), having a banner or triangle-headed standard on its back (S- 262, 22, 122), a sun or star mark on the back (S-537), or seated or standing on an arched hill (S-350-350a, 613) cannot be regarded as the theriomorphic representation of Śiva or even of his mount Nandi. One can't be sure even about the independent figures of bull (like S-46, 58, 82, 234, 338) as representing them. Symbol 539[24] has been described by Gupta and Hardaker as 'Bull right with standing rider who holds long stick in right hand' is noteworthy. It occurs on the coins of Series VIII (nos. 606-607) which are dated to second century BCE. The human figure with a queer head-dress or helmet holding a long scepter in one hand and a water pot in the other (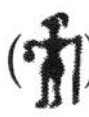) described and discussed in the first chapter occurs for the first time on Type 566 of Series VIb tentatively dated to the accession of Aśoka. But this human figure is nowhere associated with the bull on punch-marked silver coins. Similar anthropomorphic figure holding a *daṇḍa* 'sceptre' and water-pot in the two hands is depicted on Ujjain coins also. Ujjain region issued abundant base metal coinage imitating Type 566 in the post-Mauryan period, probably after the disintegration of the empire after the death of Pushyamitra Śuṅga in 148 BCE. It is on these billon punch-marked coins of Mathurā and Ujjain that we find the bull associated with this helmeted human figure for the first time. It is, however, to be noted that the bull, without or with a standing human figure on it, figures even on brass or base metal Mathurā punch-marked coins of Series VIII which show Saṃkarshaṇa-Balarāma holding pestle and plough in his upraised hands alone or along with club and wheel wielding Vāsudeva-Kṛishṇa clearly indicating that the

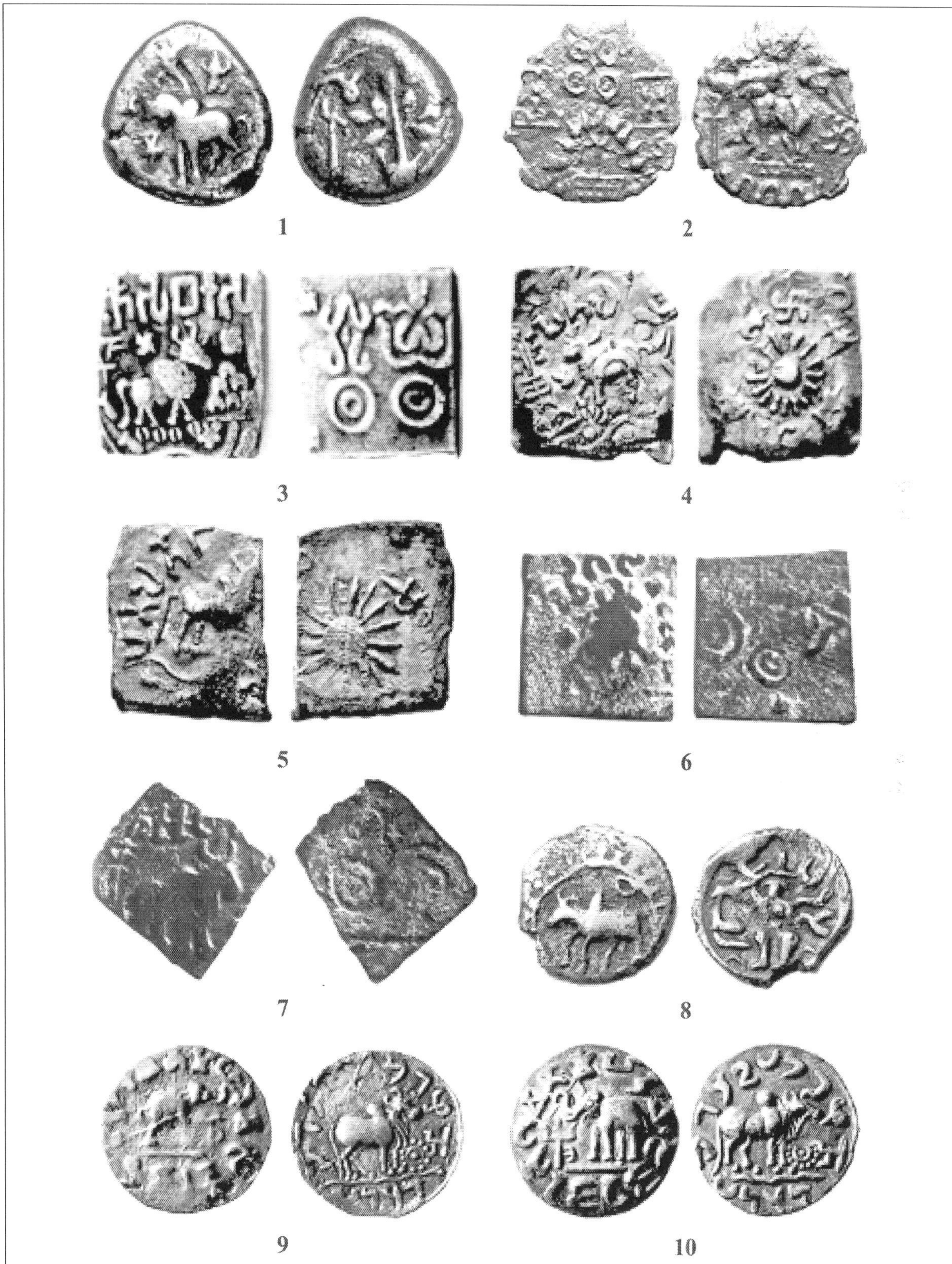

Fig. 62. Bull on coins.

bull had not yet been recognized as the mount of Śiva.[25] Many other die-struck Ujjain copper coins also show such a figure with a bull looking at him (*devavīkshaṇatatparaḥ*) on the basis of which Banerjea has identified the human figures with Śiva as referred to above. Wilfried Pieper[26] has illustrated a billon punch-marked coin of Mathurā with a trident at the back of the bull. It thus seems probable that bull had come to be recognized as the vehicle of Śiva sometime in the post-Mauryan period, most probably in the latter half of second century BCE or even slightly later.

The elephant is also shown with a rider[27] on *kārshāpaṇas* and may be taken as representing Indra on Airāvata, his vehicle. Since Series Va is associated with the accession of Chandragupta Maurya this variety may be dated to the last quarter of the 4th century BCE. Indra is regarded as *devādhideva* 'god or king of gods' in Hindu mythology. The elephant may have thus been a symbol of royalty or a very powerful ruler.

India came in contact with the Greeks and their coins from the time of Alexander's invasion. The king of Taxila at the time of Alexander's invasion was Sophytes (Saubhūti) who struck silver coins following the Greek pattern by putting his head to right on the obverse with the Greek legend ΣΩΦΫΤΟΥ and caduceus or owl on the reverse.[28] Diodotus I and Euthydemus I who ruled over Bactria also put their heads on the obverse and a deity or its theriomorphic or religious symbol on the reverse.[29] Demetrius, son and successor of the latter, is generally connected with the conquest of India and followed the same pattern on his silver specie but issued his bronze coins putting bust of Herakles/Artemis, Gorgon head on round shield/Trident; head of elephant/caduceus on his bronze coins. Caduceus is a symbol of power that produced wealth and prosperity and an emblem of influence over the living and the dead in Greek mythology. The trident is well known as the weapon par excellence of the Hindu god Śiva. Thus these two symbols on the reverse represent the religious predilections. The substitution of the head of the king by the head of elephant, however, is interesting. The elephant head seem to have represented the king. Elephant being the most gorgeous animal, the vehicle of Indra, the king of the gods (*devādhideva*), was perhaps considered as the most appropriate symbol to represent the king or royalty. It may not be without significance that this symbol which had long been represented on punch-marked coins for a few centuries before was adopted by a Greek king who is associated with his conquest of Indian territory and occupying it. Euthydemus II, son and successor? of Demetrius, continued the Greek pattern for his silver issue but put the head of Appolo or Herakles on the obverse and tripod-lebes (a type of altar) or prancing horse on his nickel and bronze issues. Pantaleon, son and successor? of Demetrius, issued nickel and bronze coins like his predecessor with a deity on the obverse and panther or lion on the reverse. He was the first Indo-Greek ruler to put Brāhmī legend *Rājine Paṃtalevasa* on the obverse of his square bronze coins along with a female figure in Indian dress holding flower in her right hand (Lakshmī). The next ruler Agathocles issued various types of coins including the square bronze type of his predecessor with the goddess holding flower in her right hand and Brāhmī legend (*Rājine Agathukleyasa*) on the obverse. Coins found in

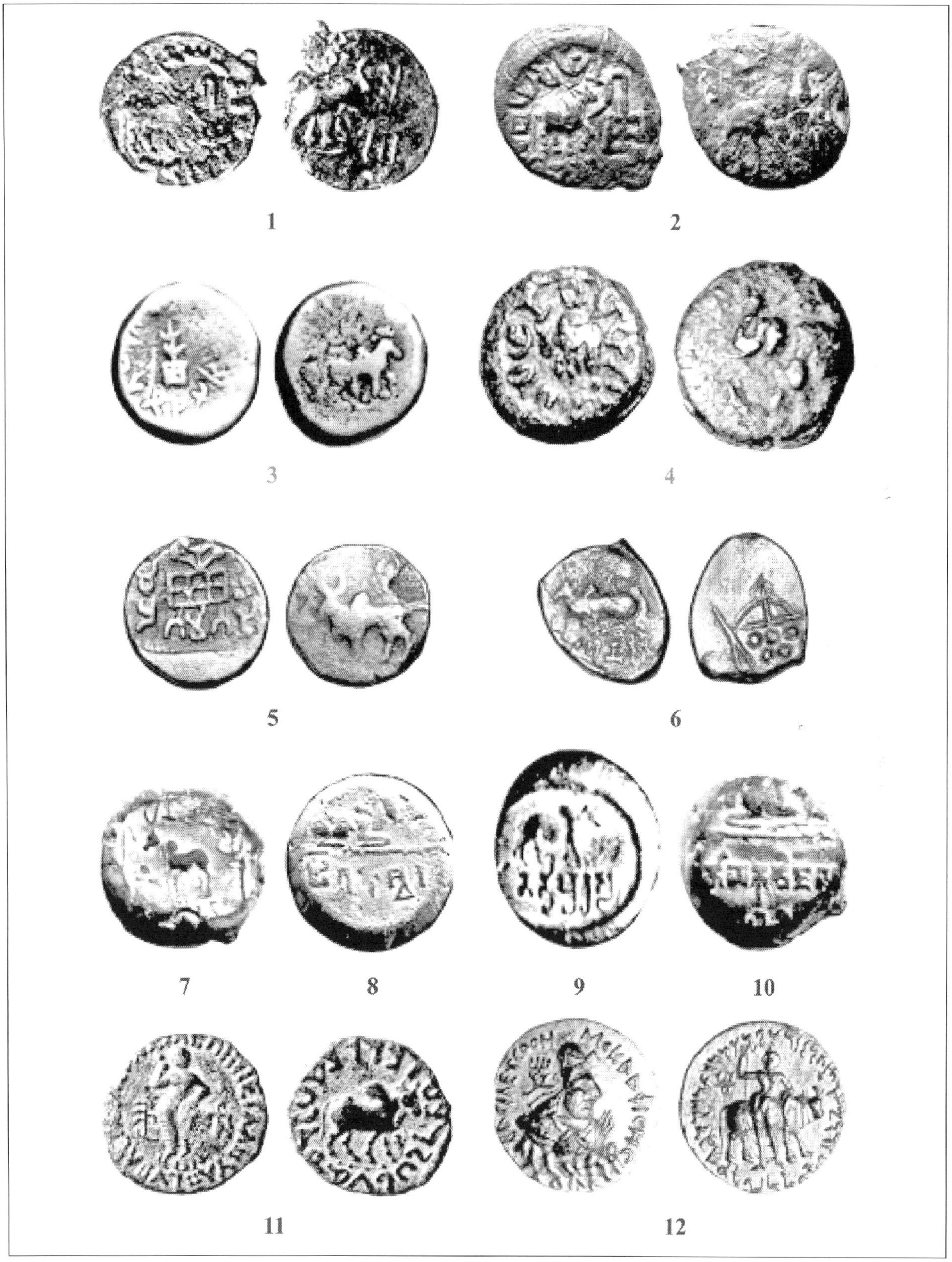

Fig. 63. Bull on coins and sealings.

excavations at Ai-Khanoum, however, are the most important as they show on the reverse the Hindu deities Vāsudeva-Kṛishṇa and Saṃkarshaṇa-Balarāma. We thus see that though there are some exceptions, the general pattern of the Greek coins was to put the head of the king on the obverse and a deity or a religious symbol on the reverse. This pattern was followed by most of the Indo-Greek rulers but Heliocles substituted the head of the king on the obverse by an elephant to right and put Indian bull on the reverse. Diomedes again put the Dioscuri on the obverse and bull to right on the reverse leaving it to Apollodotus I to finally substitute the head or bust to elephant with bull on the reverse even of his silver coins (Fig. 61.4-7).[30] I feel inclined to regard elephant on the obverse as the representation of the king and bull as the religious symbol, the theriomorphic representation or vehicle of Śiva. Philoxenus, Azes (Fig. 63.11), Azilises, Artemidorus, Gondophares, Aspavarman, Wema Kadphises (Fig. 63.12) from whose time bull becomes an important adjunct of Śiva. Vāsudeva Kushāṇa put the Indian humped bull on his different coin-types which served as a model for some post-Kushāṇa series as well. Mahādeva type silver coins (Fig. 62.9-10) which are similar to the Vemaka coins too carry elephant and bull devices. The names Rudravarman, Bhavavarman, Śivaghosha and the legend *Mahādevasa* (or *Māhādevasa*) on these coins clearly shows that the bull here represented Śiva or his vehicle Nandi. Post-Kushāṇa Kota coins continue to carry the crude figure of Śiva with bull on the pattern of Kushāṇa coins.

Maues (*circa* 95 – 60 BCE) is regarded to have represented Poseidon (Greek god of waters, rivers) or Śiva with a trident in his left hand putting his right foot on a human figure (apasmāra-purusha?) as the first alien ruler to have been inclined towards Śaivism. His Artemis/Bull type coins seem to corroborate this possibility. Some scholars, however, believe that the figure under Poseidon's feet represents a river deity and the motif signifies the conquest of a river valley (Indus and Punjab river valleys) by Maues. The Bactrian humped bull is considered as a symbol of Bactria and elephant as a symbol of Punjab which he also conquered.[31]

The bull is represented on the coins of various dynasties, tribes and places.[32] It occurs on the coins of some Almora rulers[33] along with a symbol of a circle connected with a wavy line which I feel inclined to identify as representing Śiva-liṅga with flowing lustral water[34] indicating the bull to be Nandi. This is corroborated by the Śaivite names of the kings like Śivadatta, Śivapālita, etc.

Bull may be seen on Agra (Fig. 63.4) and Ārjunāyana coins. The Agras issued not only the bull type coins but also those of lion, composite animal, Lakshmī, *chakra*, temple and *chaitya* types[35] also which betray their respect towards all sects including Śaivism. On some Ārjunāyana coins the animal stands before a *yūpa* 'sacrificial post' (described by Allan as *liṅgam*), clearly indicating the Śūlagava sacrifice (Fig. 54.1).[36] Performance of śūlagava is indicated by quite a few terracotta sealings of Dhanadeva found from Rajghat near Varanasi (Fig. 63.7) and many others. The couchant bull on the terracotta sealing with the legend *Mātaṅgeśvara* (Fig. 63.8) and another reading *Nāyaka-dvijasya* (Fig. 63.10) of unknown provenances correspond to the Śaivite *īśvara*-ending name or epithet and the personal faith of an individual. The bull has been

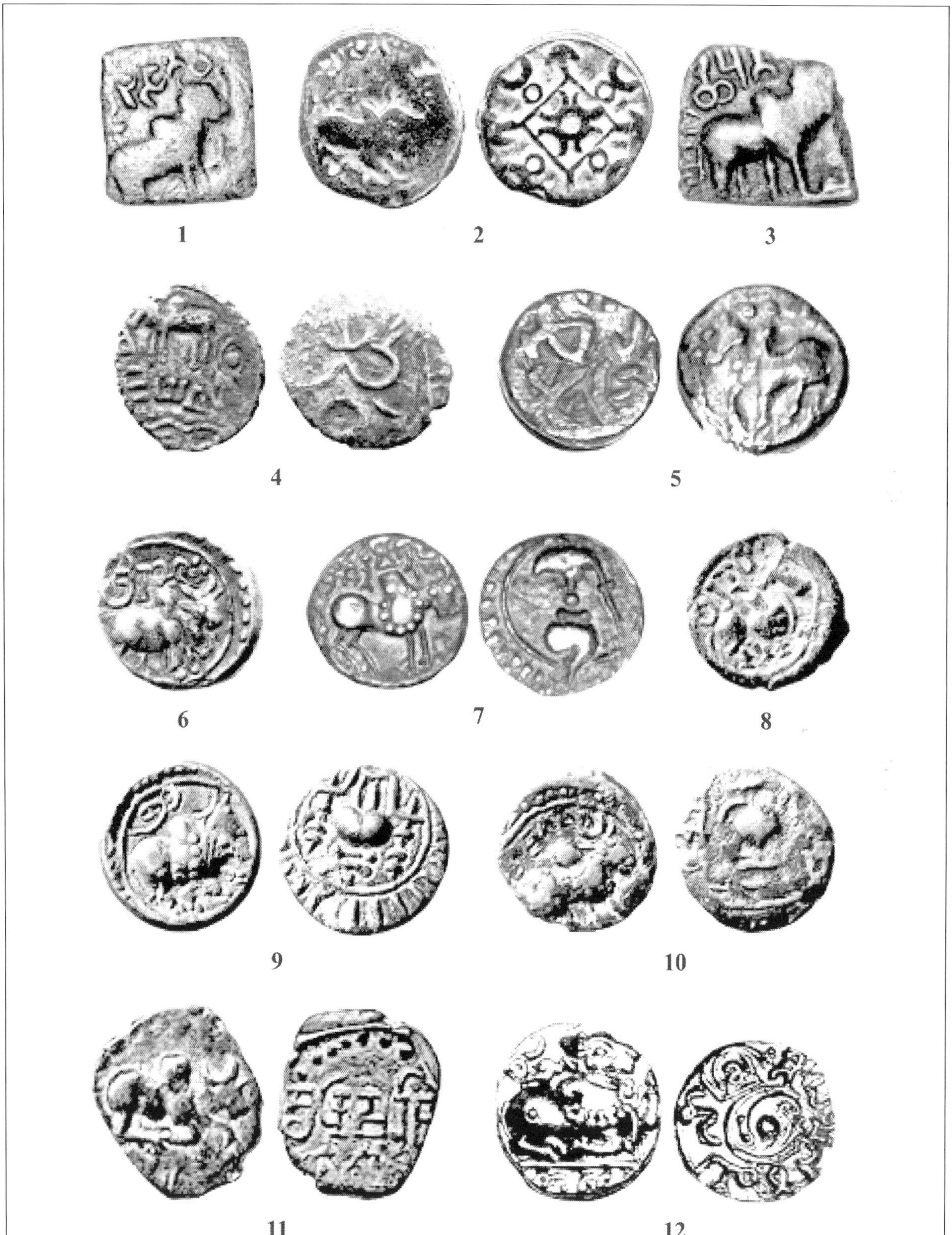

Fig. 64. Bull on coins.

quite a popular motif on early historic seals/sealings, often suggesting the Śaivite leanings of the owners.[37]

The bull figures on the coins of a ruler of the name of Dhanadeva also found from Kauśāmbī and Ayodhyā who may have been different kings as the symbols and legend patterns of their coins indicate. Many other rulers of Ayodhyā have also issued coins carrying the figure of the bull. The Maghas of Kauśāmbī too continued to put the bull on their coins. Mālava coins too show a bull amongst many other devices.

Some pre-Sātavāhana copper coins from Vidarbha, and those belonging to king Sebaka (Fig. 62.3), Vigra (?Fig. 62.6), Pātālatārita (Fig. 62.4-5), Kukkuṭapāda (Fig. 62.7) and Mitra-Bhadra rulers like Dāmabhadra, Dharmabhadra, Sachabhadra, Bhūmimitra, Sūryamitra (Fig. 61.13), etc. also carry the prominent figure of a bull, sometimes with Śiva.[38] The Yaudheya seals/sealings and coins also show a bull (Fig. 63.3) betraying the cultic affiliation of the tribe. Their bull/elephant type coins depict the bull before a sacrificial post (Fig. 63.2) indicating Śūlagava like the Ārjunāyana coins. Many rulers of Ayodhyā also issued, among others, coins with the bull device which may be interpreted as their predilection towards Śaivism. The Rājanyas provided a special status to the bull by putting it in a rayed circle (Fig. 62.8). The bull thus seems to have been the theriomorphic representation of Śiva on their coins. Bull occurs on Eran (Fig. 61.12) and Ujjain coins (Fig. 61.8-11 & 14) in various forms, facing a *bilva* tree (sacred to Śiva) to right or left, looking at Śiva holding the trident, with Śiva holding *daṇḍa* and water pot in the hands seated or standing before the latter, and is generally accepted as representing Śiva's mount. On the reverse of a coin of Pushyamitra of Ujjain (wrongly identified with Pushyamitra Śuṅga) the bull figures before a tree in railing with a lotus bud and triangle-headed standard above.[39] We know that Ujjayinī was a great centre of Śaivism in ancient times. So the bull indicates the popularity of the sect in the Ujjain region rather than the personal sectarian symbol of Pushyamitra Śuṅga. The animal is popularly depicted on Kauśāmbī coins as lanky bull or as a natural animal (Fig. 62.1-2; 63.5-6). Bull on a coin type of Mathurā ruler Gomitra II carries a reflection of the name of the ruler. Rāmadatta and Kāmadatta of Mathurā have also issued some coins with this device though Lakshmī has been the most important deity represented on Mathurā coins even by the Śaka rulers Rājuvula and Ṣoḍāsa. The Rājanyas have provided a special status to the bull by putting it in a rayed circle on their coins to signify that the bull represented Śiva. Coins of Taxila reveal the depiction of animals like elephant, lion, horse as well as bull on their different coin types. The Pauravas in their vicinity seem to have followed the Taxila rulers in representing different animals on their coins. King Jayavarman probably of the Garhwal region has also issued coins with a prominent bull on the obverse (Fig. 64.4).

Some city states like the Bhāgilā, Erikachha, Kosambi, etc. have also shown their predilection towards the bull. Mahāraṭhi and Mahātalavara coins also featured the bull.[40] Sātavāhana coins bearing the name of Sātavāhana and Sātakarṇi (I), Sundara Sātakarṇi and Kautsīputra (Kochhiputa) Sātakarṇi bear the figure of a bull to right (Fig. 64.1-3).[41] Post-Sātavāhana coins of Andhra/Karnataka also bear the figure of bull. Śālaṅkāyana coins too bear the figure of bull. The Pallava coins are well known for their bull figures on the obverse, often with auspicious symbols like *śrīvatsa*, conch, crescent, lotus, double fish on the obverse or reverse. The Gupta kings were the followers of the Bhāgavata cult but a lead coin of Kumāragupta struck on Western Satrap prototype with bull on one side and his name on the other is unique to indicate his respect for Śaivism too.[42] Skandagupta too struck some silver coins on Western Indian model with bull on the reverse.[43] The animal occurs on some coin types of the Western Kshatrapas[44], Nāgas of Padmāvatī (Fig. 64.5)[45], Rudrila of Malwa[46], Kadamba coins of Banavasi, post-Gupta lead coins of western central India, almost invariably on Vishṇukuṇḍin type coins (Fig. 64.6-10), Kalachuri coins particularly of Kṛishṇarāja (Fig. 64.11) who calls himself as *Parama-Māheśvara* on one of his coin-types, Alchon and Indian Hūṇas[47], the repousse gold coins of the Nala kings of Chhattisgarh[48], Harshavardhana (with Śiva and Pārvatī seated on it)[49], Śaśāṅka of Gauḍa (with Śiva seated on it)[50], on the Harikela series of Bengal[51] and coins of the Hindu Shāhis.[52] The Bull/Horseman type coins have been found from various places in Himachal Pradesh either alone or in association with those of the Katoch rulers of Kangra who also adopted the Bull/Horseman type.[53] Coins of Spalapatideva and Sāmantadeva have been found from Uttar Pradesh and Rajasthan also. The type was continued by some of the Rajput states[54] as also by the Ghaznavis and the Ghoris. The Tomara kings of Delhi namely Mahipāla, Anaṅgapāla (1049-79 CE), Sallakshaṇapāladeva and Madanapāladeva struck Bull/Horseman type in billon.[55] The Chauhan king Vigraharāja III Vīsaladeva, Someśvara (1162-66 CE) and Pṛithvīrāja III (1166-92 CE) also copied this type.[56] Various contemporary dynasties and even the Delhi sultans continued to put the bull on their coins[57] though it was not because of any religious leanings but for numismatic tradition. In south India, Nolamba coins carry the figure of couchant bull to right with sun, crescent and conch above on the obverse (Fig. 64.12).[58] The zodiac coins of Jahangir include Taurus on which the animal has been depicted artistically.[59] It is just possible that some of the kings who may have been born during the zodiacal period of Vṛisha or Taurus depicted bull on their coins. Bull figures even on the coins of the Republic of India.

Bull is depicted even on the coins of neighbouring countries like Sri Lanka[60], Myanmar[61], Nepal (which has been a great centre of the worship of Paśupatinātha), etc. influenced by Indian culture and religion.

We thus see that on early punch-marked coins the elephant and bull were the most popular of all the faunal representations and that the latter also figured as a yoked animal for agriculture, and also probably for transport, carrying weight and various other domestic chores. Indo-Greek ruler Apollodotus I adopted these two animals as the obverse and reverse devices of his coins meant for circulation in India and that these two animals substituted the head/bust of the king and the deity on the obverse and reverse of Graeco-Bactrian coins in general and may have thus signified the king or royalty by the obverse device and deity or religious affiliation of the issuers by the reverse one. Some dynasties and cities adopted the bull (and perhaps other animals like the elephant also) as their insignia. Independent or prominent figure of the bull with a sign of respectability like its being shown in a rayed circle represented the god Śiva in theriomorphic form or his vehicle Nandi betraying the cultic affiliations of the rulers and probably also most of their subjects. Representation of bull before a sacrificial post indicated the performance of Śūlagava sacrifice. Kings desirous of divine favours, progeny and renown may have put the bull before sacrificial post as the required device on their coins. Since the bull was regarded as a symbol of strength, vigour and excellence the potentates desirous of these qualities or those who regarded themselves as possessing them put the figure of the bull on their specie. It was used as an auspicious symbol also. As one of the various devices it generally betrayed the cultic propensities. Sometimes, however, it was adopted by the conquerors on their coins because of expediency and numismatic tradition of the region and the people.

NOTES AND REFERENCES

1. *Annual Report of the Archaeological Survey of India*, 1934-35, pp. 95, 98-99, figs. 3 & 6.
2. Banerji, Arundhati (1994), *Early Indian Terracotta Art*, New Delhi: Harman Publishing House.
3. *Rām.*, V.8, 8: *karāla-kṛishṇa-piṅgala/vāmano vikaṭo muṇḍī nandī hrasvabhujābalaḥ / /.*
4. *Mahābhārata kī Nāmānukramaṇikā*, Gita Press, Gorakhpur, VS 2016, p. 351.
5. Joshi, N.P. (1972), *Catalogue of the Brahmanical Sculptures in the State Museum, Lucknow*, Part I, Lucknow: State Museum, pp. 38-39, line drawing 43.
6. Apte (1959), p. 531.
7. Jolly, Julius (1966), *The Institution of Viṣṇu*, Sacred Books of the East Series, Vol. 7 (reprinted Delhi: MLBD, pp. 260-63.
8. Joshi, N.P. (1965), *Mathurā kī Mūrti-Kalā*, Mathura: Archaeological Museum, Fig. 85.
9. Sahni, D.R. (1933), *Guide to the Buddhist Remains at Sarnath*, Delhi: ASI, p. 40.
10. Majumdar, B. (1947), *Guide to Sarnath*, 2nd ed., Delhi: ASI, p. 46.
11. Coomaraswamy, A.K. (1927), *History of Indian and Indonesian Art*, New York: Dover Publications, p. 17.
12. Bloch, T. (1908), *Z.D.M.G.*, LXII, pp. 653-56.
13. Smith, V.A. (1911), *History of Fine Arts in India and Ceylon*, Oxford, pp. 59-60.
14. *DHI*, p. 171.
15. *Mahābhārata kī Nāmānukramaṇikā*, p. 351.
16. Agrawala, V.S. (1954), 'Terracottas from Ahichchhatra', *Ancient India*, No. 4.
17. Agrawala, V.S. (1936), 'Mathura Terracottas', *JUPHS*, Vol. IX (II), pp. 6-38; Joshi, M.C. *et al.* (1976-77), 'Some Terracottas from Excavations at Mathura: A Study', *JISOA*, New Series, Vol. VIII, pp. 16-31.
18. Handa, Devendra (2021), *Facets of Indian Art, Iconography and Numismatics*, New Delhi, pp. 18-50.
19. Daivakarṇi, Virjānanda (2008), *Agrohā kī Mṛinmūrtiyāṃ*, Jhajjar: Gurukula, p. 26, figs. 336 ff.
20. Coomaraswamy (1927), *op. cit.*, p. 44.
21. Gupta, P.L. & T.R. Hafdaker (2014), *Punchmarked Coinage of the Indian Subcontinent Magadha-Mauryan Series*, Anjaneri: IIRNS Publications Pvt. Ltd., pp. 114-15, nos. 94a – 95r.
22. *Ibid.*, p. 110, nos. 65m – 66b.
23. *Ibid.*, p. 278: q.v. Bull.

24. *Ibid.*, p. 251.
25. *Ibid.*, p. 191, Types 604-608.
26. Pieper (2013), pp. 170-71, no. 153. Cp. Gupta and Hardaker, Var. 497.
27. Symbol 105 of Gupta and Hardaker, Series Va, Var. 490.
28. Gardener (1966), p. 2, Pl. I.3.
29. *Ibid.*, pp. 3-7, Pls. I.4-11 – III.1-2. All subsequent references to Indo-Greek coins are from this work unless otherwise stated.
30. *Ibid.*, pp. 34-36, Pl. IX.8-9. Bopearachchi, O. (1991). *Monnaies Greco-Bactriennes et Indo-Greques, Catalogue Raissone.*
31. Cunningham, Alexander (1892-95), *Coins of Indo-Scythian, Śakas and Kusāṇas*, pp. 21-49, Pls. II, III and VI; Lily Srivastava, 'Historical Significnce of the Figures of Kings and Deities found on the coins of Indo-Scythian, Parthian and Kushāṇa Kings', in K.D. Bajpai, *et al.* (Eds.), *Gleanings of Indian Archaeology, History & Culture: Prof. R.N. Mehta Commemoration Volume*, I, Jaipur: Publication Scheme, 2000, pp. 243-56.
32. Srivastava, Prashant (2011), *Encyclopaedia of Indian Coins*, Delhi: Agam Kala Prakashan, Vol. I, pp. 87-88.
33. Allan, *BMCAI*, pp. lxxx-lxxxi and 120, Pl. XIV.7-9.
34. Handa (2007), *TCAI*, p. 260.
35. *Ibid.*, pp. 6-12, Pls. I-III.
36. *Ibid.*, pp. 20-21, Pl. V.3, 6-9.
37. For details see Thaplyal (1972), *SAIS*.
38. Kulkarni, Prashant P. (2011), 'Pusad Hoard of Pre-Sātavāhana Coins: A Treasure' in Reddy, P. Chenna (ED.), *Numismatica Indica Festscrift to Prof. D. Raja Reddy*, New Delhi: Research India Press, pp. 43-59.
39. Kulkarni (2009-2010), 'Coinage of Pusyamitra Sunga', *JAINS*, Vol. XXXIII-XXXIV, pp. 5-9.
40. Rapson (1908), p. 57, Pl. VIII.
41. Dutta, Mala (1990), *A Study of the Sātavāhana Coinage*, New Delhi: Harman Publishing House, pp. 90-91, Pls. I.2-3; III.11; IV.13-16; V.18; etc.
42. Pieper (2013), *op. cit.*, pp. 326-27, no. 888.
43. Maheshwari, K.K. (June 1981), 'Western Type Silver Coins of Skandagupta', *ND*, Vol. V (I), pp. 29-30.
44. Rapson (1908), p. 76: Jayadāman, p. 85: Jīvadāman, p. 93: Rudrasiṃha, and p. 187: Rudrasena III.
45. Trivedi, H.V. (1957), *Catalogue of the Coins of the Nāga Kings of Padmāvatī*, Gwalior: Department of Archaeology and Museums.
46. Kothari (2006), p. 118, Types 85-86.
47. Tandon, Pankaj (2013), 'Notes on the Evolution of Alchon Coins', *Journal of the Oriental Numismatic Society*, No. 216, pp. 24-34; Vondrovec, Klaus, 'Numismatic Evidence of the Alchon Huns reconsidered', *BUFM* 50, pp. 25-
48. Jain, Balchandra (1978), 'New Hoards of Repousse Gold Coins', *JNSI*, XL, pp. 108-10, Pl. III.4-6.
49. Bajpai, K.D. (1965), *JNSI*, XXVII, pp. 103-106.
50. Mukherjee, B.N. (1993), *Coins and Currency Systems of Post-Gupta Bengal (c. AD 550 – 700)*, New Delhi: Harman Publishing House, pp. 40-41, Pls. I.6-9, II.1-5.
51. Mukherjee, B.N. (1976-77), "Harikela and Related Coinages", *Journal of Ancient Indian History*, Calcutta, Vol. X, pp. 166-71; (1956), "The Coin Legend Harikela", *Journal of the Asiatic Society*, Vol. XVIII, pp. 99-101; (2008), "Early Bengal Numismatics: The Scope of Study", *Coin – 2008*; etc.

52. Smith, *IMC*, I, pp. 243-46; Gopal, Lallanji (1966), *Early Medieval Coin-Types of Northern India*, Varanasi: NSI, pp. 28-30; etc.
53. Gupta, P.L. (1988), *Numismatic History of Himachal Pradesh*, Delhi: B.R. Publishing Corporation, pp. 38 & 124-29, Pls. XVI.8-15, XVII-XVIII; Jha, A.K. and Sanjay Garg (1991), *A Catalogue of the Coins of the Katoch Rulers of Kangra*, Anjaneri: IIRNS.
54. Gopal (1966), p. 28.
55. Cunningham, Alexander (1894), *Coins of Medieval India* ((reprint, New Delhi: Orient Print, 1967), pp. 66 f, 92-95; *IMC*, I, pp. 262ff; Tye, Robert & Monica (1995), *Jitals*, Isle of South Uist: Robert Tye; etc.
56. *Ibid.*
57. Gopal, *op. cit.*, 34-35 and 68-69, Pls. VII.12-13, Pl. VIII.1-2 &VII.15-17; Tye, *loc. cit.*
58. Girijapathy, M. (2011), 'The History and Coinage of the Nolambas', in Reddy, P. Chenna (Ed.), *Numismatica Indica Festschrift to Prof. D. Raja Reddy*, New Delhi: Research India Press, pp. 191-96.
59. Mukherjee, B.N. (1990), *The Indian Gold*, Calcutta: Indian Museum, p. 64, no. 106.
60. Pieper (2013), pp. 300-301, no. 779.
61. Angal, Devadutta G. (2007), 'Three More Coins from South East Asia', *JNSI*, LXIX, pp. 162-63; Angal, Narendra D. (2011), 'Bull Type Gold Coin from Myanmar', *JNSI*, LXXIII, p. 104.

XVII

Pañchāla Coins
Sovereigns, Symbols and Significance

Pañchāla was one of the prominent Mahājanapadas 'great states' in Buddha's time. The *Mahābhārata*, the Jātakas and the *Divyāvadāna* refer to the division of Pañchāla into two parts – northern and southern, of which Ahichhatra and Kāmpilya respectively were the capitals.[1] Pañchāla was conquered by Mahāpadma Nanda in about 350 BCE and amalgamated with the Magadhan Empire like many other Mahājanapadas. Numismatic evidence, however, reveals the existence of an independent dynasty in Northern Pañchāla from about the death of Pushyamitra Śuṅga to the rise of the Guptas covering a period of about four centuries from *circa* 150 BCE to 320 CE except the period of Kushāṇa supremacy. Pañchāla coins form one of the longest and most uniform series of ancient Indian coins. Cunningham[2] had found these coins in "Rohilkhand and chiefly at Ahichhatra, Aonla and Badaon" and considered Northern Pañchāla (with Ahichhatra as the capital) as their provenance. Smith[3] states that they are "common in Eastern Oudh and in the Basti district" (where Carlleyle also obtained about a hundred coins of Agnimitra and Indramitra at Bhuila).[4] Though a coin of Indramitra has been found as far east as Kumrahar (Pāṭaliputra)[5] it has rightly been remarked by Bela Lahiri that "though the territories of some of the Pañchāla rulers might have included parts of Kośala, it could not have been permanently included within the kingdom of Pañchāla, as we know that Ayodhyā was also ruled by a local dynasty of princes during this period".[6]

Made of copper and perhaps some alloy of copper, Pañchāla coins are characterized by three symbols ( ) on the obverse with the king's name below in the genitive in a square die impressed on a round coin forming a characteristic incuse, and a deity or a symbol or attribute of the deity on a kind of platform corresponding generally to king's name[7], e.g. Vishṇu on Vishṇumitra's coin, Indra on Indramitra's coin, Bhūmi (Earth) on Bhūmimitra's coin, Phālgunī star on Phālgunīmitra's coin, solar disc on the coins of Sūryamitra and Bhānumitra, sacrificial altar on the coins of

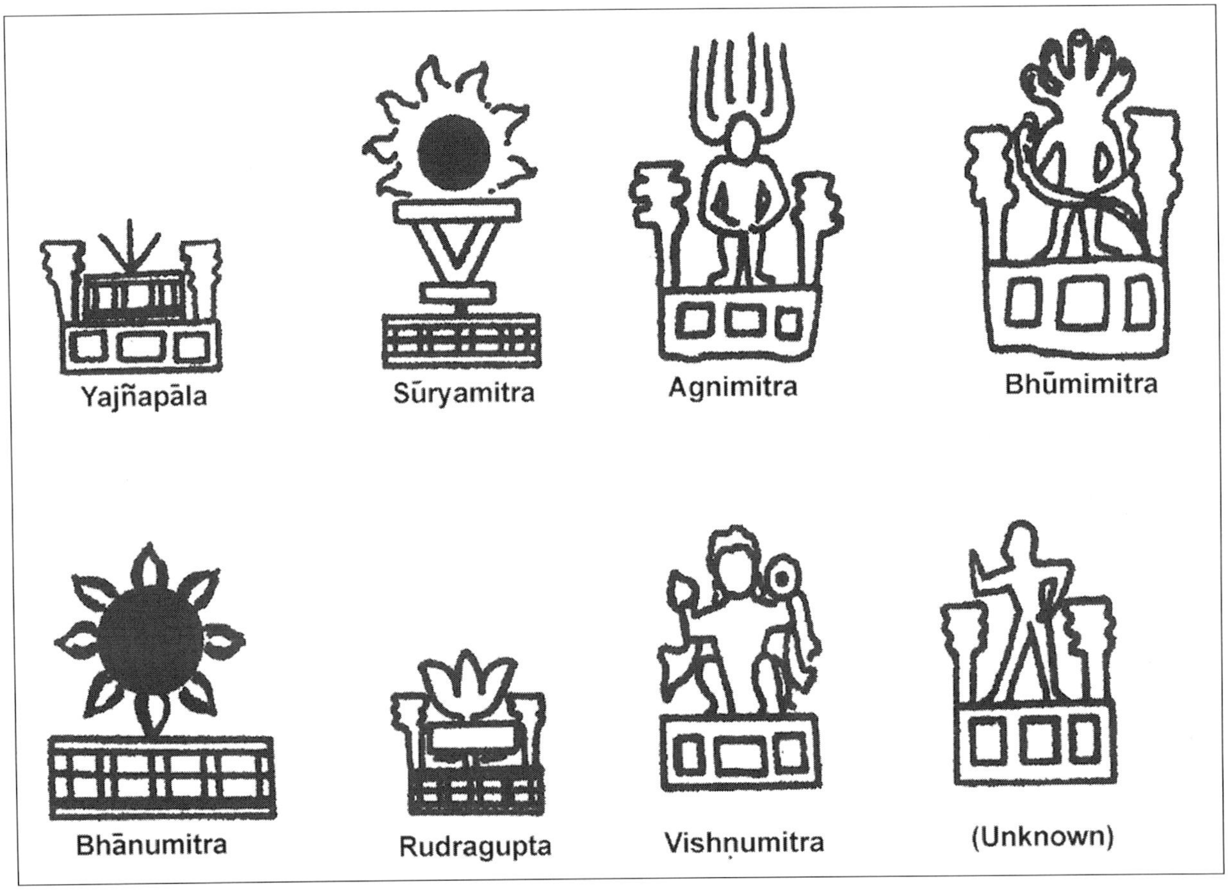

Fig. 65. Reverse devices of Pañchāla coins.

Yajñapāla, and so on. The reverses of Pañchāla coins (Fig. 65) are thus of special interest to the students of Hindu iconography and architecture.

Allan had noted a coin of Agnimitra countermarked by a standing female figure.[8] K.L. Shrimali has noted a symbol 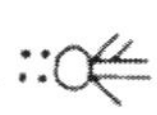 or 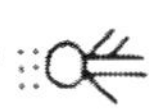 on some coins of Indramitra (along with the symbol 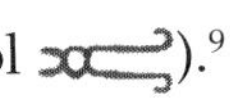).[9] He seems to have drawn the symbol 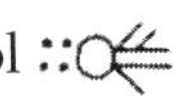 after Bela Lahiri but has given its variant 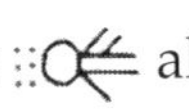 also. The coins being small and not always very clear he probably could not determine the exact form of the symbol. Shailendra Bhandare and Ralf Althoff have brought to light two very fine specimens of Pañchāla coins of Bhānumitra and Agnimitra from Köhler-Osbahr collection (Fig. 66.3-4) on which they see the two symbols above the name of the rulers on the obverse as 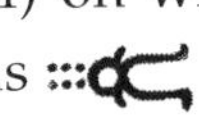 and 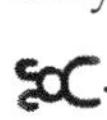.[10] We have thus three variations of the first symbol: 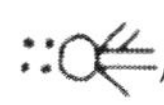, 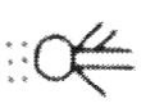 and 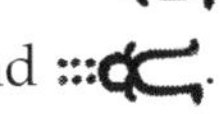. The slanting strokes with the parallel horizontal arms are certainly wrongly drawn by Bela Lahiri and Shrimali. Shailendra and Althoff seem to be closer to the actual symbol in drawing the strokes appended to the right or leg side of the symbol. A careful perusal of the two specimens illustrated by them and numerous others examined by me, however, shows that there are seven dots to the left or head side (or above in its vertical position) arranged in two rows of three and one on left or above:

or . This symbol occurs on the coins of Bhānumitra, Agnimitra and Indramitra as noted above and may be checked up in the two coins illustrated by Shailendra Bhandare and Althoff as well as on the coin of Sūryamitra in Jan Lingen's collection referred to by them and illustrated here for the first time (Fig. 66.6).[11] A coin of Agimita (Agnimitra) illustrated by Sushma Arya[12] leaves absolutely no doubt to its exact form with seven dots as noted above (Fig. 67.1). So I suggest that only the exact form of this symbol (or) should be used now onwards. I think that represents Agni and the seven headed figure on Agnimitra's coins () may be Agni's spouse Svāhā having seven tongues or flames.

The occurrence of this symbol is evidently not exclusive to any one ruler as it is found on the coins of Bhānumitra, Sūryamitra, Agnimitra and Indramitra (along with the second symbol) and is equally enigmatic. The occurrence of the two symbols side by side gives the impression of their being the stylized representation of a couple or two individuals the correct identification and interpretation of which has defied satisfactory explanation. The symbol without dots seems to me to be the stylized figure of the deity whose name occurs on the coin and the figure with seven dots may have stood for the Śakti (power, spouse) of the deity. The seven-headed figure on the coins of Bhānumitra and Sūryamitra probably represents the personification of the *sapta-raśmi* or *saptāśva* (seven rays or horses) aspect of the Sun. The allegorical reference of Indra vanquishing Sūrya[13] and taking away his power may perhaps be the reason for depicting Sūrya's powers on Indramitra's coins. His association with seven *gaṇas* (hosts, groups) of Maruts (winds) of which he is considered as the Lord may have been the other explanation.

The second symbol has been drawn as by Shrimali and as by Bhandare and Althoff. On Jan Lingen's coin of Sūryamitra it looks like or in its vertical form. On the clay sealings of Āshāḍhaghosha and Meghaka[14] also it looks like leaving little doubt to its being a Pañchāla symbol. It shows slight variations but its Brāhmī *mya*-like form in vertical position or its lateral form and with stunted or elongated legs may be accepted as noted by different scholars. The symbol occurs on some un-inscribed pieces of Pañchāla. Both and occur on the coins of Dāmagupta.[15] Sushma Arya reads the name of Dāmabhūti (Fig. 66.7-9) in stead of Dāmagupta.[16] On no coin, however, is the medial vowel *i* clearly seen and the coins indicate the name to have been inscribed as 'Damagutasa'. One specimen shows a small vertical stroke parallel to the vertical upper part of the letter 'ta' giving the impression of its being a part of 'pa' joined with 'ta' (Fig. 66.10). So till some better examples are available with clear letters, the legend 'Damagutasa' should be upheld. A somewhat controversial piece brought to light long back was rightly interpreted by Bela Lahiri as the coin of Dāmagupta over struck by Vaṅgapāla and not the vice versa.[17] Recently more coins of Vaṅgapāla with clear legends have come

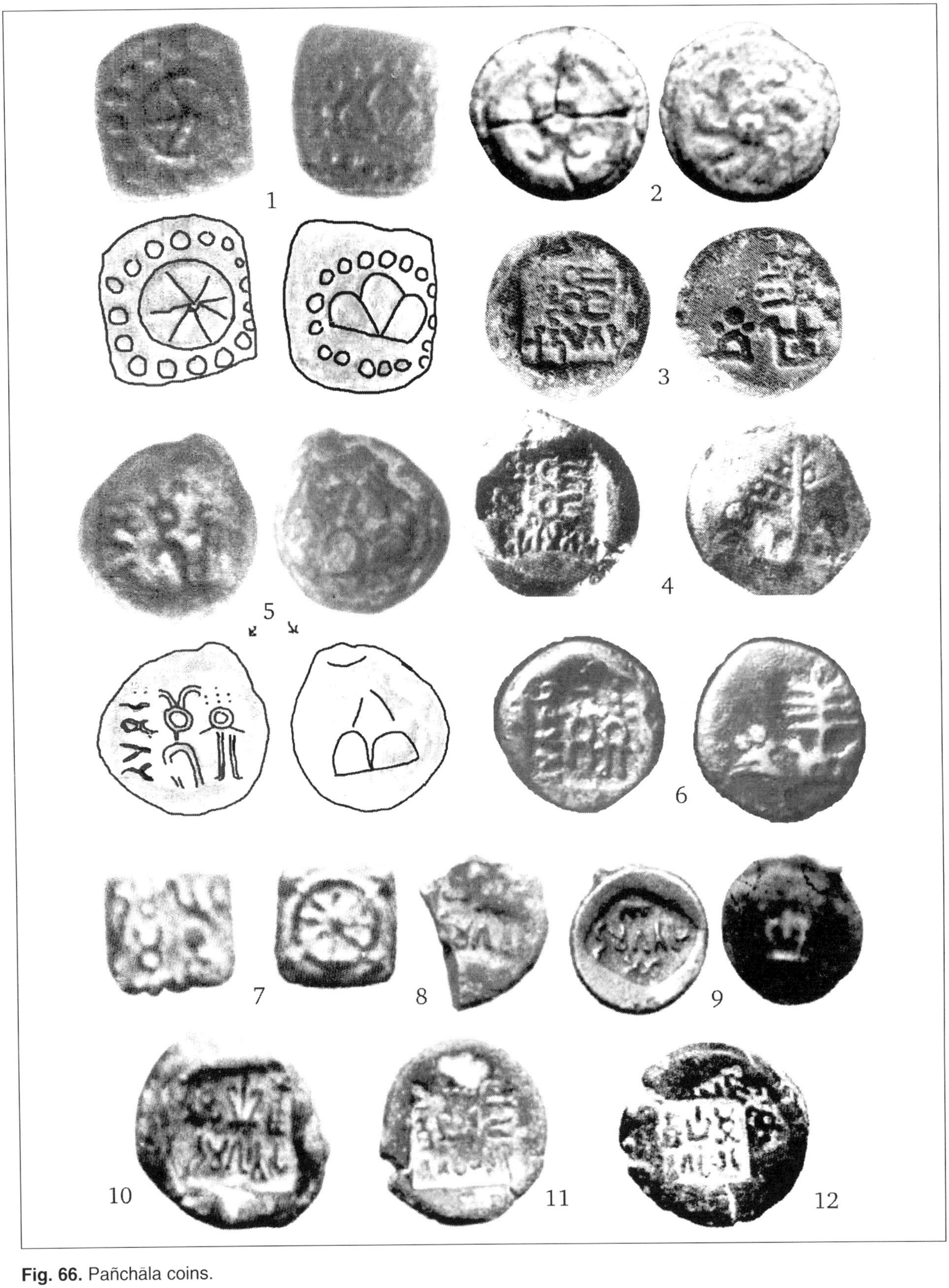

Fig. 66. Pañchāla coins.

to light (Fig. 66.11) including those on which the counter marking done by Vaṅgapāla is very clear (Fig. 66.12).[18]

I draw the attention of scholars to a Pañchāla coin in the British Museum (Fig. 66.5). Roundish in shape and measuring 1.35 X 1.2 cm, it shows the two symbols or figures resembling those of the coins of Bhānumitra, Sūryamitra, Agnimitra and Indramitra as noted above but the name of the king is unfortunately not very clear except the 'mitasa' ending. I am biased to read the name of the ruler as Iṃdramitra [I(ṃ)damitasa]. Its reverse presents a three arched hill or *chaitya* with a crescent above, which is altogether a new reverse device not noticed on any Pañchāla coin as yet. It adds to the repertoire of Pañchāla coin types. It is interesting to note that the arched symbol occurs on the reverse of another coin in the British Museum collection, placed just next to the above mentioned coin indicating the same source. But the arched *chaitya* here is shown with dots all around on a square piece of 1.0 cm. On the other side is depicted a wheel of six spokes within a dotted border (Fig. 66.1).[19] This reminds us of the coins of Dāmagupta with a similar wheel device (Fig. 66.7). Another coin from Ahichhatra shows  on one side and a wheel or whorl-like symbol on the other (Fig. 66.2). Dāmagupta was the earliest Pañchāla ruler in the group. This un-inscribed coin may thus have preceded the coinage of the Pañchāla rulers under discussion.

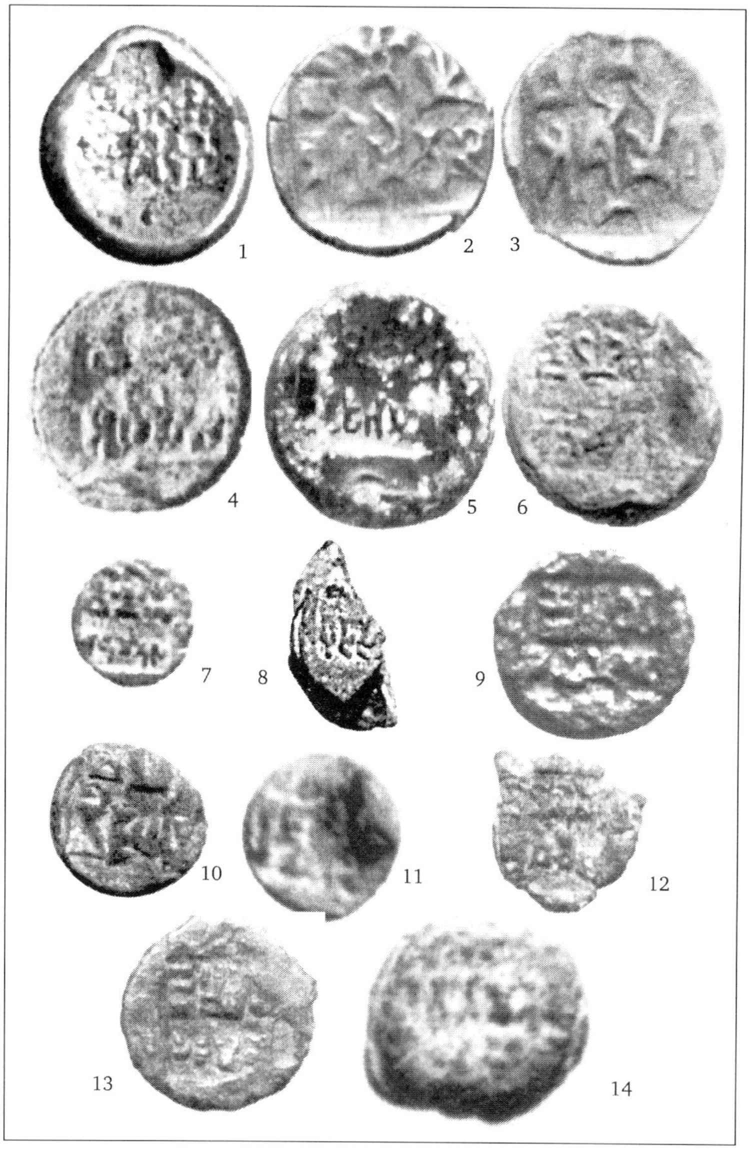

Fig. 67. Pañchāla coins.

As far as the commonly found three symbols of the obverse on most of the coins are concerned, Cunningham simply referred to them as 'three Panchāla symbols' and Allan just gave their drawings 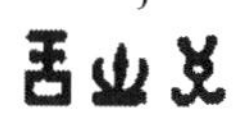 without naming them. No scholar has explained their significance. They may have been auspicious symbols. That at least one of them, the middle one, was so is clear from a coin of Dāmagupta illustrated by Sushma Arya

(Fig. 66.10).[20] Here even the order of the three symbols has been reversed and the middle one looks like a crown. It may have been symbolic of royalty or Rāja-Lakshmī. It figures as 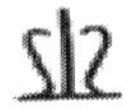 and may also be compared with a *Śrīvatsa* symbol. The order of the three characteristic Pañchāla symbols has been changed on a coin of Viśvagupta.[21] King Prajāpatimitra is known to have used only the first symbol[22] which is absent from the coins of Anamitra and Śivanandī and appears on the reverse, and not on the obverse as usual, on Śrīnandī's coin. The second and third symbols also do not appear on the coins of these three rulers. Dāmagupta makes use of the three characteristic symbols but optionally uses only the third symbol on his coins and sealing.[23] Many Pañchāla coins show counter striking also, e.g. Dāmagupta's coins have been over struck by Vaṅgapāla (Fig. 66.12), Agnimitra's coin shows countermark of a lion[24] as also of a female figure[25], the latter one appearing on the coins of Bhānumitra, Sūryamitra, etc. also.[26] Numerous coins of some hitherto unknown Pañchāla rulers like Vṛishabhamitra (Fig. 67.5), Revatīmitra (Fig. 67.14), Pushyasena (Fig. 67.8), Bhadramitra (Fig. 67.6-7), Vijayamitra (Fig. 67.10), Vasumitra (Fig. 67.9), Yajñamitra (Fig. 67.13), Śivamitra (Fig. 67.12), Yajñabala, Rājyamitra (Fig. 67.11), etc. collected by Virjānanda Daivakarṇi and now housed in the Gurukula Museum at Jhajjar[27] and many others in personal and institutional collections are awaiting systematic study. I myself have seen a hoard of Pañchāla coins including one of Dharmamitra with the three Pañchāla symbols in square incuse with a Delhi dealer. An inscription from Pabhosa near Kauśāmbī refers to king Bahasatimitra son of Gopālī while another one from the same place tells us of Śonakāyana's son king Vaṅgapāla, his son Tevaṇīputra Bhāgavata, and his son Vaihidarīputra Āshāḍhasena.[28] A brick from Erich (ancient Erikachchha, 70 km northeast of Jhansi in Uttar Pradesh) refers to 'Raño Baṃbikasa Dāmamitasa Poṃḍarīka'.[29] A clay sealing from Ahichhatra in the Jhajjar museum gives us the names of four rulers of Gomi dynasty as Vasumitra, Sūryamitra, Pṛithavīmitra and Achyuta – *Gomikulagotragṛihīta-Mahārāja / Śrī-Vasumitra- Mahārāja (Sūryami-) / tra-Mahārāja-Śrī-Pṛithavīmi- / tra Śrī-Mahārāj=Āchyuta(sya).*[30] The Pañchāla rulers obviously did not belong to one but perhaps many different dynasties. Many coins hoards found from Ahichhatra and the surrounding region from time to time contain coins of Pañchāla rulers and others suggestive of their chronology and relationships. Very important are the hoards with following contents –

1. Cast copper coins + Indramitra + Vishṇumitra + Jayamitra + Prajāpatimitra + Rudragupta + Dhruvamitra + Kanishka
2. Rudragupta + Dhruvamitra + Vāsudeva (Kushāṇa)
3. Agnimitra + Indramitra + Vishṇumitra + Jayamitra + Rudragupta[31]

These coin hoards furnish important evidence regarding the chronological proximity of the rulers whose coins are found together. Similar devices used by different rulers also provide clues to their relationships as does orthography, palaeography, phonology and language. The conjuncts and long vowels used in the names of Vṛishabhamitra, Bhadramitra, Agnimitra, Vasumitra, I(ṃ)dramitra, Yajñamitra, Rājyamitra, Vishṇumitra, Prajāpatimitra, Dhruvamitra, Rudragupta,

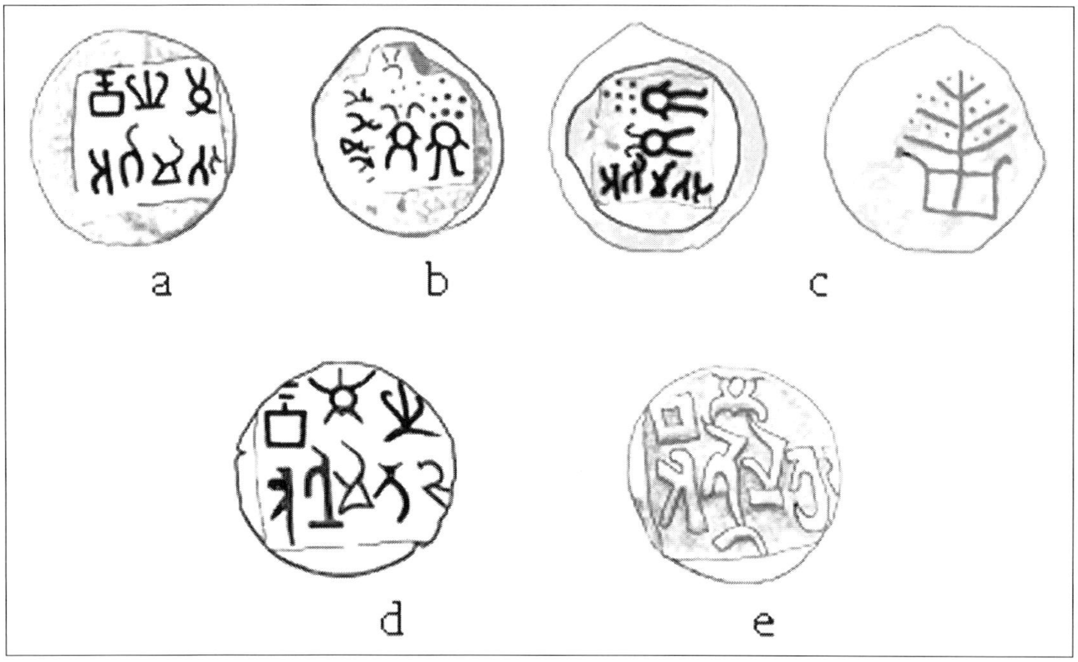

Fig. 68. Coins of Agnimitra showing differences in devices and palaeography.

Rājña Vishṇumi(tra), Pṛithivīmitra, etc. indicate the growing impact of Sanskritization and hence of a later date than others.[32] So the coins of Agimita and Agnimitra (Fig. 67.2-3), Suyamita and Sūryamitra, Idamita and I(ṃ)dramitra, etc. and those showing partial or different devices may belong to different homonymous rulers (Fig. 68.a-e):[33]

The list of Pañchāla rulers who issued coins has swelled from thirteen known to Allan in 1936 to more than forty now. A fresh study and reassessment of the available material regarding Pañchāla coins and sigils is thus a great desideratum now.

NOTES AND REFERENCES

1. Raychaudhuri (1953), *Political History of Ancient India*, 6th ed., Calcutta, pp. 58, 134-35; Shrimali, K.M. (1985), *History of Pañchāla*, Vol. I, New Delhi, pp. 30 ff.
2. *CAI*, p. 75.
3. *IMC*, I, p. 184.
4. *JASB*, 1880, p. 21.
5. *Archaeological Survey of India, Annual Report*, 1912-13, p. 85.
6. Lahiri, *ISNI*, p. 171.
7. *BMCAI*, pp. cxvi-cxxi, 192-204, Pls. XXVII-XXVIII, XXIX.1-9. Allan listed the coins of thirteen rulers.
8. *Ibid.*, p. 201, no. 79, Pl. XLVI.16.
9. Shrimali (1985), *History of Pañchāla*, Vol. II, pp. 78-80, nos. 96-102 and 103-35. Shrimali studied 170 coins of Agnimitra which show a fair diversity in their weight standards, devices and palaeography. He places Agnimitra in *circa* 80-100 CE and has classified them into ten types: A – J (pp. 88-90, Pls. I.9-15, II.1-20 & III.1-4).
10. *ONSNL No. 155* (Winter 1998), p. 17.

11. I am thankful to Jan Lingen for kindly sending the photograph of this coin and allowing me to use it.
12. Arya, Sushma (2001), *Paṃchāla Rājya Kā Itihāsa* (Hindi), New Delhi, pp. 81-82, Fig. 137(a).
13. *Ṛigveda*, X.7, 5.
14. Srivastava, O.P.L. (1995), "Sealings of Three Unknown Kings of Panchala", *ND*, vol. 19, pp. 205-07.
15. Arya (2001), Fig. 127.
16. *Ibid.*, pp. 82-83.
17. *ISNI*, pp. 174-75.
18. Arya (2001), *op. cit.*, p. 84, Fig. 130.
19. British Museum, London, neg. no. CAB 15, P.J.D. 4136, nos. 44-45. See also *Pañchāla*, XI, pp. 48-49.
20. Arya (2001), *op. cit.*, Fig. 130.
21. Srivastava, O.P.L. and Rajiv Rawat (2007), "Coin of an Unknown Pañchāla Ruler: Viśvagupta", *JNSI*, LXIX, pp. 41-42, Pl. I.1.
22. *JNSI*, III, pp. 79-81.
23. Bajpai (1976), *INS*, p. 80, fn. 23; Shrimali (1985), *op. cit.*, Vol. II, p. 26, fn. 3. Vaṅgapāla also used the third symbol on his sealing found from Ahichhatra [Saraswati, Swami Omanand (VS 2031), *Ancient Seals of Haryana*, Jhajjar, VS 2031, no. 285] but all the three symbols on his coins.
24. *BMCAI*, p. 201, Pl. XLVI.15.
25. *Ibid.*, Pl. XLVI.16.
26. Lahiri, Bela (1968), "Typological Study of the Local Coins of Northern India", in Narain, A.K. *et al.* (eds.) (1968), *Seminar Papers on the Local Coins of Northern India c. 300 B. C. to 300 A. D.*, Varanasi, p. 46.
27. *Arya* (2001), *op. cit.*, p. 85.
28. *Ibid.*, pp. 99-100, figs. 199-200.
29. Srivastava, *O.P.L.* (1991), *Archaeology of Erich: Discovery of New Dynasties*, Varanasi, p. 7, Pl. I.2.
30. *Ibid.*, p. 86, Fig. 172. A clay sealing of Pṛithivīmitra is also known from Ahichhatra (*Ibid.*, Fig. 173).
31. *Ibid.*, pp. 87 and 109.
32. Cf. Shrimali, K.L. (1977), "The Chronological Implications of the Language and Palaeography of Pañchāla Coins", *JNSI*, XXXIX, pp.42-48.
33. Cf. Srivastava, O.P.L. (1995), "Pañchāla ke Navīna Śāsaka – Agnimitra I aura Indramitra I", *Pañchāla*, VIII, pp. 3-4 and (200-01), *JNSI*, LXII-LXIII pp. 49-51 where the author distinguishes Dāmagupta I and II, Vaṅgapāla I and II, Agnimitra I and II, Indramitra I and II, and so on and establishes the relationship of various kings on the basis of the symbology of their coins.

XVIII

Some Interesting Ayodhyā Coins

1. A UNIQUE UN-INSCRIBED COPPER COIN

Un-inscribed copper coins of Ayodhyā, ascribed to circa third-second century BCE, are quite rare.[1] Of the seven coins catalogued by Allan, the first two Types are represented by one coin each and Type 3 by five specimens. Allan has, however, rightly observed that the unique piece of Type 1 may not be a coin at all.[2] Type 3, being the commonest, is known from two specimens in the Indian Museum, Kolkata also.[3] All these coins are cast, round in shape and 0.5 inch in diameter. They show on the obverse a *svastika* over a fish and on the reverse a steelyard (or axe) with a taurine above. A new anonymous type of this series has come to our notice[4]

Æ, round, 1.45 cm, weight not taken.

Obv. An animal (probably a bull) to left.

Rev. Steelyard (or axe) with taurine above and another symbol below. (Fig. 69.1)

It may be pointed out that that H. Rivett-Carnac[5] had published a square copper coin with a *svastika* on obverse and bull on reverse, which Allan feels to be a coin of this series.[6] The determination of the obverse and reverse of this series by different scholars is only arbitrary. The bull has been one of the prominent devices of even the subsequent inscribed coins of Ayodhyā.

The coin published here may doubtlessly be connected with the series of un-inscribed copper coins of Allan with which it betrays the similarity of the reverse device. The steelyard or axe on this coin, however, shows the free end to the right unlike Allan's coins of Type 3 which all show its free end to left. The symbol below the steelyard looks like the Brāhmī letter *sa* if viewed from an angle in which the steelyard points upwards. It may be triskeles or a small *svastika* with one arm lost. Unlike the coins of this series which are all cast, this specimen is die struck. As such,

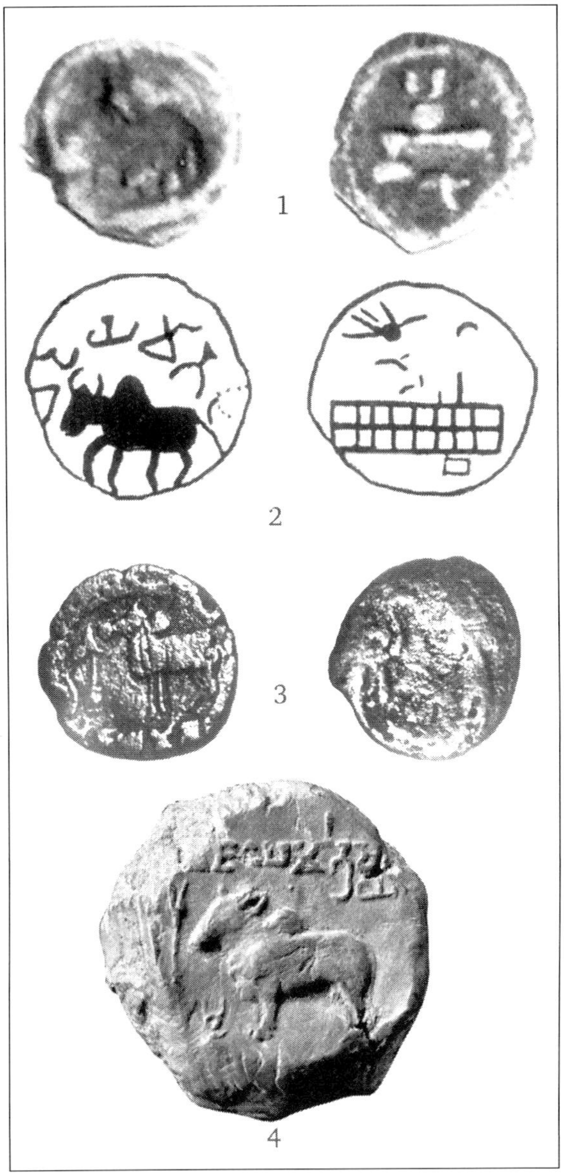

Fig. 69. Ayodhya coins: Anonymous 1, Vijayamitra 2-3, clay sealing of Vijayamitra.

it may represent the last stage of the coins of this series. The coin, however, is unique and has remained unnoticed so far.

2. AN UNPUBLISHED COIN OF VIJAYAMITRA OF AYODHYĀ

The British Museum collection contains the following interesting Ayodhyā coin of king Vijayamitra (Fig. 69.2):

Copper, 16 mm, weight not recorded.[7]

Obv. Humped bull walking to left, Brāhmī legend around from about 8 to 3 o'clock *V(i)jayamitasa*.

Rev. Obliterated but the pedestal with two rows of eight compartments each and traces of other devices above and below it may also be made out.

The coin does not pose any problem of identification as the known Ayodhyā coins of Vijayamitra also carry a bull, generally on the obverse but sometimes on the reverse also, and a similar compartmented pedestal on some specimens of the reverse.[8] All these coins, however, show the legend placed horizontally below the main device or along the margin in the lower half part of the obverse. The present coin is the first specimen to show the legend above the bull around the margin in the upper half part of the obverse. Saṃghamitra is the only other Ayodhyā ruler whose coins carry the legends above the bull on the obverse.[9] It may be pointed out here that a clay sealing in the Allahabad museum belonging to Vijayamitra (Acc. No. K/305) shows the bull to left facing an *Indradhvaja* with a Brāhmī *mya*-like symbol ( ) below in the fiels and the legend placed above the bull in a horizontal line (Fig. 69.4).[10] The temporal proximity of the two rulers is thus evident. Since Saṃghamitra does not use 'the cock on post and tree' as the reverse device, which Vijayamitra adopted and became characteristic reverse device for other Mitra rulers who followed him, chronologically Vijayamitra has to be placed after Saṃghamitra.[11]

3. ANOTHER COIN OF VIJAYAMITRA OF AYODHYĀ

Another copper coin of Vijayamitra in the collection of Dr. Major M.K. Gupta (Burhanpur)[12] may be described as follows –

Æ, round, 1.5 cm, 2.0 g.

Obv. Bull to left before standard, Brāhmī legend *Vijayamitasa* below.

Rev. Cock on left, tree on right. (Fig. 69.3)

The type is well known from the coins of Vijayamitra of Ayodhyā. This coin, however, deserves some special attention for its well preserved obverse device which shows the bull as caparisoned and the standard in front as rising from a pitcher placed on a pedestal. It is just not the bull before the standard but shows some ceremonial event.

NOTES AND REFERENCES

1. *BMCAI*, p. lxxxvii.
2. *Ibid.*, p. 129, Pl. XVI.6-10.
3. *IMC*, I, p. 149, nos. 12-13. See also *JASB*, 1880, Pl. XVII.15.
4. It belongs to the British Museum (Neg. No. CAB 14A, P.J.D. 4118, coin no. 37).
5. *JASB*, 1880, Pl. XVII.15.
6. *BMCAI*, p. lxxxviii.
7. Neg. No. CAB 14A, P.J.D. 4118.38.
8. *BMCAI*, p. 139, Pl. XVIII.2, 4 & 5.
9. *Ibid.*, p. 138, no. 69, Pl. XVI.21.
10. Thaplyal (1972), *op. cit.*, p. 32; Vijay Kumar *et al.* (2021), 'Seals & Sealings kept at Allahabad Museum, District Prayagraj, Uttar Pradesh', *Indian Journal of Archaeology*, Vol. 6, No. 3, p. 135, Fig. 19.
11. Cf. Lahiri, *ISNI*, 143-144. Saṃghamitra may have adopted this pattern of placing the legend at the top on the obverse from the earlier indigenous rulers of Ayodhyā who issued square cast copper coins putting the legend on the top of the main device on the obverse. See *BMCAI*, pp. 130-35, Pls. XVI.11-18, XVII.1-7 and XVIII.4-8.
12. *ND*, Vol. 29-30 (2005-06), p. 46.

XIX

Some Observations on the Square Copper Coins of Ayodhyā

Allan's Catalogue[1] is a monumental work for the study of ancient Indian coins. Most of the scholars, particularly Indian, have been studying ancient Indian coins through this work as it presents the most comprehensive treatment of the various series and coin types. The other monumental works are by Alexander Cunningham [2] and Vincent Smith.[3] Since actual coins are not available to many of the scholars, they rely only on what is available in print. As such, many mistakes committed by stalwarts like Cunningham and Allan, have persisted all through. Without any intention of belittling the great contribution of these great scholars and even those who have followed them, we offer below some of our observations on the inscribed square copper coins of Ayodhyā in the hope that it will lead to a better understanding and analysis of the series.

MŪLADEVA

Allan has described three coins (nos. 8-10) of Mūladeva, second-first century BCE. Made of copper and square in shape, they are almost similar and have been described as following by Allan[4] –

Obv. Bull r.; uncertain object in front, Brāhmī legend *Mūladevasa* above.

Rev. 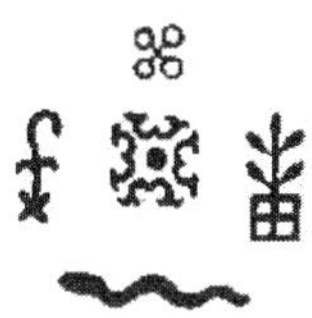 (?)

Cunningham had referred to the animal on the obverse as elephant moving to left and the uncertain object in front as the Buddhist symbol.[5] It may be pointed out here that Allan had rightly recognized the animal as bull.[6] The uncertain object in front, however, is the *nandipada* or *triratna* symbol with Ujjain symbol below.

Both Allan and Cunningham, and all other scholars following them have missed a symbol which exists at the back of the bull. It is . This symbol exists under the deer on the reverse of a Chitreśvara type coin in the British Museum.[7] The symbols on the reverse, however, have not been represented fully and correctly. The exact form of the first symbol on left above the wavy line is not as drawn by Allan but . We feel that it is this form which exists on most of the Ayodhyā coins. Allan has also missed a triangle-headed staff (*Indra-dhvaja*) above this symbol as also a *svastika* above the tree on right. The central symbol (generally known as Taxila symbol) as visible on the second and third coin is actually a circular symbol with a pellet in the centre and having a beaded rim. The whole configuration on the reverse being 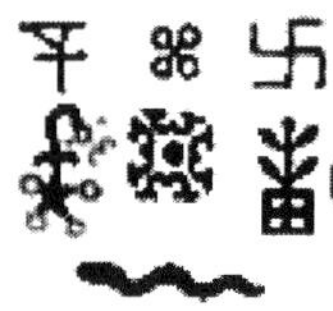.

VĀYUDEVA

Allan has listed four coins of Vāyudeva belonging two each to Var. *a* and *b*. The former variety shows an elephant to left, uncertain object in front and the legend *Vāyudevasa* above. Allan has missed a symbol on the back of the elephant which is *nandipada* or *triratna*. The uncertain object in front of the elephant seems to be , i.e., a square with an umbrella and *Indra-dhvaja* above capped by a crescent in stead of the symbol as drawn by Allan . It is an unusual combination but the coin itself is not very clear to ascertain the exact form. The configuration of the symbols on the reverse, however, is 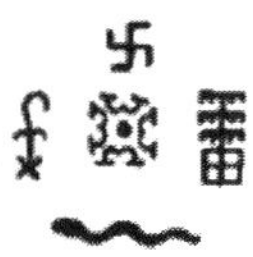 in stead of 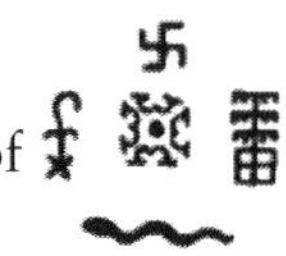 as given by Allan. The wavy line on the reverse seems more likely to be a snake. Also noteworthy is the form of the tree in railing with three horizontal branches having drooping leaves which is typical of the Kuṇinda and Yaudheya coins of Shaḍānana-Shashṭhī and Shaḍānana-Deer type (Class 3 of Allan).[8]

One coin of Var. *b* has been illustrated by Allan. He describes it as bearing on the obverse a bull to right before on right and legend (-)*yudevasa* above. There are traces of an Ujjain symbol on the back of the bull. The symbol in front is also slightly different – it consists of an *Indra-dhvaja* placed on a three arched hill or *chaitya* as seen on the coins of Dhanadeva as discussed below. The legend too does not seem to have been given correctly by Allan. The first visible letter (or symbol?) on the coin is followed by and then *devasa*. The circular symbol may at best be read as *tha* followed by ma indicating the legend to be *thama-devasa*. If we presume that the first letter is out of flan or missing, it may be visualized to have been *Pra*. The whole legend would then be restored as *Prathamadevasa*, giving us an alternate and altogether new name.

The second coin of this variety (coin no. 14) has not been illustrated by Allan. The obverse of this coin is fairly clear and shows the humped and horned bull to right with a symbol which looks like a three arched hill or *chaitya* surmounted by a triangle-headed standard (*Indra-dhvaja*) in front and Ujjain symbol on its back, but the legend is actually *Dhanadevasa*. The coin should, therefore, be attributed to Dhanadeva and not Vāyudeva.

VIŚĀKHADEVA

Allan has given the configuration of the reverse symbols of Var. *a* of Viśākhadeva as

but the symbol on the upper corner on the right hand above the tree in railing is a *nandipada* and not the inverted multi-arched hill or *chaitya* as shown by Allan, the whole configuration thus being

.

Var. b has been described by Allan as follows –

Obv. Bull l.; uncertain object in front, Brāhmī legend *Visa – devasa.*

Rev.

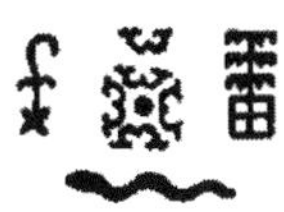

There seems to be an inverted *nandipada* on the back of the bull and the uncertain object in front is an Ujjain symbol with a taurine above it on the obverse.

DHANADEVA

The coins of Dhanadeva belong to two varieties – *a* and *b*. On the coins of Var. a, Allan shows bull to right before symbol on right, but this symbol is actually a three arched hill or *chaitya* surmounted by a triangle-headed standard on the obverse. On the obverse of Var. b, Allan referred to a 'small uncertain object in front' of the bull to left. It is a small *nandipada*.

It may also be pointed out here that the legend on coin no. 27 with elephant to left on the obverse and Abhisheka-Lakshmī in an oval on the reverse was wrongly deciphered as *Sivadatasa* whereas it actually is *Dhanadevasa*. Bela Lahiri has rightly attributed this coin to Dhanadeva.[9]

ŚIVADATTA

Allan could not make out properly the symbols on Vars. *c* and *d* of the coins of Śivadatta and referred to them as a 'Group of uncertain symbols, including and a variety of tree in railing'. The three symbols on his coin no. 35 of the latter variety seem to be tree in railing, *śrīvatsa* and a curved post above an Ujjain symbol from left to right, with a wavy or serpentine line below.

POTHADEVA

Allan described three coins (nos. 37-39) under 'Uncertain' category but their legends indicate that they may be attributed to king Pothadeva. On the reverse of coin no. 37, Allan describes tree in centre, 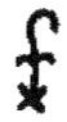 on right (actually left), uncertain on right and serpentine line below. The uncertain symbol on the right is a *svastika*.

NOTES AND REFERENCES

1. Allan, *BMCAI*.
2. *CAI*.
3. *IMC*, I.
4. *BMCAI*, p. 130, nos. 8-10, Pl. XVI.11-12.
5. *CAI*, pp. 91-92, Pl. IX.4.
6. It is very clear on all the three coins listed by Allan.
7. *BMCAI*, p. 168, no. 78, Pl. XXIII.11.
8. *BMCAI*, pp. 159-68, Pls. XXII-XXIII; pp. 270-75, Pls. XXXIX.19-21, XL.11-15.
9. *ISNI*, p. 141, fn. 175. See also *JNSI*, XIII, p. 197.

XX

A New Type Coin of Śivaghoshaka

A large number of Hindu rulers are known from coins discovered at and around Mathurā – Gomitra, Sūryamitra, Brahmamitra, Dṛiḍhamitra, Vishṇumitra, Purushadatta, Rāmadatta, Uttamadatta, Kāmadatta, Bhavadatta, Śeshadatta, Balabhūti, etc. who were followed by the Śaka Kshatrapas Śivaghosha, Śivadatta, Hagāmāsha (or Hagāmasha) and Hagāna, Mahākshatrapa Rājuvula and his son Śoḍāsa.[1] The coins of Śivaghosha and Śivadatta are very rare, the former represented by a unique specimen in Sir Richard Burn's collection and the latter also by a unique piece in the British Museum.[2] They have been described by Allan as following.

Śivadatta

Æ, round, 0.7 inch, 65.0 grains (=4.2 g).

Obv. Lakshmī standing facing, below, on right, on left, Brāhmī legend 𑀔𑀢𑀧𑀲 𑀰𑀺𑀯𑀤𑀢[𑀲] (*Khatapasa Śivadatasa*) around from 7 to 3 o'clock.

Rev. Horse to left.[3]

Śivaghosha

Æ, round, 0.75 inch, 81.4 grains (=5.3 g).

Obv. Lakshmī and tree, Brāhmī legend 𑀔𑀢𑀧𑀲 𑀰𑀺𑀯𑀖𑁄𑀱𑀲 (*Khatapasa Śivaghoshasa*) around.

Rev. Horse to left.

This coin of Śivaghosha is known to us from Allan's description and has been illustrated by Mitchiner and Senior.[4]

Published here is a new coin of Śivaghoshaka:

Æ[5], round, 2.0 cm, 5.7 g (= 88 grains or 49 *rattīs* approximately), find spot: Ahrwan near Palwal.

Obv. Brāhmī legend *Śivaghoshakasa* in bold letters in a deep round incuse.

Rev. Obliterated (Fig. 70).

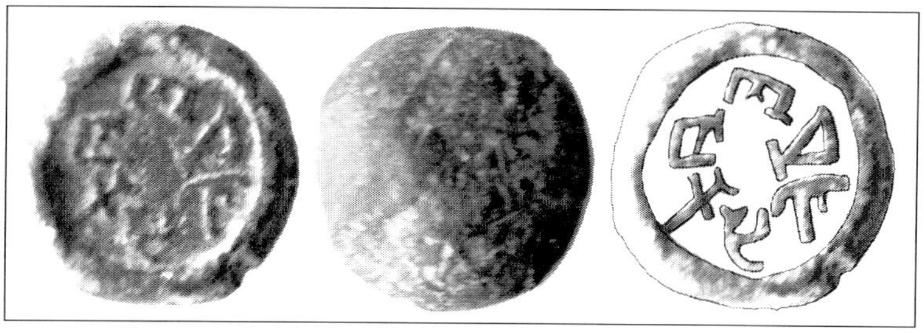

Fig. 70. Coin of Śivaghoshaka.

The coin seems to have been struck on an earlier piece by heating that to a high degree and striking it with a hammer die resulting in a deep incuse on the obverse. The piece has also turned slightly cup shaped obliterating the earlier device(s) of which only traces are left on the reverse. The traces indicate that there existed perhaps a horse or a bull to right and a ladder-like symbol below. There are faint traces of river with fishes and some other symbols on this side but one cannot be very sure of these for they are very vague. The bull finds depiction on the coins of Rāmadatta and Kāmadatta but as a very small figure along with various other motifs and the latter symbol occurs on the coins of Gomitra, Uttamadatta, Rāmadatta and Kāmadatta.[6] Śivaghoshaka obviously used the coin of some earlier ruler for striking this piece. The coin is quite corroded but the legend is clearly visible. Notable, however, is the fact that the legend runs anti-clockwise in contradistinction to the earlier Kshatrapa coins where it is to be read clockwise from inside. The disposition of the legend also differs and the crescent-shaped serif marks are a characteristic of the Brāhmī characters which cannot be assigned to a period earlier than the first century CE. The obverse does not show any device except the legend.

The coin has been found from the ancient mound of Ahrwan located about 12 km southwest of Palwal on road to Hathin in district Palwal, Haryana (Fig. 71).[7] The old mound extends over an area of about 40 acres and is nearly 12 meters high. Painted Grey Ware, early historic and medieval plain red ware sherds, sprinklers, votive tanks, copper coins of Hagāmāsha and Śoḍāsa, an inscribed clay sealing with the Brāhmī legend 'Śamaṇasa' in the characters of *circa* second century BCE, bricks measuring 36 X 22 X 7 cm, Kushāṇa seated Buddha in red sandstone, fragments of spotted red sandstone Kushāṇa Buddhist images and railing, Kushāṇa terracotta depicting Pañchaka and Hāritī, early and medieval images of Hindu and Jaina faiths, etc. have been picked up from the mound from time to time during the past.[8]

The symbol of a conventional tree occurs on all the coins of the Hindu rulers as well as the Kshatrapas except Rājuvula, the Ujjayinī symbol exists on the coins of the Mitras but is replaced by a Brāhmī *śa*-like symbol on the coins of the Dattas. The Śaka Kshatrapas belonged to two distinct groups as revealed by the reverses of their coins – Rājuvula and Śoḍāsa forming one group[9] and Hagāna, Hagāmāsha, Śivadatta and Śivaghosha forming the other. Rājuvula made use of Greek and Kharoshṭhī scripts on his coins of Class I but replaced the former with Brāhmī subsequently. Śoḍāsa discarded even Kharoshṭhī.

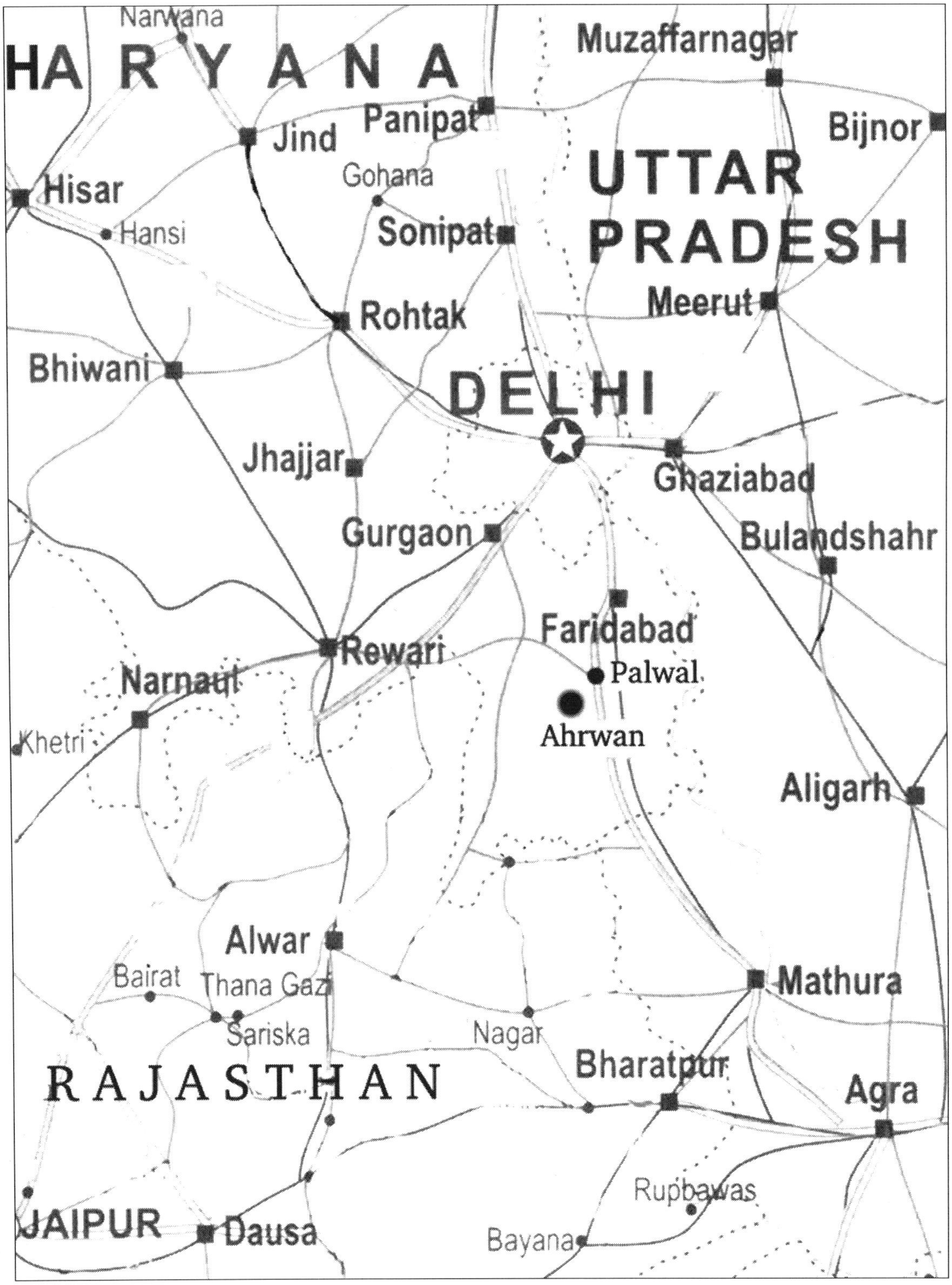

Fig. 71. Location of Ahrwan.

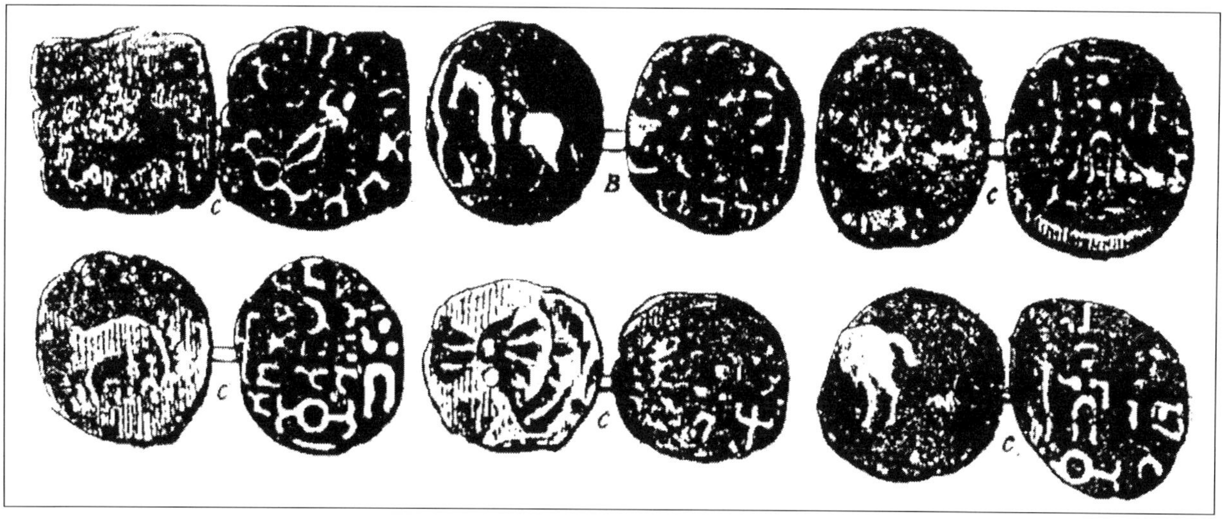

Fig. 72. Coins of later Mathura Kshatrapas.

Rulers of the latter group are distinguished by the use of horse as the reverse device and 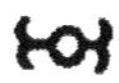 symbol on the obverse (Fig. 72).[10]

Scytho-Parthian rule was extended to Mathurā during the period of Azilises and Rājuvula served him at Taxila and slightly later perhaps to the east and south of the Jhelum including Mathurā.[11] Rājuvula issued coins of Bust of king/Pallas type (Class I of Allan) using Greek and Kharoshṭhī and Lakshmī/Abhisheka-Lakshmī type (Allan's Class II) with legend only in the Brāhmī script on the obverse.

Coins of the former type bespeak of his connection with the northwest India which is also indicated by his 'Mounted king/Zeus Nikephoros' type[12] while the latter seem to have been issued continuing the local type at Mathurā.[13] His coins of Lion/Hercules type (Allan's Class III) with traces of the Greek script on the obverse and Kharoshṭhī on the reverse along with some allied types like Bust of king/Pallas type not represented in the British Museum collection but collected by Talbot, Rodgers, Rawlins and Whitehead (all Punjab collectors) were perhaps originally meant for the region between Taxila and Mathurā, a fact substantiated by finds from Hoshiarpur, Amritsar, Nurmahal, Sultanpur Lodi, etc.[14] Some scholars[15] regarded Rājuvula as the successor of Hagāmāsha and Hagāna but a careful study of the evolution of the local types of Mathurā coins showing the adoption of the devices of Hindu rulers of Mathurā and exclusive use of Brāhmī by his son Śoḍāsa on his coins and in his inscriptions clearly indicates that the rule of Hagāna and Hagāmāsha is to be placed later than that of Rājuvula and Śoḍāsa as was aptly pointed out by J.N. Banerjea.[16] The find-spots of the epigraphs and coins of Rājuvula's son Śoḍāsa (bearing the Brāhmī legends *Rājuvulaputasa khatapasa Śoḍāsasa* and *Mahākhatapasa Śoḍāsasa*) suggest that his rule was restricted only to the Mathurā and its surrounding region. His power and dominions seem to have suffered substantially because of the growing power of Gondophares I whose coins have been discovered from Ajaram (district Hoshiarpur); Sirhind and Brass (district Patiala); Rohira (district Sangrur); Sunet, Jagraon, Bahlolpur and Kheri Naudh Singh (district Ludhiana); Sanghol (district

Fatehgarh Sahib); Nurpur (district Jalandhar); Pathankot; etc. in Punjab and Ambala, Bari Kohori, Naraingarh, Thanesar, etc. in Haryana.[17] Unfortunately we do not know for how long did Śoḍāsa rule but there is enough of numismatic evidence to show the continuity of Satrapal rule at Mathurā. The coin of Kshatrapa To[/Bha]raṇaḍāsa referred to by Allan[18] from Richard Burn's collection bearing the Brāhmī legend *Mahakhatapasa putasa khatapasa* [*T*(*o*)*ra*]*ṇaḍāsasa* (𑀫𑀳𑀔𑀢𑀧𑀲𑀧𑀼𑀢𑀲𑀔𑀢𑀧𑀲[𑀢𑁄𑀭]𑀡𑀟𑀸𑀲𑀲卐) with a *svastika* at the end of the legend like those of the coins of Rājuvula and Śoḍāsa and showing Lakshmī with conventional tree on the obverse and Abhisheka Lakshmī on the reverse has also to be grouped with Rājuvula and Śoḍāsa for being similar to their coins. It has been suggested that he may have been the unnamed son of Rājuvula of the Morā well inscription.[19] Allan thought that he was perhaps the elder son of Rājuvula who predeceased his father as a result of which Śoḍāsa was made Kshatrapa under his father[20] but Richard Salomon thinks that this coin belongs to Śoṇaḍāsa which is only a variant of the name of Śoḍāsa.[21]

As noted above, the coins of the later rulers are distinguished by the horse to left on the reverse and the symbol on the obverse. B.N. Mukherjee has published another Kshatrapa coin from Mathurā showing a tree in railing in the centre, standing wavy line on right and symbol below with Brāhmī legend from 7 to 4 o'clock *Khatapasa vaja*(*ā*)*tatajama* on the obverse and a horse prancing to left on the reverse (Fig. 73).[22]

B.N. Mukherjee takes the symbol as comparable to the Gondopharian symbol and thinks that the Mathurā Kshatrapas using this symbol on their coins owed allegiance to Gondophares whose influence extended to Mathurā after Śoḍāsa.[23] He observes that "Typologically the obverse devices of the coins of Śivadatta, Śivaghosha and a class of specie of Hagāmasha are related to those of the group of coins of Rājuvula and of the coins of Śoḍāsa and so-called Toraṇaḍāsa or Bharaṇaḍāsa. On another group of Hagāmasha's coins we can notice a wavy line and a stylized version of "a tree within railing" device, but not the representation of a standing goddess (which forms the principal obverse type of the Mathuran coins of the group of Rājuvula). On the other hand, neither the obverse device(s) nor the reverse type of the joint coinage of Hagāna and Hagāmasha can be related to the group of Rājuvula. These considerations", he continues, "suggest that the coins of the group of Rājuvula were followed by those of Śivadatta and Śivaghosha (or of Śivaghosha and Śivadatta) and then by the specie of Hagāmasha."[24] Bela Lahiri, however, observes that "The names of the two rulers of the

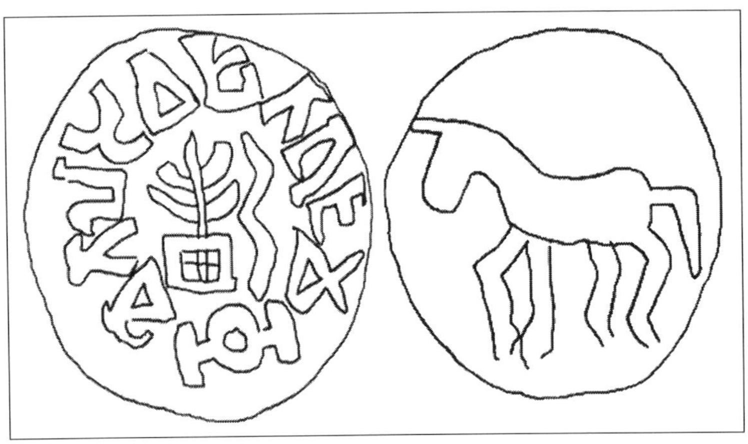

Fig. 73. A coin of Mathura Kshatrapas.

Hagāna-Hagāmāsha group, viz. Śivaghosha and Śivadatta, suggest that they flourished at a time when the process of Hinduisation of the Śakas was complete, and that they were probably the latest of the Satraps".[25] When she wrote she did not know of the coin of Vajatatajama as it was published later. Nor was the coin of Śivaghoshaka published here known to any of the authors to be discussed by them. I concur with Bela Lahiri to regard Śivadatta and Śivaghosha to be the latest of the Kshatrapas of the second group known till then. The coin of Śivaghosha in Sir Richard Burn's collection described by Allan shows that he discarded the symbol 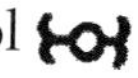 ending allegiance, even nominal if any, to the Gondopharian overlord. Vajatatajama, who may have been a scion of the Hagāmasha-Hagāna family as the name suggests, probably took control for some time, may be with some help from his Gondopharian overlord, and issued coins of the type illustrated above with the Gondophrian symbol 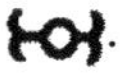. Śivaghosha seems to have overthrown him at a time when his overlord could not come to his succor being himself overrun by the Kushāṇa supremacy.

Our coin, however, poses another difficulty. The legend on this coin is *Śivaghoshakasa* without the title *Khatapasa* (*Kshatrapasa*). Though quite likely yet it is difficult to prove in the present state of our knowledge that he was none else than Śivaghosha who having been victorious against Vajatatajama, issued his coins of the type published by Allan and soon declared independence and struck his currency with his name as Śivaghoshaka discarding the satrapal title. The weight of Śivaghosha's coin published by Allan (5.3 g) approximates to the coin of Śivaghoshaka (5.7 g) and both the coins seem to have been struck on the 48-*rattī* weight standard. Though the evidence of one or two coins does not permit of a definite conclusion yet it may be suggested that discarding of the Gondopharian symbol and horse device indicate that Śivaghosha(ka) may have been the last of the rulers of Mathurā who was probably subjugated in about the middle of the first century CE by the Kushāṇas whose large number of coins and inscriptions are found at Mathurā.[26]

NOTES AND REFERENCES

1. *CAI*, pp. 85-90, Pl. VIII; *BMCAI*, pp. cviii-cxvi & 169-91, Pls. XXIV-XXVI, XLIII.15-21, XLIV.1-5; *IMC*, I, p. 193. A coin of Satamita of Mathurā (Satyamitra according to K.D. Bajpai) has also been published in the *JNSI*, vol. XXVIII, 1966, p. 42, Pl. II.7. Some kings (Gomitra, Vishṇumitra, Sūryamitra, Dhanabhūti, etc.) are known from inscriptions also. A coin of Kshatrapa Toraṇaḍāsa or Bharaṇaḍāsa, son of a Mahākshatrapa, is also known from Sir Richard Burn's collection (*Allan*, *BMCAI*, p. cxii). For the typological, symbological and chronological analysis of these coins see Lahiri, *ISNI*, pp. 151-69.
2. *BMCAI*, p. cxii.
3. *Ibid.*, p. 183, Pl. XXV.26. Allan dates Śivadatta to *circa* 60 – 50 BCE.
4. Mitchiner, Michael [(1978), *Oriental Coins and their Values: The Ancient and Classical World (600 B.C. – A.D. 650)*, Hawkins Publications, London, p. 572, # 4532] dated it to *circa* 50 CE. Senior, R.C. [(2001), *Indo-Scythian Coins And History: The Illustrated Catalogue of Indo-Scythian and Indo-Parthian Coins*, 3 volumes, Lancaster-Pennsylvania-London: Classical Numismatic Group, Inc., Vol. II, p. 128, no. 157.2] gives its exact weight as 5.27 g. Bela Lahiri (*ISNI*, p. 165, fn. 116) thinks that an uncertain coin listed by Smith in the Indian Museum collection (*IMC*,

I, p. 194, Uncertain, no. 1) also belongs to Śivaghosha. The coin has not been illustrated and cannot be checked up.

5. The coin looks to be made of copper but in the absence of any scientific test it is difficult to say if it was not alloyed with any other metal.
6. Allan, *BMCAI*, pp. 170-71, Pl. XXV.2-7 (Gomitra II); p. 177, Pl. XXIV.15-17 (Uttamadatta); pp. 179-80, Pl. XXIV.5-8 & 12-13 (Rāmadatta) and p. 182, Pl. XXIV.18 (Kāmadatta).
7. I am thankful to Dr. Lal Singh of Faridabad for bringing it to my notice and also sending me its details and scans.
8. Handa, Devendra (2006), *Sculptures From Haryana (Iconography & Style)*, Shimla-New Delhi, pp. 3, 76-77, 131, 228, 250 and 267; (2007), "A Terracotta Seal from Ahrwan (District Palwal, Haryana)", *ICSNL*, No. 45, pp. 107-09; (2010), "Archaeological Remains from Ahrwan, District Palwal, Haryana", *Purātattva*, No. 40, pp. 205-07, Pls. 1-5.
9. Allan (*BMCAI*, pp. 183-91) dates Rājuvula between *circa* 40 – 20 BCE and Śoḍāsa between circa 20 – 10 BCE and places Hagāmasha in circa 50 – 40 BCE after Śivadatta (*c.* 60 – 50 BCE). Senior places Rajuvula in c. 25 – 15 BCE and has observed that Hagamasha and Hagana follow Śoḍāsa (and his horse type coins) and occupy the period up to the Kushāṇa conquest under Soter Megas [Senior, R.C. (2001), pp. 100-101].
10. Prinsep, James (1858), *Essays on Indian Antiquities*, edited by E. Thomas, London, Pl. XLIV.
11. Mukherjee, B.N. (1969), *An Agrippan Source – A Study in Indo-Parthian History*, Calcutta, p. 219.
12. Mukherjee, B.N. (1981), *Mathurā and Its Society – the Śaka-Pahlava Phase*, Calcutta, p. 9, Pl. I.1.
13. Allan, *BMCAI*, pp. 185-90.
14. *Ibid.*, p. 118, nos. 118 & 120; *CASR*, XIV, pp. 62 & 67. Some of his coins have been found from western Uttar Pradesh also.
15. Rapson, E.J. (Ed.) (1968), *op. cit.*, p. 527; Raychaudhuri (1953), *op. cit.*, p. 445; Allan, *BMCAI*, p. cxi; etc.
16. Banerjea, J.N. (1957), "The Satraps of Northern and Western India", in K.A. Nilkanta Sastri (ed.), *A Comprehensive History of India*, Vol. II, Calcutta, p. 268. Sircar (1968, p.313) holds that the mention of Hagāna before Hagāmasha in their joint issues (*Khatapāna Hagānasa Hagāmashasa*) indicates that Hagāna was the senior partner.
17. *CASR*, XIV, p. 116; Rodgers, C.J. (1891), *Report of the Panjab Circle of the Archaeological Survey of India for 1888-89*, List of Coins (Appendix), p. 2; *Purātattva*, No. 12, 1980-81, p. 127; Sharma and Kumar (1986), pp. 44-50.
18. Allan, *BMCAI*, p. cxii.
19. *CASR*, XX, p. 49, Pl. V.4; *Archaeological Survey of India, Annual Report*, 1911-12, p. 127.
20. *BMCAI, loc. cit.*
21. Salomon, Richard (1975), "Re-identification of the Coin of Kshatrapa Toraṇaḍāsa", *JNSI*, XXXVII, pp, 147-49.
22. Mukherjee, B.N. (1976), "A Unique Satrapal Coin", *JNSI*, XXXVIII, Part II, pp. 60-61, Pl. I.3 and (1981), *op. cit.*, p. 30, Pl. III.23-23A. I feel inclined to restore the legend as *Khatapasa V(i)j(i)ta-gajama* as the form of the letter 'ta' preceding 'jama' of the legend *Khatapasa Vajātatajama* differs from 'ta' occurring twice earlier on this coin.
23. *JNSI*, XXXVIII, p. 61.
24. Mukherjee (1981), *op. cit.*, pp. 30-31. Mukherjee thinks that the coins struck jointly by Hagāmasha and Hagāna should be placed after the pieces struck by Hagāmasha alone.
25. Lahiri, *ISNI*, p. 167.
26. Raychaudhuri (1953), *op. cit.*, p. 473.

XXI

Social Mobility and the Migration of a Numismatic Motif

The Vṛishṇis were known to us as a very ancient people from literary sources[1] but it was Alexander Cunningham who discovered their unique silver coin in 1891[2] which was subsequently placed in the British Museum.[3] Cunningham did not record its exact provenance and published it along with the coins of the Audumbaras. The subsequent scholars therefore differ regarding the original home of the Vṛishṇis. Bela Lahiri[4] places them in the Punjab from where they later shifted to Mathura and afterwards to Dvārakā but Asim Kumar Chatterjee[5] and K.K. Dasgupta[6] differ from her. The circular coin has a diameter of 1.5 cm and weighs 2.073 g (32 grains). It bears on the obverse a sort of *nandipada* standard in railing with a composite animal, half-lion and half-elephant, in front and the circular Brāhmī legend *Vṛishṇi-rājajña-gaṇasya tra(ā)ta(ā)rasya* of *circa* second-first century BCE while the reverse shows an elaborate twelve-spoked wheel and the circular Kharoshṭhī legend *Vṛishṇi-rājaṇṇa-(gaṇasa)-tra(tarasa)* within a pellet border (Fig. 74.1-2). Early literary evidence, the use of Kharoshṭhī and grouping it with the Audumbara coins certainly point to its Punjab provenance.[7]

Chakra 'wheel' (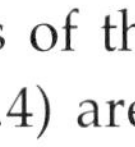) and half-lion and half-elephant (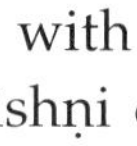) seem to have been the special symbols of the Vṛishṇis. These symbols along with *mūsala* 'pestle' and *gadā* 'club' (Fig. 74.4) are found on the post-Kushāṇa Vṛishṇi clay sealings found from Sunet in Punjab brought to light by Swami Omanand Saraswati. Found amongst the Sunet sealings were five pieces which carried the legend *Jitaṃ Bhagavatā* or a part thereof with Vṛishṇi symbols. Three sealings showed only the symbols including the conch shell.[8] Vṛishṇi symbols were found on a Sunet sealing with the legend *Siddhaṃ. . . Jaya/Pañchanāyakānāṃ* also.[9] The form of the wheel, pestle, club and half-lion and half-elephant symbols seems to have undergone changes at different times and at the hands of different artists. The wheel was sometimes represented by pellets and so also the club (as pellets placed one on the other) as for example on a sealing bearing the legend *Yogeśvaraḥ* seen by me with an antiquity dealer many years back (Fig. 74.5). Another sealing from Sunet bearing the legend *Jitaṃ Bhagavatā* shows the Vṛishṇi symbols of wheel, club and pestle but the wheel has fellies (Fig. 74.6).[10] These sealings indicate that sometimes only a few of the symbols were also used.

An interesting coin said to have been found from Hisar was published by Prashant P. Kulkarni some time back.[11] It bears the early Brāhmī legend *Pusamitasa* on the obverse and a wheel, club, Ujjayinī symbol, plough and pestle on the reverse, the first three in the upper row and the last two in the lower row(Fig. 74.7). To me this seems to be a Vṛishṇi coin issued by some local ruler named Pushyamitra carrying the usual five Vṛishṇi symbols but with the half-lion and half-elephant symbol substituted by the Ujjain symbol.

A sealing from Naurangabad near Bhiwani carries the wheel and the stylized half-lion-half-elephant symbols on post on left and right (Fig. 74.3.[12] As noted above Sunet sealings show that the wheel and half-lion and half-elephant were sometimes fused and shown on two different posts placed in railing (Fig. 74.4).[13] Anyway, all these pieces point to the location of the Vṛishṇis in the Punjab.

The Śaka conquest of Punjab is variously attributed by scholars to Maues (*c.* 85 – 60 BCE)[14], Azes (*c.* 60 – 20 BCE)[15] and Rājuvula (*c.* 25 BCE – c. 5 CE).[16] The Greeks were definitely expelled from Taxila and Punjab region in about 55 BCE when Azes dethroned Hippostratos, the last Greek king to rule over Taxila and western Punjab. The Śakas subsequently extended their sway to the Mathura region. Coins of Azes[17] have been found from Amritsar and Kaithal[18] and his satrap Rājuvula from Sultanpur and Nurmahal in the Jalandhar Doab and from Mathura and some other sites in western Uttar Pradesh.[19] Early incursions of the Śakas seem to have put an end to the indigenous rule in Punjab and Haryana and pushed the Vṛishṇis to Mathurā where they are found settled according to the Mora Well Inscription of Rājuvula's successor Śoḍāśa which mentions the installation of the images of the five heroes of the Vṛishṇi clan in a stone shrine.[20] The five Vṛishṇi heroes are identified with Saṃkarshaṇa (Balrāma), Vāsudeva (Kṛishṇa), Pradymna, Sāmba and Aniruddha. *Chakra* is associated with Vāsudeva, plough and pestle with Saṃkarashaṇa, and the latter with Sāmba also. Does it indicate that the symbols were associated with the Vṛishṇi heroes?

Mathurā, according to the *Mahābhārata* (Sabhā Parva, XIV.44) was the city of the Yādavas and the place of birth of Kṛishṇa who became the chief of the confederation formed by the Andhakas and the Vṛishṇis. As per the numismatic evidence the Vṛishṇis may have shifted from Punjab-Haryana region where they issued their coins during the second-first century BCE to Mathurā under foreign pressure and may have made it their home. In due course it seems to have become their stronghold.

Interestingly, the Vṛishṇi symbol of *chakra* and stylized half-lion and half-elephant on post occurs with Brāhmī and Kharoshṭhī legend on the reverse of the coins of Kshaharāta Kshatrapa Ābhīraka (Fig. 74.8 & 75.1)[21] which show on the obverse

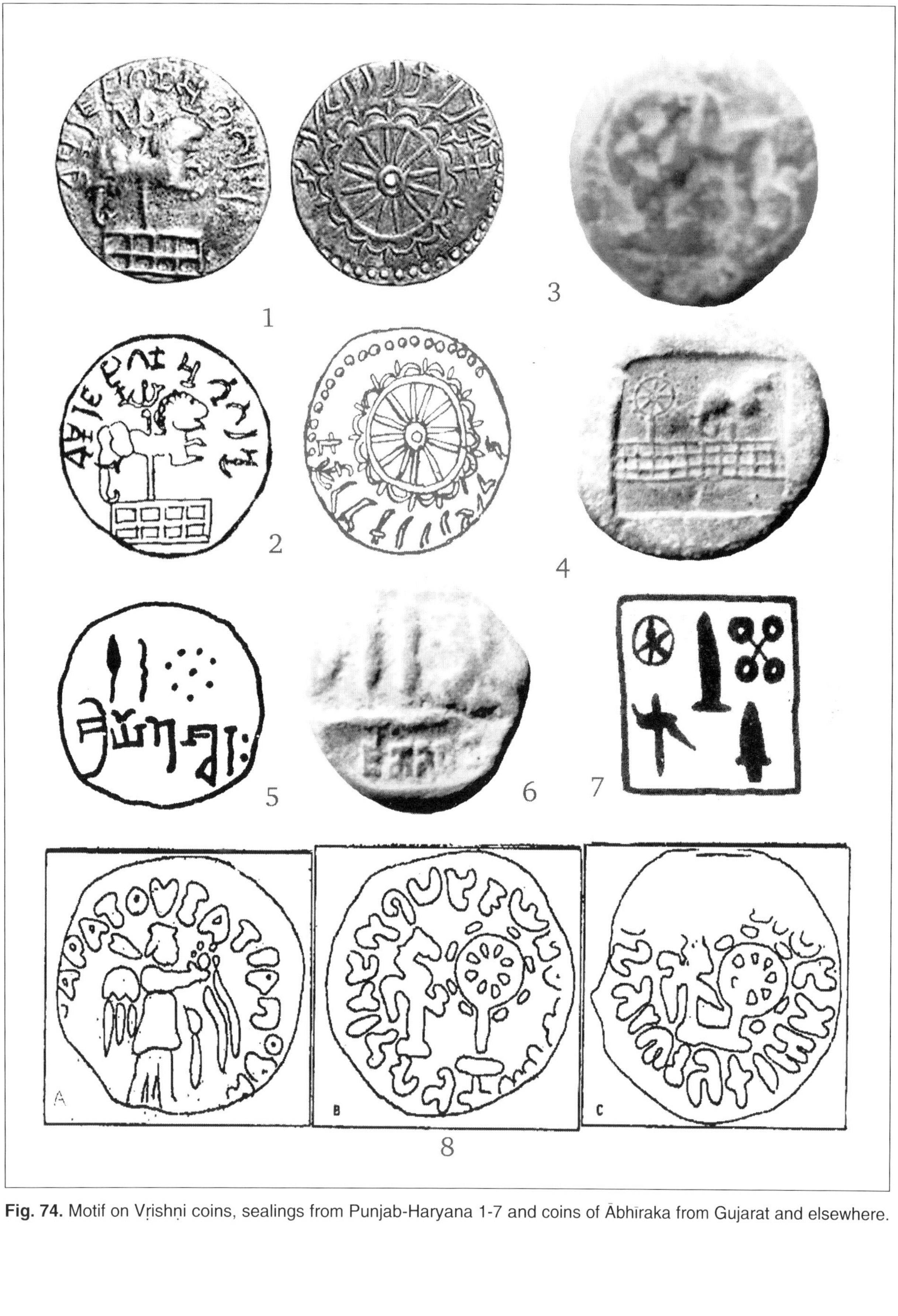

Fig. 74. Motif on Vṛishṇi coins, sealings from Punjab-Haryana 1-7 and coins of Ābhīraka from Gujarat and elsewhere.

winged Nike standing to right, holding wreath and the not very clear Greek legend (. . . *ΑΡΑΤΟΥ ΣΑΤΡΑΠΟΥ Α*· · ·). His descendant Bhūmaka also continued to use it on his coins.[22] It is probable that after conq uering the Ujjain region Azes appointed his satraps in Gujarat to rule over that territory. The adoption of winged Nike and the use of both Greek and Kharoshṭhī on his coins furnish definite evidence of the northwestern origin of Ābhīraka. The Taxila copper plate of Patika mentions Liaka Kusulaka as a kshatrapa of Chhaharāta and Chuksha and it seems probable that like Chuksha, Chhaharāta (=Kshaharāta) was also the name of a locality or region near Taxila. The Kshaharātas may have thus hailed from this region.[23] Greek and Kharoshṭhī were not intelligible to the people in western India, so in due course they disappeared and only Brāhmī was used on the coins.

As the associates or generals of Azes, the Kshaharātas probably came to Mathurā with him as is indicated by the fragmentary Ganeshra (Mathurā) inscription which mentions the erection of a *stūpa* by some female relative of Kshaharāta Kshatrapa Ghaṭāka.[24] While at Mathurā, the Kshaharātas may have adopted the cult of the Vṛishṇis. The Great Epic (Sabhā Parva, XIV. 48 f) refers to the migration of the Vṛishṇis from Mathurā to Dvārakā out of the fear of Jarāsandha. Was it the Parthian pressure under Gondophares? Likely, but corroborative evidence is still a desideratum. The migration may also be related to the expansion of Śaka dominions to central and western India under Azes who is credited with the foundation of the Vikrama era of 57 BCE according to some scholars.[25] Kshaharāta Ābhīraka may have thus taken the Vṛishṇi symbol of wheel and half-lion-half-elephant to Saurashtra in Gujarat where he started issuing his coins as a satrap of Azes adopting it as a motif on his coins. His successor Bhūmaka also continued its use (Fig. 75.2-4). This motif thus became fairly known to the masses.

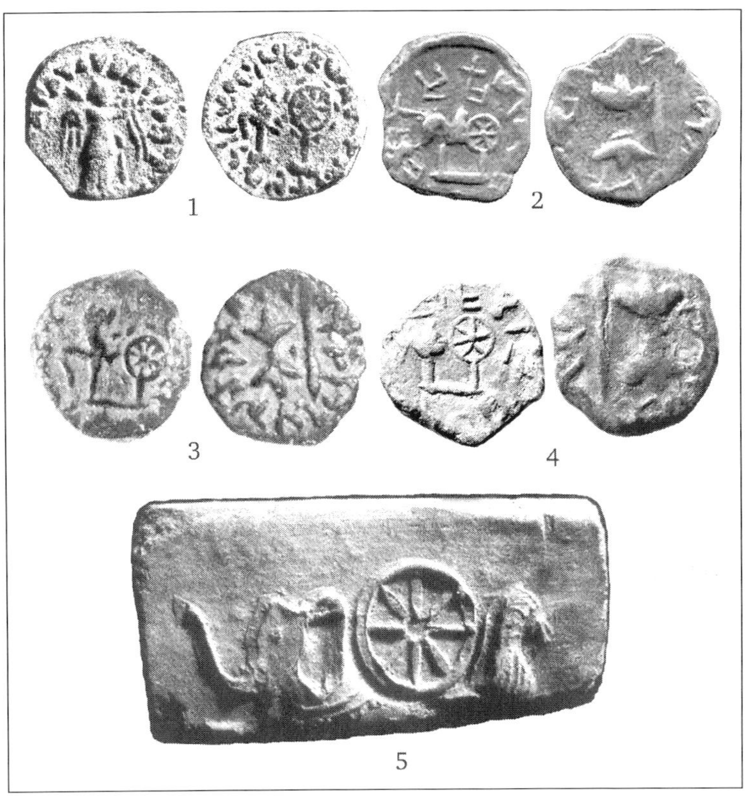

Fig. 75. Coins of Ābhīraka 1, Bhūmaka 2-4 and Sātavāhana terracotta from Paithan 5.

Well-established in power Bhūmaka's successor Nahapāna also used lion and wheel standard atop a pillar on some of his copper coins and continued the arrow and thunderbolt device on the reverse as it was one of the popular device of Bhūmaka's copper and lead coins. He came in conflict with the Sātavāhana ruler Gautamīputra Sātakarṇī and counter-struck his coins and issued his own silver coins with his bust on the obverse and also adopted many other devices.[26] An un-inscribed terracotta tablet of 4.7 X 2.3 cm found from the Sātavāhana capital of Paithan showing half-elephant on left and half-lion on right with a wheel between the heads of the two animals (Fig. 75.5) provides evidence of the further migration of this motif to the Sātavāhana dominions in Maharashtra.[27]

According to the *Mahābhārata*[28] and the *Bhāgavata Purāṇa*[29] Arjuna shifted the Vṛishṇis after the death of Vāsudeva (Kṛishṇa) to Indraprastha and installed his grandson Vajra on the throne. The *Vishṇu Purāṇa*, however, states very explicitly that Arjuna settled the Vṛishṇis in the fertile Pañchanada country.[30] Pañchanada is the exact Sanskrit equivalent of Punjab.[31] In the death of Vāsudeva (Kṛishṇa) is there any allusion to the death of the last imperial Kushāṇa ruler Vāsudeva? It is after the death of Kushāṇa Vāsudeva that the Vṛishṇis and Yaudheyas rose to power again and we find them issuing their coins and making use of their seals and sealings with their typical symbols and motifs as noted above.

The wheel and half-lion and half-elephant device of the Vṛishṇi coins thus presents an interesting story of its migration from Punjab-Haryana region to Maharashtra and betrays the socio-political and religious mobility during the early centuries BCE/CE. Back home it continued to be popular to the post-Kushāṇa period with a Scytho-Parthian-Kushāṇa interregnum.

NOTES AND REFERENCES

1. For details see Handa (2007), *TCAI*, pp. 137 ff.
2. *CAI*, p. 70, Pl. IV.15.
3. *BMCAI*, pp. civ-vii and 282, Pl. XVI.5.
4. Lahiri, Bela (1970), "The Location of Certain Tribes and the Evidence of Coins", in D.C. Sircar (Ed), *The Bhakti Cult and Ancient Indian Geography*, Calcutta, pp. 194-97.
5. Chatterjee, Asim Kumar (1972), "The Vrishnis", *JNSI*, XXXIV.
6. *THAI*, p. 189.
7. Cunningham, *loc. cit.*
8. *JNSI*, XXXV, pp. 95-100; Daivakarani, Virjanand (2010), *Bhārata ke Prāchīna Mudrāṅka*, Part II, Jhajjar, p. 26, no. 101.
9. *JNSI*, XL, pp. 87-91, Pl. VII.1.
10. Daivakarani (2010), *op. cit.*, p. 28, no. 143.
11. *ICSNL*, No. 38, Jan-March 2006, pp. 4-7. Kulkarni seems to feel inclined to relate this coin to Pushyamitra Śuṅga. See also Kulkarni (2009-2010), *JAINS* XXIII-XXIV, pp. 5-9 and (2005), *JONS*, No. 205, pp. 4-15. The original procurer of this lead coin told me (on 30. 06. 2011 at Kurukshetra) that the piece was found from Uklana in district Hisar along with the other round lead coin bearing a human figure and the legend *Patiṭhānaṃ* in early Brāhmī characters on the obverse and a tree in railing flanked by an arched hill symbol on left and *svastika* on right on the reverse counter struck on both sides. Coins of these types have also been procured by Shri R.K. Aggarwal of Ambala from Mughalpura (Uklana).
12. Daivakarani (2010), *op. cit.*, p. 17, no. 32.
13. *Ibid.*, p. 26, nos. 102-03.
14. Raychaudhuri (1953), p. 437.

15. Bopearachchi, Osmund (2007), "Some Observations on the Chronology of the Early Kushans", Des Indo-Grecs aux Sassanides: donnees pour l'histoire et la geographie historique, *Res Orientales*, Vol. XVII, p. 56.
16. Chattopadhyaya, Sudhakar (1958), *Early History of North India*. Calcutta, p. 62.
17. Senior, R.C. (2001), "Gondophares-Sases, St. Thomas and Era of Kanishka", *Numismatic Studies*. Vol. 6. New Delhi, p. 88 refers to a hoard of coins which surfaced with a dealer in Delhi who had acquired a few tetra drachms from another dealer from Ambala. It contained a tetradrachm of Maues (enthroned deity type), two of Apollodotus II, one of Artemidoros and a Hippostratos tetradrachm while a second dealer in Delhi had drachms of Maues and Vonones. The coins of this hoard later appeared in London and in a subsequent visit Senior saw more coins of this hoard in Srinagar. From personal information I know that the Ambala dealer had acquired a part of the big hoard found originally in Kashmir or Pakistan.
18. Rodgers (1891), *op. cit.*, List of Coins, p. 2.
19. *BMCAI*, p. cxv.
20. *Epigraphia Indica*, XXIV, pp. 187 ff. They are mentioned in the *Vāyu Purāṇa* (97.1-2) and *Matsya Purāṇa* (47.23) also.
21. His coins were known earlier also and the name was read erroneously as Aghudaka and Abhedaka. The complete legend read on his coins is *Kshaharātasa Kshatrapasa Ābhīrakasa Jayatasa*. See for details Senior, R.C. (1993), "Aghudaka? A new discovery gives a clearer reading", *Numismatic Studies*, Vol. 3, New Delhi, pp. 35-38. See also Jha and Rajgor (1994), pp. 79-80.
22. Rapson, E.J. (1908), *Catalogue of the Coins of the Andhra Dynasty, the Western Kṣatrapas, the Traikūṭaka Dynasty and the Bodhi Dynasty [in the British Museum]*, London; Jha and Rajgor (1994), *op. cit.*, pp. 80-84.
23. A.S. Altekar as quoted by Jha and Rajgor (1994), *op. cit.*, p. 17, fn. 16.
24. Lüders, H. (1961), *Mathurā Inscriptions* (edited by K.L. Janert), Gottingen, p. 158.
25. Senior (2001), *op. cit.*, pp. 59-121.
26. Jha and Rajgor (1994), *op. cit.*, pp. 85-109.
27. *JNSI*, LXIV-V (2002-03), p. 19, Pl. II.2.
28. Mausal Parva, VII. 32; VII.51-72.
29. X.60, 37-38; XI.15, 39; XI.31, 25.
30. *Vishṇu Purāṇa*, V.38, 12.
31. *Mahābhārata*, Sabhā Parva, XXXII.11: *Tataḥ Pañchanadaṃ chaiva kṛitsnaṃ cha Kuru-jāṅgalam/ Tathā Rohitakāraṇyaṃ maru-bhūmiścha kevalā* / /. Pañchanada is also the name of a pilgrimage in Kurukshetra (Vana Parva, LXXXIII, 16-17). See also Dey (1971), *op. cit.*, pp. 145-46.

XXII

Coins of King Magha

The Megha dynasty of Kosala consisting of nine powerful rulers referred to in some of the Purāṇas[1] is now generally accepted to be the Magha dynasty known through its epigraphic and numismatic records.[2] Some of the Magha kings seem to have minted extensively and actually more than nine chiefs are are known from their coins. These coins are generally made of a base metal, have irregular shapes, vary in sizes, are die-struck and their planchets have been cut from the sheets of metal.[3] Though uniface specimens are also known yet mostly these coins bear a three-peaked hill, tree-in-railing, issuers name in bold angular Brāhmī characters with legends generally only partially accommodated, and a ladder-like design on the obverse and a humped bull, sometimes with some auxiliary devices, on the reverse. Prof. Ajay Mitra Shastri has observed that "a chief named Magha . . . may be justifiably credited with the establishment of the line which came to be designated ater him even as the Bodhi dynasty was so called after its progenitor Bodhi or Śrībodhi and the Gupta dynasty was after its founder Gupta or Śrīgupta."[4] In a hoard of 2942 Magha coins from Kauśāmbī, he discovered for the first time a coin of king Magha – round, 1.5 cm, 1.7 gm, with the usual Magha devices and the Brāhmī legend [*Ma*]*hārāja* [*Ma*][*gha*]*.[5] He thinks that a coin from another Kauśāmbī hoard referred to by Dr. P.L. Gupta and bearing the legend *Rājā Magha* or *Rāja Magha*,[6] too, may have belonged to king Magha.[7]

Prof. Shastri referred to another coin in the collection of the Allahabad Museum in 1984 which was similar in fabric and typology with the legend *Mahārāja Ma* fully accommodated on that and beyond any doubt.[8] Prof. S.N. Roy also published a note illustrating two coins from the collection of Shri R.C. Vyas of Allahabad containing the legends *rājama* (*Rāja Magha*) and *hārājama* (*Mahārāja Magha*)[9] leaving little doubt to the existence of a ruler of the name of Magha.

While studying the photographs of some important ancient Indian coins sent to us graciously by Mr. Jan Lingen (Bergambacht, Netherlands), we have found the following interesting piece (Fig. 76)–

Æ, irregular in shape, approximately 1.6 cm, 3.800 g.

Obv. Three-peaked hill (slightly damaged on left) and a railed tree (with its uppermost leaf slightly out of flan and right hand side branches obliterated) in the upper part, Brāhmī legend *Magha* in the centre and the ladder-like design below.

Rev. Humped bull to right with a part of the face out of flan and with back flattened, horizontally placed auxiliary devices resembling a conch and a snake above the back of the animal.

The coin partakes of all the characteristics of the Magha coins described above. The legend does not contain the title *Mahārāja* as found on Shastri's coin.[10] Coins referred to by Dr. P.L. Gupta and S.N. Roy may have also borne this title. It, however, seems strange as to why did he forsake his title *Mahārāja* as on the present coin? If he issued coins initially only with his name and adopted the title later, why did his successor or even any subsequent member of his dynasty not adopt it? It is logical to think that king Magha may have started issuing his coins without any title and it was later when he grew somewhat powerful that he assumed the title *Mahārāja*. No coin of this ruler, however, was known without the title. The coin from Lingen's collection is thus of great interest and importance.

Allan had listed amongst the Magha coins of Kauśāmbī a piece which he described as 0.8 inch, 74.0 grains, showing a bull to right with trident on the back on the obverse and having illegible reverse. Since Allan did not illustrate the reverse of this coin no attempt has ever been made to read the legend. We had an opportunity of examining this coin in the British Museum and read the legend on it as Magha and feel that it corroborates our view that Magha issued coins initially without any title. Both the sides of this coin are illustrated here for the first time (Fig. 76).[12]

The obverse[13] showing the trident on the back of the bull connects this coin with a coin of Dhanadeva, which shows similar device with a three-arched hill in front. Allan had observed that "The very common coins with the types of Dhanadeva with incomplete and apparently meaningless legends represent the last stage of the coinage of Kauśāmbī, and must belong to the early centuries A.D."[14] It is not improbable that king Magha took over from where Dhanadeva or his weak successors left.

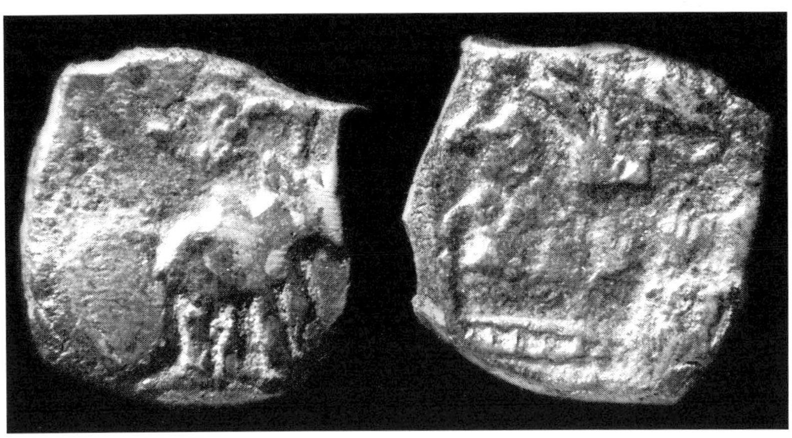

Fig. 76. Coin of King Magha.

NOTES AND REFERENCES

1. Pargiter, F.E. (1913), *Purāṇa Text of the Dynasties of the Kali Age*, London, p. 51.
2. Shastri, Ajay Mitra (1979), *Kauśāmbī Hoard Of Magha Coins*, Nagpur, p. xi.
3. *Ibid.*, pp. 5 ff.
4. *Ibid.*, p. 10.
5. *Ibid.*, pp. 41-42, Pl. I.1. The hoard studied by Prof. Shastri contained 406 unattributed coins and nine pieces of an hitherto unknown ruler Vijayanandin who may have preceded the Maghas (*Ibid.*, pp. 12-16).
6. *JNSI*, XXXVIII (i), p. 52.
7. Shastri (1979), *op. cit.*, p. 57.
8. *JNSI*, XLVI, pp. 26-27.
9. *Ibid.*, pp. 28-30, Pl. VI.2-3.
10. The title *rājā / rājño* has been read on three coins of Bhīmasena (Shastri, *op. cit.*, Appendix I, p. 93) besides the one referred to by Dr. P.L. Gupta. The illustrations of the two coins of Bhīmasena published by Prof. K.D. Bajapai [*INC*, III (i), 1962, p. 13, Pl. between pp. 20-21] are not at all clear to check the legends properly.
11. *BMCAI*, p. 158, no. 73, Pl. XXI.15.
12. We are thankful to the Trustees of the British Museum for the photograph published here obtained through our friend Mrs. Ann Shankar.
13. We take this side to be the reverse and the side with the legend as the obverse. Also, the letter *ma* used here is of rounded base whereas this letter on the coin of Lingen's collection shows triangular base. But the use of different varieties of letters on the coins of a single ruler is not something very peculiar; it is met with on the coins of other rulers also.
14. *BMCAI*, p. xcvii.

XXIII

Seals and Sealings from Haryana

"A seal is an engraved stamp bearing, singly or collectively, a device, mark or letters pertaining to the owner"[1] and the sealing is an impression of a seal. Seals and sealings constitute an important primary source of history and culture of a country or a region. Besides furnishing significant historical information "they throw interesting light on art, iconography and religious beliefs of the past, on ancient trade and commerce, on systems of education and educational institutions and on the chronology of kings and general administration".[2] Literature bears ample evidence to their use in India and numerous specimens of varied materials and sizes, legends and devices have actually come down to us. Made of gold, ivory, silver (very rarely), copper/bronze/brass, lead, crystal, carnelian, glass, shell, stone, slate, bone, or terracotta, seals are scarce for obvious reasons and sealings abundant. They are generally found at important centres of administration, religion, trade and commerce.[3] Published here are some seals and sealings which have been recovered from such centres in Haryana.

AGROHA

Agroha is situated about 22 km north-northwest of Hisar on the Delhi – Sirsa highway in Hisar district of Haryana (Fig. 77) and is a well known historical and archaeological site. Many old mounds lying to the northwest of the fast expanding present town, the largest of them being about 87 feet high and occupying an area of nearly 650 acres[4], are indicative of the past glory, importance and expanse of the ancient city.

Dr. Satyaketu has recorded an interesting tradition in his Hindi book entitled *Agravāla Jāti kā Prāchīna Itihāsa* ascribing the foundation of Agroha to an eponymous king Agra (later named as Agrasena), from whom the Agravāla (Agrawal/ Agrawala/Aggarwal) *banias* (mercantile class of people) derive their descent.[5] The dilapidated fort on the top of the mound is pointed out to be the residence of king

Agrasena. In reality, however, it was got built by Diwan Nannomal, an Agrawal employee of king Amar Singh (Current Era 1765 – 81) of Patiala.[6] The name Agroha can certainly be said to be the corrupt form of the old Sanskrit name Agrodaka which is met with twice in the Buddhist text *Mahāmāyūrī*[7] and on the old coins found from here bearing the Brāhmī legend *Agodaka Agācha janapadasa* '(coin of the) Agratya tribe of Agrodaka'.[8] L.D. Barnett gives another derivation also: (Sanskrit) Agra-rodhaka > (Prakrit) Agga-rohaya > Agroha.[9] But the derivation from Agrodaka seems to be more logical because of the literary and numismatic evidence. It is corroborated by a medieval inscription of 1328 CE which mentions the place as Agrotaka.[10] The Pabhosa inscription dated Saṃvat 1881 (= 1824 CE) also mentions the donor of a Jaina temple as belonging to Agrotakānvaya.[11] Agrodaka lay on the trade route which connected Takshaśilā (Taxila) with the Gaṅgā Valley via Mathura in ancient times.[12]

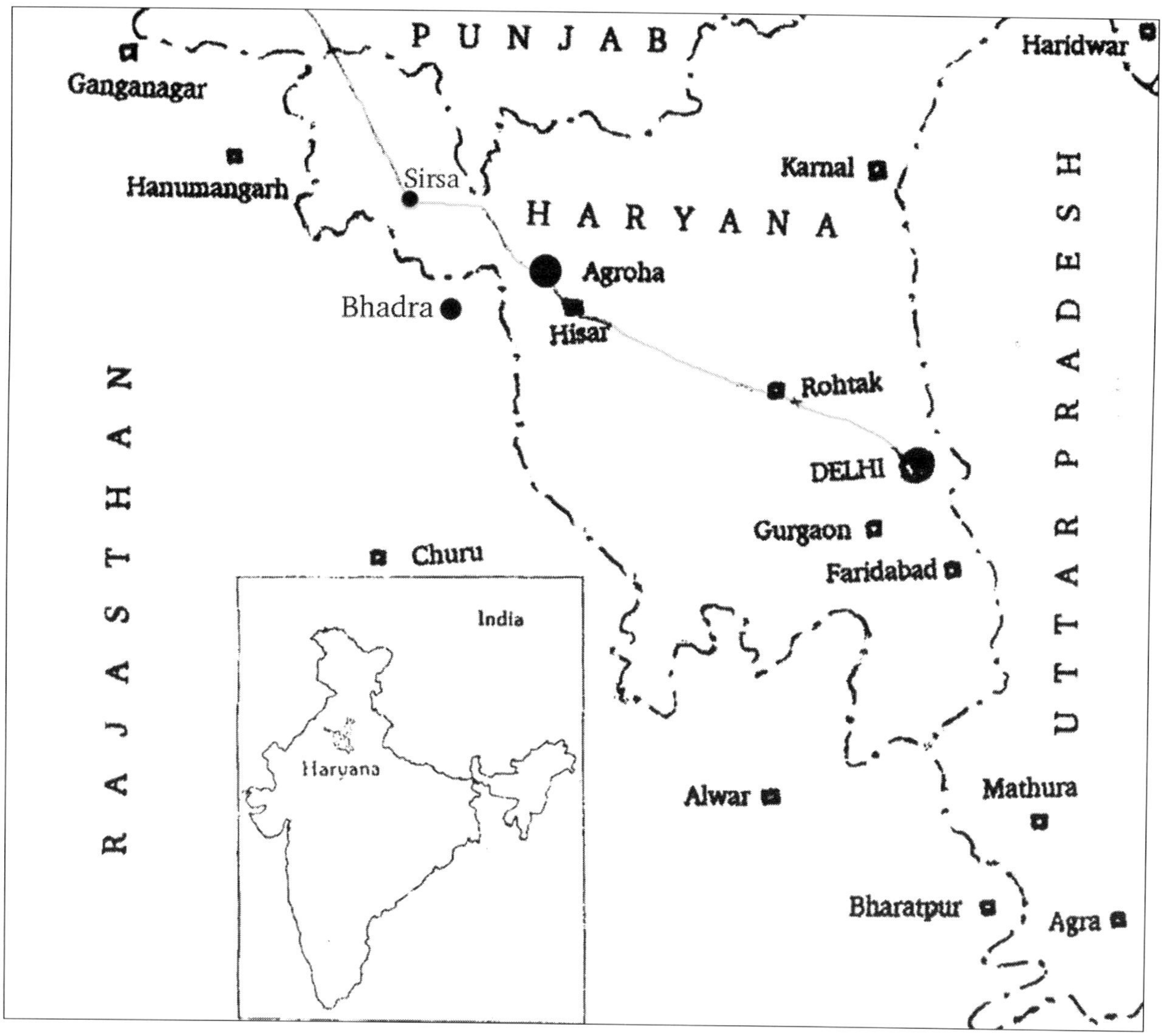

Fig. 77. Location of Agroha.

In a Tibetan version of the *Vinaya* of the Mūla-Sarvātivādins (*Dulva*, III.629), Buddha is stated to have lived at "*bab chu rab-tu bzan-mo' Gramdu*" (= on the bank of the River Excellent), on his itinerary from Bhaddiya (Bhadraṃkara, i.e., Śākala = Sialkot) to Sāvatthi (= Śrāvastī). M.J. Przyluski thinks that the Tibetan translators had before them probably the original Sanskrit word 'Agrodaka'.[13] The place mentioned as A-kia-lou-t'o (Agroda) on the Chinese traveler Tche Mang's journey from Śākala to Rohitaka (= modern Rohtak) is also very probably our Agrodaka.[14] Aṅguttarāpa and Aggaḷapura found in the *Vinaya* and mentioned in the itineraries of Meṇḍhaka and Revata[15] are the distortions of the place-name Agrodaka according to Przyluski: "Agroda (or Agrodaka) may be the Sanskrit name of the city which is called in Pāli Aggaḷapura or Aṅguttarāpa. Aṅgutta, Agoda and Agroda could then be derived from the same place-name modified by the popular etymology in order to obtain a sense in Pāli or in Sanskrit: Aṅguttara, aggaḷapura, agra+udaka".[16] Barnett supports Przyluski's identification of Aggaḷapura with Agrodaka though on different ground. He thinks that Aggaḷa-pura signifies 'Town of Aggaḷas' and that Aggaḷas is synonymous with Agācha-janapada of the coins found from Agroha.[17] Barnett takes both the names, Aggaḷa-pura and Agrodaka[18], to be the name of one town, i.e., Agroha.[19] The Sanskrit word '*agra*' has different connotations like 'first, foremost, chief, best, principal, topmost, excessive' etc.[20] and '*udaka*' means water. As such Agrodaka itself is liable to be interpreted differently but the references in the *Mahāmāyūrī* regarding the worship of Buddhist *yakshas* at different places and amongst different tribes or peoples certainly indicate that the word Agrodaka stood for a place-name and the inhabitants of the city of Agrodaka: *Agrodake Mālyadharaḥ* (Line 8) and *Agrodake Muñjakeśaḥ* (Line 70).

That there were *udaka*-ending names in ancient India is exemplified by some other names also. Pṛithūdaka, modern Pehowa on the river Sarasvatī about 25 km west of Kurukshetra (Haryana) has been mentioned in the *Mahābhārata* and various Purāṇas as an important *tīrtha* 'pilgrimage'.[21] The great epic mentions another *tīrtha* on the Sarasvatī as Kālodaka.[22] The name of Amaroha near Moradabad in Uttar Pradesh is popularly derived from Āmrodaka. Prashant P. Kulkarni has recently brought to light coins of an ancient city-state Hathodaka.[23]

Pṛithūdaka got its name from King Pṛithu who sat here on the bank of the Sarasvatī offering water to all comers for twelve days after performing the usual funerary rites of his father Vena (a scion of Hiraṇyakaśipu).[24] Umpteen are the towns in India known after kings or their inhabitants. If Pṛithūdaka is connected with king Pṛithu, Agrodaka could also be connected with king Agra(sena) as believed by the Agrawals but there is hardly any evidence of the existence of any ruler of this name known to history in the region. The *udaka*-ending of the name makes it more probable that it was connected with water. Agrodaka, therefore, seems to have been a derivative name connected with some water body or store or tank at Agra, which may have been the original name of the place.[25] This Agra may be identified with Ptolemy's Agara.[26]

From the word Agācha of the legend '*Agodaka Agācha janapadasa*' found on Agroha coins[27] Barnett deduces the existence here of an oligarchic tribal state of the

Agācha *janapada*.[28] He derives Agācha from Sanskrit *Agrā-tya* or *Agrāt-tya* meaning 'The inhabitants of Agra'. Barnett identified the Agras or Aggaḷas with the Agalasseis (also spelt as Agalassoi)[29], a tribe in Punjab, which fought fiercely against the Greeks with their 40,000 foot soldiers and 3,000 horses, as we learn from Quintus Cutius, and when the Macedonians could not resist they burnt their houses and killed their women and children.[30] Diodorus (XVII.96) tells us that the Agalasseis lived in the neighborhood of the Siboi, i.e., the Śibis who dwelt in and around Śivapura, identified with Shorkot in Jhang district of Pakistan.[31] In Alexander's time, both the Siboi and the Agalasseis were large tribes who probably occupied spacious area extending far beyond Shorkot and Agroha and possibly included between them the interjacent region.[32] According to Barnett, the name Agalasseis itself supplies some evidence as it was probably translated from the common word Aggaḷāso or Aggaḷāse, a nominative plural of Aggaḷa in Pāli.[33] The *Mahābhārata* (Vana Parva, 254/20) refers to these people as Āgreyas, a derivative from Agra, in association with the Bhadras, Rohitakas, and Mālavas, who were conquered by Karṇa during his western expedition –

Bhadrān Rohitakāṃśchaiva Āgreyān Mālavānapi /
Gaṇān sarvān vinirjitya nītikṛit prahasannive //

This passage gives us an idea of the geographical location of the Āgreyas (the people of Agra) in the vicinity of Bhadras (the inhabitants of modern Bhādarā located about 65 km west of Hisar), the inhabitants of Rohtak (nearly 90 km southeast of Hisar) and the Mālavas (who may have then been located at Malab (nearly 200 km southeast of Hisar) in district Faridabad.

Archaeological excavations conducted at Agroha by Charles J. Rodgers (1888-89)[34], H.L. Srivastava (1938-39)[35], and the Department of Archaeology and Museums, Haryana, now at Panchkula (1979-85)[36] have brought to light very important and interesting relics which throw very welcome light on the history of the town and the life of the people living in it for about the last two and a half millennia. Having been founded sometime during the late phase of the Painted Grey Ware, roughly around Buddha's time, it was fortified some time later and a moat was dug around it. During the Mauryan period it seems to have been an important place and probably Aśoka set up a pillar here. Śuṅga style terracottas, particularly of Kubera, the god of wealth, indicate the love for riches of the inhabitants. The Agras seem to have occupied it at the weakening of the Maurya hold. After a period of Śaka-Kushāṇa ascendancy it came under the Yaudheyas who probably made it an administrative headquarters as is indicated by an important sigil found from here. During the Gupta period it must have been an elegant city with beautiful temples bedecked with terracotta figurines. Subsequently it came under the Pushyabhūtis, Hūṇas, Pratīhāras, Chāhamānas and the Muslims. During the reign of Muhammad Tughlaq it was deserted because of a severe famine[37] and the Hindu temples and other important buildings of this place were got demolished and their material utilized by Firuz Tughlaq in constructing Hisar-i-Firuza.[38] The deserted town was, however, reoccupied after some time but could never attain its pristine glory. The site is quite rich in antiquities and numerous individuals and even institutions have made big hauls of old coins, beads, terracotta figurines, sculptures, etc. from here, including, of course, seals and sealings.

Amongst the important antiquities brought to light by Srivastava's partial excavations in 1938-39 of the high and extensive mound immediately to the south of the road were punch-marked and Indo-Greek coins in a vase, a hoard of 51, mostly rectangular coins of the Agācha *janapada* in another clay vase, and a clay seal with the Brāhmī legend in two lines (*Pāvanesa Rudra/dha*[*m*]*ma*?) below the bull seated to right palaeographically ascribable to *circa* second-third century CE.[39] The depiction of the Nandī (bull, the vehicle of Śiva) and the word Rudra are important clues to indicate the Śaivite proclivity of the owner of the seal and its affiliation to the Yaudheyas who have all their important seals and sealings with the figure of the bull.[40] The palaeography also points to this ascription. A similar sealing was discovered and published later by Swami Omanand Saraswati also.[41]

A very important oval clay sealing from Agroha measuring 70 X 62 mm was brought to light in 1970 by Bhagwan Deva Acharya (later known as Swami Omanand Saraswati) from the collection of the Gurukula Museum, Jhajjar[42] founded by him. It shows in the upper one-third part a humped bull trotting to left above a horizontal line below which is the five-line legend deciphered as following by Swamiji –

Line 1. *Yaudheyagaṇapuraskṛitasya Śaṅkara-rā-*
Line 2. *ja-Mahākshatrapa-Mahāsenāpater=Indra-*
Line 3. *mitra-gṛihītasya Mahārāja-Mahākshatrapa-*
Line 4. *Senāpater=apratihata-śāsanasya*
Line 5. *Dharmamitra-Nandavarmmaṇaḥ*

Swamiji's Hindi translation of the sigil may be rendered into English thus: "(This is the seal) of a friend of righteousness (*dharma-mitra*), *Mahārāja* (the great king), *Mahākshatrapa* (the great satrap) and *Senāpati* (commander) of the Yaudheya tribe Nandavarma who overpowered Indramitra and has an uninterrupted reign and has succeeded *Mahārāja, Mahākshatrapa, Mahāsenāpati* Śaṅkararāja."

P.L. Gupta[43], in his editorial note observed that what has been read by the author as *Śaṅkararāja* is most likely *Mahārāja* and referred to the author's letter to him admitting that the reading *Śaṅkara* was by no means certain but that he does not think it to be *Mahā*. P.L. Gupta rightly remarked that "Whatever be the true reading, here a proper name is out of context and the word could only be an epithet. Then there is no mention of any enemy here. The word *grihīta*, has probably led to the author to stretch his imagination; but it is a well known term used by Chandra Gupta II in his inscriptions in relation to his father. It only means adopted or selected as successor. The true rendering of the inscription would be: '(The seal) of one who is appointed by (*puraskrita*) Yaudheya *gaṇa*; of one who was adopted (*grihīta*) by (*Mahārāja*) *Mahākshatrapa Mahāsenāpati* Indramitra; of one who was *Mahārāja Mahākshatrapa, Senāpati* and *Apratihata-śāsana*; and of Dharmamitra Nandavarmana'."[44] Dr. Gupta also felt that 'Dharmamitra may also be an epithet meaning 'friend of the righteousness'.[45]

Swamiji seems to have kept Dr. P.L. Gupta's remarks in mind as he changed his reading when he republished this sealing four years later in his book on *Ancient Seals of Haryana* in 1974.[46] Dr. Yogānanda Shastri also included this important document with a much better illustration in his Hindi book on the Yaudheyas telling us that it was he who discovered it originally on 14 August 1969.[47] The image and revised transcription (eye-copy) and reading of the legend as given by these scholars are given below –

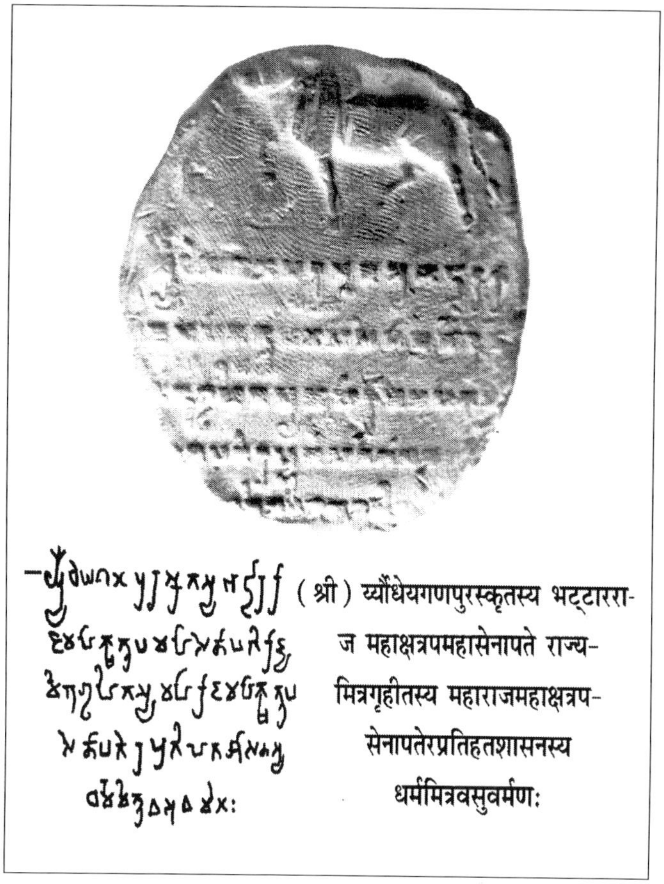

Fig. 78. Agroha sealing, transcription and reading.

We thus see that the original reading Śaṅkara-rāja has been changed to Bhaṭṭāra-rāja, Indramitra has given place to Rājyamitra and it has been rightly observed that the existence of superscript *r* visible on the initial syllable *Yau* indicates that the legend started with the word *Śrī* which has been lost in the molded edge.[48] The changed reading and rendering has been presented thus: "(This is the seal) of *Mahārāja Senāpati* Dharmamitra Vasuvarman who has an uninterrupted reign and has been appointed (*puraskṛita*) by the illustrious Yaudheya-gaṇa and accepted (*gṛihīta*) by *Bhaṭṭāra-rāja Mahākshatrapa Mahāsenāpati* Rājyamitra".[49]

A careful look, however, indicates that the first line of the legend ends not with the letter *ra* but *ka* and the initial letter of the second line partially lost but still recoverable in traces is *rā* followed by *ja*. We, therefore, think that the reading should be *Bhaṭṭāraka-rāja* in stead of *Bhaṭṭāra-rāja*. It is, however, worth noting that this title has been used here in place of the title *Mahārāja* which occurs on the Bijaygarh inscription (Fig. 79) of the Yaudheyas – [*Siddham*] *Yaudheya-gaṇa-puraskṛitasya Mahārāja Mahāsenāpateḥ pu . . ./ Brāhmaṇa-purogaṃ chādhishṭṝhitaṃ śarīrādi-kuśalaṃ prishṝvā likhatyastirasmā/. . .* [50]

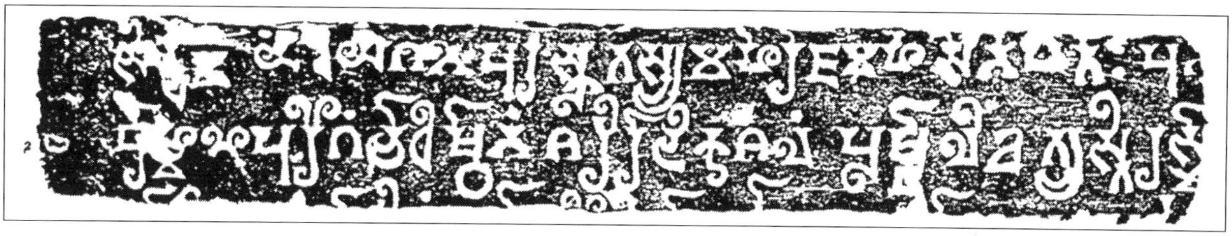

Fig. 79. Bijaygarh inscription.

The use of the title '*Bhaṭṭāra(ka)-rāja*' is met with on any sigil, and particularly of the Yaudheyas, for the first time. *Bhaṭṭāraka* 'worshipful one' occurs on a seal from Bhita and others from Basarh.[51] It was generally applied to feudatory chiefs and *yuvarājas* 'crown princes' though *parama-bhaṭṭāraka* is applied to *mahārājādhirājas* also denoting their independent status. Does this sealing represent a stage when the Yaudheyas had been defeated by Samudragupta and rendered *karada* 'tax-paying' though autonomous? Unfortunately, however, it is very difficult to determine the exact year of the use of this document to ascertain whether it belongs to a stage before their defeat at the hands of Samudragupta or after that. The employment of the title of mahākshatrapa is equally interesting and significant. It certainly seems to have been adopted from the Western Kshatrapas after the defeat of the Yaudheyas at the hands of Rudradāman as mentioned in his Junagarh *praśasti: Sarvva-kshatrāvishkṛita-vīra-śabda-jātotsekāvidheyānāṃ Yaudheyānāṃ prasahyotsāda-kena. . .* .[52] I think that the Yaudheyas adopted the system of selecting the successors by the ruling chiefs (*mahākshatrapas*) from the Western Kshatrapas but the successor had to be approved by the *Gaṇa*. The term '*gṛihīta*' seems to have been adopted under the impact of the Guptas whose sovereigns used to select and approve the crown prince.

The sealing shows some interesting linguistic peculiarities also. The honorific title *Śrī* has been used with *visarga* in the beginning and the following consonant '*Ya*' has been doubled. Here the nominative of the noun *Śrī* is governing the following genitive compound form. Though the Nāgarī transcription of the text does not show it the letter '*ta*' in '*kshattrapa*' and '*mittra*' (in Dharma-mitra only) has also been doubled in the eye-copy of the inscription. One would expect such a duplication of '*ta*' in Rājyamitra's name and of '*ma*' in the word 'Dharmamitra' also. Since the legend in the sealing is not very clear the exact forms of the words noted above cannot be determined with certainty. Thaplyal has observed that "Mostly, the legends on pre-Gupta seals are either in Prakrit or in mixed Sanskrit but the Gupta and post-Gupta ones, with the exception of a few irregular formations, are in Sanskrit".[53] The use of Sanskrit is notable as we generally find the early documents in Prākṛita or influenced by Prākṛita.

The sealing is of great importance as it shows that the successor for the Yaudheya kingdom was nominated by the ruling chief of the tribe who used to be the *Mahārāja*, *Mahākshatrapa* and *Senāpati* or *Mahāsenāpati* and that the nomination made by him had to be approved by the *gaṇa*.

Besides the important sealing described and discussed above, Swamiji published from Agroha the following sigils also in 1974 with details of legends and devices as given below –

1. *Pitṛidatta* with temple above (Fig. 80.2)
2. Śrī-Sādhuvṛiddhisya
3. *Śaṅkaramalasya* with seated Nandi to left above
4. Nūnakusalā
5. *Visapālakasa/tapuvidaśane* (copper signet ring)
6. *Śrī-Yākasa* (clay pot ornamented with *svastikas*, flower-pot, creeper in bloom and other designs) (Fig. 80.1)

7. Hāleta/geyā
8. Siṃhasa
9. Bhadrasya
10. *Pāvanesa Rudre/Dhama* with Nandi sitting to right
11. *Ju/Ju* (on both sides)
12. Śrī-Śivadarajaḥ
13. *Dadākasya* (Fig. 80.3)
14. *Tutuṇya* (copper seal) (Fig. 80.4)
15. Mu/cha
16. Clay seal with a person entreating an equestrian
17. Clay seal with *svastika* and *chakra* designs
18. Clay seal with *svastika*, tree, weapons, etc.
19. *Śrīr=Dhruvā. . . ra. . . mitra* (copper seal)

We thus see that Swamiji brought to light twenty seals and sealings including one inscribed clay pot from Agroha of which only one (no. 10 with the legend *Pāvanesa Rudre / Dhama*) was known earlier from Srivastava's excavation of the site as referred to above. We have already discussed the Yaudheya sealing (Swamiji's no. 31) in detail above and now take up the others (Swamiji's nos. 32-50) one by one.

Swamiji has deciphered the legend *Pitṛidatta* of sigil no. 1 (Swamiji's no. 32) correctly and referred to the figure above the legend as that of a temple (Fig. 80.2). The eye-copy of the figure looks like 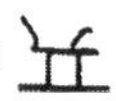 which is more akin to sacrificial altars than temples. Such altars, of course with many variations, are found on the coins of the Kushāṇas and the Guptas as well as on some sealings.[54] Quite often seals and sealings are found as containing not only the legend but also some device or devices, connected with the names or religious affiliations of their owners, though not necessarily. It will, however, be hazardous to say that Pitṛidatta got his seal prepared at the time of the performance of a *Pitṛi-yajña* (filial sacrifice).

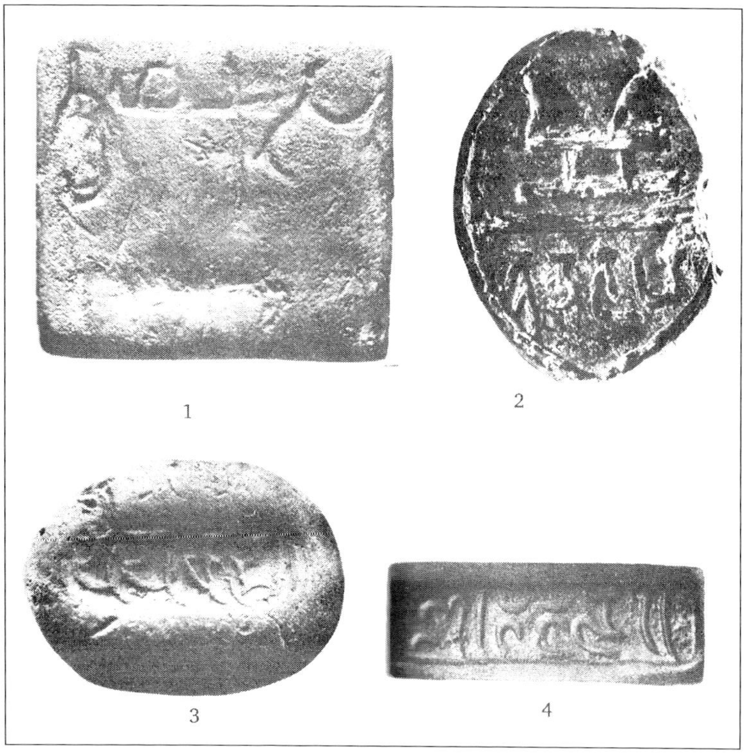

Fig. 80. Agroha sealings.

Sealings with the legend *Śrī-Sādhuvṛiddhisya* are quite common at Agroha. Besides the one published by Swamiji, three more specimens are known from Agroha. One of them measuring 3.25 x 2.87 cm was obtained during the excavations of the site

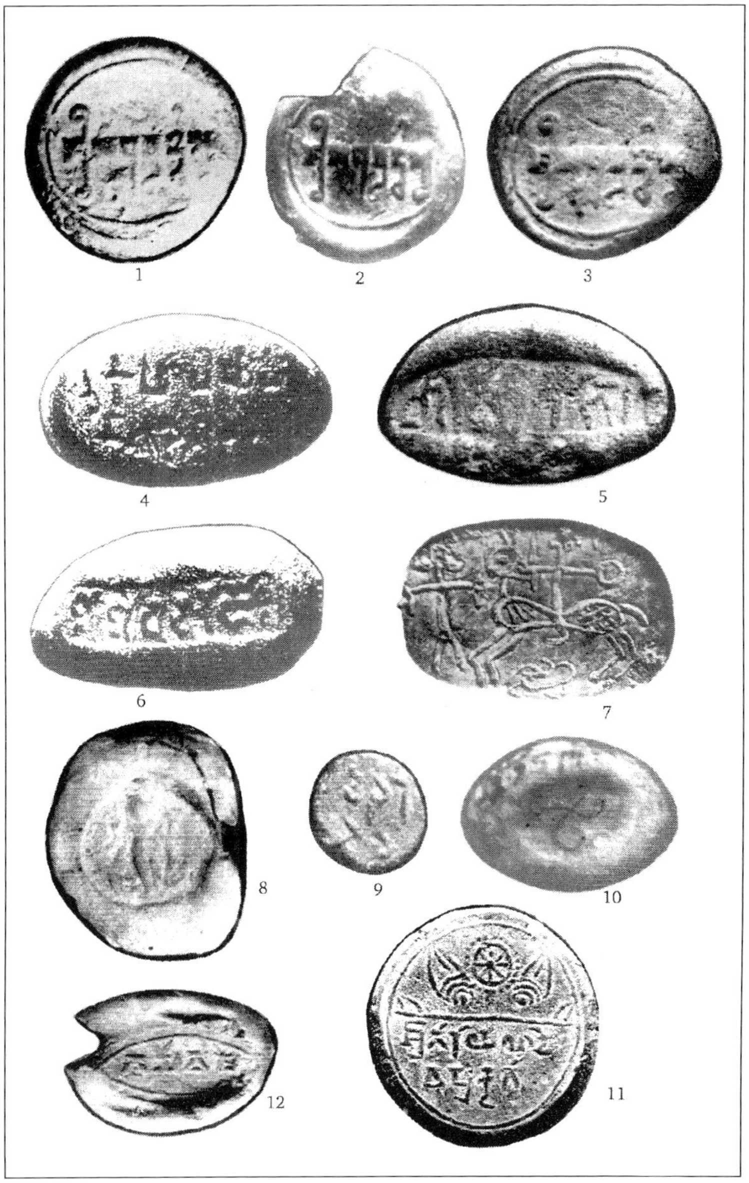

Fig. 81. Sealings from Agroha.

in 1985 from Trench No. WA-26, Quadrant IV, layer 2, at a depth of 30 cm. It contains the Brāhmī legend *Śrī-Sādhuvṛiddhisya* in a lined circle engraved in the typical Gupta characters of *circa* fourth century CE (Fig. 81.1). Another similar but smaller in size and slightly damaged on the edge (Fig. 81.2) and a third one, complete and measuring 3.0 X 2.5 cm (Fig. 81.3), were recovered from the surface. The occurrence of so many specimens of Sādhuvṛiddhi's sealings at Agroha indicates that he may have been an important administrative official of the Yaudheyas or a highly placed denizen of Agroha. The legend *Śrī-Sādhuvṛiddhisya* is influenced by Prākṛita and is grammatically incorrect from the viewpoint of Sanskrit. There are, however, numerous examples of Prākṛita influenced case-endings, e.g., *Mahāsenāpatisya*, *Pushyahasthisya*, *Śrī-Nandasirisya*, *Buddhivasusya*, etc. on the seals and sealings from Punjab and Haryana published by Swamiji.[55]

Swamiji's third sealing with the legend *Śaṅkaramalasya* contains the figure of a humped bull quite in conformance of the name Śaṅkara (Śiva) and his vehicle Nandi. Swamiji has read the legend on the next sealing as '*Nūnakusalā*' and given the eye-copy of the legend as 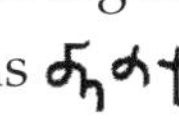. Swamiji's reading does not make any sense. The letters as drawn by Swamiji also seem to be somewhat anachronistic as the second letter '*na*' shows a developed form; the following '*ka*' and '*sa*' betray earlier forms. The last letter looks more like '*hā*'. There are no serif marks. The sealing may have belonged to *circa* first century BCE. The first letter seems to be a conjunct with subscript '*ña*'. Considering the fact that all the letters of the legend are not very clear on the sealing and allowing for some discrepancy in drawing their eye-copies, I think that the legend may have been *Jñānakusala*.[56]

The next piece is a copper signet ring the legend *Visapālakasa/Tapuvidaśane* (Fig. 81.4) is again an example of misreading. The illustration shows the first letter as '*va*' and the second as 'sva/*chha*'. So I prefer to read the legend in the upper line as 'Visva or *Vachha-pālakasa*' (i.e., the seal of Viśva/Vatsapālaka). The second line also does not give a sensible reading but since the initial letters are not clear it is very difficult to decipher them correctly. However, the last letter of the second line looks like '*ke*' to suggest a very tentative reading as '*Tipuavideśake*' (*Tripuravideśake*). The palaeography indicates a first century BCE/CE date for Viśva/Vatsapālaka. The use of copper for the signet ring indicates more abundant use and perhaps a little higher status of the owner.

The name of Yāka has been read on a clay pot. A surface find during 1985 presents the specimen of his sealing (Fig. 81.5) on which very clear serif mark on the last letter suggests a second century CE date for him. The sealing also shows a stroke over '*ka*' looking like a medial vowel-mark. The preceding letter '*ya or śa*' is just traceable but the vowel mark if any attached to it is lost. There is the possibility of the name starting with *Śā* and the full name being Śāka (Shāka), which as compared to the unknown name Yāka seems to be more likely. Swamiji's reading of the next specimen as '*Hāleta-geyā*' is again unintelligible.

Nos. 8 and 9 belong to Siṃha and Bhadra. These names are known to us from the sealings obtained from Rajghat.[57] Sealings bearing the legend *Pāvanesa Rudra(/e)/dhama* and Nandi have already been commented upon above. The piece bearing only one letter *Ju* on both sides is interesting and seems to show the use of abbreviated name. One letter abbreviation is found for the first time on any sealing. Swamiji's reading *Śrī-Śivadarajaḥ* on the next sealing (Fig. 81.6) seems to have resulted from partial damage to one of the letters (his '*da*') and wrong decipherment of the last letter as '*ja*' for '*ṇa*'. Swamiji has given the eye-copy of the legend as 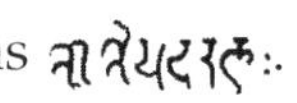. The vertical stroke of the fourth letter of the legend has suffered some mutilation and looks like '*da*' whereas actually with the complete vertical stroke it should have been '*cha*'. If we restore this letter the eye-copy will be 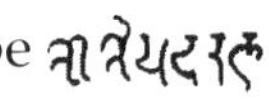, which can be deciphered as *śrī-Śivacharaṇaḥ*, more sensible and meaningful reading than *Śivadarajaḥ*. The name here occurs in the nominative case which though met with on other examples also is rather rare. Dadākasya (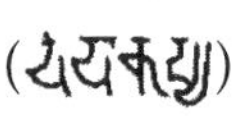) read on another sealing (Fig. 80.3) is again a misreading. The letter '*ka*' in the legend indicates an early medieval form. We decipher the legend as *Śaśā(ṃ)kasya*. Similarly *Śrī-Tutuṇya* on a copper seal (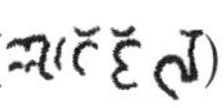) does not make any sense (Fig. 80.4); we read the legend as *Śrī-Titṛila* (= *Śrī-Tittrila*). The sealing with the legend *Mucha* is almost modern written in the form of a monogram with '*mu*' above '*cha*'. These letters may have been the initials of the name of the owner.

The seal or sealing showing a linear equestrian facing a human figure (Fig. 81.7) is characterized by folk art and it is very difficult to determine its exact date. The two clay seals with *svastika* and *chakra* and *svastika*, tree, etc. are early historical pieces. The copper seal shows the legend as 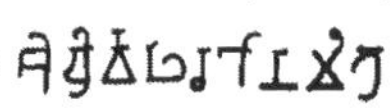 which has been deciphered by Swamiji as *Śrīr=Dhruvā. . . ra. . . mitra*?. The question mark put by Swamiji at the end of his reading indicates his dissidence about the decipherment. To me it again seems to be a case of faulty eye-copy and reading. The superscript *'r'* over *'va'* indicates that the conjunct has to be read as *'rva'*. The legend therefore cannot be *'Dhruvā'*. The letter after *Śrī* seems to have been copied wrongly. It was perhaps *'Pū'*. The unread letters are also there which look like *'Phā/r(l)/ga/na'*. The original legend may have been *Śrī-Pūrvaphālgunimitra* palaeographically ascribable to *circa* third century CE. We have the comparable name of Phālgunimitra who was a ruler of Ayodhya and has also left for us a sealing bearing his name.[58] A Pañchāla ruler of this name is also known. Pūrva-Phālguni is the eleventh *nakshatra* 'lunar mansion' (containing two stars). A *nakshatra* presiding at the time of the birth of a child was often chosen as the name of the new-born in the historical period. The name on this sealing has been left without case-ending.

Agroha was excavated by the Department of Archaeology and Museum, Haryana during 1979-85 and quite a good number of seals and sealings were recovered in excavations and as surface finds as mentioned in case of the three sealings bearing the legend *Śrī-Sādhuvṛiddhisya* described above and illustrated here. Quite a few more are preserved in the said Department and are comparatively little known.[59] They are described and discussed below.

1. One sealing in the above-mentioned institution, baked almost black and slightly damaged on its right side bears a light circular impression of a female figure facing to front (Fig. 81.8). The contours of her body are quite attractive and graceful but unfortunately the details of the physical features are irretrievably lost. She seems to bear four hands, the normal ones hanging (*pralamba*) and the additional ones raised to the level of the shoulders and probably holding lotus flowers with long stalks. Multiplicity of arms and the presence of lotuses in her hands suggests that she may be identified with Lakshmī, the goddess of fortune, and the favorite of the Agravālas. It may be pointed out that Lakshmī has been depicted on a variety of the coins of the Agra *janapada* also.[60] Stylistically, the sealing may be assigned to *circa* second-first century BCE.
2. From the surface of the mound at Agroha has been collected a small sealing of nearly 9 mm diameter bearing a Kharoshṭhī legend in first century BCE characters in two lines (Fig. 81.9), read for me by Prof. B.N. Mukherjee as *'Vasamuti'*.[61] The legend probably stands for Vasumatī. If it be so the sealing may be taken to belong to some lady bearing this name. Going by the literal meaning, she may have been quite a rich lady. Be as it may, the very fact that her sealing has survived, makes her important for us. Since seals and sealings bearing the names of the females are almost unknown in India[62], the discovery becomes all the more significant. Also notable is the fact that this is the only sealing from Agroha known so far to carry the legend in Kharoshṭhī.
3. A diminutive sealing but great in importance comes from Trench No. AGR, XC-8, Quadrant IV, layer 13, from a depth of 5. 05 meters during the excavations in 1984. It is irregular in shape and bears a tree in railing in the

centre and Brāhmī legend from X to II which reads *Agodaka ka(u)la / dra(u)ma* in characters assignable to *circa* first century CE.[63] The depiction of the tree in railing and the legend indicate it to be the family tree of the nucleus Agrodaka tribe. In Pāṇini's time the *kula* 'family' was represented by its eldest member (*vṛiddha*) on all important occasions and functions and he used to be the *rājanya* 'consecrated to kingship'. The *janapadas* which were originally named after the peoples settled in them, dropped their tribal significance and figured as territorial units or regions consisting of heterogeneous population.[64] The mention of *Agrodaka-kula druma* here seems to refer to the original settlers and *rājanyas*, whose family tree has been depicted on the sealing. And very important is the fact that the coins of the Agra *janapada* invariably show a tree in railing on the obverse. The coins were issued by the ruling aristocracy belonging to the Agra *janapada* and hence the tree in railing is the sacred tree or plant of the tribe. The fact that it has been shown in railing indicates its respectability and sanctity. Though it is difficult to identify this tree or plant with certainty it may have been the Tulasī plant which symbolizes goddess Lakshmī and continues to be worshipped in traditional Hindu families till date. A tree anointed by two elephants depicted on a coin-type of the Agra *janapada*[65] almost corroborates it.

4. A small round sealing was recovered from Trench No. WA-26, Quadrant II, layer 12, from a depth of 3.65 meters in 1985. It is baked black. The device in the upper half is completely worn out but the Brāhmī legend in the lower half may be read as *Śrī-G(o)da(ttasya)*. On palaeographic ground it may be dated to *circa* late first or early second century CE.
5. From Trench No. WA-30, Quadrant III, layer 11, depth 2.25 meters was found another small round sealing bearing a *svastika* as the central device (Fig. 81.10). There is no legend. It may be dated to *circa* second century CE. *Svastika* is an auspicious symbol and met with commonly on early Indian coins also.
6. Trench No. XC-7, Quadrant II yielded a sealing from layer 2 at a depth of 1.60 meters. It shows a *chakra* in the upper half. The legend below may be read as *Śrī-Vishṇumitra*. There is a double dividing line between the wheel and the legend. The glyptic provides a perfect example of characteristic connection between the name and the device. The sealing is broken on the left. On palaeographic grounds, it may be dated to about the second-third century CE.
7. Obtained from Trench No. 26, Quadrant I, layer 8, at a depth of 2.15 meters, this sealing is not in a good state of preservation. The device in the upper half is not clear. The Brāhmī legend below separated from the device by a horizontal line, too, is not clear but for its second part which reads *Svāmī*. The first part of the legend amy be tentatively restored on the basis of the traces of two letters with which the legend begins, as *Gṛiha* or *Guṇa*, the complete legend thus being *Gṛiha-svāmī* or *Guṇa-svāmī*.[66]

8. This well baked sealing (Fig. 81.11) is slightly oval and measures 7.0 X 6.2 cm. Having a lined border, it shows in the upper half a wheel of eight spokes surrounded by a circle of 24 dots, flanked on either side by a slantingly placed conch with spiral head resting downwards.[67] A horizontal line with parapet- or banner-like appendages near their ends (as usually found on the fire or sacrificial altars) separates the two-line legend below from the device. The legend in the Brāhmī characters of the northern variety ascribable to *circa* third-fourth century CE reads –

   Line 1. *Śrī-Nārāyaṇa-de-*
   2. *va-prakṛitā*

   The legend may be translated as '(something indicated by feminine gender) made (or created) by the illustrious Nārāyaṇadeva'.

   The motif of wheel flanked by conches is quite in conformity with the name of the owner of the sigil Śrī Nārāyaṇadeva. It certainly furnishes evidence of the popularity of Vaishṇavism in Haryana during the third century CE. It is, however, the legend which is very rare and interesting. The word prakṛitā consisting of the prefix *pra* (*prakarsheṇa*) and the root *kṛi* (*karaṇe*) seems to be significant. Amongst the various meanings of the root *kṛi* one intended here seems to have been 'to make' or 'to create'. The prefix *pra* stands for *prakarsha* and does not change the meaning except adding force to making or creating. We have a very large number of images where the word *kārita/kāritam* is often used in the sense of 'caused to be made'. The legend, thus, may well be compared to modern trade marks like 'Manufactured by so and so'. Nārāyaṇadeva of this sealing appears to have specialized in creating/manufacturing something (indicated by a feminine gender) and may have been making use of his seal while selling and sending his commodity elsewhere. There is every ikelihood that Agroha continued to be a flourishing trade centre during the third-fourth century CE where people like Nārāyaṇadeva specialized in the manufacture of certain commodities which they sold under their trade mark.

9. This interesting sealing on a lump of clay (Fig. 80.12) broken on the left was obtained in the excavations during 1985 from Trench No. WA-27, Quadrant IV, layer 3 at a depth of 8.50 meters. It measures 3.6 X 2.8 cm. It contains the Brāhmī legend *Namo Vishṇau* within eye-shaped lined space in the characters of 3rd-4th century CE. It is a sectarian sealing belonging to the category of motto seals[68] and corroborates the popularity of Vaishṇavism in the region.

   The legend is grammatically incorrect as the locative case has been used for the dative.

   We thus see that 33 seals and sealings are known from Agroha so far and like other glyptics from other parts of the country they throw very welcome and fresh light on various aspects of the history, culture, religion, polity, administration, rituals, names and naming of children, art, trade, auspicious symbols, etc. of the people of Agroha from about the second century BCE to the beginning of the early medieval period.

NAURANGABAD

We have referred to the Yaudheya sealing from Agroha. The earliest coins of Bull/ Elephant type of this warrior tribe have come down to us in substantial numbers from Rohtak and Naurangabad ((about 35 km northwest of Rohtak and 11 km southeast of Bhiwani on Rohtak-Bhiwani road). It seems that like many other tribes, they declared independence after the death of Pushyamitra Śuṅga in about the middle of the second century BCE. Patañjali, a contemporary of Pushyamitra Śuṅga, refers to them in his *Mahābhāshya* (IV.1, 117). The Yaudheyas seem to have suffered a set back at the hands of the Indo-Greeks, under Menander probably, when even their capital Rohtak may have been devastated. The discovery of hundreds of Indo-Greek coins from Rohtak indicates this. The Greek sway was very short-lived and when the Yaudheyas regained power they made Naurangabad (about 35 km northwest of Rohtak and 11 km southeast of Bhiwani on Rohtak-Bhiwani road) their capital and also set up their mint there. Bhagwan Dev Acharya (later Swami Omananda Saraswati) discovered a well-baked reddish oval (6.0 X 4.9 cm) clay seal with a knob at the back bearing the finger impressions of probably the maker from Naurangabad which has four-lined legend in 1st century BCE/CE Brāhmī characters beginning with a hooked railed symbol (Fig. 82). [69] It was read by him as following –

Swamiji deciphered the legend as given below –

Rapata
Yodheya janapa-
Da prakṛitānāka-
Nagara

Swamiji pointed out the similarity of the sacrificial symbol in the beginning of the legend with the symbol occurring on the Bull/Elephant type Yaudheya coins and restored the first word as *'raipati'*. In 1970, however, he suggested that the seal belonged to *Rapata* (or *Rapati*) who was probably an official of the Yaudheya tribe of Prakṛitānākanagara which he identified with Naurangabad. He also mentioned that some friends suggested that the first letter was not *'ra'* but *'ha'* and interpreted *'hapata'* in the sense of *'hayapati'*, i.e. 'the master of horses'. Swamiji observed that the word *'gavāśvaṃ'* occurs as a variant of *'gavāḍhyaṃ'* in a verse of the *Mahābhārata* describing Nakula's conquest of the Western Quarter

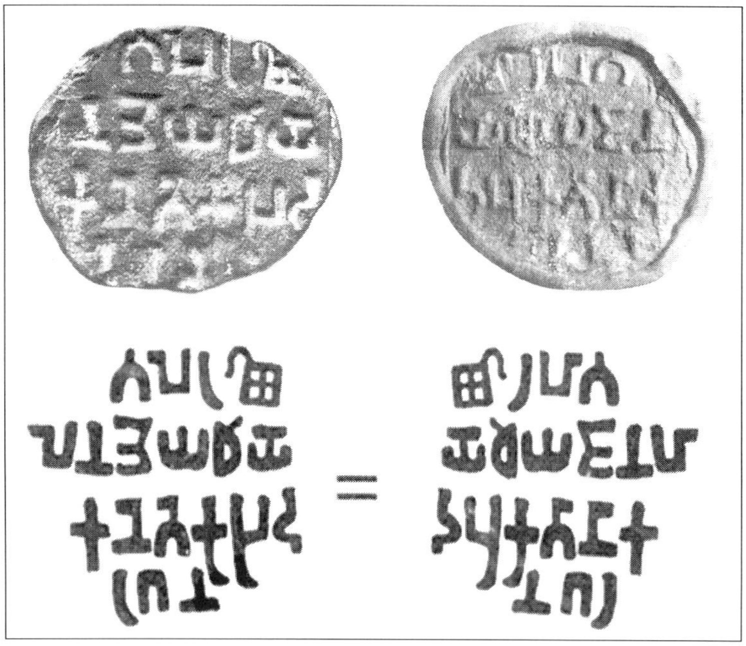

Fig. 82. Clay seal from Naurangabad with mirror view.

(*'Tato bahudhanaṃ . . .'* as quoted above) and thought that like Rohitaka (modern Rohtak) the second city of the Yaudheyas (i.e. Prakṛitānākanagara, the find spot of the seal) too may have been rich in horses. Prof. Ajay Mitra Shastri rightly pointed out that because of the truncation of the upper parts of the three letters in the top line, the word has wrongly been deciphered as *Ra(i)pat(i)* or *Hayapati*; the actual word should be read as *R(o)h(ī)ta*, the Prakrit version of the Sanskrit word *Rauhīta*. "Thus the seal inscription", he observed, "refers to the town of Prakṛitānākanagara of the Yaudheya Janapada of Rohita or Rohtak".[70] Unaware of Prof. Shastri's suggestion, Silak Ram referred to *Śukranītisāra* (IV.7, 24 ff) which uses the word *'prakṛitis'* in the sense of ministers and officers suggested that the seal belonged to the city where the ministers and officers lived. "If the interpretation is accepted", he observed, "it would show that the seal does not belong to the city of 'Prakṛitānākanagara' as taken by Bhagwandev Acharya, but that it belonged to the city or, more probably the capital of the Yaudheyas where the ministers and officers lived".[71] Silak Ram was perhaps not aware of the fact that the *Śukranītisāra* is a very late text[72] and it will not be logical to adduce its evidence for the Yaudheya polity. Even if, for the sake of argument, one agrees to the explanation of the word *'prakṛiti'* as given in that text, it is not understandable as to how does this word change to Prakṛitānāka. Silak Ram has not explained it. It will not be irrelevant to refer to the Agroha sealing which shows a *chakra* 'wheel' flanked by a conch on either side in the upper half and the two-lined Brāhmī legend below which reads *'Śrī Nārāyaṇade/va-prakṛitā'* as discussed above. The word 'prakṛita' (*Taddhita* or past participle of the prefix *'pra'* + *'√kṛi'*) was used in the sense of 'made' or 'created'. I think that the legend of the seal under consideration is the Prakrit version of *'Rauhīta Yaudheya-janapada- prakṛit=ānāka-nagara(sya)'* meaning '(the seal of the) Ānāka-nagara made capital (*prakṛita*, i.e. created or founded or renovated) by the Yaudheya-*janapada* of Rohtak'. The Yaudheya-*janapada* made this new town its capital because the old capital Rohtak was perhaps devastated during an attack of Menander as noted above.[73]

Besides 80 moulds of punch-marked coins, 100 of the Indo-Greeks and more than 2000 of Kushāṇa coins, nearly 8500 coin-moulds of the Yaudheyas of Bull/ Elephant type or Class 2 (*Yaudheyānāṃ Bahudhāñake*) have been recovered from Naurangabad and housed in the Gurukula Museum at Jhajjar.[74] Five sigils - one copper seal, one lead seal, one lead sealing and two clay sealings, all bearing the legend *'Yaudheyānāṃ'* above a bull walking to right or left and at least two clay sealings bearing the legend *'Yaudheyānāṃ jaya-mantradharānāṃ'* above the bull found from Naurangabad vouch for its continued importance as a Yaudheya town.

AHRWAN (DISTRICT PALWAL, HARYANA)

Ahrwan is located about 10 km southwest of Palwal on road to Hathin in district Palwal (formerly in district Faridabad), Haryana (Fig. 71).[75] It was in July 1883 that a red sandstone seated Buddha image measuring 1.20 X 1.00 X 0.49 m and belonging to the Kushāṇa period was acquired by the Lahore Museum (No. H 671) from this

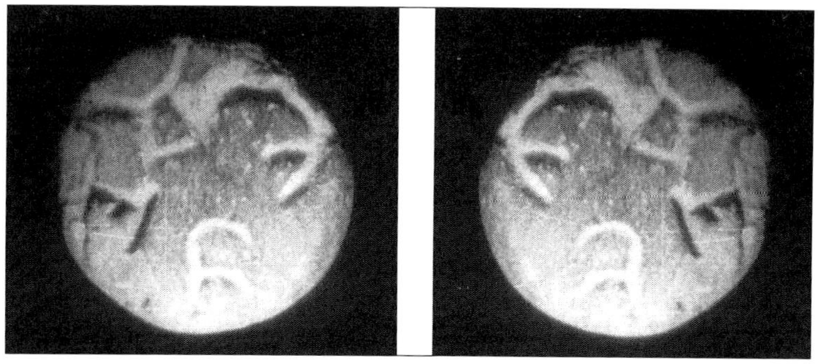

Fig. 83. Ahrwan seal.

village then falling in District Gurgaon in Punjab.[76] There is an extensive old mound near Ahrwan which extends over an area of about 40 acres and is nearly 12 meters high. Half of the mound on the eastern side is occupied by the village. Local people connect it with the Mahābhārata. Painted Grey Ware, Northern Black Polished Ware, early historic (Śuṅga-Kushāṇa) and medieval plain red and Muslim glazed ware sherds, sprinklers, votive tanks, copper coins of Brahmamitra, Hagāmāsha and Śoḍāsa, Vāsudeva Kushāṇa (with Oesho and Ardoksho reverse), Kota coins, an inscribed clay sealing, bricks measuring 36-37 X 22-23 X 6-7 and 30 X 20-21 X 6-6.5 cm sometimes marked with three straight or curved lines, early and medieval Hindu images, etc. have been picked up from the mound from time to time during the past.[77]

The credit of finding an important clay seal from Ahrwan goes to G.B. Sharma and Dharampal Singh Punia but unfortunately it has remained confined to the latter's unpublished thesis.[78] Baked red, the seal is conical in shape with a hole for passing a string on the back. Its significance remains to be discussed and ascertained. This small circular seal bears four Brāhmī letters engraved anti-clockwise along the margin reading *Śamaṇasa* in the characters of *circa* second century BCE (Fig. 83, seal with mirror view).

The legend is a Prakrit version of the Sanskrit *Śramaṇasya* 'of Śramaṇa'. The word *Śramaṇa* in Sanskrit means an ascetic or religious mendicant or devotee in general. It has also been used for both, the Buddha and Mahāvīra, the last Jaina *tīrthaṅkara* 'path maker', in Indian literature. It was popularly used for Buddhist ascetics and sometimes for Jaina monks also. A Sātavāhana inscription refers to a *Śramaṇa mahāmātra* of Nasik in the days of early Sātavāhana king Kṛishṇa.[79] Dr. A.S Altekar opined that in the Sātavāhana period *Śramaṇa mahāmātras* performed the same functions and duties as the *Dharma-mahāmātras* of Aśoka in the Maurya period.[80] The Buddhist work *Milindapañho* (IV.6, 49) refers to *Samaṇa* Kolañña, king of Kaliṅga. We do not come across *Śramaṇa* as a proper name in literature and rule out the possibility of this seal as belonging to a person of this name. Did it then belong to a Jaina or a Buddhist monk? Since no early Jaina relics are known from Ahrwan, the possibility of this seal belonging to a Jaina monk is also negated. We are thus left with the option of taking this seal to have belonged to a Buddhist monk. The Buddhist association of this site in the early period has already been pointed out above. The Buddhist monks cannot be expected to run any private or commercial activities to use such seals but its use by a monk to send some confidential messages or materials to other or higher monks or teachers cannot be ruled out altogether. A large number of sealings of the *Nālandā-mahāvihā*ra[81] testify to the use of such seals by the religious establishments and personae. The seal under review thus corroborates the evidence of the red sandstone seated Buddha image in the Lahore Museum[82] and indicates that Ahrwan was an important centre of Buddhism in the second century BCE where a Buddhist establishment worked under a *Śramaṇa*. The word *Śramaṇa* may well be compared with the designations of the present day heads of departments or gazetted officers who make use of their stamps (seals) as per their designations and not in their personal names.

KURUKSHETRA

Kurukshetra 'the field of Kuru' is well known as the cradle of Vedic culture and the battlefield of the Mahābhārata war. Geographically defined as the country lying between the two divine rivers Sarasvatī in the north and the Dṛishadvatī in the south it is equated with heaven (*Mahābhārata*, Vana Parva, 81.175):

Dakshiṇena Sarasvatyā uttareṇa Dṛishadvatī /
Ye vasanti Kurukshetre te vasanti trivishṭape //

The name first occurs in the *Maitrāyaṇī Saṃhitā* (II.1, 4) as the venue of sacrifices by gods and sages and is repeatedly referred to as a holy land in subsequent literature. *Śrīmad-Bhagavad-Gītā* (I.1) calls it *dharma-kshetra* 'the land of righteousness'.

The *Ṛigveda* refers to the Śaryaṇāvat Lake on the edge of Kurukshetra in the legends relating to the Soma plant the fermented juice of which helped Indra to kill the Vṛitras with the thunderbolt designed with the bones of sage Dadhyañcha.[83] The *Sāmaveda* (II.4.2, 11; III.1.8, 20, *Yajurveda* (Maitrāyaṇī Saṃhitā, II.13.6, 23-25) and *Atharvaveda* (XX.41.1, 2) also recognized the importance of Śaryaṇāvat similarly and the story has also been recounted in *Śatapatha Brāhmaṇa* (XIV.1, 1) and the *Śaunakīya Bṛihaddevatā* (III.23) where the lake Śaryaṇāvat figures. German scholar Hillebrandt[84] have identified Śaryaṇāvat in Kashmir but Datta and Phadke[85] have rightly observed that 'The close association of the sage Dadhīcha with the Sarasvatī (*Mbh*, III.98, 12-18), and with Indra's killing of Vṛitra on her banks (*RV*, VI.61, 7 where Sarasvatī is called *Vṛitraghnī*) and the existence of Dadhīchi *tīrtha* at Kurukshetra establishes the connection of Śaryaṇāvat with Kurukshetra'. Sāyaṇa[86] has also identified Śaryaṇāvat with the holy tank of Kurukshetra now called Brahma Sara or Brahma Sarovara, which has also loosely been called Vinaśana (*Trikāṇḍaśesha*, II.17: *Kurukshetraṃ Vinaśanaṃ*), Samantapañchaka, Rāmahrada, etc. (*Vīramitrodaya*: 462) –

dyaṃ Brahmasaraḥ puṇyaṃ tato Rāmahradaḥ smṛitaḥ /
Kuruṇā kṛishiṇā kṛishṭaṃ Kurukshetraṃ tataḥ smṛitaḥ //

Al-Biruni spoke highly of its sanctity.[87] The great tank measures about 1300 x 630 m is a landmark in the city and has been renovated in the recent years by Kurukshetra Development Board. The renovation and construction of *pucca ghats* now separates Brahma Sarovara from Sannihita Sarovara but in ancient times it was probably a single aquatic entity. Desiccation or draught in ancient times may have divided it into two parts, the smaller one still known as Sannihita and the larger part to its southwest as Brahma Sarovara. Sannihita is regarded as the redort of Brahmā, Vishṇu and Maheśa.

Clearance work at a *stūpa* site near the Department of Fine Arts, Kurukshetra University, Kurukshetra close to the western end of the Brahma Sarovara during the last two years has revealed the existence here of the foundations of a temple, *tri-ratha* in plan, about 50 meters northeast of the *stūpa* and at a level nearly 2-3 meters below. The bricks used measure 36-38 x 23-24 x 6-7 cm and seem to belong to the late Kushāṇa or the Yaudhaeya period. A sherd of the Rang Mahal type[88] bowl bearing beautiful peacock designs corroborates this date and also indicate that people from Rajasthan used to visit this place of pilgrimage and stand evidence to the movement of people including trades, existence of caravan routes and system of communication. Sharma[89] has rightly observed that the wide distribution of Rang Mahal ware "is linked with the continuous movement of people, traders and craftsmen from one place to another and also presuppose well-knit caravan routes and communication system between various parts of north-western India." At almost the same level nearly 100 meters south of it existed another temple, and another one, rectangular on plan, having a circumambulatory around with later structures above, utilizing Kushāṇa and carved bricks and brickbats. These temples may have been destroyed during the Hūṇa depredations. Mud extracted from cleaning the Brahma Sarovara also seems to have been deposited here when the temples had fallen in disuse. The whole area may thus have got the look of elevated ground.

Probably during the reign of *Parama-saugata* Rājyavardhana, or more probably of Harshavardhana, a *stūpa* was built over this naturally elevated edge of the Brahma Sarovara making use of the available bricks and brick-bats strewn around for its core. Some old Hindu temples too may have been renovated or built afresh in the area as indicated by the discovery of some clay sealings obtained in the clearance work.

The best preserved sealing (Fig. 84.1) shows in the upper half portion a nimbate two-handed goddess wearing *karṇa-kuṇḍalas* 'earrings', a cross-shaped necklace, wristlets and lower garment covering the legs above the knees and secured by a girdle, standing slightly turned to her left, holding a *bījapūraka* in her right hand bent at the elbow and raised to the level of the shoulder and probably a garland of flowers in her *pralamba* 'suspended' left hand. Her long and wide cloak bearing lined strip design is spread behind her and the ground. The facial features are not very clear. On her right side is shown a trident with big flaring outer spikes. All the three spikes and the base of the shaft of this slantingly placed trident are marked by prominent pellets. On her left lies a horizontally placed conch at the level of her feet and a big flower-like object above. It shows a cross within a circlet enclosed in a linear circle at the periphery of which may be seen parasol-like spacers.

The lower half portion of the sealing is marked by a horizontal line, below which is carved Brāhmī legend in two lines beginning with two vertical strokes, representing an auspicious symbol. The legend in the first line reads *Śrīḥ Sanni-hitā-devī*. The second line is also separated from the first by a horizontal line and has three letters *Kāha*[*ña*?]. There is a lined circle all around the sealing. The characters belong to *circa* sixth or early seventh century CE.

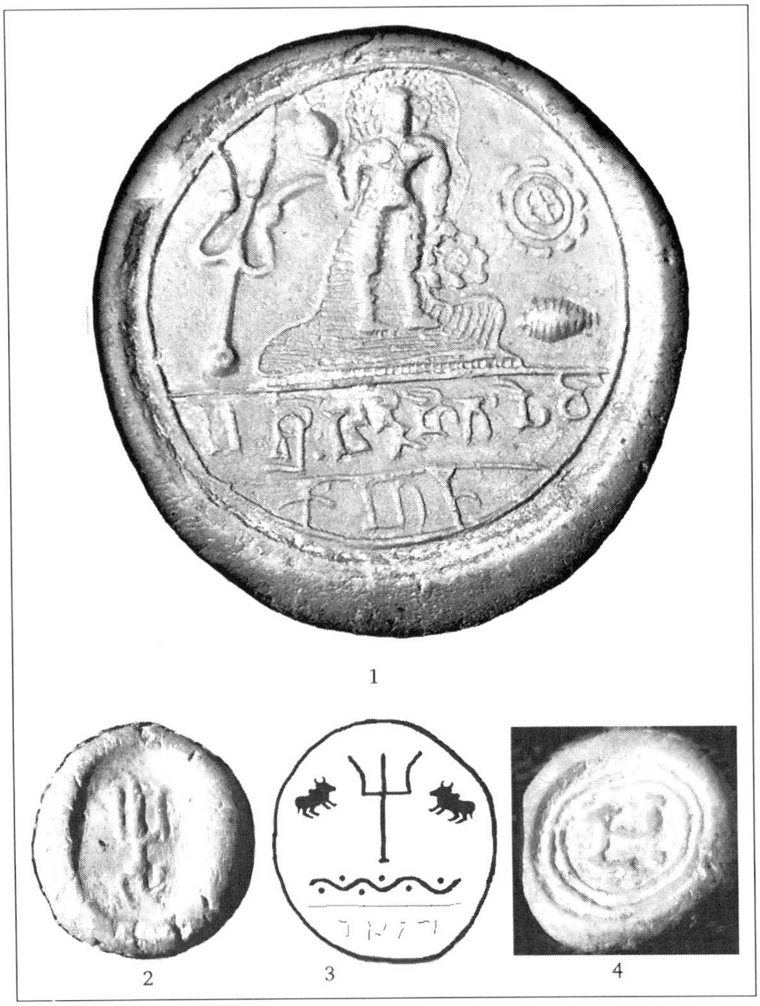

Fig. 84. Sealings from Kurukshetra.

While the second line of the legend is not clear the first line gives us the name of the deity represented in the upper half as Sannihitā-devī. It seems to be the deification of the lake near the Brahma-Sarovara called Sannihita/Sannihitā/Sannihati, etc. in the *Mahābhārata* and the Purāṇas. The name seems to have been derived from the popular tradition or belief of the convergence of the *tīrthaṣ* into this holy lake every month on no-moon day. A bath in this *tīrtha* on Amāvasyā and solar eclipse is particularly sanctifying and performance of *śrāddha* 'obsequies' on this occasion is said to bring merit accruing from the performance of a thousand Aśvamedhas 'horse sacrifices'.[90]

The *Vāmana Purāṇa*[91] echoes the same statement. We know that the rivers are deified in our religious texts but this perhaps is the first instance of the deification of a lake or pool. The deity must have been set up in a temple for the visitors to Sannihita-sarovara at the time of the Amāvasyā and solar eclipses and for the performance of obsequies of their ancestors. The presence of the trident, conch, wheel, lotus and garland indicates that the goddess Sannihitā was conceived as a syncretistic deity to attract all pilgrims without any bias of sectarian feeling. The *bījapūraka* in her right hand indicates that she was also regarded as the mother of all creatures as the *Vishṇudharmottara* (III.48, 12B-13A) explains –

Jagadbījasya sarvasya ye rājanparamāṇavaḥ //
Taiḥ pūrṇaṃ bījapūravaṃ bhhairavasya kare smṛitam/

Three more sealings bearing this legend but only with trident, wheel and flower symbol in the upper portion have been recovered from the site indicating that such sealings may have been given along with the *prasāda* 'propitiation favour' to the devotees. The legends on these sealings are not very clear but the visible marks in the upper portions resemble those of the sealing described above. Another sealing shows a trident in the upper portion flanked by a bull on either side resembling the *abhisheka* 'lustration' type figures of Lakshmī and some other deities. There is an undulating line below with dots in the curves, probably indicating fish or tortoises in the water of the river, probably Sarasvatī. There is a horizontal line dividing the flan of the sealing into two parts. The legend in the lower portion of the sealing is unfortunately so rubbed off that nothing can be made out (Fig. 84.3). I do not know of any sealing or sculpture where the trident has been shown with slantingly placed bulls flanking it in the stance of lustrating it. The trident here seems to represent Śiva.

One more sealing shows the Brāhmī letter 'sa' joined to the trident above (Fig. 84.2) while another bears only the Brāhmī letter 'sa' within a double lined circle (Fig. 84.4). These sealings indicate the existence of Śaiva shrines at the site. The existence of the Śaiva shrines in the vicinity of the Buddhist *stūpa* reveals the religious harmony practiced by the people at that time. Regular excavations in the area are a great desideratum to know more about the life of the people and to throw light on history of the site before even this part of the area falls a prey to expanding urban activities.

The significance of seals and sealings was well recognized by Thaplyal who observed that "They throw interesting light on art, iconography and religious beliefs of the past, on ancient trade and commerce, on system of education and educational institutions and on the chronology of kings and general administration. They provide data which corroborate, supplement and also alter known facts of history and, at times, supply new information not available from any other source."[92] Though quite a good number of seals and sealings in copper, lead and terracotta are known from Haryana[93] yet new material continues to surface every now and then and needs to be brought to light.

ROHTAK

More than a quarter of century back I had seen a clay sealing with a trader who told me to have obtained the piece from Khokhrakot mound at Rohtak. Since it has not surfaced since then I publish it with the eye-copy which I had prepared when I saw it (as illustrated in Fig. 74.5 above):

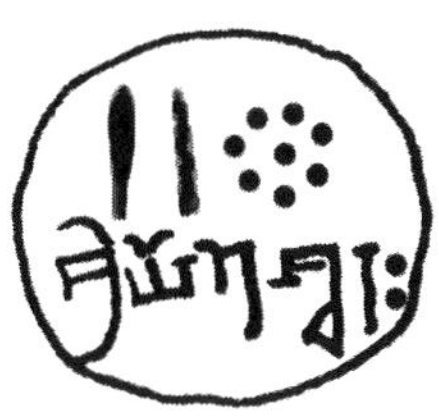

It shows a staff slightly thickened in the upper portion, a vertical column which seems to have been made of pitchers placed one over the other[94] and a dotted circle with a pellet in the centre in a row from left to right in the upper half of the sealing above and the Brāhmī legend in early Gupta characters reading 'Śrī-Yogeśvaraḥ' 'the illustrious Yogeśvara'. Yogeśvara means 'the master of Yoga'. It is also an epithet of Śiva.[95] The legend in nominative singular classes it with some rare sealings as generally the legends end in the genitive.[96] Thaplyal has referred to several sealings from Rajghat bearing the legend Yogeśvara with devices like a crescent enclosing a dot, long-necked water-vessel, trident-axe, serpent, rosary, conches, etc. Most of these symbols are Śaivite. Rosary and water-vessel are especially indicative of his yogic character.[97] V.S. Agrawala published a sealing with the legend Yogeśvarasvāmi and suggested that it belonged to a shrine of Śiva which was a centre of yogic discipline.[98]

Swami Omanand Saraswati brought to light a sealing from Achchhej (10 km southwest of Beri on road to Dadri in district Rohtak) bearing the legend *Karavīreśvarasya* showing a trident, another from Daulatpur (15 km east of Kurukshetra) bearing the legend *Sthāneśvarasya* with a trident-axe preceding the legend, and one from Sunet (now forming part of Ludhiana) having trident-axe above the legend *Maheśvara*.[99] The devices above the legend on the sealing under discussion, however, are comparable to the *musala* 'pestle', *gadā* 'club' and *chakra* 'wheel' of the Vṛishṇi sealings published by Swamiji.[100] Though the half-lion-half elephant on post in railing device (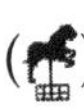) is missing the club made of round pellets piled upon one another on the sealing under discussion is in particular very similar to the one depicted on Vṛishṇi sealings. As such, this sealing should also belong to a person/official of the Vṛishṇi clan. All the Vṛishṇi seals/sealings known to us till now have been recovered from Sunet[101] except one from Naurangabad near Bhiwani.[102] So I doubt the statement of the trader regarding the provenance and feel that this piece too may have been obtained either from Sunet or freom Naurangabad. Nothing, however, is known about the owner of this sealing from any other source.

JIND

Another clay sealing allegedly found from Jind in Haryana seen with a trader long back showed a *triratna* or *Nandipada* symbol in the centre, the *svastika* symbol at about VI o' clock position with the early Brāhmī legend along the margin beginning from VII and ending at about IV o' clock position reading *Balayaśasa* in the characters of about second-first century BCE (Fig. 85.1).[103]

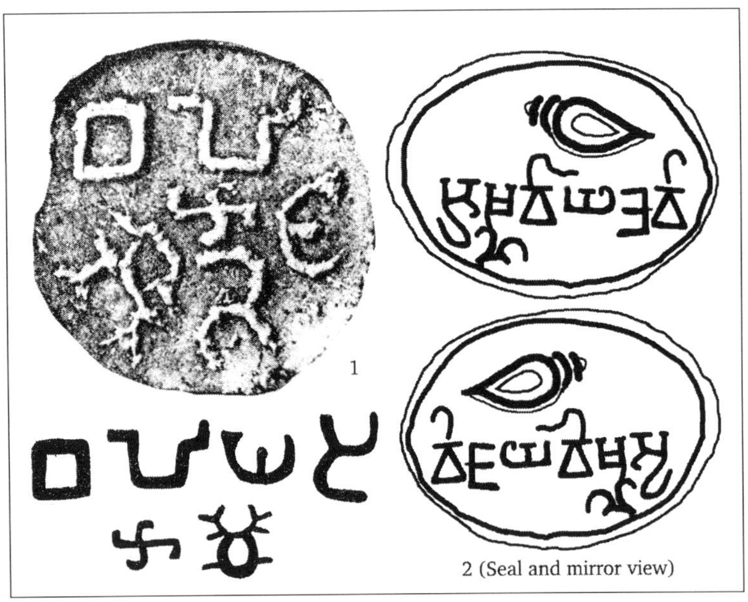

Fig. 85. Sealing from Jind and a copper seal.

Iyal did not come across this name on any seal or sealing. Nothing, however, is known about him. The piece provides a new name.

Another piece, a seal made of copper which seems to have detached from a ring, seen recently with a trader from Haryana region bears the Gupta

Brāhmī legend *Vijayavishṇusya* ('of Vijayavishṇu') with a conch engraved above (Fig. 85.2).

Though names like Dhanyavishṇu, Mātṛivishṇu, Indravishṇu, Varuṇavishṇu and Harivishṇu are known to us from inscriptions[104] a name like Vijayavishṇu is not known to us earlier from any other source. The conch goes well with the name. That he used a copper ring for putting his impressions indicates his somewhat elevated position in the social order.

The glyptic pieces described above thus add to our existing knowledge, bit by bit though.

NOTES AND REFERENCES

1. Thaplyal (1971), *SAIS*, p. 1.
2. *Ibid.*, pp. 1-2.
3. *Ibid.*
4. Rodgers (1891), *op. cit.*, pp. 41-43; Srivastava, H.L. (1952), *Excavations at Agroha (Punjab)*, Memoirs of the Archaeological Survey of India, No. 61, Delhi, p. 1.
5. *The Imperial Gazetteer of India*, Vol. I, p. 242; P.L. Gupta (1942), "Identification of Agācha on Agroha Coins", *JNSI*, IV, pp. 49-52.
6. Srivastava (1952), *loc. cit.*
7. *Journal Asiatique*, 1915, pp. 19-138.
8. Allan, *BMCAI*, pp. cliii-viii, p. 279, no. 1, Pl. XLV.9; pp. 282-83, nos. 22-29, Pl. XLV.21-24; Mitchiner, Michael (1976), *Indo-Greek And Indo-Scythian Coinage*, Vol. 7, London, p. 649; Handa, Devendra (2007), *op. cit.*, pp. 1-17, Pls. I-III.
9. Barnett, L.D. (1940), "Another Ancient Tribe of the Punjab", *BSOAS*, Vol. X, pp. 277-84.
10. *Epigraphia Indica*, Vol. I, pp. 293 ff.
11. *Ibid.*, Vol. II, p. 234.
12. Chandra, Moti (1953), *Sārthavāha* (Hindi), Patna, p. 15.
13. Przyluski, M.J. (1962), *Ancient Peoples of the Panjab*, English tr. By Chitrabhanu Sen, Calcutta, p. 9.
14. *Ibid.*
15. Malasekhera, G.P (1960), *Dictionary of Pāli Proper Names*, London, pp. 9 and 22.
16. Przyluski, *op. cit.*, p. 11. Cf. Upadhyaya, Bharat Singh (VS 2018), *Buddha-Kālīna Bhāratīya Bhūgola* (Hindi), Prayāga, p. 12, who locates Aṅguttarāpa in the Aṅga-deśa.
17. Barnett, *loc. cit*; Cf. Sircar (1968), *op. cit.*, pp. 213-214.
18. The name actually found on the coins from Agroha.
19. Barnett, *loc. cit.*
20. Apte (1959), *op. cit.*, p. 4.
21. Handa, Devendra (2004), *An Epic Pilgrimage - History and Archaeology of Pehowa: Ancient Pṛithūdaka (A Mahābhārata Site on the Sarasvatī)*, New Delhi.
22. *Mahābhārata*, Gita Press ed, XII/152.12-13.
23. Kulkarni (2007), *ICSNL*, No. 37, pp. 3-21.
24. Handa (2004), *op. cit.*, p. 3.
25. Altekar, A.S. (1942), 'Editorial Note' to P.L. Gupta's article in the *JNSI*, IV, p. 54.
26. Srivastava (1952), *loc. cit.*; Bajpai, K.D. (Gen. Ed.) (1965), *The Geographical Encyclopaedia of Ancient and Medieval India*, Part I, Varanasi, p. 8.
27. For a discussion of the legends on Agra coins see Handa (2007), *op. cit.*, pp. 12-14.

28. Barnett, *loc. cit.* Gupta (1942) has identified it with Agra of Pāṇini (IV.1, 99).
29. Barnett, *loc. cit.*
30. McCrindle, J.W. (1901), *Invasion of India by Alexander the Great*, Westminster, p. 232.
31. *JRAS*, 1903, pp. 685 ff.
32. Lahiri (1974), *ISNI*, p. 248, however, feels that since Agroha is far separated from Jhang the identification seems to be doubtful. It is possible that like many other tribes the Agras shifted from their original home to Agrodaka (Agroha) under the pressure of the Indo-Greeks during the second century BCE.
33. Barnett, *loc. cit.*
34. Rodgers, *loc. cit.*
35. Srivastava (1952), *op. cit.*, pp. 1 ff.
36. *Indian Archaeology – A Review 1981-82* onwards; Handa, Devendra (1989), "Agroha Revisited", in Bhattacharyya, D.C. and Devendra Handa (Eds.), *Prācī-Prabhā" Perspectives in Indology* (*Essays in honour of Prof. B.N. Mukherjee*), New Delhi, pp. 239-51, Pls. 24-43.
37. Haig, Wolseley (1958), *Cambridge History of India*, Vol. III, Delhi, p. 153.
38. *Ibid.*, p. 175.
39. Srivastava (1952), *loc. cit.*
40. Handa (2007), *op. cit.*, Pl. XXXV.
41. Saraswati, Swami Omanand (VS 2031), *Ancient Seals of Haryana*, Jhajjar (henceforth *ASH*), p. 41.
42. *JNSI*, XXXII (ii), p. 154, Pl. V.1.
43. *Ibid.*, pp. 156-57.
44. *Ibid.*
45. *Ibid.*
46. *ASH*, no. 31.
47. Shastri, Yogānanda (1999), *Prāchīna Bhārata meṃ Yaudheya Gaṇarājya* (Hindi), New Delhi, pp. 102 & 132-33, Pl. 13.
48. *Ibid.*
49. Swamiji's reading Rājyamātra is an obvious typological mistake.
50. *Corpus Inscriptionum Indicarum*, III, p. 8.
51. Thaplyal (1972), *op. cit.*, p. 89.
52. *Epigraphia Indica*, VIII, p. 44, lines 11-12.
53. Thaplyal (1972), *op. cit.*, p. 7.
54. *Ibid.*, p. 191, Pl. XX.1.
55. *ASH*, nos. 1, 20, 89, 76 respectively from Rohtak, Naurangabad, Sunet and Sanghol.
56. Some of the readings of Swamiji were amended by me vide Handa, Devendra (1988), "On the Reading of Some Ancient Seals and Sealings", *JAINS*, Vol. VI, pp. 76-81.The name Jñānakusala has been given with the case ending. Such examples do exist but are rare. Cf. Thaplyal (1972), *op. cit.*, p. 3.
57. Thaplyal (1972), *op. cit.*, pp. 311, no. 366a and 297, nos. 42-43 respectively.
58. *Ibid.*, p. 32, Pl. V.3.
59. Handa, Devendra (1992), "Some More Sealings from Agroha", *Panjab University Research Bulletin* (*Arts*), Chandigarh, Vol. XXIII (1), pp. 111-15, Pl. I.
60. Handa (2007), *TCAI*, pp. 9-10, Pl. IV.3-5.
61. Handa (1989), *op. cit.*, p. 243, Pl. 33.
62. Thaplyal (1972), *op. cit.*, p. 295. The only sealing belonging to a female which has come to our notice is from Sunet bearing the figure of a lion and wheel with the legend '*Svāmigupta-bhāryā Śrī-Rudradevyā*' below (*ASH*, no. 142).

63. The letters are comparable to those found in the coin-legends of the Agras. We are sorry that we could not obtain the relevant photographs and illustrate some of the important sealings discussed here, like the present one.
64. Agrawala (1963), *op. cit.*, pp. 49-64 and 426-30.
65. Handa (2007), *op. cit.*, p. 10, Pl. IV.5.
66. For other glyptics with the name-ending Svāmī, see Thaplyal (1972), *op. cit.*, p. 288.
67. There are many instances of the depiction of two *śaṅkhas* 'conches' with a *charka* or a *kalaśa* 'vase'. For details see *ibid.*, p. 157, fn. 3.
68. *Ibid.*, pp. 162 ff.
69. Acharya, Bhagwan Deva (1965), *Vīra-Bhūmi Harayāṇā* (Hindi), Jhajjar, pp. 143-51. The author, however, did not reveal the provenance of the seal in this book. The seal attracted the attention of the scholars when it was republished five years later in the *JNSI*, Vol. XXXII, Part II (1970), p. 155, Pl. V.2-3 mentioning the find spot for the first time and again in 1974 in his monumental work on *Ancient Seals Of Haryana*, Jhajjar, VS 2031, pp. 45 ff and Pl. XI.
70. *JNSI*, XXXVIII (1976), pp. 117-19.
71. Ram, Silak (1972), *Archaeology of Hissar and Rohtak Districts*, Unpublished Ph. D. Thesis, Kurukshetra University, p. 275 and (March, 1976), "Some Important Seals of the Yaudheyas", *Vishveshvaranand Indological Journal*, Hoshiarpur, Vol. XIV, Pt. I, pp. 93-95.
72. Lallanji Gopal (*BSOAS*, Vol. XXX) has put forth convincing arguments to prove that it was compiled in the early 19th century.
73. Handa, Devendra (1988), "An Interesting Yaudheya Seal from Naurangabad", *Journal of the Epigraphical Society of India*, Vol. 15, pp. 81-85, Pl. VIII. Nisar Ahmad reads the legend as '*Rohitaka Yaudheya Jana rupakritana(n)katakasa*' and interprets it as the "(seal) of the mint-house of the Yaudheya republic in Rohtak". For details see Ahmad, Nisar (1996), "A Yaudheya Clay Seal: Some Observations", in Sharma, R.K. and K.K. Tripathi (eds.), *Recent Perspectives On Prehistoric Art In India And Allied Subjects*, New Delhi, pp. 230-31.
74. *AMH*, pp. 25 ff and 109.
75. Palwal has now been declared to be a new district of Haryana. As a result of the partition in 1947, the state of Punjab was divided between India and Pakistan and on November 1, 1966 Indian Punjab was further divided and the state of Haryana was carved out of it.
76. Dar, Saifur Rehman (2004), "Fifty Years of Research in Gandhāra Art (1947 – 1997)", in Sharma, R.C. and Pranati Ghosal (eds.), *Buddhism and Gandhāra Art*, Shimla-Varanasi-New Delhi, p. 23, fn. 2.
77. Punia, Dharampal Singh (1976), *Archaeology of Mahendragarh and Gurgaon Districts [Haryana]*, Unpublished Thesis, Kurukshetra University, Kurukshetra, pp. 157 ff; Handa, Devendra (2006), *Sculptures From Haryana (Iconography & Style)*, Shimla-New Delhi, pp. 3, 76-77, 131, 228, 250 and 267. Recently a Kushāṇa terracotta votive tank, a copper coin of the Mathurā Kshatrapa Śivaghosha and a *Gani* of Rukn-ud-Din Ibrahim Shah I (son of Firuz Khilji who was put on the throne by his mother after Firuz's death but fled to Multan when attacked by Ala-ud-Din Khilji, AH 695 = 1295-96 CE) have been picked up by Dr. Lal Singh of Faridabad from this site.
78. Punia, *loc. cit.*
79. *Lüder's List*, Inscription no. 1144.
80. Altekar, A.S. (1958), *State and Government in Ancient India*, 3rd ed., Delhi, p. 205.
81. *Memoirs of the Archaeological Survey of India*, No. 66, p. 27. For rock crystal Kharoshṭhī seals of the Buddhist monasteries (*Saṃgha-mudre*) from Rawalpindi and Peshawar see also *Numismatic Chronicle*, 6th Series, Vol. X (1950), pp. 23 ff and Schlingloff, D. (1969), "Stamp Seal of a Buddhist Monastery", *JNSI*, XXXI (I), pp. 69-70, Pls. VII.1-2 & VIII.1.
82. Foe details see Handa, Devendra (2021), *Facets of Indian Art, Iconography and Numismatics*, New Delhi: Aryan Books International, p. 77, Pl. XLVII.

83. Satavaḷekar, S.D. (Ed.), *Ṛigveda* (Pardi): 58, 472-73, 530, 586, 625, 655, etc.
84. Keith, A.B. & A.A. MacDonell (1912). *Vedic Index of Names and Subjects*, Oxford: OUP (Reprint, Delhi, 1967), 2 vols., p. 364; Bhargava, M.L. (1971), *India in the Vedic Age*, Lucknow: Upper India Publishing House, pp. 76-77; Phadke, H.A. (1974), 'Śaryaṇāvat', *Proceedings, All India Oriental Conference*, Poona: Bhandarkar Oriental Research Institute, pp. 6-7.
85. Datta, V.N. and H.A. Phadke (1984). *History of Kurukshetra*, Kurukshetra: Vishal Publications, pp. 367-74;
86. *Ibid.*; *CASR*, Vol. II (reprint, New Delhi: ASI, 2000), pp. 218-19; Rodgers (1891). *Op. cit.*, p. 8.
87. Datta and Phadke (1984), *op. cit.*, p. 167.
88. Rydh, Hanna (1959), *Rangmahal*, The Swedish Archaeological Expedition to India, 1952-54, Lund: Acta Archaeology.
89. Sharma, Y.D. (1961), "Explorations in historical sites", *Ancient India*, No. 9, pp. 123 ff.
90. *Mahābhārata*, Vana Parva, 83.195-197: *Māsi māsi nara-vyāghra Sannihatyāṃ na saṃśayaḥ / Tīrtha-saṃnihanādeva Sannihatyeti viśrutā / / Amāvasyāṃ tu tatraiva Rāhu-graste divakare /Yaḥ śrāddhaṃ kurute martyaḥ tasya puṇya-phalaṃ śriṇu /Aśvamedha-saharasya samyagishṭasya yat-phalam / /*
91. *Vāmana Purāṇa*, 13.50 and 20.9.
92. Thaplyal (1972), *SAIS*, pp. 1-2.
93. *ASH*; Daivakarani, Virjanand (2010), *Bhārata ke Prāchīna Mudrāṃka* (Hindi), Jhajjar, 2010; Handa, Devendra (October 2007), "Seals and Sealings from Agroha", *Nidhi*, Vol. II, pp. 35-51.
94. Some images of Vishṇu and other deities carry a mace similar to this one which is generally described as knotted mace. M. Mariottini Spagnoli has traced the antiquity of knotted mace in Indian art from the Śuṅga period (*East and West*, XVII. 1967, pp. 248-67 and figures). A similar mace is shown in the lower right hand of Vishṇu on a unique gold coin of the Kushāṇa ruler Vāsudeva (B.N. Mukherjee, "Lord Vāsudeva on a Coin of King Vāsudeva I", *JNSI*, XLIX, 1987, pp. 44-45, Pl. IV.4B). The tradition of the knotted mace seems to have continued, though intermittently and irregularly, to the 6th-7th century CE as evidenced by an image of a yaksha in the National Museum (Acc. No. 67.106) holding the knotted mace horizontally placed on his knees published by R.C. Agrawala (*Ibid.*, New Series, Vol. 20 – No. 3, September 1970, pp. 351-52, Fig. 1).
95. For the meanings of this word see Apte (1959), *op. cit.*, p. 460.
96. Thaplyal (1972), *op. cit.*, p. 6.
97. *Ibid.*, pp. 142-43.
98. *JNSI*, XXIII (1961), p. 408. Varanasi was a great centre of Śaivism and Motichandra has referred to some other Śaiva seals from Rajghat bearing the legends *Bhogeśvara*, *Gaṅ(/r)geśvara*, etc. (Moti Chandra, *Kāśī kā Itihāsa*, Bombay, 1962, p. 97).
99. *ASH*, nos. 8, 52, 166 respectively. A seal from Sanghol bearing the legend *Śrī-Gomīśvarasya*, however, carried a conch and *śrīvatsa* above the legend (*Ibid.*, no. 72). It is interesting to note that another sealing, square in shape, has been recovered from Sunet which also bears the legend *Sthāneśvarasya* with a motif above which looks like a flower on the obverse and the name *Rudraśarma* on the reverse [Daivakarni (2010), *op. cit.*, p. p. 27, Fig. 112].
100. *JNSI*, XXXV (1973), pp. 95 ff, Pl. X.
101. *Ibid.*, XL (1978), pp. 87-91, Pl. VII.1; Daivakarani (2010), *op. cit.*, pp. 25-28, figs. 101-03.
102. Daivakarani (2010), *op. cit.*, Fig. 32.
103. It was purchased by Swamiji and has been illustrated at the end of his book (*ASH*) as no. 478 telling us that it was actually found frm Naurangabad.
104. Sircar (1965), *Select Inscriptions*, pp. 34-36, 334-36, 421, etc; Thaplyal (1972), *op. cit.*, p. 285, fn. 2.

XXIV

An Interesting Gupta Clay Sealing from Kauśāmbī

Kauśāmbī, mentioned in the later Vedic literature as the capital of the Vatsa *Mahājanapada* 'Great State', is identified with the modern village Kosam located about 65 km southwest of Allahabad on the northern bank of the Yamunā river. A Pauranic tradition states that when Hastināpura, the capital city of the Pāṇḍavas, was washed away by the floods in the Gaṅgā during the reign of king Nichakshu, the grandson of Arjuna's son Abhimanyu, he shifted his capital to Kauśāmbī. Excavation of the old mound at Kosam has confirmed its antiquity revealing twenty-five structural phases, beginning around 1165 BCE and lasting to 580 CE according to the excavator. It was subjected to destruction by the Hūṇas in the sixth century. The site has yielded evidence of the existence of a fire-altar of the form of a flying eagle (*śyena-chiti*) of the type described in the *Śatapatha Brāhmaṇa* and other ritualistic texts; an extensive stone palace covering an area of 315 by 150 meters built according to the excavator by king Udayana, a contemporary of Buddha; remains of a monastery called Ghoshitārāma as confirmed by inscriptional evidence, which was the scene of many a sermon of Buddha, consisting of a courtyard with rooms and a large *stūpa*, described also by the Chinese pilgrim Xuanzang; and many other significant remains It is thus one of the oldest and very important cities of India which has yielded year after year a rich range of iron implements, ivory objects, sculptures, human and animal terracotta figurines, coins, moulds, stone inscriptions and copper-plates, beads, bangles, seals and sealings and numerous other antiques.[1] Kauśāmbī is exceptionally rich in seals and sealings hundreds of which have been recovered from the site. 218 of them are now preserved in the Gurukula Museum at Jhajjar in Haryana.[2] Of these, an interesting Gupta clay sealing (Fig. 86) forms the subject matter of this note.

This well-baked broken clay sealing measuring about 3.4 X 3.0 cm in its extant form shows standing to front on a lined pedestal a human figure unfortunately broken

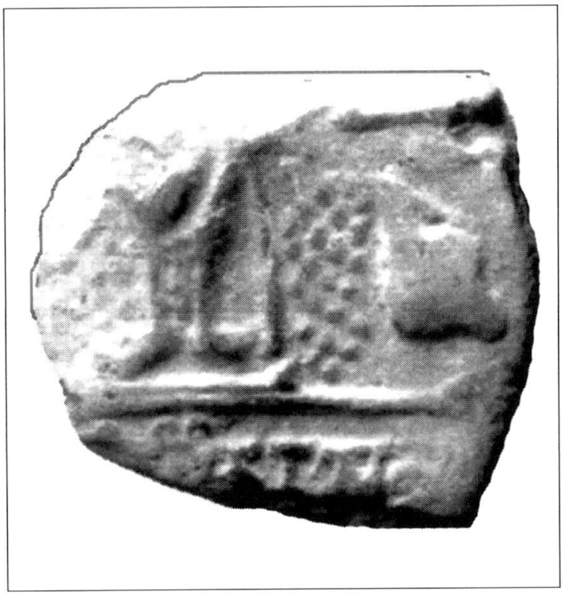

Fig. 86. Gupta clay sealing from Kauśāmbī.

above the thighs. A part of the *dhotī* worn by him covering the right thigh with free end suspended between his legs has survived. Part of a long almost vertical shaft or scepter held by him in his left hand is also visible. His feet are splayed outwards in the Kushāṇa style. A slantingly placed conch with spiral head down right is depicted on the right but what is very interesting is that a large number of globules are coming out of its groove and raining on the earth. It is not the ordinary conch but the Śaṅkha-nidhi 'conch-shaped treasure' of Kubera, the god of wealth.[3] On the proper right hand side of the standing human figure also there are some traces of some device with rows of similar globules below. It is quite possible that originally there may have been the Padma-nidhi here. The globules obviously are the *suvarṇas* 'golds' (gold coins). It is well-known that yakshas were considered as the presiding genii of wealth and were associated with Vaiśravaṇa-Kubera, the god of wealth, who is often depicted as holding a mongoose-shaped purse (*nidhi*) in his left hand in the icons. A horizontal line divides the area of the sealing into two parts, the lower one carries the legend in Brāhmī characters of the Gupta period. The legend is unfortunately truncated and only [*syā*]*dhikaraṇasya* has survived indicating that this sealing belonged to some office. The depiction of Śaṅkha-nidhi, however, provides the clue of its being connected with revenue but it is difficult to identify properly the human figure with the scepter.

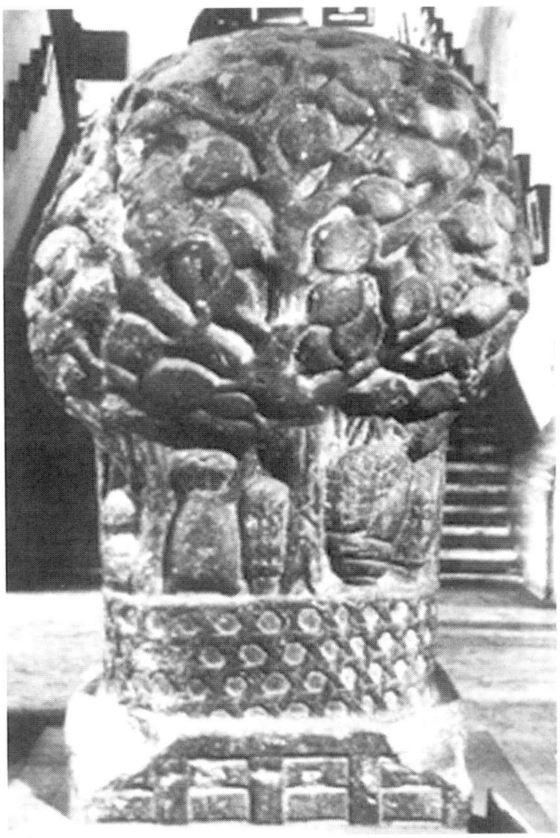

Fig. 87. Pillar capital with *Kalpavṛiksha*, Vidiśā.

It is interesting to note that a pillar capital (*Dhvaja-stambha*) from Besnagar (Vidiśā) representing Kalpa-vṛiksha 'wish-fulfilling tree', ascribable to third century BCE and pointed out to be the capital of a column of Kubera by Coomaraswamy, shows a pot and two bags overflowing with money as hanging between its aerial roots with a lotus and a conch exuding punch-marked coins on the corresponding other side (Fig. 87).[4] A similar representation of a vertically placed conch (winged in this case) with spiral head upwards exuding coins from its

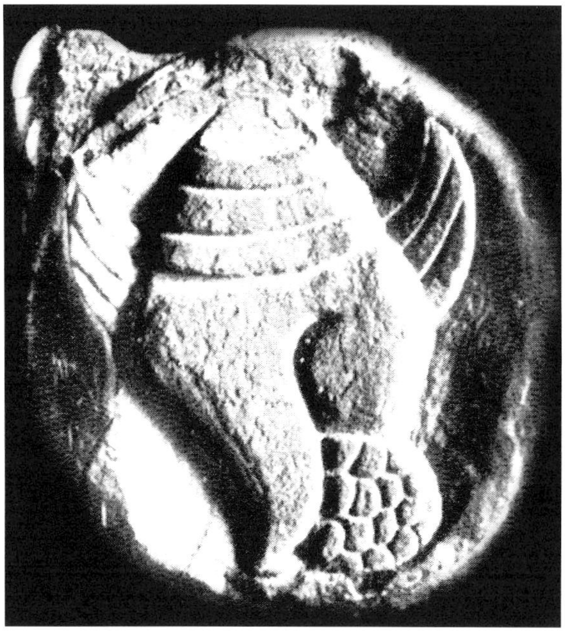

Fig. 88. Winged conch from Mathurā exuding coins.

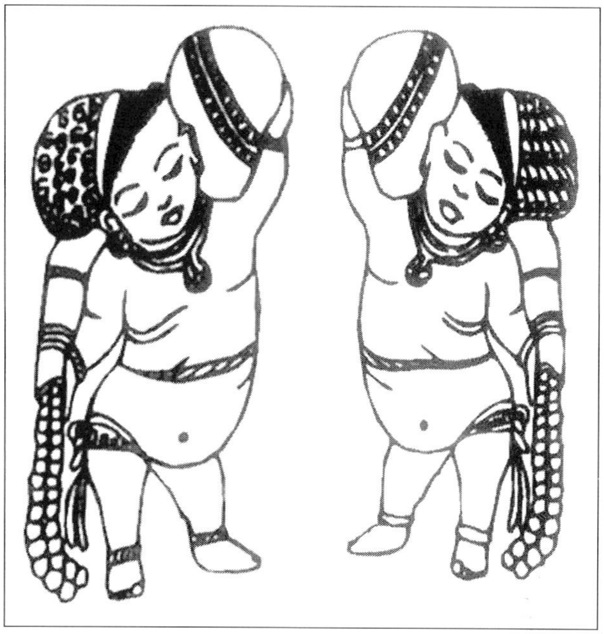

Fig. 89. Padma and Śaṅkha *nidhi.*

groove exists on a cross-bar of the railing of Kaṅkālī Ṭīlā Jaina Stūpa at Mathurā belonging to *circa* second century BCE (Fig. 88).[5]

The tradition of representing Śaṅkha and Padma *nidhis* continued subsequently also and we have a good example from The Kevala-Narasiṃha Temple at Ramtek in district Nagpur belonging to the Vākāṭaka period which shows two dwarfish figures (*gaṇas*) carved on the door-jambs pouring coins from bags held on their shoulders (Fig. 89).[6]

Lakshmī scattering coins depicted on Gupta coins[7] corroborates the continuity of the old tradition. The intense and varied numismatic activity of the reign of Kumāragupta I evinces that conch and lotus shown on some of his coins[8] may have been the symbolic representations of the Śaṅkha and Padma *nidhis* of Kubera. These two symbols are actually found on a large variety of coins issued by various kings and dynasties and may have signified the treasures of the god of wealth in many cases if not all.

NOTES AND REFERENCES

1. Sharma, G.R. (1969), *Excavations at Kausambi* (1949-50), New Delhi: ASI; *Indian Archaeology – A Review*, 1954-55 to 1966-67, relevant pages.
2. *ASH*; Daivakarani (2010), *op. cit.*, pp. 34-37, nos. 218-309 & figs.
3. Daivakarani (2010), *op. cit.*, no. 288. He has described the motifs on the sealing as human figure, bunch of grapes (?) and conch.
4. Coomaraswamy, A.K. (1971), *Yakṣas*, Part I, Delhi (reprint), Pl. 10, Fig. 10; Part II, pp. 72 & 83, Pls. 1 & 46.
5. *Ibid.*, p. 72, Pl. 46.3.

6. Jamkhedkar, A.P. (1987), "A Newly Discovered Vakataka Temple at Ramtek, Dist. Nagpur", in Rao, M.S. Nagaraja (Ed), *Kusumāñjali New Interpretation of Indian Art & Culture: Sh. C. Sivaramamurti Commemoration Volume*, Delhi: Agam Kala Prakashan, Vol. I, pp. 217-23, Figs. 4, 6-7 and 11. The *nidhi* figures have been adopted by the Indian Coin Society as its logo for its research journal named *Nidhi* and the line-drawings are after this logo.
7. Altekar (1957), *op. cit.*, pp. 126, 173, Pls. VIII.3, X.6, etc.
8. *Ibid.*, pp. 172, 220-21, Pls. X.5, XVII.1-6.

XXV

The Aulikaras and Their Associates

Recent Numismatic Evidence

The dynastic name Aulikara is now well known to the savants and students of Indian history. It was in 1886 that this name was first encountered and published by John Faithful Fleet when he deciphered an inscription of Yaśodharman Vishṇuvardhana from Mandsaur (25°04' North, 75°04' East), where it featured in a description of Yaśodharman's dynasty in the phrase *prakhyāta aulikara-lāñchhana-ātma-vaṅśo*.[1] This inscription was included in Fleet's *Corpus Inscriptionum Indicarum*, Volume III also in 1888.[2] There was some confusion in the interpretation of the expression *aulikara-lāñchhana-ātma-vaṅśo* and the words *kara* (meaning ray, i.e. hot among others) was taken to signify sun and *auli* meaning 'cold' signifying moon were interpreted as the royal marks or symbols (*lāñchhana*) of the dynasty. The Risthal Inscription discovered in 1983 refers to Drapavardhana as the ornament of the entire Aulikara dynasty (*sakalasyaulikarasya lakshma*) corroborating the fact that Aulikara was the dynastic name.[3] This renders the interpretation of the word 'lāñchhana' as mark, symbol or crest as unacceptable.[4]

In 1942 was published the Bihar Kotra (about 200 km east-southeast of Mandsaur in District Rajgarh, Madhya Pradesh) stone inscription of Kṛita (Mālava) year 474 (now preserved in the store of Chhatrapati Shivaji Maharaj Vastu Sangrahalaya, Mumbai) which refers to the ruler as *Śrī[r]-mmahārāja-Naravarmmaṇaḥ Olikarasya* in its first line making it clear that Olikara was the name of the dynasty to which he belonged (Fig. 90).[5]

The in situ Bihar Kotra cave inscription of the same year (417 CE) and of the time of Naravarmman[6] also refers to him as Olikara - *Śrīr-mmahārāja-Siṅhavarmmaṇassatputtrasya Śrīr-mmahārā/ja-Naravarmmasyolikarasya* (*saṃdhi* rule transgressed here). . . . (Fig. 91).

Most of the historians have used Aulikara as the dynastic name. The term Aulikara is a derivative form of Olikara meaning 'descendant of or belonging or related to Olikara'. So both the forms Olikara and its derivative Aulikara are correct.

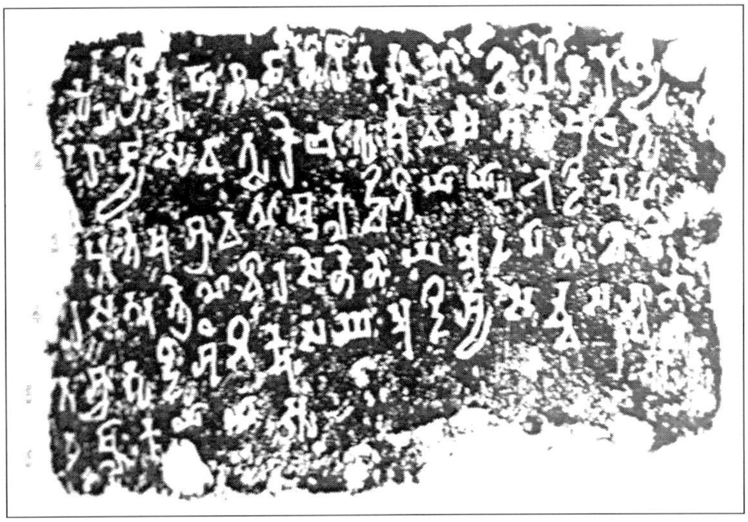

Fig. 90. Bihar Kotra inscription of the time of Naravarmman.

Daniel Balogh thinks that since Olikara has been used by Naravarmman only, it was his personal epithet. What does O/ Aulikara mean? Balogh states that "*oli* could be a vernacular form cognate to Sanskrit *āvali*, a word frequently used in the sense of "dynasty." Thus, olikara could be synonymous to *vaṃśakāra*, "founder of a dynasty."[7] Mandsaur Inscription of the Kṛita (Mālava) Era 461 (= 404 CE) discovered while ploughing a field near the Fort Gate of Mandsaur close to the Shivna river in 1912 commemorates the construction of a temple of Kṛishṇa and refers to his grandfather king (*narendra, devendra-vikrame* – valiant as Indra of the gods) Jayavarmman and father Siṅhavarmman (*siṅha-vikrānta-gāmini* – having the gait or stride of a lion).[8] Aware of the fact that Naravarman has mentioned two of his ancestors (Jayavarmman and Siṃhavarmman) in the above mentioned Mandsaur inscription of Mālava Saṃvat 461 (verses 6-7a) he avers that since these ancestors did not issue any inscriptions and no record of their achievements have been recorded in the inscriptions of their descendants they were only local chieftains and it was Naravarman who attained substantial power and proclaimed himself as the progenitor of the dynasty.[9] It is to be noted that Balog himself has referred to Bihar Kotra graffiti recording *Mahārāja*-Jaya(varmman) (?*mahārāja-jaya* and *Śrīr-mmahārāja-Siṅhavarmmaṇa[ḥ]* as graffiti 2 and 3).[10] There is no doubt that Naravarman has been designated as *Mahārāja* in his inscription but the evidence of the graffiti and the fact that Jayavarman has been referred to as *narendra* (lord of men, king) and Siṅhavarmman as *kshitīśa* (lord of earth, i.e. king) should not be set aside altogether. Issuing inscriptions is no criterion for greatness as even some of the great rulers have not done so and their achievements have not been recorded even by their descendents in their records. Balogh feels that the mention of the date of Bihar Kotra inscription in his own reign was the proud assertion of Naravarman as an independent king.[11]

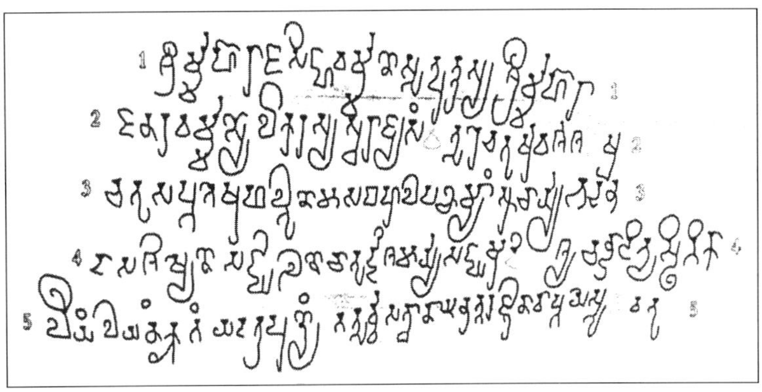

Fig. 91. Bihar Kotra cave inscription.

The Aulikara inscriptions found from Mandsaur and the area around (Fig. 92) throw

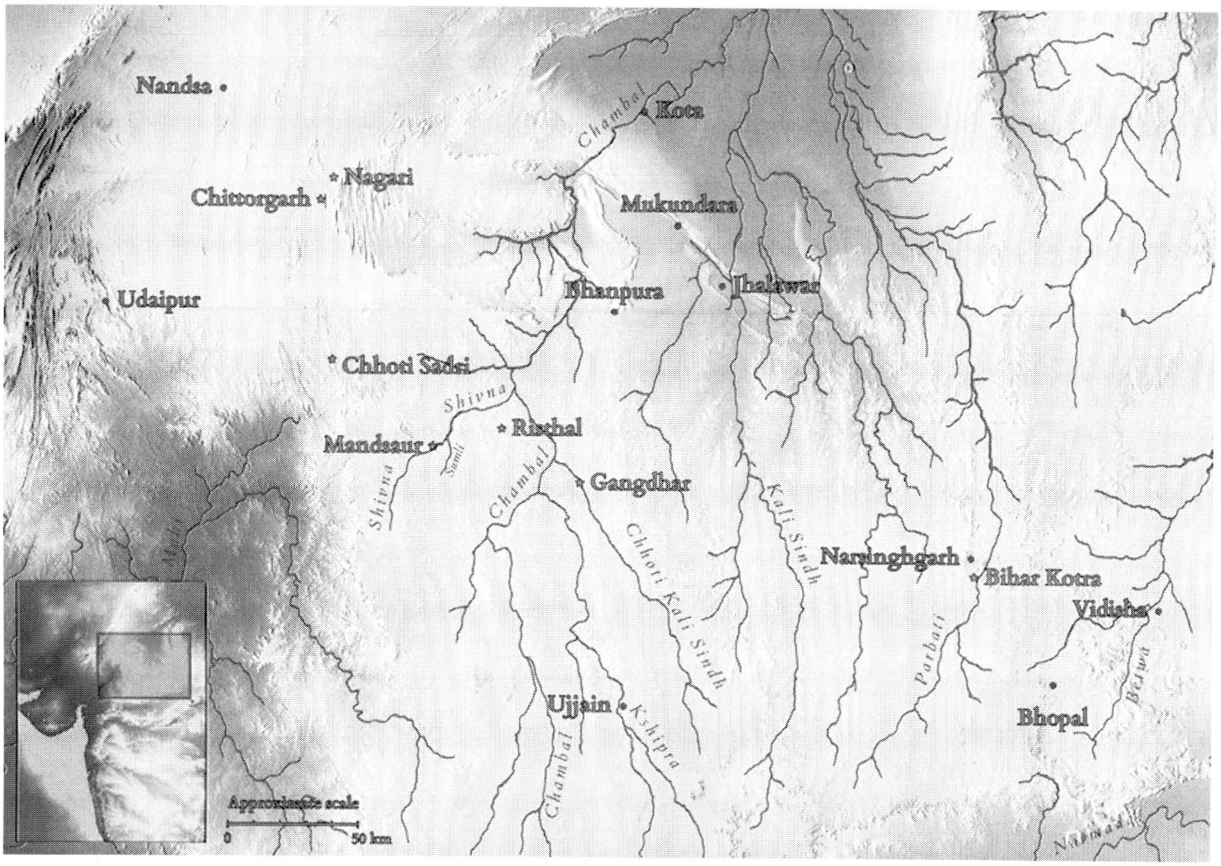

Fig. 92. Map showing important Aulikara and allied sites.

important light on the history of the dynasty and activities of its rulers who held sway in the region from about the latter half of the fourth through sixth century or seventh century with Mandsaur as their capital.[12]

Since Naravarmman is known from inscriptions to have ruled from 404 to 417 CE, his grandfather Jayavarmman may have started ruling over some territory in northwest Malwa sometime during the latter half of the fourth century CE. Naravarmman's son and successor Viśvavarmman is mentioned in the Gangdhar (Lat. 23° 56' North, Long. 75° 41' East, nearly 60 km east of Mandsaur in Disrict Jhalawar of Rajasthan) stone inscription dated Mālava year 480 (= 423 CE) when he was ruling. It records the construction of a Vishṇu temple and a shrine of the divine mothers (*Ḍākinīs*) by Mayūrāksha, a minister of Viśvavarman.[13] Viśvavarman's successor was Bandhuvarman known from Mandsaur stone inscription of Mālava Samvat 493 (= 436-37 CE) which also mentions his overlord Kumāragupta I of the imperial Gupta dynasty.[14] We thus have a complete genealogy of the Aulikara rulers from inscriptions found from Mandsaur: Jayavarmman, Siṃhavarmman, Naravarmman, Viśvavarmman and Bandhuvarmman.

The later history of the Aulikaras is not very clear. Some other inscriptions found from Mandsaur and other sites in the region furnish evidence of the existence of another line of rulers. Mandsaur inscription of MS 524 (= 467 CE) refers to king

Prabhākara as "a destroyer of the enemies of the Gupta house" (*Guptānvayāri-druma-dhūmaketuḥ*). It praises Kumāragupta I and Govindagupta indicating Prabhākara's feudatory status.[15] Chhoti Sadri stone inscription of MS 547 (= 490 CE) and a Mandsaur

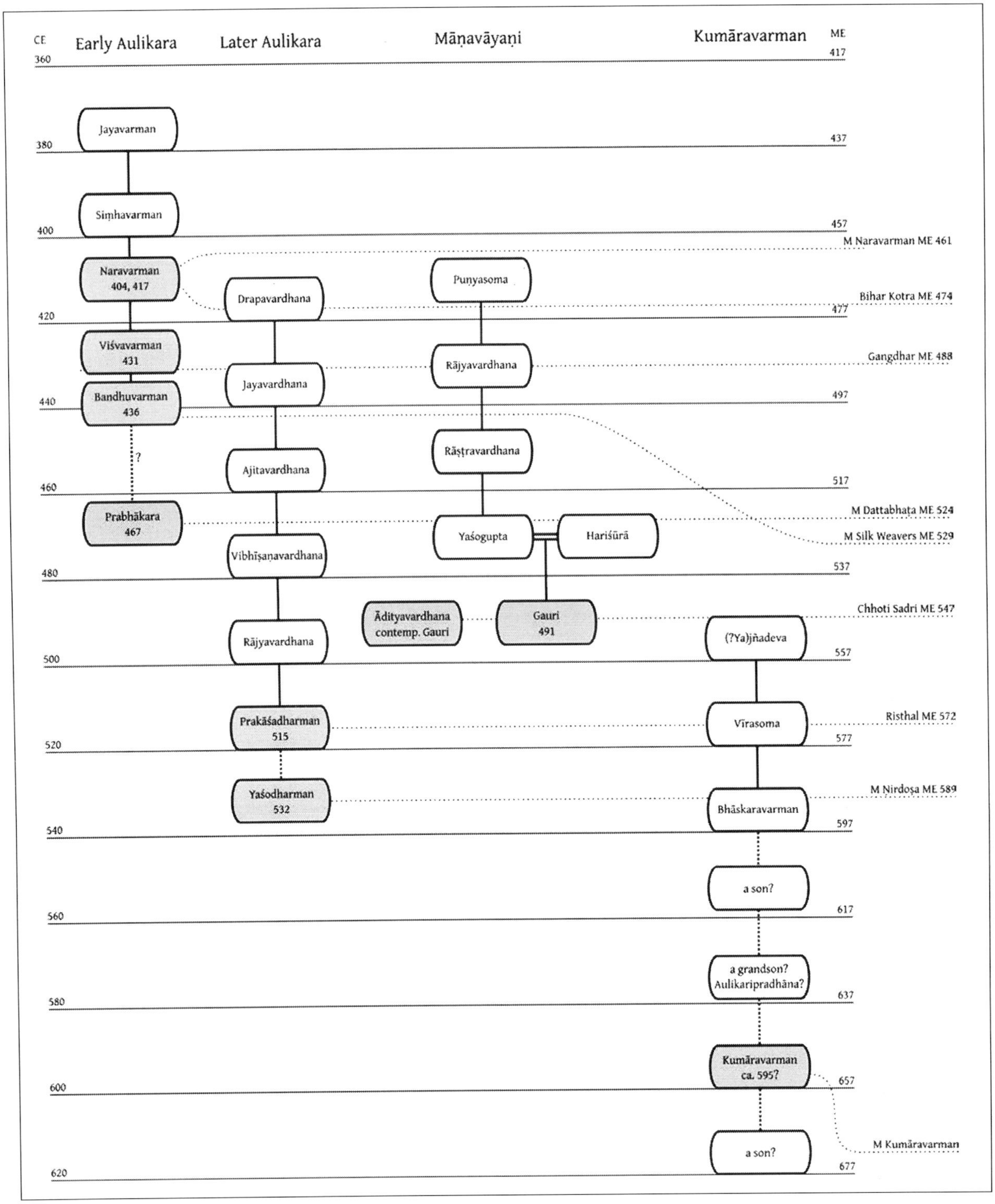

Fig. 93. Genealogies of Aulikara and associated ruling houses.

Fragmentary Inscription refer to *Mahārāja* Gaurī of Mānavāyanī *gotra* 'sept' but of unknown dynasty ruling over the region in the time of king (*Narendra*) Ādityavardhana.[16] Though their exact relationship with the above-said Aulikaras is not known yet it is generally believed that they may have belonged to a collateral branch of the family. Their generally vardhana-ending names differed from the varmman-ending names of the main dynasty.

Risthal Stone Slab Inscription of Prakāśadharmman of MS 572 (= 515 CE) describes at length his conquest over the Hūṇa emperor Toramāṇa and other achievements. He is also known from two glass seals from Mandsaur. Two inscriptions from Mandsaur give a graphic account of the prestige, prowess and conquests of Yaśodharmman. He is described to have defeated Hūṇa emperor Mihirakula and is designated as *Rājādhirāja* and *Parameśvara* having a large number of feudatories.[17] His son and successor Yaśodharmman-Vishṇuvardhana continued to rule from Daśapura (an old name of Mandsaur) to 532 CE at least.

The inscriptions refer to some members of the Mānavāyanī 'sept' who may have been the virtual rulers and also the family/dynasty of Kumāravarman who held sway over some region in the seventh century CE. The Naigamas are described in some epigraphs to have worked as 'rājasthānīyas' (provincial governors, 'Chancellors' according to Balog) under the Aulikaras. Relying on all available and latest evidence Balog has suggested the following genealogies of Aulikara and associated ruling houses (Fig. 93).[18]

There are numerous gaps in our knowledge and the above figure is based on possibilities and probabilities. Some of these gaps are likely to be filled up by recent and future discoveries. Some of the recent numismatic discoveries have been discussed below.

AULIKARA COINS, SEALS/SEALINGS AND SIGNET RINGS

Quite a good number of lead pieces (coins or tokens) with the Gupta Brāhmī legend *Jitam bhagavatā padmanābhena* with a crescent and dot above on one side and *Śrīvatsa* as the central device with *śaṅkha* 'conch', *chakra* 'wheel', *gadā* 'mace' and *padma* 'lotus' on the other sides have been found from Mandsaur, the capital of the Aulikaras (Fig. 94).

Thaplyal[19] has referred to a copper coin bearing this legend and alludes to this expression occurring in some inscriptions also. The legend may be compared to clay seals bearing the legends in Gupta Brāhmī characters *Jitaṃ bhagavatā Vāsudevena* and *Jitaṃ bhagavatā svāmi-Nārāyaṇena*. Prof. K.D. Bajpai[20](1976, 150-51, Pl. IX.16) attributed a variant of these coins to Chandragupta II, Bhatt and Johri[21] regard these pieces as the coins of Govindagupta, son of Chandragupta II, with dissidence of course. Had these coins been issued by Chandragupta II or Govindagupta, they would certainly have a wider circulation; but most of the pieces of known provenience come from Mandsaur and had only local circulation. Jai Prakash Singh[22] had rightly observed that they are temple tokens. Had these coins been issued by Chandragupta II or Govindagupta, they would certainly have a wider circulation; but most of the

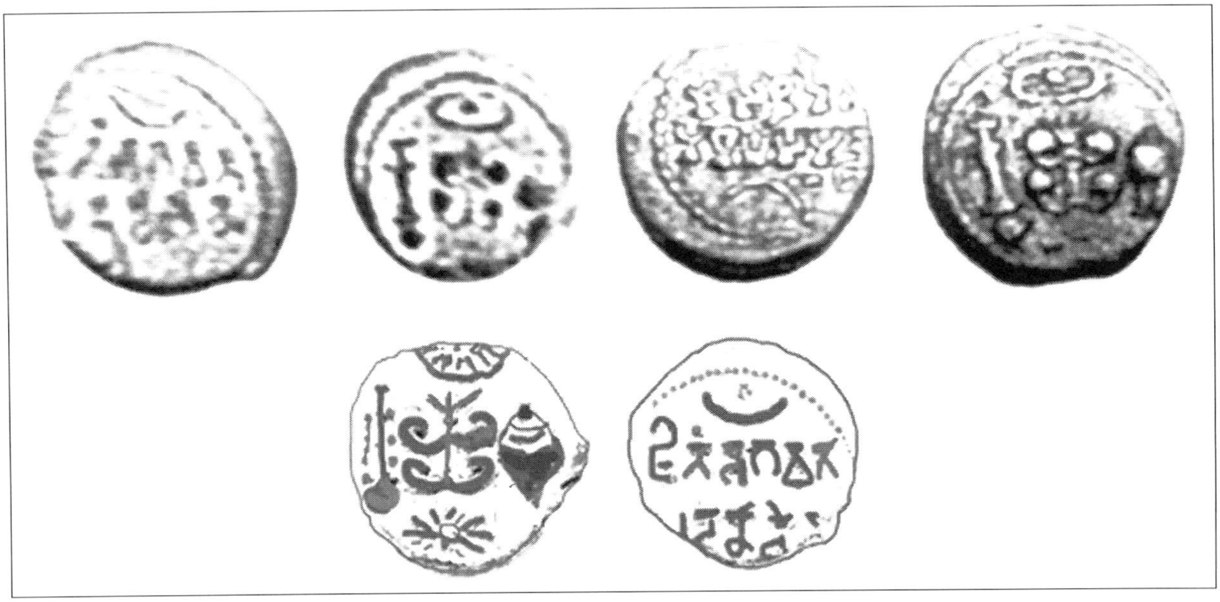

Fig. 94. Lead temple tokens.

pieces of known provenience come from Mandsaur and had only local circulation.They corroborate the popularity of Vaishṇavism amongst the Aulikaras. Interestingly the Mandsaur inscription of Kṛita year 461 (= 404 CE) opens after the customary auspicious word *Siddham* with homage to Śeshśāyī Vishṇu, i.e. Padmanābha (Fig. 84), and the epigraph seems to have been engraved at the time of the completion of a temple dedicated to Vāsudeva Vishṇu/Kṛishṇa (*Sahasraśīrshe tasmai purushāyāmitātmne[/] chatussamudraparyyaṅkatoya nidrālaye namaḥ* [//])[23] (Fig. 95).

So it is probable that the lead coins/tokens may have been issued at the time of the inauguration of this temple. That Naravarmman too professed this faith is

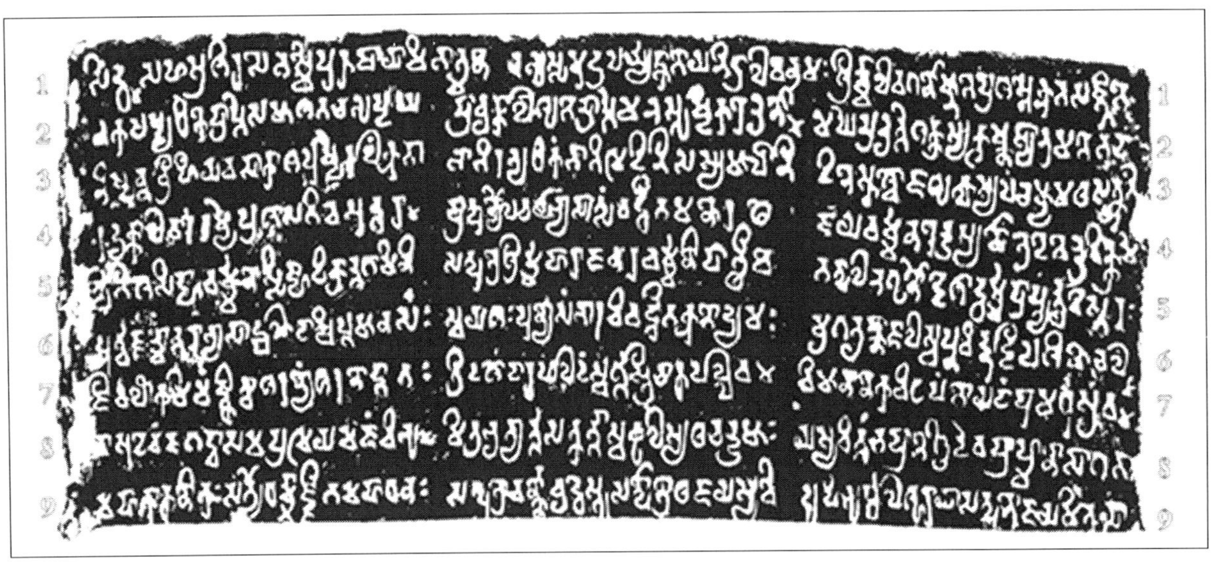

Fig. 95. Mandsaur inscription of Kṛita year 461.

exemplified by the existence of wheel, lotus and other Vaishṇava attributes on his coin discussed in the sequel.

COPPER COIN OF SIṂHAVARMAN

No coins definitely attributable to the Aulikaras were known till 2016 when I came across an interesting coin in a private collection (Fig. 96)[24] which bears the following details -

Metal : copper[25]
Shape : oval
Size : 18 x 24 mm
Weight : 3.98 g
Obverse : Traces of a bull (or lion?) to right walking on an undulating track, legend *Śrī Siṃhavarma* below in the Northern Brāhmī characters of the latter half of fourth century CE
Reverse : *Śrīvatsa* symbol with partially visible lined frame around

Below the last two letters of the legend on the obverse may be seen a part of another syllable which is not very clear but may have been the nominative singular suffix *sya* attached to the name of the king. Balog feels that 'it is more likely to be a subscript *m* attached to the main consonant and pushed to the left to accommodate the curve of the coin'.[26] The name of the issuer of this coin can easily be restored as Siṃhavarman. The lion on the obverse is in consonance of the name of the issuer and the bold *Śrīvatsa* symbol on the reverse betrays his Vaishṇava predilection. The definite provenance is not known but since it has been obtained in trade from Indore the original find-spot may have been somewhere in western Malwa.

Though in an indifferent state of preservation, yet being the first definite Aulikara coin to come to light, it forms an important discovery and revives the hope of more important discoveries in future. The issuance of a coin betrays the independent status of the king and the *Śrīvatsa* on the reverse indicates the popularity of Vaishṇavism which seems to have flourished during Siṃhavarmman's reign.

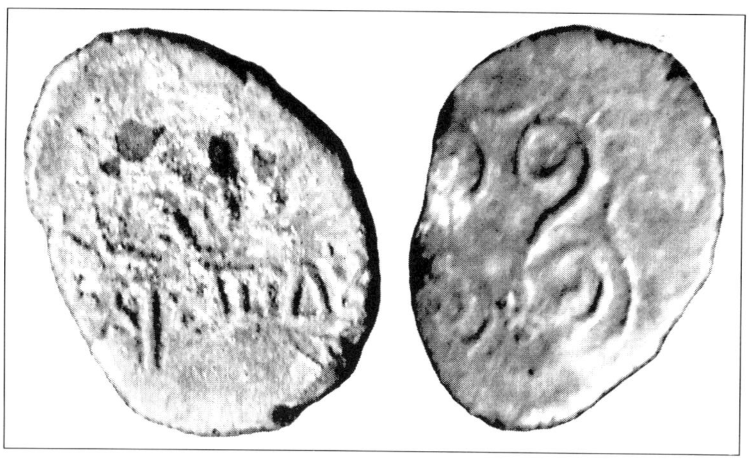

Fig. 96. Copper coin of Siṃhavarman.

UN-INSCRIBED COPPER COIN

Another un-inscribed copper coin (5.31 g) from Mandsaur in possession of Rajnarayan Maurya of Ahmedabad (Fig. 97) shows a lion to left with a prominent symbol which looks like sun and moon or a *Śrīvatsa* on the obverse and a taurine on the reverse too

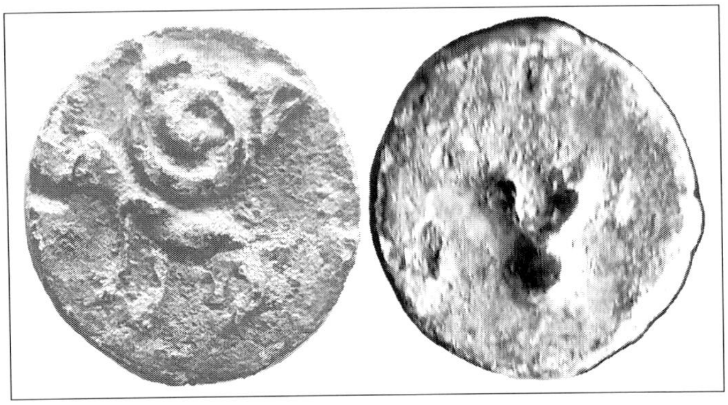

Fig. 97. Un-inscribed copper coin.

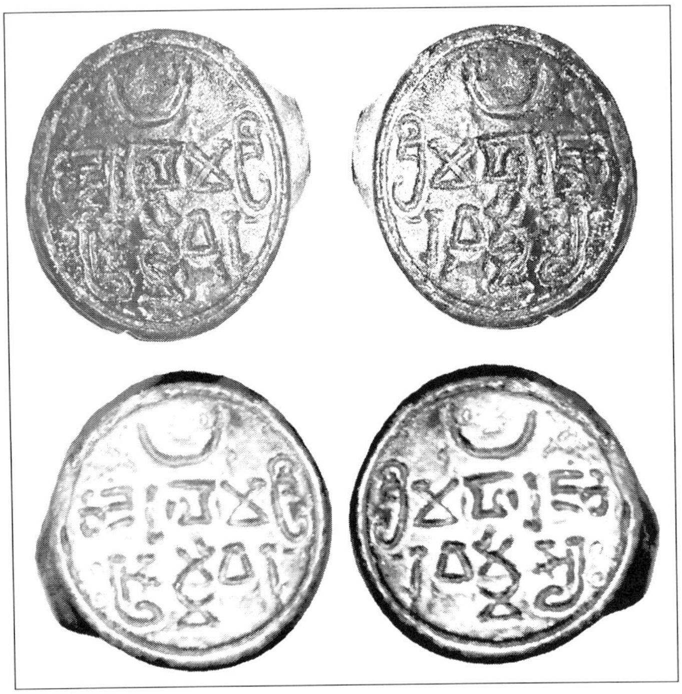

Fig. 98. Signet ring of Naravarmman and its mirror impression.

may have probably been issued by Siṃhavarmman initially during the early phase of his rule as suggested by the device and the provenience:

SIGNET RING OF NARAVARMMAN

Some time back a copper signet-ring wrongly deciphered and identified as that of Kuruvarmmā was put on the net.[27] The motif in the upper half of the ring shows what looks like a crescent with a small sun or star mark and the lower half engraved in the Brāhmī characters of fifth century CE containing the name of its master in two lines which I read as 'Śrī Mahārāja-Na/ravarmmasya' followed by two dots, one upon the other, just like the Sanskrit *visargas*[28] (Fig. 98):

The title *Mahārāja* following the honorific *Śrī* 'the illustrious' and preceding the proper name of its possessor clearly indicates it to be a royal ring. Since the legend has been engraved negatively this ring was obviously used as the royal seal. Being the first royal Aulikara signet ring to come to light it is an important historical document of the dynasty.

COPPER COIN OF NARAVARMMAN

On November 25/December 15, 2015, a round die struck copper coin (780 mg, 12.5 mm) was floated on the Facebook by the well known collector Shri Dau Lal Johri of Indore (Fig. 99):

I identified this coin as an issue of the Aulikara king Naravarmman of Mandsaur.[29] It bears on the obverse a dotted circle with the two-lined Brāhmī legend 'Śrī Mahārāja-Na/ravarm(masya*)' in the Gupta characters of *circa* fifth century CE. The reverse shows a wheel in profile placed on a lotus with fillets flowing from the axels. The placement of the wheel with ribbons on a lotus indicates its sanctity and divinity and may be interpreted as a representation of Vishṇu's attribute. The presence of dotted wheel may be compared with the crescent with dot motif on Naravarmman's signet ring.

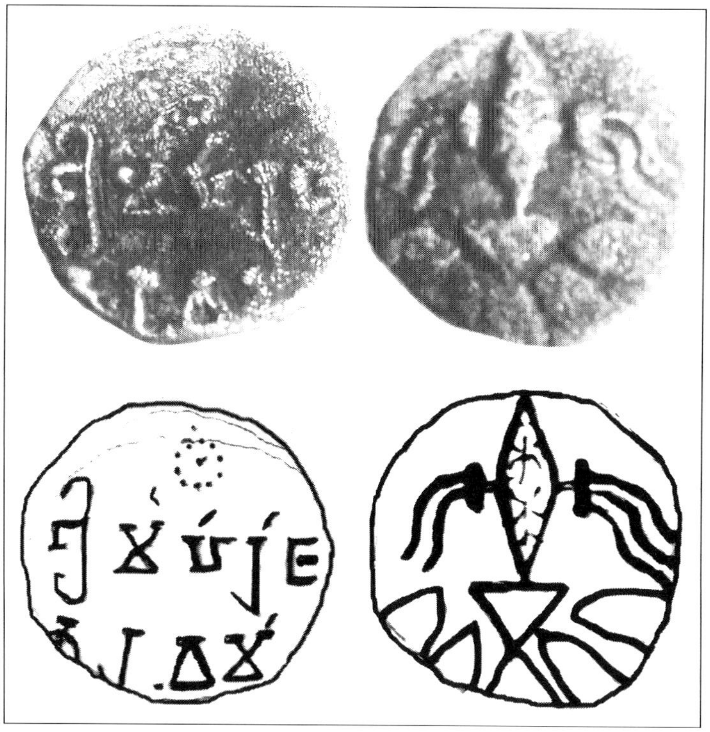

Fig. 99. Copper coin of Naravarmman.

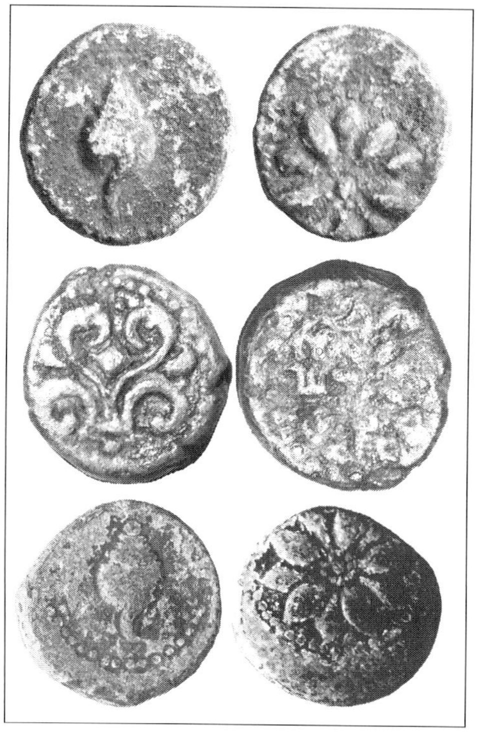

Fig. 100. Mandsaur coins with conch and lotus 1 & 3, with *Śrīvatsa* 2.

UN-INSCRIBED LEAD COINS

An un-inscribed lead coin (4.56 g) from Dashpur in possession of Mr. Deepak Jain (Fig. 100.1) and another piece in the same metal weighing 3.27 g in the collection of Shri R.N Maurya of Ahmedabad (Fig. 100.3) bear a prominent conch on the obverse and a ten-petal lotus on the reverse. The devices and provenience suggest its attribution to the Aulikaras and the example of the preceding coin betrays that it may have been struck by Naravarmman, probably for distribution to the devotees at the occasion of the inauguration of the Vishṇu/Kṛishṇa temple referred to in Mandsaur stone inscription of Kṛita year 481 cited above. The depiction of the lotus on the first coin is very similar to a beautiful piece in possession of Shri Girish Sharma which shows an elaborate and decorative *Śrīvatsa* on the obverse and lotus with the legend *Jitaṃ bhagavatā [Padmanābhena]* around on the reverse (Fig. 100.2) corroborating our surmise–

LEAD COIN OF NARAVARMMAN

Another coin (1.5 g) brought to light recently by Rajnarayan Maurya and rightly identified by well known numismatists Bhushan Kapadia and Shailendra Bhandare as that of Naravarman further confirms Olikara as the dynastic name (Fig. 101). A part of the legend on this coin has been read as *[Mahārāja-Śrī]-Naravarm(m?)asya Olikarasya* from about 9 to 7 o'clock position:

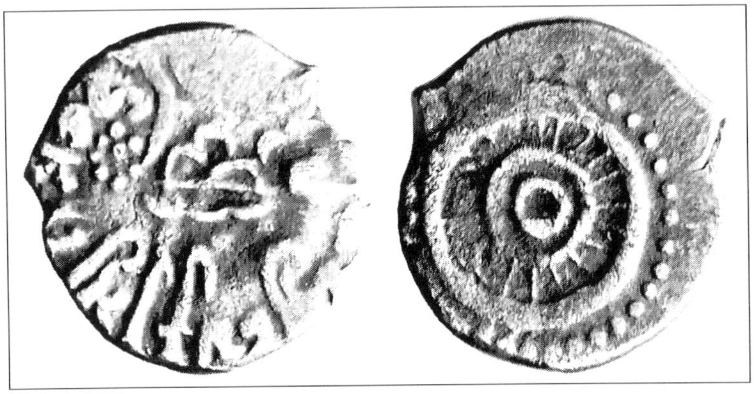

Fig. 101. Copper coin of Naravarman Olikara.

This coin contains the central device of three-arched (crescented?) hill or *chaitya* with a wavy line below and sun and crescent symbols flanking it on the left and right on the obverse adopted from the coins of the Western Kshatrapas indicating clearly that Naravarman won an important war against the Western Kshatrapas and annexed some territory previously occupied by them. The wheel within dotted border on the reverse betrays his Vaishnavite leanings. It may be a representation of Sudarúana-*chakra* of Kṛishṇa whose temple was constructed at Mandsaur as referred to in the Mandsaur inscription of Mālava Samvat 461 (= 404 CE) cited above.

These coins and temple tokens together with the inscriptional evidence make it clear that These early Aulikara rulers were inclined towards Vaishnavism from the beginning and may have come to grab power from being important warrior chiefs of a particular or various clans then occupying parts of northwestern Malwa and southern Rajasthan after Samudragupta's campaign. In all likelihood besides occupying their original area of habitat they may have annexed some adjoining areas of Western Kshatrapa dominions as indicated by their coins listed above.

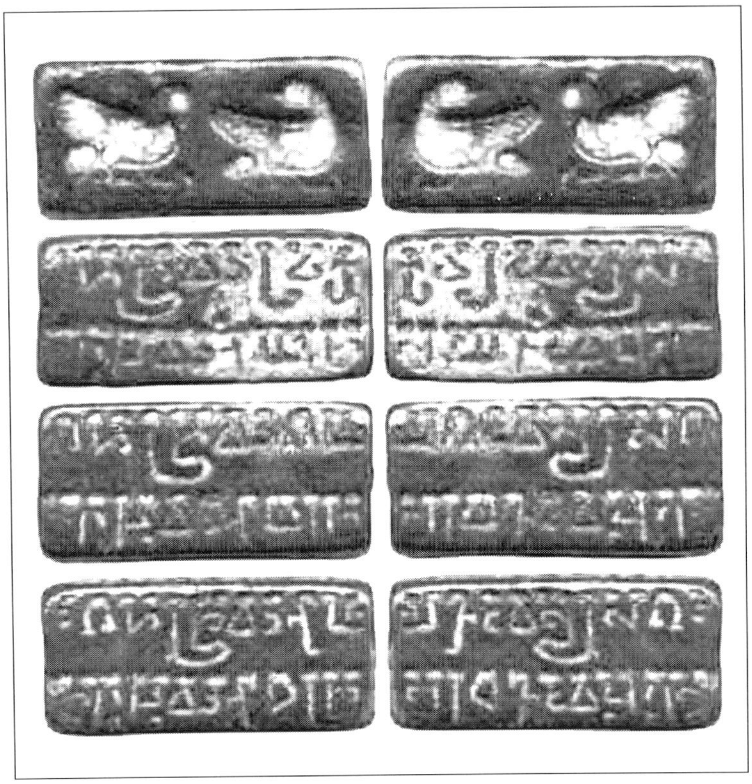

Fig. 102. Copper seal of Yañadeva and his sons Yaśadeva and Kumāradeva with mirror views.

COPPER SEAL OF YAÑADEVA SOGI AND HIS SONS

Some time back the well known collector and numismatist Shri Girish Sharma of Indore[30] put on the net the following copper seal with its mirror impression (Fig. 102).

It is a square sectioned rectangular seal measuring 18 x 8 mm in size and 13.88 g in weight. It has a transverse hole for stringing it. It shows two ducks with one turning its head backwards towards the other on one side with each of the other three facets bearing the Brāhmī legend in two lines which he deciphered almost correctly except the term 'saga-/sya' qualifying the names of the users of this seal. Earlier I preferred to read and amend this word as Sagajasya thinking that the users of this seal were connected with elephant maintenance or elephant force and that this term represented the title or name of the post held by the users.[31] With the coming into light some more seals/sealings discussed in the sequel I read the legends as following:

1. Kumāradevasya sog(i)-/sya Yañadevaputrasya
2. Yaśadevasya sog(i)-/sya Yañadevaputrasya
3. Yañadevasya sog(i)-/sya Dhañadevaputrasya

The seal also provides interesting orthographic evidence of the use of *ña* both for *na* or *nya*[2] and *jña*.[32]

The legends thus furnish the evidence of three generations –

Dhañadeva (Dhanadeva or Dhanyadeva)
|
Yañadeva (Yajñadeva) Sogi
|
Yaśadeva Sogi — Kumāradeva Sogi

The seal as per the legend seems to have belonged to and used by two generations, i.e., by Yañadeva, son of Dhañadeva, and two sons of Yañadeva namely Yaśadeva and Kumāradeva of the Sogi clan. It is rather difficult to determine as to who was elder and succeeded his father first, Yaśadeva or Kumāradeva.

In 1979 a large but fragmentary stone inscription of a post-Aulikara ruler named Kumāravarmā was found while digging for the foundation of a building for the weavers of Mandasor. V.V. Mirashi[33] dated him to circa 580-610 CE. The preserved portion of the inscription traces the lineage of Kumāravarmā from [Ya]jñadeva as following –

[Ya]jñadeva
!
Vīrasoma
!
Bhāskaravarmā
!
Kumāravarmā

The purpose of the inscription was evidently to register the performance of some charitable work such as the construction of a tank at Mandasor. Mirashi believed that Yajñadeva was a feudatory of the Aulikaras who rose to power in circa 540 CE. He was probably the founder of Kumāravarman's dynasty. The verse describing Bhāskaravarman is imperfectly preserved, but it seems to have described his victory over an illustrious king of the Aulikara family. It is well known that Aulikara was the name of the family of Yaśodharman. Bhāskaravarman thus seems to have defeated a successor of Yaśodharman and ousted him from the Mandasor Ujjain region. Kumāravarman was the son of someone described as the foremost Aulikara and had become heir-apparent (*yuvarāja*) at a tender age. The name of his family does not occur in the preserved portion of this Mandasor inscription.

Yajñadeva's son Vīrasoma was a ruler of peaceful disposition. If the Yajñadeva of the fragmentary Mandsaur inscription was the son of Dhanadeva of the above-mentioned seal he may be regarded as having three sons - Yaśadeva, Kumāradeva and Vīrasoma. The genealogy also makes it clear that the name-endings in a family were not fixed and could vary. Also Kumāradeva could be mentioned as Kumāravarmā in different records. Another important information yielded by the copper seal is that the family of Yajñadeva belonged to the Sogi clan.

It is interesting to note that Nandsa (25° 14' 56" N, 74° 16' 49" E, District Bhilwara, Rajasthan) Yūpa inscriptions commemorate the tremendous sixty-one day long sacrifice (*?aikashashṭi-rātramatisatram*) held by Śrīsoma or Nandisoma, son of Jayasoma, grandson of Jayanartana or Bhṛiguvardhana and great grandson of Jayatsena, who belonged to the Sogi clan. The sacrifice was performed in the Kṛita era 282 (=225-6 CE) to celebrate a victory against a Śaka ruler.[34] Another inscription from the same site refers to a *mahāsenāpati* Bhaṭṭisoma Sogi. The Sogis of the seal under discussion may have descended from the Sogis of Nandsa or have a common heritage. These names again tell us that the scions of a family could have different name-endings and that it will not always be very prudent to suppose linkages between persons having similar name-endings.

SIGNET RING OF MITRAVARMAN SOGI

Kumāravarmā was a scion (probably the grandson or great grandson) of Bhāskaravarman. He was attacked by 'a son of Krishṇa' whom he defeated and killed capturing his elephants. Shri Girish Sharma possesses a beautiful signet ring of Mitravarmā of Sogi clan bearing two-line legend reading *Mitrava(r)ma/sya Sogisya* (Fig. 103).

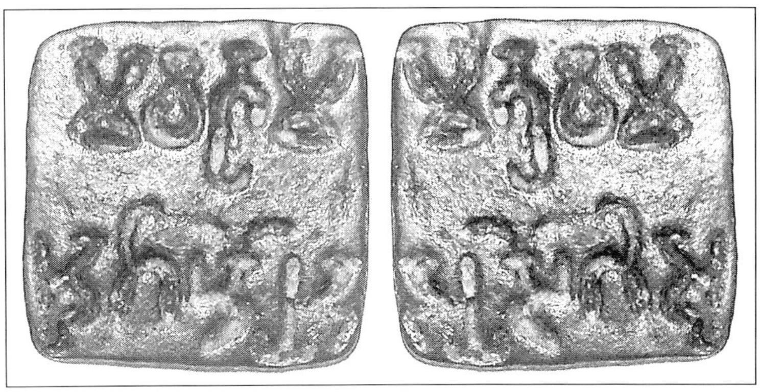

Fig. 103. Copper signet ring of Mitravarman Sogi and its mirror view.

This Mitravarman Sogi may have been a scion of Bhāskaravarman but his exact relationship cannot be established definitely in the present state of our knowledge. Definitely, however, he was not the father of Kumāravarmā's father who is described as the foremost Aulikara.

COPPER SEAL OF SOGI DEVASOMA AND PRIYASOMA

Kumāravarmā (or his son? was attacked by 'a son of Krishṇa' whom he defeated and killed capturing his elephants. Another copper seal (Fig. 104)[35] used jointly or successively by Devasoma Sogi, son of Kanha, and his brother, Priyasoma (?) Sogi, son of Kanha, has come to light recently indicating their joint or successive rule as the inscriptions reading *Devasomasya Sog(i)/sya Kanhaputrasya* and *Priyasomasya So/g(i)sya Kanhaputrasya* respectively occur on two facets of the seal alternating with the depiction of bull figures which betray their Śaivite affiliation.

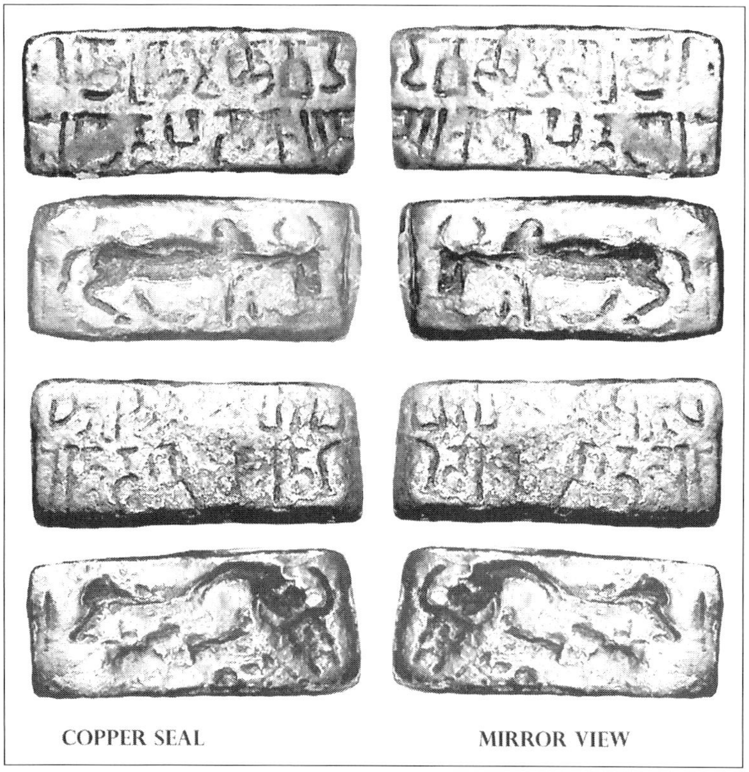

Fig. 104. Copper seal of Kanha-putra Devasoma and Priyasoma with mirror views.

The name-ending Soma reminds us of Nandisoma and *mahāsenāpati* Bhaṭṭisoma Sogi of the Nandsa pillar inscriptions, *Mahārāja* Gaurī's ancestor Puṇyasoma, Kumāravarman's ancestor Vīrasoma, the commissioner of Chhoti Sadri inscription Bhramarasoma and his father Mitrasoma. Since the bull alternating with Priyasoma's name is counter struck by another animal looking like a hyena he seems to have been defeated by someone. Kumāravarmman? Since he (or his successor) was probably captured by an enemy, from whom he escaped and re-conquered Daśapura from his enemies who are probably referred to as *dasyu* 'demonic'. Since Yajñadeva's family to which Kumāravarmā or his son belonged was the Sogi family and so also of Kanha-putras Devasoma and Priyasoma, an internecine war seems to have taken place. After being victorious finally Kumāravarmā or his son performed *Pauṇḍarīka* sacrifice and made donations to the Brāhmaṇas as referred to in the fragmentary Mandsaur inscription of the time of Kumāravarmā.

The present seal, however, confirms the genealogy of Yajñadeva known from Kumāravarmā's fragmentary inscription.

COPPER SEAL OF LOHATAKA SŪRYAVARMAN

The copper seal in the Ashwini Śodha Saṃsthāna, Mehidpur too is similar in shape and contains on all its four facets the two-lined similar legend which reads "Sū(r)yava(r)masya L[o]hataka/sya Jayava(r)dhanaputrasya"[(This is the seal) of Lohataka Sūryavarman, son of Jayavardhana] (Fig. 105).[36]

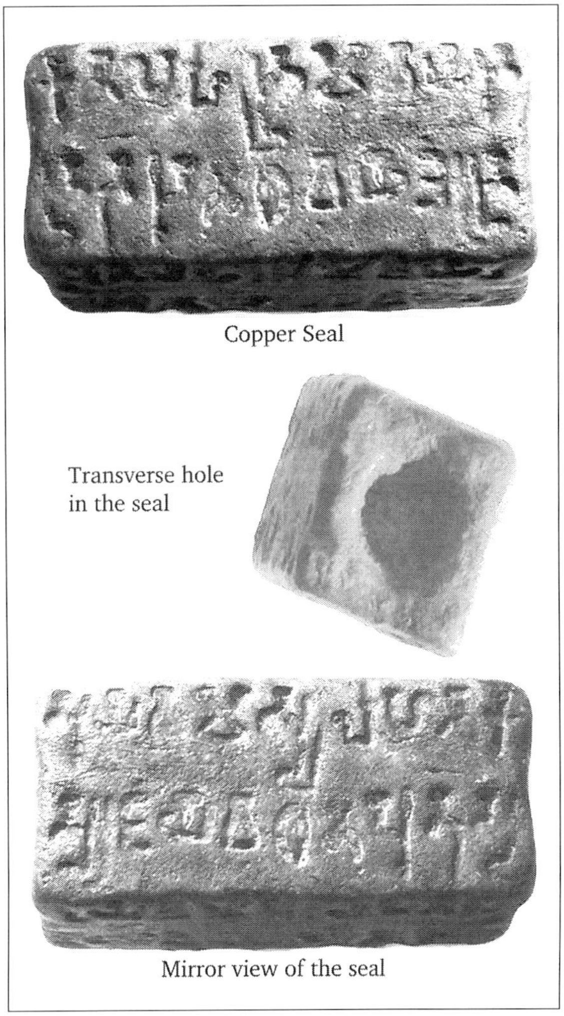

Fig. 105. Copper seal of Sūryavarman, son of Jayavardhana.

Earlier I had taken the term Lohataka as an administrative post[37] but on the analogy of many of the seals/sealings discussed here now I feel that it may have been the clan name.

The Risthal Inscription describes Jayavardhana as the son of *Senāpati* Drapavardhana[38] who commanded great armies and was a conqueror and progenitor of Prakāśadharman's dynasty.

On epigraphic evidence, the genealogy of the Later Aulikara dynasty of Drapa(Druma)vardhana as reconstructed by Mirashi is as following[39] –

CE	Ruler
400-420	Drapavardhana
	!
420-440	Jayavardhana
	!
440-460	Ajitavardhana
	!
460-480	Vibhīshaṇavardhana
	!
480-500	Rājyavardhana
	!
500-520	Prakāśadharman
	!
520-532	Yaśodharman [Mandsor Insc. of MS 589]

The present seal thus refers to Jayavardhana's second son Sūryavardhana who was an important functionary of the state sometime during the fifth century CE. Taking clue from the legend pattern of the seals described above, if we take the word Lohataka as the clan name like the Sogi, it formed part of the Aulikaras. All these seals are square sectioned rectangular seals with transverse perforation for stringing. In all these the legend is engraved in two lines giving us the name of the issuer or user with his official title or post followed by his father's name. Strangely enough the official title of the issuer/user is not very clear in all these examples. All have motifs or legends on all the four faces. The style of putting the legend is similar in all these. The honorific *Śrī* does not precede the names of users/issuers or of their fathers. The palaeography too shows similitude. These similarities leave little doubt to the first seal belonging to the Aulikaras and coming from Aulikara dominions.

COPPER SEAL OF VIJAYA-PUTRA ŚIVA

Ashwani Shodha Samsthana, Mahidpur possesses a copper seal weighing 9.9 g and 19 mm long with a breadth of about 9 mm, bearing the Brāhmī legend *Vijaya-putra/sya Śivasya*(?) in two lines on its main facet (Fig. 106a and its plasticene impression 106e), lion (Fig. 106b), a retrorse bird followed by another (Fig. 106c and its plasticene impression 106f) and a boar (Fig. 106d) on the other facets with transverse hole through its length (Fig. 106g-h).

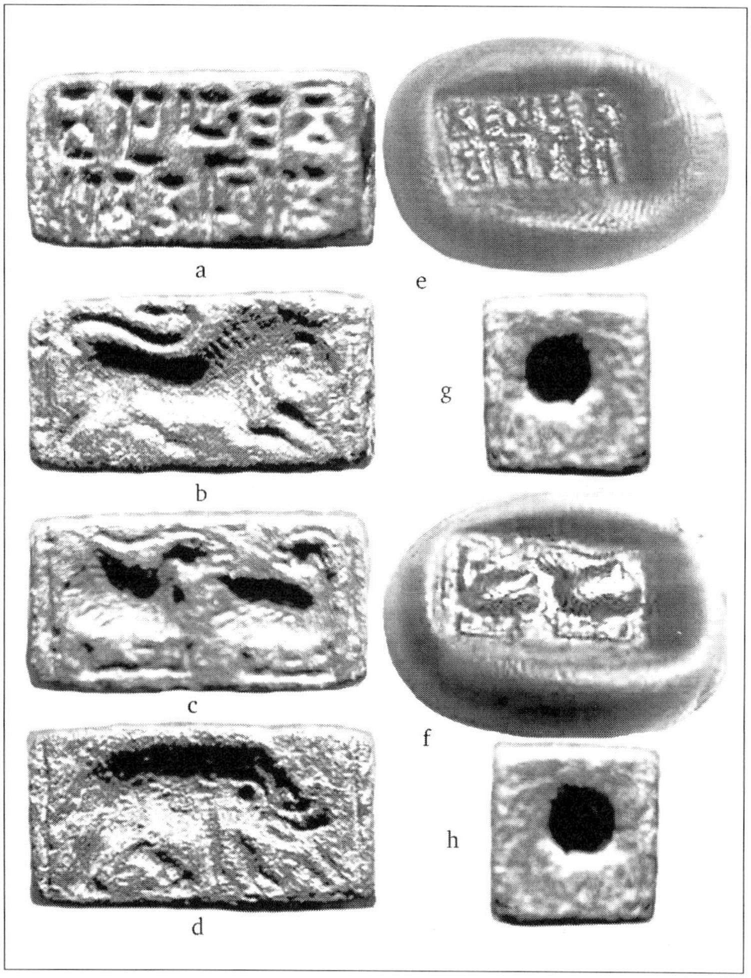

Fig. 106. Copper seal of Vijaya-putra Śiva.

In the present state of our knowledge it is difficult to establish the relationship of the possessor of this seal with any Aulikara chief. The absence of any honorific title indicates his common stature. The legend pattern and the depiction of birds and animals on its different facets, however, class it with the seals/ sealings of the Aulikaras or their associates. The presence of a retrorse bird with another following that, however, indicates some connection with the seal of Yajñadeva and his sons described above (Fig. 102), the depiction of animals brings to our mind the seal of Kanha-putra Devasoma and Priyasoma (Fig. 104) while the transverse hole through its length is similar to the copper seal of Sūryavarman (Fig. 105).

GOLD SEAL OF VISHṆUVARMMAN

In July 2015, Dr. S.K. Bhatt (Director, Academy of Indian Numismatics & Sigillography, Indore) kindly referred to and passed on to me the available details and scans of a gold seal (Fig. 107) which some denizen of Mandsaur brought to him for identification some time back.[40] The gold seal under reference is square in shape, about one inch in size and approximately 14.0 g in weight. It does not have any knob to handle it and bears the legend and designs on four rectangular sides of its thickness which is nearly 0.3 of an inch.

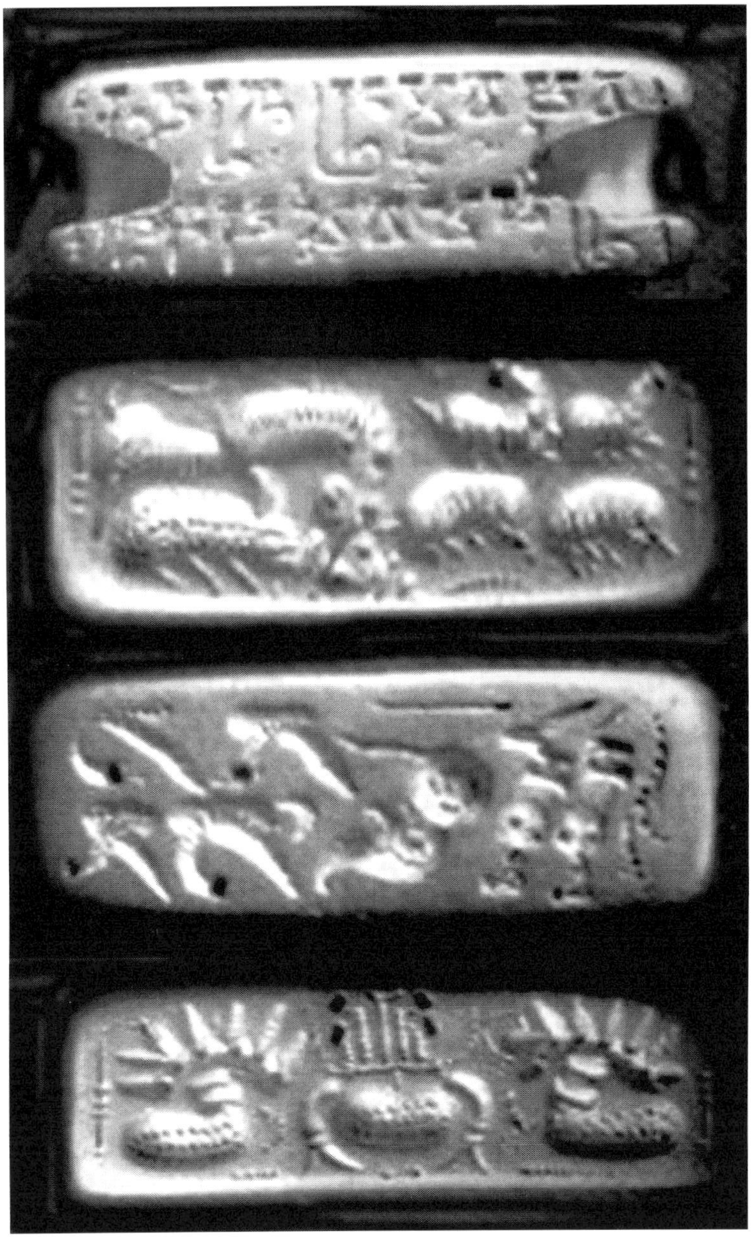

Fig. 107. Aulikara gold seal of Vishṇuvarmman.

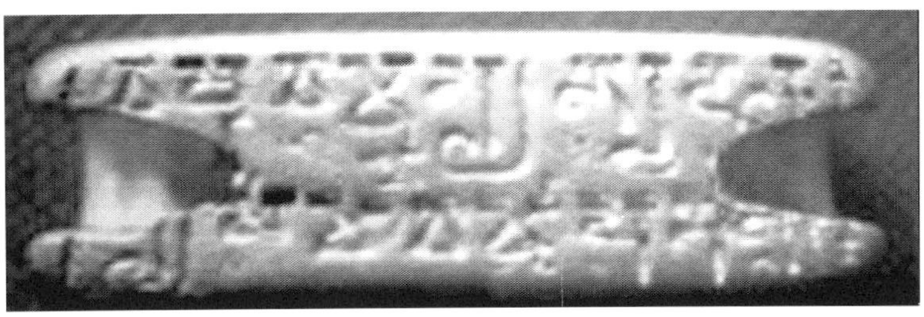

Fig. 108. Mirror image of the inscribed facet of the Aulikara gold seal.

The legend has been engraved in intaglio or negative letters to give a positive impression when stamped (Fig. 108).

The legend is engraved in two lines and I read it tentatively as following: *[Śrī?] V(i)sh(ṇu)va(r)mmasya kāryahāraka(?)/sya Somavarmma-putrasya* [followed probably by a symbol].

The characters belong to the central Indian Gupta Brāhmī of *circa* fifth century CE. The superscript letter (*r*) and vowel marks on some letters of the upper line are not visible. As on the copper signet ring of Naravarmman and inscriptions of the main dynasty, *m* has been doubled after superscript *r* in the names of Vishṇuvarmman and Somavarmman. The language used is Sanskrit using the genitive singular suffix *sya* (instead of *ṇaḥ*) as we find also on the coin of Siṃhavarmman and signet ring of Naravarmman. On both sides of the legend portion there are apsidal cuts, made subsequently, which have erased portions of some letters also. It was done to make a hole for hanging this seal after use. The names of Somavarmman and Vishṇuvarmman, use of Sanskrit, similar orthography and palaeography leave hardly any doubt to its being the seal of a scion of the Aulikara family of Mandsaur who may have occupied an important executive office. Earlier I took the term *kāryahāraka*[41] as an executive officer but taking into consideration the evidence of various other seals described above, I feel inclined to regard it as a clan name.

The other three sides of this square seal carry some obscure designs. The designs cannot be explained with definiteness but the side ones probably portray hunting scenes. In one of them we see different animals and in the other one an animal, probably a baby elephant, being hunted by an animal-rider assisted by two soldiers. Between these hunting scenes on the sides there seems to be a vase with foliage flanked by laterally placed floral garlands covered with seven-rayed objects on the fourth facet of the seal. Vase with foliage is an auspicious symbol signifying richness, opulence, abundance, plenty, etc. It was popularly used in ancient Indian art. It is difficult to explain satisfactorily as to why different designs were engraved on the four facets of this seal. They may have served decorative purpose but it is also likely that they had different functions and were used to stamp the documents of different departments under the charge of Vishṇuvarmman. His name betrays the popularity of Vaishnavism amongst the masses.

GOLD SIGNET RING OF *MAHĀRĀJA* PRABHĀKARA

As noted above Mandsaur Stone Inscription of Mālava Year 524 (467 CE) refers to a ruler named Prabhākara who has been described as a bonfire to the trees that are the enemies of the Gupta dynasty (*guptanvayāridhūmaketuḥ prabhākaro bhūmipatiḥ*). Prabhākara made Dattabhaṭa, son of Vāyurakshita, the commander of his forces out of regard for his qualities (*sveshāṃ balānāṃ baldeva-vīryyaṃ guṇānurāgādadhipaṃ chakāra*). Vāyurakshita was a general (*senāpati*) of Govindagupta, son of Chandragupta (II) of the Gupta dynasty. Though the inscription likens Dattabhaṭa to his father and describes him as an abode of virtues and renown, vigorous as Baladeva, Kubera in largesse (*dāne dhaneśaṃ*), Bṛihaspati in intellect, Kāma in bed, and Yama in battle, it does not give any factual details about Prabhākara, nor does it give his pedigree. The provenience of the record however indicates that Mandsaur (Daśapura) was under his control in 467-68 CE. Whether it was the royal seat or not is not known and it is likely that he ruled from another city. Nothing more is known about him except the information provided by the said inscription.

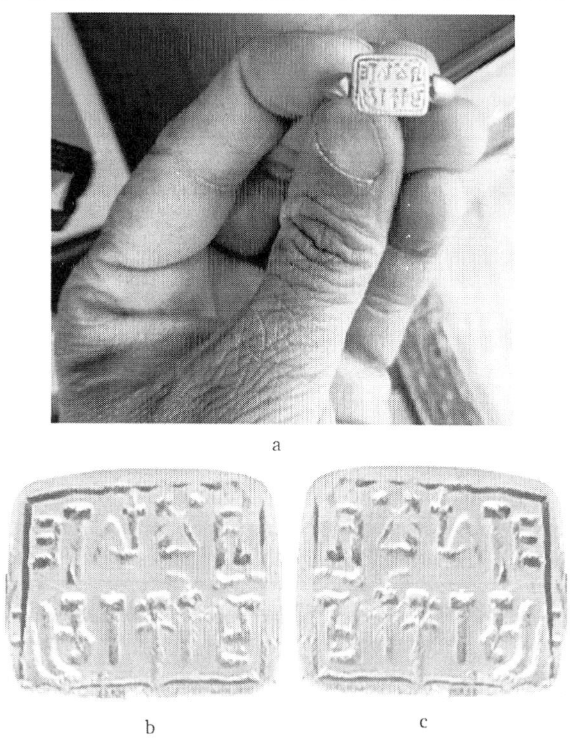

Fig. 109. Gold signet ring of Prabhākara (a), engraved part (b), mirror view (c).

Some time back Shri Ranavijay Singh of Lucknow procured a gold signet ring of about 13.23 g (Fig. 109a) and as per his information, it came from Chittor-Jhalawar region in southern Rajasthan.[42] On the rectangular signet part it bears in intaglio the Gupta Brāhmī legend (Fig. 109b) which may easily be deciphered from its mirror view (Fig. 109c) as *Śrī-Mahārāja/Prabhākarasya* (of the illustrious king Prabhākara) split into two lines.

The dynastic affiliation of Prabhākara has been a subject of great controversy and speculation with the historians. D.C. Sircar[43], K.C. Jain[44] and many others including V.V. Mirashi[45] regarded him as a successor of Bandhuvarman. Richard Salomon[46] also thinks that Prabhākaravardhana's name has been shortened to Prabhākara and that he was an Aulikara. Jagannath Agrawal[47] opined that he was not an Aulikara and was placed in control of Western Malwa by the Guptas. M.B. Garde[48], Hans Bakker[49] and Daniel Balogh[50] have also supported Jagannath Agrawal's view though on slightly different grounds. Definite evidence to determine whether he was an Aulikara or not is still a great desideratum but the provenience of his gold signet ring from southern Rajasthan indicates that Daśapura was not his capital and he may not have been an Aulikara.

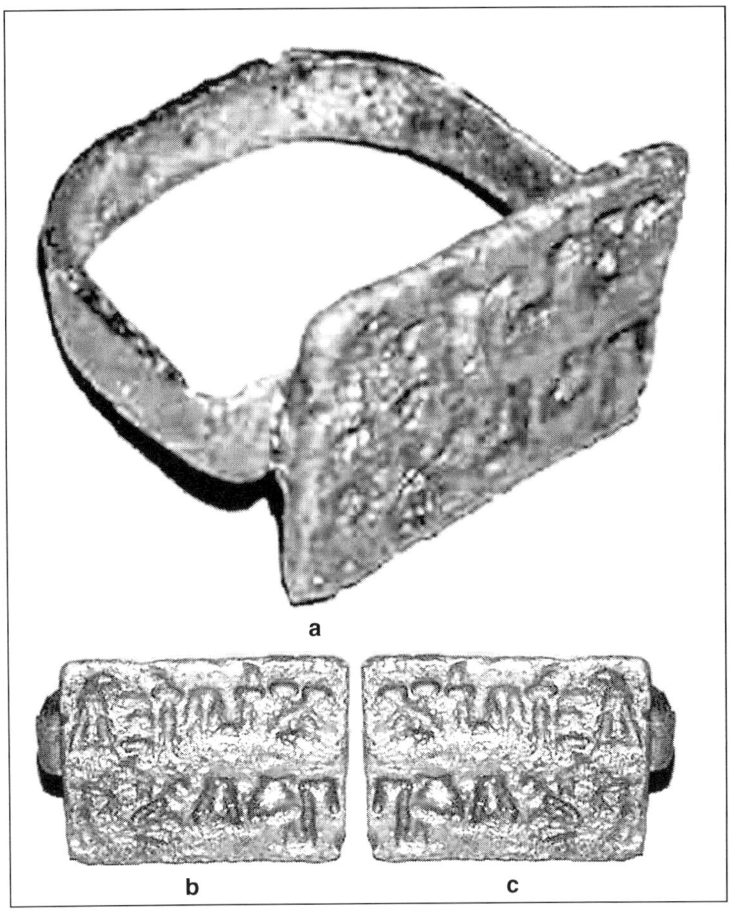

Fig. 110. Signet ring of King Vigrahavarman (a), engraved portion (b), mirror view (c).

SIGNET RING OF VIGRAHAVARMAN

Dr. Satish Karandikar possesses a signet ring of king Vigrahavarman who is unknown to us from any other source (Fig. 110a). Engraved in intaglio (Fig. 110b) in circa sixth century Brāhmī letters its mirror view (Fig. 110c) gives the reading *Mahārāja-Vi-/grahavarm(m?)asya*. There is no honorific *Śrī* prefixed to the name. This signer ring, however, adds a new name to the Aulikara associates. It is hoped that some future discovery will enable us to know more about this potentate.

A NEW GOLD SIGNET RING

Another new gold signet documented in trade belongs to Bhavavarmman (Fig. 111). The complete legend in two lines reads *Bhavadeva-putra-/sya Bhavavarmmasya* in Gupta Brāhmī

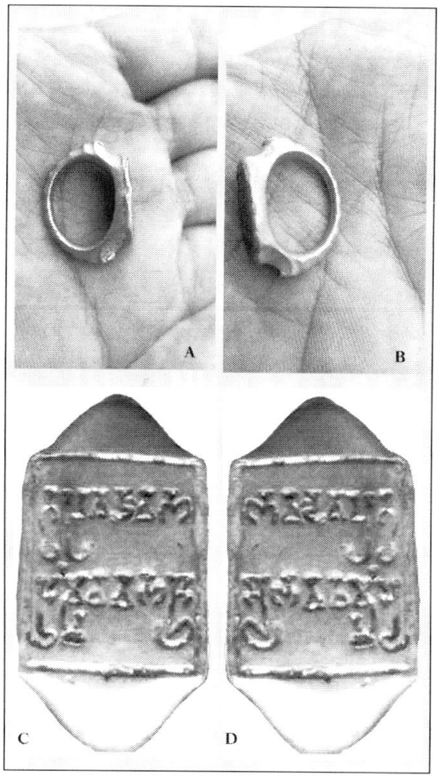

Fig. 111. Gold signet ring of Bhavavarmman, side views (A-B), engraved part (C) and mirror view (D).

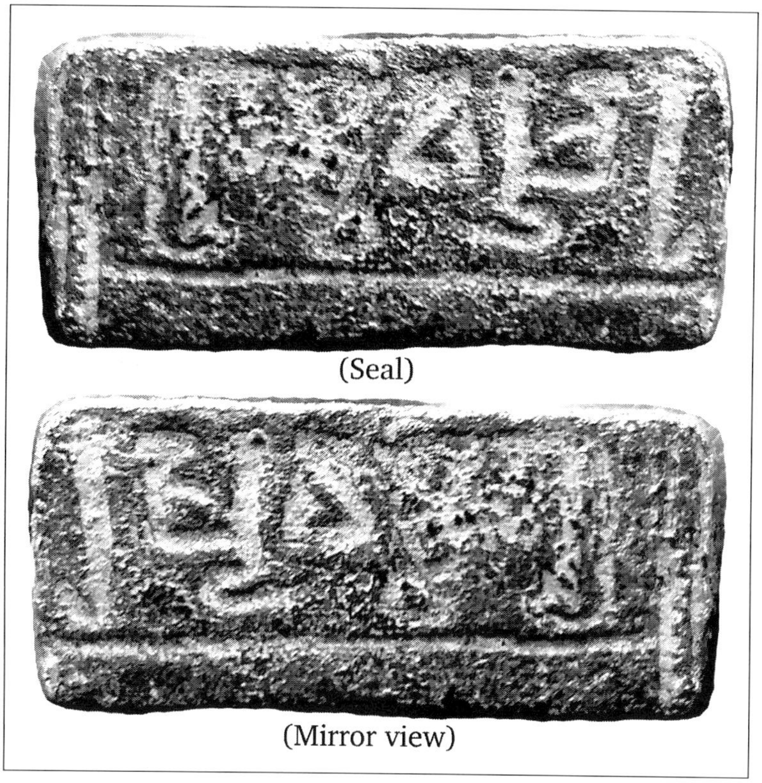

Fig. 112. Seal of Rāshṭravarmman and its mirror impression.

characters of late fifth century CE. Nothing is known about Bhavavarmman or his father Bhavadeva but the palaeography and legend pattern betray its association with the Aulikaras. The metal used for the signet-ring indicates Bhavavarmman's high status.

COPPER SEAL OF RĀSHṬRAVARMMAN

Chhoti Sadri inscription of Gaurī of Malava era 547 (= 490 CE) records the construction of a Devī temple and refers to the genealogy of the ruler mentioning the name of Punyasoma (for Puṇyasoma) of the Mānavāyanī *kula* 'clan' as the glorious progenitor of the dynasty, his successor Rājyavardhana followed by Rāshṭra (probably shortened for Rāshṭravardhana), then Yaśagupta (Yaśogupta) and Gaurī. The way in which the names of Rāshṭra and Yaśagupta, mentioned actually as Rāshṭravardhana and Yaśogupta in the Mandsaur fragmentary inscription of Gaurī, have been put indicates that sometimes changes were made by the engravers or other authorities in recording them. We have come across a rectangular copper seal bearing in intaglio the Brāhmī legend *Rāshṭ(r)avarmmasya* (Fig. 112).

It is difficult to determine whether this is the seal of Rāshṭravardhana mentioned as Rāshṭravarmman or it belongs to a different person. The absence of the honorific *Śrī* and the title *mahārāja*, however, favors the latter possibility.

COPPER SEAL OF SHASHṬIDĀSA

A copper seal bearing the Brāhmī legend *Śrī-Shasht(i)dāhasya* in box-headed characters of Gupta-Vākāṭaka period and its impression on plasticine were put on the internet by an inquisitive collector quite some time back (Fig. 113).

The orthographic peculiarity of using *ha* for *sa*, particularly popular in western India, is noticeable here. Shashṭidatta - the pious, wealthy person, progenitor of the Naigama clan and an eminent retainer of Yaśodharman's ancestors - is well known to us from the Mandsaur Inscription of Nirdosha dated Mālava *saṃvat* 589 (- 532 CE). The name on our seal differs using *dāsa* as the name-ending instead of *datta*, but indicating the popularity of the goddess Shashṭhī, the protector of children. The name thus has socio-religious significance.

The feudal status of the Aulikaras, has been quite controversial.[51] Bhandarkar[52] and S.R. Goyal[53] consider all the rulers of the family as Gupta feudatories. P.L. Gupta[54] thought that Bandhuvarmmā was the first Mālava ruler who accepted Gupta suzerainty. The titles *Narendra, Kshitīśa, Nṛipa,* etc. are of little consequence in this regard. They simply mean a king and have been applied to petty local potentates as well as to independent rulers. The title *Mahārāja*, however, seems to be more important as it has been used extensively from the Kushāṇa period onwards initially for subordinate rulers and subsequently for both, feudatory and independent rulers. If the use of this title by king Gaurī ruling under Ādityavardhana is indicative of his subordinate status, Naravarmman too may be taken as a feudatory of the Gupta emperor Chandragupta II who, according to the Udaigiri cave inscription of Vīrasena Śāba, undertook the conquest of the whole earth (*kṛitsna-pṛithvī-jayārtthena*) in order to consolidate his position and strengthen his hold on the empire.[55] This is further supported by the account of his achievements given in the Mehrauli iron pillar inscription which is assigned to him by most of the scholars and corroborated by the Mandsaur stone inscription of MS 524.[56] The Rāmagupta episode and Chandragupta II's expedition against the Śakas who held sway over Gujarat and parts of Malwa also indicate in this direction. The adoption of arched hill with sun and crescent flanking it by Naravarmman too indicates that he participated in the war against the Śakas and annexed some of their territory to his dominions. The adoption of filleted wheel on a lotus which is also found on his copper coin further supports his association with the Guptas and betrays that Vaishnavism had become more popular in Malwa during the reign of Chandragupta II. We may also refer here to the Mandsaur inscription of MS 524 which records the excavation of a well and the construction of a *stūpa*, *prapā* (step-well) and an *ārāma* (garden) by

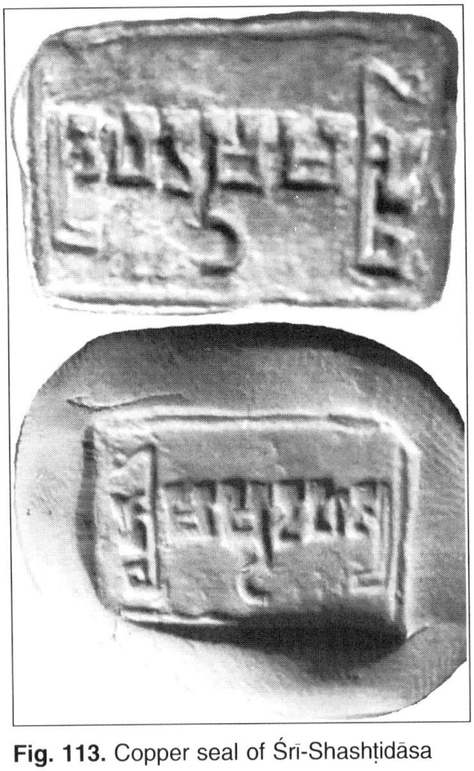

Fig. 113. Copper seal of Śrī-Shashṭidāsa and its plasticine impression.

Dattabhaṭa, the commander of the army of king Prabhākara. This inscription also plays glorious tributes to Chandragupta II and his son Govindagupta and tells us that Dattabhaṭa's father Vāyurakshita was the commander-in-chief of the forces of Govindagupta. Evidently the commander-in-chief must have been selected from amongst the subjects of the Guptas themselves or those of their allies. This clearly evinces to the fact that Mandsaur rulers served as the feudatories of the Guptas from the reign of Chandragupta II onwards.

We may also refer here to the chance discovery of a hoard of twenty-eight (one broken) copper plates in a huge copper container covered with a copper lid in a field near the settlement of Risavala near the well known Gupta cave site of Bagh in Madhya Pradesh in 1982. These plates belonging to king Bhuluṇḍa (Year 47 - 57 = 367 - 377 CE), Svāmīdāsa (Year 63 - 65 = 383- 385 CE), Rudradāsa (Year 67 - 69 = 387 - 389 CE), Bhaṭṭāraka and Nāgabhaṭṭa of Valkhā region were studied and edited by K.V. Ramesh and S.P. Tewari in 1990.[57] Valkhā was spread on both sides of the river Narmadā as indicated by the grants. There is no clue in these copper plates to confirm whether all these rulers were genetically connected and belonged to one or different families but they all have used the title *Mahārāja*, follow similar pattern of recording the charters (using probably the Gupta reckoning as indicated by palaeography), open with the expression *paramabhaṭṭāraka-pād=ānudhyāta* acknowledging the supremacy of *paramabhaṭṭāraka*. Since such an expression had become a common political idiom and was popularly used in the epigraphs of many of the feudatories of the period[24] the reference in all possibility may have been to the Gupta emperors.

We know that Eran (Airikiṇa) and eastern Malwa around it had come under the Gupta rule in the time of Samudragupta (*circa* 335 – 375 CE) and continued to be associated with the Gupta realm till the reign of Budhagupta (*circa* 475 – 496/ 500 CE). The presence of Chandragupta II (*circa* 375 – 414 CE) in eastern Malwa with the ardent desire of conquering the whole world further furnishes evidence of his victories in the west up to parts of Gujarat. Since no other Gupta emperor is known to have undertaken any expedition to Malwa and western India after Chandragupta II the Aulikara rulers may have recognized the suzerainty of the Guptas from his times onwards. Siṃhavarmman seems to have issued coins as an independent ruler and Naravarmman may have been the first Aulikara king to accept Gupta suzerainty as evinced by his coin motif of filleted wheel on lotus. That scions of the royal family occupied high administrative offices is indicated by the gold seal of Vishṇuvarmman, son of Somavarmman.

We have brought to the notice of scholars hitherto unknown coins and seals/ sealings of the Aulikaras and their associates from the Mandsaur region. The gold signet ring of *Mahārāja* Prabhākara and Vigrahavarmman, seals/sealings of the Sogis and others are important relics belonging to them. It is true that we do not know much about many of the owners and users of these in the present state of our knowledge but it is hoped that future discoveries will surely put them in a definite historical perspective and highlight their significance.

NOTES AND REFERENCES

1. Fleet, John Faithful (1886), 'Sanskrit and Old Kanarese Inscriptions No. 163. Mandsor Inscription of Yasodharaman and Vishnuvardhana, The Malava Year 589', *The Indian Antiquary*, Vol. 15, pp. 222-28.
2. Fleet, John Faithful (1888), *Inscriptions of the Early Gupta Kings and Their Successors*, Calcutta: Superintendent of Government Printing, pp. 151 ff; Chhabra B. Ch. and G. S. Gai (Eds.) (1981), *Inscriptions of the Early Gupta Kings and Their Successors* (revised by D.R. Bhandarkar), *Corpus Inscriptionum Indiacrum*, Vol. III, New Delhi, pp. 261 ff.
3. Ramesh, K.V. and S.P. Tewari (1983), 'Risthal Inscription of Aulikara Prakasadharmma, [Vikrama] Year 572', *Journal of the Epigraphical Society of India (Bharatiya Puralekha Patrika)*, Vol. 10, pp. 96-103, line 2.
4. Balogh, Daniel (2019), *Inscriptions of the Aulikaras and Their Associates*, Berlin/Boston: De Gruyter, p. 24. This is the latest work on the history and inscriptions of the Aulikaras and I have drawn much from this publication. Most of the references to the Aulikara epigraphs are from this work.
5. Chakravarti, S.N. (1942), 'Bihar Kotra Inscription of Naravarman's Time; [Malava] Year 474', *Epigraphia Indica*, Vol. 26, pp. 130-32; Balogh, pp. 46-49.
6. Balogh, pp. 50-53.
7. *Ibid.*
8. Bhandarkar, pp. 261 ff: *Jayavarmma-narendrasya pautre devendra-vikrame// Kshitīśe Siṃhavarmmaṇas=siṃha-vikrānta-gāmini/Sat-putra Śrīr=Mmahārāja-Naravarmmaṇi pārtthive//.* Bhandarkar interpreted it as 'the follower of 'Siṃha-vikrānta' and equated the expression with *Siṃha-vikrama*, the title of Chandragupta II found on his coins. Jagannath Agrawal [as quoted by Agrawal, Ashvini (1989), *Rise and Fall of the Gupta Empire*, Delhi: Motilal Banarsidass, p. 262, fn. 6], however, interpreted it as 'one who moves with the stride of a lion'.
9. Balogh, p.24.
10. *Ibid.*, pp. 229-30.
11. *Ibid.*
12. Besides the works cited above see Mirashi, V. V. (1960), *Studies in Indology*, Vol. I, Nagpur, p. 227 and (1984), *Studies in Ancient Indian History*, Nagpur, pp. 33 ff.; Sircar, D. C. (1969), *Ancient Malwa and the Vikramāditya Tradition*, Delhi, p. 13; Jain, K. C. (1972), *Malwa Through the Ages*, Delhi, p. 251-52; Salomon, Richard (1989), 'New Inscriptional Evidence for the History of the Aulikaras of Mandasor', *Indo-Iranian Journal*, 32, pp. 1-36; Ojha, N.K. (2001), *The Aulikaras of Central India History and Inscriptions*, Chandigarh: Arun Publishing House Pvt. Ltd.
13. Balog, pp. 54 ff.
14. *Ibid.*, pp. 76 ff.
15. Garde, M.B. (1912-13), *Progress Report of the Archaeological Survey of India, Western Circle*, p. 58; *Indian Antiquary*, XLII, pp. 161 ff; *Archaeological Survey of India, Annual Report*, 1922-23, p. 187; *Epigraphia Indica*, XII, pp. 315 ff; Sircar, D.C. (1965), *Select Inscriptions*, pp. 397-98; Bhandarkar (1981), pp. 263-65.
16. *Epigraphia Indica*, XXX, pp. 120 ff.
17. Agrawal, Ashvini (1989), *loc. cit.*; Ojha, *loc. cit.*
18. Balog, p. 28.
19. Thaplyal (1972), *SAIS*, pp. 164-65.
20. Bajpai [(1976), *INS*, pp. 150-51, Pl. IX.16] attributed a variant of these coins to Chandragupta II.

21. Bhatt, S.K. and D.L. Johri [(2014-15), 'Inscribed Lead Coins of Govindagupta? From Dashpur (Mandsaur)', *JAINS*, Vol. XXVIII-XXIX, pp. 43-45.
22. Singh, Jai Prakash (1972), 'Gupta Copper Coin or Temple Medal?', *JNSI*, XXXIV, pp. 253-57. I am thankful to Dr. Suken Shah (Pune) for making available to me a scanned copy of Jai Prakash Singh's article.
23. Balogh, 42.
24. Handa, Devendra (2016), 'Fresh Light on the Aulikaras', *ND*, Volume 40, pp. 78-85.
25. The coin is in a corroded state and the exact metallic composition may be determined only after assaying it.
26. Balogh, p. 231, fn. 414.
27. Handa, Devendra (2014), 'A Copper Ring of the Aulikara King Naravarmman', *History Today*, No. 15 (2014), pp. 147-48, Pl. I; (2014-15), *JAINS*, Vol. XXVIII-XXIX, pp. 40-42; (2016), *ND*, Vol. 40, p. 81.
28. Earlier I thought that there is a symbol of full vase at the end of the legend but Balog (p. 233) rightly recognized it as *visarga* which is clearly so in a better visual of its mirror impression.
29. Handa (2016), *loc. cit.*
30. Shri Girish Sharma has informed me that he purchased this seal in an auction and the exact provenance is not known. It is, however, not difficult to ascribe it to the Aulikara dominions as the shape, format, style, legend pattern, palaeography and naming the users with their fathers' names corresponds perfectly with the gold and copper square sectioned rectangular Aulikara seals with transverse holes known from Mandsaur now preserved in an unknown collection and the other in the Ashwini Śodha Saṃsthāna, Mehidpur (District Mandsaur) and discussed below.
31. Handa, Devendra (2018), 'Some Recently Discovered Aulikara Seals', *JAINS*, Vol. XXXII, pp. 91-92.
32. On some ancient Indian coins also *ña* has been used for *nya* and *jña*, e.g. Rajaña *and* Brahmaña on the coins of Rājanyas aand Yaudheyas and for *jña* on the coins of Yajña Sātakarni.
33. Mirashi, V.V. (1982),"Mandasor Fragmentary Inscription of Kumāravarmam," *Journal of the Oriental Institute*, Baroda, Vol. XXXII, pp. 70-75.
34. Altekar (1948), 'Nandsa Yupa Inscriptions', *Epigraphia Indica*, Vol. XXVII, pp. 252-67. Later M. Venkataramayya (1953, 'The Ancient Mālavas: Some New Royal Names', *Indian Historical Quarterly*, vol. XXIX, pp. 80-83) corrected the names Śrīsoma to Nandisoma and Jayanartana to Bhṛiguvardhana.
35. Handa (2018), *loc. cit.*
36. *Ibid.*, pp.93-94.
37. Handa, Devendra (2020), 'An Interesting Copper Seal from Mandsaur', *ND*, 42, pp. 79-84.
38. Drumavardhana according to Mirashi ('Risthal Stone Inscription of Prakāśadharman', *Studies in Ancient Indian History*, Bombay, 1984, pp. 21 ff.).
39. *Ibid.*
40. Handa (2018), pp. 92-93.
41. Balogh (pp. 241-43) suggested *Nirvāhaka*.
42. It now belongs to Aman Siddiqi of Lucknow.
43. Sircar (1965), *Select Inscriptions*, p. 406, note1.
44. Jain, K.C. (1972), *Malwa Through the Ages*, Delhi: Motilal Banarsidass, pp. 251-52.
45. Mirashi, V.V. [(1980), 'Further Light on Yasodharman-Visnuvardhana', *Bharati-Bhanam (Light of Indology) Being Dr. K.V. Sarma Felicitation Volume*, edited by Bhaskaran Nair, Hoshiarpur: Vishveshvaranand Vishva Bandhu Institute, pp. 405-26; (1984), *Studies in Ancient Indian History*, Bombay: Maharashtra State Board for Literaure and Culture, pp. 104-05.

46. Salomon, Richard (1989), pp. 20 ff.
47. Agrawal, Jagannath (1946a), 'Govindagupta, a New Gupta Emperor', *Indian Historical Quarterly*, Vol. 22, pp. 286-90; (1946b), *Proceedings of the Indian History Congress, Ninth Session, Patna University, Patna*, Allahabad: Indian History Congress, pp. 78-82.
48. Garde (1948), *op. cit.*, pp. 12-18.
49. Bakker, Hans I. (2006), 'A Theatre of Broken Dreams', in *Interrogating History, Essays for Hermann Kulke*, edited by Brandtner, Martin and Shishir Kumar Panda, Delhi: Manohar, pp. 170-72; (2014), *The World of Skandapurana: Northern India in the Sixth and Seventh Centuries*, Leiden: Brill, p. 34.
50. *Ibid.*, pp. 81-82.
51. Mankodi, K.L. (2015), "The Mandasor Silk Weavers' Inscription of 437 CE and Temples of the Aulikaras", in Verghese, Anila and Dillapiccola, Anna L. (Eds.), *Art, Icon and Architecture in South Asia: Essays in Honour of Dr. Devangana Desai*, New Delhi: Aryan Books International, 2 vols, II, pp. 305-16.
52. Ojha, *loc. cit.* and Thaplyal, K.K. (2012), *The Imperial Guptas A Political Study*, New Delhi: Aryan Books International.
53. Bhandarkar (1981), pp. 66-67.
54. Goyal, S. R. (1987), *Gupta Sāmrājya kā Itihāsa* (Hindi), Jodhpur, p. 215.
55. Gupta, P. L. (1998), *The Imperial Guptas*, Varanasi, p. 311.
56. Agrawal, Ashvini (1989), *op. cit.*, p. 160.
57. Ramesh, K.V. and S.P. Tewari (1990), *A Copper-Plate Hoard of the Gupta Period from Bagh, Madhya Pradesh*, New Delhi: ASI.

XXVI

Lion as the Vehicle of Śiva on Kashmir Coins

Śiva is one of the most influential members of the orthodox Brahmanical triad and his worship is traced to very old times in India. The so-called Paśupati of the Harappan seal and the Vedic Rudra are regarded as his prototypes. In the Ṛigvedic hymns, Rudra is usually said to be armed with bow and arrow[1] which continued to be associated with him even in the *Mahābhārata* as is evident from his epithets Dhanvī, Pinākadhṛit, Pinākagoptā, Pinākahasta, Pinākapāṇi and Pinākī. The *Śatarudrīya* text of the *Śukla Yajurveda* of the *Vājasaneyi Saṃhitā* also refers to his bow and arrows and at many places in the *Atharvaveda* he is called an archer. Once in the *Rigveda* (II.33, 3) he is said to have held the thunderbolt in his arm. Elsewhere in this and other later Vedic texts his bow, arrow, bolt, or club are frequently referred to.[2] Epithets like Bhava, Śarva (arrow-wielder or tormenter of misery), Paśupati (lord of animals), Ugra (terrific), Mahādeva (the great god) and Īśāna assigned to him in the *Atharvaveda* presuppose his rise to the position of the supreme god. The *Śatapatha* and *Kauśītaki Brāhmaṇas* add Aśani to these epithets indicating his association with the thunderbolt. One hundred names of Rudra enumerated in the *Śatarudrīya* mention him as Giritra 'one living in the hills', Kṛittivāsa 'having animal hide as his garment', Kapardī 'having the crown of snail-shell like matted locks on the head' (*kapardo'sya jaṭājūṭaḥ, Amarakosha*), Śatadhanvan 'having hundred bows', Sudhanvan 'good bowman', Iśumat 'possessing arrows', Bilmin 'helmeted', Nishaṅgin 'having a sword', Śiva 'auspicious' (*kalyāṇarūpaḥ*), Śaṅkara 'causing worldly happiness', Śambhu 'one who causes good or happiness' (*śaṃ sukhaṃ bhāvayatīti Śambhuḥ*), etc. which characterize his personality.[3]

The *Mahābhārata* often refers to *śūla* 'spike, lance', and sometimes a *triśūla* 'trident' also, as the weapon of Śiva as indicated by his names/epithets like Śūlabhṛit, Śūladhara, Śūladhṛik, Śūlahasta, Śūlāṅka, Śūlapāṇi and Śūlī[4]; (*Rāmāyaṇa*: V.6, 30; 17, 9 & 15; 46, 35; VI.7, 2; 9, 4; 31, 22; 37, 11; 42, 42;45, 14; 51, 24;58, 7; 59, 101 &

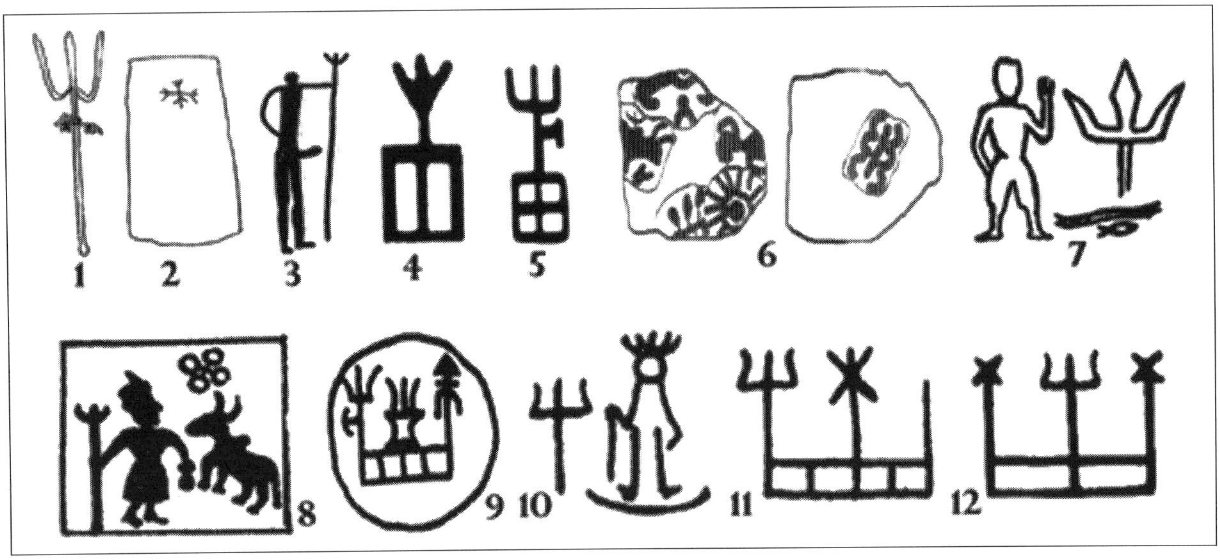

Fig. 114. Trident on early Indian artefacts and coins.

137; 60, 140; 65, 38; 67, 16; 67, 38; 67, 61; 67, 63-64; 67, 66; 69, 53; 75, 55; 82, 18; 86, 21; 90, 59; 95, 25; VII.32, 34; 61, 6; etc.) and Triśūlahasta and Triśūlapāṇi (*Mbh*, XII.14, 231-33) also. Since *trisula* does not find mention anywhere in early literature or on Indian indigenous coins and art as Śiva's attribute, Rosenfield[5] held that it has a Graeco-Bactrian provenance and was adopted by Indians from the trident held in the hand of the Greek god Poseidon. Albert Gail[6] has made a very significant observation that "It was only when this weapon was transferred to Siva that the Indians found a proper name for it: *triśūla*. *Triśūla* is in fact first traceable to the late sectarian text of the Mahābhārata. . . . . any Sanskrit text using the term *triśūla* cannot be written before the Kusana period". Recently Laura Giuliano[7] has also endorsed this view. I have discussed the antiquity of the trident in Indian art and the problem of the appearance of trident as Śiva's attribute elsewhere[8] and have shown its antiquity going back to the megalithic period if not earlier and its depiction as an attribute of Śiva going back to at least the second century BCE if not prior to that as it occurs on punch-marked, Audumbara, Ujjain, Pañchāla and other coins which all predate the Kushan period (Fig. 114) –

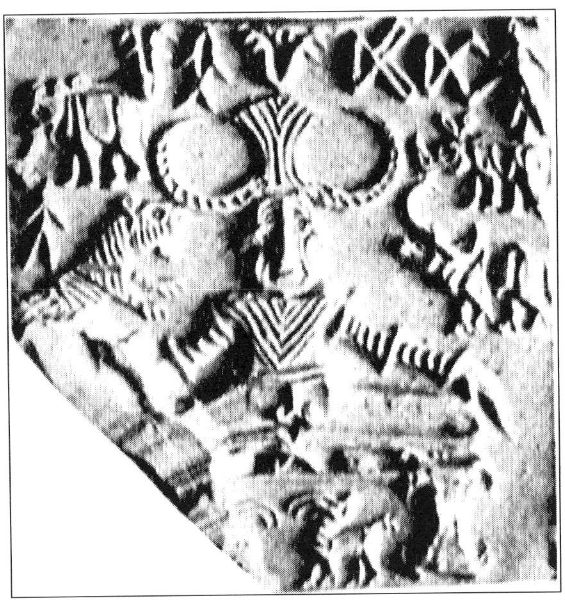

Fig. 115. Paśupati seal.

Nandī, the bull, is now almost an invariable and popular adjunct of Śiva's figures. It does not figure on the well known Harappan seal of Paśupati amongst the five distinct species of animals - lion, elephant, rhinoceros, buffalo and deer (Fig. 115).

Rudra is mentioned in the *Ṛigveda*[9], the oldest Hindu scripture and the earliest literary work of the world. He got various names and epithets like Dhanvī, Bhava, Śarva, Paśupati, Ugra, Mahādeva, Īśāna, Aśani, Giritra, Girīśa, Kṛittivāsa, Śūlahasta, Śaṅkara, Śambhu, etc. in the subsequent literature. Some of these provide clues to his iconographic traits also. Though bow, arrow and lance are often mentioned as his weapons in early literature, the later literature and art bespeak of trident as his attribute and bull as his vehicle par excellence.

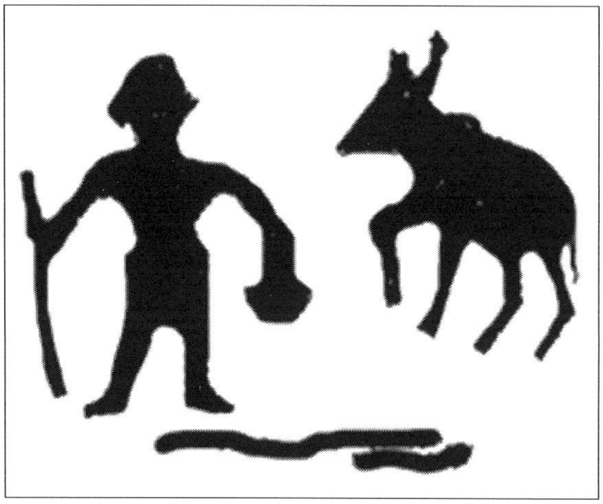

Fig. 116. Śiva with Nandi on Ujjain coins.

J.N. Banerjea[10] had observed that "Śiva appears for the first time in an anthropomorphic form on the coins hailing from Ujjayinī and its environs. The single standing figure on many of these coins can be definitely identified with him. . . . Any doubt whatsoever is set at rest by the testimony of another variety of the same series of coins which show a bull slightly prancing up and looking at the deity, *devavīkshaṇatatparaḥ* as described in the *Matsyapurāṇa*" (Fig. 116).

From Kushan period onwards we see the Nandi bull depicted popularly as Śiva's vehicle in numismatic and plastic art. In later art, however, the bull as the vehicle of Śiva becomes ubiquitous. He is said to be the second Śaṅkara (*dvitīyamiva Śaṅkaraḥ*). According to the *Mahābhārata* (XIII.77, 27-28) Daksha Prajāpati gave to Śiva a bull which became his mount and banner-mark. The epic refers to Śiva as Govṛishāṅka, Govṛisha-dhvaja, Govṛishottama-vāhana, Rishabhaketu, Vṛisha, Vṛishāṅka, Vṛisha-dhvaja, Vṛishaketana, Vṛishavāhana, Vṛishabha, Vṛishabhāṅka, Vṛishabha-dhvaja, Vṛishabhaketans, Nandīśvara, etc.[11] indicating that by the time of the great epic, the bull had firmly been associated with Śiva as his banner-mark and mount. Naturally the related verses belong to a period posterior to the above said date.

It is interesting to note that lion is shown with the figure of Śiva on two recently published Kashmir electrum (debased gold) *dinars* (7.37 & 7.05 g, 23 mm) of Meghamaḥ (Meghavāhana of Kalhaṇa's *Rājataraṅginī*) datable to sixth century CE indicating that there was a tradition of the association of lion with Śiva in Kashmir (Fig. 117.1-2).[12] A third coin of Meghavāhana exists in the collection of Shri Ranvijay Singh of Lucknow (Fig. 117.3). Haloed Śiva is shown as standing slightly turned towards his right holding a flower in his right hand and resting his left hand at his left hip, holding a trident with curved outer prongs above upturned crescent across the shaft over his left shoulder. Behind the god's legs lion standing towards the god's right, with raised tail and raised left paw and head turned towards the god. The legend in Gupta Brāhmī characters reading *śrī-meghamaḥ* may be seen in the upper left field from 11 to 9 o'clock position to be read from outside. The reverse shows the goddess with round nimbus around her head seated frontally on lotus, slightly turned towards her left with right arm raised to the level of her shoulder supporting a lotus

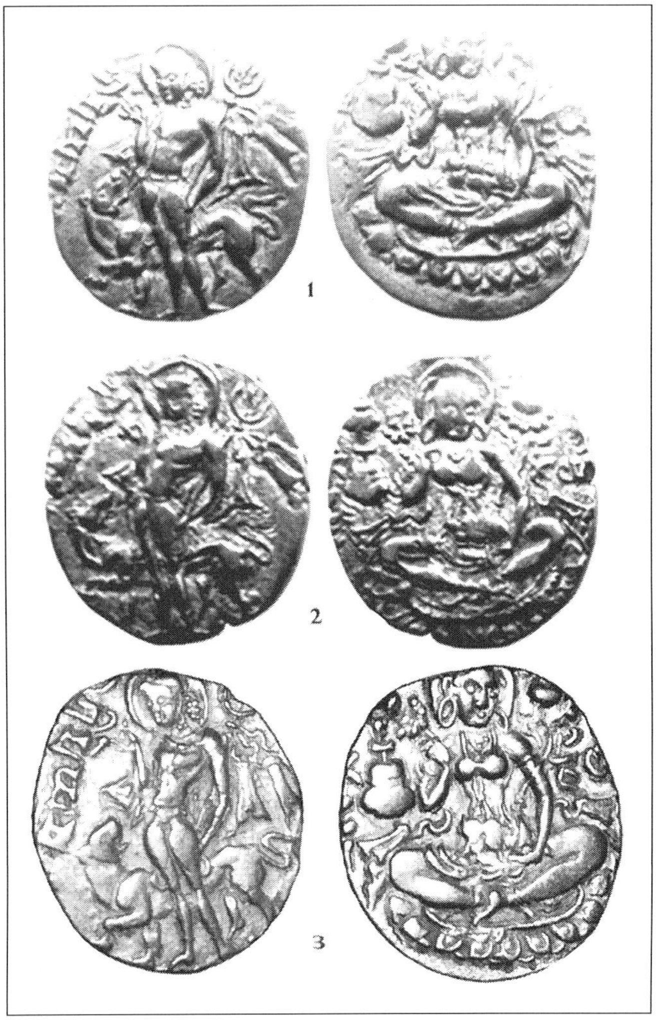

Fig. 117. Lion as the vehicle of Śiva on Kashmir coins of Meghavāhana.

blossom and her left hand resting in her lap holding a long stemmed fully blossomed *pūrṇa-ghaṭa* (vase of plenty) like lotus. A water pot with narrow neck surmounted by a conch may be seen to the right of her shoulder. Traces of the Brāhmī legend *kidara* written vertically on her right and clearly visible horizontally inscribed *jaya(ti)* on her left may also be seen. Joe Cribb has identified the goddess as Śrī Lakshmī but the coins of Toramāṇa and Pravarasena showing the goddess with similar attributes seated on lion[5] indicates that she may be Durgā-Pārvatī.

Śiva with the vehicle lion is interesting. Long back, N.P. Joshi[13] had published from Musanagar, 67 km from Kanpur towards Punkharaya, an almost five feet high corner railing pillar of red sandstone carved on two adjacent sides with third side (and probably fourth one also now fixed in the wall) bearing mortise holes to receive cross-bars, datable between 50 BCE and 50 CE. Both the carved sides of the pillar have been divided vertically in three panels each bordered by miniature pillars with octagonal shafts having vase-like base, inverted lotus capitals surmounted by winged animals with curved brackets depicting honey-suckle designs. The lower two panels show amorous couples but the topmost panel of the front side of this corner pillar shows two-handed crowned ithyphallic (*ūrdhvameḍhra*) male figure seated in *lalitāsana* on a couch wearing fluted headgear, earrings, bracelets, dhoti, etc. The ithyphallic figure obviously belongs to Śiva. Interestingly two figures emerge from his body from the shoulders and one behind his head which holds sun and crescent in the hands raised above. Below the seat is depicted a lion which interests us here (Fig. 118). The other facet of this pillar also shows standing ithyphallic Śiva with a retrorse lion looking towards him (Fig. 119). Dr. Joshi observed that lion with Śiva is a very uncommon feature.

R.C. Agrawala[14] also published a four feet high spotted red sandstone Śivaliṅga from Chauma, about 14 km from Bharatpur on road to Sikri in district Mathura, bearing a vase with foliage in front (east), a couchant lion, a female head and a pot-bellied Yaksha or Gaṇa on other sides at the base, datable to the beginning of the Common Era.

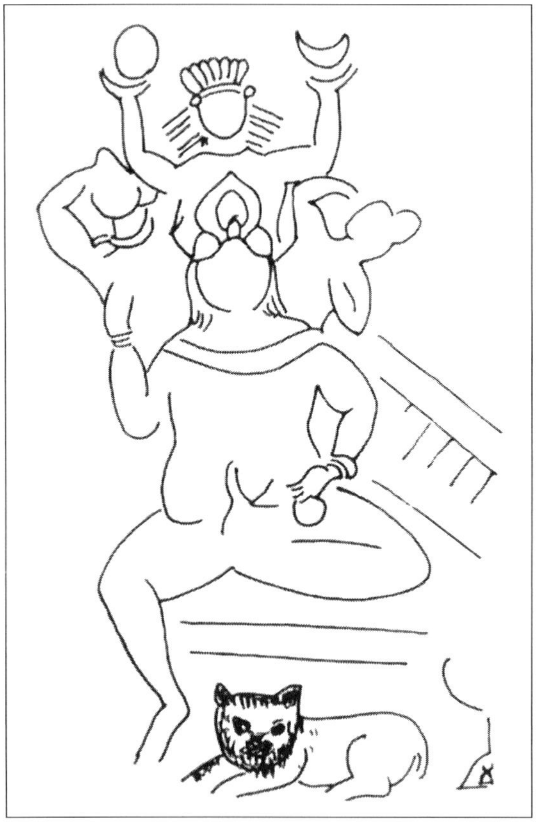

Fig. 118. Railing pillar from Musanagar.

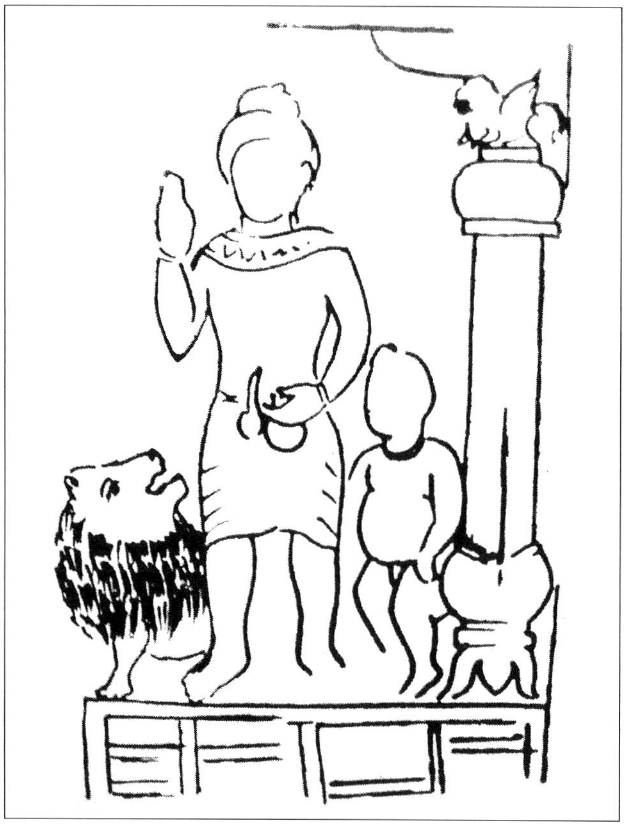

Fig. 119. Other side of the pillar.

The only literary reference to Śiva's association with lion known to us is from the *Vāyu Purāṇa* (Upasaṃhāra, 101.291-98) which tells us that being insulted by Daksha on the occasion of his sacrifice and after hearing the news of Sati's immolation by jumping into the sacred fire of the sacrificial pit Śiva became so furious that his wrath appeared in the form of a lion and disturbed Daksha's sacrifice. Later Śiva restrained his personified wrath to save the world from destruction and kept it with him. The presence of lion with Śiva in the referred reliefs may thus be explained to represent his destructive power (*saṃhāra-śakti*) as the god is well known in the Hindu mythology as the divine Destroyer (Saṃhāra-kartā).

Preserved in the State Museum, Shimla are some sculptures from Masrur (32°4′ 213 N and 76°8′ 133 E), famous for its magnificent and colossal unfinished monolithic rock cut temple of circa eighth century CE.[15] Important amongst these sculptures is an image of Śiva seated gracefully on a lion (Fig. 120).[16]

The god is three-faced with Aghora and probably Vāmadeva or Umāvaktra faces attached to the serene central face in profile on left and right. The locks of hair are combed upwards tied with a pearl band and bedecked with jewels. He wears large beaded earrings, double-stringed torque, nether garment secured by double-stringed beaded waist-band and anklets. The dhoti covers his left thigh and bears engraved lines to mark the folds. The right leg of the god is folded and the left one dangles down with foot splayed outwards. The back of the couchant lion to left is

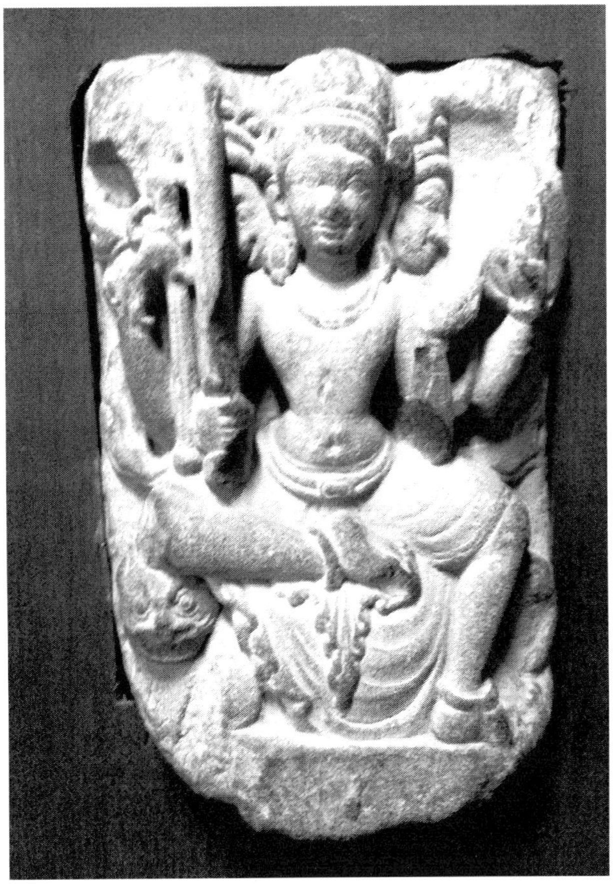

Fig. 120. Śiva seated on lion vehicle, Masrur (H.P.).

covered with a looping sheet having a decorative corner falling in the centre. Lion's face under the right knee of the god is shown as enfacing with wide open goggle eyes and moustaches indicating fierceness. The normal right hand of the god holds a sword, slightly broken above the handle, while the additional right hand supports the trident which too has suffered diminution of the prongs. The upper left hand carries a shield while the natural left held upwards to the level of the shoulder has lost its attribute. The existence of sword and shield in Śiva's hands are interesting features. A comparable image of Śiva's spouse Umā or Durgā-Pārvatī from the same site is also preserved in the museum.[17] Both these images seem to have been the creation of a single artist.

Nowhere in medieval Indian sculptures is lion depicted as the vehicle of the god. As noted above, amongst the various names and epithets of Śiva, we find expressions like Paśupati (Lord of the beasts), Kṛittivāsa (having animal hide as his garment), Giritra (living in the hills/mountains), Giriśa/Girīśa (Lord of the hills/mountains), etc. The *Kirātārjunīya* episode betrays his association with forests where wild animals abound. Lion is regarded as the king of animals and Śiva as the Lord of the mountains may have naturally got associated with him in the early period. The Anuśāsanaparva of the *Mahābhārata* describes Śiva not only as having the roar and fangs of a lion but also as having the lion as his vehicle: *Siṃhanādaḥ siṃhadaṃshṭraḥ siṃhagaḥ siṃhavāhanaḥ//.*[18] Sword and shield were given to Śiva by Brahmā to destroy the demons (*Mbh,* Śāntiparva, 166.45-66). Though the bull had become Śiva's vehicle par excellence from the Kushan period onwards and the tradition of depicting lion as Śiva's vehicle was forgotten in most parts of the country in the medieval period yet the portraiture of lion as the vehicle of the god on Kashmir coins and Masrur image reveals that the tradition of the Vedic and Mahābhārata period lingered on in the hill region of western Himalayas till the early medieval period.

NOTES AND REFERENCES

1. Keith, A.B. (1925), *The Religion of the Veda and Upanishads*, 2 vols, Cambridge: Harvard Oriental Series, I, p. 143.
2. Macdonell, A.A. (1971), *Vedic Mythology*, Varanasi-Delhi: Indological Book House (reprint), p.76.

3. Sivaramamurti, C. (1976), *Śatarudrīya: Vibhūti of Śiva's Iconography*, New Delhi: Abhinav Publications.
4. Anon, *Mahābhārata kī Nāmānukramaṇikā*, Gita Press, Gorakhpur, VS 2016, p. 351.
5. Rosenfield, J.M. (1967), *The Dynastic Arts of the Kushans*, Berkeley – Los Angeles, p. 93.
6. Gail, A. (1993), "On the Beginning of Figurative Representations in Indian Art", *South Asian Archaeology, 1991*, Proceedings of the Eleventh International Conference of the Association of South Asian Archaeologists in Western Europe held in Berlin 1 – 5 July 1991, edited by Gail, A.J., G.J.R. Mevissen with the assistance of B. Zehmake, Stuttgart, pp. 427-36.
7. Giuliano, Laura (2004), "Studies in Early Śaiva Iconography: the Origin of the Triśūla and Some Related Problems," *Silk Road Art & Archaeology*, Vol. 10, p. 51.
8. Handa, Devendra (2014-2015), 'Śiva, Bull, Trident and Phallus – Numismatic Evidence', *Jñāna-Pravāha Research Journal*, Number XVIII, pp. 23-40.
9. Keith (1925), *loc. cit.*; Macdonell (1971), *loc.cit.*
10. Banerjea (1956), *DHI*, p. 117.
11. Anon (VS 2016), *op. cit.*, p. 351.
12. Cribb, Joe (2016), 'Early Medieval Kashmir Coinage – A New Hoard and An Anomaly', *ND*, Vol. 40, pp. 86-112. Joe Cribb had referred to the existence of lion with Śiva even on a Kushan image earlier though he hid not illustrate that [Cribb, Joe (1997), 'Shiva images on Kushan and Kushano-Sasanian coins', *Studies in Silk Road Coins and Culture: Papers in honour of Professor Ikuo Hirayama on his 65th birthday* (ed. Tanabe, K., Cribb, J. & Wang, H.), p. 31].
13. Joshi, N.P. (June 1969), 'A Unique Figure of Śiva from Mūsānagar, Distt. Kanpur', *Bulletin of Museums & Archaeology in U.P.*, No. 3, pp. 25-30.
14. Agrawala, R.C. (June 1971), 'A Unique Śiva Liṅga near Bharatpur', *Bulletin of Museums & Archaeology in U.P.*, No. 7, pp. 22-24, Figs. 1-4.
15. Shuttleworth, H.L. (1915), 'Note on the Rock-Hewn Vaishnava Temple at Masrur, 'Dehra Tehsil, Kangra District, Punjab', *The Indian Antiquary*, Vol. 44, pp. 19-23; Hargreaves, H. (1918), 'The Monolithic Temples of Masrur', *Annual Report of the Archaeological Survey of India*, 1915-16, (Calcutta), pp. 39-48; Meister, Michael W. (2006), 'Mountain Temples and Temple Mountains: Masrur', *Journal of the Society of Architectural Historians*, Philadelphia, Vol. 65 (1), pp. 26-49; (2009), 'India's Angkor Siva's Temple at Masrur', in Desai, Devangana & Arundhati Banerji, (Eds.), *Kalādarpaṇa, The Mirror of Indian Art: Essays in Memory of Shri Krishna Deva*, New Delhi: Aryan Books International, pp. 30-43.
16. Handa, Devendra (2017), 'A Rare Image of Siṃhavāhana Śiva from Masrur', *Manimahesh*, Vol. VIII, pp. 56-63.
17. Handa, Devendra (2018), *Monolithic Rock-Cut Temple, Masrur*, Shimla: State Museum, Pl. XXXII.
18. *Mahābhārata* (Gita Press, Gorakhpur), XVII.111b, page 5523.

XXVII

Interesting Clay Sealings of Bhavarāja

Some time back Sanjay Godbole published an interesting clay sealing, round in shape having a diameter of about 2.0 cm, bearing an inverted *Nandipada* or *Triratna* symbol ( ) above the legend in two lines in the Brāhmī characters of fifth-sixth century which he read as 'Arahana Dvi (followed by a trident)/ putrasya Bhavarajasya'.[1] A similar sealing exists in the collection of Dr. Major M.K. Gupta (Fig. 120).[2] Sanjay Godbole has, however, missed the *vajra* 'thunderbolt' symbol at the beginning of the first line of the legend. The trident at the end of the first line is also of the shape of , slightly different than what the author has drawn. It is quite in keeping with the name of Bhavarāja (Bhava = Śiva). We shall have the occasion to discuss the significance of the *vajra* symbol subsequently. Unfortunately Godbole has not given the find spot or even the region of its procurement and has not identified Bhavarāja whose seal impression it is except that he was the son of Arahana as mentioned in the legend. Godbole belongs to Pune and has actively been collecting coins, seals/sealings and other antiques from Maharashtra, particularly from Paithan[3], which too may have been the probable site from where this sealing could have come. What for does the word '*dvi*' stand, has not been explained. We feel that '*dv*i' was followed by '*ja*' in the beginning of the second line whose lower most slanting horizontal stroke is partially visible on the sealing (Fig. 121). We thus restore the legend as *Arahana-dvi/ja-putrasya Bhavarājasya* meaning "(this is the seal) of Bhavarāja son of the Brāhmaṇa (*dvija*) Arahana."[4]

Bhava is well known in Sanskrit as a name of Śiva and also having different other meanings like 'existence, world, prosperity, etc.' Bhavabhūti is a well known Sanskrit poet. There are numerous individuals and kings of the name of Bhava (with or without some name-ending) known to us from coins, glyptics and epigraphs. King Bhavadatta ruled from Mathurā in first century BCE.[5] A silver coin of a new

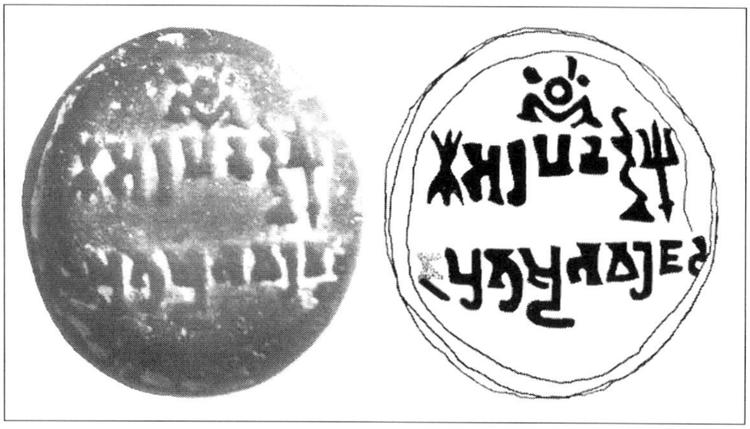

Fig. 121. Clay sealing of Bhavarāja and its eye-copy.

Vemaka king Bhavavarman who ruled over the Kangra-Palampur region of Himachal Pradesh in first century BCE/CE has been brought to light recently.[6] King Bhavasena, father of Vishṇumitra of Ayodhyā of *circa* first-second century CE, is known from a Rajghat sealing now preserved in the Bharat Kala Bhavan, Varanasi.[7] Excavations at Bhokardan (ancient Bhogavardhana in district Jalna, Maharashtra) yielded a copper coin bearing in bold Brāhmī characters of *circa* second century CE the legend 'Bhavasa'.[8] Bhava is the name of a Bhāraśiva Nāga ruler of Padmāvatī (*circa* 310-45 CE) also.[9] Persons bearing names like Bhavadāsa, Bhavadeva, Bhavaghosha and Bhavasena are known to us from their sealings found from Basarh, Nandpur, Besnagar and Basarh/Rajghat respectively.[10] One Bhavvirāja finds mention in an inscription in Cave No. XXVI at Ajanta[11] and a Bhavagopa has been referred to in an epigraph of Cave No. XX from Nashik.[12] Names after Śiva, Rudra, Īśāna, Īśvara, Maheśvara, Śaṅkara, Paśupati (all synonyms of Bhava), etc.[13] are so common and numerous to need any details.

Who was this Bhavarāja of the seal impression under discussion? Was he a commoner or a king or some important individual? It is difficult to give any definite answer to these questions in the absence of any regal title with the name except its name-ending *rāja*. As per the evidence of the Gṛihyasūtras and Manu the general practice was to name the Brāhmaṇas as ending in *deva* or *śarman*, Kshatriyas in *varman*, *rāja* and *trāta*, Vaiśyas in *gupta*, *bhūti* and *datta* and Śūdras in *bhṛitya* and *dāsa*[14] but the practice does not seem to have always been adhered to as we know that the famous Sanskrit poet and dramatist Kālidāsa was not a Śūdra and Bhavabhūti was not a Vaiśya; Dhanadeva, Mūladeva, Vāyudeva, Viśākhadeva, Jyeshṭhadatta, Naradatta and Śivadatta were the rulers of Ayodhyā; Amoghabhūti was a Kuṇinda king and Mṛigabhūti ruled over Almora; Balabhūti, Bhavadatta, Kāmadatta, Rāmadatta, etc. were the rulers of Mathurā; and so on.[15] No definite conclusion may thus be derived merely from the name Bhavarāja occurring on the sealing. If our restoration of his father's name as Arahana-dvija is correct, he may have been a Brāhmaṇa. Still his definite status and identity eludes us.

We have just referred to 'Bhavvirāja' mentioned in a cave inscription at Ajanta. Bhavarāja and Bhavvirāja stand very close linguistically. It is interesting to note that Bhavvirāja was a Minister (*Mantrin*) of the King of Aśmaka in whose memory the said cave was excavated.[16] Aśmaka has variously been equated with Assaka, Alaka or Mūlaka and generally identified with Marathwada region of Maharashtra between the Narbada and the Godavari rivers covering the present districts of Nashik, Dhule,

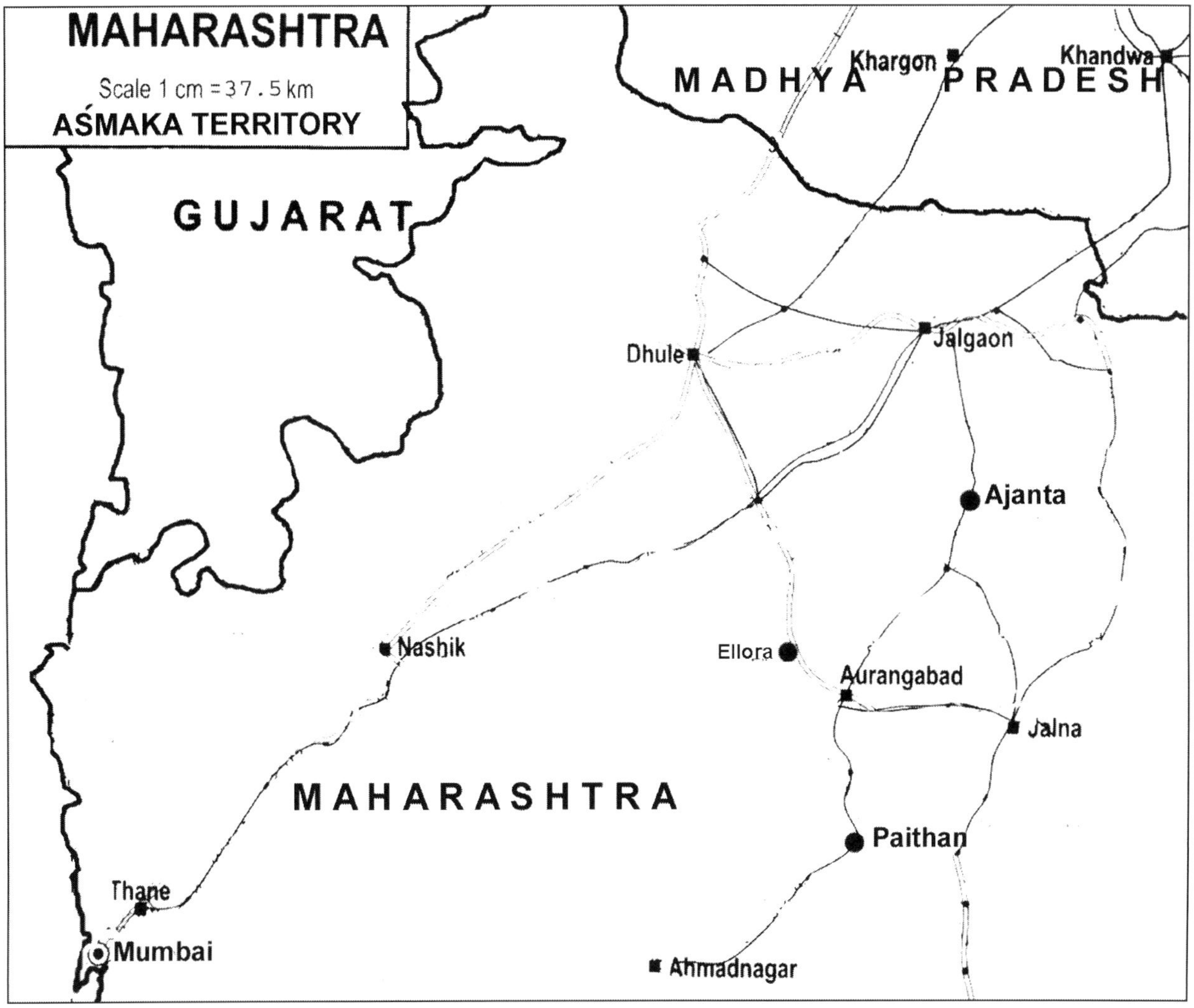

Fig. 122. Aśmaka territory and the location of Ajanta and Paithan.

Jalgaon and Aurangabad with its capital at Pratishṭhāna, modern Paithan (Fig. 122).[17] The location of Ajanta fits very well in this equation. The inscription of Cave No. XXVI at Ajanta is not dated specifically and its date is conjectured purely on its palaeography. Burgess and Indraji dated it to the latter half of the sixth or the beginning of the seventh century.[18] It is to be noted that Percy Brown has also dated the *chaitya* hall of Cave No. XXVI at Ajanta to 550-600 CE purely on architectural development of cave architecture.[19] Walter Spink who has focused his academic life in studying the architectural and sculptural activities at Ajanta is of the view that the Mahāyāna phase at Ajanta dates entirely from the reign of Vākāṭaka emperor Harisheṇa and roughly covers a period of *circa* 462-80 CE. The undertakings of this phase were disrupted for some time because of the conflict between his Ṛishīka and Aśmaka feudatories in about 472 CE and was cut short suddenly by the death of Harisheṇa in about 477 CE where after the Aśmaka feudatory and the chief monk Buddhabhadra performed some intrusive work in Cave No. XXVI.[20] B.Ch. Chhabra and N.P. Chakravarty place the record between 450 and 552 CE.[21] This period is quite close to the date of our sealing based on its palaeography.[22]

Buddhabhadra, the chief monk of the Ajanta monastery, was a friend and junior contemporary of Bhavvirāja, the minister of the Aśmaka king, mentioned in the inscription. When Cave No. XXVI (Fig. 123) was being excavated Bhavvirāja passed away but his son Devarāja succeeded him as the minister of the Aśmaka king and provided the desired financial assistance for the excavation of the cave. Our restoration of the word 'dvija' in the legend goes very well with Bhavvirāja and his son Devarāja being ministers of the king of Aśmaka. The sealing under consideration, probably obtained from Paithan, may thus be related to the Aśmaka minister Bhavvirāja of the Ajanta Cave No. XXVI inscription, which can now be dated to the last quarter of the fifth century. The use of the *vajra* symbol in the beginning of the legend also seems to be significant and indicative of Bhavarāja's belief in Buddhism. Originally the thunder and lightning bolt of the Hindu god Indra, "the vajra is also interpreted as a diamond because it resembles the purity, firmness, indestructibility, and enlightenment power of absolute truth and the immutable, adamantine essence of all being. The vajra is thus identical with the Buddha and the Buddha nature; it can

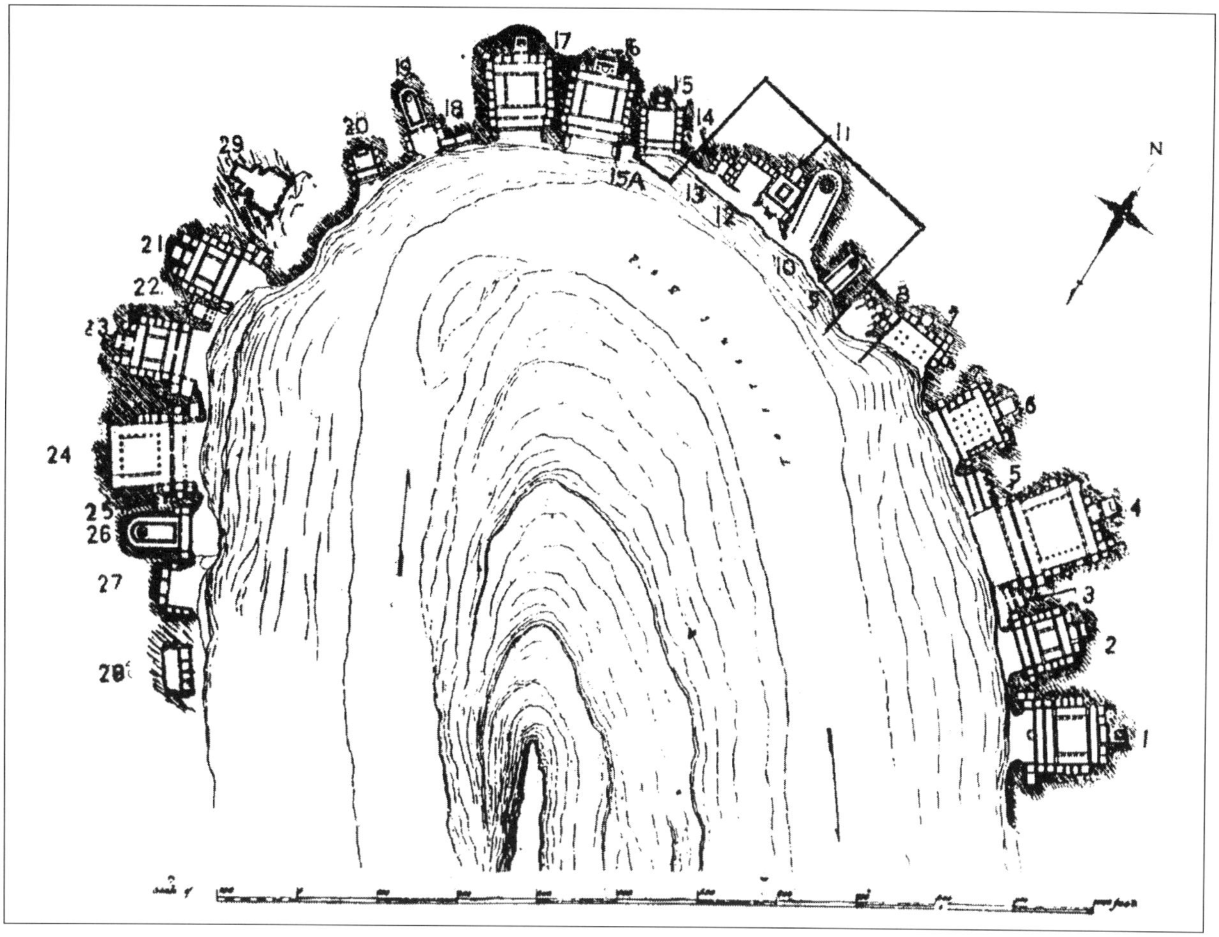

Fig. 123. Location of Cave XXVI at Ajanta; marked line denotes Hīnayāna activity at the site (after Burgess).

represent them as an aniconic symbol, for it is the symbol of the pure << suchness>> (*tathatā*) standing beyond all differentiation. The Buddha manifests Nirvāṇa in personal form; the vajra manifests it in non-personal form".[23] The seat of Buddha at the time of his 'Great Enlightenment' (Mahāsambodhi) is called *vajrāsana* 'adamantine seat'. Even Yuan Chwang mentioned it.[24] *Vajra* occurs on a unique *Buddhapāda* sculpture from Amaravatī.[25] Sculptures of Buddha seated on *vajra*-marked seat are found in considerable numbers in the prominent Buddhist centres of India. Buddha images from Bodh Gaya in the Patna Museum, Bilheri (Madhya Pradesh), Ujani (Dacca Museum), Sarnath Museum (inscribed) and crowned basalt Buddha in Victoria & Albert Museum, all in *Bhūmisparśa* posture, are a good examples thereof.[26] Later, *vajra* came to represent *vajrāsana* and even Buddha himself. *Vajra* appears prominently in Buddhist *maṇḍalas* (a kind of mystical diagrams used in invoking a divinity), and its name appears in the term Vajrayāna (Thunderbolt Vehicle), which is a synonym for Esoteric Buddhism.[27] Avalokiteśvara Vajrapāṇi is so well known in Buddhist iconography to need any elucidation. *Vajra* is thus intimately connected with Buddhism and its existence on the seal of a Buddhist like Bhavarāja closely connected with the excavation of Buddhist caves at Ajanta as a minister of the Aśmaka king should therefore be no surprise.

We thus see that this sealing of Bhavarāja is an important document which can be dated on palaeographic evidence to the last quarter of the 5th century CE, *circa* 475 – 480 CE to be more precise as borne out by the historical events, a date supported by architectural development of Cave No. XXVI at Ajanta (Fig. 122) which has a colossal image of the Mahāparinirvaṇa of Buddha, perhaps hinting at the death of Bhavarāja whose son Devarāja got this cave completed after his father's demise. It also helps us indirectly to almost precisely date the cave inscription about which there has been a great difference of opinion.

NOTES AND REFERENCES

1. *JNSI*, LXVIII, 2006, p. 64, Pl. III.3. Many duplicate sealings pepared from a seal have come to light in the recent years.
2. I am thankful to Dr. Major M.K. Gupta for supplying and allowing me to utilize the photograph of the sealing.
3. *JNSI*, LXVIII, pp. 62-63, Pls. II.2-4, III.1; LXIV-LXV, 2003-03, pp. 18-19, Pls. II.1-3 & III.1. For a 'Reappraisal of Inscribed Sealings from Paithan (Ancient Pratishthana)' by Amarendra Nath see *JNSI*, LVII 2005, pp. 50-52. Paithan has been excavated quite a few times during 1936-37, 1965-66 and 1995-96 to 1998-99 and a brief account of the excavations may be seen in Yazdani, G. (1936-37), *Annual Report, Hyderabad Archaeological Department*, pp. 18-22; *IAR*, 1965-66, pp. 28-29, Pl. XIII, A-B; 1995-96, p. 56; 1996-97, p. 70; 1997-98, pp. 125-29; 1998-99, pp. 107-12. Many individuals too have made good collections of antiquities from Paithan.
4. Arahana seems to be the Prakrit version of Arihan meaning the 'destroyer of enemies', cf. Arihanta, Śatrughna. Philosophically speaking, the enemies are what bind the soul to the cycle of birth and death. *Suhṛillekha* of the Buddhist philosopher Nāgārjuna mentions avarice (*mātsaryya*), deceit (*śāṭhya*), duplicity (*māyā*), lust, indolence (*kausīdya*), pride (*māna*), greed (*rāga*), hatred (*dvesha*) and intoxication (*mada*) as the enemies of human beings causing

bondage [Dasgupta, Surendranath (1975), *A History of Indian Philosophy*, Vol. I, First Indian Edition, Delhi, p. 144].

5. Allan, *BMCAI*, p. cxi.
6. Handa (2007), *TCAI*, pp. 130-32, Pl. XXXIV.3.
7. Thaplyal (1972), *SAIS*, p. 33, Pl. V.2.
8. Shastri, Ajay Mitra (1974) in Deo, S.B. and R.S. Gupte (Eds.), *Excavations at Bhokardan 1973*, Nagpur-Aurangabad, p. 61.
9. Trivedi (1957), *op. cit.*, pp. xviii-xx & 27-37, Pl. III.4-38.
10. Thaplyal (1972), *SAIS*, p. 298.
11. Burgess, James and Bhagwanlal Indraji (1881), *Inscriptions from the Cave Temples of Western India*, No. 9, pp. 77-79.
12. Mirashi, V.V. (1991), *History and Inscriptions of the Sātavāhanas and the Western Kshatrapas*, Bombay, No. 26. H.S. Thosar identifies Bhavvirāja with Bhavagopa ("Identity of King Bhava of the Bhokardan Coin", *JNSI*, LIV, 1992, pp. 119-23).
13. Thaplyal (1972), *SAIS*, p. 283.
14. Hastings, James (Ed.) (1967), *Encyclopaedia of Religion and Ethics*, New York, Vol. IX, p. 130.
15. For details see Allan, *BMCAI*.
16. Burgess and Indraji, *loc. cit.*
17. De (1971), *op. cit.*, pp. 12-13.
18. Burgess and Indraji, *loc. cit.*
19. Brown, Percy (1959), *Indian Architecture (Buddhist and Hindu Periods)*, Bombay, p. 57.
20. Spink, W. (1981), "Ajanta's Chronology: Politics and Patronage", *Kalādarśana*, ed. Joanna Williams, New Delhi, pp. 109-26; (1992), "The Achievement of Ajanta", in *The Age of the Vākāṭakas*, ed. Ajay Mitra Shastri, New Delhi, pp. 177-202; (2006), "Ajanta's History", in *Hari Smṛiti: Studies on Art Archaeology and Indology – Papers Presented in Memory of Dr. Haribishnu Sarkar*, edited by Arundhati Banerji, Vol. I, New Delhi, pp. 91-98.
21. Yazdani, G. (Ed.) (1940), *Ajanta*, Part IV, Oxford, pp. 114-20.
22. Thosar (*loc. cit.*) has stretched his imagination too far to date this inscription to the third century to match it with the possible date of king Bhava known from a coin from Bhokardan excavations.
23. Dietrich, Seckel (2004), *Before and Beyond the Image: Aniconic Symbolism in Buddhist Art*, Artibus Asiae Publishers, Zürich, p. 69.
24. Watters, *op. cit.*, pp. II.114, 126, 137, etc.
25. Prasad, P.R.K. (1991), "A Unique Buddhapāda Sculpture from Amaravatī", in Margabandhu, C., K.S. Ramachandran *et al.* (Eds.), *Indian Archaeological Heritage (Sh. K.V. Soundara Rajan Felicitation Volume)*, Delhi, Vol. II, pp. 607-13, Pl. 87.1.
26. Nath, Jitendra (1991), "Buddha on Vajra-Marked Seat", *Ibid.*, pp. 621-24, Pl. 89.1-5.
27. Dietrich, *loc. cit.*

XXVIII

Two Interesting Sealings of Rājāmātyas

Paithan (19°39' 19'' North Longitude & 75°26' 2'' East Latitude), situated about 50 km south of Aurangabad on the right bank of the river Godavari in Maharashtra, is a well known archaeological site which has yielded numerous and some very significant relics. The present name comes from Pratishṭhāna as it was known in ancient times. Located strategically at the point of the convergence of the hinterland routes of Uttarāpatha and Dakshiṇāpatha, it flourished as a great trading centre during the Sātavāhana period.

Amongst the four terracotta sealings from Paithan published some years ago by Sanjay Godbole[1] was a piece (Fig. 124) showing a *nandipada*, *śrīvatsa*, triangle-headed standard and *svastika* arranged in two rows in the *pradakshiṇā* order (from top left) in the centre with the Brāhmī legend around of about 1st century BCE/CE read as *Mahasenadata Siri Ach Masa* by the author.

Amarendra Nath assigned first century CE date to this sealing on palaeographic considerations and feeling that the legend had not been deciphered satisfactorily by Godbole, he observed that "It reads: ma h(a) s(e) n(a) pa t(i) si ri (u) v(a) cha sa: Mahasenapati Sriuvachasya i.e. (sealing) 'of Mahasenapati Uvacha'".[2] It has to be admitted that the upper portions of some of the letters have rubbed off or have suffered diminution and the vowel marks, if any, attached to the letters are not clear and visible. Explaining his decipherment Amarendra Nath observes that "The beginning part of legend Mahasenapati has been restored on the basis of the reading of preceding (Maha) and succeeding (pati) portions of the word. Besides, existing lower portions of letters se and na have also helped in restoring the legend. Likewise, the lower portions of letters u and v(a) assisted in reading – uvacha – the name of Mahasenapati."[3] *Uvācha* is a Sanskrit word no doubt, but it is a verbal form meaning 'spoke' (past tense) and not a noun. Such a name is unknown in Sanskrit. So I don't think that the reading of the sealing suggested by Amarendra Nath is appropriate and correct.

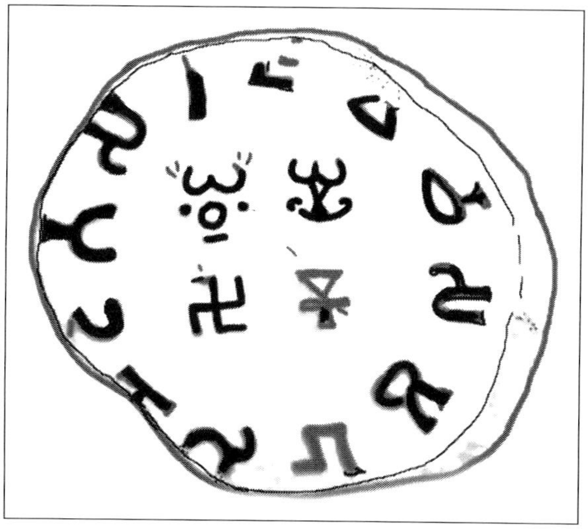

Fig. 124. Sātavāhana clay sealing.

Sanjay Godbole's reading is certainly unsatisfactory as what he has taken as A after r (of what he has read as *Siri*) shows the horizontal line with a perpendicular stroke on its left end and cannot therefore be accepted as A. His reading of the first letter of *Masa* is also unacceptable as its form differs from the Ma letter of *Mahasenadata*. Amarendra Nath's reading *Mahasenapati* in stead of *Mahasenadata* cannot be taken as correct as what he has deciphered as pa is definitely da with its slanting top-stroke truncated. This form of da occurs on many other coins, sealings and epigraphs. I feel that the letter deciphered as A by Sanjay and U by Amarendra Nath is the lower part of the letter ja with its upper part on the edge gone. The following letter deciphered as va by both the scholars is only the lower triangular part of the original ma with upper part damaged as can be judged even from the illustration of the sealing. The next letter seems to have rightly been deciphered as cha by Amarendra Nath. Thus taking into consideration the right disposition of the central symbols, I read the legend starting from about XI o'clock position as *Rajamachasa Mahasenadatasa*, i.e. the Prakrit version of Sanskrit *Rājāmātyasya Mahāsenadattasya*, '(this is the seal) of *Rājāmātya* Mahāsenadatta'.

Amātyas (*Amachchas*/*Amachas*) or *sachivas* were a class of civil officers who served as counselors or ministers.[4] Sealings of quite a few *Amātyas*, including one bearing the legend *Amacha-Hatthikasa* in Kushāṇa Brāhmī letters from Rajghat near Varanasi, and *Kumārāmātyas* are known from various places.[5] The term *Kumārāmātya* has remained quite popular in ancient times and has been used with various connotations.[6] The principal ministers of the state were called *Rājāmātyas* or *Rājāmachas*. U.N. Ghoshal has observed that the term *Kumārāmātya* and its interpretation as 'the prince's or heir-apparent's minister' "apparently has its historical justification in the title *rāyāmātya* (Skt. *rājāmātya*) known to the administration of the Sātavāhana rulers of Western India".[7] It is interesting to note that the term *rājamachcha* actually occurs in the Jātakas in the sense of a royal minister.[8] Paithan was the capital of the Sātavāhanas and it is no wonder if *Rājāmātya* Mahāsenadatta was living there. As such the sealing under consideration is an important document. Seals/sealings and epigraphs mentioning the title *Kumārāmātya* are known in considerable numbers[9] but it is one of the rare sealing referring to the title *rājāmātya*.

Another interesting terracotta sealing from Erich[10] (<Erikachcha), located on the right bank of the Betwa in district Jhansi, has been published by Prashant P. Kulkarni[11] (Fig. 125) showing four *nandipada* symbols around a central circlet with the first century Brāhmī legend around read as *Rājā Maṭhisagoti putasa Sivalasa* which he has translated as 'the seal of king Sivala, the son of Maṭhisagoti'.

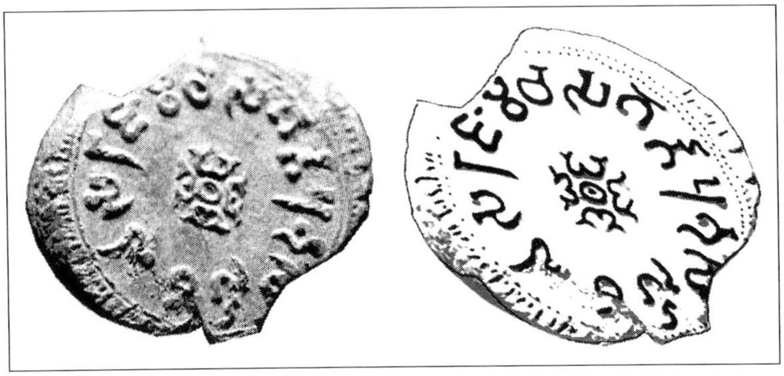

Fig. 125. Clay sealing from Erich.

Maṭhisagoti is an unusual and un-meaningful name. Kulkarni seems to have erred in deciphering as ṭhi the letter which follows Ma. What has been taken as the vowel-mark i differs from this mark as seen with ti of Goti and Si of Sivala as deciphered by Kulkarni. It is the serif mark and not the vowel-mark. This letter is very clear on the sealing and is certainly cha. The ta of *putasa* differs from the ta of Goti. The lengthening of the right leg of this letter with a curved downward flourish indicates that it is the conjunct tra. I would therefore decipher the legend as *Rājāmachasa Goti-putrasa Sivalasa* and render it as '(the seal) of *rājāmātya* Sivala, son of Goti'.[12]

The legend is in Prakrit and the name Goti needs a comment. Interestingly an inscription from Bharhut also mentions a 'Gotiputasa Agarajasa'.[13] It seems to be the Prakrit version of the Sanskrit word *Goptṛi* which means 'protector, preserver, guardian' and is also an epithet of Vishṇu.[14] Goti also gives an impression of being a female name. Interestingly some brick inscriptions found from Erich reveal the use of mother's name before that of *Senāpati* Āshāḍhamitra, king of Daśārṇa.[15] Goti may also be derived from the Sanskrit word *Goptrī* which is the feminine form of *Goptṛi*. So it becomes difficult to decide whether Goti is the name of Sivala's father or mother. A look at the inscriptions recovered from Erich reveals that when the name of the ruler or commander is preceded by father's name it is not compounded with the latter but when it is referred to with mother's name it is compounded with that.[16] So with expressions like *Gotamiputasa*, *Vāsiṭhiputasa*, etc. in mind, I would like to take Goti (<Goptrī) as the name of Sivala's mother.

Coins, epigraphs and seals/sealings found from Erich (<Erikachcha) indicate it to have remained the capital city during the early centuries BCE/CE.[17] Naturally thus the city must have been inhabited by kings, commanders and ministers.[18] This sealing belonging to a *rājāmātya*, 'the State Minister', is therefore no surprise. It is, however, important for providing the name of another State Minister and illustrating the use of the title *rājāmacha* (Skt. *Rājāmātya*) corroborating the evidence of the Paithan sealing discussed above. Two sealings of *Amātya* Āshāḍhasena and *Amātya* Kshatikāyā[19] recovered from Erich, however, indicate that the two titles of *Amātya* and *Rājāmātya* refer to distinct categories of ministers as noted above.

The two sealings reviewed here furnish for the first time clear-cut evidence of the use of the title *rājāmātya* during the first century CE not only at Paithan in the Deccan but also as north as Erich near Jhansi in North India.

NOTES AND REFERENCES

1. *JNSI*, LXIV-V (2002-03), p. 19, Pl. III.1.
2. *Ibid.*, LXVII (2005), p. 51.
3. *Ibid.*
4. Raychaudhari (1953), *op. cit.*, p. 521.
5. Thaplyal (1972), *SAIS*, pp. 100 ff.
6. *Ibid.*, pp. 103 ff.
7. Ghoshal, U.N. (1957), *Studies in Indian History and Culture*, Bombay-Calcutta-Madras, p. 446. The title *rājāmātya* occurs in a Pāla epigraph also (*Epigraphia Indica*, XVII, p. 32).
8. *The Jataka or the Stories of the Buddha's Former Births*, (English translation) Cowell, E.W., R. Chalmers, H.T. Francis *et al.*, Cambridge: CUP, 1895-1907, I. 262; V. 444.
9. Thaplyal (1972), *loc. cit.*
10. Srivastava, O.P.L. (1991), *Archaeology of Erich Discovery of New Dynasties*, Varanasi; Gupta, Mohan Lal (2000), *Erich an Ancient City on River Betwa: its History, Coinage and Discovery of New Dynasties*, Jhansi.
11. Kulkarni, Prashant P. (October 2007), "Important Seals and Sealings from Central India", *Nidhi*, Vol. II, pp. 25-26 and colour plate on p. 140.
12. The letter *va* following *sa* of the name Sivala is somewhat damaged and the possibility of its being a different letter or conjunct cannot be ruled out altogether.
13. Luders, H. (1998), *CII*, Vol. II, Part II, ASI, New Delhi, Pl. A.1.
14. Apte (1959), *op. cit.*, p. 25.
15. Srivastava (2020), *op. cit.*, pp. 8 and 10, Pls. II.3 and IV.3 respectively.
16. E.g. – *Mūlamitrasya putreṇa senāpatinā Ashāḍhamitreṇa* and *Daśārṇādhipateḥ Mūlamitrasya putreṇa senāpatinā Daśārṇeśvareṇa Vāsishṭhīputreṇa Ashāḍhamitreṇa* (*Ibid.*, p. 10, Pl. IV.2-3).
17. *Ibid.*; Gupta, Mohan Lal, *loc. cit.*
18. Bhandare, Shailendre, "Kings, Commanders and Ministers from Erich", *ONS Newsletter*, No. 175, pp. 11-17.
19. Kulkarni (October 2007), *op. cit.*, pp. 25-26.

XXIX

A Copper Seal of Dhavalapa

Shri Girish Sharma of Indore is a well-known public figure, famous as a numismatist for his rich and wonderful collection of coins, seals and sealings besides other antiquities. Quite some time back he put on the Facebook the following copper seal which is illustrated here with its mirror view (Fig. 126) for ease of decipherment.

It shows the legend *Śrī-Dhavalapa* in characters belonging to the northern class of alphabets, commonly known as Kuṭila script, with the figure of a boar below. There is a crescent mark above the letter *la*. The first letter *Dha* of the proper name seems to be smaller and constricted as compared to the other bold letters of the legend.

We know of Dhavala as a Rāshṭrakūṭa king of Hastikuṇḍī whose Bijapur inscription (tehsil and district Pali, Rajasthan) of Vikrama Saṃvat 1053 (996-997 CE) tells us that he had given refuge to king Mahendra of Nadol when Durlabharāja II of Śākambharī attacked him and had also protected Paramāra Dharaṇivarāha of Ābū and Kirātakūpa (Kirāḍu). He helped the Chalukya ruler Mūlarāja too when Vākpati-Muñja Paramāra of Malwa stormed Āghāṭa (Ahad near Udaipur, Rajasthan) with his elephant force to recover a part of his dominion. Inspired by his preceptor he constructed a Jaina temple dedicated to the first pontiff and abdicated the throne for his son Bāla Prasāda who too enhanced the glory of his family.[1] It is interesting to note that two diminutive silver coins weighing 0.39 and 0.45 g and having a diameter of 8 and 7 mm bearing the figure of a boar to left standing on a platform with a lotus below and a crescent having a dot above shown in a dotted border on the obverse and Brāhmī legend *Śrī Nīrava/Dhavala* in two lines with dotted crescent above in a border of dots around on the reverse has been published recently (Fig. 127)[2].

Nīrava Dhavala is not known from any other source. Besides the Imperial Rāshṭrakūṭas who were initially the feudatories of the Chalukyas of Badami, we know of the Rāshṭrakūṭas of Manapura (Manyakhet in Maharashtra), Rāshṭrakūṭas of Achalapura (Elichpur), and two branches of Gujarat Rāshṭrakūṭas. Garuḍa was the royal emblem of all these Rāshṭrakūṭas. Though most of the Rāshṭrakūṭa copper plates and coins bear the emblem of Garuḍa[3] the silver coins of Nīrava Dhavala show the boar which occurs on the silver coins of Guṇatuṅga(?) and copper issues of Prabhūtava(r)sha also.[4] Boar was the typical emblem of the Chalukyas. The occurrence of boar on Rāshṭrakūṭa coins may be the result of Nīrava Dhavala conquering some Chalukya territory and following the age-old numismatic tradition of issuing coins bearing the insignia of the conquered ruler and striking the type popular in the vanquished territory. Nīrava Dhavala, however, cannot be identified as the owner of our seal as his name differs from the one put on the seal. The palaeography of the coins and seal too is different as the letters on the seal are angular and bear serif marks clearly showing spacio-temporal differences. Nīrava Dhavala's achievements are not known from any other source to have adopted a grandiloquent title.

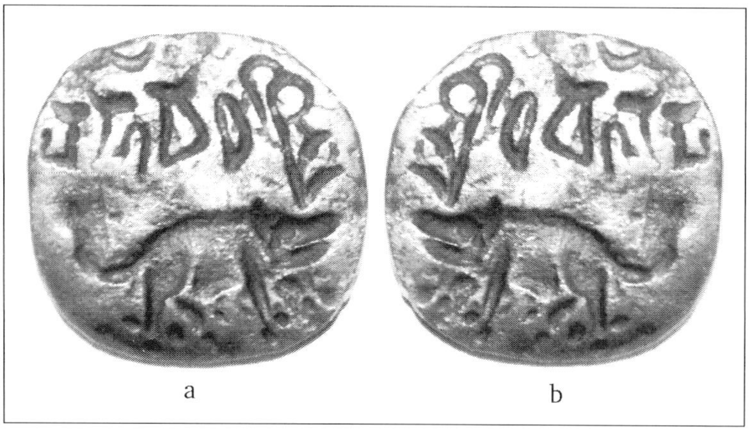

Fig. 126. Copper seal of Dhavalapa (a), mirror view (b).

Another ruler named Dhavalappadeva is mentioned in the Ḍhōḍ inscription of Gupta year 407 (727 CE) in old Udaipur state of Rajasthan. It mentions *Paramabhaṭṭāraka-Mahārājādhirāja-Parameśvara Dhavalappadeva* as the overlord of Guhilaputra Dhanika.[5] He might be the Maurya ruler Dhavala of Chittore known from the Kanswa (old Kota state) inscription of VS 795 (738 CE) of the Brāhmaṇa prince Śivagaṇa who mentions him as his friend.[6] One Dhanika, son of Guhila, is known from his Nagar inscription of Saṃvat 741 (=684 CE) which is quite poetical and betrays impact of Kālidāsa. It refers to the construction of a step-well by him at Nagar (in the Uniyārā estate of the old Jaipur state) for the use of his subjects, for the performance of the *abhisheka* of Śaṅkara and for the acquisition of religious merit.[7] Dr. D.R. Bhandarkar, however, identifies him with Dhanika of the Ḍhōḍ inscription

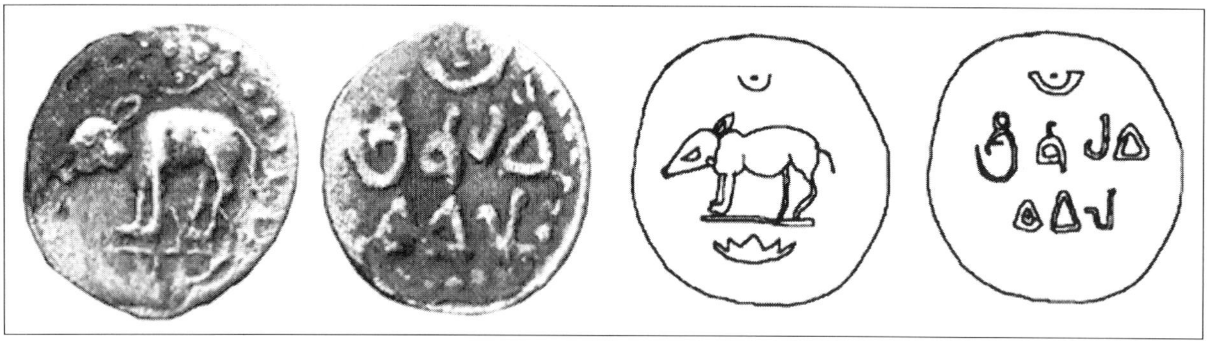

Fig. 127. Coin of Rāshṭrakūṭa Nīrava Dhavalapa and its line-drawing.

which states that during the reign of *Paramabhaṭṭāraka Mahārājādhirāja Parameśvara Dhavalappadeva*, *Vaidya* Gīyaka, son of Nāgadāma of the Kāyastha family and an inhabitant of Dhavagartā (modern Ḍhōḍ), which was being ruled over by Guhilaputra Dhanika, made endowments to the temples of Mahāmaheśvara and Durgādevī, previously established by *Vaidya* Yaśodeva.[8] The date of this inscription has been read as 207 by R.R. Halder as belonging to Harsha era (606=207= 813 CE). Halder edited the epigraph from an ink impression which was not very clear and he himself recorded that "the reading is not free from doubt in several places".[9] Halder noted that the names ending in *ppa* generally denote the names of persons of South India, for instance, Tailappa, Dhōrappa, Dhāḍiyappa, etc. So he thought that "the Rāshṭrakūṭas of Dhanōp, which is near Mewar, were related to the Rāshṭrakūṭas of the Deccan, and Dhavalappadeva may also have been related to them."[10] Dr. R.C. Majumdar rejected this reading of 207 observing that Dhanika "could not have flourished in 207 H.E. (AD 813) as Harṣarāja, fourth in descent from him, was a contemporary of Bhōja I."[11] Bhandarkar deciphered the date of this inscription as 407 and referred to it as belonging to the Gupta era according to which the record may be dated to (407+319) 726 CE. This date clearly indicates that this Dhanika is nearer in date to Dhanika of the Kanswa inscription of Vikrama saṃvat 795 (=728 CE) and that he is different from Dhanika of the Nagar inscription. Dr. Dasharatha Sharma rightly observed that if we equate the two, we should expect the name of Dhavalappa as Dhanika's sovereign in the Nagar inscription and "finally we have to keep in view the distance between Ḍhōḍ and Nagar. A clan which ruled over both these places was more likely to be independent than dependent."[12] Dhavalapa of our seal should thus be identified with the Mauryan ruler Dhavala of the Kamswa inscription and the overlord of Guhillaputra Dhanika of the Ḍhōḍ inscription. The palaeography of this seal belongs to about the eighth century and is quite close to the characters of the Ḍhōḍ inscription. This negates its attribution to the Rāshṭrakūṭa ruler Dhavala of Hastikuṇḍī.

The figure of a boar, the royal emblem of the Chalukyas, occurs on the coins of some Rāshṭrakūṭa rulers as noted above. So it is possible that Dhavalapa of our seal conquered some Chalukya or Rāshṭrakūṭa ruler and adopted this symbol. Dhavalapa may have adopted the grandiloquent and high sounding title of *Paramabhaṭṭāraka-Mahārājādhirāja-Parameśvara* after subjugating some lesser potentates like Dhanika and some Chalukya and/or Rāshṭrakūṭa potentate. The only other possibility is that Dhavalapa had his personal inclination to Vaishṇavism and the boar incarnation of Vishṇu. It is quite likely that this *Paramabhaṭṭāraka-Mahārājādhirāja-Parameśvara* regarded himself as the savior of the earth like the boar incarnation of Vishṇu. Dhavalapa did not issue any coins probably because abundant Indo-Sasanian species were already circulating in Rajasthan, Malwa and elsewhere in India at that time.[13]

NOTES AND REFERENCES

1. Ram Karna, Pandit, "Bijapur Inscription of Dhavala of Hastikundi; Vikrama Samvat 1053", *Epigraphia Indica*, X, pp. 20-21, verses 9 ff.

2. Jantakal, Gautam, Bhushan Kapadia & Prakash Jinjunvadiya (2019), *History and Coinage of the Rashtrakutas*, Mumbai-Anjaneri: IIRNS, p. 42.
3. Gai, G.S. (1965), 'On the Seals of the Rashtrakutas', in *Felicitation Volume presented to Mahamahopadhyaya Dr. V.V. Mirashi*, Nagpur: Vidarbha Samshodhan Mandal, p. 388.
4. Jantakal *et al.*, *op. cit*, pp. 43 & 61 respectively. Fishman (RA8.1), as quoted by Pieper (2021, p. 634, No. 3782) reads the legend as *Śrī Naravai/dhavala* and takes Naravai dhavala as a title as it is comparable with the titles such as Atiśayadhavala and Tribhuvanadhavala datable to the time of Govinda III or Amoghavarsha I, i.e. late 8th to mid 9th century CE.
5. Bhandarkar, D.R., "Chatsu Inscription of Baladitya," *Epigraphia Indica*, XII, p. 11; *Inscriptions of Northern India*, No. 1371. This title is used by the Maitraka rulers too from Siladitya II (662-684) onwards (Sircar (1965), *op. cit.*, p. 334.
6. Kielhorn, F. (1890), "Sanskrit and Old Kanarese Inscriptions 176-213", *Indian Antiquary*, XIX (Reprint, Swati Prakashan, 1985), p. 10.
7. Guleri, S.S. (1945), "The Nāgar Inscription", *Bhārata-Kaumudī* (*Studies in Indology in honour of Dr. Radha Kumud Mookerji*), Part I, Allahabad: The Indian Press Ltd., pp. 269 and 276 ff (book source: Digital Library of India, 2015.98278dc); Sharma, Dasharatha (Gen. Ed.) (1966), *Rajasthan Through the Ages*, Bikaner: Rajasthan State Archives, p. 523.
8. *Supra* fn. 2.
9. Halder, R.R., "Ḍābōk Inscription of the time of Dhavalappadeva [Harsha-] Samvat 207", *Epigraphia Indica*, XX, pp. 122-25.
10. *Ibid.*, p. 123.
11. Majumdar, R.C. *et al.* (eds.) (1954), *The Classical Age*, Bombay, p. 160, fn. 2.
12. *Rajasthan Through the Ages*, p. 212.
13. Maheshwari, K.K. (2010), *Imitations in Continuity: Tracking the Silver Coinage of Early Medieval India*, Anjaneri: IIRNS Publications.

XXX

A Unique Gold Coin of King Śūra-Varmmaṇa–I of Kashmir

The SKANDA collection of Indian gold coins' which was auctioned some years back included an interesting piece (Fig. 128) described as follows in a sale catalogue: "Palas or contemporaries: uncertain ruler (probably 9th century), AV inar (8.01 gm), inscribed *Sri Sri Ra*(?) *Varmman La/parmmi Samire*(?) in typical 9th-10th century script. There are no pictorial types, only the inscription divided between two faces of the coin. The correct reading of the legend as well as the identity of the issuer remains to be determined. Good, very fine, unpublished, and presumed unique."[1]

There is no doubt that it is a very fine and unique coin and that it can be assigned to the tenth century CE on palaeographic grounds. The script used is the northern variety of the early Nāgarī, known as Śāradā to be precise, prevalent in northern during the early medieval period, and the legend is clear enough to be deciphered undoubtedly as given below:

Obv. *Śrī Śūra/Varmmaṇa-*

Rev. *Dharmmātma/Meroḥ*//

The legend is in chaste Sanskrit and may be rendered as "(coin) of Śrī Śūra-Varmmaṇa, (the mount) Meru[2] of piety, justice or righteousness".

The coin may be attributed to a virtuous king Śūra-Varmmaṇa who ruled somewhere in northern India. The use of the Śāradā script was restricted generally to Kashmir and Himachal Pradesh and though kings with Varmmaṇ-ending names ruled in the Chamba region yet none with the name of Śūravarmmaṇa is known from the latter state. My choice naturally fell upon Kashmir. The *Rājataraṅgiṇī*[3], the famous Chronicle of Kashmir, written by Kalhaṇa during the Śaka years 1070-72 (= 1148-50 CE), refers to two kings of this name both belonging to the Utpala dynasty and known to the historians as Śūra-Varmmaṇa I and II.[4] The former was the son of Nirjita-Varman (Paṅgu, the Lame), born from Mṛigāvatī. The Tantrins (a band of powerful people organized militarily who played an important role in the history of

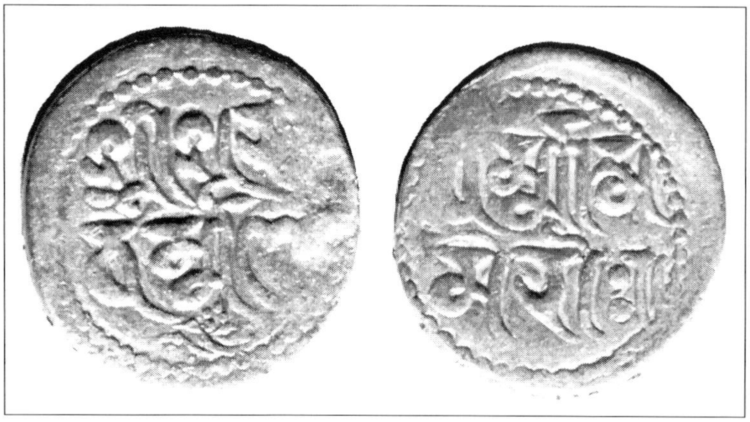

Fig. 128. Gold coin of Śūra-Varmmaṇa I of Kashmir.

Kashmir comparable to the 'Praetorian Guards' of the Roman Empire and the Turks under the Caliphs of Baghdad) put him on throne in the Laukika era 4009 (933-34 CE). During the rule of the Utpalas, the Tantrins rose to such supreme power that their favour and support virtually decided the succession to the Kashmir throne. Bribery, corruption and maladministration became rampant under their influence.[5] The ministers and officials of the state, together with the members of the royal family, contrived to bring about a rift between Śūra-Varmmaṇa I and the Tantrins. Kalhaṇa (V.294) describes Śūra-Varmmaṇa I as a man of caliber and character[6], but he became a victim of circumstances and was dethroned after a rule of about one year as he could not meet the exorbitant demands of the Tantrins who having received big promises now restored Pārtha, a brother of Śūra-Varmmaṇa I, on throne.[7]

Power passed on quickly from the hands of Pārtha (*circa* 934-35 CE) to Chakra-Varman (*c.* 935 CE), Śambhu-Vardhana (*c.* 935-36 CE), again to Chakra-Varman (*c.* 936 CE), and then to Unmattāvanti, i.e. Avanti-Varman (*c.* 937-39 CE), a vain and wicked person who liked vicious and licentious people for his company.[8] Licentious of habits, he died of consumption in *c.* 939 CE after putting his supposititious son Śūra-Varmmaṇa II on the throne, entrusting him (still a child) to the care of his loyal ministers, feudatories, Tantrins and Ekāṅgas (a body of soldiers performing the duties of royal bodyguards).[9] On hearing the news of the death of Unmattāvanti, Kamala-Vardhana, the commander-in-chief, who had distinguished himself against the Ḍāmaras and was staying in Maḍva-rājya, marched on the capital, defeated the Ekāṅgas and the Tantrins, and entered the palace, and put the rule of the Utpala dynasty to an end.[10]

The present coin may thus be assigned to king Śūra-Varmmaṇa I (c. 933-34 CE) with some certainty. The palaeography, Kalhaṇa's reference to his caliber and character and the legend of this coin corroborate this attribution. Śūra-Varmmaṇa I may have started issuing gold coins to meet the heavy, illegal and unethical demands of the Tantrins and others on the one hand and to oppose them on the other by attracting the support of the virtuous subjects and officials through the message of his coin-legend.

Unlike the Kashmir coins which generally follow the Kushāṇa pattern and carry the figure of the standing king and legend on the obverse and seated goddess on the reverse the legend on both the sides of our coin is arranged in two lines within a border of dots and the field under *mma* of the word *Varmmaṇa* on the obverse is bedecked with floral design. The die impression discernible on the reverse indicates the coin to have been a die-struck one. Complete impressions of the dies on both the sides reveal that the dies were smaller than the flan of the coin. The paucity of his coins may be attributed to the brevity of his rule. Śūra-Varmmaṇa I, however, seems to have been innovative in introducing a simple but altogether a new and hitherto unique type bearing only the legend on both sides and not following the usual crude figures of king and the goddess.

The weight of the coin 8.01 g (= 123.5 grains) indicates that the Kushāṇa weight standard continued to be followed in Kashmir till the early medieval period. A coin of Śūravarman belonging to Mr. Spinner (AV, 0.9 inch. 123.5 grains) was referred to by Rapson in 1900 CE.[11] The exactly corresponding weight of 123.5 grains indicates that the said coin ultimately reached the SKANDA collection. Taking into consideration the general paucity of gold coinage in the early medieval period the coin is an important piece, the first and the only one of Śūravarman-I known so far.[12]

NOTES AND REFERENCES

1. *Singapore Coin Auction, Spink-Taisei Catalogue 9*, 1991, p. 25, no. 164. The estimated price of this coin was $ 4,000 – 5,000.
2. Meru in Indian mythology is a fabulous mountain consisting of gold and gems and around which all the planets are said to revolve [Apte (1959), op. cit., p. 458 sv.].
3. *Rājataraṅgiṇī*, translated into English by Ranjit Sitaram Pandit, Sahitya Akademi, New Delhi (Reprint, 1959), p. xiii.
4. For details, see Saxena, K.S. (1974), *Political History of Kshmir*, Lucknow: The Upper India Publishing House Pvt. Ltd., pp. 111 ff; Jagannath (1981), "Kashmir", in Majumdar, R.C. and K.K. Dasgupta (eds.), *A Comprehensive History of India*, Vol. III, Part I (A.D. 300 – 985), New Delhi: People's Publishing House, pp. 539-47. Besides these, another Śūra-Varman, a half-brother of the illustrious Kashmir king Avantivarman, who was also made a yuvarāja 'heir-apparent' by the latter, is well-known. See Saxena, *op. cit.*, pp. 111-12; Jagannath, *op. cit.*, p. 539.
5. Saxena (1974), *op. cit.*, p. 121.
6. *Rājataraṅgiṇī*, V.294.
7. Saxena (1974), *op. cit.*, pp. 128-29.
8. *Ibid.*, pp. 129-31.
9. *Ibid.*; Jagannath, *op. cit.*, pp. 546-47.
10. *Ibid.*
11. Rapson, E.J. (1900), "Notes on Indian Coins and Seals, Part I", *JRAS*, pp. 124-25, Pl. I.20. Rapson deciphered the name as Śaravarman and tried to connect it with Śarajanman, i.e., Kārttikeya. He, however, recorded that "This coin, which is noteworthy in many ways, was sent to the British Museum for examination by Mr. Daniel Howorth, of Ashton-under-Lyne, in February, 1889. There is, apparently no other Indian gold coin known of the period to which it belongs – probably ninth or tenth century A.D." (*Ibid.*, p. 124).
12. I wrote a note on the identification of this coin from the published reference in the above-mentioned Auction Catalogue for *Spink Numismatic Circular* [CI (5), June 1993, p. 154] and it was referred to Nicholas Rhodes, an authority on Himalayan coinages. Nick informed me (vide his letter dated 23rd January 1993) that the coin did not sell at Singapore and was reoffered for sale in Steve's Album, Price List No. 90, Sept 1992 and was acquired by him. I am thankful to him for this information and the fine photograph of this coin sent to me by him and illustrated here.

XXXI

A Diminutive Silver Coin of Śāraṅgapāṇideva

In the history of the Yādavas of Devagiri, also known as Seunas after the first ruler Seuṇachandra I (c. 880-900 CE), not much is known about Śāraṅgapāṇideva, son of Siṅghaṇa II (1210-46 CE) and younger brother of Jaitugī II. In the annals of the Yādava dynasty, the reign of Siṅghaṇa II was the most eventful during which the dynasty reached the zenith of its power. As heir-apparent, he had received fruitful training in administration and martial campaigns, particularly against the Kakatiyas of Warangal, which later helped him in his campaigns against the Hoysalas, Śilāharas, Paramāras, etc. His son Jaitugī (also known as Jaitrapāla) from Chilādevī, 'a veritable moon full of all the digits' seems to have predeceased the father. Though his qualities and heroic exploits are referred to in the later Yādava inscriptions no epigraphic records of Jaitugī's reign are available and Hemādri's *Vratakhaṇḍa* (which is an important source of Yādava history) does not mention him at all. After Siṅghaṇa II, we are told that the throne passed on to his grandson Kṛishṇa (Kānhaḍa) and then to the latter's younger brother Mahādeva.[1]

In the Arjunavada inscription of Śaka year 1182, Kṛishṇa states that he was the son of Siṅghaṇa's eldest son.[2] This means that Siṅghaṇa had more than one son. From a Kakatiya record we know the name of Śāraṅgapāṇideva, another son of Singhaṇa from Tanudasammādevī.[3] Neither *Vratakhaṇḍa* nor any Yādava epigraphs, however, mention Śāraṅgapāṇideva. It is probable that after Siṅghaṇa's death a civil war broke out between Jaitugi's brother Śāraṅgapāṇideva and his son Kṛishṇa for the imperial throne. A gold padma-ṭaṅkā issued by Kānhaḍadeva which surfaced some time back shows the usual Yādava punches with his name at the top on the obverse and depicts on the reverse a battle scene indicating his upper hand (Fig. 129).

Śāraṅgapāṇideva was compelled to leave the Yādava kingdom. The Kakatiyas, who were sworn enemies of the Yādavas having been defeated by Siṅghaṇa earlier,

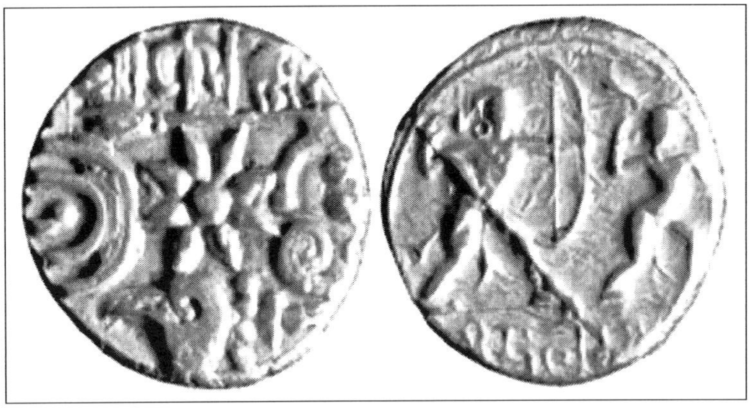

Fig. 129. Kānhaḍadeva's padma-ṭaṅkā depicting battle scene.

may have been sympathetic to him and extended to him their helping hand. It is probable that Śāraṅgapāṇideva nurtured rebellious thoughts in his mind against his nephew Kṛishṇa (1247-1261 CE) but the latter seems to have held the reins of power firmly in his hands. Kṛishṇa was succeeded by his younger brother Mahādeva (1261-1271 CE), probably because his son Rāmachandra (Rāmadeva as mentioned later on his coins) was too young to ascend the throne. In 1267 CE, however, we find Śāraṅgapāṇideva ruling over Panungal, as a feudatory of the Kakatiya ruler Manumarudra of Anumkonda.[4] According to Penungallu (Panugala) inscription Śāraṅga claimed victory over Kokalladeva, Jājalladeva and the Turushkas. This inscription is dated in Śaka year 1189, Prabhava Saṃvatsara, Adhika Jyeshṭha Pūrṇimā, i.e. Monday, Solar eclipse (May 15, 1267 CE).[5] The Mannepalli copper-plate purports to register the establishment of an *agrahāra* village called Śāraṅgapuram and its donation to forty-seven Brāhmaṇas.[6] Śāraṅgapāṇi was a contemporary of the Kakatiya ruler Rudra. Here is published and discussed for the first time a unique small silver coin, unfortunately badly broken and damaged, from the collection of Shri Girish Sharma of Indore which I think belongs to him. Like the silver coins of his near contemporary Yādava rulers Kṛishṇa and Mahādeva, it weighs slightly less than a gram and is less than a centimeter in size. On the obverse it bears Nāgarī legend Śri-Śāra(ṃ)/gapā[ṇi] in two lines (deva in the third line seems to have been lost in damage) and a boar to left within a linear and dotted circle on the reverse (Fig. 130).

It is interesting to note that R. Subramanyam had noticed a boar as one of the punches along the edge of a couple of gold coins included in the Rachapatnam hoard and took it to be a countermark put by the Kakatiya queen Rudrammādevī to mark her victory over Mahādeva who according to the Telugu work *Pratāpacharitramu* of Ekāmranātha, was defeated by her.[7] On the other hand Hemādri claims victory for Mahādeva who defeated her but did not kill her as she was a woman.[8] It is quite likely that Śāraṅgapāṇideva may have been a part of this campaign against Yādava Mahādeva and the battle may have been inconclusive with both sides claiming victory. Coins of Mahādeva show a boar to left on the obverse along with the legend and the usual Yādava

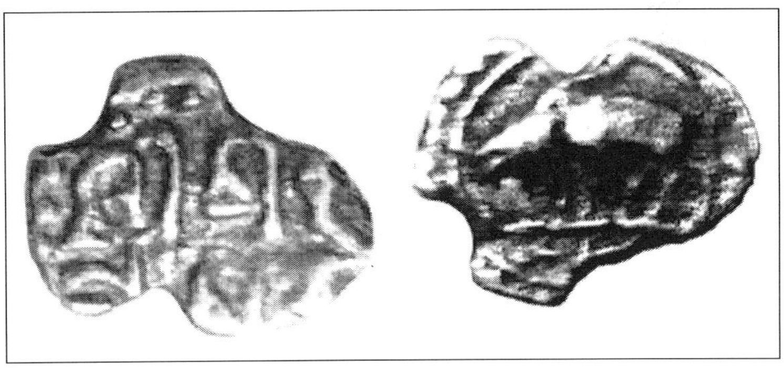

Fig. 130. Silver coin of Śāraṅgapāṇi.

dynastic insignia of lion on the reverse. Ajay Mitra Shastri, however, thinks that Mahādeva placed this device on his coins to express his devotion to god Vishṇu from whom the Yādavas trace their descent.[9]

It is well known that the Kakatiyas had adopted Boar mark from their Western Chālukya overlords. Their coins show this device.[10] Śāraṅgapāṇideva seems to have adopted it on his coinage to show his subservience to the Kakatiyas. Since numismatic symbols were generally adopted by the victors from the vanquished enemies it is likely that Mahādeva adopted it on his coins to pronounce his victory in the inconclusive skirmishes with the Kakatiyas of which Śāraṅgapāṇideva was also a part.[11]

NOTES AND REFERENCES

1. Verma, Onkar Prasad (1970), *The Yadavas and their Times*, Nagpur, pp. 78 ff. I am thankful to Dr. Pradeep Meshram (Nagpur) for kindly making this work available to me. See also Altekar, A.S. (1967), *Maharashtra State Gazetteer*, History, Part I, Bombay, Ch. 10, pp. 355-374; Ritti, S.H. (1973), *The Seunas*, Dharwad.
2. *Epigraphia Indica*, XXI, p. 15.
3. *Hyderabad Archaeological Series*, No. XIII, pp. 98-102.
4. *Ibid.*; Verma, *op. cit.*, p. 113.
5. *Hyderabad Archaeological Series, loc. cit.*
6. Butterworth, Allan and V. Venugopal Chetty, *A Collection of Inscriptions on copper-plates and stones in Nellore District*, pp. 1038, 1059 1064, etc.
7. Subramanyam, R., *A Catalogue of the Yadava Coins in the Andhra Pradesh State Museum*, Hyderabad, p. 22, nos. 70-71.
8. Bhandarkar, R.G., *Early History of the Deccan* (*Collected Works of Sir R.G. Bhandarkar*, Poona, Vol. III), pp. 196-97.
9. Shastri, Ajay Mitra (1990), "Some More Interesting Yadava Silver Coins", *ND*, Vol. 14, pp. 38-40.
10. Chattopadhyaya, B.D. (1977), *Coins and Currency Systems in South India c. AD 225-1300*, pp. 295-96.
11. I am thankful to Shri Girish Sharma for the scan of the coin and (late) Dr. Brahmanand Deshpande for detailed information and references about the epigraphs referring to Śāraṅgapāṇideva received through Dr. Chandra Shekhar Gupta with whom I had the occasion to discuss this ascription in some detail.

Bibliography

ORIGINAL SOURCES

Anargharāghava
Ashṭādhyāyī
Arthaśāstra
Bhāgavata Purāṇa
Brahma Purāṇa
Bṛihatsaṃhitā
Daśakumāracharita
Dīgha Nikāya
Garuḍapurāṇa
Liṅga Purāṇa
Mahābhārata (Gita Press edn.)
Mahābhāshya
Mahāmāyūrī
Mārkaṇḍeya Purāṇa
Matsya Purāṇa
Padma Purāṇa
Rājataraṅgiṇī
Rāmāyaṇa
Ṛigveda
Śiva Purāṇa
Skanda Purāṇa
Vāmana Purāṇa
Vishṇu Purāṇa

SECONARY SOURCES

Acharya, Bhagwan Deva (1965), *Vīra-Bhūmi Harayāṇā* (Hindi), Jhajjar.
Agrawal, Ashvini (1989), *Rise and Fall of the Imperial Guptas*, Delhi.

Agrawal, D.P. and S. Kusumgar (1974), *Prehistoric Chronology and Radiocarbon Dating in India*, Delhi.

Agrawala, V.S. (1963), *India as Known to Pāṇini*, 2nd edn., Varanasi.

Allan, John (1936), *Catalogue of the Coins of Ancient India*, London: British Museum.

Altekar, A.S. (1957), *The Coinage of the Gupta Empire*, Varanasi.

—— (1958), *State and Government in Ancient India*, 3rd ed., Delhi.

Anon (VS 2016), *Mahābhārata kī Nāmānukramaṇikā*, Gorakhpur: Gita Press.

Apte, V.S. (1959), *The Student's Sanskrit-English Dictionary*, Delhi-Patna-Varanasi.

Arya, Sushma (2001), *Paṃchāla Rājya Kā Itihāsa* (Hindi), New Delhi.

Bajpai, K.D. (Gen. Ed.) (1965), *The Geographical Encyclopaedia of Ancient and Medieval India*, Part I, Varanasi.

—— (1972), *Indian Numismatic Studies*, New Delhi.

—— (1976), *Indian Numismatic Studies*, New Delhi.

Bajpai, *et al.* (Eds.) (2000), *Gleanings of Indian Archaeology, History & Culture: Prof. R.N. Mehta Commemoration Volume*, I, Jaipur: Publication Scheme.

Bakker, Hans I. (2014), *The World of Skandapurana: Northern India in the Sixth and Seventh Centuries*, Leiden: Brill.

Ball, Valentine (1881), *Manual of the Geology of India, Part III, Economic Geology*, Calcutta.

Balogh, Daniel (2019), *Inscriptions of the Aulikaras and Their Associates*, Berlin/Boston: De Gruyter.

Banerji, Arundhati (1994), *Early Indian Terracotta Art*, New Delhi: Harman Publishing House.

Barbara A. (2009), *Encyclopaedia of the Peoples of Asia and Oceanica*, Infobase Publishing.

Berkson, Carmel. 2000. *The Life of Forms in Indian Sculpture*. New Delhi: Abhinav Publications.

Bhandarkar, D.R. (1921), *The Carmichael Lectures on Ancient Indian Numismatics*, Calcutta (Reprint, Patna, 1984).

Bhandarkar, R.G., *Early History of the Deccan* (*Collected Works of Sir R.G. Bhandarkar*), Poona, Vol. III.

Bhan, Suraj (1977), "Report of Excavations at Sugh (1964 and 1965)", *Journal of Haryana Studies*, Vol. IX, Nos. 1-2, pp. 1-49.

Bhargava, M.L. (1971), *India in the Vedic Age*, Lucknow: Upper India Publishing House.

Bhattacharyya, D.C. and Devendra Handa (Eds.) (1989), *Prācī-Prabhā: Perspectives in Indology* (*Essays in Honour of Prof. B.N. Mukherjee*), New Delhi.

Biswas, Arun Kumar and S. Biswas (1996), *Minerals and Metals in Ancient India*, Vol. I, New Delhi.

Bopearachchi, O. (1991). *Monnaies Greco-Bactriennes et Indo-Greques, Catalogue Raissone.*

Brown, Percy (1959), *Indian Architecture (Buddhist and Hindu Periods)*, Bombay.

Burgess, James and Bhagwanlal Indraji (1881), *Inscriptions from the Cave Temples of Western India*, No. 9.

Chakrabarti, Dilip K. and Makkhan Lal (Eds.) (2014), *History of Ancient India, III, The Texts, Political History and Administration Till c. 200 BC*, New Delhi: Vivekananda International Foundation & Aryan Books International.

Chakrabortty, S.K. (1931), *Ancient Indian Numismatics*, Mymensingh.

Chandra, Moti (1953), *Sārthavāha* (Hindi), Patna.

—— (1962), *Kāśī kā Itihāsa*, Bombay.

Chattopadhyaya, B.D. (1977), *Coins and Currency Systems in South India c. AD 225-1300.*

Chattopadhyay, Bhaskar (1977), *Coins and Icons A Study of Myths and Symbols in Indian Numismatic Art*, Calcutta.

Chattopadhyaya, Sudhakar (1958), *Early History of North India*, Calcutta.

Chhabra B. Ch. and G.S. Gai (Eds.) (1981), *Inscriptions of the Early Gupta Kings and Their Successors* (revised by D.R. Bhandarkar), *Corpus Inscriptionum Indiacrum*, Vol. III, New Delhi.

Choudhury, S.B. (1955), *Ethnic Settlements in Ancient India, A Study on the Puranic Lists of Peoples of Bharatavarsa*, General Printers and Publishers.

Coomaraswamy, A.K. (1927), *History of Indian and Indonesian Art*, New York: Dover Publications.

—— (1971), *Yakṣas*, Part I, Delhi (reprint).

Cunningham, Alexander, *Archaeological Survey Report*, Vols. II, V, XIV, etc.

—— (1891), *Coins of Ancient India*, London (Reprint, Varanasi, 1963).

—— (1893-95), *Later Indo-Scythians*, London.

—— (1894), *Coins of Medieval India* (reprint, New Delhi: Orient Print, 1967).

—— (1963), *The Ancient Geography of India*, Varanasi: Indological Book House.

Daivakarṇi, Virjānanda (2008), *Agrohā kī Mṛinmūrtiyāṃ*, Jhajjar: Gurukula.

—— (2010), *Bhārata ke Prāchīna Mudrāṅka*, Part II, Jhajjar.

Dani, Ahmad Hasan *et al.* (1999), *History of Civilizations of Central Asia*, UNESCO.

Dasgupta, K.K. (1974), *Tribal History of Ancient India: A Numismatic Approach*, Calcutta.

Dasgupta, Surendranath (1975), *A History of Indian Philosophy*, Vol. I, First Indian Edition, Delhi.

Datta, V.N. and H.A. Phadke (1984). *History of Kurukshetra*, Kurukshetra: Vishal Publications.

Davids, Rhys, T.W. (1903), *Buddhist India* (Reprint, Delhi, 1999).

Deo, S.B. and R.S. Gupte (Eds.) (1974), *Excavations at Bhokardan*, Nagpur.

Dey, N.L. (1927), *The Geographical Dictionary of Ancient and Medieval India*, London (Reprint, New Delhi, 1971).

Dhavalikar, M.K. (2016), *Gaṇeśa, the God of Asia*, New Delhi: Aryan Books International.

Dietrich, Seckel (2004), *Before and Beyond the Image: Aniconic Symbolism in Buddhist Art*, Zürich: Artibus Asiae Publishers.

Dutta, Mala (1990), *A Study of the Sātavāhana Coinage*, New Delhi.

East Nimar Gazetteer, Bombay, 1908.

Elliot, W. (1975), *Coins of Southern India* (Reprint).

Fausboll, V. (1963), *The Jātaka*, London, Vol. IV.

Fleet, John Faithful (1888), *Inscriptions of the Early Gupta Kings and Their Successors*, Calcutta: Superintendent of Government Printing.

Gopal, Lallanji (1966), *Early Medieval Coin-Types of Northern India*, Varanasi: NSI.

Gardner, Percy (1966), *Coin of Greek and Scythic Kings of Bactria and India in the British Museum*, Chicago (reprint).

Ghoshal, U.N. (1957), *Studies in Indian History and Culture*, Bombay-Calcutta-Madras.

Goffer, Z. (1980), *Archaeological Chemistry*, New York: John Willey and Sons.

Goyal, S. R. (1987), *Gupta Sāmrājya kā Itihāsa* (Hindi), Jodhpur.

Gupta, Mohan Lal (2000), *Erich an Ancient City on River Betwa: its History, Coinage and Discovery of New Dynasties*, Jhansi.

Gupta, Parmanand (1989), *Geography from Ancient Indian Coins and Seals*, Kurukshetra: Concept Publishing Company.

Gupta, P.L. (1959), *Punchmarked Coins of Ancient India*, Unpublished Ph.D. Thesis submitted to the Banares Hindu University.

—— (1974), *The Imperial Guptas*, Varanasi.

—— (1988), *Numismatic History of Himachal Pradesh*, Delhi: B.R. Publishing Corporation.

Gupta, P.L. and T.R. Hardaker (1985), *Ancient Indian Silver Punch-marked Coins of the Magadha-Maurya Kārshāpana Series*, Anjaneri.

—— (2014), *Punchmarked Coinage of the Indian Subcontinent Magadha-Mauryan Series*, Anjaneri: IIRNS Publications Pvt. Ltd.

Gupta, P.L. and A.K. Jha (Eds.) (1987), *Numismatics & Archaeology*, Anjaneri: IIRNS.

Haaff, P. Anne van't (2004), *Saurashtra (c. 450 – 50 BC) Surasena (c. 500 – 350 BC) Silver Punchmarked Coinage*, Anjaneri: IIRNS.

Haig, Wolseley (1958), *Cambridge History of India*, Vol. III, Delhi.

Handa, Devendra (1984), *Osian History Archaeology Art and Architecture*, Delhi.

—— (1985), *Studies in Indian Coins and Seals*, Delhi.

—— (Ed.) (1987), *Ajaya-Śrī – Recent Studies in Indology (Prof. Ajay Mitra Shastri Felicitation Volume)*, 2 vols., Delhi.

—— (2004), *An Epic Pilgrimage – History and Antiquit of Pehowa: Ancient Pṛithūdaka,* New Delhi.

—— (2006), *Sculptures from Haryana (Iconography & Style)*, Shimla-New Delhi.

—— (2006), *Early Indian Coins from Sugh*, New Delhi.

—— (2007), *Coins and Temples: Numismatic Evidence on the Evolution of Temple Architecture*, Mumbai: Reesha Books International.

—— (2007), *Tribal Coins of Ancient India*, New Delhi.

—— (2018), *Monolithic Rock-cut Temple, Masrur*, Shimla: State Museum.

—— (2021), *Facets of Indian Art, Iconography and Numismatics*, New Delhi: Aryan Books International.

Handa, Devendra and Major Dr. M.K. Gupta (2012), *Numismatic Gleanings*, Delhi: Agam Kala Prakashan.

Hardaker, Terry (1999), *The Mashaka Fractional Coinage of Ancient India: A Type Catalogue*, Anjaneri: IIRNS.

—— (2019), *Punchmarked Coinage of the Indian Subcontinent: Non-Imperial Series North of the Deccan*, Nasik: IIRNS Publications.

Hastings, James (Ed.) (1967), *Encyclopaedia of Religion and Ethics*, New York, Vol. IX.

Hirano, Shinji (2007), *The Ghaghra-Gandak River Region: c. 600 – 300 BC Archaic Silver Punchmarked Coinage*, Anjaneri: IIRNS.

Hutchison, J. and J. PH. Vogel (1933), *History of the Punjab Hill States*, Lahore.

Jain, K.C. (1972), *Malwa through the Ages*, Delhi.

Jantakal, Gautam, Bhushan Kapadia & Prakash Jinjunvadiya (2019), *History and Coinage of the Rashtrakutas*, Mumbai-Anjaneri: IIRNS.

Jha, Amiteshwar (2003), *Bhāratīya Sikke Eka Aitihāsika Parichaya* (Hindi), Anjaneri.

Jha, Amiteshwar and Dilip Rajgor (1994), *Studies in the Coinage of the Western Kṣatrapas*, Anjaneri: IIRNS.

Jha, A.K. and Sanjay Garg (1991), *A Catalogue of the Coins of the Katoch Rulers of Kangra*, Anjaneri: IIRNS.

Jolly, Julius (1966), *The Institution of Viṣṇu*, Sacred Books of the East Series, Vol. 7 (reprinted Delhi: MLBD.

Joshi, N.P. (1965), *Mathurā kī Mūrti-Kalā*, Mathura: Archaeological Museum.

—— (1972), *Catalogue of the Brahmanical Sculptures in the State Museum, Lucknow*, Part I, Lucknow: State Museum.

Keith, A.B. (1925), *The Religion of the Veda and Upanishads*, 2 vols, Cambridge: Harvard Oriental Series.

Keith, A.B. & A.A. MacDonell (1912). *Vedic Index of Names and Subjects*, Oxford: OUP (Reprint, Delhi, 1967), 2 vols.

Kern, H. (1895), *Bṛihatsaṃhitā of Varāhamihira with Utpala Bhaṭṭa's Commentary*, Benares.

Khare, M.D. (Ed.) (1981), *Malwa Through the Ages*, Bhopal

Kothari, Narendra (2006), *Ujjayini Coins* (edited by Dilip Rajgor), Mumbai: Reesha Books International.

Kramrisch, Stella (1976), *The Hindu Temple*, Calcutta, 1946 (reprinted Delhi)

Lahiri, Bela (1974), *Indigenous States of Northern India*, Calcutta.

Law, B.C. (1973), *Tribes in Ancient India*, 2nd ed., Poona.

Lüders, H. (1961), *Mathurā Inscriptions* (edited by K.L. Janert), Gottingen.
Macdonell, A.A. (1971), *Vedic Mythology*, Varanasi-Delhi: Indological Book House (reprint).
Mackay, E.J.H. *Chanhu-daro Excavations 1935-36* (reprint, Varanasi).
—— (1938), *Further Excavations at Mohenjodaro*, Delhi.
Maheshwari, K.K. (2010), *Imitations in Continuity: Tracking the Silver Coinage of Early Medieval India*, Anjaneri: IIRNS Publications.
Maheshwari, K.K. and Biswajeet Rath (Eds.) (1996), *Numismatic Panorama (Essays in Honour of Late Sh. S.M. Shukla)*, New Delhi.
Majumdar, B. (1947), *Guide to Sarnath*, 2nd edn., Delhi: ASI.
Majumdar, R.C. (1952), *Ancient India*, Delhi: MLBD (Reprint, 1977).
Majumdar, R.C. *et al.* (eds.) (1954), *The Classical Age*, Bombay.
Majumdar, R.C. and K.K. Dasgupta (eds.) (1981), *A Comprehensive History of India*, Vol. III, Part I (A.D. 300 – 985), New Delhi: People's Publishing House.
Majumdar, Sushmita Bose (2000), *Local Coins of Ancient India – A New Series: Coins of Malhār*, Anjaneri: IIRNS.
Malasekhera, G.P. (1960), *Dictionary of Pāli Proper Names*, London.
Mangalam, S.J. and Pushpa Tiwari (2001), *Shankar Tiwari Collection of Early Coins from the Narmada Valley*, Bhopal.
Margabandhu, C., K.S. Ramachandran *et al.* (Eds.) (1991), *Indian Archaeological Heritage (Sh. K.V. Soundara Rajan Felicitation Volume)*, 2 vols., Delhi.
Marshall, John (1931), *Mohenjodaro and the Indus Civilization*, Vol. III, London.
—— (2012), *The Buddhist Art of Gandhāra*, Cambridge, 1960 (Reprint, Delhi: Munshiram Manoharlal).
—— (Ed.) (1973), *Mohenjo-daro and the Indus Civilisation* (reprint, Delhi).
—— (1975), *Taxila*, 2 vols. (reprinted Varanasi).
McCrindle, J.W. (1896), *Invasion of India by Alexander the Great*, Westminster.
Mehta, R.N. and S.N. Chowdhary (1966), *Excavations at Devnimori*, Baroda.
Mehta, R.N. and A.J. Patel (1967), *Excavations at Shamalaji*, Baroda.
Mirashi, V.V. (1960), *Studies in Indology*, Vol. I, Nagpur.
—— (1984), *Studies in Ancient Indian History*, Nagpur.
—— (1991), *History and Inscriptions of the Sātavāhanas and the Western Kshatrapas*, Bombay.
Miscellaneous Publication, No. 27: Exploration and Development of Non-ferrous Metals in India, Calcutta: Geological Survey of India, 1977.
Mitchiner, M.B. (1976), *Indo-Greek and Indo-Scythian Coinage*, Vol. 9, London.
—— (1978), *Oriental Coins and Their Values, II: The Ancient and Classical World*, London: Hawkins Publications.
—— (2004), *Ancient Trade and Early Coinage*, Vol. 2, Hawkins Publication.
Mukherjee, B.N. (1969), *An Agrippan Source – A Study in Indo-Parthian History*, Calcutta.
—— (1981), *Mathurā and Its Society – the Śaka-Pahlava Phase*, Calcutta.
—— (1990), *The Indian Gold*, Calcutta: Indian Museum.
—— (1993), *Coins and Currency Systems of Post-Gupta Bengal (c. AD 550 – 700)*, New Delhi: Harman Publishing House.
Murphy, Paul (2001), *Kosala State Region, c. 600-470 BCE: Silver Punchmarked Coinage*, Nasik: IIRNS Publications.
Narain, A.K. (Ed.) (1966), *Seminar Papers on the Chronology of Punchmarked Coins*, Varanasi.
—— (1968), *Seminar Papers on the Local Coins of Northern India c. 300 B.C. to 300 A.D.*, Varanasi.
Ojha, N.K. (2001), *The Aulikaras of Central India: History and Inscriptions*, Chandigarh: Arun Publishing House Pvt. Ltd.
Pargiter, F.E. (1913), *Purāṇa Text of the Dynasties of the Kali Age*, London.

Pieper, Wilfried (2013), *Ancient Indian Coins Revisited*, Lancaster-London.
—— (2021), *Ancient Indian Coins: A Comprehensive Catalogue*, Mumbai: IIRNS.
Pliny, *Naturalis Historia*, edited by C. Mayhoff, Leipzig, 1892-1909.
Prinsep, James (1858), *Essays on Indian Antiquities*, edited by E. Thomas, London.
Pande, B.M. and B.D. Chattopadhyaya (Eds.) (1987), *Archaeology and History: Essays in Memory of Shri A. Ghosh*, 2 vols., Delhi: Agam Kala Prakashan
Przyluski, James (1962), *Ancient Peoples of the Panjab*, English tr. by Chitrabhanu Sen, Calcutta.
Puri, K.N. (no date), *Excavations at Rairh*, Jaipur.
Rajgor, Dilip (2001), *Punch-marked Coins of Early Historic India*, California.
Ramalakshman, A. (2002), *Andhra Pradesh Archaeology – A Review, 1987 – 2001*, Dept. of Archaeology and Museums, Govt. of Andhra Pradesh, Hyderabad.
Ramesh, K.V. and S.P. Tewari (1990), *A Copper-Plate Hoard of the Gupta Period from Bagh, Madhya Pradesh*, New Delhi: Archaeological Survey of India.
Rao, M.S. Nagaraja (Ed.) (1987), *Kusumāñjali: New Interpretation of Indian Art & Culture: Sh. C. Sivaramamurti Commemoration Volume*, Delhi: Agam Kala Prakashan
Rao, M. Rama (1961), *Satavahana Coins in the Andhra Pradesh Govt. Museum*, Hyderabad.
Rao, S.R. (1966), *Excavations at Amreli*, Baroda.
Rapson, James (1908), *Catalogue of the Coins of the Andhra Dynasty the Western Kṣatrapas the Traikūṭaka Dynasty and the "Bodhi" Dynasty*, (reprinted 1967), London: British Museum.
—— (Ed.) (1922), *Cambridge History of India*, Vol. I, (reprint, Delhi, 1968).
Raychaudhuri, Hemchandra (1953), *Political History of Ancient India*, 6th edition, Calcutta.
Reddy, D. Raja and P. Suryanarayana Reddy (1984), *Uninscribed Coins of Andhra*, Hyderabad Numismatic Society, Hyderabad.
—— (1987), *Kotalingala Coinage of the Satavahanas and Other Rulers – A Profile*, Hyderabad.
—— (1993), *Coins of the Meghavahana Dynasty of Coastal Andhra*, Numismatic Society of Hydrabad, Hyderabad.
Reddy, P. Chenna (ED.) (2011), *Numismatica Indica: Festscrift to Prof. D. Raja Reddy*, New Delhi: Research India Press.
Reu, B.N. (1946), *Coins of Marwar*, Jodhpur.
Ritti, S.H. (1973), *The Seunas*, Dharwad.
Rosenfield, J.M. (1967), *The Dynastic Arts of the Kushans*, Berkeley – Los Angeles.
Rydh, Hanna (1959), *Rangmahal*, The Swedish Archaeological Expedition to India, 1952-54, Lund: Acta Archaeology.
Sahni, D.R. (1933), *Guide to the Buddhist Remains at Sarnath*, Delhi: ASI.
Sankalia, H.D. and M.G. Dikshit (1957), *Excavations at Brahmapurī (Kolhapur), 1945-46*, Poona.
Sankalia, H.D., B. Subbarao and S.B. Deo (1958), *The Excavations at Maheshwar and Navdatoli*, Poona-Baroda.
Sankalia, H.D. *et al.* (1960), *From History to Pre-history at Nevasa (1954-56)*, Poona.
Saraswati, Swami Omanand (VS 2031), *Ancient Seals of Haryana*, Jhajjar, VS 2031.
Sarma, I.K. (1980), *Coinage of the Sātavāhana Empire*, Delhi.
—— (1992), *South Indian Coinage – A Review of Recent Discoveries*, Madras: New Era Publications.
Śāstrī, Yogānanda (1999), *Prāchīna Bhārata meṃ Yaudheya Gaṇarājya* (Hindi), New Delhi.
Sastry, T.V.G. (1983), *Vaddamanu Excavations and Explorations in Krishna Valley*, BACRI, Hyderabad.
Sastry, T.V.G., M. Kasturibai and J.V.P. Rao (1984), *Veerapuram: A Type Site for Cultural Study in the Krishna Valley*, BACRI, Hyderabad.
Satyaprakash and N.S. Rawat (1965), *Chemical Study of Some Indian Archaeological Antiquities*, Bombay.
Satya Prakash and Rajendra Singh (1968), *Coinage of Ancient India*, Delhi.

Saxena, K.S. (1974), *Political History of Kashmir*, Lucknow: The Upper India Publishing House Pvt. Ltd.

Schroff, W.H. (1912), *The Periplus of the Erythrean Sea*, London.

Senior, R.C. (2001), *Indo-Scythian Coins And History: The Illustrated Catalogue of Indo-Scythian and Indo-Parthian Coins*, 3 volumes, Lancaster-Pennsylvania-London: Classical Numismatic Group, Inc.

Sharma, Dasharatha (Gen Ed.) (1966), *Rajasthan Through The Ages*, Vol. I, Bikaner.

Sharma, G.B. and Manmohan Kumar (1966), *Coins Seals and Sealings from Sanghol*, Chandigarh.

Sharma, G.R. (1969), *Excavations at Kauśāmbī* (1949-50), New Delhi: ASI.

Sharma, R.C. and Pranati Ghosal (eds.) (2004), *Buddhism and Gandhāra Art*, Shimla-Varanasi-New Delhi.

Sharma, R.K. (2011), *Coinage of Central India with Special Reference to Early Coins from the Narbada Valley*, New Delhi.

Sharma, R.K. and K.K. Tripathi (eds.) (1996), *Recent Perspectives on Prehistoric Art In India And Allied Subjects*, New Delhi.

Shastri, Ajay Mitra (Ed.) (1972), *Coinage of the Sātavāhanas and Coins from Excavations*, Nagpur.

—— (1979), *Kauśāmbī Hoard of Magha Coins*, Nagpur.

—— (1992), *The Age of the Vākāṭakas*, New Delhi: Harman Publishimg House.

Shrimali, K.M. (1985), *History of Pañchāla*, 2 vols., New Delhi.

Singapore Coin Auction, Spink-Taisei Catalogue 9, 1991.

Singh, Bharat (VS 2018), *Buddha-Kālīna Bhāratīya Bhūgola* (Hindi), Prayāga.

Singh, Jai Prakash and Nisar Ahmad (Eds.) (1977), *Seminar Papers on the Tribal Coins of Anciet India (c 200 B.C. to 400 A.D.)*, Varanasi.

Sircar, D.C. (1965), *Select Inscriptions Bearing on Indian History and Civilization*, Vol. I, 2nd edn., Calcutta.

—— (1968), *Studies in Indian Coins*, Delhi.

—— (1969), *Ancient Malwa and the Vikramāditya Tradition*, Delhi.

—— (Ed.) (1970), *The Bhakti Cult and Ancient Indian Geography*, Calcutta.

—— (Ed.) (1970), *Early Indian Indigenous Coins*, Calcutta.

—— (1971), *Studies in the Geography of Ancient and Medieval India*, 2nd ed., Delhi.

Sivaramamurti, C. (1976), *Śatarudrīya: Vibhūti of Śiva's Iconography*, New Delhi: Abhinav Publications.

Smith, Vincent A. (1906), *Indian Museum Catalogue*, I, Oxford.

—— (1911), *History of Fine Arts in India and Ceylon*, Oxford.

Srivastava, H.L. (1952), *Excavations at Agroha (Punjab)*, Memoirs of the Archaeological Survey of India, No. 61, Delhi.

Srivastava, O.P.L. (1991), *Archaeology of Erich Discovery of New Dynasties*, Varanasi.

—— (2020), *Erach Rediscovered: Coins, Inscriptions, Seals and Sealings*, Mumbai: Rajgor's Heritage Hub.

Srivastava, Prashant (2011), *Encyclopaedia of Indian Coins*, Delhi: Agam Kala Prakashan.

Subramayam, R. (1962), *A Catalogue of Ikshvaku Coins in A.P. Govt. Museum*, Museum Series, No. 5, Hyderabad.

—— *A Catalogue of the Yadava Coins in the Andhra Pradesh State Museum*, Hyderabad.

—— (1964,), *Salihundam*, Hyderabad.

Thaplyal, K.K. (1972), *Studies in Ancient Indian Seals*, Lucknow: Akhila Bharatiya Sanskrit Parishad.

—— (2012), *The Imperial Guptas: A Political Study*, New Delhi: Aryan Books International.

Tiwari, M.N.P. 1981. *Jaina Pratimā-vijñāna* (Hindi). Varanasi: Pārśvanātha Vidyāśrama Śodha-Saṃsthāna.

Trivedi, H.V. (1957), *Catalogue of the Coins of Nāga Kings of Padmāvatī*, Gwalior.

Tye, Robert and Monica (1995), *Jitals*, Isle of South Uist: Robert Tye.

Utgikar, N.B. (Ed.) (1929), *Collected Works of Sir R.G. Bhandarkar*, III, Poona: BORI, pp. 13-14.

Van't Haaff, P.A. (2004), *Saurashtra and Surasena Silver Punchmarked Coinage*, Nasik: IIRNS Publications.

Vats, M.S. (1940), *Excavations at Harappa*, New Delhi.

Verghese, Anila and Anna L. Dillapiccola (Eds.), *Art, Icon and Architecture in South Asia: Essays in Honour of Dr. Devangana Desai*, 2 vols., New Delhi: Aryan Books International.

Verma, Onkar Prasad (1970), *The Yadavas and their Times*, Nagpur.

Wadia, D.N. (1975), *Geology of India*, Delhi.

Warmington, E.H. (1974), *The Commerce between the Roman Empire and India*, Delhi.

Watters, Thomas (1961), *On Yuan Chwang's Travels in India*, Delhi: Munshiram Manoharlal.

Yazdani, G. (Ed.) (1940), *Ajanta*, Part IV, Oxford.

IMPORTANT PAPERS

Agrawal, Jagannath (1946a), "Govindagupta, a New Gupta Emperor", *Indian Historical Quarterly*, Vol. 22, pp. 286-90.

—— (1946b), *Proceedings of the Indian History Congress, Ninth Session, Patna University, Patna*, Allahabad: Indian History Congress, pp. 78-82.

Agrawala, R.C. (June 1971), "A Unique Siva Linga near Bharatpur", *Bulletin of Museums & Archaeology in U.P.*, No. 7, pp. 22-24, Figs. 1-4.

Agrawala, V.S. (1936), "Mathura Terracottas", *Journal of the U.P. Historical Society*, Vol. IX (II), pp. 6-38.

—— (1969), "Dravya-parīkshā of Ṭhakkura Pheru" (English Translation) *INC*, Vol. VII.

Ahmad, Nisar (1966), "The Bearing of the Archaeological Evidence from Maheshwar on the Chronology of Punch-Marked Coins", in *Seminar Papers on the Chronology of the Punch-Marked Coins* edited by A.K. Narain, Varanasi.

—— (1968), "On the Local Coins of Maheshwar and Navdatoli Excavations", in A.K. Narain (Ed.), *Seminar Papers on the Local Coins of Northern India c. 300 B.C. to 300 A.D.*, Varanasi.

Altekar, A.S. (1948), "Nandsa Yupa Inscriptions", *Epigraphia Indica*, Vol. XXVII, pp. 252-67.

Altekar, A.S. and D.B. Diskalkar (1946), "Kasarwad Hoard of Ujjain Coins", *JNSI*, VIII (ii).

Bajpai, K.D. (October 1975), "New Excavated Numismatic Material bearing on the History of Malwa", *Research Journal: Humanities & Social Sciences*, University of Indore, Vol. IV, No. 2.

Bakker, Hans I. (2006), "A Theatre of Broken Dreams", in *Interrogating History, Essays for Hermann Kulke*, edited by Martin Brandtner and Shishir Kumar Panda, Delhi: Manohar.

Banerjea, J.N. (1957), "The Satraps of Northern and Western India", in K.A. Nilkanta Sastri (ed.), *A Comprehensive History of India*, Vol. II, Calcutta.

Barnett, L.D. (1940), "Another Ancient Tribe of the Punjab", *BSOAS*, Vol. X, pp. 277-84.

Bhandare, Shailendra, "Kings, Commanders and Ministers from Erich", *ONS Newsletter*, No. 175, pp. 11-17.

Bopearachchi, Osmund (2007), "Some Observations on the Chronology of the Early Kushans", Des Indo-Grecs aux Sassanides: donnees pour l'histoire et la geographie historique, *Res Orientales*, Vol. XVII.

Chakrabortty, S.K. (1935-36), "The Tribal Coins of Northern India", *Numismatic Supplement (NS)*, XLVI, pp. 69-70.

Cribb, Joe (1997), "Shiva images on Kushan and Kushano-Sasanian coins", *Studies in Silk Road Coins and Culture: Papers in Honour of Professor Ikuo Hirayama on his 65th birthday* (eds. K. Tanabe, J. Cribb & H. Wang).

Saifur Rehman Dar (2004), "Fifty Years of Research in Gandhāra Art (1947 – 1997)", in R.C. Sharma and Pranati Ghosal (eds.), *Buddhism and Gandhāra Art*, Shimla-Varanasi-New Delhi, p. 23, fn. 2.

Dasgupta, K.K. (1972), "The Aśvakas: an Early Indian Tribe", *East and West*, Vol. 22 (1-2), pp. 33-40.

Das, Rai Krishna (1973-74), "Rāma-Siya mudrā evaṃ tatkālīna samāja aura Tulasī Dāsa kā Prabhāva", *Prajñā*, Varanasi.

Dhavalikar, M.K. (1987), "Ganesa in Mathura", in B.M. Pande & B.D. Chattopadhyaya (Eds.), *Archaeology and History: Essays in Memory of Sh. A. Ghosh*, 2 vols, Delhi: Agam Kala Prakashan, Vol. II, pp. 471-78.

—— (1990), "Origin of Gaṇeśa", *Annals of the Bhandarkar Oriental Research Institute*, Vol. LXXI, pp. 1-24.

Gai, G.S. (1965), "On the Seals of the Rashtrakutas", in *Felicitation Volume presented to Mahamahopadhyaya Dr. V.V. Mirashi*, Nagpur: Vidarbha Samshodhan Mandal.

Giuliano, Laura (2004), "Studies in Early Saiva Iconography: The Origin of the Trisula and Some Related Problems", *Silk Road Art & Archaeology*, Vol. 10.

Guleri, S.S. (1945), "The Nāgar Inscription", *Bhārata-Kaumudī (Studies in Indology in Honour of Dr. Radha Kumud Mookerji)*, Part I, Allahabad: The Indian Press Ltd., pp. 269 and 276 ff (book source: Digital Library of India, 2015.98278dc).

Gupta, Chandrashekhar (January 1991), "Sīsa-Kahāpaṇa: The Lead Punch-marked Coin", *ICSNL*, No. 6.

Gupta, P.L. (1955-57), "Sātavāhana Coins from Brahmapuri (Kolhapur)", *Bulletin of the Prince of Wales Museum*, No. 5, pp. 62 ff.

Handa, Devendra (1992), "Some More Sealings from Agroha", *Panjab University Research Bulletin (Arts)*, Chandigarh, Vol. XXIII (1), pp. 111-15.

—— (2008-2009), "Numismatic Imagery and Beyond: Some Observations", *JPRJ*, Volume XII.

—— (2009), "Coins of the City-State of Māhiṣmatī", *Prajñādhara: Essays on Asian Art History Epigraphy and Culture in Honour of Gouriswar Bhattacharya* (edited by Gerd J.R. Mevissen and Arundhati Banerji), Vol. I, New Delhi, pp. 149-57.

—— (2011-2012), "The Earliest Representation of Brahmā: Numismatic Evidence", *Jñāna-Pravāha Research Journal (JPRJ)*, No. XV, pp. 38-45.

—— (2012). "Divinities on Ujjain Coins", *ICSNL*, No. 51, pp. 29-30.

—— (2012-2013), "Portrayal and Deification of Hanumān and Rāma – Fresh Evidence", *Jñāna-Pravāha Resarch Journal*, No. XVI, pp. 1-16.

—— (n.d.), "Sugh" in Dilip K. Chakrabarti and Makhan Lal (Editors), *History of Ancient India-III, The Texts, Political History and Administration Till c. 200 BC*, New Delhi: Vivekanand Research Foundation and Aryan Books International, no date, pp. 635-42.

Hegde, K.T.M. (1968), "Source of the metal in lead coins of Kshatrapa periods", *Current Science*, Vol. XXXVII, No. 18.

Joshi, M.C. *et al.* (1976-77), "Some Terracottas from Excavations at Mathura: A Study", *JISOA*, New Series, Vol. VIII, pp. 16-31.

Joshi, N.P. (June 1969), "A Unique Figure of Siva from Musanagar, Distt. Kanpur", *Bulletin of Museums & Archaeology in U.P.*, No. 3, pp. 25-30.

Kamalkar, G. and M. Veerender, "Coins from Veerapuram Excavations", *Numismatic Bulletin*, No. 3, BACRI, Hyderabad.

Kielhorn, F. (1890), "Sanskrit and Old Kanarese Inscriptions 176-213", *Indian Antiquary*, XIX (Reprint, Swati Prakashan, 1985).

Kulkarni, Prashant P. (2005), "New Discoveries in Coins from Narmda Valley: Geographical and Historical Implications", *ICSNL*, No. 17.

Kumar, Manmohan (2001), "Historical Geography of Some Tribes of Ancient India", *Numismatic Studies*, Vol. 6.

Mahalingam, T.V. 1968. "The Bearing of the Local Coins on the Religious Conditions of Central India", in A.K. Narain (Ed.), *Seminar Papers on the Local Coins of Northern India: C. 300 B.C. to 300 A.D.* Varanasi: Department of Ancient Indian History, Culture & Archaeology, Banaras Hindu University. pp. 54-58.

Maheshwari, K.K. (June 1977), "Some Interesting Coins from Andhra Pradesh", *ND*, Vol. 1, Part 1, pp. 5-6, Pl. I.7-11.

Mirashi, V.V. (1980), "Further Light on Yasodharman-Visnuvardhana", *Bharati-Bhanam (Light of Indology) Being Dr. K.V. Sarma Felicitation Volume*, edited by Bhaskaran Nair, Hoshiarpur: Vishveshvaranand Vishva Bandhu Institute.

—— (1982), "Mandasor Fragmentary Inscription of Kumāravarmam", *Journal of the Oriental Institute*, Baroda, Vol. XXXII, pp. 70-75.

Mitchiner, Michael (1983), "India: Minute Silver Coins of the Early Mauryan Empire", *East and West*, New Series, Vol. 33, Nos. 1 4, pp. 113-23.

—— (July 1994), "Mauryan-Sunga Punch-marked One Ratti Coinage: 128 Silver-Plated Copper Specimens", *ICSNL*, No. 27, pp. 1-4.

Mukherjee, B.N. (1976-77), "Harikela and Related Coinages", *Journal of Ancient Indian History*, Calcutta, Vol. X, pp. 166-71.

Nanda, Rajni and Dilip K. Chakrabarti (July 1981 – January 1982), "Lead in Early India: A Study of the Geological, Archaeological and Literary Data", *The Indian Historical Review*, New Delhi, Vol. III, Nos. 1-2, pp. 1-18.

Pieper, Wilfried (1994), "The Local Copper Currency of Ujjain in Ancient Central India (ca. 200 BC – ca. 50 BC)", *ONS Newsletter*, No. 142, pp. 6-9.

—— (2015), "The Earliest Śaivite Images on Ancient Indian Coins", *Numismatic Digest*, Volume 39, pp. 66-71.

—— (2016), "The deity with crested hairstyle and the first identification of the serpent goddess Manasā Devi on ancient Indian coins", *Ibid.*, Vol. 40, pp. 21-26.

Pramanik, S. (2004), "Hathab: An Early Historic Port on the Gulf of Khambat", *Journal of the Indian Ocean Archaeology*, Vol. I, pp. 133-40.

Prasad, Durga (1934), "Classification and Significance of the Symbols of the Silver Punch-marked Coins of Ancient India", *Journal of the Asiatic Society of Bengal, Numismatic Supplement*, No. XLV, pp. 16-55.

—— (1939), "Shamiwala (Bijnor District) Hoard of Punch-marked Coins", *Journal of the Numismatic Society of India*, Vol. I, pp. 1-4.

Raghunathan, K.R., B.K. Rao, Dhruva and M.L. Singhal (1981), "Exploration for copper, lead and zinc ores in India", *Bulletin of the Geological Survey of India Series A – Economic Geology*, No. 47, Calcutta.

Rajgor, Dilip (1996), "History and Coinage of Saurashtra Janapada (c. 400-350 BCE)", *Journal of the Oriental Institute*, Baroda, Vol. 45 (3-4), pp. 195-214.

Ramesh, K.V. and S.P. Tewari (1983), "Risthal Inscription of Aulikara Prakasadharmma, [Vikrama] Year 572", *Journal of the Epigraphical Society of India (Bharatiya Puralekha Patrika)*, Vol. 10, pp. 96-103.

Reedy, C.L. (1997), "Technical Studies of Gandhāran Art", in Bridget Allchin *et al.* (Eds.), *Gandhara Art in Contaxt: East West Exchange at Cross-roads of Asia*, New Delhi, pp. 267-81.

Salomon, Richard (1989), "New Inscriptional Evidence for the History of the Aulikaras of Mandasor", *Indo-Iranian Journal*, 32, pp. 1-36.

Sethi, R.R. (1985-86), "Ring and Ball Symbol on Ujjayini Coins" in S.K. Bhatt (Ed.). *Professor Ajay Mitra Shastri Felicitation Volume: Journal of the Academy of Indian Numismatics & Sigillography*, Vol. VI. Indore: Academy of Indian Numismatics & Sigillography, pp. 45-57.

Sharma, Sharad and Shinji Hirano (2018), "Two New Local Types of Silver Punchmarked Coins From Loni", *Numismatic Digest*, Vol. 42, pp. 1-7.

Sharma, Varsha S. (October 2007), "Lead Punch-Marked Coins from Central India", *Nidhi*, Nagpur, Vol. II, pp. 21-23.

Shastri, Ajay Mitra (1968), "Religious Study of Symbols on the Local Coins of Central India", in Narain (Ed), *Seminar Papers on Local Coins*, pp. 70-86.

—— (1996), "Junnar: A Mint-Town of the Sātavāhanas", *Studies in South Indian Coins*, V, pp. 51-56.

Sohoni, S.V. (1964-65), Text of *Dravya-parīkshā*, *The Indian Numismatic Chronicle*, Vol. IV, Part I, pp. 75-94.

Thakur, Ashok Singh and Rajesh Somkuwar (April, 2005), "An Un-inscribed Lead Coin of Vidarbha", *Chandrapur Coin Society News Bulletin*, Chandrapur, No. 3.

Thapar, B.K. (1957), "Maski 1954: A Chalcolithic Site of the Southern Deccan", *Ancient India*, No. 13.

Venkataramayya, M. (1953, "The Ancient Mālavas: Some New Royal Names", *Indian Historical Quarterly*, Vol. XXIX, pp. 80-83.

Wakankar, V.S. (1964-65), "Coins from Ujjain", *The Indian Numismatic Chronicle*, Vol. III, Part II & Vol. IV, Part I, pp. 182-88, Pl. I.

—— (1975), "Coins of Mitra Dynasty from Ujjain", *The Journal of the Numismatic Society of Madhya Pradesh*, Vol. II, vol. 25

Wheeler, R.E.M. (1947-48), "Brahmagiri and Chandravalli 1947", *Ancient India*, Bulletin of the Archaeological Survey of India, New Delhi, No. 4, pp. 287 ff.

JOURNALS

Ancient India (Bulletin of the Archaeological Survey of India, New Delhi)
Journal of Ancient Indian History, Calcutta
Annals of the Bhandarkar Oriental Research Institute, Poona (Pune)
Annual Report, Archaelogical Survey of India
Bulletin of the Geological Survey of India, Calcutta
Bulletin of Museums & Archaeology in U.P.
Bulletin of the Deccan College Research Institute
Bulletin of the Prince of Wales Museum
Bulletin of the School of Oriental and African Studies
Chandrapur Coin Society News Bulletin, Chandrapur
Current Science
East and West
Epigraphia India
History Today
IIRNS Newsline
Indian Antiquary
Indian Archaeology – A Review
Indian Coin Society Newsletter
Indian Historical Quarterly
Indian Historical Review
Indian Journal of Archaeology
Indian Numismatic Chronicle
Indo-Iranian Journal

Jñāna-Pravāha Resarch Journal, Varanasi
Journal Asiatique
Journal of the Academy of Numismatics and Sigillography, Indore
Journal of the Asiatic Society
Journal of the Asiatic Society of Bengal
Journal of the Bihar and Orissa Research Society
Journal of the Asiatic Society of Bengal
Journal of the Bhandarkar Oriental Research Institute
Journal of the Epigraphical Society of India
Journal of the Indian Ocean Archaeology
Journal of the Numismatic Society of India
Journal of the Oriental Institute, Baroda
Journal of the Oriental Numismatic Society
Journal of the Royal Asiatic Society
Journal of the United Provinces Historical Society
Manimahesh, A Journal of Himalayan Studies, Shimla
Nidhi, Nagpur
Numismatic Bulletin, Hyderabad
Numismatic Digest
Numismatic International Bulletin, Dallas
Numismatic Studies
Numismatic Supplement
ONS Newsletter
Pañchāla, Kanpur
Panjab University Research Bulletin (*Arts*), Chandigarh
Proceedings of the Indian History Congress
Purātattva
Res Orientales
Spink Numismatic Circular
Studies in South Indian Coins
Vishveshvaranand Indological Journal, Hoshiarpur

FB /Internet/WhattsApp/Wikipedia

AUCTION CATALOGUES

Kohinoor Auctions
Oswal Antiques' Auctions
Todywalla's Auctions

Index